HISTORICAL DICTIONARIES OF LITERATURE AND THE ARTS
Jon Woronoff, Series Editor

Science Fiction Literature, by Brian Stableford, 2004.
Horror Literature, by John Clute, 2005.
American Radio Soap Operas, by Jim Cox, 2005.
Japanese Traditional Theatre, by Samuel L. Leiter, 2005.
Fantasy Literature, by Brian Stableford, 2005.

Historical Dictionary of Fantasy Literature

Brian Stableford

Historical Dictionaries of Literature and the Arts, No. 5

The Scarecrow Press, Inc.
Lanham, Maryland • Toronto • Oxford
2005

SCARECROW PRESS, INC.

Published in the United States of America
by Scarecrow Press, Inc.
A wholly owned subsidiary of
The Rowman & Littlefield Publishing Group, Inc.
4501 Forbes Boulevard, Suite 200, Lanham, Maryland 20706
www.scarecrowpress.com

PO Box 317
Oxford
OX2 9RU, UK

British Library Cataloguing in Publication Information Available

Library of Congress Cataloging-in-Publication Data

Stableford, Brian M.
Historical dictionary of fantasy literature / Brian Stableford.
p. cm. — (Historical dictionaries of literature and the arts ; no. 5)
Includes bibliographical references.
ISBN 0-8108-4944-5 (hardcover : alk. paper)
1. Fantasy fiction—Dictionaries. 2. Fantasy fiction—Bio-bibliography.
I. Title. II. Series.

PN3435.S82 2005
809'.915—dc22 2005000099

∞™ The paper used in this publication meets the minimum requirements of American National Standard for Information Sciences—Permanence of Paper for Printed Library Materials, ANSI/NISO Z39.48-1992.
Manufactured in the United States of America.

Contents

Foreword

This latest addition to the series of Historical Dictionaries of Literature and the Arts is fairly large—and it has to be. For fantasy literature, while rather young in terms of scholarly classification, is as old as they come in reality. Myths and folktales, fairy tales and fables were around even before there was much of a written literature, and once put on paper this category just kept growing, and growing, and growing. Over the centuries it has reached in all possible directions, backward into the mythical past, forward into science fiction, and sideways into all sorts of parallel worlds. Works can portray hate and war or love and romance; they can solve all our pressing problems or leave most unsolved; they can be cautionary and didactic or humorous and, yes, fantastic. They can and do reflect the situation in all cultures and civilizations the world has ever seen, plus many it is never likely to see. Thus, even the most concise compilation must cover a lot of ground, given the vast numbers of books and shorter works, authors, illustrators, and publishers, and of types, and categories.

Fortunately, any presentation of fantasy literature is facilitated by the form adopted by this and other books in the series, since it can focus on many significant individual features in the dictionary section, which includes entries on literally hundreds of authors, dozens of types and categories, a broad array of standard themes and stock characters (many of which are periodically recycled), and the situation in different countries and cultures. The history of fantasy literature is traced in the chronology. The introduction, which might best be read after perusing some of the entries, explains the phenomenal, if almost inevitable, growth of the field and its increasingly complex categorization—this in scholarly terms but quite accessibly to ordinary readers. For those who want to know more, the bibliography provides a wide range of further reading resources.

This *Historical Dictionary of Fantasy Literature* was written by Brian Stableford, who is presently lecturer in creative writing in the School of Cultural Studies, University College Winchester, where he teaches creative writing and writing for children. He has also taught at other universities in the past, but the bulk of his time was devoted to writing, and more specifically, writing of fantasy literature, with some predilection for science fiction. He has produced several dozen novels and other works of fiction while also translating and editing books in the same field. Dr. Stableford has also contributed to a number of reference works, before publishing the *Historical Dictionary of Science Fiction Literature,* the first volume in this series. Such a combination of scholarly knowledge and hands-on writing experience is hard to find, and the advantages will quickly become evident.

Jon Woronoff
Series Editor

Acknowledgments

I would like to thank the following people: Neil Barron, for commissioning the work on his library guide to fantasy literature, which enabled me to lay the groundwork for my studies in the history of fantasy; Farah Mendlesohn, whose correspondence relating to the taxonomic system she developed was very helpful; John Clute, who generously provided information regarding the entry list of his *Historical Dictionary of Horror Literature*; and Faren Miller, who kindly read and commented on the typescript in advance of its submission.

Acronyms and Abbreviations

abr	abridged
aka	also known as
BBC	British Broadcasting Corporation
BFA	British Fantasy Award
BFS	British Fantasy Society
Clute/Grant *Encyclopedia*	*The Encyclopedia of Fantasy,* edited by John Clute and Peter Nicholls
D&D	*Dungeons and Dragons*
ed	edited by
exp	expanded version
FA	*Fantastic Adventures*
HDHL	*Historical Dictionary of Horror Literature*
HDSFL	*Historical Dictionary of Science Fiction Literature*
IAFA	The International Association for the Fantastic in the Arts
ICFA	The International Conference on the Fantastic in the Arts
F&SF	*The Magazine of Fantasy and Science Fiction*
MUD	multi-user dungeon
pub	publication
rev	revised
RPG	role-playing game
sf	science fiction
SFWA	originally the Science Fiction Writers of America, after 1992 the Science-Fiction and Fantasy Writers of America

tr	translated
TV	television
US	United States (of America)
WFC	World Fantasy Convention

Chronology

8th century BC The Homeric epics are recorded, establishing the notion of literary genius and launching the tradition of fantasy literature. The works of Hesiod, including the *Theogony,* record the wider substance of classical mythology.

6th century BC The fables credited to Aesop are recorded.

5th century BC Aeschylus founds the tradition of tragic drama; his notable works include a post–Trojan War trilogy featuring Orestes, whose tribulations are further described by Euripides. Sophocles contributes a trilogy about Oedipus. In 423 B.C., Aristophanes' ground-breaking humorous fantasy *The Clouds* wins one of his several prizes for satirical comedy.

19 BC Virgil's *Aeneid* imports Roman ideals into a sequel to the Homeric epics.

c10 AD Ovid compiles *Metamorphoses,* a theme anthology recycling mythical tales, including the story of Perseus and Andromeda.

c65 The wandering protagonist of Petronius's *Satyricon* encounters various leftovers of classical mythology.

c150 Lucian satirizes traveler's tales in the "True History" and writes "Lucius; or, The Ass," a licentious tale.

c165 Apuleius's transfiguration of Lucian's "Lucius," *The Golden Ass*, elaborates the story considerably, interpolating the original allegory of "Cupid and Psyche."

c425 Longus writes the Arcadian fantasy *Daphnis and Chloe*.

c725 *Beowulf,* written in a language ancestral to English, provides a key example of a local hero-myth.

c850 *The Voyage of St. Brendan* offers an account of an Irish expedition to a series of marvelous islands, providing a popular exemplar of a traveler's tale with quest elements.

c1090 The Elder Edda provides a poetic version of the foundations of Nordic fantasy.

c1130 The earliest surviving manuscript of *The Song of Roland,* transfigures the defeat of Charlemagne's army by Basque forces in 778, describing a valiant but hopeless rearguard action by Roland and his comrades.

c1135 Geoffrey of Monmouth's pioneering exercise in scholarly fantasy, *History of the Kings of Britain,* supplies the primal seed of Arthurian fantasy. Geffrei Gaimar's similarly imaginary *History of the English* includes the story of Havelok the Dane.

1165 A letter is allegedly received by the Holy Roman Emperor, Frederick Barbarossa, signed by Prester John, the ruler of a Christian kingdom in India. The fake letter—an instrument of propaganda intended to drum up support for the Crusades—is widely copied, its account of Prester John's kingdom provoking a good deal of scholarly fantasy.

c1170 Marie de France produces her Breton lays, many of which employ the Arthurian court as a backcloth; *Sir Orfeo* hybridizes Arthurian romance with the classical materials that provide the other major inspiration of French verse romance. A clerk known as Thomas writes *The Romance of Horn,* an account of unjust dispossession followed by heroic exploits, culminating in eventual reinstatement. The earliest texts composing the *Roman de Renart* lay the foundations of modern animal fantasy in their elaboration of fabular accounts of Reynard the Fox.

c1185 Chrétien de Troyes dies, leaving *The Story of the Grail* (aka *Perceval*) tantalizingly unfinished and awkwardly entangled with the similarly unfinished *Gawain,* provoking the production of thousands of literary fantasies and hundreds of scholarly fantasies.

c1210 Wolfram von Eschenbach's *Parzifal* imports Chrétien's account of the grail into German, co-opting Prester John as the grail's guardian and making him a cousin of Parzifal's son Lohengrin. A French Cistercian monk expands Chrétien's story vastly in *The Quest of the Holy Grail,* making the grail quest a major endeavor of Arthur's court.

c1220 Snorri Sturluson's Icelandic *Prose Edda,* together with the Germanic *Niebelunglied* and Scandinavian *Volsunga Saga,* completes the foundations of Nordic fantasy. The French romance of *Huon of Bordeaux* introduces a chivalrous hero to the fairy king Oberon.

c1225 Guillaume de Lorris begins composition of *The Romance of the Rose,* an allegorical visionary fantasy based in classical sources.

c1275 Jean De Meun completes a much-expanded version of *The Romance of the Rose,* which is extensively copied.

1298 The death of Jacobus de Voragine, the compiler of *The Golden Legend* and the inspiration of much subsequent Christian fantasy.

c1300 *The White Book of Rhydderch* provides the earliest written source for the substance of Celtic fantasy.

1307 **13th October:** Knights Templar throughout France are arrested, charged with heresy, and tortured by crown inquisitors to force confessions, providing the seeds of countless secret histories and fantasies of diabolism.

c1320 Dante's *Divine Comedy* provides a key model for afterlife fantasy.

c1355 *The Marvellous Adventures of Sir John Maundeville* exemplifies the fantasized traveler's tale.

c1370 The story of *Gawain and the Green Knight* provides a key exemplar of English Arthuriana and a significant exercise in obscure allegory.

c1375 *The Red Book of Hergest* adds the second foundation stone of Celtic fantasy; it includes "Peredur of Evrawc," which recycles Chrétien's Perceval.

c1387 Geoffrey Chaucer's *The Canterbury Tales* introduces fantasy—as well as naturalism—into the nascent tradition of English literature; the tales display a clear understanding of the various functions of calculated fabulation.

Early 15th century The first version of the chivalric fantasy *Amadis of Gaul* is written, probably in Portugal; the original is lost but serially expanded versions in Spanish and French boost the novel-length version to international popularity.

1485 *Le Morte d'Arthur,* bylined Thomas Malory, refashions the massive body of Anglo-Norman Arthuriana into a continuous and more-or-less coherent prose narrative, deemphasizing its supernatural elements but providing modern fantasy with its most important taproot text and exemplar.

1492 Christopher Columbus's "discovery" of the New World demonstrates that not all traveler's tales are ludicrous.

1494 Matteo Boiardo dies, leaving his epic poem *Orlando Innamorato* unfinished.

1515 The lifestyle fantasist styling himself "Nostradamus" publishes his first set of quatrains, laying down a rich vintage for future scholarly fantasists.

1516 Ludovico Ariosto's *Orlando Furioso* picks up where Boiardo left off, taking chivalric romance to new extremes of elaboration and exoticism, spicing them with sophisticated wit.

1532 François Rabelais's *Pantagruel* begins a series of parodic satires that provides a crucial exemplar for Swiftian satire and Voltairean *contes philosophiques,* and for lifestyle fantasists avid to adopt the guiding motto of the Abbey of Thelema ("Do As Thou Wilt").

1550 Gianfrancesco Straparola's *Nights* offers literary versions of 20 folktales, including texts of Puss-in-Boots and Beauty and the Beast.

1587 Johann Spies publishes a fantasized account of the career of an obscure German scholar, founding the genre of Faustian fantasy.

1590 Edmund Spenser publishes the first part of *The Faerie Queene,* allegorizing contemporary culture in the form of a fairy romance. Sir Philip Sidney performs a similar allegorical service for the myth of *Arcadia.*

1593 Christopher Marlowe is murdered, leaving behind *The Tragical History of Dr. Faustus,* a transfiguration of Spies's *Faust Book.*

c1595 William Shakespeare's *A Midsummer Night's Dream* offers a new blueprint for English fairy literature.

1605 Miguel de Cervantes's *Don Quixote* pillories chivalric romance as a kind of folly, but concedes that if nostalgia is a mental disease there is a tragic dimension in its cure.

c1611 Shakespeare's *The Tempest* produces a key model of the figure of the Enchanter—an important archetype of philosophically inclined wizards—and supplies him with an equally influential exemplary household.

1634 Giambattista Basile's *Pentamerone* recycles many folktales recorded by Straparola and adds many others, including versions of Snow White, Cinderella, and Rapunzel.

1654 Justus van den Vondel's epic drama of the rebellion in heaven, *Lucifer,* is couched as a complaint against Puritanism.

1667 John Milton's epic account of the rebellion in heaven, *Paradise Lost,* turns the ideological tables on Vondel.

1668 Jean de la Fontaine's *Fables* recycles works by Aesop and Pilpay, supplementing them with many new examples in a more cynical and satirical vein.

1678–79 The first part of John Bunyan's *Pilgrim's Progress* revives and modernizes the tradition of medieval Christian allegory.

1691 Robert Kirk writes his account of *The Secret Commonwealth of Elves, Fauns and Fairies*, which languishes unpublished until 1893.

1696–98 Madame d'Aulnoy's sophisticated satirical fairy tales found a fanciful tradition in French literature.

1697 Charles Perrault's collection of moralistic tales adapts folklore to the function of "civilizing" children.

1701 Antoine Galland's translation of the adventures of Sinbad the Sailor adds a vital new element to Madame d'Aulnoy's brand of fantasy.

1704–16 Galland's *Thousand and One Nights* provides the foundation stone of Arabian fantasy.

1707 Alain-René Lesage's *Asmodeus; or, The Devil on Two Sticks* displays considerable sympathy for the eponymous devil and provides an important model for supernaturally assisted tours.

1726 Jonathan Swift's *Travels into Several Remote Nations of the World . . . by Lemuel Gulliver* sets a crucial precedent for English satirical fantasy.

1730 The posthumous publication of tales by the exiled Count Anthony Hamilton—who had died in 1720—provides significant exemplars for French writers of Gallandesque satires and entertainments.

1746 Voltaire's "The World as It Is" pioneers the tradition of fanciful *contes philosophiques*.

1752 Sir Francis Dashwood establishes the Friars of St. Francis of Wycombe (nicknamed the Hell-Fire Club by its detractors) at Medmenham Abbey, setting an important precedent for modern lifestyle fantasists.

1757 Edmund Burke's *A Philosophical Enquiry into the Origin of Our Ideas of the Sublime and Beautiful* considers the venturesome exercise of the imagination as a psychological necessity.

1764 James Ridley imports Gallandesque fantasy into English in *Tales of the Genii,* bylined Charles Morell. Horace Walpole represents the moralistic Gothic fantasy *The Castle of Otranto* as a translation of an Italian manuscript.

1765 Thomas Percy's *Reliques of Ancient English Poetry* provides a classic compendium of English ballads.

1768 Voltaire's "The Princess of Babylon" leavens a *conte philosophique* with fantasy for entertainment's sake.

1772 Jacques Cazotte's *The Devil in Love* provides a crucial example of sympathy for a seductive devil.

1782 Johann Musäus issues the first volume of his collection of *German Folktales,* prompting the brothers Grimm to start their collection.

1785 Rudolf Eric Raspe's Baron Münchhausen provides the tall story with its literary paradigm.

1786 William Beckford's *Vathek* gives Arabian fantasy a decadent twist.

1787 Charles Garnier's collection of *Imaginary Voyages* is launched, providing a library of philosophically informed traveler's tales.

1793 William Blake publishes the first of his "prophetic books."

1795 Johann von Goethe publishes his *Märchen,* providing a key model for the "art fairy tale."

1797 Ludwig Tieck's "The Faithful Eckhart" transfigures material from Musäus to create a new German hero-myth.

1798 Nathan Drake's *Literary Hours* describes the "sportive" element of Gothic fiction. Samuel Taylor Coleridge's *The Rime of the Ancient Mariner* appears in the first edition of *Lyrical Ballads,* exemplifying the fantastic aspect of British Romanticism.

1799 William Godwin's *St. Leon* introduces moralistic alchemical romance to the medium of the three-decker novel.

1801 M. G. Lewis's *Tales of Wonder* collects ballads with a supernatural theme, adding several new compositions.

1802 Walter Scott's *Minstrelsy of the Scottish Border* provides a significant supplement to Percy's *Reliques*.

1803 Robert Southey's translation of *Amadis de Gaul* imports chivalric romance into 19th-century Britain.

1805 Walter Scott's "Lay of the Last Minstrel" consolidates the Romantic image of the wizard in its depiction of Michael Scott.

1808 Goethe publishes the first part of his definitive allegorical version of *Faust*.

1811 Friedrich de la Motte Fouqué's *Undine* and Ludwig Tieck's "The Elves" provide the paradigm examples of the German art fairy tale.

1812 Jakob and Wilhelm Grimm issue the first volume of their *Children's and Household Tales,* firmly establishing the notion of folktales as tales told by adults to children.

1813 Fouqué's *The Magic Ring* revives the tradition of chivalric romance within the novel format. Percy Shelley's "Queen Mab" establishes an important precedent for the 19th-century English revival of fairy art and literature.

1814 The first volume of E. T. A. Hoffmann's *Tales in the Manner of Callot* and Adalbert von Chamisso's *Peter Schlemihl* introduce a note of sinister grotesquerie into the German art fairy tale.

1818 Mary Shelley's *Frankenstein* creates an important template for tales of man-made monsters.

1819 Washington Irving's "Rip van Winkle" and "The Legend of Sleepy Hollow" pioneer the invention of American "fakelore." John Polidori's "The Vampyre" supernaturalizes Lord Byron.

1820 John Keats's "Lamia" and "La Belle Dame Sans Merci" reintroduce two carefully re-eroticized classic motifs into English Romantic fantasy. Shelley's *Prometheus Unbound* provides a model of disguised literary satanism.

1822 Charles Nodier's *Trilby* imagines a goblin in love with a human woman.

1824 Walter Scott's "Wandering Willie's Tale" renders the substance of a fantastic ballad into prose. William Austin's "Peter Rugg—the Missing Man" Americanizes a European folktale as an allegory of history.

1828 Thomas Keightley's *Fairy Mythology* provides a Bible for the English vogue; excerpts appear in the *Athenaeum,* assisting John Sterling's experiments in fantasy fiction.

1831 Honoré de Balzac's account of *The Wild Ass's Skin* provides a paradigm example of modern moralistic fantasy. Nikolai Gogol's *Evenings on a Farm near Dikanka* give literary form to Russian folklore.

1832–33 Benjamin Disraeli's "Ixion in Heaven" exemplifies the use of classical fantasy as political allegory.

1833 James Dalton's *The Invisible Gentleman* attempts to adapt humorous moralistic fantasy to the three-decker format.

1834 The diffusionist thesis of Keightley's *Tales and Popular Fictions* emphasizes the contribution of recycling and transfiguration to the heritage of modern fantasy.

1835 Elias Lonnrott compiles the *Kalevala,* synthesizing a Finnish "epic" from fragmentary folk songs. Hans Christian Andersen begins publishing his synthetic fairy tales.

1836 Théophile Gautier's "Clarimonde" breaks new ground in erotic fantasy. Gogol's "The Nose" reinvents absurdist satire.

1837 Sara Coleridge's *Phantasmion* provides a significant example of an allegorical fairy romance with elements of heroic fantasy. Nathaniel Hawthorne's "Dr Heidegger's Experiment" assists the foundation of an American tradition of fantastic *contes philosophiques*. Andersen's "The Little Mermaid" warns young women of the dangers of standing on their own two feet.

1838 John Sterling's *The Onyx Ring* attempts to found an English tradition of experimental *contes philosophiques* in novel form.

1839 Captain Marryat's account of *The Phantom Ship* transfigures the myth of the Flying Dutchman.

1840 Edgar Allan Poe's *Tales of the Grotesque and Arabesque* takes up where John Sterling left off in demonstrating the breadth and versatility of the fantasy spectrum. The first series of R. H. Barham's *Ingoldsby Legends* provides a crucial exemplar for English humorous fantasy.

1842 Edward Bulwer-Lytton's *Zanoni* provides a key exemplar of occult fantasy and launches a thousand lifestyle fantasies. Poe's "The Masque of the Red Death" establishes a paradigm of decadent fantasy. Robert Browning's "The Pied Piper of Hamelin" recycles a famous folktale in hectic rhyme.

1843 Charles Dickens's *A Christmas Carol* creates the tradition of moralistic Christmas fantasy. Richard Wagner's "The Flying Dutchman" begins his development of fantasy in musical form.

1844 Dickens's *The Chimes* attempts to strike a great blow for the poor but exposes the limitations of moralistic fantasy. Nathaniel Hawthorne's account of "Rappaccini's Daughter" aims at a softer target.

1845 Andersen's "The Ugly Duckling" gives an archetypal form to a hopeful modern myth. Heinrich Hoffmann's *Struwwelpeter* takes the tactics of parental moral terrorism to a new extreme.

1846 Andersen's "The Snow Queen" lays down a template for modern Orphean fantasy. Edward Lear's *The Book of Nonsense* takes up arms against the tyranny of "common sense."

1848–49 Gustave Flaubert writes the first version of *The Temptation of Saint Anthony,* working toward a modern conception of the Devil. Douglas Jerrold's *A Man Made of Money* demonstrates the literary potential of literalized puns.

1850 Nathaniel Hawthorne's "Ethan Brand" embarks upon a perverse quest for the unpardonable sin.

1851 John Ruskin's *King of the Golden River* provides the cardinal English example of an art fairy tale.

1853 Richard Wagner begins his operatic transfiguration of Nordic fantasy in *The Rheingold.*

1854–56 Éliphas Lévi's *Dogma and Ritual of Transcendental Magic* provides a handbook for modern lifestyle fantasy.

1855 Robert Browning's "Childe Roland to the Dark Tower Came" furnishes a key source of enigmatic imagery.

1856 William Morris's account of "The Hollow Land" lays down a template for the design and decoration of secondary worlds.

1857 Charles Baudelaire's *Les Fleurs du Mal* pioneers decadent style.

1858 George MacDonald's *Phantastes* lays down a template for didactic portal fantasy.

1859 Éliphas Lévi's *History of Magic* completes his couplet of scholarly fantasies, adding theory to practice.

1860 Paul Féval's multilayered and chimerical *Knightshade* demonstrates the elasticity of metafiction.

1861 Bulwer-Lytton's *A Strange Story* reclaims, with interest, what Éliphas Lévi had borrowed from *Zanoni*.

1862 Christina Rossetti's "Goblin Market" explores the symbolism of "forbidden fruit." Jules Michelet's *La Sorcière* demonstrates that real historians can fake history more skillfully and more extravagantly than mere pretenders.

1863 Charles Kingsley's *The Water Babies* explores the utility of phantasmagoric imagery in Christian fantasy.

1865 In response to George MacDonald's suggestion that he too might produce something akin to *The Water Babies,* Lewis Carroll prepares *Alice's Adventures in Wonderland* for publication, achieving something quite different.

1866 Sabine Baring-Gould's *Curious Myths of the Middle Ages* provides easily accessible imaginative fuel for contemporary fantasists. Théophile Gautier's *Spirite* pioneers paranormal romance. William Gilbert's *The Magic Mirror* exemplifies the Victorian attitude to wish-fulfillment fantasies.

1867 Henrik Ibsen's *Peer Gynt* demonstrates the difficulty of putting fantasy on stage.

1869 Jean Ingelow's *Mopsa the Fairy* exemplifies the sentimental aspects of the Victorian fascination with fairies.

1870 Frank R. Stockton's *Ting-a-Ling* founds an American tradition of children's fantasy.

1871 Carroll's *Through the Looking-Glass* takes "nonsense" to new extremes of logical effect.

1872 George MacDonald's *The Princess and the Goblin* exemplifies the darker aspects of the Victorian fascination with fairies.

1874 Gustave Flaubert publishes the revised version of *The Temptation of Saint Anthony,* featuring a more comprehensively modernized image of the Devil.

1876 Carroll's *The Hunting of the Snark* gives nonsense its verse epic.

1877 Madame Blavatsky's *Isis Unveiled* lays the foundation for a scholarly and lifestyle fantasy of unprecedented complexity. Mrs. Molesworth's *The Cuckoo Clock* refines didactic portal fantasy for children.

1878 Max Adeler's "Mr Skinner's Night in the Underworld" adds an American irreverence to humorous fantasy.

1880 Vernon Lee's "Faustus and Helena" sets out a new theory of the functions of the supernatural in literature.

1882 F. Anstey's *Vice Versa* employs humorous fantasy to expose the follies and impostures of Victorian attitudes. Gilbert and Sullivan's light opera *Iolanthe* arranges a cultural exchange between the fairy court and the House of Lords. Wagner's heavy opera "Parsifal" completes the set of his mythical dramatizations.

1883 Carlo Collodi's *Pinocchio* explains the difficulties involved in becoming human.

1884 Oscar Wilde's "The Sphinx" takes a tour of the cosmos of the contemporary imagination.

1886 Rider Haggard's *She* takes the lost race story into new fantastic territory. Marie Corelli's *A Romance of Two Worlds* pretends to revitalize religious fantasy while luxuriating in wish fulfillment.

1887 Oscar Wilde's account of "The Canterville Ghost" sophisticates the humorous ghost story.

1888 Richard Garnett's *The Twilight of the Gods* displays the scope of *contes philosophiques* dressed with a sharp satirical wit and a blithely decadent style. Robert Louis Stevenson's *Strange Tale of Dr. Jekyll and Mr. Hyde* adds a new dimension to moralistic fantasy. A. E. Waite's *Elfin Music* summarizes the tradition of English fairy poetry.

1889 Mark Twain's *A Connecticut Yankee in King Arthur's Court* breaks new ground in didactic timeslip fantasy.

1890 James Frazer publishes the first version of *The Golden Bough,* supplying a mythical account of the evolution of magic and religion destined to inform countless historical fantasies. Anatole France's *Thaïs* brings the ideals of Christianity and Epicureanism into sharp conflict. Andrew Lang's *Blue Fairy Book* launches an encyclopedia of the sources of modern children's fantasy. William Morris's *The Story of the Glittering Plain* brings the Hollow Land up to date.

1891 George du Maurier's *Peter Ibbetson* celebrates the power of dreams to activate wish fulfillment. Oscar Wilde exemplifies the thesis of "The Decay of Lying" by publishing *The House of Pomegranates* and *The Picture of Dorian Gray*.

1892 "Amour Dure" and "Dionea," in Vernon Lee's *Hauntings,* set new standards in decadent erotic fantasy.

1893 W. B. Yeats's *The Celtic Twilight* celebrates the mystical survival, in spirit, of the Irish Arcadia.

1894 Fiona MacLeod's *The Sin Eater and Other Tales and Episodes* argues that Scotland was also part of Britain's Arcadia, although William Morris removes it to *The Wood beyond the World*. Rudyard Kipling's *The Jungle Book* brings animal fantasy to a new pitch of sophistication.

1895 H. G. Wells's *The Wonderful Visit* employs an angel as a critical observer of Victorian folkways. John Kendrick Bangs's *A Houseboat on the Styx* credits Dante's *Inferno* with New York's urbanity. Marie Corelli's *The Sorrows of Satan* sympathizes with the Devil's aristocratic ennui.

1896 M. P. Shiel's *Shapes in the Fire* and Laurence Housman's *All-Fellows* deploy decadent style in very different ways. Gerhardt Hauptmann's *The Sunken Bell* struggles heroically with the problems of staging fantasy.

1897 Bram Stoker's *Dracula* invents a monster of unparalleled seductiveness.

1898 Aleister Crowley joins the Hermetic Order of the Golden Dawn, bringing a dash of Rabelais to the world of English lifestyle fantasy. H. G. Wells's "The Man Who Could Work Miracles" offers a definitive analysis of the tragedy of wish fulfillment.

1899 Charles Godfrey Leland's *Aradia* mixes Michelet and Frazer into a heady new cocktail for scholarly and lifestyle fantasists.

1900 Sigmund Freud publishes *The Interpretation of Dreams,* issuing a caution to all lovers of hallucinatory fantasy. F. Anstey's *The Brass Bottle* toys with the idea of letting an intrusive fantasy get out of hand. L. Frank Baum's *The Wonderful Wizard of Oz* suggests that if you live in Kansas, the grass might be greener on the other side of the portal.

1902 Kipling's *Just So Stories* inject a healthy dose of nonsense into the business of fabulation. E. Nesbit's *Five Children and It* adapts Ansteyan fantasy for young readers. Arthur Machen's *Hieroglyphics* explores the ecstatic dimension of enchantment.

1904 J. M. Barrie's *Peter Pan* explores the psychological politics of escapism. W. H. Hudson's *Green Mansions* and H. G. Wells's "The Country of the Blind" bid farewell to lost races.

1905 Lord Dunsany's *The Gods of Pegana* goes in for secondary creation on a large scale in lapidary form. The launch of Winsor McCay's comic strip *Little Nemo in Slumberland* adapts fantasy to a new and exceedingly hospitable medium.

1907 George Sterling's "A Wine of Wizardry" sets out a manifesto for fantasy in a suitably decadent style and demonstrates that the readers of *Cosmopolitan* are small-town folk at heart.

1908 G. K. Chesterton's *The Man Who Was Thursday* demonstrates that the spy story is an unsuitable medium for religious allegory. Kenneth Grahame's *The Wind in the Willows* demonstrates that animal fantasy is the last viable refuge of Arcadian fantasy. Dunsany's "The Sword of Welleran" attempts to recast chivalric romance in the mold of heroic fantasy. William Hope Hodgson's *The House on the Borderland* demonstrates the utility of leaky portals.

1909 Maurice Maeterlinck's *The Blue Bird* demonstrates that fantasy is stageable, provided that one takes a sufficiently impressionistic approach.

1910 Walter de la Mare's *The Return* and Algernon Blackwood's *The Human Chord* fuse occult and existentialist fantasy.

1912 James Stephens's *The Crock of Gold* revisits the Irish Arcadia and finds it slightly tarnished. Edgar Rice Burroughs's *Tarzan of the Apes* provides a key model of the Noble Savage.

1914 Anatole France's *The Revolt of the Angels* provides literary satanism with its masterpiece, shortly before the outbreak of the Great War in August; shortly thereafter, Arthur Machen's "The Bowmen" illustrates the hazards of fantastic indulgence in a time of great social stress. The Vorticist periodical *Blast* is founded, taking esoteric allegory to new extremes.

1915 Gustav Meyrink's *The Golem* and Franz Kafka's *Metamorphosis* illustrate the anxieties bred by war. Jack London's *The Star Rover* celebrates escapism. Machen's *The Great Return* suggests that Wales was never in greater need of a grail.

1917 James Branch Cabell's *The Cream of the Jest* employs portal fantasy to mock the follies of American mores.

1918 A. Merritt's "The Moon Pool" employs a definitive portal fantasy to issue a manifesto for escapist fantasy in pulp fiction. The Great War ends in November.

1919 Stella Benson's *Living Alone* indicates the need for postwar re-enchantment. James Branch Cabell's *Jurgen* continues his symbolist satirization of American mores and is fortunate enough to excite stern opposition.

1920 David Lindsay's *A Voyage to Arcturus* modernizes metaphysical allegory. The Ĉapek brothers' *Insect Play* and Hugh Lofting's *The Story of Dr. Doolittle* provide contrasting templates for modern animal fantasy. Jessie Weston's scholarly fantasy *From Ritual to Record* makes an important contribution to the ideology of Celtic Arthurian fantasy.

1921 Barry Pain's *Going Home* takes sentimental fantasy to a new extreme.

1922 Eric Rucker Eddison's *The Worm Ouroboros* demonstrates several new extremes to which transfiguration of epic materials might go. David Garnett's *Lady into Fox* modernizes theriomorphic fantasy. Ben Hecht's *Fantazius Mallare* celebrates the perversities of delusionary fantasy.

1923 *Weird Tales* begins publication.

1924 Dunsany's *The King of Elfland's Daughter* gives Faerie a crucial symbolic role in the politics of re-enchantment.

1925 Margaret Irwin's *These Mortals* and Christopher Morley's *Thunder on the Left* reverse the conventional direction of portal fantasy in order to highlight the moral effects of disenchantment.

1926 Ronald Fraser's *Flower Phantoms* considers the metaphysical implications of erotic fantasy. Hope Mirrlees's *Lud-in-the-Mist* revisits the symbolism of forbidden fruit. Thorne Smith's *Topper* adapts Ansteyan fantasy to an American milieu. Sylvia Townsend Warner's *Lolly Willowes* casts the Devil as a loving huntsman.

1927 John Erskine's *Adam and Eve* adapts Edenic fantasy to the purposes of modern satire. Herman Hesse's *Steppenwolf* suggests that the magical Theatre of the Imagination might hold the answer to problems of alienation. T. F. Powys's *Mr. Weston's Good Wine* offers a revised account of divine benevolence.

1928 Wyndham Lewis's *The Childermass* transfigures Dantean fantasy for the modernist era. Robert Nathan's *The Bishop's Wife* imagines that even angels can fall in love. George Sylvester Viereck and Paul Eldridge's *My First Two Thousand Years* explores the ways in which an accursed wanderer might profitably employ an extended sojourn in the world. Lewis Spence's *The Mysteries of Britain* collates the scholarly fantasies underlying modern Celtic fantasy.

1929 Aleister Crowley's *Moonchild* provides a key example of occult fantasy informed by scholarly and lifestyle fantasies. Robert E. Howard's "The Shadow Kingdom" offers a tentative template for sword and sorcery fiction.

1930 Charles Williams's *War in Heaven* demonstrates that genre thrillers might benefit from a dash of religious fantasy.

1931 T. F. Powys's "The Only Penitent" suggests that the moral rearmament of the confessional might work both ways.

1932 Robert E. Howard's first Conan story establishes a more authoritative exemplar for sword-and-sorcery fiction. John Cowper Powys's *A Glastonbury Romance* explores the potential of reckless mythological syncresis.

1933 C. L. Moore's "Shambleau" hybridizes planetary romance and mythical fantasy. James Hilton's *Lost Horizon* establishes a new escapist myth.

1934 C. L. Moore's "Black God's Kiss" feminizes sword and sorcery fiction in graphic fashion.

1935 Charles G. Finney's *The Circus of Dr Lao* employs a circus as a mirror to various hidden aspects of the American Dream. Herbert Read's *The Green Child* remodels the underworld of Faerie in surreal fashion.

1936 Evangeline Walton's *The Virgin and the Swine* demonstrates the utility of Celtic fantasy in the dramatization of post-Frazerian scholarly fantasy.

1937 J. R. R. Tolkien's *The Hobbit; or, There and Back Again* sets a crucial precedent for modern immersive fantasy. Stephen Vincent Benét's "The Devil and Daniel Webster" sets up a crucial title fight between the Devil and an American lawyer.

1938 T. H. White's *The Sword in the Stone* provides significant new models of education and wizardry. Mikhail Bulgakov writes *The Master and Margarita,* knowing that he will be unable to publish its satanic rebellion against Stalinism. J. R. R. Tolkien's lecture "On Fairy Tales" offers an unprecedentedly robust apologia for fantasy literature.

1939 *Unknown* provides a vital arena for the development of chimerical fantasy. Flann O'Brien's *At Swim-Two-Birds* takes metafiction to new extremes. James Thurber's "The Secret Life of Walter Mitty" provides a classic description of everyday escapism. World War II begins in September.

1940 Jorge Luis Borges, Adolfo Bioy Casares, and Silvina Ocampo compile a showcase anthology of international fantasy literature. Robert Nathan's *Portrait of Jennie* provides a key example of sentimental fantasy.

1941 The United States becomes embroiled in World War II in December.

1942 C. S. Lewis's *The Screwtape Letters* breaks new tactical ground in propagandistic Christian fantasy.

1943 Antoine de Saint-Exupéry's *The Little Prince* provides a parable of enchantment destined to become the best-selling book of the 20th century.

1944 Neil M. Gunn's *The Green Isle of the Great Deep* wonders whether heaven itself might be endangered by the spirit of Fascism.

1945 C. S. Lewis's *The Great Divorce* redraws the map of Dantean fantasy in a calculatedly unmelodramatic style. George Orwell's *Animal Farm* adapts animal fantasy to modern political allegory. Charles Williams's *All Hallows' Eve* places the war-torn world in a melodramatic metaphysical context. In August, World War II is concluded with an unprecedented melodramatic flourish.

1946 Mervyn Peake's *Titus Groan* sets a new standard in Gothic grotesquerie. Mervyn Wall's *The Unfortunate Fursey* lends a new sophistication to humorous fantasy.

1948 Fletcher Pratt's *The Well of the Unicorn* begins the sophistication of American heroic fantasy.

1949 Joseph Campbell's *The Hero with a Thousand Faces* maps the essential features of the heroic quest. *The Magazine of Fantasy* is launched (becoming *The Magazine of Fantasy Science Fiction* after its second issue).

1950 Jack Vance's *The Dying Earth* finds the marketplace not yet ready for decadent far-futuristic fantasy. C. S. Lewis's *The Lion, the Witch and the Wardrobe* establishes a crucial exemplar in children's portal fantasy. James Thurber's *The Thirteen Clocks* introduces a decadent flamboyance into children's fantasy.

1951 L. Sprague de Camp introduces a lighter note to sword and sorcery in *The Tritonian Ring*.

1952 Italo Calvino's *The Cloven Viscount* accommodates the substance of chivalric romance to modern fabulation. Mary Norton's *The Borrowers* explores the narrative potential of miniaturization. E. B. White's *Charlotte's Web* introduces the oddest couple in animal fantasy.

1954 Poul Anderson's *The Broken Sword* and J. R. R. Tolkien's *The Fellowship of the Ring* give the elves of Nordic mythology a thorough makeover, conclusively revising the imagery of heroic fantasy. Harry Blamires's *The Devil's Hunting Grounds* restores Purgatory to the Dantean scheme.

1956 C. S. Lewis's *Till We Have Faces* modernizes Apuleius's story of Cupid and Psyche.

1958 T. H. White's *The Once and Future King* updates Malory's Matter of Britain. Philippa Pearce's *Tom's Midnight Garden* adds a new metaphorical dimension to children's timeslip fantasy.

1960 Peter S. Beagle's *A Fine and Private Place* sustains the tradition of American sentimental fantasy. Alan Garner's *The Weirdstone of Brisingamen* imports a new energy to children's Celtic fantasy.

1961 Michael Moorcock's "The Dreaming City" undertakes a new departure in sword and sorcery fiction.

1962 Ray Bradbury's *Something Wicked This Way Comes* finds further employment for the circus as a mirror of dreams. Thomas Burnett Swann's "Where Is the Bird of Fire?" demonstrates the unreadiness of the American market to accommodate classical fantasy. Norton Juster's *The Phantom Tollbooth* modernizes didactic portal fantasy. Moorcock's "The Eternal Champion" takes Joseph Campbell's notion of the ubiquitous hero on to a multiversal stage.

1963 L. Sprague de Camp's *Swords and Sorcery* provides a definitive showcase for the subgenre. Andre Norton's *Witch World* draws hybrid science-fantasy further into the realms of magical fantasy. Maurice Sendak's *Where the Wild Things Are* inverts the logic of parental moral terrorism.

1964 Lloyd Alexander's *The Book of Three* Americanizes the Matter of Britain. Roald Dahl's *Charlie and the Chocolate Factory* adds a phantasmagoric flamboyance to moralistic fantasy.

1966 The Ace and Ballantine paperback editions of *The Lord of the Rings* become best-sellers, setting the text en route to becoming the most highly regarded text of 20th-century popular fiction.

1967 Robert Scholes's *The Fabulators* popularizes the notion of modern fantastic fiction as metafictional fabulation. Gabriel Garcia Marquez's *One Hundred Years of Solitude* establishes the definitive text of "magic realism." Russell Hoban's *The Mouse and His Child* demonstrates that toy animals can be as effectively anthropomorphized as real ones.

1968 Ursula le Guin's *The Wizard of Earthsea* sets a crucial precedent for the employment of immersive fantasies set in sophisticated secondary worlds in the field of "young adult" literature. Leon Garfield's "Mr. Corbett's Ghost" updates the moral outlook of Christmas fantasy.

1969 Ballantine Adult Fantasy Series is given its own label, retrospectively taking aboard books published in the wake of *The Lord of the Rings;* its range and ambitions are defined by Lin Carter's exemplary anthology showcasing *The Young Magicians*. Vera Chapman founds the Tolkien Society.

1970 Jack Finney's *Time and Again* provides a paradigm example of timeslip romance. Katherine Kurtz's *Deryni Rising* illustrates the potential of Tolkienesque commodified fantasy. Roger Zelazny's *Nine Princes in Amber* expands the reach of portal fantasy to embrace the recent recomplication of secondary worlds.

1972 Richard Adams's *Watership Down* recycles the *Aeneid* as an ecological and political fable about dispossessed rabbits. Angela Carter's *The Infernal Desire Machines of Dr. Hoffman* provides an analytical account of the seductions of erotic fantasy.

1973 William Goldman's *The Princess Bride* celebrates the magnificent follies of recycled fantasy. Lin Carter's *Imaginary Worlds: The Art of Fantasy* attempts a theoreticized account of the nascent commercial genre.

1974 The role-playing game of Dungeons and Dragons is launched, adding a new dimension to the commodification of fantasy.

1975 Pierre Kast's *The Vampires of Alfama* and Fred Saberhagen's *The Dracula Tape* pioneer revisionist vampire fiction.

1976 Anne Rice's *Interview with the Vampire* adds an intensely Romantic dimension to revisionist vampire fiction.

1977 J. R. R. Tolkien's *The Silmarillion* is published four years after the author's death, as the closest contrivable approximation of his "lost epic" of pre-Norman England. Piers Anthony's *A Spell for Chameleon,* Terry Brooks's *The Sword of Shannara,* and Stephen R. Donaldson's *Chronicles of Thomas Covenant* demonstrate the best-selling potential of commodified fantasy. Sylvia Townsend Warner's *The Kingdoms of Elfin* Balkanizes Faerie in a spirit of modernization. Raymond Briggs's *Fungus the Bogeyman* takes adversarial existentialism to a parodic extreme. Diana Wynne Jones's *Charmed Life* introduces a new paradigm of the philosopher-wizard.

1979 Angela Carter's *The Bloody Chamber* adds a sharp feminist twist to transfigurations of familiar fairy tales. Samuel R. Delany's *Tales of Nevèrÿon* brings a new sophistication to the sexual politics of heroic fantasy. *Thieves' World* demonstrates the commercial potential of shared world fantasylands and encourages the proliferation of picaresque fantasy. Jack Zipes's *Breaking the Magic Spell* explores the political ideologies underlying fairy tales.

1980 Gene Wolfe's *The Shadow of the Torturer* adds a new sophistication to messianic heroic fantasy.

1981 John Crowley's *Little, Big* juxtaposes contemporary America with a distinctive version of Faerie. Nancy Willard's *A Visit to William Blake's Inn* achieves a new poetic fusion of innocence and experience.

1982 Marion Zimmer Bradley's *The Mists of Avalon* provides a definitive feminization of the Arthurian mythos. The International Association for the Fantastic in the Arts is founded.

1983 Mark Helprin's *Winter's Tale* mythologizes the history of New York. Terry Pratchett's *The Colour of Magic* establishes a new milieu for serious humorous fantasy.

1984 Robert Holdstock's *Mythago Wood* establishes a new means of making archetypal imagery manifest. Tom Robbins's *Jitterbug Perfume* introduces modern America to Pan. Margaret Weis and Tracy Hickman's *Dragons of Autumn Twilight* demonstrate that the literary borrowings of Dungeons and Dragons can be recycled into textual form to produce the ultimate in commodified fantasy.

1985 Guy Gavriel King's *The Summer Tree* begins the development of an exceptionally detailed secondary world.

1986 Freda Warrington's *A Blackbird in Silver* demonstrates the potential of secondary world fantasy as a milieu for generic romantic fiction.

1987 John Crowley's *Aegypt* launches an exceptionally extended project in historical fantasy.

1988 Salman Rushdie's *The Satanic Verses* proves that religious fantasy is still capable of exciting murderous intolerance. Terri Windling's contribution to a new *Year's Best Fantasy and Horror* series establishes an invaluable annual summary of the field. Tad Williams launches the Memory, Sorrow, and Thorn trilogy, intended as an ideological corrective to Tolkien.

1989 Lindsay Clarke's *The Chymical Wedding* testifies to the imaginative authority still possessed by the elements of occult fantasy. Tim Powers's *The Stress of Her Regard* introduces modern melodrama to the Romantic Agony.

1990 Robert Jordan's *The Eye of the World* sets out to take commodified fantasy to record lengths. James Morrow's *Only Begotten Daughter* brings a combative skepticism to Christian fantasy. Harcourt Books establish Jane Yolen Books, appointing a new icon of American children's fantasy.

1991 Jostein Gaarder's *Sophie's World* enlarges the didactic ambitions of children's fantasy.

1992 Kim Newman's *Anno Dracula* tests the limits of alternative history. Tim Powers's *Last Call* demonstrates the literary utility of esoteric scholarly fantasy.

1993 Michael Swanwick's *The Iron Dragon's Daughter* explores the functions of modern fantasy literature. Laurel K. Hamilton's *Guilty Pleasures* finds appropriate contemporary employment for a fey princess. Ellen Datlow and Terri Windling's *Snow White, Rose Red* begins a series of anthologies demonstrating the contemporary relevance of transfigured fairy tales.

1994 Michael Bishop's *Brittle Innings* explores the difficulties of becoming truly human. A. S. Byatt's "The Djinn in the Nightingale's Eye" demonstrates the continued literary utility of traditional fabulation. James Morrow's *Towing Jehovah* asks how far God would have to go to prove His irrelevance. Michael Swanwick's "In the Tradition . . ." suggests that fantasy literature resembles an archipelago rather than a continent, even though no book is an island unto itself.

1995 Philip Pullman's *Northern Lights* takes advantage of the booming market in children's fantasy to embark on a bold experiment in theodicy. Gregory Maguire's *The Life and Times of the Wicked Witch of the West* suggests that Oz was not as far removed from Kansas as Dorothy imagined.

1996 Richard Grant's *Tex and Molly in the Afterlife* updates the tradition of posthumous fantasy.

1997 J. K. Rowling's *Harry Potter and the Philosopher's Stone* sparks a worldwide fad of a kind never previously associated with a book.

1998 Patricia McKillip's *Song for the Basilisk* demonstrates that a commodified genre can play host to extraordinary literary ambition. Sophie Masson's *The Lady of the Pool* brings the work of Marie de France up to date.

1999 Jan Siegel's *Prospero's Children* revitalizes Atlantean fantasy. The boom in apocalyptic fantasies reaches its peak, demonstrating the awful extent of contemporary innumeracy.

2000 China Miéville's *Perdido Street Station* provides a cardinal example of the "new weird."

2001 Eoin Colfer's *Artemis Fowl* suggests that Faerie's technological development may have been more rapid than ours. Neil Gaiman's *American Gods* examines the fate of traditional icons in modern America.

2002 Lisa Goldstein's *The Alchemist's Door* reassesses the significance of John Dee's expedition to Rabbi Loew's Prague.

2003 K. J. Bishop's *The Etched City* offers a new iconic image of decadent civilization. Robin McKinley's *Sunshine* examines the social aftermath of the Voodoo Wars. Catherine Webb's *Waywalkers* considers the education of the Son of Time.

2004 Elizabeth Hand's *Mortal Love* explores the work of the Muse during the last two centuries. Gene Wolfe's *The Knight* and *The Wizard* reassess the crucial roles of modern heroic fantasy. Susannah Clarke's *Jonathan Strange and Mr Norrell* tracks a heroic attempt to reintroduce magic into 19th-century England for the benefit of generations to come.

Introduction

ONCE UPON A TIME

Fantasy is the faculty by which simulacra of sensible objects can be reproduced in the mind: the process of imagination. What we generally mean when we speak of "a fantasy" in psychological terms is, however, derived from an exclusive rather than an inclusive definition of the term. The difference between mental images of objects and the objects themselves is dramatically emphasized by the fact that mental images can be formulated for which no actual equivalents exist; it is these images that first spring to mind in association with the idea of fantasy, because they represent fantasy at its purest.

For this reason, Geoffrey Chaucer, the first writer known to us who worked in a language recognizably akin to modern English, uses the word *fantasye* to refer to strange and bizarre notions that have no basis in everyday experience, and this is the sense in which it is usually used today when one speaks of "fantasy literature." Nor is the word a mere description in Chaucer's usage; it has pejorative implications. Any dalliance with "fantasye" in the Chaucerian sense tends to be regarded as self-indulgent folly, whether it is a purely psychological phenomenon (a fanciful aspect of "daydreaming") or a literary one.

This attitude is peculiar, if not paradoxical. There is no thought without fantasy, and the faculty of fantasizing may well be the evolutionary raison d'être of consciousness—and yet, the notion of "fantasy" comes ready-tainted with implications of unworthiness, of a failure of some alleged duty of the human mind to concentrate on the realities of existence. It is partly for this reason that the notion of "fantasy" as a literary genre is so recent. Before 1969, the description "fantasy," with respect to literary works, was usually only applied to a variety of *children*'s fiction, the implication being that the folly of fantasizing was something that adults ought put away with other childish things.

The paradoxicality of common attitudes to fantasy is powerfully reflected in the idea of fantasy literature. Although it is the most recent genre of literature to acquire a marketing label, it is also the most ancient genre that is readily identifiable. Storytelling is much older than literature—although, by definition, it has no history other than its literary history—and the overwhelming majority of the stories that became visible to history once writing had been invented were fantasies in the Chaucerian sense: strange and supernatural. Anthropological observations suggest that all human cultures are alike in this respect. The stories that cultures possess before acquiring the faculty of writing, and the stories that provide the foundations of literary culture when they do acquire it, are almost all fantastic.

Before anthropologists had refined their scientific stance, they often took the inference that the fantastic aspects of preliterate culture implied that preliterate cultures were in some sense "childish" or "primitive," having not yet evolved to a state of mental maturity—but those early anthropologists were contemporaries of many other men who believed that "Enlightenment" would surely banish "superstition" from the world and that there would be no such thing in the future (which is to say, our present) as false belief, let alone fantasy literature. We know better now.

The prehistory of stories retains a good deal of its mystery, but we can now understand the situation of stories in preliterate societies. We understand that stories seem to exist in oral cultures independently of their tellers; their tellers inevitably seem to be "passing them on," or "handing them down." We understand that many tellers must have routinely modified the stories they told and that some must occasionally have made up new ones—but that when they did, they posed as mere transmitters, surrendering all their "authority" to the story itself, which had to take on an independent existence if it was to survive within the culture from day to day, let alone from generation to generation.

One corollary of the logic of this situation is that almost all of a preliterate culture's stories would be heard for the first time in childhood; their acquisition would be part and parcel of the process of growing up. That is one reason why the kinds of story preserved and maintained by oral transmission are commonly seen as "children's stories." Another corollary is that all of a preliterate culture's stories are set in the past. Their authority and value is often intricately bound up with their seeming antiquity; that is, the apparent guarantee of their independence and power.

The "past" of a preliterate culture is not, however, the past of history; by definition, preliterary cultures have no history. The "past" in which a preliterate culture's stories are set is a construction of myth and legend: a past that was different in kind and quality from the present. It is, invariably, a magical past, which imagines the world in the process of creation and ordering—in a time when its present conformation was still in the process of being worked out. Only a minority of a preliterate culture's stories are explicitly concerned with processes of creation and ordering, but even those that are not partake of the processes of origination and organization.

It is intrinsic to the nature of preliterate storytelling, therefore, that stories should be set in a world that is not the everyday world of the present day but in a world of myth and magic: the world of "once upon a time." Even stories in which no magic is worked and nothing supernatural occurs must, if the illusion of antiquity is to be retained, have such possibilities as a context. We understand all this partly because we can still observe something similar, insofar as a vestigial oral culture survives alongside our literary culture.

The traditional tales we still possess—and that "everybody knows"—include a considerable number that are among the oldest ever to be written down and may well have the most extended prehistories. These are the deepest roots of modern fantasy literature. Now, as always, the tales are frequently altered in the retelling—"transfigured," as the analytical language of this dictionary has it—but the process and perception of transfiguration depends on the notion of there being something underneath that is definitive, ancient, and eternal: something that is endlessly "recycled" without ever being fundamentally transformed.

We can also observe the processes of recycling and transfiguration in what remains to us of writing, whose early preservation depended on ceaseless copying. We can see that certain items of writing were preserved as faithfully as possible because they were considered sacred and unalterable (although that did not prevent variant versions of scriptures being generated). We can also see that items treated with less reverence—or a different kind of reverence—were routinely modified and often expanded by many of the copyists through whose hands they passed. The modifications made to some of the early classics of fantasy literature produced for amusement—the chivalric romance of *Amadis of Gaul,* for instance, as it migrated from Portuguese into Spanish, French, and English—were truly prodigious; extant versions are sometimes the result of inordinately complex serial collaborations.

The complex combination of the processes of recycling and transfiguration gives rise to confused perceptions. The fact that fantasy literature continues to recycle stories that have been told for countless generations makes it seem repetitive and unoriginal as well as unrealistic—but it is the implication of "deep-rootedness" that gives fantasy literature its unique qualities and utilities, both culturally and psychologically. The fact that fantasy literature deals with the fictitious past of "once upon a time" makes it seem quaint and old-fashioned by comparison with stories that deal with the experienced world or the past of history—but our perceptions of who and what we are, and ought to be attempting to become, owe at least as much to our notions of that fictitious past as to our theories regarding the actual one.

In the days when anthropologists thought that preliterate cultures were "primitive," some of the people who thought that Enlightenment would exterminate Chaucerian "fantasye" in all its forms and manifestations also thought that traditional notions of "once upon a time" would be replaced by modern equivalents—that the imaginary past of myth and magic would be replaced by the "real" past of history, archaeology, paleontology, and geology. The notion also emerged, albeit somewhat belatedly, that writers might, and perhaps ought to, manufacture a new kind of Chaucerian fantasye, one that would draw its wonders from hypothetical futures and alien worlds rather than imaginary pasts. The proposal was therefore put about that the old kinds of fantasy literature might be replaceable by a new and distinctively modern kind: "science fiction."

This is significant, because one of the reasons why "fantasy" took so long to appear as a commercial label was that the market space it might have occupied had already been colonized by something that seemed more "advanced." We can now see easily enough that this was an illusion, although it is understandable that many early observers of science fiction thought that the development of that genre was the sensible way to free fantasy literature from its dependence on the assumption of a mythical past—the ideative prison of "once upon a time." The history of modern fantasy literature demonstrates, however, that the themes and mannerisms of naturalistic fiction (including historical fiction) and science fiction were not the only escape routes that storytellers could follow in wriggling free of the restraints of the mythical past.

Modern fantasy literature has evolved numerous strategies that allow fantasy literature to deal with the historical rather than the mythical past, and the present (or future) rather than any kind of past. In the process, writers who have expanded the scope and ambition of fantasy literature have continued to recycle as well as transfigure the material they inherited from literary prehistory. Their extensive adventures in fabulation and metafiction have celebrated the continuation of recycling and transfiguration as well as pointed out that neither naturalistic fiction nor science fiction ever really escaped the necessity of recycling and transfiguring old stories. These same adventures also serve to remind us that the distinction between the mythical and historical pasts has never been clear and that much of what passes for history is, in fact, merely a concatenation of legends that we have chosen, for one reason or another, to believe.

FANTASY VERSUS THE FANTASTIC

"Fantasy" became firmly established as the label for a popular commercial genre of adult fiction in the 1970s. As with the two other popular genres whose contents were also nonmimetic—horror fiction and science fiction (sf)—the creation of the label involved the invention of a generic history: a myth of creation and organization, complete with legendary heroes. Fantasy's two rival genre labels—both of which represent subgenres of the broader field—tend to base their claims to modern relevance on myths of relatively recent creation; the mythical past of horror fiction situates the origins of the definable genre in the gothic novels of the late 18th century, while the mythical past of sf places the development of its recognizable literary method in the 19th century.

Some definers of genre fantasy have adopted a similar course; while admitting that genre fantasy takes its definitive themes and images from myth, legend, and folklore—raw materials older than literature itself—they nevertheless insist that "fantasy literature" is something relatively new that needs to be distinguished from the literature of earlier eras despite the many elements they have in common. The reasons for this are complex, but it is primarily an attempt to avoid stigmatization; the desire to distinguish from "folktales" and "children's fantasy" a "fantasy literature" fit for the consumption of modern adults is natural enough, although attempts to implement it in this way generate further complications.

The strategy that represents "fantasy literature" as something relatively new is summarized and reinforced by John Clute in *The Encyclopedia of Fantasy* (1997, coedited with John Grant), which is the closest thing to a definitive text the genre currently has. The argument alleges that we should not speak of "fantasy literature" as having existed before the Age of Enlightenment, because "fantasy literature" is an essentially contradictory notion, formed in dialectical opposition to the notion of "realistic (or naturalistic) literature." Before the Enlightenment, there was allegedly no such manifest opposition, because the realistic and fantastic elements of literature coexisted harmoniously, free of any apparent tension or enmity. "The fantastic," in this view, could not qualify as a genre, because it was not significantly separate or distinct from other raw materials of story making.

Critics employing this argument sometimes find it convenient to separate "fantasy" and "the fantastic" in a contemporary context as well as a historical one, because it helps them to identify contemporary literary forms that they wish to save from the pejorative connotations routinely attached to the notion of "fantasy," or at least to give diplomatic recognition to the fact that many writers and other critics wish to make such saving moves. Thus, Brian Attebery begins his study of *Strategies of Fantasy* (1992)—which is one of the leading contenders in an ongoing struggle to present a coherent theory of the genre—by contrasting "fantasy as genre" (which he sees as an essentially modern phenomenon) with both "fantasy as formula" (an essentially commercial phenomenon) and the much more generalized "fantasy as mode"—which, he asserts, still extends into "the vast, unformed realm of the fantastic."

The Clute/Attebery strategy must, however, be contrasted with the strategy, adopted in showcase anthologies, by which Lin Carter sought to describe and identify the genre of "adult fantasy" in the 1970s, a strategy that was tacitly adopted by such reference books as Neil Barron's guide to *Fantasy Literature* (1990). These texts and others like them extend the history of modern fantasy literature all the way back to Homer, in a more or less unbroken evolutionary chain.

This dictionary will, inevitably, have to document both these strategies and the terminologies spun off therefrom, but it will also have to choose between them in order to permit its own organization. Readers of the chronology will already have noted that it favors the Carter/Barron strategy; it does so on the grounds that the Clute/Attebery strategy creates more confusion than it dispels.

Any attempt to introduce a crucial category distinction between a noun and its adjectival form is probably doomed to founder on the rock of linguistic necessity, but the attempted differentiation of "fantasy" from "the fantastic" is further compromised by other special meanings that critics have attached to the term "fantastic"—particularly those derived from French deployments of *fantastique*. Even if this were not the case, the improvisation of a historical divide between modern fantasy literature and earlier manifestations of the materials that it recycles and transfigures is a brutal artifice. To claim that there was no manifest opposition between the real and the imaginary before the 18th century is to imply far too much; it is true that the Enlightenment refined ideas about the definition and determination of "reality," but it is certainly not true that previous storytellers were unaware of any contrast or tension between the naturalistic and supernatural elements of their stories.

Critics who do not accept the distinction between "fantasy" and "the fantastic" take it for granted that the history of "fantasy literature" should begin with the origins of writing. A strong case can be made for this assertion by considering the formation of the reputation of the first significant author of fantasy literature thus defined, Homer. Homer is probably a fantasy himself, a legendary hero invented by the preservers of the *Iliad* and the *Odyssey;* what is important about those two works, however, is precisely the fact that their preservers thought it necessary to invent an individual author for them, irrespective of whether they actually had one. Whether he existed or not, the *idea* of Homer was so powerful that no less than seven Greek cities claimed the privilege of being his birthplace. According to those who sang his praises, he was unlike all those who had gone before him, in being no mere transmitter of independent stories but a literary genius—*the* literary genius, in an era and culture that had as yet produced no other.

The myth of Homer illustrates the fact that writing immediately called into being the notion of *the writer*. Homer was an *originator,* not in the sense that he was the inventor of the characters and events he wrote about, let alone their metaphysical context, but in the senses that he was a transfigurer first and a recycler second, and that his transfiguration enjoyed a special status. Homer the narrator does not represent himself in this way; when he calls upon the unnamed Muse, it is not for inventive inspiration but for the gift of memory so that he might correctly remember the lines he must sing. Those who formulated his myth, however, also suggested that he was blind, subtly implying that he did not know his own nature. To those who fabricated his legend, Homer was an orderer and formulator in his own right; he was also an archetypal model for others to imitate, the very definition of a *literateur.*

There is no doubt that Homer was a fantasist, in every sense of the word. Whether or not he or his inventors believed in the real existence of the gods they intruded into his canonical accounts of the fall of Troy or of the monsters encountered by Odysseus, they knew perfectly well that there was a difference between the supernatural aspects of the stories and the naturalistic ones. They understood such concepts as symbolism and metaphor, because they knew—how could they possibly not?—that the mind can produce images as well as reproduce them, imagine things that have no actual existence as well as things that do. They knew, even though they had as yet no history, that the mythical past was indeed mythical. They knew, even though they had as yet no naturalistic fiction with which to contrast them, that the *Iliad* and the *Odyssey* were works of fantasy literature.

The most important thing to understand about the nature of fantasy—in its literary forms as in its psychological ones—in the view adopted by this dictionary is that its definition has nothing at all to do with belief. To believe in miracles—or magic, ghosts, or fairies—is not to transfer such entities from the category of Chaucerian fantasye into that of reality; they still remain outside the range of ordinary events and actions, and beyond the scope of everyday causes and effects. Belief does not affect the boundary between the natural and the supernatural, nor does the slight fuzziness of that boundary confuse the pattern of discrimination unduly. Chaucerian fantasyes that people believe in are still strange and bizarre, and recognizably so; once this is admitted, it is easy to see that the reach of Chaucerian fantasye extends far beyond the limits of literature, into scholarly writing and social action. It is necessary to understand, if the pattern of fantasy literature's evolution is to be properly understood, that there are scholarly fantasies and lifestyle fantasies as well as literary fantasies.

The extent to which storytellers prior to the 18th century may or may not have believed in magic, divination, fairies, witches, ghosts, legendary heroes, or mythical gods is not a significant factor in the decision as to whether to classify stories about such ideas and individuals as fantasy. Prior to the 18th century, supernatural elements were much more likely to be mingled with naturalistic ones in works of literature, but that does not mean that meaningful distinctions could not then be made as to which were which, and as to what narrative functions the supernatural elements were supposed to perform. It is for these reasons that the descriptions contained in this dictionary will accept that fantasy literature is as old as literature itself and that its elements of fantasy are much older. This assumption should assist the task of explaining how the components of modern fantasy literature evolved and why they have come into the various configurations evident within and without the commercial genre.

THE THEORY OF FANTASY LITERATURE

The pioneer of modern aesthetic philosophy, Alexander Baumgarten (1714–62), argued that the creation of a literary work is a process of "secondary creation" analogous to the primary process by which the world was made. He also argued that the best kind of secondary creation is rigorously mimetic, restricted to the faithful and artful reproduction of the world of primary creation, and that any attempt to create "heterocosmically" is necessarily inferior.

It was natural that Baumgarten should believe this, because he was a follower of Gottfried Leibniz (1646–1716), whose assertion that God's creation had produced the best of all possible worlds had not yet been shamed by the mockery of Voltaire's *Candide*. It is not so obvious why other literary creators and critics—especially those who were later to side with Voltaire in regard to the merits of Leibnizian optimism—should have agreed with Baumgarten, but the majority was on his side in 1760 and remained there for the next two centuries and more.

Baumgarten's view contrasts sharply with the contemporary opinion of Edmund Burke, whose *Philosophical Enquiry into the Origin of Our Ideas of the Sublime and Beautiful* (1757) argues that the imagination requires exercise just as the body requires physical exercise if the mind is to develop in a healthy manner, capable of sustaining and benefiting from the full range of the emotions. Although Burke's ideas paved the way for the development of Romanticism and excused gothic indulgence in terror and horror, it was Baumgarten's view that had the greater support—with the result that anyone seeking to celebrate "heterocosmic" creativity had to begin by defending it, building defensive walls capable of withstanding an ideative siege. The assertiveness of Burke's championship of imaginative ambition was rarely replicated, let alone carried forward; since the publication of the *Philosophical Enquiry,* discussion of fantasy literature has been almost entirely a matter of resistance to disdain rather than the celebration of innovation.

Baumgarten's *Aesthetika* was published—not entirely coincidentally—when the novel was making great strides toward its establishment as the dominant form of literary endeavor. Although it was still reckoned less meritorious than poetry throughout the 19th century, the novel's potential seemed as great as its popularity, and the techniques of narrative realism that novelists developed to facilitate their work came to seem wondrously powerful. The invention of printing had standardized the shapes of whole words, thus opening up the potential for people to read "by eye" rather than "by ear"—which is to say, to absorb the meaning of a word or phrase directly rather than by translating it into a set of phonemes. Poetry is essentially geared to reading by ear, making use as it does of such devices as rhyme, scansion, and alliteration; all poetry is, in effect, designed to be read "aloud," even if the words are only sounded within the privacy of the reader's mind. Prose, on the other hand, can be read without figuratively moving one's lips; a page of prose can be scanned, and its meaning taken up, far more economically than a page of verse.

The possibility of reading by eye rather than by ear facilitated the development of the devices of narrative realism: the prose writer's ability to draw the reader "into" a story, so that it becomes something more like a lived experience than an observed artifact. Inevitably, the education of readers in this kind of surrogate experience—and the education of writers in the skills of its production—initially concentrated on simulation and mimesis. The first task and first test of the techniques of novel writing were bound to be that of facilitating the reader's illusion that the world within the texts was *the* world, because that was the only way that the reader could feel entirely at home there, as fully immersed as was possible.

It was, however, realized almost immediately that the techniques facilitating this immersion, and the conviction they carried, could be used satirically. Jonathan Swift's account of Lemuel Gulliver's travels mimicked the form of novelistic traveler's tales that had already taken full advantage of the power of incidental detail, a seemingly candid first-person narrative voice and the seemingly accurate mapping of time and space within the story, but it used such devices teasingly and flippantly. As soon as the novel form had been invented, the potential was there for the creation of "immersive fantasies"—but the business of educating readers to experience exotic worlds within texts with the same degree of conviction, and the same sense of "being at home," as could be obtained from naturalistic narratives was never going to be easy. The history of fantasy literature is, to a large extent, the history of that educative process; the recent emergence of a commercial genre of fantasy is the proof of its success. In the interim, however, it was inevitable that a defensive frame of mind would continue to dominate writing about fantasy literature.

Theorists who prefer to think of fantasy literature as a contradictory product of the Enlightenment inevitably seek its origins in the Romantic movement, which became the Enlightenment's loyal opposition. Some members of that movement did indeed make great strides in the rehabilitation of traditional fantasy materials and the adoption into contemporary literature of real and imitation folktales, and it was their justifications for so doing that laid the apologetic foundations of modern fantasy theory. Because they were couched so defensively, however, the ideas the Romantics formulated showed no conspicuous evolution for a long time. The 18th-century opinions of Johann Musäus, Madame d'Aulnoy, Charles Perrault, Antoine Galland, Voltaire, Nathan Drake, and Samuel Taylor Coleridge regarding the utility and potential of literary fantasy were not much extended by the 19th-century and early 20th-century theorists who came after them, whose English representatives included Edward Bulwer-Lytton, Charles Dickens, Oscar Wilde, Arthur Machen, and G. K. Chesterton. Even critics who refused to consider fantasy literature as a subdivision of children's literature were forced to begin their work by arguing long and fiercely against opponents who insisted that it was.

The definers of modern "adult fantasy" had to start from that position; the fundamental document of modern fantasy theory originated in 1938 as a lecture, then entitled "On Fairy Tales," given by J. R. R. Tolkien, who in it asserted his conviction that fairy tales—and the whole literary field of which they had become archetypal—were far too useful in psychological terms to be considered unfit for adults. The essay "On Fairy-stories" that Tolkien developed from his lecture proposed that fantasies modeled on fairy stories performed three fundamental and vital psychological functions: recovery, escape, and consolation.

The first of these three terms, in Tolkien's usage, proposes that reality cannot be clearly seen or fully appreciated without an imaginative sidestep that extracts the observer from imprisonment therein and that standpoints located in imaginary worlds allow readers to recover a proper sense of perspective. The second proposes that the pejorative connotations frequently attached to the notion of "escapism" are unwarranted and that temporary escapes from the burden of maintaining one's public image and conduct are entirely healthy, by no means symptomatic of cowardice or laziness; well-constructed fantasies, Tolkien suggests, provide ideal places of refuge for the stressed imagination. The third proposes that there is valuable moral rearmament to be obtained from the climactic "eucatastrophes" that typically set things right in fantasy stories.

It is partly because Tolkien practiced what he preached in his essay that the modern commercial genre of fantasy came into being when it did and in the format that became typical of it. Tolkien was its Homer, *The Lord of the Rings* its *Iliad* and *Odyssey*. When the genre's most conspicuous advocate in the commercial publishing arena, Lin Carter, attempted to describe and delimit the field, he called his first book on the subject *Tolkien: A Look behind* The Lord of the Rings (1969); *Imaginary Worlds: The Art of Fantasy* (1973) was a sequel and extrapolation.

The territory thus claimed and staked out was swiftly colonized by academic writers; such surveys as Colin Manlove's *Modern Fantasy* (1975), Eric S. Rabkin's *The Fantastic in Literature* (1976), Roger C. Schlobin's *The Literature of Fantasy* (1979), and Marshall B. Tymn, Kenneth J. Zahorski, and Robert H. Boyer's *Fantasy Literature* (1979) supplemented Carter's mapping, with appropriate supportive arguments, while such texts as L. Sprague de Camp's *Literary Swordsmen and Sorcerers* (1976), Marion Lochhead's *The Renaissance of Wonder in Children's Literature* (1977), Roger Sale's *Fairy Tales and After* (1978), Diana Waggoner's *The Hills of Faraway: A Guide to Fantasy* (1978), and Stephen Prickett's *Victorian Fantasy* (1979) retraced and reemphasized the genre's connections with earlier forms of popular fiction. Within a decade, the commercial genre was up and running and its history (mythical as well as actual) had been thoroughly mapped out, summarized in a five-volume *Survey of Modern Fantasy Literature* (1983), compiled by Keith Neilson on behalf of Frank Magill's Salem Press. It was then that theoreticians began the serious work of contesting and refining definitions, and trying to figure out where the potential limits of the genre might and ought to lie.

The astonishing rapidity with which the idea of the new genre asserted itself, in both the marketplace and the academy, seemed akin to a dam burst. When John Clute planned his *Encyclopedia of Fantasy* in the mid-1990s, he envisaged it as a smaller and more tightly focused volume than the recently updated *The Encyclopedia of Science Fiction;* it ended up as a sprawling leviathan almost twice as large as originally intended. The immense difficulty Clute and Grant had in setting boundaries to the project and in discovering an adequate descriptive terminology for comparative and taxonomic purposes provides a graphic illustration of the manner in which the historical and critical writings of the 1970s had created more problems than they had solved. The *Encyclopedia* writers' heroic attempts to solve the problems in question complicated the situation even farther, as well as clarifying some of the essential issues.

It would have been possible, in constructing this dictionary, simply to reproduce and attempt to use the terminology coined and deployed in the Clute/Grant *Encyclopedia,* but that would imply the existence of a consensus that has not yet been solidified and acceptance of several other judgments that are as manifestly dubious as the judgment that it makes sense to draw a clear distinction between "fantasy" and "the fantastic." For this reason, many of the terms used in the *Encyclopedia,* although defined here, are left unused in discussion of authors and their works, while other terms that now seem more useful have been drafted from other sources. It would be foolishly optimistic to hope that this volume can possibly provide the last set of words on the subject, but it is worth insisting that progress is being made and that this dictionary will ideally be part of it.

READING FANTASY LITERATURE

Many writers, readers, and critics still express a preference as strong as Baumgarten's for naturalistic novels, not on the grounds that the experienced world is the best of all possible worlds, but on the grounds that it is, after all, the one in which we are condemned to exist, about the transactions and possibilities whose we need to be as fully aware as possible. The illusion that the characters in novels might be actual people cultivates the further illusion that by standing in their shoes—thus getting to know them far more intimately and completely than it is possible to know any actual person—readers are actually enhancing their understanding of the world of experience, in a way that identification with characters involved in strange and bizarre encounters and adventures never could.

There may be some truth in the first stage of this argument, although it is probably dangerous to assume that the people who actually surround us can be understood as if they were literary characters. There is, however, none in the second; there is not the slightest reason why we cannot learn just as much from hypothetical encounters and adventures of various improbable and impossible kinds as from thoroughly mundane ones. Even so, most fantasy novels begin naturalistically, adopting the pretense that the worlds they contain are simulations of some aspect of the reader's experienced world, albeit one that is carefully distanced geographically, and perhaps historically. In the most discreet variety of fantasy literature, a singular element of fantasy is introduced into this seemingly mimetic context so that its disturbing effect can be observed and measured.

This kind of exercise is what Farah Mendlesohn calls an "intrusive fantasy." The modus operandi is convenient in several ways; most importantly, it allows readers to orientate themselves quickly and easily within the text. It is easier for author and reader to establish and maintain comfortable communication if they are working from a set of common assumptions, and it is useful to both if the reader can be snugly accommodated within the text before strange and bizarre things start to happen.

In traditional intrusive fantasies, the intrusions usually arise as relics of the mythical past, and the tacit assumption that such relics might exist serves as a reminder that the present state of worldly affairs is assumed by traditional fantasy to be the result of a long process of erosion that has removed supernatural and magical aspects from contemporary normality. In *The Encyclopedia of Fantasy*, Clute calls this process "thinning," and he finds an acute consciousness of it very widely distributed in modern fantasy.

This representation of the primary world as a product of long-term magical erosion contrasts sharply with the representation of the primary world as the product of progress, one in which a wealth of knowledge and technological apparatus has been accumulated. This is the principal reason why science fiction and fantasy seem to many observers to be contradictory categories, despite the fact that the stories they tell are often formulated in exactly the same way; the intrusive fantasies of sf draw their intrusions from the present rather than the past, as irruptions from alien worlds or as new discoveries made by inventive scientists. This makes traditional intrusive fantasies seem rather old-fashioned to the modern eye, and it is a significant factor in the evolutionary process that has made other fundamental categories of fantasy more fashionable.

The most obvious alternative to the narrative pattern in which our world is disturbed by a fantastic intrusion is the pattern in which the reader is led away from the mimetic world-within-the-text into a "secondary" world, either by undertaking a journey into terra incognita or by passing through some kind of portal, akin to the Gates of Ivory and Horn that were once alleged to admit sleepers into the world of dreams. This kind of fantasy is often known as "portal fantasy"; under that label, it makes up a second major category of Mendlesohn's classification of fantasy stories. The third principal category of that classification, which Mendlesohn calls "immersive fantasies," consists of novels that adopt the much more difficult task of substituting an entire fantasy world for the simulacrum of the real world that readers usually expect to discover when they embark upon the task of immersing themselves in a novel.

This is, in a sense, the ultimate challenge for the writer, the reader, and the techniques of narrative realism: to allow the reader to move directly into a wholehearted heterocosmic creation, without warning or guidance, and to establish facilities that will enable the reader to feel quite at home there in spite of its strangeness. This seems, and is, a difficult thing to accomplish—and yet, if we forget novels for a moment and return to an earlier phase of literary evolution, there was a time when almost all fantasy fiction was "immersive" in Mendlesohn's sense, although it did not seek to immerse the reader in the fashion typical of novels. Oral narratives and recorded stories that resemble folktales in the manner of their narration are necessarily represented as having taken place "once upon a time," in milieux that are unlike the experienced world in various fundamental ways.

There is, in consequence, a sense in which the evolution of modern fantasy literature toward a renaissance of "immersive fantasy"—which is to say, the evolution of the fantasy novel—has been a process of recovery: accommodating the magical and mythical materials of folklore to the novel form. This was not a simple process, and its complications need to be appreciated if the history and nature of fantasy literature are to be understood. It is important to observe that the process does not end with recovery. Once accommodated within the novel form, the materials of folkloristic fantasy became far more flexible and imaginatively powerful than they had ever been in their "natural habitat"; this flexibility and power has already changed the nature of fantasy literature dramatically, and it will determine its future prospects.

The literary art of designing mimetic simulacra is dependent on the fact that a text, unlike a painting, which can be seen as a whole, is the product of a linear string of information. The words making up a literary text build an image *gradually* in the minds and memories of its readers. The literary image has to be *assembled* in such a way that readers can be eased into its details and complexities, while being provided with sufficient narrative momentum to motivate them to follow the informative thread to its terminus.

This process of assembly is greatly assisted in mimetic fiction by the reader's awareness that the partial picture offered by the informational string can be filled out—however vaguely—from stocks of knowledge relating to the actual world. As soon as it is indicated to the reader that the world within the text is a secondary world rather than a simulacrum of the primary one, however, the utility of those preexistent stocks becomes uncertain and problematic. The burden of informing the reader about the nature, population, and history of a secondary world is likely to be considerable, unless shortcuts can be devised. The notion of "once upon a time" is one such shortcut.

The assumption that there was a mythical past beyond the reach of memory, when magic worked, miracles occurred, supernatural beings coexisted and interacted with humankind, and animals had the power of speech, forms the basis for a second store of "knowledge" that coexists with the ones people build up concerning the actual world. One of the reasons why it seems to belong to childhood is that people generally master this alternative stock of knowledge more rapidly than they can master stocks of knowledge about the actual world, because it is as simple as it is fanciful. It is also limited and relatively changeless—unlike the actual world, which is so complicated and subject to such sweeping changes that stocks of knowledge relating to it are often obsolete as soon as they are formed.

As Michel Butor has pointed out, this is the main reason why folktales and their clones are uniquely *useful* as stories told to children by adults. Because a child's experience of the primary world differs so drastically from an adult's, it is difficult for parents and their offspring to draw upon common stocks of knowledge in constructing simulacra of that world; the simplified secondary world of folktales is much easier to grasp, and it provides common ground in which adults can meet with children almost as equals, each knowing the same things about the world within the story—especially if the story seems to have an existence of its own independent of any particular teller or hearer.

Since the advent of the novel, writers have developed a complex armory of transferable narrative techniques, by means of which literary mimesis can be cultivated—most obviously, the development of the "third person limited" viewpoint. This device is uniquely conducive to the facilitation of a reader's intimate identification with the viewpoint character—a degree of intimacy impossible in any medium other than text read "by eye." Readers are not passive participants in the process of mimetic simulation; the most sophisticated among them have become experts in picking up the cues that writers distribute within their texts, just as writers have become experts in crafting and placing those cues. As literary history has unfolded, therefore, mature readers have become increasingly sensitive to the cultivation of resemblance; as the skills of mimetic reading have been honed and mimetic writing has become more demanding of those skills, many skilled readers have become specialists in that kind of collaboration. To them, the devices of folktales—the assumptions wrapped up in the phrase "once upon a time"—seem implicitly primitive, no matter how ingenious they may be in serving their own purposes.

Given that observers of literary history have to be highly skilled readers, it is only natural that they consider the triumphant advances of novelistic technique to be literature's principal progressive component. From this standpoint, heterocosmic modifications may be easily seen as flaws. Although the main trend in painting during the last two centuries has been opposite in its direction—moving away from the cultivation of accurate resemblance toward impressionism, expressionism, abstraction, and surrealism—there have been relatively few literary critics who have been prepared to tolerate, let alone laud, the artistry of heterocosmic secondary creation. It has seemed to many observers that there is a fundamental contradiction and incompatibility between the novelistic devices of narrative realism and the pretense of "once upon a time."

Heterocosmic creators, understandably, tend to see things differently. They do not see the nonmimetic elements of their work as flaws; on the contrary, they consider that it is the heterocosmic aspects of their creativity that demonstrate the ingenuity and originality of their work. No matter how defiantly they take this stance, though, heterocosmic creators must acknowledge that the problems involved in accommodating readers comfortably within their fictitious worlds are far more awkward than the problems faced by creators of literary simulacra, and that this awkwardness may easily infect the fictional worlds themselves. From the viewpoint of heterocosmic creators, the assumptions bundled up in the "once upon a time" device are as inconveniently limiting as the constraints of rigorous mimesis; they represent something to be escaped, challenged, or transfigured—but that requires sacrificing the utility of the device and discovering other ways by which readers might be quickly and comfortably accommodated within secondary worlds.

A heterocosmic creator cannot organize the informational thread of a text in the same way as can the creator of simulacra. The reader's attention must be drawn to similarities *and differences* between the world within the text and the primary world. The heterocosmic creator must not only work hard to establish the relevance of *some* aspects of the readers' preexistent stocks of knowledge into the text, but must work at least as hard to ensure that certain other aspects are definitively excluded. The heterocosmic creator must separate into two distinct parts the readers' ready-made understanding of the way a world might work and must then compensate for the part ruled irrelevant by supplying a new understanding to take its place. Even in its simplest variants, this process requires considerable skill and versatility on the part of the writer; it also requires considerable skill and versatility—as well as an uncommon generosity—on the part of the reader.

The skills that writers and readers must bring to the navigation of complex heterocosmic constructions are different in kind, as well as degree, from those required in the navigation of mimetic texts. Instead of requiring to be persuaded that the heterocosmic construction is as perfect a simulacrum of the primary world as can reasonably be contrived, readers of nonmimetic fiction require to be persuaded that a world within a text is plausible and interesting *in spite of* its marked differences from the primary world: differences that might pertain, as a set, uniquely to the world within a particular text. This kind of reading requires not only special skills but a special kind of willingness to be persuaded. Samuel Taylor Coleridge called it "the willing suspension of disbelief," while J. R. R. Tolkien preferred to represent it as a kind of "secondary belief" uniquely appropriate to secondary worlds—but Tolkien also called it "enchantment," and some other theorists have gone even farther than that in representing it as an altered state of consciousness.

As with the skills involved in reading mimetic fiction, there has been a gradual evolution during the last two centuries in the skills required in reading heterocosmic constructions. Many individual readers have extended both ranges of skills, and a few have doubtless achieved equal expertise in both; they are not, after all, mutually exclusive opposites. The construction of both mimetic and heterocosmic creations has to proceed from the same common ground: the writer's and reader's shared understanding of the primary world. The differences between them are matters of replication on the one hand and variation on the other—but variation can occur in different ways and at different rates; it may involve supplementation, reduction, transfiguration, hybridization, chimerization, and the careful management of ambiguity, or any admixture thereof.

These variations are relatively easy to manage in intrusive fantasies; the stocks of knowledge that the writer and reader share can be mobilized in their entirety and modified in an orderly linear fashion. The predominance of horror stories and farcical comedies within this category is a corollary of the nature of intrusive fantasy. As Mendlesohn observes, a supernatural intrusion is bound to function within a simulacrum of the primary world as a "bringer of chaos": it is disturbing by definition, and disturbance has two typical forms, generating either anxiety or humor, or some combination of the two. The close relationship between horror and comedy is, of course, very evident in the evolution of the horror fiction genre, as well as the evolution of "black comedy."

Intrusive fantasy also has the advantage of a seemingly "natural" story arc. The solution to the problem posed by a bringer of chaos is self-evident: order must be restored. The seeming naturalness of this story arc is, however, dependent on the assumption that "normality" is a privileged state, whose recovery is imperative. In a mimetic text, this seems to be a viable contention, because the simulacrum of the primary world not only reflects but supports the prescriptive definition of social order; it relies upon the "common sense" of that order to engage and consummate its fundamental marriage of minds. In a heterocosmic construction, that foundation becomes uncertain and negotiable. An intrusive fantasy must, by definition, begin its story in a simulacrum of the primary world, but the moment the intrusive element appears, the possibility emerges that the simulacrum might be permanently transformed into something else. Indeed, it is arguable that from the moment the intrusive element appears, the simulacrum has already been transformed—and that normality cannot possibly be restored to it, because the possibility of further intrusions can no longer be ruled out. The history of intrusive fantasy clearly exhibits a growing awareness of this argument and its consequences.

Like intrusive fantasies, portal fantasies also begin by cultivating simulacra of the primary world, but their protagonists often do not remain in those simulacra for very long. Instead of fantastic elements merely intruding upon their home territory, the protagonists of portal fantasies are physically removed to unfamiliar ground, into a secondary world. The great advantage of the portal fantasy method, so far as writers and readers are concerned, is that readers can be guided from one world to the other in a conveniently linear fashion. The reader enters the secondary world in the intimate company of a protagonist to whom it is equally unfamiliar; as the character learns about the secondary world, the reader learns too, sharing the character's astonishment, inquisitiveness, and gradually increasing ability to feel at home.

As with intrusive fantasies, the seemingly "natural" story arc of a portal fantasy is a normalizing one; dream fantasies can have no other ending, because every sleeper eventually wakes. The same problems apply, however; once Gulliver has been to the land of the Houyhnhnms, or Dorothy to Oz, England and Kansas can never be the same again. There is, moreover, a sense in which every individual portal implies an infinite array of potentially accessible secondary worlds, all of them "beside" our own—sideways being a much more expansive direction than the single temporal thread that connects the present to the past. The utility of "once upon a time" as a facilitating device hinged on the fact that it was indeed *once*—that there was only a single mythical past, which could be securely known in its basics if not its details. Modern intrusive fantasies began by bringing most of their intrusions out of that mythical past, but they eventually moved on to other sources. Modern portal fantasies were always far more versatile, as the examples of Gulliver and Lewis Carroll's Alice readily exemplify.

From the viewpoint of a reader, a book is itself a kind of portal, in a metaphorical sense extravagantly literalized in such flamboyant works as Michael Ende's *The Neverending Story*. The metaphor in question is sturdier than the notion of the gates of ivory and horn; a book is a physical object, which the reader opens in order to gain access. Having done so, the reader ceases to use the sense of sight in the manner for which nature designed it; even if the text is read "by ear" rather than "by eye," the eyes are employed as an input port for the decoding of a long string of symbols—which, if cleverly interpreted, will convey the reader into an imaginary arena with its own decor, its own population, and its own standards of normality. This too serves to emphasize that the employment of a normalizing story arc in a portal fantasy cannot simply restore a privileged status quo. Once a character and a reader have stepped into the infinite array of possible worlds, there is a sense in which they are there forever, even when the character has come home and the reader has closed the book. There are always more books to be read.

Mendlesohn observes that portal fantasies, unlike intrusive fantasies, are usually didactic. Intrusive fantasies usually present mysteries to be unraveled, traps to be escaped, and adversaries to be exorcized, in the interests of temporary excitement. Portal fantasies usually present obstacle courses to be ingeniously negotiated, quests to be bravely carried out, and—most importantly—lessons to be permanently learned. This is a subtle transformation of the standard normalizing story arc; the point is not that the dreamer-cum-traveler returns home but that he or she returns home intellectually *better equipped* and morally rearmed.

The situation of individual portal fantasies within a potentially infinite array emphasizes the supposition that imaginary travel broadens the mind, that life in the actual world may be enhanced, not merely by particular intrusions of magic or trips into secondary worlds, but by a wide acquaintance with a range of such experiences. If so, that process can obviously be further assisted by the cultivation of the skills required for the navigation of secondary worlds *without* the kind of step-by-step guidance that portal fantasies supply. This pressure has been the principal evolutionary force governing the development of modern immersive fantasies.

THE RENAISSANCE OF IMMERSIVE FANTASY

Portal fantasies sometimes serve as precursors of immersive fantasies, as in the series developed from the best known portal fantasy of the 19th century, L. Frank Baum's *The Wonderful Wizard of Oz*. As the sequence extended, Dorothy eventually left Kansas permanently in order to live in Oz, and the later volumes make increasing use of native protagonists who have never lived anywhere else. This development was facilitated by the fact that followers of the series no longer needed to be guided into Oz and introduced to its eccentricities; they already knew the way and already felt quite at home there—perhaps, like Dorothy, *more* at home there than they could ever hope to feel in the primary world.

This last observation sounds alarm bells in the minds of many unsympathetic observers, for exactly the same reason that the didactic elements of portal fantasies soothe anxieties. Critics who will grant, gladly or reluctantly, that portal fantasies can and sometimes do offer a precious cargo of useful lessons to be transported back into the primary world by their protagonists often take a dimmer view of immersive fantasies, whose protagonists seek their goals and find their destinies *within* imaginary worlds. That kind of "escapism" seems to them to be dangerously untemporary, even though the reader must still return through the portal that is the book.

The most important narrative consequence of total immersion in a secondary world, as Mendlesohn points out, is that viewpoint characters in immersive fantasies have to take the fantastic elements by which they are surrounded entirely for granted; the reader's fantasy is their normality, the reader's secondary world their primary. This tends to weaken, or even to negate, the "sense of wonder" associated with fantastic manifestations in intrusive or portal fantasies, by requiring the reader to share the viewpoint character's assumed familiarity.

Such dissonant association is what Darko Suvin calls "cognitive estrangement," although his use of the term restricts it to science-fictional immersive fantasies, whose secondary worlds are constructed on allegedly rational principles. The reading skills involved in this kind of imaginative identification are markedly different from those associated with reading mimetic fiction; they involve an effect that Tolkien—whose policy of critical exclusion is the converse of Suvin's, applauding fairy tales while remaining suspicious of sf—calls "enchantment." In speaking of enchantment and secondary belief, however, Tolkien was thinking in terms of "once upon a time": of a syncretic mythical past to which all fairy tales—no matter how far they have traveled from one culture to another or how drastically they have been transfigured by a modern teller—always refer. He did not believe that modern fantasy literature could escape from the constraints of that assumption, or even that it ought to try. Suvin, by contrast, argues that if modern fantastic literature is to be worthwhile it not only can but must escape, and that the way to do it is to discard the follies of once-upon-a-time in favor of the rational extrapolations of sf.

There is, of course, no *logical* reason why the secondary worlds of immersive fantasy cannot simply be resituated in the same kind of infinite—and infinitely various—array as the secondary worlds of portal fantasy, but there are practical reasons. How are readers supposed to accommodate themselves within imaginary worlds without some set of default assumptions on which to draw so as to "fill in the gaps" that writers have perforce to leave? This problem affects all the subgenres of fantasy, but the writers who had the most obvious incentive for trying to solve it, in the late 19th and early 20th centuries, were those interested in exploring hypothetical futures rather than hypothetical pasts—and it is for this reason that Suvin and critics of a similar stripe consider sf to be innately superior to other kinds of fantasy.

Writers ambitious to use the future and other planets as imaginative spaces for speculation could not be content with the narrative frameworks of intrusive fantasy and portal fantasy, although they had perforce to put up with them for a while; they *had* to develop means of using viewpoint characters native to their heterocosmic constructions rather than always displacing them from the here-and-now by means of spaceships and time machines. In order to make that possible, on any considerable scale, they had to educate readers in the skills necessary to navigate immersive fantasies.

This process of education was difficult, and it was slow. A few 19th-century texts dealing with the future do take the form of immersive fantasies, but they go to great pains to explain in advance to the reader what they are doing, usually by embedding a prefatory essay into the text. Such devices seem clumsy nowadays, when they are routinely stigmatized as "info dumps," but they were necessary in their day, and they laid valuable groundwork in preparing readers to take futuristic settings aboard without such careful preparation. The headway made in the early 20th century was gradual, but a crucial breakthrough came when magazines appeared that specialized in sf. The label itself had the effect of informing readers, even before they began to read, that the story they were about to enter might not be set in the primary world; it functioned, in effect, as a minimal metanarrative preface.

Many of the stories in the early sf magazines retained intrusive fantasy and portal fantasy frameworks; those that did not soon began to reproduce a pattern reminiscent of folktales. The future began to be vaguely manifest in the sf magazines as a kind of syncretic consensus in which certain common elements began to fill the same cartographic role as the default assumptions of once-upon-a-time. In a sense, the creation of this third set of default assumptions completed a natural set, in which the experienced present was supplemented by imaginary extensions backward and forward in time. As with the world of once-upon-a-time, though, the imaginative common ground established in this hypothetical future initially subtracted more from the experienced world than it added.

Although it always remained nebulous, the formulation of this consensual image of the future was based in the myth of the "space age," which saw the future history of humankind in terms of a phased colonialist expansion into the universe. The same myth facilitated the development of a similar consensual frame in which alien worlds could be held: the "galactic empire." Unlike the world of once-upon-a-time, however, the future of the space age was capable of infinite extension, and it eventually began to acquire the complexity it had initially sacrificed in the interests of laying foundations. In the latter half of the 20th century, sf writers and readers left behind the necessity of invoking a set of default assumptions; the ability to map and navigate immersive fantasies without the aid of any such rough-hewn crutch became increasingly widespread.

In retrospect, it is easy to see why science fiction emerged as a popular genre before fantasy, and why it had to take such pains to develop the narrative skills required to read immersive fantasy. By the same token, it is easy to see *now* that once those skills had been sufficiently refined, the scope would be opened up for a renaissance in fantasy literature, which would apply them not merely to rationally plausible hypothetical futures and a fairly narrow range of alternative pasts and parallel dimensions but to the whole range of imaginable pasts, alternative presents, and conceivable futures.

The development of immersive fantasy by sf writers facilitated the simultaneous redevelopment of immersive fantasies of other kinds, initially in the pages of such specialist magazines as *Weird Tales* and *Unknown*—but the fantasy subgenres thus encouraged lived a fugitive existence in the margins of the sf field for half a century, because they seemed to lack the conspicuous modernity of sf. Many fans of sf assumed that the principles of rational explanation supposedly guiding science-fictional visions of the future and alien worlds were the principal justification for the genre's existence and a key element of its reader appeal. That was the basis of the apologies and manifestoes written by the genre's leading ideologists.

Much of the fiction published under the sf label, however, never made any serious attempt to live up to the ideals of rational extrapolation, and many of its readers showed no sign of caring. By the early 1950s, critics found it necessary to distinguish "hard" science fiction from various other materials sheltering under the label, but the coinage of the term was eloquent testimony to the fact that hard sf had already lost the battle for the hearts and minds of the majority of readers. The first sf book to break out of the critical and commercial "ghetto" to which the genre had long seemed confined was Ray Bradbury's *The Martian Chronicles,* whose image of Mars was stubbornly archaic and nostalgic, deliberately fusing the imagery of the space age with elements drawn from the well of once-upon-a-time. Within three years of its publication, Tolkien's *Lord of the Rings* supplied a much more powerful exemplar.

To some extent, Tolkien's Middle-earth was merely one more once-upon-a-time—albeit one developed in extraordinary and unprecedented detail—but its secondary world seemed entirely self-contained, quite independent of the primary world rather than reproductive of a mythical past. *The Lord of the Rings* was by no means unprecedented; it was itself a sequel to *The Hobbit,* similarly formatted as an immersive fantasy, which had managed to pass in 1937 as an unusually elaborate once-upon-a-time fantasy for children. When Lin Carter took his "look behind" the trilogy, he was able to identify a whole series of august predecessors, including works by Lord Dunsany, William Morris, and George MacDonald. All those earlier works had, however, remained esoteric, designed for and consumed by tiny coteries of highly atypical readers. When *The Lord of the Rings* became a huge paperback best seller in the 1960s—or, to be strictly accurate, when slavish imitations of its narrative method proved in the 1970s that its salability was not an unrepeatable fluke—it changed the face of modern publishing.

The early imitations of *The Lord of the Rings* contrived in the 1970s and 1980s had to be slavish in order to exploit the particular expectations generated by Tolkien's work in readers who had not previously been exposed to immersive fantasy. The first effect of Middle-earth's success was that a host of new genre writers soon produced a syncretic "fantasyland" similar to the traditional once-upon-a-time of fairy tales or the newer orthodoxy of the space age—whose instant clichés were mercilessly satirized in Diana Wynne Jones's *Tough Guide to Fantasyland*.

The establishment of this Tolkien-refined once-upon-a-time as the archetype of a commodified genre seemed to many observers to be a bad thing. Critics like Ursula Le Guin loudly condemned "commodified fantasy" as something crudely imitative and wholly devoid of imagination, by contrast with "real" fantasy, whose principal claim to intellectual seriousness was the originality of its designs and internal dynamic. As Le Guin's own example demonstrates, however, the establishment of Middle-earth as a key model of a secondary world permitted transfiguration—and hence diversification—as well as recycling. The process of cloning Middle-earths by the score (or, as rapidly became the case, by the thousand) did indeed result in a vast array of smudged carbon copies—but it also resulted in a fringe of calculated modifications that grew and extended as quickly as the genre's imitative core. Le Guin's Earthsea recycled many elements of Middle-earth, but it also modified them, and the more Earthsea grew from text to text the more far-reaching its modifications became.

It is probably true that most inexperienced readers who acquire a taste for fantasy rely on a rapidly accumulated stock of knowledge about "fantasyland" to navigate their way through texts; such readers undoubtedly sustain a core of formularized material whose wide appeal is entirely dependent on its unoriginality. It is, however, almost certainly true that many such readers make substantial progress in the skills required to read immersive fantasies and that they free themselves soon enough from the prisoning effects of that initial stock. Those who want to move on from the fantasyland of commodified fantasy to fresher pastures—including the works of Diana Wynne Jones and Ursula Le Guin—are assisted to do so rather than inhibited. As a steadily increasing population of readers developed, between the 1970s and the present day, the ability to accommodate and orient themselves in such worlds without undue difficulty, the scope of genre fantasy's variation and ambition increased dramatically. The debt owed by genre fantasy to the training accomplished by sf is clearly reflected in the manner in which genre sf has largely forsaken its ambitions of "hardness" in favor of reckless experiments in chimerization, experiments that strongly emphasize the fact that sf was always a subgenre of fantasy literature.

THE AESTHETICS OF IMMERSIVE FANTASY

In addition to the status of their viewpoint characters, there is another significant factor distinguishing immersive fantasies from intrusive and portal fantasies: that they have no seemingly "natural" story arc built into them. Because immersive fantasies do not begin in the primary world, they cannot return to it; "normalization" is not an option. Traditional immersive fantasies, being set in a past that had supposedly produced the present, had mirrored the ambitions of the present—most fairy tales, like most early novels, end with a wedding and an inheritance—but the constraints of this kind of conventional reward became as dispensable as the other constraints of once-upon-a-time.

Not all writers of modern fantasy, of course, wanted to dispense with such conventional rewards, but even those who did not tended to exaggerate them. Tolkien was prepared to dabble in weddings and inheritances, and even with climactic returns home, but they seemed trivial by comparison with the opportunity to redeem whole worlds within texts from evil. His apology for fairy tales makes this potential aspect a key element of their utility, in the notion that consolatory "eucatastrophes" are imperative if they are to provide the reward that justifies their existence. It is for this reason that Tolkien considered immersive fantasy potentially far more valuable to readers than intrusive fantasies or portal fantasies—and the eventual success of *The Lord of the Rings* lent a great deal of weight to his argument. The more expansive a eucatastrophe is, the more intense a reader's experience might become; that is why some critics have been eager to move beyond Tolkien's notion of "enchantment" to some more grandiose notion, like Arthur Machen's "ecstasy."

In claiming that existing fairy tales routinely led to "eucatastrophes," Tolkien was overstating his case somewhat. The endings of many actual folktales were so bleak and cruel that Perrault and other adaptors for children felt obliged to censor them; pioneering synthesists like Hans Christian Andersen often attached endings that were rather harrowing. Many traditional immersive fantasies dealing with extraordinary rewards take the form of cautionary tales, warning their characters—and hence their readers—that there is no use dreaming that their more ambitious wishes might be granted, because something would inevitably go wrong.

The reason for this occasional cautiousness is easy enough to understand; the reader, unlike the character, has to return to the primary world, closing the book-as-portal when the magical string of words reaches its final period. Even so, it is not obvious that secondary worlds need to be as disappointing as the actual one in order to provide rewarding experiences, and it is obviously not the case that readers prefer to visit innately disappointing secondary worlds because the real one continually lets them down. The most popular tales are, indeed, the ones in which clones of Cinderella marry Prince Charming, poor boys run away with geese that lay golden eggs, and ugly ducklings turn out to be swans. In spite of his overstatement, Tolkien was broadly correct: there *is* a great deal of consolation to be obtained even from temporary escapes to worlds where rewards impossible of achievement in the actual world are generously on offer.

Tolkien was correct too in his attempt to emphasize—by coining the word "eucatastrophe"—that there is something to be gained from imaginative participation in rewards that go far beyond the simple desire of the individual for the heritable and marriable materials of personal happiness. In immersive fantasy, the characters with whom the reader identifies may achieve much more; that is why so many of them are heroes and so much immersive fantasy takes the form of heroic fantasy. There is a sense in which Tolkien-clone fantasy is heroic fantasy, but one of the problems afflicting the construction of a historical dictionary of fantasy literature is that the phrase was already in use as a label for a rather different kind of fantasy, already established in the commercial marketplace of the 1970s as a fugitive but manifest presence.

This other kind of "heroic fantasy" was more familiarly known as "sword and sorcery" fiction. As with Tolkienesque "epic fantasy," sword and sorcery had one principal model, in the story series by Robert E. Howard featuring Conan. Howard had pioneered a new frontier in action/adventure fiction by borrowing imaginary prehistoric civilizations from the scholarly fantasies of theosophy and centralizing a new kind of Noble Savage as protagonist. Sword-and-sorcery fiction was reliant on a mythical past in exactly the same way that fairy tales were—Howard called his once-upon-a-time the "Hyborian Age"—but it was a more brutal and cynical once-upon-a-time that bore a closer resemblance to the once-upon-a-time of the western genre than that of Middle-earth. Sword and sorcery's elder races were more loathsome than Tolkien's aristocratic elves, its dragons more monstrous, its wizards less academically inclined, and—most importantly—its swords more akin to gunslingers' revolvers than to emblems of chivalric knighthood. Sword-and-sorcery fiction *was* heroic, but it had a notion of heroism that was more physical than that enshrined in epic fantasy. It was partly to distinguish Tolkien-cloned fantasy from sword-and-sorcery fiction that some of the other labels routinely applied to it were cloned, including "high fantasy" and "quest fantasy."

It is certainly arguable that the description of sword-and-sorcery fiction as "heroic fantasy" is mistaken; if one accepts Joseph Campbell's description of the "monomyth" that defines the quintessence heroism, Conan and his clones do not seem to fit. Their ambitions are usually selfish and modest, in consequence of which their achievements are rarely as prodigious as those of the messianic heroes of epic fantasy. Nevertheless, they fall into the same spectrum, and they function as ideological counterweights to the temptations of casual excess that afflict every deus ex machina or holy grail that beckons to the world savers of epic fantasy. One of the virtues of the diversity of modern fantasy is that it forbids writers to take the nature or the goals of heroism too much for granted.

In fact, the diversity of modern secondary worlds, by comparison with the narrow horizons of any particular once-upon-a-time, is bound to call everything into question. Although it is perfectly possible to write immersive fantasies in which the characters' rewards are perfectly ordinary or conventionally stereotyped—and the multiple cloning of Middle-earth immediately brought conventions into being that reduced the vast ambitions of its eucatastrophe to mere cliché—their situation within a genre can hardly help creating pressure to explore the possibility of finding alternative rewards or raising the possibility of finding alternative routes to the familiar ones. The formation of a new "fantasy" genre out of disparate materials—even materials whose fundamental assumptions about the mythical past were as broadly similar as those of epic fantasy and sword and sorcery—inevitably created a tension that immediately began to modify the processes of imitation and recycling. As more materials were gathered into the new genre, especially the varieties of "contemporary fantasy" that sought to renew and revitalize the intrusive-fantasy format, as well as various kinds of didactic portal fantasy, the tensions between the newly defined genre's various components were considerably complicated.

For this reason, the tendency of commodified fantasy toward formularization was always problematic; there were simply too many formulas available. As Michael Swanwick observed in a perceptive analysis of the workings of fantasy tradition, the genre looks more like an archipelago than a continent—but every island in the archipelago exercises a modifying influence on the others, so that every recycling of an influential model tends to be at least slightly shifted by the example of at least one other. In more adventurous examples, writers deliberately set out to mix different formulas together, rejoicing in the new syntheses that emerge from the unlikeliest combinations. One of the most striking attributes of the emergent genre of commodified fantasy has been its hospitability to chimerical combinations.

Interestingly, this is not a tendency that is confined within the genre. It was natural enough, given the stark contrast between their tacit worldviews on the one hand and the close alliance between their narrative forms on the other, that chimerical combinations of fantasy and sf should appear at a very early stage in their history, and that one of the few specialist fantasy magazines of the pulp era, *Unknown,* should be largely devoted to the exploration of the possibilities inherent in such chimerization. What is slightly more surprising, however, is that the establishment of a commercial fantasy genre should have given such swift and spectacular birth to crossovers with other popular genres. There had always been hybrid crossovers between fantasy and detective fiction, in the subgenre of "occult detective stories," and there had always been a considerable enclave of love stories within fantasy, especially in the subgenre of "timeslip romances," but the revitalization and recomplication of the various subgenres of fantasy detective story and "paranormal romance" in the last decade has been remarkable. Whereas the long-established crossovers were hybrid subgenres rather than chimerical ones, the proliferation of new kinds of crossover has relied much more heavily on exaggerating the contrasts between the elements fed into the mix rather than smoothing them.

These phenomena, together with a dramatic recent increase in the use of fantastic materials in literary fiction, emphasize the fact that the history of fantasy literature should not be viewed in isolation, as if it were something self-enclosed. Because all literature is fantasy of a sort, trends within generic fantasy can easily overflow into other genres. The energy and vitality of commodified fantasy is clearly demonstrable in the way in which it has helped to refresh other commodified genres whose formulas had become a trifle stale; the utility of the skills involved in reading sophisticated immersive fantasy is clearly demonstrable in the manner in which literary fiction has become much more flexible in its use of fantasy tropes.

We have also been able to observe in recent years that the establishment of a fantasy genre, however carefully commodified its central examples may be, is bound to create a sceptical interrogation of the nature and functions of fantasy itself—to encourage the growth of fantasies about fantasy: self-conscious exercises in fabulation and metafiction. Such endeavors may appear to be exercises in sophistication, likely to be confined to the more esoteric realms of literary fiction, but that has never been the case. Children's fantasy has always accommodated fantasies about fantasy quite readily, and as soon as fantasy became a commercial genre it made the same ready accommodation.

The most conspicuous examples of fantasies about fantasy are humorous, but even the humorous examples routinely serve as *contes philosophiques,* and the most serious examples aspire to sentimental as well as philosophical depth. There is, in fact, a sense in which the high status of all the finest works of modern fantasy literature is dependent on their commentary on the politics of fantasy, no matter what other aesthetic merits they may have in addition to their metafictional implications. This is where their own realism becomes manifest, and important. Secondary worlds may function in several kinds of interesting and realistically significant ways, related to the real one logically, satirically, or allegorically, but the function they can fulfill most intricately, most cleverly, and most artistically is that of questioning and reevaluating their own conventional forms.

There are several reasons why a reader might benefit from cultivating the skills required to read immersive fantasy, only three of which are outlined in Tolkien's celebration of recovery, escape, and consolation. None are to be despised, even if they extend no farther than ritual uses of commodified fantasy—the core works of commodified fantasy are not all badly written, and painters long ago proved that there is an art in imitation as well as invention—but it is arguable that their greatest possible reward is the ability to construe fantasies about fantasies, to participate fully in the joys of fabulation.

This is a useful kind of mental flexibility, valuable not only in the everyday routines of psychological fantasization but also in reminding us that the summary past of history is really no more than another once-upon-a-time. It might be the most accurate estimate we can presently contrive of what really did happen (although one is perfectly free to doubt that), but even if so, it is certainly not a record of the best of all possible worlds. The opportunity to explore others in the imagination can only increase the possibility that we might find better ways to exist as individuals in the actual world, and perhaps the possibility that we might find better ways collectively to change the actual world in ways that will improve it.

THE SCOPE OF THE DICTIONARY

Because fantasy literature, as defined here, is as old as writing, this guide to its contents has to be very selective, especially in terms of the authors annotated. Authors have been selected for individual attention according to the historical significance, rather than the number, of their contributions to the genre. The lists of titles credited to individual authors are often selective, on the same basis; for instance, the importance of fantasy within children's literature necessitates the listing of a great deal of fiction marketed for older children, but stories for younger children are usually left unlisted. Biographical information has been kept to a minimum. Authors who are also annotated in the *Historical Dictionary of Science Fiction Literature* are cross-referenced thereto by the indicator (refer to *HDSFL*), and those to be annotated in John Clute's forthcoming *Historical Dictionary of Horror Literature* are cross-referenced thereto by the indicator (refer to *HDHL*).

The great majority of the terms defined herein have been included because of the frequency of their use or their particular significance within the discourse of contemporary fantasy criticism, but because that criticism is still too thin on the ground for any substantial consensus to have arisen regarding the most useful category distinctions, considerable improvisation has been necessary. Although new emphasis has been lent to such relatively transparent and commonplace terms as "recycling" and "transfiguration," the invention of new jargon has been minimized. Some of the more esoteric terms introduced in the Clute/Grant *Encyclopedia* have either been omitted or restricted to brief definitions, in the interests of maintaining as much clarity as the complexity of the phenomena will allow.

In order to list as many relevant titles as possible, descriptions of all but the most important have been restricted to succinct categorization, and the bibliographical information relating to them has usually been limited to the dates of original publication, variant titles, and indications of significant expansion or revision.

The Dictionary

– A –

ABBEY, LYNN (1948–). U.S. writer best known for her coeditorship with **Robert Lynn Asprin** of the *Thieves' World* **shared world** project (1979–89), which stimulated the production of **picaresque/commodified fantasy**. Her early novels featured **goddess**-worshipping **witches** battling patriarchal black **magic** in quasi-medieval settings. Examples include the couplets comprising *Daughter of the Bright Moon* (1979) and *The Black Flame* (1980), *Unicorn and Dragon* (1987) and *Conquest* (1988; aka *The Green Man*), and *The Wooden Sword* (1991) and *Beneath the Web* (1994). *Siege of Shadows* (1996) and *Jerlayne* (1999) are **quest** fantasies; the heroine of the latter leaves **Faerie** in order to find out why her family are misfits. The Orion's Children series, which began with *Out of Time* (2000), *Behind Time* (2001), and *Taking Time* (2004), is a lively **contemporary fantasy** featuring a librarian who develops extraordinary powers.

ACKROYD, PETER (1949–). British writer of literary fiction whose preoccupation with **secret histories** of London is reflected in characters obsessed or haunted by their past equivalents, as in the Dickensian fantasy *The Great Fire of London* (1982) and the **occult fantasies** *Hawksmoor* (1985) and *The House of Doctor Dee* (1993) (refer to *HDHL*). *First Light* (1989) and *English Music* (1993) employ similar transhistorical links and narrative movements. *Milton in America* (1996) is an **alternative history** in which the poet funds a utopian community. In the **satire** *The Plato Papers* (1999), the great philosopher comments on "the Mouldwarp era" (1500–2300 A.D.) from the viewpoint of 3700 A.D., blithely misinterpreting its haphazard relics.

ADAMS, RICHARD (1920–). British writer whose **animal fantasy** *Watership Down* (1972)—a heartfelt ecological morality play modeled on Virgil's *Aeneid*—revived the subgenre when it became a best seller. *The Plague Dogs* (1977) and the satirical *Traveller* (1988) stretched the subgenre's conventions, but *Tales from Watership Down* (1996) reverted to safer ground. *Shardik* (1974) and *Maia* (1984) are **dark/historical fantasies** with elements of **political fantasy**. *The Girl in a Swing* (1980) is a **sentimental/ghost story**. *The Legend of Te Tuna* (1986) and the tales in *The Iron Wolf and Other Stories* (1980) are **recycled** folktales.

ADELER, MAX (1841–1915). Pseudonym of U.S. writer Charles Heber Clark, whose collections of **humorous** stories include several **hallucinatory fantasies**, notably "Mr Skinner's Night in the Underworld" in *Random Shots* (1878), the **Arthurian fantasy** "Professor Baffin's Island" (1880; aka "The Fortunate Island") in *An Old Fogey and Other Stories* (1881; aka *The Fortunate Island and Other Stories*), and the two novellas making up *Transformations, Containing* Mrs Shelmire's Djinn *and* A Desperate Adventure (1883). "Professor Baffin's Island" anticipates **Mark Twain**'s *Connecticut Yankee,* and *Transformations* anticipates the work of **F. Anstey**.

AFTERLIFE FANTASY. The subgenre of fantasy featuring **secondary worlds** in which humans are reincarnated after death. Its cardinal examples are the Infernos—and occasional Paradisos and Purgatorios—of **Dante**'s fantasy, including the spinoff subgenre of **infernal comedy**. Various other traditional images—whose variety is mocked in such comedies as **Andrew Lang**'s "In the Wrong Paradise"—are also featured, but modern afterlife fantasy tends to be much more inventive and adventurous in designing scenarios in which the moral accounts left in conspicuous debit by life on earth might be ingeniously balanced. Afterlife fantasy overlaps **posthumous fantasy**, which situates its lives after death within the **primary world**. Earnest **religious fantasies** featuring afterlives include a large subset of credulous **spiritualist fantasies**, but **satire** predominates in literary fiction.

War tends to stimulate the production of afterlife fantasy; the evolution of the genre can be measured by contrasting the boom in spiritualist fantasies produced by World War I with the more philosophically innovative fantasies produced by World War II, of which Beth Brown's *Universal Station* (1944), Ketti Frings's *God's Front Porch* (1944), and **C. S. Lewis**'s *The Great Divorce* are notable examples. The broader context of the 20th century is represented by such examples as Evelyn Underhill's *The Grey World* (1904), A. E. Coppard's "Clorinda Walks in Heaven," Oliver Claxton's *Heavens Above!* (1933), Marjorie Livingston's *The Future of Mr Purdew* (1935), Marc Connelly's *Green Pastures* (1929), Wyndham Lewis's Human Age sequence (1928–55), **Robert Nathan**'s *There Is Another Heaven,* and Lady Saltoun's *After* (1930). Satirical examples became more sarcastic in the latter years, as in Michael Frayn's *Sweet Dreams* (1973), Stanley Elkin's *The Living End* (1979), **Robert A. Heinlein**'s *Job,* Shere Hite's *The Divine Comedy of Ariadne and Jupiter* (1994), Mick Farren's *Jim Morrison's Adventures in the Afterlife* (1999), and Cynthia Rylant's *The Heavenly Village* (1999).

Commodified fantasy took the subgenre aboard in the graphic **shared world** series begun with *Heroes in Hell* (1986) and Lloyd Arthur Eshbach's **portal fantasy** collection, comprising *The Land beyond the Gate* (1984), *The Armlet of the Gods* (1986), *The Sorceress of Skath* (1988), and *The Scroll of Lucifer* (1990). The establishment of genre fantasy assisted the imagistic diversification of such idiosyncratic works as Alex Shearer's *Great Blue Yonder* (2002), **Louise Cusack**'s *Destiny of the Light,* Jeffrey Thomas's *Letters from Hades* (2003), and Martin Chatterton's *Michigan Moorcroft, R.I.P.* (2003). Characters in afterlife locations sometimes interfere with life on earth, as in Art Buchwald's *Stella in Heaven* (2000), or are featured as detached observers, as in Alice Sebold's *The Lovely Bones* (2002). Artificial afterlives are featured in numerous **science-fantasies**, notably Philip José Farmer's "Riverworld" series.

AIKEN, JOAN (1924–2004). British writer from a notable literary family, the daughter of Conrad Aiken and the sister of John Aiken and Jane Aiken Hodge (all of whom made minor contributions to fantasy literature). Her novels for adults use fantastic motifs very sparingly and marginally, but her works for children, from *The Kingdom and the Cave* (1960) onward, make much freer use of such devices. Her short fiction for adults and children includes such **horror** stories (refer to *HDHL*).

The series begun with *The Wolves of Willoughby Chase* (1962) and *Black Hearts in Battersea* (1964) employs an **alternative history** to license vivid adventures in melodrama. *Nightbirds on Nantucket* (1966) and *The Cuckoo Tree* (1971) shift the focus from the original protagonists to their exotic helper Dido Twite, whose far-ranging exploits are continued in *The Stolen Lake* (1981), *Dido and Pa* (1986), *Is* (1992; aka

Is Underground), *Cold Shoulder Road* (1995), *Dangerous Games* (1999; aka *Limbo Lodge*), and *Midwinter Nightingale* (2003). Alongside this serie, Aiken produced the effective **allegories** of maturation comprising *The Whispering Mountain* (1968), *Midnight Is a Place* (1974), and *The Shadow Guests* (1980); a trilogy similar in spirit to the alternative history series, comprising *Go Saddle the Sea* (1977), *Bridle the Wind* (1983), and *The Teeth of the Gale* (1988); two plays issued in an omnibus as Winterthing *and* The Mooncusser's Daughter (1973).

Many of Aiken's short story collections are dominated by horror stories, but those foregrounding fantasies include *A Necklace of Raindrops* (1968), *A Small Pinch of Weather* (1969), *Smoke from Cromwell's Time and Other Stories* (1970), *The Kingdom under the Sea* (1971), *A Harp of Fishbones* (1972), *More than You Bargained For* (1974), *Not What You Expected* (1974), *Arabel's Raven* (1974), *A Bundle of Nerves* (1976), *The Faithless Lollybird* (1977), *Fog Hounds, Wind Cats, Sea Mice* (1984), and *The Last Slice of Rainbow* (1985). *The Winter Sleepwalker and Other Stories* (1994), *Shadows & Moonshine* (2001), and the novella *The Scream* (2002) are more smoothly hybridized.

ALCHEMICAL FANTASY A subgenre of **occult fantasy**. Alchemy was the name given in Western Europe from the 12th century to a mystical proto-chemistry whose traditions were allegedly handed down from antiquity, although its earlier history is almost entirely an artifact of **scholarly fantasy**. Its central quests for the elixir of life and the philosopher's stone (the secret of transmuting "base metal" into gold) have been considerable inspirations to literary fantasists. Alchemical writings of the Renaissance tend to be couched in elaborate symbolism, encouraging later commentators, especially **Rosicrucian/lifestyle fantasists**, to argue that alchemical endeavor is best regarded as a quest for spiritual enlightenment, whose confusion with hopes of vulgar gain was unfortunate—a notion avidly taken up by such alchemical fantasists as **Vladimir Odoevsky**.

Alchemists were initially featured in literature as confidence tricksters, as in **Geoffrey Chaucer**'s "The Canon's Yeoman's Tale" and Ben Jonson's *The Alchemist* (1610), and they proved useful as mistaken pursuers of futile dreams in **moralistic fantasies** like William Godwin's *St. Leon* (1799) and **Honoré de Balzac**'s *Quest for the Absolute*. Even when they were not mistaken, early literary alchemists were usually frustrated in their quests—as in Balzac's "The Elixir of Life," **Alexandre Dumas**'s *Joseph Balsamo*, **Edward Bulwer-Lytton**'s *A Strange*

Story, **Nathaniel Hawthorne**'s "Dr Heidegger's Experiment" and *Septimius,* Alexander de Comeau's *Monk's Magic* (1931), and **Vincent Starrett**'s *Seaports in the Moon*—but the 19th-century occult revival inspired a more reverent interest, widely reflected in the work of such writers as **Arthur Machen**, **Gustav Meyrink**, **John Cowper Powys**, and **Charles Williams** and such individual items as Ithell Colquhoun's *Goose of Hermogenes* (1961) and **Avram Davidson**'s *The Phoenix and the Mirror*.

The alchemist who had the greatest influence on fantasy literature was Theophrastus von Hohenheim (c1493–1541), nicknamed Paracelsus, who is the central figure in a philosophical fantasy by **Robert Browning**. Paracelsus recorded a recipe for manufacturing a homunculus—an artificial man in miniature—whose successful application is imagined in such works as John Hargrave's *The Artificial Man* (1931) and **David H. Keller**'s *The Homunculus*. Histories of alchemical scholarly fantasy such as **Mircea Eliade**'s *The Forge and the Crucible* (1956; tr. 1962) and Frances Yates's *The Rosicrucian Enlightenment* (1972) provided further inspiration, extrapolated in such works as **Annie Dalton**'s *Night Maze*, **Lindsay Clarke**'s *The Chymical Wedding*, **Margaret Yourcenar**'s *The Abyss*, **John Crowley**'s series begun with *Aegypt,* Neal Barrett, Jr.'s *The Prophecy Machine* (2000), Kate Thompson's *The Alchemist's Apprentice* (2002), and **Lisa Goldstein**'s *The Alchemist's Door*. Alchemists are frequently integrated into the **secret histories** featured in conspiracy theory novels; Neal Stephenson's trilogy begun with *Cryptonomicon* (1999) features **John Milton** as a alchemist.

The failure of alchemy to inspire 20th-century **lifestyle fantasy** has limited its appeal mainly to the field of **historical fantasy**, although Ian Watson's **science fantasy** *The Gardens of Delight* (1980) and Patrick Harpur's *Mercurius; or The Marriage of Heaven and Earth* (1990) are conspicuous exceptions to the rule. Chinese alchemy—with an ancient tradition better documented than any Western equivalent—is featured in Frank Owen's "Dr Shen Fu" (1938). **Science fiction** stories featuring technologies that emulate alchemical gold manufacture sometimes retain an ironic fantasy element, as in Charles Harness's "The Alchemist" (1966). The **wizards** of modern **commodified fantasy** often have alchemical apparatus in their workrooms, and alchemy is usually on the syllabus of their educational institutions. **Anne McCaffrey**'s *Alchemy and Academe* is a showcase **anthology**. *See also* IMMORTALITY.

ALDISS, BRIAN W. (1925–). British writer best known for **sf** (refer to *HDSFL*). There are elements of fantasy in some of his **planetary romances**, but his purest fantasy novels are the **decadent** fantasy *The Malacia Tapestry* (1976) and the **humorous fantasy** *Affairs at Hampden Ferrers: An English Romance* (2004). His relevant short fiction is mostly assembled in *A Romance of the Equator: Best Fantasy Stories* (1989), although most of his later short fiction shows the influence of **magic realism**. He edited the early showcase **anthology** *Best Fantasy Stories* (1962).

ALEXANDER, LLOYD (1924–). U.S. writer for children who published *Time Cat* (1963) before embarking on his major fantasy project, the **Celtic fantasy** Chronicles of Prydain, comprising *The Book of Three* (1964), *The Black Cauldron* (1965), *The Castle of Llyr* (1966), *Taran Wanderer* (1967), and *The High King* (1968); associated short fiction is collected in *The Foundling and Other Tales of Prydain* (1973). Like **T. H. White**'s *Once and Future King*, the Prydain series matured along with its hero, and it became a significant model for subsequent heroic fantasies designed for the **young adult** market. *The Marvelous Misadventures of Sebastian* (1970), *The Cat Who Wished to Be a Man* (1973), *The Wizard in the Tree* (1975), and *The First Two Lives of Lukas-Kasha* (1978) are in a lighter vein. Many of Alexander's later works moved their fantastic devices to the margins of adventure stories, but the **Oriental fantasy** *The Remarkable Journey of Prince Jen* (1991), the **Arcadian fantasy** *The Arkadians* (1995), and the **Hindu myth**–based *The Iron Ring* (1997) form a set with backgrounds that are calculatedly far-ranging. *The Rope Trick* (2002) describes a frustrating **quest** for the eponymous secret.

ALLEGORY. A narrative with a sequence of events that encodes or symbolizes a distinct pattern of ideas. The most famous classical example is the allegory of the cave in Plato's *Republic*. Religious allegory was popular in medieval times. In 1225, Guillaume de Lorris began work on *Le Roman de la Rose* [*The Romance of the Rose*], an allegorical **visionary fantasy** whose completed version by Jean de Meun (c1275) was the most widely copied work of medieval French literature. It was highly influential partly because of its erotic content and partly because it lent itself to different interpretations—it was probably the inspiration of the **Rosicrucian** rose—although its significance as a model for **Christian fantasy** was eventually surpassed by John Bunyan's *Pilgrim's Progress*.

Chrétien de Troyes's allegory in *Le Conte du Graal*—whose lack of an ending left it undecoded—has been enormously influential in **scholarly fantasy** and has provided the most important archetype of **quest** fantasy. Allegorical short fiction was still popular in the 19th century, exemplified in the **moralistic fantasies** of writers as various as **Nathaniel Hawthorne** and **Hans Christian Andersen**. **George MacDonald**'s of allegorical form as a medium of philosophical and spiritual exploration was carried forward by **William Morris** and Henry Newbolt's *Aladore* (1914).

Andersen's "Ugly Duckling" exemplifies the manner in which **animal fantasy** routinely employs animal life as an allegory of human life; the **Ĉapek** brothers' *Insect Play* and George Orwell's *Animal Farm: A Fairy Story* (1945) are modern examples, the latter being cleverly transfigured in Scott Bradfield's *Animal Planet* (1995) and John Reed's *Snowball's Chance* (2003). Gerald Heard's *Gabriel and the Creatures* (1952; aka *Wishing Well*) employs animal fantasy to allegorize unorthodox ideas about evolution. In much the same way, modern **recyclings** and **transfigurations** of **myths** and **fairy tales** often employ their characters as allegorical representations of modern types, in the satirical manner of **John Erskine** and **Osbert Sitwell**. Apart from the convenient improvisations of routine transfiguration, and literary **dreams** that embed brief but ingenious allegorical sequences within longer works, the construction of elaborate allegorical schemes is rare in 20th-century fiction; notable exceptions to the rule include **Wyndham Lewis**'s *The Enemy of the Stars,* **David Lindsay**'s *A Voyage to Arcturus,* Brian Moore's *The Great Victorian Collection* (1975), **Robert Silverberg**'s *Son of Man,* and Jill Paton Walsh's *Knowledge of Angels* (1994).

ALLENDE, ISABEL (1942–). Peruvian-born writer resident in the United States. The novel translated as *The House of the Spirits* (1982; tr. 1985) is a key example of **magic realism**. *Eva Luna* (1987; tr. 1988) is a celebration of the transformative power of storytelling. *City of the Beasts* (2002) and its sequel *Kingdom of the Golden Dragon* (2004) launched an elaborate **Odyssean fantasy** series aimed at younger readers.

ALTERNATIVE HISTORY. An account of a hypothetical past or present that might have been actualized had a crucial historical event worked out differently, or a false belief had an authentic foundation in reality. Exercises of the former kind are usually categorized as **sf** (refer to

HDSFL) but **historical fantasies** in which workable magic is introduced into a variant of recorded history routinely break free from the confined narrative spaces of **secret history** to create alternative worlds.

Modestly reconfigured alternative histories make a convenient frame for mildly fantasized texts, as in **Joan Aiken**'s series begun with *The Wolves of Willoughby Chase,* but those more central to fantasy literature use magic much more decisively to modify the pattern of historical development, as in the series by **Orson Scott Card** and **Sara Douglass**. The popularization of the chimerical "steampunk" subgenre of **science fantasy** in the 1980s encouraged a dramatic increase in extravagant alternative histories accommodating practical magical disciplines; notable examples include the series by **J. Gregory Keyes** and **Kelley Armstrong** and such works as S. Andrew Swann's *Broken Crescent* (2004). A popular variant of the strategy of adding workable magic to the pattern of history is to confer actual existence on fictitious characters, as in many relatively modest examples of **metafiction**.

Many **secondary worlds** mirror their **primary** model closely enough to qualify as alternatives of a sort, especially if they feature **transfigured** versions of actual cities or nations; notable examples include **Michael Moorcock**'s *Gloriana*, various works by **John Whitbourn**, and Jonathan Stroud's Bartimaeus series (launched 2003), set in alternative Englands, and Mary Hoffman's Stravaganza series (launched 2002), set in an alternative Italy.

AMAZON. A member of a mythical tribe of warrior women featured in **classical fantasy**. Heracles and Theseus engaged them in battle, and they featured in Homer's *Iliad* as allies of the Trojans. They became significant emblems of female independence, acquiring iconic status in lesbian **erotic fantasy**, although the tenor of their representation differs markedly in such proto-feminist **historical fantasies** as Maude Meagher's *The Green Scamander* (1934) and male equivalents like Ivor Bannet's *The Amazons* (1948).

Modern fantasies featuring the orignal Amazons include **Jane Yolen** and Robert J. Harris's *Hippolyta and the Curse of the Amazons*, **Theresa Tomlinson**'s *The Moon Riders,* and **Judith Tarr**'s *Queen of the Amazons*, but by the time **commodified fantasy** was established in the marketplace the term had been promiscuously broadened to refer to any violently inclined female. That usage was promptly redeemed by its application to female heroes of **sword and sorcery**, such as those featured in **Jessica Amanda Salmonson**'s *Amazons* **anthologies**, various works by **Sharon Green**, and **Megan Lindholm**'s *Harpy's Flight*. In spite of the key example provided by **Marion Zimmer Bradley**'s Darkover series, many of the stories in her Sword and Sorceress series featured feminized models of female heroism, and those in **Esther Friesner**'s Chicks series are mostly parodic. Salmonson's *Encyclopedia of Amazons* (1991) is a thoroughgoing analysis of the history of the idea.

AMBIGUOUS TEXTS. Texts whose generic status is difficult to determine because the status of the premises they employ is unclear or calculatedly obscured. Many stories attempt to boost the plausibility of their fantastic devices by claiming that what seems to be magic actually consists of natural mental powers not yet understood by science or admitted as realities by sceptics. Such rationales can draw on a prodigious legacy of **scholarly fantasy** in the field of the "paranormal," which allow many **occult fantasies** to claim ambiguous status. Tzvetan Todorov made the refusal to resolve ambiguities between literal and delusional interpretations of disturbing events the definitive feature of his genre of the ***fantastique***, and ambiguity is also crucial to the French-originated genre of **surrealism**.

Far-futuristic fantasies routinely excuse magical devices as relics of decadent superscience but rarely trade on the ambiguity. **Chimerical** and **hybrid** texts are more common nowadays across the entire spectrum of fantasy literature, partly because fantastic devices no longer require the kind of apologetic disguise to which they are subject in such conscientiously ambiguous accounts of exotic intrusion as **Paul Féval**'s *The Vampire Countess* and **Jerome K. Jerome**'s "The Passing of the Third Floor Back" or accounts of witchcraft like Ethel Mannin's *Lucifer and the Child* (1945) and **Frank Baker's** *Talk of the Devil* (1956), but mainly because hybridization and chimerization lend themselves to more dramatic narrative effects.

ANDERSEN, HANS CHRISTIAN (1805–1875). Danish writer. He produced six novels—including an account of the **Wandering Jew**—and several volumes of autobiography in addition to the synthetic **fairy tales** that secured his reputation, which he began to write in 1829 and to publish in 1835. He recycled a few items, including "The Princess and the Pea" (1835), but the vast majority of is works were original. Some, like "The Emperor's New Clothes" (1837), are **satirical**; others, like "The Little Mermaid" (1837) and "The Little Match Girl" (1848), are **sentimental**; several, like "The Ugly Duckling" (1845) are **allegorical**. More earnest philosophical allegories like "The Nightingale" (1845) and "The Shadow" (1847) are sometimes omitted from child-oriented collections, although critics often rate them very highly. "The Snow Queen" (1846) is the most extended. A 20-volume Hans Andersen Library issued in the United Kingdom between 1869 and 1887 is nearly complete; the most comprehensive modern collection is *The Complete Fairy Tales and Stories* (Anchor, 1974).

Andersen's tales had an enormous influence on subsequent writers; **Oscar Wilde**'s fairy tales are obvious extrapolations of Andersen originals. "The Snow Queen" is the most frequently **transfigured**; notable examples include Kelly Link's "Travels with the Snow Queen" (1997) and Eileen Kernaghan's *The Snow Queen* (2000). Variants of "The Little Mermaid" range from Wilde's "The Fisherman and his Soul" to Debbie Viguié's *Midnight Pearls* (2003) and variants of "The Nightingale" from Wilde's "The Nightingale and the Rose" to **Kara Dalkey**'s Sagamore couplet.

ANDERSON, MARGARET J. (1931–). Scottish-born U.S. writer, most active as a popularizer of science. Most of her fantasies are **timeslip** stories; they include *To Nowhere and Back* (1975); the trilogy comprising *In the Keep of Time* (1977), *In the Circle of Time* (1979), and *The Mists of Time* (1984); and *The Druid's Gift* (1989). *The Ghost inside the Monitor* (1990) is an account of a haunted computer.

ANDERSON, POUL (1926–2001). U.S. writer best known for **sf** (refer to *HDSFL*). His fantasies are routinely leavened with doses of rational analysis that obtain **hybrid** or **chimerical** effects, sometimes lightheartedly—as in *Three Hearts and Three Lions* (1953; exp. book 1961) and the couplet comprising *Operation Chaos* (1971) and *Operation Luna* (1999)—but sometimes with a bittersweet regret for the inevitability of **thinning**, as in the elegiac mosaic *The Merman's Children* (1979).

The Broken Sword (1954; rev. 1971) is a **dark/heroic fantasy** wherein recovery of a traditional image of Nordic **elves** is similar in intent to the simultaneous efforts of **J. R. R. Tolkien**'s *Lord of the Rings*. The Viking romances *Hrolf Kraki's Saga* (1973), *The Demon of Scattery* (1979 with Mildred Downey Broxon), and *War of the Gods* (1997) also reflect Anderson's interest in his Scandinavian ancestry; the **historical fantasy** *Mother of Kings* (2001) is a more earnest exploration of his cultural roots. *A Midsummer Tempest* (1974) is a Shakespearean fantasy set in an **alternative history**. His shorter fantasies are collected in *Fantasy* (1981) and *The Armies of Elfland* (1992).

In collaboration with his wife, Karen (1932–), Anderson wrote the elaborate historical fantasy series The King of Ys, comprising *Roma Mater* (1986), *Gallicenae* (1987), *Dahut* (1988), and *The Dog and the Wolf* (1988); their other collaborations are collected in *The Unicorn Trade* (1984).

ANDOM, R. (1869–1920). Pseudonym of British writer Alfred Walter Barrett, who wrote a great deal of **humorous** fiction, much of it for boys' papers, including several Ansteyan fantasies. The title story of *The Strange Adventure of Roger Wilkins and Other Stories* (1985), *The Identity Exchange* (1902; aka *The Marvellous Adventures of Me*), and the second of the two novellas making up The Magic Bowl *and* The Blue-Stone Ring (1909) all recycle the central motif of *Vice Versa*. In *The Enchanted Ship* (1908), a pirate ship is plagued by ghosts.

ANGELIC FANTASY. In Judaic, Christian, and Islamic scripture, angels are divine messengers. According to various apocryphal texts, some were expelled from heaven after a rebellion led by Lucifer, thus becoming "fallen angels." Some Christian sects assert that every human is attended by a "guardian angel."

All of these ideas are very abundantly reflected in literature. **John Milton**'s rebuttal in *Paradise Lost* of Vondel's account of the war in heaven established a significant **taproot text**, to which such revisionist accounts as Jonathan Daniels's *Clash of Angels* (1930), **John Cowper Powys**'s *Lucifer*, Edward Pearson's *Chamiel* (1973), Stefan Heym's *The Wandering Jew* (1981; tr. 1983), **Steven Brust**'s *To Reign in Hell* (1984), and **Philip Pullman**'s *The Amber Spyglass* are overt ripostes. Notable accounts of fallen angels on earth include **Anatole France**'s *The Revolt of the Angels*, **Helen Beauclerk**'s *The Love of the Foolish Angel*, **Garry Kilworth**'s *Angel*, **Nancy Springer**'s *Metal Angel*, Harry Mulisch's *The Discovery of Heaven* (1996), Nancy Collins's *Angels on Fire* (1998), L. A. Marzulli's *Nephilim* (1999), and Peter Lord-Wolff's *The Silence in Heaven* (2000). The notion that fallen (and sometimes unfallen) angels interbred with humankind, producing "nephilim" offspring, is explored by **Storm Constantine** and Thomas E. Sniegoski's series begun with *The Fallen* (2003). Ambiguous angels of other kinds are featured in Elizabeth Knox's *The Vintner's Luck* (1998) and Cameron Rogers's *The Music of Razors* (2001).

Angelic messengers and guardians are notably featured in the works of **Marie Corelli**, Guy Thorne's *The Angel* (1908), **Frank Baker**'s *Sweet Chariot*, *Inez and Her Angel* (1954) by Georgina Sime and Frank Nicholson, Vassilis Vassilikos's "The Angel" (1961; tr. 1964), **Robert Nathan**'s *Heaven and Hell and the Megas Factor,* **James Morrow**'s *Towing Jehovah*, Frederick Buechner's *On the Road with the Archangel* (1997), A. Manette Ansay's *River Angel* (1998), Elizabeth Brownrigg's *Falling to Earth* (1998), Cecelia Holland's *The Angel and the Sword* (2000), and Stephanie Bedwell-Grime's *Guardian Angel* (2003). Angelic fantasies giving priority to the Judaic tradition include **Ben Hecht**'s "Remember Thy Creator" and Bernard Malamud's "Angel Levine" (1955).

Sceptical fantasies representing angels as agents of divine tyranny include **Marcus Donnelly**'s *Prophets for the End of Time,* and Jeffrey Thomas's *Letters from Hades* (2003). Various other sceptical analyses of the notion are featured in **H. G. Wells**'s *The Wonderful Visit*, David Almond's *Skellig,* and *The Man on the Ceiling* (2000) by Steve Rasnic Tem and Melanie Tem, but modern belief in the reality of angels and their continued involvement in human affairs remains very strong, especially in the United States, assisting a recent flood of credulous **Christian fantasies**; this phenomenon sharpens the piquancy of such sceptical **satires** as David Sosnowski's *Rapture* (1996), Lyda Morehouse's chimerical trilogy comprising *Archangel Protocol* (2001), *Fallen Host* (2002), and *Messiah Node* (2003), and Robert Deveraux's *A Flight of Storks and Angels* (2004).

Artists have routinely assumed that angelic messengers would need wings to travel between heaven and earth; angelic wings are often featured as symbolic badges of virtue, in such works as **Barry Pain**'s *Going Home*, **Mervyn Peake**'s *Mr Pye,* and **Nancy Willard**'s *Sister Water*, which overlap with secular fantasies of **flight**. In a rare instance of fantasy literature borrowing inspiration from the **cinema**, the notion that dead people might serve an apprenticeship to earn angelic status—popularized in Frank Capra's *It's a Wonderful Life* (1946)—frequently crops up in modern angelic fantasy, as in **Donna Jo Napoli**'s Angelwings series and **Annie Dalton**'s Angels Unlimited series. As with **fairies**, representations of angels in art provided a convenient vehicle for eroticization in Victorian times—an inspiration carried flamboyantly forward by **Jacqueline Carey**. Peter Crowther's *Heaven Sent* (1995) is a notable showcase **anthology**.

ANIMAL FANTASY A story with characters that include sentient animals credited with the ability to communicate with others of their own species, and sometimes members of other species, but usually not with humans. Fantasies featuring human/animal communication—from Edgar Allan Poe's *The Raven* through the principal works of **Hugh Lofting**, Shirley Rousseau Murphy, and **Mary Brown** to M. Coleman Easton's *Masters of Glass* (1985) and *The Fisherman's Curse* (1987), **Paul Auster**'s *Timbuktu* (1999) and Donald Harington's *With* (2004)—may also be subsumed under the heading, as may **theriomorphic fantasies**, but they are essentially separate categories, with only slight overlaps. Accounts of entirely hypothetical species, like **Tove Jansson**'s moomintrolls and **Elisabeth Beresford**'s wombles also belong to a different category, although they sometimes mimic key features of animal fantasy, as in **Robin Wayne Bailey**'s accounts of the dragonkin. Didactic works that credit sentience to animals whose exploits are otherwise naturalistic—for example, Anna Sewell's *Black Beauty* (1877) and Henry Williamson's *Tarka the Otter* (1927)—are also marginal.

Animal fantasy is rooted in **allegorical** and **satirical** beast **fables**, which range from those credited to Aesop and Pilpay through such medieval tales as the 12th-century *Roman de Renart,* featuring Reynard the Fox, and Wu Ch'eng-en's 16th-century *Journey to the West* (aka *Monkey*) to Joel Chandler Harris's 19th-century tales of Brer Rabbit; the purer literary extensions of the tradition include **Rudyard Kipling**'s *Jungle Books*, **Kenneth Grahame**'s *The Wind in the Willows*, Manfred Kyber's works collected in *Among Animals* (1912–26; tr. 1967), John Lambourne's *The Kingdom That Was* (1931), the principal works of **Walter Wangerin** and **Richard Bach**, and Philip J. Davis's *Thomas Gray, Philosopher Cat* (1988).

Some of these works became significantly influential in their own right, especially *The Wind in the Willows,* which echoes in a good deal of subsequent British fantasy, including the works of **Beatrix Potter**, and such successors as Alison Uttley and such exercises in calculated quaintness as Beverley Nichols's series begun with *The Tree That Sat Down* (1945). The nearest American equivalent is found in the works of George Selden, author of *A Cricket in Times Square* (1961). Grahame's eccentric juxtapositions of species are further represented in fantasies featuring odd couples, including **Algernon Blackwood**'s *Dudley and Gilderoy,* Don Marquis's tales of *archy and mehitabel* (1927), and **E. B. White**'s *Charlotte's Web*.

Although animal fantasy was perennially popular in **children's fiction**, especially for younger readers, the subgenre was dramatically repopularized by the success of **Richard Adams**'s rabbit fantasy *Watership Down,* an example followed by such writers as **William Horwood** (featuring moles), **Garry Kilworth** (wolves, foxes, and weasels), **Brian Jacques** and **Robin Jarvis** (mice), and **William Kotzwinkle** and **David Henry Wilson** (rats). Adams's **quest** template was adapted to **commodified fantasy** by Niel Hancock's Circle of Light sequence, *Greyfax Grimwald, Faragon Fairingay, Calix Stay,* and *Squaring the Circle* (all 1977). Other notable examples of post-Adamsian animal fantasy include Robert Westall's *The Cats of Seroster* (1984) and *Urn Burial* (1987), Meredith Hooper's *The Journal of Watkin Stench* (1988; rats), Stephen Moore's *Tooth and Claw* (1998; cats), Donald Harington's *The Cockroaches of Stay More* (1989), **Tad Williams**'s *Tailchaser's Song,* Michael H. Payne's *The Blood Jaguar* (1998), David Clement-Davies's *Fore Bringer* (1999; deer), Michael Hoeye's *Time Stops for No Mouse* (2000), **Cherith Baldry**'s Eaglesmount trilogy, Livi Michael's *Frank and the Black Hamster of Narkiz* (2002), Dale C. Willard's *The Linnet's Tale* (2002), S. F. Said's *Varjak Paw* (2003; cats), Melissa Haber's *The Heroic Adventures of Hercules Amsterdam* (2003; mice), and Carter Crocker's *The Tale of the Swamp Rat* (2003).

ANSTEY, F. (1856–1934). Pseudonym of British writer Thomas Anstey Guthrie, who popularized a new subgenre of **humorous/intrusive fantasy** with a sequence of novels begun with the classic **identity exchange** story *Vice Versa; or, A Lesson to Fathers* (1882). The teasing **erotic fantasy** *The Tinted Venus* (1885) extrapolates an anecdote from Richard Burton's *Anatomy of Melancholy,* using a misplaced engagement ring to bring a **classical** figure, the **goddess** of love, into the unsuitable moral environment of Victorian England. *A Fallen Idol* (1886) imports a sinister Jain idol with similar but darker effect. In *Tourmalin's Time Cheques* (1885; aka *The Time Bargain*), a young man who banks the time spent on a long sea voyage finds himself in paradoxical difficulties when he begins cashing the cheques. In *The Brass Bottle*, an exceedingly grateful **djinn** causes severe embarrassment to his releaser.

Anstey reversed his formula in *Only Toys* (1903) and *In Brief Authority* (1915), the latter taking a Victorian matron and her family into the **Brothers Grimm**'s *Märchenland.* His shorter fantasies are collected, with other material, in *The Black Poodle and Other Tales* (1884), *The Talking Horse* (1891), *Paleface and Redskin* (1898), *Salted Almonds*

(1906), *Percy and Others* (1915), and *The Last Load* (1925). The works reprinted in the omnibus *Humour and Fantasy* (1931) became the definitive models of "Ansteyan fantasy," although most of the notable examples thereof had already appeared, including "Sir Jocelyn's Cap" by **Walter Besant** and **Walter Herries Pollock**, various works by **R. Andom** and Richard Marsh, and *The Rejuvenation of Miss Semaphore* (1900) by "Hal Godfrey" (C. O'Conor Eccles). The formula lost its bite once Victorian moralism had weakened, although various works by **W. A. Darlington**, Kennedy Bruce's *The Fakir's Curse* (1931), Ladbroke Black's *The Gorgon's Head* (1932), Josephine Leslie's *The Ghost and Mrs Muir* (1945 as by R. A. Dick), and Ernest Elmore's *The Lumpton Gobbelings* (1954) maintained the tradition until the eve of the permissive 1960s.

ANTHOLOGY. Many early collections of myths and legends are, in essence, anthologies, and such widely sourced collections as **Chaucer**'s *Canterbury Tales* (c1387) and Straparola's *Nights* (1550–53) played a key role in converting the substance of **folktales** into literature, as did collections of **ballads**. Classic collections of folktales assembled by such writers as **Charles Perrault** and the **Brothers Grimm** helped to normalize the practices of literary **recycling** and **transfiguration**. When books began to be compiled with contents that were credited to an assortment of authors judiciously sampled by an editor—at the end of the 18th century—the format was frequently used as a showcase for fantastic materials, as in the volume of *Tales of the East* (1812) compiled for **Walter Scott** by his assistant Henry Weber, who also assembled *Popular Romances* (1812), an anthology of **fantastic voyages** modeled on Charles Garnier's 36-volume collection of *Voyages imaginaires, songes, visions, et romans cabalistiques* (1787–89). Other significant 19th-century samplers included Thomas Carlyle's *German Romances* (4 vols., 1827), poetry anthologies like **A. E. Waite**'s *Elfin Music*, numerous anthologies of fairy tales, including **Andrew Lang**'s classic series, and a series of U.S. anthologies edited by Thomas H. Mosher, *The Bibelot* (20 vols., 1895–1914), which reprinted a good deal of fantasy by **William Morris**, **Fiona MacLeod**, **Vernon Lee**, **Oscar Wilde**, and others.

Anthologies of **ghost** and **horror** stories became very popular in the early part of the 20th century, but fantasy anthologies were usually marketed as children's literature. The anthology translated as *The Book of Fantasy* (1940; tr. 1976), ed. Jorge Luis Borges, Silvino Ocampo, and

Adolfo Bioy Casares, broke that mold, probably helping to inspire *Pause to Wonder* (1944) and *Strange to Tell* (1946), ed. Marjorie Fischer and Rolfe Humphries, two significant showcases displaying the full range of fantastic fiction to English readers. A further set of three was assembled by Kay Dick (two of them bylined Jeremy Scott) in 1946–50, while Donald A. Wollheim began issuing a series of *Avon Fantasy Readers* in 1949. The literary end of the spectrum, including early examples of **surrealism** and **magic realism**, was showcased in *A Night with Jupiter and Other Fantastic Stories* (1947), ed. Charles Henri Ford.

The 1960s paperback boom created market space for **L. Sprague de Camp**'s subgenre-defining *Swords and Sorcery* and its sequels, which soon spawned numerous imitations, clearing the way for **Lin Carter** to begin his crucial genre-defining exploits in such texts as *The Young Magicians* and *Dragons, Elves and Heroes*. Showcase anthologies compiled by other interested editors supplemented and amended Carter's, the most notable being Robert H. Boyer and **Kenneth Zahorski**'s *The Fantastic Imagination*, **Terri Windling**'s *Elsewhere* couplet, Terry Carr's *A Treasury of Modern Fantasy* (1981), Maxim Jakubowski's *Lands of Never* (1983) and *Beyond Lands of Never* (1984), David Hartwell's *Masterpieces of Fantasy and Enchantment* (1988) and *Masterpieces of Fantasy and Wonder* (1989), and Martin H. Greenberg's **Tolkien** memorial *After the King* (1992).

The commercial genre's domination by long novels and novel series ensured, however, that there would be a significant role still to be played by showcases of shorter works. The international dimensions of the genre are extravagantly displayed by Alberto Manguel in *Black Water* (1983) and *Black Water 2* (1990; aka *White Fire*), by Franz Rottensteiner in *The Slaying of the Dragon: Modern Tales of the Playful Imagination* (1984), and numerous **Dedalus** samplers. The literary pretensions of the genre are also exhibited by such anthologies as Tom Shippey's *Oxford Book of Fantasy Stories* (1994) and *The Penguin Book of Modern Fantasy by Women* (1995), ed. A. Susan Williams and Richard Glyn Jones. The remarkable eclecticism of Windling's fantasy section of the *Year's Best* series she edited with Ellen Datlow, until she was replaced by **Kelly Link** and Glenn Grant, continues to exemplify the full range of the genre. Other significant showcase anthologies include the 1996 *Fantasy* volume of the Bending the Landscape series, ed. Nicola Griffiths and Stephen Pagel, **Robert Silverberg**'s *Legends* couplet, and Al Sarrantonio's *Flights: Extreme Visions of Fantasy* (2004).

ANTHONY, MARK (1966–). U.S. writer. The Last Rune series, comprising *Beyond the Pale* (1998), *The Keep of Fire* (1999), *The Dark Remains* (2001), *Blood of Mystery* (2002), *The Gates of Winter* (2003), and *The First Stone* (2004), is a sophisticated **portal fantasy** that juxtaposes the city of Denver with the **secondary world** of Eldh, providing opportunities for far-ranging adventures—the fourth volume **timeslips** to the Wild West—and the examination of various philosophical and political issues, including problems of **prophecy**.

ANTHONY, PIERS (1934–). U.S. writer. His early work was mostly **sf** or **ambiguous/science fantasy** (refer to *HDSFL*). The **humorous fantasy** *A Spell for Chameleon* (1977) launched the best-selling Xanth series, continued in *The Source of Magic* (1979), *Castle Roogna* (1979), *Centaur Aisle* (1981), *Ogre, Ogre* (1982), *Night Mare* (1982), *Dragon on a Pedestal* (1983), *Crewel Lye* (1985), *Golem in the Gears* (1986), *Vale of the Vole* (1987), *Heaven Cent* (1988), *Man from Mundania* (1989), *Isle of View* (1990), *Question Quest* (1991), *The Color of Her Panties* (1992), *Demons Don't Dream* (1993), *Harpy Thyme* (1993), *Geis of the Gargoyle* (1994), *Roc and a Hard Place* (1995), *Yon Ill Wind* (1996), *Faun and Games* (1997), *Zombie Lover* (1998), *Xone of Contention* (1999), *The Dastard* (2000), *Fell Swoop* (2001), *Up in a Heaval* (2002), and *Cube Route* (2003), which mixes wordplay (literalizing metaphors on a wholesale basis) with mildly **sentimental**, heroic quests in an unusually turbulent melting pot.

In the **chimerical** Apprentice Adept series, comprising *Split Infinity* (1980), *Blue Adept* (1981), *Juxtaposition* (1982), *Out of Phaze* (1987), *Robot Adept* (1988), *Unicorn Point* (1989), and *Phaze Doubt* (1990), magic and science are required to maintain a careful balance. The more earnest Incarnations of Immortality series comprises *On a Pale Horse* (1983), *Bearing an Hourglass* (1984), *With a Tangled Skein* (1985), *Wielding a Red Sword* (1986), *Being a Green Mother* (1987), *For Love of Evil* (1988), and *And Eternity* (1990). The Geodyssey series, which uses serial reincarnation to track the prehistory of humankind, comprises *Isle of Woman* (1993), *Shame of Man* (1994), *Hope of Earth* (1997), and *Muse of Art* (1999).

Hasan (1977) is an **Arabian fantasy**. *Shade of the Tree* (1986) is a **dark fantasy**. *Tatham Mound* (1991) is a historical novel with some marginal fantasy content. *The Willing Spirit* (1996) is a humorous fantasy. Anthony's collaborative work includes a stereotyped **heroic fantasy** series written with Robert E. Margroff, comprising *Dragon's Gold* (1987), *Serpent's Silver* (1988), *Chimaera's Copper* (1990), *Orc's Opal* (1991), and *Mouvar's Magic* (1992). *Through the Ice* (1989 with Robert Kornwise) is a posthumous completion of a novel by a teenager. *If I Pay Thee Not in Gold* (1993, with **Mercedes Lackey**) features a magically sustained matriarchy. *Quest for the Fallen Star* (1998, with James Richey and Alan Riggs) is a **quest** fantasy. *Dream a Little Dream* (1999) is a **hallucinatory fantasy** based on dream-journals written by Julie Brady. *The Secret of Spring* (2000, with Jo Anne Tauesch) is a humorous chimerical fantasy. In *The Gutbucket Quest* (2000, with Ron Leming), the blues feature as magical **music**.

APOCALYPTIC FANTASY. Apocalyptic literature was produced in considerable abundance between 200 BC and 200 AD, when Jews and Christians responded to political persecution by envisaging a cataclysmic divine intervention in earthly affairs that would put an end to history and settle outstanding moral accounts. The example accepted into the New Testament as the Revelation of St. John the Divine became enormously influential as a **taproot text**, dominating the imagery of a subgenre that has broadened its scope to encompass any abrupt "end of the world [as we know it]."

Favorite motifs from Revelation include the mysterious Beast whose number is 666; the four horsemen who spread Famine, Pestilence, War, and Death; and the field of Armageddon, on which the kings of the earth are drawn to battle. The four horsemen have become part of the standard apparatus of **humorous fantasy**, lavishly employed by **Terry Pratchett**, who produced a comprehensive comic fantasy version of Revelation in collaboration with **Neil Gaiman**, *Good Omens*. The sounding of trumpets following the removal of the seventh seal of the book binding the world together also became a familiar comedy motif, as featured in **H. G. Wells**'s "The Story of the Last Trump" and **Lord Berners**'s *Count Omega*. More earnest **transfigurations** of Revelation include Sydney Watson's trilogy begun with *"Scarlet and Purple"* (1913) and Joseph B. Burroughs's *Titan, Son of Saturn* (1921).

The modern subgenre belongs as much to **sf** (refer to *HDSFL*) as to fantasy, continuing a syncretic tradition that began with such **hybrid** works as Cousin de Grainville's *The Last Man* (1805: tr. 2003); further examples include R. H. Benson's *The Lord of the World* (1906), Robert Nichols's "Golgotha & Co." (1923), **John Cowper Powys**'s *Up and Out*, Bernard MacLaren's *Day of Misjudgment* (1956), and James Blish's *The Devil's Day* (1968–72).

Apocalyptic fantasy enjoyed a spectacular renaissance as the end of the second millennium approached, a flourishing represented in such pious **religious/horror stories** (refer to *HDHL*) as Tim LaHaye and Jerry B. Jenkins's best-selling Left Behind series (1995–2003) and Michael D. O'Brien's *Father Elijah: An Apocalypse* (1996); such **satires** as Andrei Codrescu's *Messiah* (1999), Melvin Jules Bukiet's *Signs and Wonders* (1999), and Lyda Morehouse's *Apocalypse Array* (2004); and such melodramas as **Mark Chadbourn**'s Age of Misrule sequence and the climactic volume of Charles E. Grant's Millennium Quartet, *Riders in the Sky* (1999). The fashionability of the theme continued into the 21st century in such works as **Marcos Donnelly**'s *Prophets for the End of Time.*

The **secondary worlds** of **commodified fantasy** are often threatened with apocalyptic termination, but the formulaic plots of commodified versions usually require that the apocalypses be aborted in the nick of time. Thrillers employing the apocalypse as the ultimate instrument of **melodramatic inflation** are compelled to do likewise, as in **George R. R. Martin**'s *The Armageddon Rag*. Some secondary world fantasies, however, such as R. Scott Bakker's Prince of Nothing trilogy, begun with *The Darkness That Comes Before* (2003), gain valuable narrative energy from such apocalyptic threats. Ancient apocalypses are sometimes featured in **historical fantasies**, as in Pauline J. Alama's *The Eye of Night* (2002).

APOLLINAIRE, GUILLAUME (1880–1918). Pseudonym of Italian-born French poet Wilhelm de Kostrowitzky, the great pioneer of **surrealism**. His fiction includes the title novella (1904) of *L'Enchanteur pourrissant* (1909), featuring an attempt to resurrect **Merlin**, the items translated in *The Heresiarch and Co.* and *The Wandering Jew and Other Stories* (1910; tr. 1965), and *The Poet Assassinated and Other Stories* (tr. 1985).

APPLEGATE, K. A. (1956–). U.S. writer best known for the Animorphs series of educational **animal fantasies**, launched in 1996, which runs to more than 60 volumes. Her other fantasy project, the Everworld series, is an **Odyssean fantasy** in which a group of children are displaced into a parallel universe where they encounter the apparatus of **fairy tales**, **classical** mythology, **Atlantean fantasy**, and various other motifs; it comprises *Search for Senna* (1999), *Land of Loss* (1999), *Enter the Enchanted* (1999), *Realm of the Reaper* (1999), *Discover the Destroyer* (1999), *Fear the Fantastic* (2000), *Gateway to the Gods* (2000), *Brave* *the Betrayal* (2000), *Inside the Illusion* (2000), *Understanding the Unknown* (2000), *Mystify the Magician* (2001), and *Entertain the End* (2001).

APULEIUS. Carthaginian writer, sometimes called Lucius Apuleius, who flourished in the second century A.D. *Metamorphoses, or The Golden Ass*—based on the slightly earlier *Lucius; or The Ass* by the Greek satirist **Lucian**—is a bawdy, **picaresque fantasy** that might qualify as the first fantasy novel. Similarly, the interpolated tale of Cupid and Psyche might be regarded as the first **art fairy tale**; it was frequently **recycled**, most notably in Molière's *Psiché* (1671), Thomas Shadwell's *Psyche* (1675), Louis Couperus' *Psyche* (1898), and **C. S. Lewis**'s *Till We Have Faces*. *The Golden Ass* survived the Dark Ages in spite of its flamboyant licentiousness, with the assistance of blatantly hypocritical attempts to construe it as a Christian **allegory**.

ARABIAN FANTASY. A subcategory of **Oriental fantasy** founded in **Antoine Galland**'s version of *The Arabian Nights;* the motif most widely deployed in fantasy literature is the **djinn**, although magic carpets are also commonplace and the framing device of **Scheherazade**'s life-saving efforts as a storyteller has generated its own mini-genre. The erotic content of Galland's tales, bowdlerized in some translations and exaggerated in others, recommended them for use in the kind of sophisticated fantasy that became commonplace in subsequent French fiction; notable examples include **Anthony Hamilton**'s *The Four Facardins,* Augustin-Paradis de Moncrif's *The Adventures of Zeloide and Amanzarifdine* (1715; tr. 1929), Jacques-Rochette de la Morlière's *Angola: An Eastern Tale* (1746; tr. 1751), **Voltaire**'s *Zadig,* Stanislaus-Jean de Boufflers's "The Dervish" (1810; tr. 1926) and two novellas by **Gérard de Nerval**. English pastiches include Samuel Johnson's *Rasselas* (1759), **William Beckford**'s *Vathek*, G. P. R. James's *The String of Pearls* (1832), George Meredith's *The Shaving of Shagpat* (1855), H. N. Crellin's *Tales of the Caliph* (1887), and **F. Marion Crawford**'s *Khaled*.

The fashionability of Arabian fantasy waned in the 19th century, but the subgenre survived into the 20th in such examples as Frank Heller's *The Thousand and Second Night* (1924 in Swedish; tr. 1926), Noel Langley's *The Tale of the Land of Green Ginger* (1937; aka *The Land of Green Ginger*), and Arthur Lee Gould's *An Airplane in the Arabian Nights* (1947) before its absorption into **commodified fantasy** in the wake of **Piers Anthony**'s *Hasan*. Notable examples include Graham Diamond's *Marrakesh* (1981) and *Marrakesh Nights* (1984), M. Coleman Easton's *Iskiir* (1986), Seamus Cullen's *A Noose of Light* and *The Sultan's Turret* (both 1986), Lillian Stewart Carl's *Wings of Power* (1989), and works by **Chaz Brenchley**, **Esther Friesner**, **Richard Matheson**, and **Ray Bradbury**. Works by **Salman Rushdie**, **A. S. Byatt**, and Anna Kashina's *The Princess of Dhagabad* (2000) assisted in its reintroduction into the field of literary fiction. A notable showcase is the **anthology** couplet *Arabesques: More Tales of the Arabian Nights,* ed. Susan Schwartz.

Arabian fantasy originating in the Middle East is rare in translation; notable exceptions include Naguib Mahfouz's *Arabian Nights and Days* (1979; tr. 1995), Bahiyyih Nakhjavani's *The Saddlebag* (2000), and Raja Alem's *Fatma: A Novel of Arabia* (2003; co-credited to translator Tom McDonough).

ARCADIAN FANTASY. A subgenre consisting of fantasies based on the hypothesis that there was once a pastoral "Golden Age" of social harmony and languid ease. Its core is a subcategory of **classical fantasy** relating to the myth of Arcadia, which was elevated by the Roman poet Virgil to archetypal status as a pastoral paradise; the notion was essentially nostalgic even then. The paradigm example of Roman Arcadian fantasy is Longus's *Daphnis and Chloe* (5th century); the subgenre reappeared in the Renaissance in such works as Giovanni Boccaccio's *The Nymph of Fiesole* (Italy, c1350; tr. 1959), Jacopo Sannazaro's *Arcadia* (Italy, 1504), Jorge de Montemayor's *La Diana* (Spain, 1559), Sir Philip Sidney's posthumously published *Arcadia* (England, 1590) and Honoré d'Urfé's *L'Astrée* (France 1607–27).

Arcadian fantasy is complementary to Utopian fantasy, contesting the notion that civilization, technological development, and political reorganization can provide a route to ideal human existence. It was unfashionable during the era of **romanticism**, because its harmonious imagery of benign nature seemed too tame to the followers of that movement, the German origins of which had a more sinister and menacing notion of wilderness; in the post-Romantic 19th century, however, there was a dramatic revival of interest in the god of Arcadia, **Pan**, an ambivalent figure who could be invested with menace as well as nostalgia. Ford Madox Ford's *The Young Lovell* (1913) features a rare Arcadian **timeslip**. There was also a conspicuous Arcadian spirit in pre-Raphaelism, as exemplified by the works of **William Morris**, and the literature of the

Celtic revival, although even its fervent participants could not imagine ancient Ireland, Scotland, or Wales as lands overflowing with natural bounty.

There are significant elements of Arcadian fantasy in the work of many 20th-century writers, notably **W. H. Hudson**, **Eleanor Farjeon**, **E. R. Eddison**, **Eden Phillpotts**, and **Thomas Burnett Swann**; its perennial nostalgic appeal was reinforced in the latter part of the century by ecological anxieties and the growth of ecological mysticism (refer to *HDSFL*). Ecological fantasies often focus intently on forests, which are essentially hospitable in Arcadian fantasy, as in Nancy Kress's *The Golden Grove* (1984), **David B. Coe**'s Tobyn-Ser series, **Richard Grant**'s *Rumours of Spring*, Kate Atkinson's *Human Croquet* (1997), Mindy L. Klasky's *Season of Sacrifice* (2002), and Susan Britton's *The Treekeepers* (2003).

ARDEN, TOM (1961–). Pseudonym of Australian writer David Rain, resident in Britain since 1990. The Orokon series is a **chimerical** amalgam of **dark** and **humorous** fantasy set in a **secondary world** resembling an **alternative** 18th century; it comprises *The Harlequin's Dance* (1997), *The King and Queen of Swords* (1998), *Sultan of the Moon and Stars* (1999), *Sisterhood of the Blue Storm* (2000), and *Empress of the Endless Dream* (2001). The range of its mythical and folkloristic sources expands in the final volume to take in literary reflections like the legendary lamasery of *Found Horizon* and echoes of **Mervyn Peake**. *Shadow Black* (2002) is a similarly inclined **Gothic**/**Satire**.

ARIOSTO, LODOVICO (1474–1533). Italian poet whose crucial contribution to the development of prose romance, *Orlando Furioso* (1516; exp. 1532), picked up the thread of Matteo Boiardo's incomplete *Orlando Innamorato* (1487). Such celebrated passages as Astolpho's hippogriff-flight to the moon, in search of Orlando's lost wits, exemplify an inventive exhilaration that became central to the appeal of modern fantasy fiction. The author and his creation are deftly transformed in **Chelsea Quinn Yarbro**'s **alternative history** novel *Ariosto*.

ARMSTRONG, ANTHONY (1897–1976). British writer best known as a humorist, in which vein he produced two volumes of parodic **fairy tales**, *The Prince Who Hiccupped and Other Tales* (1932) and *The Pack of Pieces* (1942; aka *The Naughty Princess*). His longer works include two **karmic romances**, *Lure of the Past* (1920) and *The Love of Prince*

Raameses (1921), the **Atlantean fantasy** *The Wine of Death* (1925), and the **doppelgänger** story *The Strange Case of Mr Pelham* (1957).

ARMSTRONG, KELLEY (1968–). Canadian writer. Her fantasies are set in an **alternative history** in which most species of "supernaturals" exist covertly. *Bitten* (2001) features the world's only female werewolf. The heroine of *Stolen* (2002) is thrown into a secret prison with a mixed population of inmates. *Dime Store Magic* (2004) and *Industrial Magic* (2004) examine the commerce of the altered world, the latter introducing a supernatural mafia.

ARNOLD, EDWIN LESTER (1857–1935). British writer. He was the son of the poet Sir Edwin Arnold, whose verse epic *The Light of Asia* (1879) dramatized the life of Buddha and who bequeathed to his son a strong interest in the ideas of **reincarnation** and karma. With **H. Rider Haggard,** Arnold Lester pioneered the subgenre of **karmic romance**. The hero of *The Wonderful Adventures of Phra the Phoenician* (1891) recalls his "awakenings" in different eras of British history, continually meeting versions of his female ideal. "Rutherford the Twice-Born" (1892) makes more explicit use of the notion of *karma*. In *Lepidus the Centurion: A Roman of To-day* (1901), a young Victorian and a resurrected Roman turn out to be fragmentary aspects of a single soul. *Lieut. Gullivar Jones: His Vacation* (1905; aka *Gulliver of Mars*) took Haggardesque adventure fiction to Mars, pioneering the subgenre of **planetary romance**.

ART FAIRY TALE. A translation of the German term *kunstmärchen*, applied by members of the German **Romantic** movement to stories that **transfigured** or mimicked **folktales** but aspired to the "higher" artistic goals of stylistic elegance and philosophical or allegorical purpose. The term was derived by analogy with a distinction drawn by the **Brothers Grimm** between *naturpoesie* (nature poetry) and *kunstpoesie* (art poetry), the former being allegedly generated by a quasi-organic process by the *volk*—the entire people—rather than by distinct individuals. Although the Grimms thought "natural" folk tales innately superior to *kunstmärchen,* their fellow Romantics did not.

Cardinal examples of art fairy tales include **J. W. Goethe**'s *Märchen*, **Johann Ludwig Tieck**'s "The Elves," and the **Baron de la Motte Fouqué**'s *Undine*. French examples were produced by **Charles Nodier** and many **Decadent** writers, notably Catulle Mendès's *Luscignole* (1892; tr. 1928). **George MacDonald**'s allegories, John Ruskin's

moralistic *The King of the Golden River* (1850), and **Oscar Wilde**'s fairy tales are among the most notable early English examples. Twentieth-century art fairy tales were produced in some profusion by **Herman Hesse**, **Michel Tournier**, and **Angela Carter**.

ARTHURIAN FANTASY. The legend of King Arthur, seeded by Geoffrey of Monmouth's **scholarly fantasy** *Historia Regum Britanniae* [*The History of the Kings of Britain*] (1136), became enormously important in French **romance** as "the Matter of Britain" following its translation and elaboration in the *Roman de Brut* (1155). Further key elaborations were added by **Chrétien de Troyes**, who popularized the story of *Lancelot* and left the **allegorical/grail** romance *Le Conte de graal* (c1180) so tantalizingly unfinished that many others—including Wolfram von Eschenbach in Germany—took it upon themselves to do so. The love story of Tristan and Iseult was also gathered into the corpus, although it remained marginal.

Arthurian romance was reclaimed by native British writers in such texts as the obscurely allegorical *Gawain and the Green Knight* (c1370). It became a key element of the Welsh legendry assembled in the source texts of **Mabinogion** before being summarized and elaborated in *Le Morte d'Arthur* (published 1485 by William Caxton), which was credited to "Sir Thomas Malory," although its originator remains stubbornly mysterious. Malory's became the definitive version of Arthurian legend and one of the most important **taproot texts** of English literature.

Arthurian fantasy was repopularized in 19th-century Britain, its legendary base fetishized by the Pre-Raphaelite Brotherhood. Thomas Love Peacock's *The Misfortunes of Elphin* (1829) led the way for Alfred Lord Tennyson's "The Lady of Shalott" (1832) and *Idylls of the King* (1859), **William Morris**'s *The Defence of Guinevere* (1858), and Algernon Swinburne's *Tristram of Lyonesse* (1882). The legends also became a central pillar of the culture developed in late-19th-century **children's literature**, notable versions being issued by **Andrew Lang** in Britain and **Howard Pyle** in the United States, where **Mark Twain**'s *A Connecticut Yankee at King Arthur's Court* had already demonstrated the subgenre's potential as a comparative exemplar.

Arthurian fantasy is the primary modern refuge of the relics of **chivalric romance**, robustly sustained in that role by such motifs as the Round Table (and the ruination of its principles by Lancelot's adultery with Guinevere) and the grail quest. Arthur's magical mentor **Merlin** became the archetype of the philosopher **wizard** who exercises power from behind the throne. The notion that Arthur's death was not final and that he is eternally ready to return in some national hour of need offers abundant scope for the subgenre's extrapolation into **contemporary fantasy**. Such allegorical works as Coningsby Dawson's *The Road to Avalon* (1911) anticipated the elaborate exploration begun in **T. H. White**'s *The Sword in the Stone*. The disenchantment reflected in White's *The Ill-Made Knight* is evident in many other works shadowed by one or other of the world wars.

A significant dialogue was established in the 20th century between such de-romanticized **historical fantasies** as **John Cowper Powys**'s *Porius*, Edward Frankland's *The Bear of Britain* (1944), Edison Marshall's *The Pagan King* (1959), Henry Treece's *Legions of the Eagle* (1954), and Nikolai Tolstoy's *The Coming of the King* (1968) and defiantly Romantic texts like **C. S. Lewis**'s *That Hideous Strength* and Dorothy James Roberts's *Kinsmen of the Grail* (1963). That conflict was productively mined by American fantasies like **Robert Nathan**'s *The Fair,* Sanders Anne Laubenthal's *Excalibur* (1973), **Thomas Berger**'s *Arthur Rex,* and Parke Godwin's trilogy comprising *Firelord* (1980), *Beloved Exile* (1984), and *The Last Rainbow* (1985), as well as by sophisticated British children's fantasies by Rosemary Sutcliff, **Alan Garner**, **William Mayne**, and **Kevin Crossley-Holland**.

The combative attitude of the defenders of Romance was **feminized** when Arthurian fantasy was adapted into **commodified fantasy** by such writers as **Vera Chapman** and **Marion Zimmer Bradley**, establishing an even greater contrast with the rugged masculinity of the de-romanticized tradition carried forward by such works as Jack Whyte's Camulod Chronicles (launched 1992), Dafydd ab Hugh's *Arthur War Lord* (1994), and Bernard Cornwell's Arthurian trilogy (1995–97). Masculine romanticization was conscientiously reenhanced by **Stephen Lawhead** and **A. A. Attanasio** but treated lightheartedly by **Gerald Morris**. Feminized Arthurian fantasies tend to foreground Guinevere rather than Arthur—as in Sharan Newman's trilogy comprising *Guinevere* (1981), *The Chessboard Queen* (1983), and *Guinevere Evermore* (1985); Rosalind Miles's *Guinevere: Queen of the Summer Country* (1999); and Nancy McKenzie's trilogy comprising *The Child Queen* (1994), *The High Queen* (1995), and *Queen of Camelot* (2002)—and to establish **Morgan le Fay** as a counterpart to Merlin.

The nationalistic aspects of Arthurian fantasy remain central to the works of **Peter Vansittart**, Patrick McCormack's Albion series, begun with *The Last Companion* (1997) and *The White Phantom* (2000), and to Michael Morpurgo's sequence begun with *Arthur, High King of Britain* (1994), which moved on from straightforward **recycling** to contemporary fantasy in *The Sleeping Sword* (2002). Twain's use of Camelot as a yardstick for American culture, incorporated into actual political rhetoric in the 1960s, is extrapolated in such fantasies as **Peter David**'s *Knight Life*, in which Arthur is re-enthroned in the White House. The subgenre was adapted to the concerns of postcolonial analysis in Elizabeth E. Wein's trilogy comprising *The Winter Prince* (1993), *A Coalition of Lions* (2003), and *The Sunbird* (2004), which export its materials to Africa.

Showcase **anthologies** of Arthurian fantasy include *Arthurian Literature by Women* (1999), ed. Alan Lupack and Barbara Tepa Lupack; several edited by **Mike Ashley**, Parke Godwin's *Invitation to Camelot,* Lawrence Schimel and Martin H. Greenberg's *Camelot Fantastic* (1998), Greenberg's *Merlin* (1999), James Lowder's *The Doom of Camelot* (2000) and *Legends of the Pendragon* (2002), **Jennifer Roberson**'s *Out of Avalon,* and **Sophie Masson**'s *The Road to Camelot*. Guides to the mythos include **Phyllis Ann Karr**'s *The Arthurian Companion*.

ASH, SARAH (1950–). British writer. *Moths to a Flame* (1995) is a **decadent fantasy** set in a "**Gothic**-Byzantine" court. *Songspinners* (1996) features magical **music** that is both a gift and a curse. *The Lost Child* (1998) is a **secondary world** murder mystery. The Tears of Artamon series, comprising *Lord of Snow and Shadows* (2003) and *Prisoner of Ironsea Tower* (2004; aka *Prisoner of the Iron Tower*), tracks an unfortunate inheritance that involves possession by a "dragon-daemon."

ASHLEY, MIKE (1948–). British scholar, whose guide to *Science Fiction, Fantasy and Weird Fiction Magazines* (1985) tracks the evolution of fantasy in popular magazines. His most substantial contribution to the genre is a series of **anthologies** of original **Arthurian fantasies** comprising *The Pendragon Chronicles* (1990), *The Camelot Chronicles* (1992), *The Merlin Chronicles* (1995), *The Chronicles of the Holy Grail* (1996; aka *Quest for the Holy Grail*), and *The Chronicles of the Round Table* (1997; aka *Tales of the Round Table*). *The Mammoth Book of Arthurian Legends* (1998) also includes some original items. His other anthologies include *Jewels of Wonder* (1981), *The Giant Book of Myths and Legends* (1995)—which **recycles** 51 items—*Classical Stories:*

Heroic Tales from Ancient Greece and Rome (1996; aka *Heroic Adventures Stories From the Golden Age of Greece and Rome*), *Fantasy Stories* (1996; aka *The Random House Book of Fantasy Stories*), *The Mammoth Book of Fairy Tales* (1997), *The Mammoth Book of Comic Fantasy* (1998), and *The Mammoth Book of Awesome Comic Fantasy* (2001). He is the biographer of **Algernon Blackwood**.

ASPRIN, ROBERT LYNN (1946–). U.S. writer. His principal contribution to the genre is a series of **humorous/Arabian fantasies** comprising *Another Fine Myth . . . .* (1978), *Myth Conceptions* (1980), *Myth Directions* (1982), *Hit or Myth* (1983), *Myth-ing Persons* (1984), *Little Myth Marker* (1985), *M.Y.T.H. Inc. Link* (1986), *Myth-Nomers and Im-perfections* (1987), *M.Y.T.H. Inc. in Action* (1990), and *Sweet Myth-tery of Life* (1994). He returned to the milieu in *Myth-ion Improbable* (2001), *Something M.Y.T.H. Inc.* (2002), *Myth Alliances* (2003, with **Jody Lynn Nye**). *Myth-Told Tales* (2003, with Nye) collects associated short stories. The best-selling 12-volume **shared world** series *Thieves' World* (launched 1979), coedited with **Lynn Abbey**, established the pattern for such marketing endeavours and helped popularize modern **picaresque fantasy**. *License Invoked* (2001, with Nye) and *E. Godz* (2003, with **Esther Friesner**) are further humorous fantasies.

ASTROLOGICAL FANTASY. Astrology is a pseudoscience based on the premise that the apparent movement of the planets through the constellations in the plane of the ecliptic influences events on Earth, permitting the personality and destiny of an individual to be investigated by means of a natal horoscope. Such beliefs were widespread in the ancient world and became briefly fashionable again during the Renaissance, but the 20th century became astrology's heyday; modern practitioners thrive by virtue of columns in magazines and newspapers and recorded telephone messages. In spite of this immense popularity, astrological fantasy is a relatively insignificant subgenre of modern fantasy, because it does not lend itself readily to narrative use.

Like alchemists, astrologers feature as minor characters in many **historical fantasies**, usually represented as charlatans; John Galt's "The Black Ferry" (c1820) and **Washington Irving**'s "Legend of the Arabian Astrologer" (1832) are exceptions. The Elizabethan magician John Dee, widely featured in historical **alchemical fantasies**, was also an astrologer, and his activities in that line are featured in such novels as Frances Sherwood's *The Book of Splendor* (2002).

Rudyard Kipling's "Children of the Zodiac" (1891), A. M. Williamson's *Children of the Zodiac* (1929), and Louis de Wohl's *Strange Daughter* (1945) toy with astrology in contemporary settings, as do Alan Griffiths's *The Passionate Astrologer*, Edward Hyams's *The Astrologer* (1950), and John Cameron's *The Astrologer* (1972), all of which examine by reductio ad absurdum what would result were the science exact. Earnest treatment of the thesis, as in Denny DeMartino's series begun with *The Astrologer: Heart of Stone* (2001) and **Michaela Roessner**'s series begun with *The Stars Dispose,* inevitably involves the construction of elaborate **alternative histories**. All treatises on astrology are **scholarly fantasies**, but *Arachne Rising* (1977) by "James Vogh" (John Sladek) is noteworthy as a hoax, which examines the properties of the long-lost 13th sign of the zodiac.

ATLANTEAN FANTASY. Atlantis—an island continent in the Atlantic allegedly sunk circa 9000 BC—was invented by Plato in the *Timaeus* and *Critias* to add dramatic zest to his model of an ideal society. The device played a major role in launching the great tradition of **scholarly fantasy**; although Plato's contemporaries and disciples treated the story as fiction, many later writers took it seriously as reportage of fact-based folklore. Scholarly fantasists from the Renaissance onward suggested many different locations for the "actual" Atlantis, which began to feature regularly in such 19th-century fantasies as Maurus Jokai's "The City of the Beast" (1856; tr. 1904) and Jules Verne's *Twenty Thousand Leagues under the Sea* (1870). The popularity of the motif was boosted by Ignatius Donnelly's best-selling scholarly fantasy *Atlantis, the Antediluvian World* (1882), which suggested that Atlantis was the ultimate source of modern civilization and that its demise offered an invaluable lesson to contemporary hubris. Donnelly's Atlantis was further transfigured in **Madame Blavatsky**'s *The Secret Doctrine* (1888), which made it a central element of **theosophical fantasy**; many subsequent **occult fantasists**, including **Dion Fortune**, similarly adapted it to their own purposes.

Donnelly's ideas were dramatized in André Laurie's *The Crystal City under the Sea* (1895; tr. 1896)—which suggested that a remnant might survive, protected by a glass dome—and C. J. Cutcliffe Hyne's pseudo-**historical fantasy** *The Lost Continent* (1900). Other literary produce of the boom included Frances Layland Barrett's "The Princess Vita" (1900), which makes Atlantis the origin of **merfolk**, D. Metchim-Bridgman's *Atlantis: The Book of Angels* (1900), and Pierre Benoît's *Atlantida* (1919; tr. 1920; aka *The Queen of Atlantis*).

Most early 20th-century Atlantean fantasy was couched as occult fantasy—including such esoterica as **John Cowper Powys**'s *Atlantis*—or marginal **sf**, although its fantasy deployments were tracked by **Lin Carter**'s **anthology** *The Magic of Atlantis*. It was quickly reclaimed by commodified fantasy, significant exemplars having been set by **Jane Gaskell** and **Marion Zimmer Bradley**. Notable modern examples include **Jan Siegel**'s *Prospero's Children,* Clive Cussler's *Atlantis Found* (2000), and **Kara Dalkey**'s Water series.

ATTANASIO, A. A. (1951–). U.S. writer whose early work was mostly **hybrid/science fantasy** (refer to *HDSFL*). *Wyvern* (1988) is a **historical fantasy** featuring a **feral child**. *Hunting the Ghost Dancer* (1991) is a **prehistoric fantasy**. The **Arthurian fantasy** *Kingdom of the Grail* (1992) prepared the ground for the series comprising *The Dragon and the Unicorn* (1994), *Arthor* (1995; aka *The Eagle and the Sword*), *The Wolf and the Crown* (1998; aka *The Perilous Order*), and *The Serpent and the Grail* (1999). *The Moon's Wife* (1993) is a **hallucinatory fantasy**. The series comprising *The Dark Shore* (1996), *The Shadow Eater* (1997), and *Octoberland* (1998) is ornately **chimerical**.

AULNOY, MADAME D' (c1650–1705). The signature used by French writer Marie-Cathérine Jumel, Comtesse d'Aulnoy, who became the hostess of a fashionable Paris salon in 1685; the custom developed there of improvising satirical versions of folktales—often drawn from Basile's *Pentamerone*—in order to comment slyly on events at Louis XIV's court, thus instituting the modern tradition of the **fairy tales/transfiguration**. "L'île de la félicité was incorporated into *L'Histoire d'Hippolyte, comte de Douglas* (1690) before her complete works were assembled in two four-volume collections, *Les contes des fées* (1696–98) and *Contes nouveaux ou les fés à la mode* (1698); a sampler of translations was issued as *Tales of the Fairys* (1699). The most famous include "The Blue Bird," "The Yellow Dwarf," and "The White Cat." Madame d'Aulnoy's contes are more substantial than Perrault's, and their didacticism is more sophisticated, but because they were not aimed at children they were not as frequently reprinted.

AUSTER, PAUL (1947–). U.S. writer of literary fiction whose novels usually have fantastic elements, frequently involving shifting identities. **Fabulation** is marginal to the trilogy of **postmodern/detective** stories, comprising *City of Glass* (1985), *Ghosts* (1986), and *The Locked Room* (1986) and to *Moon Palace* (1989), but *Mr Vertigo* (1994) is a wholehearted **allegory** of **flight**, and *Timbuktu* (1999) is an **animal fantasy** with suggestions of **reincarnation**. *The Book of Illusions* (2002) features a silent movie director who has difficulty contriving a permanent death. *Oracle Night* (2003) is a series of nested texts, the innermost of which tells the story of a clairvoyant soldier.

AUSTIN, WILLIAM (1788–1841). U.S. writer who followed examples set by **Washington Irving** in producing an Americanized version of the tale of the **Flying Dutchman**, recast as an **Odyssean fantasy**. "Peter Rugg—the Missing Man" (1824; exp. 1827) is cursed to wander the roads of New England for more than 50 years, missing the American Revolution.

AUSTRALIAN FANTASY. Australia was once a useful site for lost world stories and utopias, generating a local tradition the most notable fantasy examples of which are Robert H. Potter's **religious fantasy** *The Germ Growers* (1892) and G. Firth Scott's **theosophical fantasy** *The Last Lemurian* (1898). Little notable fantasy, however, was produced there in the first half of the 20th century. Although Australian **sf** made steady ground thereafter, fantasy was mainly restricted to the work of children's writers like **Patricia Wrightson**. The turn of the century, however, produced a remarkable flowering of fantasy literature by Australian authors, where **Keith Taylor** and **Sara Douglass** led, **Sophie Masson**, **Garth Nix**, **Tom Arden**, **Trudi Canavan**, **K. J. Bishop**, **Louise Cusack**, **Celia Dart-Thornton**, **Jennifer Fallon**, **Kate Forsythe**, **Ian Irvine**, **Josephine Pennicott**, and **Tansy Rayner Roberts** rapidly followed, assisted by immigrants like **Paul Brandon**. Fantasy elements also became more obvious in the work of literary fabulists like Peter Carey, author of *Illywhacker* (1985) and *My Life as a Fake* (2003).

Other notable fantasy writers born or based in Australia include **Mrs. Campbell Praed**, **Vernon Knowles**, **P. L. Travers**, and **Dave Luckett**; Gillian Rubenstein, author of *Foxspell* (1996), *The Fairy's Wings* (1998), and a number of **Oriental fantasies** bylined "Lian Hearn"; "Kate Jacoby" (Tracy Oliphant), author of the Elita series launched with *Exile's Return* (1998); Marele Day, author of *Lambs of God* (1998); and Marianne Curley, author of the Guardians of Time trilogy, launched with *The Named* (2002). Writers born or based in New Zealand include **Hugh Cook**, **Cherry Wilder**, **Juliet Marillier**, **Margaret Mahy,** and **Sherryl Jordan**. As in Canada, it may be that the sensation Australians have of being on the margins of English-language culture encourages an interest in exotic literary materials, although the fact that domestic publication began to flourish just as the fantasy genre was becoming commodified was undoubtedly a factor, as was the establishment of a domestic short-story market in the magazine *Aurealis*. A notable showcase **anthology** of Australian fantasy is Michael Barry's *Elsewhere: An Anthology of Incredible Places* (2003).

AWARDS. The principal annual awards for works in the fantasy genre are the Mythopoeic Awards, established by the **Mythopoeic Society** in 1971; the World Fantasy Awards, established by the **World Fantasy Convention** in 1975; and the William L. Crawford Award for best first novel in the field, established by the **International Association for the Fantastic in the Arts** in 1985. The **Locus** Awards also include a "Best Fantasy Novel" category. A Gandalf Award for lifetime contributions to fantasy by a particular writer, created by **Lin Carter** within the framework of **sf**'s Hugo Awards (for which works of fantasy are also eligible), was given from 1973 to 1980, and a similar Balrog Award from 1979 to 1985. The British Fantasy Awards, established by the British Fantasy Society in 1971, are more frequently given to **horror** fiction than fantasy (for which reason the BFA for best novel is the August Derleth Award). A **Calvino** Prize for New Writing in Speculative/Fabulist Fiction was established in 1999 by the Vermont Summer Writers' Conference.

AYMÉ, MARCEL (1902–1967). French writer whose novels of provincial life often included elements of Rabelaisian fantasy. Those translated as *The Green Mare* (1933; tr. 1938) and *The Fable and the Flesh* (1943; tr. 1949) involve apparitions based in folklore. His **fairy tales**, translated in *The Wonderful Farm* (1939; tr. 1951) and *Return to the Wonderful Farm* (1954; tr. 1954; aka *The Magic Pictures: More about the Wonderful Farm*) are slyly sophisticated. The short fiction in the samplers *Across Paris and Other Stories* (1950; aka *The Walker through Walls*) and *The Proverb and Other Stories* (1961) includes numerous fantasies.

– B –

BABBITT, NATALIE (1932–). U.S. writer and illustrator. The offbeat **quest** fantasy *The Search for Delicious* (1969) and *Kneeknock Rise*

(1970) are modeled on didactic **fairy tales**. *The Devil's Storybook* (1974) and *The Devil's Other Storybook* (1978) are **humorous** accounts of diabolical ineptitude. The sceptically meditative *Tuck Everlasting* (1975) examines the prospect of **immortality**. *Eyes of the Amaryllis* (1977) is a love story with fantastic elements.

BACH, RICHARD (1936–). U.S. writer whose motivational **animal fantasy** *Jonathan Livingston Seagull* (1970) was a best-seller. The collection *A Gift of Wings* (1974) contains some less didactically inclined works, but sentimentality and preachiness were further amalgamated in *Illusions: The Adventures of a Reluctant Messiah* (1977), *There's No Such Place as Far Away* (1979), and *One* (1988). The Ferret Chronicles, comprising *Rescue Ferrets at Sea* (2002), *Air Ferrets Aloft* (2002), *Writer Ferrets Chasing the Muse* (2002), *Rancher Ferrets on the Range* (2003), and *The Last War: Detective Ferrets and the Case of the Golden Deed* (2003) are more relaxed.

BAILEY, ROBIN WAYNE (1952–). U.S. writer. The trilogy comprising *Frost* (1983), *Skull Gate* (1985), and *Bloodsongs* (1986) follows the exploits of a warrior **witch**; the omnibus *Night's Angel* (2002) adds a new story. *Night Watch* (1990) is a fantastic mystery. The trilogy comprising *Brothers of the Dragon* (1992), *Straight on til Mourning* (1993; aka *Flames of the Dragon*), and *Triumph of the Dragon* (1995; aka *The Palace of Souls*) is a **portal fantasy** with displaced heroes who turn the tide of a war against the forces of darkness. *Shadowdance* (1996) is a **dark fantasy**. *Swords against the Shadowland* (1998) features further adventures of **Fritz Leiber**'s Fafhrd and the Grey Mouser. The trilogy begun with *Dragonkin* (2003) and *Talisman* (2004) employs dragons in an otherwise conventional **animal fantasy**.

BAIN, F. W. (1863–1940). British writer whose experiences in India gave rise to a long series of lyrically meditative stories based in **Hindu mythology**, comprising *A Digit of the Moon* (1899), *The Descent of the Sun* (1903), *A Heifer of the Dawn* (1904), *In the Great God's Hair* (1904), *A Draught of the Blue* (1905), *An Essence of the Dusk* (1906), *An Incarnation of the Snow* (1908), *A Mine of Faults* (1909), *The Ashes of a God* (191), *Bubbles of the Foam* (1912), *A Syrup of the Bees* (1914), *The Livery of Eve* (1917), and *The Substance of a Dream* (1919).

BAKER, FRANK (1908–1983). British writer. Most of his works are marginal or **ambiguous**, but three are wholehearted fantasies: *The Birds*

(1936), which externalizes personal demons; *Miss Hargreaves* (1940), a **humorous fantasy** in which a fictional character comes inconveniently to life; and *Sweet Chariot* (1942), a philosophical **angelic fantasy** of **identity exchange**. *Stories of the Strange and Sinister* (1983) mixes lighthearted fantasies with **horror** stories.

BALDRY, CHERITH (1947–). British writer. Her early work was **hybrid/science fantasy**, including a **planetary romance** trilogy comprising *The Book of the Phoenix* (1989), *A Rush of Golden Wings* (1991), and *Cradoc's Quest* (1994), which is a **quest** fantasy involving a **phoenix** and a book containing the word of God. *The Reliquary Ring* (2002), featuring a parallel Venice, is also a hybrid. *Exiled from Camelot* (2000) is an **Arthurian fantasy**, and her mystery novel *The Buried Cross* (2004) also makes use of Arthurian motifs. The Eaglesmount trilogy of **animal fantasies**, comprising *The Silver Horn* (2002), *The Emerald Throne* (2003), and *The Lake of Darkness* (2004), features pine martens. *The Roses of Roazon* (2004) is a **religious fantasy** with **allegorical** elements.

BALLADS. Ballads are the poetic repository of folklore, parallel to that of **fairy tales**; the term links their origin to French lyrics parallel to those of verse **romance**, but English and Scottish ballads often deal with distinct materials. Many examples of unknown antiquity were collected in Thomas Percy's *Reliques of Ancient English Poetry* (1765), which was much admired by leading members of the British and German Romantic movements, especially William Wordsworth, who borrowed the term for his and **Samuel Taylor Coleridge**'s collection of *Lyrical Ballads*, **Walter Scott**, who augmented it with *Minstrelsy of the Scottish Border* (1802), **M. G. Lewis**, **Ludwig Tieck**, and the **Grimms**. Similar collections of German ballads were compiled by Johann Gottfried Herder, Achim von Arnim, and Clemens Brentano. Percy's collection became the model for many subsequent projects, most notably Francis James Child's five-volume edition of *The English and Scottish Ballads* (1882–98). The ballad that has served as the most significant **taproot text** for modern fantasy tells the story of **Tam Lin**; other modern fantasies transfigured from ballads include works by **Dahlov Ipcar**, **Ellen Kushner**, **Geraldine McCaughrean**, and **Delia Sherman**, and Deborah Grabien's *The Weaver and the Factory Maid* (2003) and *The Famous Flower of Serving Men* (2004).

BALLANTINE ADULT FANTASY SERIES. A line of paperback reprints edited by **Lin Carter** that attempted to follow up the success of

Ballantine's 1965 edition of *The Lord of the Rings* by "rediscovering" other "lost classics" of a similar kind. **Eric Rucker Eddison**, **Mervyn Peake**, and **Peter S. Beagle** were among the earliest authors reprinted, in 1967–69, along with **David Lindsay**'s *A Voyage to Arcturus*, after which the series was given its own logo. Carter's showcase **anthologies** and nonfictional studies mapped out the field. **Lord Dunsany**, **William Morris**, **James Branch Cabell**, and **Clark Ashton Smith** became key exemplars, and new works soon began to appear from **Joy Chant**, **Katherine Kurtz**, and **Evangeline Walton**. Sales of these titles varied considerably, and the line viewed as a whole soon became unprofitable, with the result that the label was abandoned in 1974, although Ballantine played a leading role in developing **commodified fantasy** with its **Del Rey** imprint. The Adult Fantasy series was vitally important in determining the image of the fantasy genre and reconstructing its history; it also served as a series of experiments that determined which kinds of fantasy were commodifiable and which were not.

BALZAC, HONORÉ DE (1799–1850). French writer who wrote numerous pseudonymous **Gothic** potboilers in his early years (refer to *HDHL*), of which the most relevant is *The Last Fay* (1823; tr. 1996), but his most significant contributions to fantasy literature are in the "philosophical studies" section of the sprawling sequence comprising The Human Comedy. The classic **Faustian fantasy** is *La Peau de chagrin* (1831; tr. 1842, initially as *Luck and Leather* but more usually as *The Wild Ass's Skin* or *The Magic Skin*), whose hero reaps spectacular rewards from the eponymous object but becomes paranoid as his capital shrinks inexorably. *Louis Lambert* (1832; exp. 1833; tr. 1889) and *The Quest for the Absolute* (1834; tr. 1844; aka *The Philosopher's Stone* and *Balthazar*) are marginal, but *Séraphita* (1835; tr. 1889) features a mysterious androgynous quasi-angelic being. His short fantasies, including "The Elixir of Life" (1830), "The Unknown Masterpiece" (1831), and "Melmoth Reconciled" (1835) are didactic **fabulations**.

BANGS, JOHN KENDRICK (1862–1922). U.S. writer. Except for the **psychological fantasy** *Roger Camerden: A Strange Story* (1887), all of his genre work is **humorous**. He wrote numerous comic **ghost stories**, including *Toppleton's Ghost; or, A Spirit in Exile* (1893), and items in *The Water Ghost and Others* (1894), *Ghosts I Have Met and Some Others* (1898), and *Over the Plum Pudding* (1901). His most successful works were the **infernal comedies** *A Houseboat on the Styx* (1895), *The*

Pursuit of the Houseboat (1897), and *The Enchanted Type-Writer* (1899), in which the great men of history engage in witty conversation. Similarly laid-back material is collected in *The Dreamers: A Club* (1899), *Mr Munchausen* (1901), and *Olympian Nights* (1902). *Alice in Blunderland* (1907), *The Autobiography of Methuselah* (1909), and the belatedly assembled *Shylock Homes: His Posthumous Memoirs* (1973) are more tightly focused parodies.

BARCLAY, JAMES (1965–). British writer of **dark fantasy** whose Chronicles of the Raven, comprising *Dawnthief* (1999), *Noonshade* (2000), *Nightchild* (2001), *Elfsorrow* (2002), and *Shadowheart* (2003), track the exploits of a mercenary band of warriors, providing a sceptical antidote to conventional **heroic fantasy**. The novella *Light Stealer* (2003) is a **prequel**.

BARDIC FANTASY. Players of magical **music** are frequent protagonists of **commodified heroic fantasy**, often favored—like **healers**—by writers intent on avoiding the crude violence of swordplay. The strategy is particularly evident in the subgenre of **Celtic fantasy**, from which the term "bard" is borrowed. Although no clear boundary separates bardic fantasy from **Orphean fantasy**, the former usually features **quests** of a more conventional kind, undertaken without the necessity of journeying into an **underworld**. Although the subgenre was anticipated by **Manly Wade Wellman**'s Silver John series, the definitive examples of bardic fantasy include series by **Keith Taylor**, **Mercedes Lackey**, **Holly Lisle**, **Michael Scott**, and **Caiseal Mór**. Notable individual works include **Kristine Kathryn Rusch**'s *The White Mists of Power,* **Patricia McKillip**'s *Song for the Basilisk,* and Anne Kelleher Bush's *The Knight, the Harp and the Maiden* (1999).

BARHAM, RICHARD HARRIS (1788–1845). British writer who posed as Thomas Ingoldsby in the pages of *Bentley's Miscellany,* for which he wrote a long series of humorous pseudo-folklorish stories, poems, and sketches that were collected in three series of *The Ingoldsby Legends* (1840; 1842; 1847). Hugely popular, they were frequently reprinted, providing a crucial exemplar for subsequent Victorian writers of comic fantasy, including **Charles Dickens** and **Douglas Jerrold**.

BARING, MAURICE (1874–1945). British writer. The title story of *Orpheus in Mayfair and Other Stories and Sketches* (1909) offers appreciative guests at a house party a glimpse of the **underworld**; several other stories in the collection—which overlaps considerably with *Half a Minute's Silence and Other Stories* (1925)—provide similarly witty comments on aesthetic matters. *The Glass Mender and Other Stories* (1910; aka *The Blue Rose Fairy Book*) deploys a similarly sophisticated sensibility in **fairy tale** formats.

BARING-GOULD, SABINE (1834–1924). British writer. His own fiction is mostly irrelevant to this taxonomy, although he produced *A Book of Ghosts* (1904), three volumes of (**recycled**) **fairy tales**, and the unconventional **vampire** novella (1884) that belatedly became the title piece of *Margery of Quether and Other Weird Tales* (1999). More significantly, his collections of medieval legends became useful source books for many other writers. They include *The Book of Were-wolves* (1865), *Curious Myths of the Middle Ages* (1866; second series 1868), *Curiosities of the Olden Times* (1869), and *A Book of Folklore* (1913).

BARKER, CLIVE (1952–). British writer best known for graphic **horror** fiction (refer to *HDHL*) and work in various visual media. His first venture into genre fantasy was *Weaveworld* (1987), which miniaturizes its **secondary world** within the pattern of a carpet. His work in this vein—including items marketed for younger readers like *The Thief of Always* (1992) and the couplet comprising *Abarat* (2002) and *Days of Magic, Nights of War* (2004)—retains enough horrific material to make it virtually definitive of **dark fantasy**, albeit on an epic scale. His other relevant works include the **contemporary/metaphysical fantasy** *The Great and Secret Show* (1989) and its sequel *Everville* (1994), about the threat of the magical Quiddity, and the **quest** fantasy *Imajica* (1991; reprinted in two volumes as *The Fifth Dominion* and *The Reconciliation*). *Incarnations* (1995) and *Forms of Heaven* (1996) each collect three plays, the first forming a trilogy consisting of "Colossus," "Frankenstein in Love," and "The History of the Devil," the latter items in a **humorous** vein.

BARRIE, SIR J. M. (1860–1937). Scottish writer best known as a dramatist. His semi-autobiographical fantasy *The Little White Bird; or, Adventures in Kensington Gardens* (1902) includes an interpolation—published separately as *Peter Pan in Kensington Gardens* (1906)—about a magical boy who can fly and never grows older. A modified version of this character became the hero of the classic play *Peter Pan* (1904; novelized as *Peter and Wendy*, 1911), whose seduction of the Darling family children became a significant modern myth. *Dear Brutus* (1917) sends its cast into a magic wood so that they may sample the lives they would have led had they made crucial choices differently. *A Kiss for Cinderella* (1920) is a sarcastic farce. *Mary Rose* (1924) is a poignant **timeslip** fantasy. The novella *Farewell, Miss Julie Logan* (1931), issued as a Christmas supplement to *The Times* in memory of **Charles Dickens**'s Christmas annuals, features an ill-fated relationship between a young minister and a female ghost.

Spinoff from *Peter Pan* includes Toby Forward's *Neverland* (1989), **Penelope Farmer**'s *The Summer Birds*, **Jane Yolen**'s "Lost Girls" (1997), and Laurie Anne Fox's *The Lost Girls* (2004), which tracks later generations of Darling women.

BARRON, T. A. (1952–). U.S. writer. His fantasies include an **Arthurian** series chronicling the Lost Years of Merlin, comprising *The Lost Years of Merlin* (1996), *The Seven Songs of Merlin* (1997), *The Fires of Merlin* (1998), *The Mirror of Merlin* (1999), and *The Wings of Merlin* (2000). The Great Tree of Avalon series begun with *Child of the Dark Prophecy* (2004) carries forward its themes, focusing on ecocatastrophic threats to the "universal tree" that grows from Merlin's magical seed.

BARTH, JOHN (1930–). U.S. writer. His early novels achieved their **metafictional** objectives without recourse to supernatural apparatus, as in the **allegory** *Giles Goat-Boy; or, The Revised New Syllabus* (1966), but the shorter stories collected in *Lost in the Funhouse* (1968) and the novellas making up *Chimera* (1972) used fantasy devices more liberally. *Sabbatical* (1982) began a long sequence of carefully framed celebrations of the power of story, continued in *Tidewater Tales* (1987)—its echoes of **Scheherazade** were given more explicit expression in *The Last Voyage of Somebody the Sailor* (1991)—the **timeslip** fantasy *Once upon a Time* (1994), *On with the Story* (1996), the conscientiously **postmodern** *Coming Soon!!!* (2001), and *The Book of Ten Nights and a Night* (2004).

BARTHELME, DONALD (1931–1989). U.S. writer who dabbled extensively in conspicuous **fabulation** in short stories collected in numerous volumes, beginning with *Come Back Dr Caligari* (1964), whose contents were reassembled and further augmented in the omnibuses *Sixty Stories* (1981) and *Forty Stories* (1987). *Snow White* (1967) is a complicated **transfiguration** of the **fairy tale**. *The Dead Father* (1975) is a **metafictional** commentary on fantastic **quests**. *The King* (1990) is an

Arthurian fantasy that reverses **Mark Twain**'s timeslip strategy to bring legendary characters into World War II.

BAUDELAIRE, CHARLES (1821–1867). French poet. **Théophile Gautier** identified *Les Fleurs du Mal* (1857; exp. 1861) as the definitive example of "Decadent" literary style; its indulgent dealings with the macabre and various paeans to escapism were a great inspiration to later writers. Baudelaire was deeply influenced by the work of **Edgar Allan Poe**, whose work he began translating in 1848. His versions of Poe's tales became enormously influential in France, and a Poesque imagination is manifest in the prose poems Baudelaire intended to collect in *Le Spleen de Paris* (issued posthumously in volume 6 of *Oeuvres complètes*, 7 vols., 1868–70); the most striking include languidly mournful "Anywhere out of the World" and those translated as "The Double Room," "The Fairies' Gifts," and "The Temptations: Eros, Plutus and Fame." They played a crucial role in establishing the genre of ***contes cruels***.

BAUDINO, GAEL (1955–). U.S. writer. Her fantasies are informed by her devout neopaganism, although the **portal fantasy** trilogy comprising *Dragonsword* (1988), *Duel of Dragons* (1991), and *Dragon Death* (1992) is less propagandistically inclined than the **alternative history** series comprising *Strands of Starlight* (1989), *Maze of Moonlight* (1993), and *Shroud of Shadow* (1993). The latter extends into **contemporary fantasy** in *Strands of Sunlight* (1994); the novellas in *Spires of Spirit* (1997) are closely related. The **timeslip** fantasy *Gossamer Axe* (1990) is a **transfiguration** of **Tam Lin**. The Water trilogy, comprising *O Greenest Branch!* (1995), *The Dove Looked In* (1996), and *Branch and Crown* (1996), is a further exercise in alternative history, and *The Borders of Life* (1999 as G. A. Kathryns) another contemporary fantasy.

BAUM, L. FRANK (1856–1919). U.S. writer best known for his children's fantasies, especially the long series begun with *The Wonderful Wizard of Oz* (1900) and continued in *The Marvelous Land of Oz* (1904), *Ozma of Oz* (1907), *Dorothy and the Wizard in Oz* (1908), *The Road to Oz* (1909), *The Emerald City of Oz* (1910), *The Patchwork Girl of Oz* (1913), *Tik-Tok of Oz* (1914), *The Scarecrow of Oz* (1915), *Rinkitink in Oz* (1916), *The Lost Princess of Oz* (1917), *The Tin Woodman of Oz* (1918), *The Magic of Oz* (1919), and *Glinda of Oz* (1920), as well as in the short stories for younger readers reprinted in the omnibus *Little Wizard Stories of Oz* (1914). The first six items constitute an unusually energetic and unrepentantly **escapist** fantasy, which begins as **portal fantasy** but is gradually transformed into precedent-setting **immersive fantasy**.

Other writers continued the Oz series after Baum's death, notably Ruth Plumly Thompson and illustrator John R. Neill. The centenary of the series brought forth a new flock, including Donald Abbott's *The Amber Flute of Oz* (1998), Edward Einhorn's *Paradox in Oz* (2000), Roger S. Baum's *The Green Star of Oz* (2000), and Eloise McGraw's *The Rundelstone of Oz* (2001). Further works inspired by the series include **Geoff Ryman**'s *Was* and **Gregory Maguire**'s *The Life and Times of the Wicked Witch of the West*.

Baum's other works, which are more satirically inclined, include *American Fairy Tales* (1901), *Dot and Tot in Merryland* (1901), *The Master Key* (1901), the **Christmas fantasy** *The Life and Adventures of Santa Claus* (1902), *The Enchanted Island of Yew* (1903), *Queen Zixi of Ix* (1905), and the couplet comprising *The Sea Fairies* (1911) and *Sky Island* (1912). *The Purple Dragon* (1976) is a sampler of his short fiction.

BEAGLE, PETER S. (1939–). U.S. writer. The elegiac *A Fine and Private Place* (1960) is a stylish **sentimental fantasy** akin to the work of **Robert Nathan**, to whom "Come Lady Death" (1963) and *Tamsin* (1999) are more overt homages. *The Last Unicorn* (1968) is a **quest** fantasy splicing elements of medieval **allegory** into a **humorously** edged adventure story. The novelette *Lila the Werewolf* (1969; book 1974) brought the first phase of his career to a close; it resumed with the **dark fantasy** *The Folk of the Air* (1986), in which the lifestyle fantasists of the League for Archaic Pleasures conjure up dangerous forces.

The Innkeeper's Song (1993) is a lyrical quest fantasy with a background that is further explored in the stories in *Giant Bones* (1997). *The Unicorn Sonata* (1996) is a **portal fantasy** revisiting a fascination further extrapolated in the **anthology** *Peter S. Beagle's Immortal Unicorn* (1995), coedited with Janet Berliner and Martin H. Greenberg. *A Dance for Emilia* (2000) is an offbeat **animal fantasy**. *The Rhinoceros Who Quoted Nietzsche and Other Odd Acquaintances* (1997) mingles stories and essays.

BEARDSLEY, AUBREY (1872–1898). British artist whose **illustrations**, including famous series for Thomas Malory's *Le Morte d'Arthur* and **Oscar Wilde**'s *Salome,* encapsulated the **decadent** spirit of the Aesthetic movement. An **erotic fantasy** novel *Under the Hill* (1896–97;

reprinted in *Under the Hill and Other Essays in Prose and Verse*, 1904) transfiguring the legend of Tannhäuser was left incomplete at his death; it was reprinted with a conclusion by John Glassco in 1958 (aka *The Story of Venus and Tannhäuser*).

BEAUCLERK, HELEN (1892–1969). British writer long resident in France whose fantasy novels transpose materials borrowed from French fantastic fiction into an English mode; the **portal fantasy** *The Green Lacquer Pavilion* (1926) is a tongue-in-cheek celebration of the Gallic fascination with the Orient. *The Love of the Foolish Angel* (1929) recapitulates the heretical fantasies of **Anatole France**. The opening sequence of *The Mountain and the Tree* (1936) bases an account of the changing role of women in prehistory in Frazerian **scholarly fantasy**.

BECK, L. ADAMS (c1862–1931). Pseudonym of British writer Eliza Louisa Moresby, whose extensive travels in the Far East allowed her to cultivate a reputation as a mystic. Her fabular tales of the Orient are collected in *The Ninth Vibration and Other Stories* (1922), *The Perfume of the Rainbow and Other Stories* (1923), and *Dreams and Delights* (1926). Her novels, including *The Treasure of Ho* (1924), the **karmic romance** *The Way of Stars* (1925), *The Glory of Egypt* (1926 as by Louis Moresby), the **theosophical romance** *The House of Fulfilment* (1927), and the **Dion Fortune**–influenced occult **detective** stories in *The Openers of the Gate* (1930), were more commercially oriented.

BECKFORD, WILLIAM (1760–1844). British writer and pioneering lifestyle fantasist who squandered his fortune remodeling the extravagantly **Gothic** Fonthill Abbey. He wrote his classic novel *Vathek*—a feverish and gleefully perverse **decadent/Arabian fantasy**—in French; the English translation of 1786, initially issued as *An Arabian Tale,* is by Samuel Henley. Three novellas that Beckford intended for interpolation in the text—one of them incomplete—were discovered belatedly and translated by Frank Marzials for publication as *The Episodes of Vathek* (1912).

BELLAIRS, JOHN (1938–1991). U.S. writer. *St. Fidgeta and Other Parodies* (1966), which makes fun of religious excess, *The Pedant and Shuffly* (1968), and the humorous **historical fantasy** *The Face in the Frost* (1969) were aimed at the **young adult** market, but Bellairs's subsequent works targeted a younger age range. They follow a pattern established in *The Pedant and Shuffly,* featuring magical contests between unorthodox archetypes of good and evil. A sequence featuring Lewis Barnavelt comprises *The House with a Clock in Its Walls* (1973), *The Figure in the Shadows* (1975), *The Letter, the Witch, and the Ring* (1976); similar series featuring Anthony Monday and Johnny Dixon are less sophisticated. Numerous works that Bellairs left unfinished when he died, including the Lewis Barnavelt stories *The Ghost in the Mirror* (1993), *The Vengeance of the Witchfinder* (1993), and *The Doom of the Haunted Opera* (1995), were completed by **Brad Strickland**, who continued the series.

BEMMANN, HANS (1922–2003). German writer whose **epic** bildungsroman translated as *The Stone and the Flute* (1983; tr. 1986) includes a good deal of invented folklore. *The Broken Goddess* (1990; tr. 1993) addresses such material more directly by appointing a folklorist as its protagonist in an elaborate **portal fantasy** with a **secondary world** compounded out of **allegorical** stereotypes.

BENÉT, STEPHEN VINCENT (1898–1943). U.S. writer best known as a poet. His most notable contributions to fantasy literature are synthetic Americana of the kind pioneered by **Washington Irving**, including a classic **Faustian fantasy** featuring a clever lawyer, "The Devil and Daniel Webster" (1937). The **tall story** "Daniel Webster and the Sea Serpent" is a farcical sequel; both were reprinted in *Thirteen O'Clock: Stories of Several Worlds* (1937), alongside the similarly reconfigured folktale "The King of the Cats." *Tales before Midnight* (1939) reprints "Johnny Pye and the Fool-Killer" (1938), in which the figure of **Death** is Americanized; "O'Halloran's Luck," which transplants a leprechaun to the United States; and the **afterlife fantasy** "Doc Mellhorn and the Pearly Gates." *The Last Circle* (1946) includes a few further items in the same vein.

BENSON, STELLA (1892–1933). British writer who eventually settled in China. The quasi-autobiographical *Living Alone* (1919) spearheaded a glut of post–World War I fantasies pleading eloquently for **re-enchantment**. Her shorter fantasies—all of which, except for the **Oriental fantasy** "Kwan-yin" (1922), are in her *Collected Short Stories* (1936)—include "The Awakening" (1925), an **allegory** of divine underachievement; "The Man Who Missed the Bus" (1928), a **surreal** and **dark fantasy**; and "Christmas Formula" (1932), also reprinted in *Christmas Formula and Other Stories* (1932), a **satire** on advertising.

BERESFORD, ELISABETH (1926–). British writer, mostly for children, the daughter of novelist J. D. Beresford. Her first fully fledged fantasy was the **E. Nesbit**–inspired **intrusive fantasy** *Awkward Magic* (1964; aka *The Magic World*), the first of a series continued in *Traveling Magic* (1965; aka *The Vanishing Garden*), *Sea-Green Magic* (1968), *Vanishing Magic* (1970), *Dangerous Magic* (1972), *Invisible Magic* (1974), *Secret Magic* (1978), *Curious Magic* (1980), and *Strange Magic* (1986). Alongside these works, Beresford began chronicling the adventures of *The Wombles* (1968), furry creatures inhabiting an **underworld** beneath Wimbledon Common who recycle the upper world's rubbish more or less ingeniously. Aided by a successful TV series and various merchandising exercises, the series extended for 18 more books, with five gift-book supplements. Another miniature race of desperate conservationists, introduced in *The Tovers* (1982), failed to take off in the same spectacular manner. *The Happy Ghost* (1979), *The Ghosts of Lupus Street School* (1986), and *Emily and the Haunted Castle* (1987) feature nonthreatening apparitions.

BERGER, THOMAS (1924–). U.S. writer whose offbeat satirical work often strays into fantasy. *Little Big Man* (1964) is a marginal account of longevity, but *Return of Little Big Man* (1999) takes its **tall story** element to extremes in revealing that the protagonist faked his death (at the age of 111) before continuing his exploits. *Regiment of Women* (1973) is an unusually uncompromising fantasy of sexual role reversal. *Arthur Rex: A Legendary Novel* (1978) **recycles/Arthurian legends** with deadpan humor. The protagonists of the **wish-fulfillment** stories in *Granted Wishes* (1984) and the novels *Being Invisible* (1987) and *Changing the Past* (1989) all fail dismally to exploit the advantages of **daydream** opportunities. *Orrie's Story* (1990) **transfigures** Aeschylus's *Oresteia*. *Adventures of the Artificial Woman* (2004) transfigures Villiers de l'Isle Adam's *The Future Eve,* reversing the viewpoint.

BERNERS, LORD (Gerald Tyrwhit-Wilson) (1883–1950). British artist and writer whose eccentricity was notorious. His **surreal/delusionary fantasy** *The Camel* (1936) and his **satirical** and **apocalyptic fantasy** *Count Omega* (1941)—in which the last trump concludes a symphony—are reprinted with other items in *Collected Tales and Fantasies* (1998),

BESANT, SIR WALTER (1836–1901). British writer who wrote numerous books in collaboration with James Rice (1844–82), including *The*

Case of Mr. Lucraft and Other Tales (1876), whose title piece is a **Faustian fantasy** in which a young man leases his healthy appetite to an aged hedonist. The collection also includes some **humorous/ghost stories** and the nationalistic **allegorical/fairy tale** "Titania's Farewell." Besant also collaborated with **Walter Herries Pollock** on the Ansteyan novella "Sir Jocelyn's Cap" (1884–85; reprinted in *Uncle Jack, etc.*, 1886). His solo work includes the moralistic **identity exchange** story *The Doubts of Dives* (1889; reprinted in *Verbena Camellia Stephanotis*, 1892), in which a bored socialite changes places with an a poor friend. The dual-personality novel *The Ivory Gate* (1892) is a **psychological fantasy**.

BIBLICAL FANTASY. The mythology of the Old Testament, especially the events of Genesis, are frequently **transfigured** in stories that do not warrant description as **religious fantasy** but take advantage of the stories' familiarity; such works are often satirical. The most common variety, transfiguring the story of Adam and Eve, is a subspecies of **Edenic fantasy**. Transfigurations of the story of Noah are also common; notable examples include **H. G. Wells**'s *All Aboard for Ararat,* David Garnett's *Two by Two: A Story of Survival* (1963), Rosemary Harris's *The Moon in the Cloud* (1968), Michele Roberts's *The Book of Mrs. Noah* (1987), **Jeanette Winterson**'s *Boating for Beginners,* and **Garaldine McCaughrean**'s *It's Not the End of the World.* The Deluge also features prominently in Shamus Frazer's wide-ranging *Blow, Blow Your Trumpets* (1945) and **James Morrow**'s series of "Bible Stories for Adults." **Jenny Diski**'s *Only Human* and its sequel are similarly extensive.

Other Old Testament myths that make frequent literary appeal include the story of Job—also transfigured by Wells and Morrow—and the brief mention of the Queen of Sheba's visit to Solomon, which is also featured in **Arabian fantasy**. Examples of the latter include E. Powys Mathers's *The Queen of Sheba* (1924), Helène Eliat's's *Sheba Visits Solomon* (1930 in German; tr. 1932), and Noel de Vic Beamish's *The Quest of Love* (1960). Fantasies based in the New Testament are better considered as **Christian fantasy**, although such influential stories as those of Salome and the **Wandering Jew** are closely akin to Old Testament–based materials, which also resonate in **Jewish fantasy**. *See also* EROTIC FANTASY.

BISHOP, ANNE (1955–). U.S. writer whose fantasies are deftly **dark** edged. They include the Black Jewels trilogy, comprising *Daughter of* *the Blood* (1998), *Heir to the Shadows* (1999), and *Queen of the Darkness* (2000)—to which *The Invisible Ring* (2000) is a **prequel**—and The Tir Alainn trilogy, comprising *The Pillars of the World* (2001), *Shadows and Light* (2002), *The House of Gaian* (2003). The latter features a young witch doubly threatened by hunters and **fairies**.

BISHOP, K. J. (1972–). Australian writer and artist. Her early work for *Aurealis,* including "The Art of Dying" (1997) and "The Love of Beauty" (1999), was bylined Kirsten Bishop. The conspicuous **decadent** elements in these stories was further exaggerated in "Maldoror Abroad" (2003) in *Album Zutique* and in the elaborate novel *The Etched City* (2003), in which two former rebels follow contrasted career paths after arriving in the archetypal city of Ashamoil.

BISHOP, MICHAEL (1945–). U.S. writer best known for **sf** (refer to *HDSFL*). The 1980 title story of *One Winter in Eden* (1984) features a dragon in disguise who reacts fervently against the injustices of modern America, as Frankenstein's monster does in the poignant **sports fantasy** *Brittle Innings* (1994). *Who Made Stevie Crye* (1984) is an elaborate **metafiction** in the form of a **horror** story. *Unicorn Mountain* (1988) is a striking fabular account of interdimensional pollution. The pseudonymous author of the **Faustian fantasy** *Seven Deadly Sins* (1999) is a different person.

BISSON, TERRY (1942–). U.S. writer best known for **sf** (refer to *HDSFL*). His first two novels were the sophisticated **sword and sorcery** novel *Wyrldmaker* (1981) and the **contemporary fantasy** *Talking Man* (1986). The short stories in *Bears Discover Fire* (1993) are mostly **fabulations** that develop unlikely premises in a laconically deadpan fashion.

BLACKWOOD, ALGERNON (1869–1951). British writer, one of the foremost 20th-century writers of **horror** fiction (refer to *HDHL*). Much of his work is of fantasy interest, by virtue of its consistent employment of a quasi-animistic pantheism whose earnest metaphysical extrapolation is contained in the novels *The Human Chord* (1910), *The Centaur* (1911), *Julius Le Vallon* (1916), *The Promise of Air* (1918), *The Garden of Survival* (1918), and *The Bright Messenger* (1921), and the collections *Pan's Garden: A Volume of Nature Stories* (1912) and *Incredible Adventures* (1914). *Karma: A Reincarnation Play* (1918, with Violet Pearn) is also relevant. Blackwood also wrote **visionary fantasies** for children, including *Jimbo* (1909), *The Extra Day* (1915), and *The Fruit-Stoners* (1934). *The Education of Uncle Paul* (1909) and *A Prisoner in Fairyland* (1913) are **sentimental fantasies** about childhood. The **animal fantasy** *Dudley and Gilderoy* (1929) is satirically inclined.

BLAKE, WILLIAM (1757–1827). English poet and artist, the most innovative of the British writers associated with the **Romantic** movement. He developed an entire allegorical myth system in his **illustrated** "prophetic books," including *America: A Prophecy* (1793), *The Book of Urizen* (1794), *Europe: A Prophecy* (1794), *The Song of Los* (1795), *The Book of Los* (1795), and *The Four Zoas* (1797–1804), culminating in *Jerusalem: The Emanation of the Giant Albion* (1804–20). The tyrannical god-figure Urizen is opposed by the blacksmith (i.e., artist) Los, who eventually succeeds in binding him in chains. Los also binds the anarchic Orc, the son he fathered on Enitharmon—the inspiration that frequently deserts him—with tragic consequences. The example of this constructive labor illustrates the extremes that imaginative ambition might attain. The imagery of the earlier *Songs of Innocence* (1789) and *Songs of Experience* (1794) recurs commonly in modern parlance, especially that of "The Tyger" and "The Sick Rose" from the latter collection.

Blake's remark about **John Milton** being "of the Devil's party without knowing it" was raised by **Percy Shelley** as the banner of **literary satanism**. The esotericism of his work has not prevented the development of a small subgenre of Blakean fantasy, including R. Faraday Nelson's hybrid **science fantasy** *Blake's Progress* (1975; rev. 1985 as *Timequest*), **Nancy Willard**'s poetry collection *A Visit to William Blake's Inn,* and **Michael Williams**'s *Arcady*.

BLAMIRES, HARRY (1916–). British theologian and literary critic. His studies with **C. S. Lewis** inspired the deftly ironic but carefully reverent **Dantean fantasy** trilogy comprising *The Devil's Hunting Grounds* (1954), *Cold War in Hell* (1955), and *Blessing Unbounded* (1955), which describes Purgatory and **hell** in scathing detail but is content to map the road to Paradise without depicting it.

BLAVATSKY, MADAME (1831–1891). Russian-born **lifestyle fantasist** who became a pillar of the occult revival when she cofounded the Theosophical Society in 1875, elaborating its mythos in *Isis Unveiled* (1877) and *The Secret Doctrine* (1888). The latter's **secret history**—especially its accounts of an elaborate prehistory featuring both Atlantis and

Lemuria—became important source texts for writers of fiction ranging over a much wider spectrum than bona fide **theosophical fantasy**. Early **sword and sorcery** writers like **Robert E. Howard** and **Clark Ashton Smith** borrowed a good deal from theosophical sources. Blavatsky drew a good deal of inspiration from **Bulwer-Lytton**'s *Zanoni,* which was also plundered by the **scholarly fantasies** of **Eliphas Lévi**; the intimate relationship between literary, scholarly, and lifestyle fantasies was further demonstrated by Blavatsky's influence on **W. B. Yeats**, **Aleister Crowley**, and many others. Her own literary fantasies are collected in *Nightmare Tales* (1892).

BLAYLOCK, JAMES P. (1950–). U.S. writer. *The Elfin Ship* (1982; restored text as *The Man in the Moon*, 2002) and its sequel *The Disappearing Dwarf* (1983) are tongue-in-cheek **quest** fantasies. *The Digging Leviathan* (1984), *Homunculus* (1986), and *Lord Kelvin's Machine* (1992) are **science-fantasy** hybrids, but the fantasy ambience that reasserted itself in *Land of Dreams* (1987) became increasingly dominant in *The Last Coin* (1988), *The Paper Grail* (1991), and *All the Bells on Earth* (1995), whose plots revolve around talismanic objects: a coin paid in fee to Judas Iscariot, a peculiar version of the **grail**, and a wish-granting bluebird. *The Stone Giant* (1989) returned to the **secondary world** of *The Elfin Ship*. *The Magic Spectacles* (1991) is a **portal fantasy** for children. *Night Relics* (1994), *Winter Tides* (1997), and *The Rainy Season* (1999) tend toward **horror** fiction (refer to *HDHL*). Blaylock's short fiction is sampled in *Thirteen Phantasms and Other Stories* (2000) and *In for a Penny* (2003); two collaborations with **Tim Powers** appear in Powers's collection *Night Moves and Other Stories* (2001), and another (alongside solo stories by both writers) is in *The Devils in the Details* (2003).

BLOCH, ROBERT (1917–1994). U.S. writer best known for **horror** fiction (refer to *HDHL*). His early work, heavily influenced by the **Lovecraft** school, includes **decadent/*contes cruels***, like "Black Lotus" (1935) and "The Mandarin's Canaries" (1938). He went on to write a good deal of **humorous fantasy**; *Dragons and Nightmares* (1969) reprints the Damon Runyon pastiches "A Good Knight's Work" (1942) and "The Eager Dragon" (1943), and the **Thorne Smith** pastiches "Nursemaid to Nightmares" (1942) and "Black Barter" (1943), which had previously been combined as "Mr Margate's Mermaid" (1955). Other novellas in the latter vein are "The Devil with You" (1950; aka

"Black Magic Holiday"), "Hell's Angel" (1951), "The Miracle of Roland Weems" (1955), and "The Big Binge" (1955; book 1971 as *It's All in Your Mind*), all of which are reprinted in *The Lost Bloch* (3 vols., 1999–2002). A pun-laden series of **tall stories** from ***Fantastic Adventures*** (1942–46) was sampled in *Lost in Time and Space with Lefty Feep* (1987).

BLOCK, FRANCESCA LIA (1962–). U.S. writer. *Weetzie Bat* (1989) began a series of quirkily **surreal/urban fantasies** about a bleached-blonde punk pixie; it was continued in *Witch Baby* (1991), *Cherokee Bat and the Goat Guys* (1992), *Missing Angel Juan* (1993), and *Baby Be-Bop* (1995); *I Was a Teenage Fairy* (1998) is a **humorous fantasy** in a similar vein. *Ecstasia* (1993) and *Primavera* (1994) are ornate **Orphean fantasies**. *The Hanged Man* (1994) is a **dark** contemporary fantasy. *Echo* (2001) and *Wasteland* (2003) are marginal **delusional fantasies**. *Nymph* (2000) is a collection of **erotic fantasies**; *The Rose and the Beast: Fairy Tales Retold* (2000) features **transfigurations**.

BOK, HANNES (1914–1964). Pseudonym of U.S. illustrator and writer Wayne Woodard. His literary work was heavily influenced in manner and style by **A. Merritt**, two of whose fragmentary manuscripts he expanded into the novels *The Fox Woman and the Blue Pagoda* (1946) and *The Black Wheel* (1947). His most effective work in that vein is the **moralistic/portal fantasy** *Beyond the Golden Stair* (abr. version 1948 as "The Blue Flamingo"; book 1970); the others are "Starstone World" (1942) and *The Sorceror's Ship* (1942; book 1969). His **poetry** is collected in *Spinner of Silver and Thistle* (1972).

BOND, NELSON S. (1908–). U.S. writer whose most successful works were **humorous fantasies** in the tradition of **Thorne Smith**, most notably the 1937 title story of *Mr Mergenthwirker's Lobblies and Other Fantastic Tales* (1931), which gave rise to a series. His later collections *The Thirty-first of February* (1949) and *Nightmares and Daydreams* (1968) mingle similar works with **sf** (refer to *HDSFL*) and **horror** fiction.

BONDAGE. A term introduced by John Clute in the *Encyclopedia of Fantasy* as, allegedly, of central importance to the understanding of the genre. It refers to "a state of being contained or trapped in a particular place, time, physical shape or moral condition," resistant to or in dynamic tension with an active process of change characterizable as

"Story." The importance of such states in fantasy is connected with the manner in which fantasy can literalize and extrapolate commonplace psychological sensations of this kind, abstracting the characters from the temporal and spatial tyrannies of "real" life to contrive a kind of escape more profound and awkward in its implications than **J. R. R. Tolkien**'s. Clute suggests that a **heroic quest** is best regarded as a kind of bondage, wherein climactic attainment is release rather than reward.

BORCHARDT, ALICE (?–). U.S. writer, the sister of **Anne Rice**. Her **historical fantasies** include *Devoted* (1995), set in 10th-century France; several featuring **werewolves**, including *The Silver Wolf* (1998), *Night of the Wolf* (1999), and *The Wolf King* (2001); and the **Arthurian** Tales of Guinevere, begun with *The Dragon Queen* (2001) and *The Raven Warrior* (2003).

BORGES, JORGE LUIS (1899–1986). Argentinian writer famous for elegantly profound **metafictional/*contes philosophiques*,** many of which are collected in *Labyrinths* (1944–61; tr. 1962), *The Aleph and Other Stories* (1949; tr. 1970), and *The Book of Sand* (1975; tr. 1977). *Collected Fictions* (1999) is an omnibus. Notable examples formulated as fantasies include "The Approach to Al Mu'tasim" (1935), the **visionary fantasy** "The Circular Ruins" (1940), "The Garden of Forking Paths" (1941), the mythological fantasy "The House of Asterion" (1947), and "The Immortal" (1949). With Adolfo Bioy Casares and Silvina Ocampo, Borges compiled an 81-item showcase *Antología de la literatura fantástica* (1940; rev. 1965; further rev. 1976; tr. as *The Book of Fantasy*), which is one of fantasy literature's definitive texts. He also compiled a modern bestiary translated as *The Book of Imaginary Beings* (1957; rev. 1967; tr. 1969).

BOSTON, LUCY M. (1892–1990). British writer best known for a series of **children's fantasies** set in a house that is exceedingly prone to **timeslips**, hauntings, and other devices of **intrusive fantasy**, comprising *The Children of Green Knowe* (1954), *The Chimneys of Green Knowe* (1958; aka *Treasure of Green Knowe*), *The River at Green Knowe* (1959), *A Stranger at Green Knowe* (1961), *An Enemy at Green Knowe* (1964), and *The Stones of Green Knowe* (1976). *The Castle of Yew* (1958) is similar. *The Sea Egg* (1967) features a newborn triton.

BOYER, ELIZABETH H. (?–). U.S. writer. The **commodified** series of **heroic fantasy** comprising *The Sword and the Satchel* (1980), *The Elves* *and the Otterskin* (1981), *The Thrall and the Dragon's Heart* (1982), and *The Wizard and the Warlord* (1983) combines humor and drama; its later stages introduce warring **elves** of a **Nordic** stripe, which became central in the Wizard's War series, comprising *The Troll's Grindstone* (1986), *The Curse of Slagfid* (1989), *The Dragon's Carbuncle* (1990), and *The Lord of Chaos* (1991), and the Skyla trilogy, comprising *The Clan of the Warlord* (1992), *The Black Lynx* (1993), and *Keeper of Cats* (1995).

BOYETT, STEPHEN R. (1960–). U.S. writer. *Ariel* (1983) features an alternative history in which massive incursions from Faerie have transformed the United States. *The Architect of Sleep* (1986) is the first part of a complex portal fantasy, whose completion never appeared. *The Gnole* (1991, with Alan Aldridge) is an ecological polemic in fabular form. Boyett's short fiction is sampled in *Orphans* (2001); the earlier *Treks not Taken* (1996) parodies formularistic TV **sf**.

BRADBURY, RAY (1920–). U.S. writer whose work ranges across a very broad spectrum, much of it **hybrid** or **chimerical** (refer to *HDSFL* and *HDHL*). Many of his stories introduce **dark** elements into stories formulated and stylized as **sentimental fantasies** in a highly distinctive manner. His early fantasies included literalized allegories like "The Scythe" (1943) and a series of stories exploring the domestic life of a supernatural extended family in more earnestly sentimental terms than Charles Addams's cartoon family, begun with "Homecoming" (1946; incorporated into the mosaic *From the Dust Returned: A Family Remembrance* 2001). With the exception of his first collection, *Dark Carnival* (1947; rev. as *The October Country*, 1955), his early books were dominated by **sf** imagery, which gave way to a curious kind of fantasized autobiography in the mosaic *Dandelion Wine* (1957) and the classic dark fantasy *Something Wicked This Way Comes* (1962). Similar materials form a fugitive thread through most of his short-story collections from the 1960s to *Driving Blind* (1997) and *The Cat's Pajamas* (2004). They are more expansively developed in the children's fantasies *The Halloween Tree* (1972) and *Ahmed and the Oblivion Machines: A Fable* (1998), the latter being an Arabian fantasy.

BRADLEY, MARION ZIMMER (1930–1999). U.S. writer best known in the early phases of her career for a **science-fantasy** series set on the planet Darkover (refer to *HDSFL*), which provides a cardinal example of calculated **ambiguity** and became a key exemplar of

planetary romance. The "psi-powers" featured in the series are magic in all but name, and the world provided an arena for **sword and sorcery** adventures as well as **political fantasies**, the latter including an elaborate description of **amazon** culture. She moved toward pure fantasy in *The House between the Worlds* (1980; exp. 1981), completing the transition in the best-selling feminized **Arthurian fantasy** *The Mists of Avalon* (1982).

Web of Light (1983) and *Web of Darkness* (1984) are **Atlantean fantasies**. *Night's Daughter* (1985) **transfigures** Mozart's opera *The Magic Flute*. *The Firebrand* (1987) features the Trojan seeress Cassandra. *The Forest House* (1993) is a fantasy of **goddess** worship in Roman Britain; its sequel, *Lady of Avalon* (1997), connects it to *Mists of Avalon*. The trilogy comprising *Ghostlight* (1995), *Witchlight* (1996), and *Gravelight* (1997) is an ambiguous **contemporary fantasy**; *Heartlight* (1998) is a **prequel**.

Bradley wrote short stories set in **J. R. R. Tolkien**'s Middle-earth in the 1970s and went on to participate in a number of **shared world** enterprises, opening up her Darkover series to participation by other writers. Her work in **Robert Asprin** and **Lynn Abbey**'s Thieves' World scenario outgrew its origin, extending from the stories collected in *Lythande* (1986) to *The Gratitude of Kings* (1997; with Elisabeth Waters). With **Andre Norton** and Julian May, she wrote *Black Trillium* (1990); she made a solo contribution to the project in *Lady of the Trillium* (1995). *Tiger Burning Bright* (1995) used the same template, its other contributors being Norton and **Mercedes Lackey**. Bradley also collaborated with **Holly Lisle** on *Glenraven* (1996) and its sequel *In the Rift* (1998). Her Avalon series was continued by **Diana L. Paxson**.

Bradley was a zealous promoter of genre fantasy, especially its feminized variants, following up the original **anthologies** *Sword of Chaos* (1982) and *Greyhaven* (1983) with a series of annual anthologies, *Sword and Sorceress*, the first 20 vols. of which (1984–2003) she compiled—the final three with posthumous assistance from Elisabeth Waters—before it was taken over by Diana Paxson. In 1988, she launched *Marion Bradley's Fantasy Magazine,* which published 50 issues before folding in 2000; its spinoff included the anthology *Marion Zimmer Bradley's Fantasy Worlds* (1998; with Rachel E. Holmen).

BRADSHAW, GILLIAN (1956–). U.S. writer. The trilogy comprising *Hawk of May* (1980), *Kingdom of Summer* (1981), and *In Winter's Shadow* (1982) is an **Arthurian fantasy** foregrounding the character of

Gawain. Some of her subsequent historical fiction has marginal fantasy elements; the series of **children's fantasies** comprising *The Dragon and the Thief* (1991), *The Land of Gold* (1992), and *Beyond the North Wind* (1993) is more wholehearted. *The Wolf Hunt* (2001) is based on one of **Marie de France**'s lays. *The Alchemy of Fire* (2004) has elements of **alchemical fantasy**.

BRAMAH, ERNEST (1868–1942). British writer best known for his creation of the Chinese storyteller Kai Lung, who has **Oriental fantasy** adventures of his own in addition to those he narrates, them in a laconic yet ornate style (initially in a situation similar to **Scheherazade**'s). He features in *The Wallet of Kai Lung* (1900), *Kai Lung's Golden Hours* (1922), *Kai Lung Unrolls His Mat* (1928), *Kai Lung beneath the Mulberry Tree* (1940), and *Kai Lung: Six* (1974). Kai Lung is also credited as the teller of the **detective** story parody *The Moon of Much Gladness* (1932; aka *The Return of Kai Lung*).

BRANDON, PAUL (1971–). British writer and musician resident in Australia since 1994. *Swim the Moon* (2001) is a **hallucinatory fantasy** featuring magical **music** and selkies. *The Wild Reel* (2004) is an **urban fantasy** set in Brisbane, where the Irish **Faerie** court has taken up residence.

BRENCHLEY, CHAZ (1959–). British writer in various genres (refer to *HDHL*). His principal contribution to fantasy is the **Arabian** Outremer series, comprising *Tower of the King's Daughter* (1998; 2 vol. ed. separates first half as *The Devil in the Dust*), *Feast of the King's Shadow* (2000; 2 vol. ed. separates first half as *A Dark Way to Glory*), and *Hand of the King's Evil* (2002; 2 vol. ed separates second half as *The End of All Roads*).

BRIGGS, K. M. (1898–1980). British folklorist. Her excursions into fiction include the **children's fantasies** *The Legend of Maiden-Hair* (1915) and *The Witches' Ride* (1937), the **historical fantasy** *Hobberdy Dick* (1955), and the **psychological fantasy** *Kate Crackernuts* (1963; rev. 1979). Her nonfictional works include the useful source books *The Personnel of Fairyland: A Short Account of the Fairy People of Great Britain for Those Who Tell Stories to Children* (1953), *A Dictionary of British Folk-tales* (2 vols., 1970), *Folk Legends* (2 vols., 1971), and *A Dictionary of Fairies* (1976; aka *An Encyclopedia of Fairies*). Her critical studies include *Pale Hecate's Team: An Examination of the Beliefs* *on Witchcraft and Magic among Shakespeare's Contemporaries and His Immediate Successors* (1962), *The Fairies in Tradition and Literature* (1967), and *The Vanishing People: Fairy Lore and Legends* (1976).

BRIGGS, RAYMOND (1934–). British illustrator and writer who broke away from the conventional work he had been doing since 1961 in the satirical **comic**-strip fantasy *Fungus the Bogeyman* (1977), a portrait of a gloomy bogeyman who finds his duties as a moral terrorist onerous and absurd. The sentimental fantasy *The Snowman* (1978) was much more popular. After excursions into political satire, he returned to melancholy **existentialist fantasy** in *The Man* (1992) and *The Bear* (1994).

BROOKS, TERRY (1944–). U.S. writer. He and **Stephen R. Donaldson** were the writers who demonstrated that the commercial success of *Lord of the Rings* had not been a fluke, and that **commodified/epic fantasy** really did have potential as a mass-market genre. *The Sword of Shannara* (1977) is a dumbed-down version of **J. R. R. Tolkien**'s work, so closely imitative that **Lin Carter** described it as a "war crime of a book," but it became the foundation stone of **Ballantine**'s **Del Rey** imprint; its sequels are *The Elfstones of Shannara* (1982), *The Wishsong of Shannara* (1985), *The Scions of Shannara* (1990), *The Druid of Shannara* (1991), *The Elf Queen of Shannara* (1992), and *The Talismans of Shannara* (1993); *The First King of Shannara* (1996) is a prequel. The Voyage of the *Jerle Shannara* series, comprising *Ilse Witch* (2000), *Antrax* (2001), and *Morgawr* (2002), took up the story a generation later. The High Druid of Shannara series launched with *Jarka Ruus* (2003), and *Tanequil* (2004) moved on to a further generation. *The World of Shannara* (2001, with Teresa Patterson) is a **guide**.

Brooks's Landover series, comprising *Magic Kingdom for Sale—Sold!* (1986), *The Black Unicorn* (1987), *Wizard at Large* (1988), *The Tangle Box* (1994), and *Witches' Brew,* (1995) is a **humorous fantasy** akin to the works of **Piers Anthony**. In the **dark/contemporary fantasy** series comprising *Running with the Demon* (1997), *A Knight of the Word* (1998), and *Angel Fire East* (1999), a small town becomes the stage for an epic struggle between the Word and the Void.

BROWN, GEORGE MACKAY (1921–1996). Orcadian writer, whose fantasies are mostly based in local legend, especially the short fiction collected in *A Calendar of Love* (1957), *A Time to Keep* (1969; the 1986 book of the same title is a sampler), *Hawkfall* (1974), *The Sun's Net* (1976), *Witch* (1977), *Andrina* (1983), *Christmas Stories* (1985), *The*

Golden Bird (1987), *The Masked Fisherman* (1989), and *The Sea King's Daughter/Eureka!* (1991). *Magnus* (1973) is a longer work in the same vein. *Time in a Red Coat* (1984) is a serial **timeslip** romance. *Beside the Ocean of Time* (1994) is a **visionary fantasy** celebrating the role of storytelling in formulating history. Brown's **children's fantasies** include *The Two Fiddlers* (1974), *Pictures in the Cave* (1977), and *Keepers of the House* (1986).

BROWN, MARY (1929–). British writer. Her fantasies are distinctive; *The Unlikely Ones* (1986) and the series comprising *Pigs Don't Fly* (1994), *Master of Many Treasures* (1995), and *Dragonne's Egg* (1999) describe elaborate seriocomic **quests** undertaken by ill-matched assortments of human and animal companions.

BROWNE, N. M. (1960–). British writer who has also published under her maiden name, Nicola Matthews. The **timeslip** series begun with *Warriors of Alavna* (2000) took on an **Odyssean** slant in *Warriors of Camlann* (2003), when the characters' attempt to return home went awry. In the **psychological fantasy** *Hunted* (2002), a girl in a coma identifies with a fox living in the distant past. In *Basilisk* (2004), underworld-inhabiting "combers" reluctantly join forces with "abovers" when their rigidly stratified society is disturbed by **dreams**.

BROWNING, ROBERT (1812–1889). British poet. He was much preoccupied with **metaphysical** matters of personal evolution, concerns that are elaborated in such long poems as *Paracelsus* (1835). His most influential works, so far as fantasy literature is concerned, were "The Pied Piper of Hamelin" (1842), a lively version in verse of a famous **folktale**, and the brief and enigmatic "Childe Roland to the Dark Tower Came" (1855), which extrapolates a **chivalric** quest into an exceedingly gloomy milieu. The imagery of the latter echoes in many modern works, most elaborately in **Stephen King**'s Dark Tower series.

BRUST, STEVEN (1955–). U.S. writer. He is best known for the anti-**heroic** Taltos series, initially comprising *Jhereg* (1983), *Yendi* (1984), *Teckla* (1986), *Taltos* (1988; aka *Taltos and the Paths of the Dead*), *Phoenix* (1990), and *Athrya* (1993); *Dragon* (1998) is a **prequel**. The series continued in *Issola* (2001). An earlier historical phase of the same **secondary world** is featured in the trilogy comprising *The Phoenix Guard* (1991), *Five Hundred Years After* (1994), and *The Viscount of Ardilankha* (1994), which pays homage to **Alexandre Dumas**; this too was continued in *Paths of the Dead* (2002), *The Lord of Castle Black* (2003), and *Sethra Lavode* (2004). The **portal fantasy** *Brokedown Palace* (1986) explains the Eastern European folkloristic intrusions in the Taltos series, which are also **recycled** in *The Sun, the Moon, and the Stars* (1987) and redeployed in the **contemporary fantasy** *The Gypsy* (1992 with **Megan Lindholm**). *To Reign in Hell* (1984) is an **angelic fantasy** offering an unorthodox view of Lucifer's fall. *Agyar* (1993) is a meditative **vampire** fantasy. *Freedom & Necessity* (1997, with **Emma Bull**) is a historical novel with marginal fantasy elements.

BUCHAN, JOHN (1875–1940). Scottish writer and diplomat. The collections *Grey Weather: Moorland Tales of My Own People* (1899), *The Watcher by the Threshold and Other Tales* (1902), and *The Moon Endureth: Tales and Fancies* (1912) map his progress from **folklore**-based fantasy to the psychologically sophisticated **visionary fantasy** that he deployed in *The Dancing Floor* (1926) and *The Gap in the Curtain* (1932). *Witch Wood* (1927) is a historical novel about **devil** worship. *The Runagates Club* (1928) features fanciful **travelers' tales** narrated by the members of a dining club, including several accounts of subtle hauntings. *The Magic Walking-Stick* (1932) is a **children's/wish-fulfillment fantasy**.

BULGAKOV, MIKHAIL (1891–1940). Russian writer whose work was suppressed in the 1920s but who enjoyed a degree of protection from persecution because Stalin liked one of his plays. Many of his **satires** are framed as **sf** (refer to *HDSFL*), but the heartfelt novel translated as *The Master and Margarita* (written 1938; published 1966–67; tr. 1967)—which fuses a satirical black comedy in which the **Devil** pays a flying visit to Moscow with a poignant account of the tribulations of a writer working on an account of Christ's crucifixion—is one of the masterpieces of fantasy literature.

BULL, EMMA (1954–). U.S. writer. In 1980, she and her husband, **Will Shetterly**, founded an Interstate Writers' Workshop in Minneapolis, aka "the Scribblies," which became the parent of a **shared world** project set in the city of Liavek (1985–90). Other members of the group include **Kara Dalkey**, **Patricia Wrede**, **Stephen Brust**, and **Pamela Dean**. Bull's principal exemplification of the group's anti-modernist and pro-entertainment stance is the **urban fantasy** *The War of the Oaks* (1987). *The Princess and the Lord of Night* (1994) is a **fairy tale** fantasy. Her short fiction is sampled in *Double Feature* (1994 with Shetterly).

BULLETT, GERALD (1893–1958). British writer. His most significant venture into fantasy was the quasi-autobiographical **allegory** *Mr. Godly beside Himself* (1924), a key text in the post–World War I crusade for **re-enchantment**, in which a jaded businessman exchanges places with his fairy ***doppelgänger*** and finds **Faerie** in a state of political turmoil. A brief preparatory sketch, "The Enchanted Moment," appeared in *The Street of the Eye and Nine Other Tales* (1923); the title story is a **psychological fantasy**. A few **posthumous fantasies** are featured in *The Baker's Cart and Other Tales* (1925) and *The World in Bud and Other Tales* (1928). The title story of *Helen's Lovers and Other Tales* (1932) is a notable **timeslip** romance. *Ten Minute Tales and Some Others* (1960) and the samplers *Short Stories of To-day and Yesterday* (1929) and *Twenty Four Tales* (1938) also mingle fantasies with naturalistic works. *Eden River* (1934) is a **biblical fantasy** following the early generations of the character Adam's family. *Marden Fee* (1931) juxtaposes different eras in a melancholy romance of eternal recurrence. *Cricket in Heaven* (1949) **transfigures** the **classical myth** of Alcestis in a **contemporary** setting.

BULWER-LYTTON, EDWARD (BARON LYTTON OF KNEBWORTH) (1803–1873). British writer and politician who was plain Edward Bulwer until he inherited his mother's estate, Knebworth, and added her surname to his. He wrote numerous fantasies in his youth, including ponderous **allegories**, many of which he published while editing the *New Monthly Magazine;* these stories included *Asmodeus at Large* (1832–33; book 1833) and items collected in *The Pilgrims of the Rhine* (1834) and *The Student* (1835).

Bulwer was a highly significant writer of **occult fantasy** (refer to *HDHL*), following the tentative *Godolphin* (1833) with a novel whose aborted serial version, *Zicci* (1838), was eventually reprinted in book form despite the fact that it had been completely rewritten as *Zanoni* (1842). An enormously influential **Rosicrucian** romance, *Zanoni* won its author a reputation as an esoteric scholar that moved **Eliphas Lévi** to make a pilgrimage to Knebworth. Bulwer repaid the compliment by making some use of Lévi's ideas in the famous haunted house story "The Haunters and the Haunted" (1859; aka "The House and the Brain") and *A Strange Story* (1862).

Bulwer became more protective of his reputation once his political career took off, toning down the occult elements of the utopian romance *The Coming Race* (1871) and issuing the book anonymously. His son

Robert (1831–91), who used the pseudonym Owen Meredith as well as signing himself the Earl of Lytton, also wrote a feverish occult fantasy, *The Ring of Amasis* (1863), whose concerns foreshadowed those of **karmic romance**.

BUNYAN, JOHN (1628–1688). British Calvinist preacher. He wrote a spiritual autobiography, *Grace Abounding* (1666), while imprisoned for his evangelical endeavors; its substance was dramatically **transfigured** in the **allegory** *The Pilgrim's Progress from This World to That Which Is to Come* (first part 1678–79). A landmark text of British **Christian fantasy**—it was one of the most widely read texts in the English language, at least until 1900—its imagery has exerted a considerable influence over the structure and equipment of **quest** fantasy, where the imagery of the Slough of Despond, Doubting Castle, Vanity Fair, and so forth echoes resonantly. *The Holy War* (1682), an allegory in which the city of Mandoul has to be liberated after its seizure by Diabolus, was less successful, so Bunyan reprised his original performance by writing the second part of *The Pilgrim's Progress,* in which Christian guides his family along the route he had scouted out, thus facilitating their passage; it was added to reprints from 1684 onward.

BURDEKIN, KATHARINE (1896–1963). British writer who published the wide-ranging **historical fantasies** *The Burning Ring* (1927) and *The Rebel Passion* (1929) and the **children's fantasy** *The Children's Country* (1929) under her own name (contracted to Kay Burdekin in U.S. editions) before adopting the pseudonym Murray Constantine for two **sf** novels (refer to *HDSFL*) and the **allegory** *The Devil, Poor Devil!* (1934). In the last-named, the **Devil** wakes from dormancy to find his influence on the wane, not because of **Christian** opposition but by virtue of the emergence of rationalism, personalized as "the Independent."

BURGESS, ANTHONY (1917–1993). British writer who made occasional forays into fantasy. *The Eve of Saint Venus* (1964) recycles a common motif of **erotic fantasy** as a melancholy farce. *Beard's Roman Women* (1976) is a **sentimental fantasy** in which **ghosts** recall lost opportunities. *A Long Trip to Teatime* (1976) is a quirky **children's fantasy**. In *Any Old Iron* (1989), Excalibur is displaced from **Arthurian fantasy** into the modern world for **satirical** purposes. *Enderby's Dark Lady; or, No End to Enderby* (1985) echoes the life of **William Shakespeare**. A few fantasies are included in the collection *The Devil's Mode* (1989).

BURGESS, MELVIN (1954–). British writer for **children** whose work has often proved controversial because of its determined treatment of "adult" themes. Fantasization assists this mission in many of his works without compromising their realism, as in the elements of **animal fantasy** in *The Cry of the Wolf* (1990), the accounts of witchery in the **historical fantasy** *Burning Issy* (1992), and the **timeslip** component of *An Angel for May* (1992). Fantastic elements take on a symbolic role in *The Earth Giant* (1995), whose eponymous figure is released from the bowels of an uprooted tree, and in *Tiger, Tiger* (1996), which is based on a fake **Oriental** myth. The futuristic *Bloodtide* (1999), based on the **Nordic** Volsunga saga, is set in the ruins of London. *The Ghost behind the Wall* (2000) is an unusual account of haunting. *Lady: My Life as a Bitch* (2001) is a witty and uncompromisingly robust **theriomorphic fantasy**.

BURROUGHS, EDGAR RICE (1875–1950). U.S. writer best known for his creation of a powerful modern hero **myth** in the sequence of pulp magazine serials begun with *Tarzan of the Apes* (1912; book 1914). *The Return of Tarzan* (1913; book 1915), *The Beasts of Tarzan* (1914; book 1916), *The Son of Tarzan* (1915; book 1917), *Tarzan and the Jewels of Opar* (1916; book 1918), and the tales of Tarzan's youth collected in *Jungle Tales of Tarzan* (1919) fleshed out the myth. The series grew repetitive thereafter, and many of its elements are by other hands—although those unauthorized by his estate were quickly suppressed. The character continued his adventures in many other media, especially **cinema** and **comic** books.

Much of Burroughs's other work is formulated as **sf** (refer to *HDSFL*), although the definitive **planetary romance** series begun with *A Princess of Mars* (1912; book 1917) and its various analogues are exercises in blithely uninhibited action-adventure fantasy similar in spirit to the Tarzan novels. The others include the **lost race** stories *The Cave Girl* (1913–17; book 1925) and *The Land That Time Forgot* (1918; book 1924), and a series launched with *At the Earth's Core* (1914; book 1922) set in Pellucidar, a world within the hollow earth. Burroughs remains one of the most widely imitated writer ever to set pen to paper; his influence on the **sword and sorcery** subgenre was immense.

BYATT, A. S. (1936–). British writer. The long title story of her collection of five **art fairy tales**, *The Djinn in the Nightingale's Eye* (1994), is an **Arabian fantasy**. *Elementals: Stories of Fire and Ice* (1998) includes more items in a similar vein, most notably the novella "Cold." Some of the stories in *Sugar and Other Stories* (1987) and *The Little Black Book of Stories* (2003) feature **ghosts**. *Possession: A Romance* (1990), the two novellas in *Angels and Insects* (1993), and *Babel Tower* (1996) flirt with fantastic devices but sternly refuse commitment; *The Biographer's Tale* (2000) is more **ambiguous**.

BYRON, LORD (1788–1824). British poet. He was the most significant pioneer of English **romanticism** and the inspiration of the "Byronic" pose, whose extreme versions qualify as **lifestyle fantasy** by virtue of suggestions of diabolism. The psychology of the pose was mapped out in the quasi-autobiographical *Childe Harold's Pilgrimage* (1812–18), the **Faustian** *Manfred* (1817), and the unfinished *Don Juan* (1819–24). Forced into exile by accusations related to his sex life, Byron met up with Mary and Percy **Shelley** in the Villa Diodati in Switzerland, where a night of fevered discussions inspired Mary Shelley's *Frankenstein* (1818) and John Polidori's *The Vampyre* (1819); the latter added further fuel to the demonization by **Gothic** fiction attempted by Lady Caroline Lamb's *Glenarvon* (1816), although the notion that Byron was the prototype of the Gothic villain is ridiculous, given that the fad was over before he shot to fame.

– C –

CABELL, JAMES BRANCH (1879–1958). U.S. writer who became briefly notorious when *Jurgen: A Comedy of Justice* (1919) was labeled obscene on account of its humorous use of **erotic** symbolism. *The Cream of the Jest: A Comedy of Evasions* (1917) had already reflected sarcastically on the absurdities of contemporary prudery. Both works are part of an inordinately complex and varied series chronicling the history, influence, and genealogy of a legendary hero, Manuel; its fantasy elements are mostly set in the imaginary French province of Poictesme. The other major fantasies are *Figures of Earth: A Comedy of Appearances* (1921), *The High Place: A Comedy of Disenchantment* (1923), *The Silver Stallion: A Comedy of Redemption* (1926), *Something about Eve: A Comedy of Fig-Leaves* (1927), and the three stories in *The Witch Woman* (1948), which include "The Music from behind the Moon" (1926) and *The Way of Ecben* (separate publication 1929). There are marginal fantasy elements in many others, although Cabell's early neo-**chivalric romances**, including the items in *Gallantry* (1907) and *Chivalry* (1909) and the novel *The Soul of Melicent* (1913; rev. as *Domnei: A Comedy of Woman-Worship*, 1920), have no supernatural content.

Cabell shortened his signature to "Branch Cabell" on the **dream** fantasy trilogy *Smirt* (1934), *Smith* (1935), and *Smire* (1937), collected in the omnibus *The Nightmare Has Triplets* (1972). His late work includes two notable historical **metafictions**, *The King Was in His Counting-House: A Comedy of Common-Sense* (1938) and *Hamlet Had an Uncle: A Comedy of Honour* (1940), with themes carried forward in the nostalgic fantasies *The First Gentleman of America: A Comedy of Conquest* (1942; aka *The First American Gentleman*), *There Were Two Pirates: A Comedy of Division* (1946), and *The Devil's Own Dear Son: A Comedy of the Fatted Calf* (1949). Cabell's wit was more polished and erudite than that of his contemporary **Thorne Smith**, but its subtlety and plaintiveness do not work entirely to its advantage.

CALDECOTT, MOYRA (1927–). Pseudonym of South African–born writer Olivia Brown. The **historical fantasy** series comprising *The Tall Stones* (1977), *The Temple of the Sun* (1977), *Shadow on the Stones* (1978), and *The Silver Vortex* (1987) describes conflicts of **magic** based in rival Bronze Age religions. The trilogy comprising *Son of the Sun* (1986), *Daughter of Amun* (1989), and *Daughter of Ra* (1990) develops similar themes in an ancient Egyptian setting, with an element of **karmic romance** that is also manifest in *The Lily and the Bull* (1979)—in a Minoan setting—and the **Arthurian fantasy** *The Tower and the Emerald* (1985). The **Celtic fantasies** *The Green Lady and the King of Shadows* (1989) and *The Winged Man* (1993) are the most adventurous items in a series of **recycled** materials.

CALVINO, ITALO (1923–1985). Italian writer who became a leading practitioner of **fabulation**, comparable in status with **Jorge Luis Borges**. He first ventured into fantasy in the sophisticated mock-**chivalric romances** translated as *The Cloven Viscount* (1952; tr. 1962) and *The Non-Existent Knight* (1959; tr. 1962), which were combined with the equally witty **philosophical fantasy** *The Baron in the Trees* (1957; tr. 1959) in the omnibus *Our Ancestors* (1960; tr. 1980).

Calvino broke new ground in the cosmological fabulations collected in *Cosmicomics* (1963; tr. 1968) and *T zero* (1967; tr. 1969, aka *Time and the Hunter*); he retained its literary method, albeit in a conspicuously toned-down manner, in *Invisible Cities* (1972; tr. 1974), *The Castle of Crossed Destinies* (1973; tr. 1977), *Mr Palomar* (tr. 1985), and the incomplete *Under the Jaguar Sun* (1986; tr. 1988). *Numbers in the Dark* (1993; tr. 1995) is a posthumous assembly of fables, fragments, and other miscellaneous pieces.

The novel translated as *If on a Winter Night a Traveller* (1979; tr. 1981) is a convoluted **metafiction** exploring the complexities of the relationship between reader, texts, literary scholarship, and real life. Calvino compiled a massive compendium of *Italian Folktales* (1956; tr. 1980) and a showcase **anthology** of *Fantastic Tales: Visionary and Everyday* (2 vols. 1983; 1 vol., tr. 1997).

CAMPBELL, JOSEPH (1904–1987). U.S. scholar. *The Hero with a Thousand Faces* (1949) argues that all hero **myths** are fundamentally similar, deriving from the same archetypal "monomyth." He anatomized its structure as the hero's journey along a Road of Trials—whose challenges embody previously unrecognized aspects of his own unconscious mind. After negotiating these trials successfully, he obtains a trophy, which he offers on his return to his community so that it might enhance the lives of all. He generalized his procedure to the functional analysis of other kinds of myth in *The Masks of God* (4 vols., 1959–68), which asked that more attention be paid to the "living mythologies" of modern times.

Campbell's mythical formulas correlate very well with the formulas of **commodified fantasy**, partly due to the fact that some fantasy writers make conscious use of his ideas in planning and underpinning their endeavors, as did **Michael Moorcock** in his celebration of "the Eternal Champion."

CANADIAN FANTASY. Although David Ketterer's history of *Canadian Science Fiction and Fantasy* (1992) lists several early examples of French-Canadian *fantastique* and numerous similar supernatural fictions in English, he finds few examples of wholehearted fantasy earlier than Gwendolyn MacEwen's **occult/Christian fantasy** *Julian the Magician* (1963). A subsequent modest increase in fantastic literary fiction, exemplified by **Robertson Davies** and **W. P. Kinsella**, was followed by the more assertive appearance of such specialists as the sophisticated **epic** fantasist **Guy Gavriel Kay** and **urban fantasy** pioneer **Charles de Lint**. The magazine *On Spec* provided a useful domestic genre market, and there was a dramatic increase in the production of Canadian **sf** (refer to *HDSFL*) in both English and French, perhaps stimulated by Canada's awkward, economically marginal relationship with the United States.

As in **Australia**, there was a considerable expansion of Canadian fantasy in the 1990s, exemplified by **Kelley Armstrong**, **Terence M. Green**, **Tanya Huff**, **Sean Russell**, **Geoff Ryman**, **Sean Stewart**, and **Michelle West**, and by Matthew Hughes's **Swiftian** satires *Fools Errant* (1994) and *Fool Me Twice* (2001), Ann Marston's Rune Blade trilogy (1996–97) and Sword in Exile trilogy (1999–2000), Rebecca Bradley's Lady in Gil trilogy (1996–98), Fiona Patton's **sword and sorcery** series begun with *The Stone Prince* (1997), Yves Menard's *The Book of Knights* (1998), Dennis Jones's epic House of Pandragore series (1999–2001), Marie Jakober's **historical fantasy** *The Black Chalice* (2000), Thomas Wharton's historical fantasy *Salamander* (2001), Ursula Pflug's **portal fantasy** *Green Music* (2002), Stephanie Bedwell-Grime's **angelic fantasy** *Guardian Angel* (2003), and Janet McNaughton's historical fantasy *An Earthly Knight* (2004). Immigrants who assisted this flow included Jack Whyte, the Scottish-born author of the **Arthurian** Camulod Chronicles, and the Ethiopian Nega Mezlekia, author of *The God Who Begat a Jackal* (2002).

Showcase **anthologies** featuring Canadian fantasy include *Island Dreams: Montreal Writers of the Fantastic* (2003) and *Open Space: New Canadian Fantastic Fiction* (2003), edited by Claude Lalumière.

CANAVAN, TRUDI (1969–). Australian writer and artist, the longtime art editor of the magazine *Aurealis*. In her **picaresque** Black Magician trilogy, comprising *The Magician's Guild* (2001), *The Novice* (2002), and *The High Lord* (2003), a monopolistic guild recruits a talented woman fortunate enough to have a close friend in the Thieves' Guild.

ĈAPEK, KAREL (1890–1938). Czech writer. Much of his fantastic fiction is **sf** (refer to *HDSFL*), although the novels translated as *The Absolute at Large* (1922; tr. 1927) and *Krakatit* (1924; tr. 1925) are **hybrid** texts. His pure fantasies include two **satirical** plays written in collaboration with his brother Josef (1887–1945), the celebrated *Insect Play* (1921; first tr. as *And So ad Infinitum*, aka *The World We Live In*) and *Adam the Creator* (1927). *The Mother* (1938; tr. 1939) is a Brechtian solo work in which the dead return. He wrote numerous fantastic short stories, including some of those translated in *Money and Other Stories* (1929), *Tales from Two Pockets* (abridged 1932;

1994), *Fairy Tales* (1933; rev. as *Nine Fairy Tales*, 1990), and *Apocryphal Stories* (1949).

CARD, ORSON SCOTT (1951–). U.S. writer best known for **sf** (refer to *HDSFL*). His first fantasy, *Hart's Hope* (1983), focuses on the nullification of **magic** rather than its use. His major fantasy project is the **messianic** Alvin Maker series, set in a magic-infected **alternative history** in which the American Revolution never happened; it comprises *Seventh Son* (1987), *Red Prophet* (1988), *Prentice Alvin* (1989), *Alvin Journeyman* (1995), *Heartfire* (1998), and *The Crystal City* (2003), with further volumes to come. *Treasure Box* (1996) is a **dark fantasy**. *Enchantment* (1999) is a **timeslip** fantasy in which classic **fairy tale** motifs are darkened by their Russian setting but lightened by a **humorous** edge. Card's short fiction, including some fantasies, is collected in *Maps in a Mirror* (1990). He edited the **anthology** couplet *Dragons of Light* (1980) and *Dragons of Darkness* (1981).

CAREY, JACQUELINE (1964–). U.S. writer. Her nonfictional study of *Angels: Celestial Spirits in Legend & Art* (1997) provided some inspiration for *Kushiel's Dart* (2001), a complex **alternative history** fantasy with **religious** and **erotic** elements. It is set in Terre d'Ange, with an angel-descended population that takes a Dionysian attitude to sex; the heroine is an "anguissette" who derives ecstatic pleasure from pain; *Kushiel's Chosen* (2002) and *Kushiel's Avatar* (2003) are sequels. *Banewreaker* (2004) began a new sequence.

CARROLL, JONATHAN (1949–). U.S. writer whose work is a highly distinctive subspecies of **dark fantasy** (refer to *HDHL*). Fantastic elements, which often seem flagrantly contradictory, routinely erupt into his sentimentally inclined plots with startling abruptness and **surreal** effect. In *The Land of Laughs* (1980), two academics researching a beloved writer of children's fantasies discover the strange corollaries of his creative power. Guilt feelings are exotically dramatized in *Voice of Our Shadow* (1983). *Bones of the Moon* (1987) features **escapist dreams** infected with hidden threats. *Sleeping in Flame* (1988) incorporates a bizarre **transfiguration** of a **fairy tale**. *A Child across the Sky* (1989), *Black Cocktail* (1990), and *After Silence* (1992) are more obviously horrific, but fantasy elements are central to the equally disturbing *Outside the Dog Museum* (1991) and *From the Teeth of Angels* (1994). Some of the short fiction in *The Panic Hand* (1995) is also linked to this sequence. *Kissing the Beehive* (1998) began a new sequence continued in *The Marriage of Sticks* (1999) and *The Wooden Sea* (2000). The novella *The Heidelberg Cylinder* (2000) develops similar materials in a more relaxed, bizarrely **humorous** fashion, but *White Apples* (2002) returned to more intense imaginative territory.

CARROLL, LEWIS (1832–1898). Pseudonym of British clergyman and mathematician Charles Lutwidge Dodgson, who applied his talent for logical extrapolation to all manner of calculatedly absurd premises in the classic **children's fantasies** *Alice's Adventures in Wonderland* (1865) and *Through the Looking-Glass, and What Alice Found There* (1871; one episode dropped at the request of illustrator John Tenniel was belatedly issued as *The Wasp in a Wig*, 1977). Martin Gardner's *The Annotated Alice* (1960) offers a comprehensive commentary on the texts' sources, explaining how—following precedents set by **Edward Lear**—they mounted a defiant opposition to the didactic tendencies of Victorian children's literature, offering a particular kind of "**nonsense**" that was both exhilarating and thought provoking. The books were enormously influential, bringing about a sea change in children's fantasy. Carroll's epic **quest** fantasy in verse, *The Hunting of the Snark* (1876), is similarly brilliant, but the more moralistic couplet *Sylvie and Bruno* (1889) and *Sylvie and Bruno Concluded* (1893) is lackluster. A few more short fantasies are featured in *The Complete Works of Lewis Carroll* (1939).

Alice became an archetypal figure, recycled and transfigured in countless texts, including John Kendrick Bangs's *Alice in Blunderland: An Iridescent Dream* (1907), Gilbert Adair's *Alice through the Needle's Eye* (1984), **Emma Tennant**'s *Alice Fell*, **Jeff Noon**'s *Automated Alice*, Jeanne Purdy's *Alix in Academe* (2000), and the stories in an **anthology** by **Margaret Weis**, *Fantastic Alice*. Parallel texts range from Charles E. Carryl's *Davy and the Goblin; or, What Followed Reading "Alice's Adventures in Wonderland"* (1884) to Carol Ann Sima's *Jane's Bad Hare Day* (1995), featuring surreal adventures in Manhattan.

CARTER, ANGELA (1940–1992). British writer who became the most important English **fabulator** of the 20th century; her use of fantastic motifs is stylistically luxurious and pointedly polemical. She first edged toward fantasy in *The Magic Toyshop* (1967), a caustic **allegory** of female maturation, but her work became increasingly phantasmagorical as the **science fantasy** *Heroes and Villains* was followed by the striking **erotic fantasy** *The Infernal Desire Machines of Doctor Hoffman* (1972;

aka *War of Dreams*), the **Odyssean** *The Passion of New Eve* (1977), and the fantasy of liberating **flight** *Nights at the Circus* (1984), all of which conduct their protagonists from various models of **decadent** order to gloriously chaotic scenarios pregnant with new possibilities. The baroque **children's fantasies** *Miss Z, the Dark Young Lady* (1970) and *Moonshadow* (1982) steer in the same direction.

In the introduction to her collection *Fireworks* (1974), Carter draws a distinction between (naturalistic) "stories" and (fabular) "tales," expressing a preference for the latter that was more extravagantly developed in a collection of ideologically transfigured feminist **fairy tales**, *The Bloody Chamber and Other Stories* (1979). More items in the same vein appeared, alongside **metafictions** referring to a rich variety of literary sources, in *Black Venus* (1985; rev. as *Saints and Strangers*) and *American Ghosts and Old World Wonders* (1993). *Burning Your Boats* (1995) is an omnibus.

Carter's translation of *The Fairy Tales of Charles Perrault* (1977) and her **anthologies** *The Virago Book of Fairy Tales* (1990; aka *The Old Wives' Fairy Tale Book*) and *The Second Virago Book of Fairy Tales* (1992, aka *Strange Things Sometimes Still Happen*) acknowledge the sources of her inspiration. The radio plays collected in *Come unto These Yellow Sands* (1985) and reprinted in *The Curious Room: Plays, Film Scripts and an Opera* (1997) toy subversively with similar motifs.

CARTER, LIN (1930–1988). U.S. writer whose own fiction mostly consists of pastiches of **Edgar Rice Burroughs** and **Robert E. Howard** (to whose Conan series he added considerable material in collaboration with **L. Sprague de Camp**). They include the five-volume series begun with *The Wizard of Lemuria* (1965; aka *Thongor and the Wizard of Lemuria*), the six-volume series begun with *The Giant of World's End* (1969), the six-volume series begun with *Under the Green Star* (1972), the eight-volume series begun with *Jandar of Callisto* (1972), and the five-volume series begun with *Journey to the Underground World* (1979). His last such series, begun with *Kesrick* (1982) and continued in *Dragonrouge* (1984), *Mandricardo* (1986), and *Callipygia* (1988), was the most enterprising. His interest in the **Lovecraft** school—especially **Clark Ashton Smith**—is reflected in the pastiches collected in *The Xothic Legend Cycle* (1997), ed. Robert M. Price.

It was as an editor that Carter made a crucial contribution to the development of genre fantasy, particularly in the context of the **Ballantine Adult Fantasy series**, for which he provided such context-setting **an-**

thologies as *Dragons, Elves and Heroes* (1969), *The Young Magicians* (1969), *Golden Cities, Far* (1970), *New Worlds for Old* (1971), *Discoveries in Fantasy* (1972), and two volumes of *Great Short Novels of Adult Fantasy* (1972–73). His nonfiction studies *Tolkien: A Look behind the Lord of the Rings* (1969) and *Imaginary Worlds: The Art of Fantasy* (1973) provided these samplers with their historical context. *The Magic of Atlantis* is a showcase of modern **Atlantean** fantasy. His **sword and sorcery** anthologies include the five-volume *Flashing Swords* series (1973–81). *Kingdoms of Sorcery* (1976) and *Realms of Wizardry* (1976) range further afield, as do the six volumes of the annual sampler of *The Year's Best Fantasy* (1975–80), which he edited, and four volumes of a paperback revival of ***Weird Tales***. He also edited the Lovecraftian sampler *The Spawn of Cthulhu* (1971) and wrote *Lovecraft: A Look behind the Cthulhu Mythos* (1972).

CAZOTTE, JACQUES (1719–1792). French writer who broke significant new ground in the **Faustian** fantasy translated as *The Devil in Love* (1772), which views its winsome diabolical tempter with sufficient studied ambivalence to anticipate key developments in modern **erotic fantasy** and the emergence of **literary satanism**. Cazotte's other fantasies include the **fairy tales** "La patte du chat" ("The Cat's-Paw," 1741) and "La belle par accident" ("The Accidental Beauty," 1788), and two burlesques: *A Thousand and One Follies* (1742; tr. 1927) takes great delight in its own absurdity, while *Ollivier* (1763) parodies **chivalric romances**. In collaboration with Dom Chavis, he also contributed some alleged translations of **Arabian fantasies** to the fairy tale anthology series *Cabinet des fées* (1788–90).

CELTIC FANTASY. The overlapping terms "Celt" and "Gael" derive from the syncretic term given by the Romans to the indigenous tribes of Western Europe, most of which were gradually brought under imperial rule; the key exceptions were those that held out in Wales, Ireland, and Scotland. Those countries, along with Cornwall and Brittany, were generally supposed to have retained more Celtic culture than England, parts of which suffered also subsequent conquests by Danes and Anglo-Saxons. Celtic fantasy draws on the folklore of all these regions, sometimes separately but often collectively, using broad notions of Celtic culture and religion derived from **scholarly fantasies**, often featuring **druids**.

Celtic fantasy embraces a significant sector of **Arthurian fantasy**, by virtue of the fact that the Arthurian component of French chivalric romances was co-opted into Welsh legends before the latter were written down in such **taproot texts** as the 14th-century *The White Book of Rhydderch* and the 15th-century *The Red Book of Hergest* (selections from which were translated by Lady Charlotte Guest in 1838–49 as the ***Mabinogion***).

The literary reworking of Celtic mythology entered a new phase in Scotland with the fabrication by James Macpherson of the Ossianic verse epics *Fingal* (1762) and *Temora* (1763), which helped pave the way for various 19th-century "Celtic revivals" that gave birth to a rich subculture of scholarly fantasy as well as the production of literary fantasies. **Walter Scott**'s collections of Scottish ballads are of similarly dubious antiquity. Such writers as **Thomas Love Peacock** delighted in **transfiguring** such materials, but the likes of **W. B. Yeats** took it far more seriously.

Scottish Celtic fantasy was further complicated by layers of invention, imitative of Macpherson, heaped upon it by **James Hogg** and "**Fiona Macleod**," whose influence can be seen in the works of the Countess of Cromartie, including *The Web of the Past* (1905), W. Croft Dickinson; in his **children's fantasies** *Borrobil* (1944), *The Eildon Tree* (1947), and *The Flag from the Isles* (1951); his adult ghost stories; and in the Orcadian writer **George Mackay Brown**. Although Welsh Celtic fantasy is direly confused by its Arthurian imports, notable contributions to its development have been made by **Kenneth Morris**, **John Cowper Powys**, **Evangeline Walton**, **Vaughan Wilkins**, **Lloyd Alexander**, and **Alan Garner**. Irish Celtic fantasy has retained a more distinctive identity, exhibited by such writers as **James Stephens**, Shaw Desmond, in *Tales of the Little Sisters of St. Francis* (1929), Eimar O'Duffy, **Morgan Llywelyn**, and **Peter Tremayne**.

Notable examples of generic fantasy employing Celtic materials include Pat O'Shea's complex **portal fantasy** *The Hounds of the Morrigan* (1985); Gregory Frost's *Tain* (1986) and *Remscela* (1988); Sheila Gilluly's trilogy *The Boy from the Burren* (1990), *The Giant of Inishkerry* (1992), and *The Emperor of Earth-Above* (1993); Juilene Osborne-McKnight's *Bright Sword of Ireland* (2004); and works by **Kenneth C. Flint**, **Catherine Cooke**, **Deborah Turner Harris**, **Robert Holdstock**, and **Eoin Colfer**. Celtic materials are usually prominent in syncretic endeavors assuming a single common mythology underlying all the European variants; notable examples include numerous works by **E. Charles Vivian** and Paul Hazel's Finnbranch trilogy comprising *Yearwood*

(1980), *Undersea* (1982), and *Winterking* (1985). Some such works extend the net even farther; **Cecilia Dart-Thornton**'s Bitterbynde series includes Australian elements.

CERVANTES, MIGUEL DE (1547–1616). Spanish writer. His classic **delusional fantasy** *Don Quixote* (1605; exp. 1615) made fun of the **chivalric romances** that had retained their popularity into the previous century, although the allegation that it killed them off is probably unjustified. Don Quixote did, however, become a legendary figure in his own right, archetypal of many other deluded heroes; although the book is a comedy, the tragic dimension of his **quest**'s futility left many readers yearning for a **re-enchantment** of his **thinned**-out world.

CHABON, MICHAEL (1963–). U.S. writer. The Pulitzer Prize–winning *The Amazing Adventures of Kavalier and Clay* (2001) is a sophisticated metafiction about World War II comic-book artists whose transfigured motifs include the **Golem**. *Summerland* (2002) is a tongue-in-cheek **contemporary fantasy** with elements of **sports fantasy**. His short fiction is sampled in *Werewolves in their Youth* (1999).

CHADBOURN, MARK (1960–). British writer who worked as a journalist and wrote thrillers (refer to *HDHL*) before embarking on the Age of Misrule series of **apocalyptic fantasies** comprising *World's End* (1999), *Darkest Hour* (2000), and *Always Forever* (2001). Although the subgenre does not lend itself to sequels, he followed it up with the Dark Age series, comprising *The Devil in Green* (2002) and *The Queen of Sinister* (2004). The novella *The Fairy Feller's Master Stroke* (2002) is one of several works inspired by Bedlamite Richard Dadd's cardinal example of Victorian **fairy** art.

CHALKER, JACK L. (1944–). U.S. writer and small-press publisher. His Mirage Press specialized in writers associated with the **Lovecraft** school, including **Robert E. Howard**. His own fiction is hectic action-adventure fiction mostly formulated as a **hybrid** example of **science fantasy** (refer to *HDSFL*), his first excursion into wholehearted fantasy being *And the Devil Will Drag You Under* (1979). Series in which fantasy elements predominate include the Soul Rider sequence, comprising *Spirits of Flux and Anchor* (1984), *Empires of Flux and Anchor* (1984), *Masters of Flux and Anchor* (1985), *The Birth of Flux and Anchor* (1985), and *Children of Flux and Anchor* (1986); the four-volume Dancing Gods series begun with *The River of Dancing Gods* (1984);

the sequence comprising *Lords of the Middle Dark* (1986), *Pirates of the Thunder* (1987), *Warriors of the Storm* (1987), and *Masks of the Martyrs* (1988); and the three-decker novel comprising *When the Changewinds Blow* (1987), *Riders of the Winds* (1988), and *War of the Maelstrom* (1988).

CHANT, JOY (1945–). Pseudonym of British writer Eileen Joyce Rutter, whose **children's fantasy** *Red Moon and Black Mountain* (1970) made a significant crossover into the adult market in the United States when it was released as a paperback in the wake of **J. R. R. Tolkien**'s *Lord of the Rings* (to which it is heavily indebted). *The Grey Mane of Morning* (1977) is a sequel. *When Voiha Wakes* (1983) is more enterprising, but less successful, in its depiction of a matriarchal society. *The High Kings* (1983) **recycles** the source materials of **Arthurian fantasy**.

CHAOS. The alternative to the ex nihilo model of Creation, in which the universe emerges from a void, represents it as a process that brings order to some kind of primordial chaos. Theories of serial creation imagine ordered structures being periodically rendered back into chaos before being reordered, while theories of dynamic creation imagine a more or less permanent balance between perennially active opposed forces of order and chaos. Modern fantasy often substitutes a **dualism** of Order and Chaos for the more traditional one between Good and Evil, in order that virtue may be more evenly divided; such works as **Michael Moorcock**'s Elric series, **L. E. Modesitt**'s Recluce series and **Louise Cooper**'s Time Master series acknowledge the vigor and liberating potential of Chaos as well as the harmonizing effects of Order, thus echoing the argumentative thrust of **literary satanism**, **surrealism**, and **Alfred Jarry**'s pataphysics.

CHAPMAN, VERA (1898–1996). British writer, born Vera Fogerty, who founded the Tolkien Society in 1969. Marriage to a clergyman did not prevent her indulgence in pagan **lifestyle fantasy**, whose principal literary legacy was a groundbreaking series of feminized **Arthurian fantasies**, which anticipated **Marion Zimmer Bradley**'s work in that vein. *The Green Knight* (1975), *The King's Damosel* (1976), and *King Arthur's Daughter* (1976) were reissued in an omnibus as *The Three Damosels* (1978). *Blaedudd the Birdman* (1978) dramatizes the legend of another legendary British king, while *The Wife of Bath* (1979) **recycles** one of **Chaucer**'s *Canterbury Tales* and *The Notorious Abbess* (1998) offers synthesized **legends** starring the Abbess of Shaston. *Judy* *and Julia* (1977) and *Miranty and the Alchemist* (1983) are **children's fantasies**.

CHARNAS, SUZY McKEE (1939–). U.S. writer whose best-known works are feminist **sf** (refer to *HDSFL*). The stories comprising the mosaic *The Vampire Tapestry* (1980) made a significant contribution to the development of revisionist **vampire** fiction. A subsequent vampire romance *The Ruby Tear* (1997) was bylined "Rebecca Brand." The trilogy comprising *The Bronze King* (1985), *The Silver Glove* (1988), and *The Golden Thread* (1989) describes resistance to an invasion from a **secondary world**. *Dorothea Dreams* (1986) is a **timeslip** fantasy. *The Kingdom of Kevin Malone* (1993) features a **portal** to **Faerie**.

CHAUCER, GEOFFREY (c1340–1400). British poet, one of the first to work effectively in the hybrid version of English developed in the wake of the Norman conquest. Most of his surviving works are responses, usually ironic, to earlier literary works: *The House of Fame* is a parodic **Dantean fantasy**; *Troilus and Criseyde* is derived from **Homer**; *The Parliament of Fowls* is a satirical **animal fantasy**. The mixed collection of stories framed as *The Canterbury Tales* includes only a few fantasies, but the overall tone of the collection and the worldview it encapsulates display a clear understanding of the various functions of calculated **fabulation**.

CHERRYH, C. J. (1942–). U.S. writer best known for **sf** (refer to *HDSFL*). She made her debut with *Gate of Ivrel* (1976), an early **commodified fantasy** that retains some fugitive **hybrid** elements of **science fantasy** in its account of a **multiverse** whose connecting **portals** must be destroyed—a project continued in *Well of Shiuan* (1978), *Fires of Azeroth* (1979), and *Exile's Gate* (1988). The enterprising couplet comprising *Ealdwood* (1981; rev. as *the Dreamstone*, 1983), *The Tree of Swords and Jewels* (1983), and the connected *Faery in Shadow* (1993) is similarly syncretic, favoring elements of **Celtic fantasy** in an elegiac account of **thinning**. *The Paladin* (1988) is an **Oriental fantasy**. The trilogy comprising *Rusalka* (1989), *Chernevog* (1990), and *Yvgenie* (1991) draws on **Russian** folklore. *The Goblin Mirror* (1992) is an account of a powerful talisman. In *Fortress in the Eye of Time* (1995), a botched spell summons an enigmatic amnesiac hero, whose adventures continue in *Fortress of Eagles* (1998), *Fortress of Owls* (1999), and *Fortress of Dragons* (2000). Cherryh has also contributed to several **shared world** projects, most significantly the series begun with *Heroes in Hell* (1985), which she and **Janet E. Morris** originated.

CHESTERTON, G. K. (1874–1936). British writer whose assertive religiosity lent a baroque edge to most of his fiction, including numerous **detective** stories and a number of works that are set in the future but hardly warrant description as **sf**. His most explicit **religious fantasy** was *The Man Who Was Thursday: A Nightmare* (1908), an **allegory** absurdly shaped as a spy story; it was reprinted with some "related pieces" in 1996. *The Ball and the Cross* (1909) has a darker allegorical conclusion. The play *Magic* (1913) toys ironically with illusion. The stories in *Tales of the Long Bow* (1925) use fantasy motifs more freely, as do some of the items posthumously assembled in *The Coloured Lands* (1938) and the overlapping *Daylight and Nightmare* (1986).

CHETWIN GRACE (?–). U.S. writer, mostly for children. *On All Hallows' Eve* (1984) is a **timeslip** fantasy featuring a world ruled by **witches**. In the **chimerical** *Out of the Dark World* (1985), a boy trapped in a computer program encounters **Morgan le Fay**. The series comprising *Gom on Windy Mountain* (1986), *The Riddle and the Rune* (1987), *The Crystal Stair* (1988), and *The Starstone* (1989) features a misfit child's **quest** for personal fulfillment. The Tales of Ulm from Hesta's Hearth are set in the same milieu; *Garrad's Quest* (1998), *The Foundling of Snawbyr Grygg* (2003), and *Wycan* (2004) follow similar story arcs, but *The Fall of Aelyth-Kintalin* (2002) is more adventurous, featuring a portal to the magical realm of In Between, where dream worlds are accumulated; *Child of the Air* (1991) is a fantasy of **flight**. *Friends in Time* (1992) is a **timeslip** fantasy. *The Chimes of Alfaylen* (1993) features magical **music**. For adults, *The Burning Tower* (2000) is a Tarot fantasy. *Deathwindow* (1999) is a mystery with **dark fantasy** elements.

CHILDREN'S FICTION. Children must always have been the primary audience for the **folktales** of oral tradition, so it was entirely natural that **fairy tales** would become a core genre of children's fiction. **Charles Perrault**'s popularization of the idea that they were adaptable to the task of "civilization" was challenged by Jean-Jacques Rousseau, who asserted that children had no innate bias toward barbarism that needed correction; nevertheless, the majority of educators inevitably sided with Perrault.

A fierce assault on the suitability of fantasy as children's fiction was launched in 19th-century Britain by Christians who felt that the pagan residues in folkloristic fiction might distract children from the true faith, and by utilitarians who opined that children should not be encouraged to believe in magic; such views were sternly opposed by **Charles Dickens**, **George MacDonald**, and **Charles Kingsley**. The **moralistic** aspects of children's fiction were then counterattacked by the anarchic spirit of **Edward Lear** and **Lewis Carroll**, paving the way for unashamed exercises in whimsical indulgence by **J. M. Barrie**, **A. A. Milne**, **Kenneth Grahame**, **Walter de la Mare**, and **Beatrix Potter**. Such prejudices were less obvious in 19th-century America, so the fantastic children's fiction of **Frank R. Stockton**, **Howard Pyle**, and **L. Frank Baum** is more relaxed. Writers like Eugene Field, author of *A Little Book of Profitable Tales* (1889), established a rival camp, and Christian opposition to the paganism of Oz and its analogues grew increasingly clamorous in the 20th century. There too, however, an anarchic spirit of reckless invention arose in the works of such writers as **James Thurber** and **Dr. Seuss**.

The horrific aspects of traditional folktales—abundantly evident in those collected by the Brothers Grimm—were routinely sanitized when they were adapted into children's fiction, although the first great synthesizer of imitation folktales, **Hans Christian Andersen**, was never averse to harrowing material; the "art fairy tales" written under the aegis of the Romantic and Decadent movements often reveled in it. When the first magazines aimed at children were founded—the Victorian "boys' papers"—their editors were happy to add ghost stories to their standard repertoire, and popular horror fiction has always had a substantial readership among teenage boys.

Contemporary fantasy for children remained self-consciously artificial for most of the 19th century, represented by such **portal fantasies** as Jean Ingelow's *Mopsa the Fairy* (1869) and Mrs. Molesworth's *The Cuckoo Clock* (1877), but **E. Nesbit**'s adaptations of the kind of **intrusive fantasy** pioneered by **F. Anstey** began a new tradition, carried forward by such writers as **Elizabeth Goudge**, **Hugh Lofting**, **P. L. Travers**, **Lucy M. Boston**, **Edward Eager**, **Nicholas Stuart Gray**, **Penelope Lively**, and **Patricia Wrightson**. The use of **secondary worlds** remained cautious, in spite of the spectacular precedent set by Baum, but **portal fantasies** gradually lost their painstaking formality, greatly assisted after 1950 by the example of **C. S. Lewis**'s Narnia series. Most **immersive fantasies** for children written before 1950, save for those set in the stereotyped pseudohistorical settings of traditional folktales, were **animal fantasies**—although **J. R. R. Tolkien**'s *The Hobbit* (1937) was eventually to prove a crucial exception.

In spite of these limitations, the early 20th-century children's market provided a useful refuge for several highly idiosyncratic writers for whom little imaginative space seemed available in the adult market, including **Eleanor Farjeon** and **T. H. White**. The additional scope granted to the marketplace in the 1950s, however, accommodated a remarkable boom in sophisticated fantasy formulated as children's fiction, exemplified by **Philippa Pearce**'s *Tom's Midnight Garden,* Arthur Calder-Marshall's *The Fair to Middling* (1959), the early novels of **Alan Garner** and **Penelope Farmer**, **Norton Juster**'s *The Phantom Tollbooth*, **Lloyd Alexander**'s Chronicles of Prydain, **Susan Cooper**'s "Dark Is Rising" sequence, Paul Gallico's *The Man Who Was Magic* (1967), **Russell Hoban**'s *The Mouse and his Child,* **Ted Hughes**'s *The Iron Man,* **Ursula K. le Guin**'s Earthsea series, **Leon Garfield**'s "Mr Corbett's Ghost," and **Dahlov Ipcar**'s *The Queen of Spells*.

The opening of these floodgates brought several new fantasy subgenres in children's fiction, most significantly **psychological fantasy** adapted to the developmental phases of adolescence, as exemplified by **Catherine Storr**'s *Marianne Dreams,* **William Mayne**'s *A Game of Dark,* **Jenny Nimmo**'s *The Snow Spider,* and **Michael Ende**'s *The Neverending Story*. The effectiveness of such works in modeling teenage angst and mapping out useful processes of psychological adaptation helped to force the identification within the marketplace of a specific category of **young adult** fiction. **Heroic fantasies** involving quasi-allegorical **quests**, **timeslip** fantasies, and **ghost stories** all became more common and more sophisticated in fiction written for teenagers, and such materials began to filter down into works aimed at younger age groups via the unconstrained **wish-fulfillment fantasies** of **Roald Dahl**, the more moralistically inclined works of **Natalie Babbitt**, **Elisabeth Beresford**, and **Eva Ibbotson**, and such picture books as **Maurice Sendak**'s *Where the Wild Things Are* and **Raymond Briggs**'s *Fungus the Bogeyman*. As children began to reach puberty earlier and prepuberal children were encouraged by their consumption of ad-infested **TV** to anticipate maturation, this trend became more obvious, paving the way for **horror fiction** to be marketed to nine-to-twelve-year-olds in the late 1980s.

The spectrum of publishing opportunities was abruptly transformed by the establishment of adult fantasy as a popular genre in the late 1970s; there followed a marked outflow from the children's market in the 1980s. Some writers who felt themselves uncomfortably restricted there shifted the emphasis of their endeavor to adult fantasy—examples include **Andre Norton**, **Tanith Lee**, and **Patricia McKillip**—but many young readers also found it more appealing to read "adult fantasy" than material explicitly labeled as juvenile fare. "Crossover" material like the works of **Terry Pratchett**, which appealed equally to children and adults, thrived as never before. Many writers found, however, that work explicitly aimed at children could be more adventurously varied and more imaginatively enterprising than the deluge of Tolkien clones and **sword and sorcery** novels that initially dominated the field of **commodified fantasy**. During the 1980s and 1990s, a great deal of children's fantasy was more original, and arguably more mature, than the formularistic material aimed at adults; notable examples can be found in the works of **Diana Wynne Jones**, **Nancy Willard**, **Margaret Mahy**, **Jane Louise Curry**, and **Jane Yolen**.

Children's fiction underwent a dramatic revolution in the 1990s, first signaled by the enormous success of R. L. Stine's "Goosebumps" series (launched 1992), which completed the adaptation of horror fiction motifs for nine-to-twelve-year-olds, usually by injecting a strong element of **humor**. This helped pave the way for the even more spectacular success of **J. K. Rowling**'s Harry Potter series, with an artful combination of comedy and **dark fantasy** that proved the publishing sensation of the decade. The outflow of talent and money from the children's market was abruptly reversed, and children's fantasy embarked upon another spectacular boom, in which commercially crafted best sellers by such writers as **Eoin Colfer**, **Garth Nix**, **William Nicholson**, and **G. P. Taylor** followed hot on the heels of the more spontaneous successes of **Philip Pullman**'s *His Dark Materials* and David Almond's *Skellig* (1998).

One result of this new commercialism was an increase in the commodification of children's fantasy, reflected in a great deal of series work. The more enterprising practitioners include **K. A. Applegate**, **John Bellairs**, **Bruce Coville**, **Annie Dalton**, **Catherine Fisher**, **Dick King-Smith**, **Dave Luckett**, **Gregory Maguire**, **Donna Jo Napoli**, and **Brad Strickland**. As in the adult marketplace, however, the growth of a sturdy core permitted the rapid expansion of an experimental fringe, which provided space for adventurously innovative work by such writers as **Karen Fox**, **Cornelia Funke**, **Jostein Gaarder**, **Brian Jacques**, **Robin Jarvis**, **Michael Molloy**, **Daniel Pinkwater**, **Kathryn Reiss**, **Paul Stewart**, **Theresa Tomlinson**, **Vivian Vande Velde**, and **Laurence Yep**.

CHIMERICAL TEXTS. Texts that juxtapose motifs from very different sources or contrive other unlikely bisociations in order to derive narrative energy from the combination of apparently incompatible materials. **Nonsense** fantasy and **surreal fantasy** routinely made use of this kind of effect, as did early metafictional texts like **Walter de la Mare**'s *Henry Brocken,* before it became much more widespread in the late 20th century, led by works that applied the rationalistic outlook of **science fiction** to confrontations with entities drawn from **myths** and **fairy tales**, as in the magazine ***Unknown***. Chimerical texts need to be contrasted with **hybrid** texts, which attempt the logical reconciliation and harmonization of their materials. Chimerization is fundamental to the method of such various writers as **Tom Arden**, **Jonathan Carroll**, **Jasper Fforde**, and **Terry Pratchett**, and to such subgeneric candidates as "**hard fantasy**" and **China Miéville**'s "New Weird."

CHIVALRIC ROMANCE. Chivalry was a code of honor supposedly observed by Christian knights, whose formalization adapted a Germanic rite of passage; it became a central myth of feudalism, central to *chansons de geste* and other baronial amusements, and thus to the tradition of **Romance**. Chivalric romance was pioneered by *The Song of Roland,* sophisticated by the lays of **Marie de France** and verse romances of **Chrétien de Troyes**, and stereotyped by such proto-novels as Wolfram von Eschenbach's *Parzifal* and the 14th-century *Amadis de Gaul*.

There was always an element of self-parody in chivalric romance, but its ideals were comprehensively pilloried by Miguel Cervantes's *Don Quixote* (1605–15). It was reintroduced into the produce of the **Romantic** movement by **Friedrich de la Motte Fouqué**'s *The Magic Ring* and **Robert Southey**'s new translation of *Amadis of Gaul,* which paved the way for more experimental endeavors by **William Morris** and his imitators. Quixotic scepticism reared its head again in the work of **James Branch Cabell**, Robert Nichols's "Sir Perseus and the Fair Andromeda" (1923), William Faulkner's *Mayday* (written 1926; 1977), and **Naomi Mitchison**'s *To the Chapel Perilous,* albeit armored by a nostalgic affection carefully preserved in such revisitations as **Italo Calvino**'s *The Non-Existent Knight* and **Patricia McKillip**'s *The Tower at Stony Wood*.

The tradition connecting chivalric romance to modern fantasy is mapped out in **Lin Carter**'s showcase **anthologies**. The spirit of chivalry is carefully conserved in the Romantic sector of **Arthurian fantasy**—especially in stories dealing with **quests** for the **grail**—and reverently interrogated in a great deal of **heroic fantasy**.

CHRÉTIEN DE TROYES. The signature attached to five **Arthurian** romances written in the late 12th century, including the earliest example of the kind, *Erec et Enide;* others have apparently been lost. *Cligés*, *Le Chevalier de la Charrette* (aka *Lancelot*), and *Le Chevalier au Lion* (aka *Yvain*) are orthodox **chivalric romances**, but the work that Chrétien left incomplete at his death, *Le Conte du Graal* (aka *Perceval*), introduced the crucial **allegorical** episode of the Fisher King and the mysterious **Grail**, which helped it become an enormously influential **taproot text**.

Although the allegorical interpolation's interpretation in **Christian** terms seems perfectly straightforward, the confusions caused by the incompleteness of *Le Conte du Graal* and its fusion in extant versions with another incomplete text—featuring the adventures of Gawain—have generated an astonishing profusion of **scholarly fantasy**. Perceval's story was rapidly **recycled** in German, in Wolfram von Eschenbach's *Parzifal,* and its incorporation into the Welsh *Red Book of Hergest* engendered much speculation in Britain about a possible Celtic origin. Its pretensions were, however, parodied with equal alacrity by a tongue-in-cheek account of the adventures of Fergus of Galloway, signed Guillaume le Clerc.

CHRISTIAN FANTASY. In addition to its scriptures, the Christian faith rapidly accumulated a rich folklore, which thrived in oral culture until it was **recycled** and augmented in such documents as Jacobus de Voragine's 13th-century *Legenda aurea* [The Golden Legend], a miracle-laden **anthology** of saints' life stories. Such tales served an important inspirational purpose, often **transfiguring** preexistent folklore so that its weight could be added to the Christian cause. Pious writers conscious of the fact that they were writing fantasies routinely excused their work as **allegory**.

The most notable landmark in the early history of Christian fantasy is **Dante**'s *Divine Comedy* (c1320); the most important precedents in English literature were set by **John Milton**'s *Paradise Lost* (1667) and **John Bunyan**'s *The Pilgrim's Progress* (1678–84). Subsequent Christian fantasy, including the Christian aspects of **afterlife fantasy**, **angelic fantasy**, and **apocalyptic fantasy**, usually has an ironic aspect derived from a slightly uncomfortable awareness of its lack of literal truth. An exceedingly passionate and dogmatic faith is required to persuade a writer that angels and miracles can be accommodated in realistic fiction; those who attempt to manifest such passion—**Marie Corelli** is the most conspicuous example—often seem to be protesting too much. Pious synthetic legends such as those featured in Gottfried Keller's *Seven Legends* (1872; tr. 1911) and Eugene Field's *The Holy Cross and Other Tales* (1893) are not so very dissimilar in tone to the more sceptical offerings of **Vernon Lee**, **Anatole France,** and **Laurence Housman**, although this reflects the fact that writers who use Christian fantasy as a medium for working out their own doubts often increase their confusion rather than dispelling it and may be led reluctantly but inexorably into heresy; notable examples include **George MacDonald** and **T. F. Powys**.

Effective literary propaganda for the faith can be found in various works by **G. K. Chesterton**, **Upton Sinclair**, **C. S. Lewis**, and **Harry Blamires**, and in Arthur Calder-Marshall's *The Fair to Middling* (1959), in which inmates of a School for Incapacitated Orphans are challenged by temptations laid on by O. L. D. Scratch the Universal Provider. Effective works using the Christian mythos as a backcloth for non-evangelical purposes include examples by **M. P. Shiel**, **Charles Williams**, **Robert Nathan**, and **Mikhail Bulgakov**'s *The Master and Margarita*. Figures from the New Testament who lend themselves to use in fantasy are, however, mostly peripheral; they include Salome, the **Wandering Jew**, and two of Christ's rival miracle workers, Simon Magus—featured in Wallace Nicholls's *Simon Magus* (1946), Anita Mason's *The Illusionist* (1983)—and Apollonius of Tyana, as featured in **John Keats**'s "Lamia."

The dramatic upsurge in religious publishing in the last decades of the 20th century, which produced a good deal of propagandist **children's fantasy**, added considerably to the mass of Christian fantasy; notable examples include works by **Walter Wangerin**. Commercial publishers began to interest themselves in such material when it produced best sellers in the field of apocalyptic fantasy; Hodder Headline started a line that included such fantasies as Philip Boast's *Sion* (1999) and Anne Perry's *Tathea* (1999). There as a similar increase in the popularity of exotic thrillers irreverently involving the Vatican in complex **secret histories**, including Dan Brown's *The Da Vinci Code* (2003) and Scott McBain's *The Coins of Judas* (2001). Syncretic hybridizers occasionally include Christian fantasy in their mix, as in Elizabeth Cunningham's **Celtic** Magdalen trilogy, begun with *Daughter of the Shining Isles* (2000). Colin Manlove's*Christian Fantasy* (1992) is a useful history of the subgenre. *See also* EROTIC FANTASY.

CHRISTMAS FANTASY. Christmas annuals had been published in Britain for many years before **Charles Dickens** established a new norm for such publications, but the sequence of Christmas books launched with *A Christmas Carol* (1843) set a crucial precedent, encouraging many more periodicals to begin issuing special Christmas supplements and exerting a powerful influence on their contents. Dickens's exemplars proposed that Christmas was a time when the standards of narrative expectation that were rapidly becoming normal (favoring naturalistic fiction over anything "Gothic") could be relaxed. That special license created a valuable publishing enclave for Victorian **sentimental fantasy**, especially for **humorous/ghost** stories. Stories composed with this tradition in mind outlasted the actual magazine supplements; notable examples can be found in the work of Tom Gallon, **John Kendrick Bangs**, **Jerome K. Jerome**, **Marie Corelli**, and **Netta Syrett**. The tradition continued into the 20th century in such collections as Coningsby Dawson's *When Father Christmas Was Late* (1919), **Robertson Davies**'s *High Spirits,* and Connie Willis's *Miracle and Other Christmas Stories* (1999). Notable individual works include **J. M. Barrie**'s *Farewell Miss Julie Logan,* **Seabury Quinn**'s *Roads,* **Dr. Seuss**'s *How the Grinch Stole Christmas,* **Mervyn Wall**'s *The Garden of Echoes,* **Leon Garfield**'s "Mr. Corbett's Ghost," Robert Westall's *The Christmas Cat* (1991) and *The Christmas Ghost* (1992), Paul Hazel's *The Wealdwife's Tale* (1993), Nancy Atherton's *Aunt Dimity's Christmas* (1999), and **Jane Louise Curry**'s *The Christmas Knight*.

CINEMA. Although **horror** (refer to HDHL) and **sf** (refer to *HDSFL*) were soon established as recognizable cinematic genres, "fantasy" was rarely identified as such until very recently; the only significant attempt to construct a coherent history of cinematic fantasy is the annotated chronology contained in David Pringle's *Ultimate Encyclopedia of Fantasy* (1998). Almost all the early items listed are adaptations of books or **theater** plays, the latter serving as a stern reminder of the limitations of early movie special effects.

Cinematic ventures into such subgenres as **surreal fantasy** (*The Cabinet of Dr Caligari, Un Chien Andalou,* and René Clair's early films), **Arabian fantasy** (the 1924 and 1940 versions of *The Thief of Bagdad*), and **afterlife fantasy** (*The Green Pastures*, 1936) had little obvious impact on the development of literary fantasy, but cinematic manifestations of **angelic fantasy** in the wake of *It's a Wonderful Life* (1946) had a much greater impact and helped to encourage the remarkable subsequent growth of that subgenre. Hollywood fantasy of the 1940s was dominated by **sentimental fantasies**; another movie of the period exerting an influence that eventually proved extensive was the **Thorne Smith**–based *I Married a Witch* (1942).

Fantasy set in **secondary worlds** poses a considerable challenge to scenarists, and the 1939 version of **L. Frank Baum**'s *The Wizard of Oz* was a lonely landmark for most of the 20th century; most early adaptations of secondary world fantasies were animated, the potential of that medium being demonstrated by such Walt Disney classics as *Snow White and the Seven Dwarfs* (1937). Even **intrusive fantasies** posed considerable challenges to the artistry of the stop-motion effects employed in such movies as *King Kong* (1933) and the **classical fantasies** of the 1950s and 1960s. Although few animated films retained the production values of the early Disney classics, the opportunities and restraints of animation soon spawned a curious kind of stereotyped secondary world with its own conventions and physical laws: a distinctive fantasy milieu that quickly spilled over into **comics** and impinged tangentially on literary fantasy, most obviously in blatantly **chimerical** works such as Gary K. Wolf's *Who Censored Roger Rabbit?* (1981) and Greg Snow's *Surface Tension* (1991, aka *That's All, Folks!*).

The rapid development of computer-assisted special effects in the 1990s altered the spectrum of opportunity out of all recognition, at a time when the huge commercial successes of **Tolkien**'s *Lord of the Rings* and **J. K. Rowling**'s Harry Potter books justified the huge budgets required to made full use of such techniques. When those projects reached the screen in the early 21st century, the case for recognizing fantasy as a cinema genre was securely made; the probability that the negotiation of film rights would henceforth be a major force in the book marketplace had been demonstrated by the boosting of **Eoin Colfer**'s *Artemis Fowl* to best-seller status, allegedly on the basis of the optimistic promise that its film version would be "*Die Hard* with fairies."

CLARKE, LINDSAY (1939–). British writer. *The Chymical Wedding* (1989) employs a **timeslip** to set up an unusually elaborate and earnest **alchemical fantasy**. *Alice's Masque* (1994) similarly **recycles** materials drawn from **Frazerian/scholarly fantasy** in a **contemporary** context. *Parzival and the Stone from Heaven: A Grail Romance Retold for Our Time* (2001) recycles Wolfram von Eschenbach's version of **Chrétien**'s story. *The War at Troy* (2004) recycles **Homer**. Clarke also produced a **guide** to *Essential Celtic Mythology* (1997).

CLARKE, SUSANNAH (1961–). British writer. The mannered **historical fantasy** "The Ladies of Grace Adieu" (1996) introduced the magicians Gilbert Norrell and Jonathan Strange as the first and second "phenomena of the age"; their **quest** to restore the glories of English magic to an **alternative** 19th century, only slightly less subject to **thinning** than our own, is described in much greater detail in the massive *Jonathan Strange and Mr. Norrell* (2004).

CLASSICAL FANTASY. Fantasy based in Greek and Roman mythology. The earliest surviving Greek literature, including **Homer**'s epics and Hesiod's *Theogony* (c725 BC), already treat the **gods** as fantastic **allegorical** figures rather than objects of religious faith, and the adventures of legendary heroes as fanciful stories. There is a clear evolution of scepticism and a calculated reformulation of mythical material in surviving Greek drama; the fifth-century tragedies of Aeschylus, Euripides, and Sophocles recycle a good deal of material set in the aftermath of the Trojan War, thus providing a series of sequels to the Homeric epics; the slightly later comedies of Aristophanes, especially *The Clouds* (423 BC), *The Birds* (414 BC), and *The Frogs* (405 BC), adopted a far less reverent view of the gods. Virgil's *Aeneid* (19 BC) imported Roman imperial values into the form of Homeric epic, and Ovid's *Metamorphoses* (c10 AD) intensified the process of literary **transfiguration**. **Apuleius**'s *Golden Ass* (early second century) might have established a tradition of fantasy prose fiction had the evolutionary process not been interrupted by the creeping **decadence** that led to Christianization, collapse, and a centuries-long Dark Age.

When the Renaissance of classical learning and literature began in Europe, rival traditions of **chivalric romance** and **Christian fantasy** were already in place, but the symbolism of the Graeco-Roman pantheon and its associated imagery invaded those traditions as well as reestablishing a distinct lexicon of images and ideas for future ventures in literary fantasy. Classical imagery remained immensely powerful in **poetry**, enjoying a new phase of popularity in the 19th century in landmark works by **Percy Shelley**, **John Keats**, **Algernon Swinburne**, and many others. Its association with esoteric learning recommended it for use in sophisticated satires by such writers as **Benjamin Disraeli** and **Richard Garnett** and anti-intellectual comedies by such writers as **John Kendrick Bangs**. The renewed fashionability of **Pan** as an allegorical figure and the constant appeal of Aphrodite helped maintain the genre into the 20th century, although the nostalgia routinely attached to its imagery called forth numerous plaintive allegories of **thinning**, including Garnett's "The Twilight of the Gods," Cloudesley Brereton's *The Last Days of Olympus* (1889), and Marjorie Bowen's *The Haunted Vintage* (1922).

Classical fantasy's subsidiary categories include the core materials of **Arcadian fantasy**, **Odyssean fantasy**, **Orphean fantasy**, and **Promethean fantasy**. Writers who have made considerable use of the subgenre include **Eden Phillpotts** and **John Erskine**; individual examples fill a wide spectrum, extending from such reverent examples as C. C. Martindale's collection *The Goddess of Ghosts* (1915), George Baker's *Fidus Achates* (1944) and *Cry Hylas on the Hills* (1945), Ivor Bannet's *The Arrows of the Sun* (1949), Maurice Druon's *The Memoirs of Zeus* (1963; tr. 1964), and Frederick Raphael's *The Hidden I: A Myth Retold* (1990) to such irreverent ones as Alan Sims's *Phoinix* (1928), Thorne Smith's *The Night Life of the Gods* (1931), A. C. Malcolm's *O Men of Athens* (1947), and Susan Alice Kerby's *Mr Kronion* (1949). The basic materials do not lend themselves readily to feminization, although **Marion Zimmer Bradley**'s *The Firebrand,* which foregrounds the Trojan seeress Cassandra, and Leslie What's *Olympic Games* (2004) are heroic efforts, but the hero myths are popular objects of desupernaturalizing deflation in such works as Henry Treece's *Jason* (1961), *Electra* (1963), and *Oedipus* (1964), and Ernst Schnabel's *The Voyage Home* (1958) and *Story for Icarus* (1958; tr. 1961).

The Trojan War remains the subgenre's most popular motif, widely featured in such works as Adèle Geras's *Troy* (2000). Caroline B. Cooney's *Goddess of Yesterday* (2002) and *On the Seas to Troy* (2004), Judith Hand's *The Amazon and the Warrior* (2004), **Lindsay Clarke**'s *The War at Troy,* Clemence McLaren's *Inside the Walls of Troy* (1996) and *Waiting for Odysseus* (2004), and **Sara Douglass's** Troy Game series. Another motif that has a good deal of contemporary appeal is the minotaur of the Minoan labyrinth, featured in Peter Huby's *Pasiphae* (2000), Alan Gibbons's *Shadow of the Minotaur* (2000), Steven Sherrill's *The Minotaur Takes a Cigarette Break* (2000), John Herman's *Labyrinth* (2001), and Patrice Kindl's *Lost in the Labyrinth* (2002). *See also* EROTIC FANTASY.

COBLEY, MICHAEL (1959–). British writer. The epic trilogy launched with *ShadowKings* (2001) and *ShadowGod* (2003) feature a fallen empire in which the forces of Earthmother and Fathertree have been defeated, the Rootpower magic is gone, and order can only be restored by an enterprising warlord. His short fiction is sampled in *Iron Mosaic* (2004).

COCKAYNE, STEVE (?–). British writer whose experience with the BBC and as a lecturer in media production is clearly evident in the Legends of the Land series launched by *Wanderers and Islanders* (2002); one of its intertwined stories features Leonardo Pegasus' Multiple Empathy Machine, a kind of universal viewer. Such machines multiply, increasing their transformative and disruptive influence massively in *The Iron Chain* (2003) and *The Seagull Drovers* (2004).

COE, DAVID B. (1963–). U.S. writer. In the Lon-Tobyn Chronicle, comprising *Children of Amarid* (1997), *The Outlanders* (1998), and *Eagle-Sage* (2000), the mages who preserve order in **Arcadian** Tobyn-Ser abandon their responsibility in the face of rivalry from the hi-tech city of Lon-Ser. The Winds of the Forelands series, launched by *Rules of Ascension* (2002) and *Seeds of Betrayal* (2003), focuses on the work of unconventional **wizards** with similar sceptical intensity.

COLE, ADRIAN (1949–). British writer whose works are mostly **hybrids** of fantasy and **sf** or fantasy and **horror**. The trilogy comprising *A Plague of Nightmares* (1975), *Lord of the Nightmares* (1976), and *Bane of Nightmares* (1976), and the series comprising *A Place Among the Fallen* (1986), *Throne of Fools* (1987), *The King of Light and Shadows* (1988), and *The Gods in Anger* (1988) are **dark fantasies** framed as **planetary romances**. *Blood Red Angel* (1993) is a **far-futuristic fantasy**. *Storm over Atlantis* (2001) is a **historical fantasy** set in Egypt. His short fiction is sampled in *Oblivion Hand* (2001).

COLERIDGE, SAMUEL TAYLOR (1772–1834). British writer. With William Wordsworth, he produced *Lyrical Ballads* (1798; 2nd ed. 1800; 3rd ed. 1802), whose preface—in its ultimate version—was a crucial document in the history of English **romanticism**. While Wordsworth's verse dealt with everyday topics, Coleridge proposed to employ "persons and characters supernatural," as in "The Rime of the Ancient Mariner." The **visionary fantasy** "Kubla Khan" and "Christabel," about a female vampire, were not included because they were incomplete, but Coleridge eventually published them, only slightly augmented, in *Christabel and Other Poems* (1816). His essays on aesthetic theory in *Biographia Literaria* (1817) and *Aids to Reflection* (1825) elaborated notions from German idealist philosophy to provide foundations on which many subsequent theorists of the fantastic were to build, including the notion that reading fantasy involves a "willing suspension of disbelief" that carries no risk of confusion on the reader's part as to the limits of actual possibility. Coleridge's daughter Sara (1802–52) was also a writer, her major work being an **allegorical/fairy**

romance with elements of **heroic fantasy**, *Phantasmion, Prince of Palmland* (1837).

COLFER, EOIN (1965–). Irish writer, mostly for children. In *The Wish List* (2000), a dead teenager is given a chance at redemption. The series of blithely **chimerical** thrillers begun with *Artemis Fowl* (2001) and continued in *The Arctic Incident* (2002) and *The Eternity Code* (2003)—*The Seventh Dwarf* (2004) is a **prequel** novella—imagines that the world of **Faerie** has made technological progress at a faster rate than our own; the eponymous teenage supervillain is enthusiastic to possess himself of its secrets, but his plans are continually thwarted by a female member of its elite corps of agents, LEPrecon. *The Supernaturalist* (2004) is a futuristic fantasy featuring supernatural parasites.

COLLIER, JOHN (1901–1980). British-born writer based in the United States after 1945, best known for witty and highly polished short stories, many of which are urbane ***contes cruels*** slyly subverting the stereotypes of **sentimental fantasy** and **wish-fulfillment fantasy**. Most of the stories in *The Devil and All* (1934) are **infernal comedies**. *Presenting Moonshine* (1941)—which overlaps considerably with *The Touch of Nutmeg and More Unlikely Stories* (1943)—reprints several items from the earlier collection, alongside such classic **fabulations** as *Green Thoughts* (1932) and "Evening Primrose." Much of this material was rewritten when it was further recycled in *Fancies and Goodnights* (1951), many of whose new items were separately reprinted as *Pictures in the Fire* (1958); *The John Collier Reader* (1972) is a definitive omnibus. Collier's early novel *His Monkey Wife; or, Married to a Chimp* (1930) is a satire mocking the poses and mores of the Bloomsbury Group.

COLUM, PADRAIC (1881–1972). Irish writer. Most of his fantasies were written for **children**. *The King of Ireland's Son* (1916) was followed by a conventional **recycling** of *The Adventurous of Odysseus and the Tale of Troy* (1918), but his work became more became more adventurous in the short items collected in *The Boy Who Knew What the Birds Said* (1918) and the Cinderella **transfiguration** *The Girl Who Sat by the Ashes* (1919). *The Boy Apprenticed to an Enchanter* (1920) is a spirited account of a **quest** to locate **Merlin**. *The Children of Odin* (1920) and *The Golden Fleece and the Heroes Who Lived before Achilles* (1921) returned to straightforward recycling, but *The Children Who Followed the Piper* (1922) casts the Greek god Hermes as a Pied

Piper figure and tracks the fates of children seduced by his **music**. *At the Gateways of the Day* (1924), *The Bright Islands* (1925), and *Legends of Hawaii* (1937) are compendia of Hawaiian folklore written to commission. *The Island of the Mighty* (1924) recycled tales from the **Mabinogion**. *Orpheus: Myth of the World* (1930) returned to classical material before *The Frenzied Prince* (1943) brought Colum back to Irish mythology. He also edited *A Treasury of Irish Folklore* (1954). A few fantasies are included in his *Selected Short Stories* (1985), but most of his fantasies for adults were plays, including *The Miracle of the Corn* (1908) and *The Desert* (1912; aka *Mogu the Wanderer*).

COMICS. The early comic strips of the 1890s were almost exclusively devoted to slapstick **humor**, which began to take on fantasy elements in some strips of the 1900s, most importantly, the long-running and widely imitated series of **dream** fantasies that eventually became known as *Little Nemo in Slumberland* (1905–27), created by Winsor McCay; his young hero rides off by night on the horse Somnus to the kingdom of Morpheus, where he enjoys fabulous adventures as the playmate of the king's daughter. **Fairy tale** characters, including pixies, elves, and giants, soon became standard features of comic strips designed for children.

Comic strips also became a natural medium for **animal fantasies**, after the fashion of George Herriman's *Krazy Kat* (1916–44) and British strips like the ever-popular *Tiger Tim*—who eventually hosted his own weekly—the *Daily Mail*'s *Teddy Tail* (1915–40 and 1946–60), and the *Daily Mirror's Pip Squeak and Wilfred* (1919–40 and 1947–55). The most successful character of this kind was Rupert Bear, whose career began in 1920. American talking-animal strips eventually came to be dominated by characters created by Walt Disney, their popularity guaranteed by their starring roles in animated movies—Mickey Mouse made his debut in that medium in 1930—although non-Disney characters like Felix the Cat (launched 1943) maintained a long resistance.

The U.S. comic books spun off from the pulp magazines in the late 1930s strongly favored **sf** motifs (refer to *HDSFL*), although many superheroes were manifestly **hybrid** characters—notably Captain Marvel (launched 1940), who owed his origins to the magic word "Shazam," passed on by an aged **wizard**, and Wonder Woman (launched 1941), whose powers were carefully preserved from ancient times in the **amazon** enclave of Paradise Island. *Prince Valiant* (launched 1937) was an exceptional excursion into **Arthurian fantasy**. The comic books soon diversified into **horror** fiction, successfully enough to cause a moral panic, and it was not until they adopted the restrictive Comics Code in 1955 that the **satirical** fantasy of *Mad Magazine* became the medium's cutting edge. When the superhero comics began a new phase of evolution in the 1960s, fantasy elements continued to play a minor role, informing such characters as Marvel Comics' leftover Nordic **god** Thor and Doctor Strange, rebranded in 1963 as a "Master of the Mystic Arts."

As genre fantasy became more popular, **Robert E. Howard** became an important influence in the comic book medium; **sword and sorcery** heroes like Howard's Conan and **Michael Moorcock**'s Elric were enthusiastically co-opted into the medium. As the circulation war between D.C. Comics and Marvel heated up, borrowings from fantasy increased, encouraged by competition from such newcomers to the field as *ElfQuest* (launched 1978 by Wendy and Richard Pini). Many old characters were comprehensively revamped in frameworks that borrowed extensively from fantasy fiction, the most spectacular example being the reformulation of the Sandman in 1989 by **Neil Gaiman**, giving rise to one of the most successful series of **graphic novels**. Although fantasy narratives are much more comfortably accommodated in graphic novels, shorter strips and individual cartoons remain useful as a medium of grotesque caricature, which is a standard instrument of **political** satire, and often extends into the realms of the **surreal**.

COMMODIFIED FANTASY. A term used by **Ursula Le Guin** in the foreword of *Tales of Earthsea* to describe stereotypical and imitative genre fantasy devoid of intellectual and moral complexity. Le Guin uses the term pejoratively, but it is by no means the case that all commodified fantasy is badly written, and its stereotyping performs a useful function in providing the genre with an anchorage and a steady sales base. Literary experimentation in fantasy is to some extent parasitic—and not only in commercial terms—at the expense of the wide and consistent appeal of fantasy's commodifiable formulas. The most obvious of those formulas are the **epic** trilogy and the **sword and sorcery** action/adventure story, with the former dominating the marketplace by sheer mass as well as sales potential; **children's fiction** tends to employ simpler formulas but has reduced more subgenres to commodifiable entities, including **timeslip** fantasies and (in the wake of **J. K. Rowling**'s Harry Potter) fantasies of magical education. Best-selling writers of commodified fantasy for adults include **Terry**

Brooks, **David Eddings**, **Raymond E. Feist**, **Robert Jordan**, **Katherine Kerr**, and **Terry Goodkind**.

CONSTANTINE, STORM (1956–). British writer. Her early work was **hybrid/science fantasy** (refer to *HDSFL*); the series comprising *The Enchantments of Flesh and Spirit* (1987), *The Bewitchments of Love and Hate* (1988), *The Fulfilments of Fate and Desire* (1989), and continued in *The Wraiths of Will and Pleasure* (2003) and *The Shades of Time and Memory* (2004), extrapolates the affectations of contemporary Gothic subculture and its associated **lifestyle fantasies**. The floridly fanciful and darkly **erotic fantasies** *Hermetech* (1991), *Burying the Shadow* (1992), *Sign for the Sacred* (1993), and *Calenture* (1994) are similar in inspiration but more adventurous. The trilogy comprising *Stalking Tender Prey* (1995), *Scenting Hallowed Blood* (1996), and *Stealing Sacred Fire* (1997) is an **apocalyptic/angelic fantasy**. The Chronicles of Magravandias trilogy comprising *Sea Dragon Heir* (1999), *The Crown of Silence* (2000), and *The Way of Light* (2001) is an enterprising **epic** fantasy with spinoffs that include the title novella (1999) and other items in *The Thorn Boy & Other Dreams of Dark Desire* (2003). The collections *Three Heralds of the Storm* (1997) and *Oracle Lips* (1999) also include some fantasies. Constantine collaborated with **Michael Moorcock** on the **multiverse** fantasy *Silverheart* (2000).

CONTE CRUEL. A short-story genre that takes its name from an 1883 collection by Villiers de l'Isle Adam, although previous examples had been provided by such writers as **Edgar Allan Poe**. Some critics use the label to refer only to non-supernatural **horror stories**, especially those that have nasty climactic twists, but it is applicable to any story whose conclusion exploits the cruel aspects of "the irony of fate." There is a *conte cruel* element in many traditional **folktales**, lovingly extrapolated by many 19th-century writers in that vein, including **Hans Christian Andersen**, **Jean Lorrain**, and **Oscar Wilde**.

One way in which many modern **fabulations** seek to emphasize the fact that the velvet glove of fantasy is being used to clothe the iron fist of conscientious scepticism is by careful provision of climactic subversive twists typical of the *conte cruel;* expert practitioners include **John Collier** and **Donald Barthelme**.

CONTE PHILOSOPHIQUE. A term employed by **Voltaire** to describe his fiction, which consisted of satirical **fabulations** ironically subversive of popular delusions. It is arguable that all fantasy that aspires to intellectual seriousness must partake of this kind of relevance, but the term is usually reserved for iconoclastic works; earnest exercises in **metaphysical fantasy** and **existentialist fantasy** that are illustrative rather than combative are certainly philosophical but do not qualify as *contes*.

Voltaire cast "The Princess of Babylon" as an **Arabian fantasy** and "The White Bull" as a **biblical fantasy**; those subgenres continued to play host to a considerable number of *conte philosophiques*. Many **art fairy tales** belong to the subgenre, especially those with a **decadent** gloss; some notable examples can be found in the works of **Richard Garnett** and **Laurence Housman**. Academic philosophers who have published collections of *contes philosophiques* include L. P. Jacks, in *Among the Idolmakers* (1912) and *All Men are Ghosts* (1913), and Bertrand Russell, in *Satan in the Suburbs* (1953).

CONTEMPORARY FANTASY. All fantasies set in the present rather than the past or future are contemporary, but the term "contemporary fantasy" is usually used in a narrower sense that sets aside many **portal fantasies** and those **intrusive fantasies** in which the magical entity is a blatant anomaly. Thus narrowly defined, the subgenre focuses on works in which the mundane world is fantasized in a more pervasive but less obtrusive fashion, usually by positing an elaborate **secret history** running alongside the one reported in the newspapers and experienced by most people. Although much contemporary fantasy employs remote rural settings where the effects of **thinning** have been less corrosive, a good deal of recent work is cast as **urban fantasy** in which supernatural entities either live as outcasts in decaying inner cities or adopt polite masks in order to live in suburbia.

The subgenre is prominent in **children's fiction**—examples proliferated rapidly in the wake of **J. K. Rowling**'s Harry Potter series—and in literary fiction employing fantasy materials, as in the works of **Tom Robbins**, **Michael Chabon**'s *Summerland,* and James A. Hetley's *The Summer Country* (2002). Notable examples from genre fantasy include **John Crowley**'s *Little, Big,* **Terry Bisson**'s *Talking Man*, Marina Fitch's *The Seventh Heart* (1997), **Patricia Geary**'s *Living in Ether,* **Nina Kiriki Hoffman**'s *The Thread That Binds the Bones,* and S. Andrew Swann's *The Dragons of the Cuyahoga* (2001).

COOK, GLEN (1944–). U.S. writer in various genres, much of his work being **hybrid/science fantasy**. His early work is derivative of **Oriental**

fantasy; the Dread Empire sequence, comprising the trilogy *Shadow of All Night Falling* (1979), *October's Baby* (1980), and *All Darkness Met* (1980), the **prequel** couplet *The Fire in His Hands* (1984) and *With Mercy towards None* (1985), and the sequels *Reap the East Wind* (1987) and *An Ill Fate Marshalling* (1988), is mostly set in **secondary world** societies based on China and India. The Western reaches of the same world come to the fore in the series comprising *The Black Company* (1984), *Shadows Linger* (1984), *The White Rose* (1985), *The Silver Spike* (1989), *Shadow Games* (1989), *Dreams of Steel* (1990), *Bleak Seasons* (1996), *She Is the Darkness* (1997), and *Water Sleeps* (1999), which feature hard-bitten mercenary soldiers trashing the imaginary territories of **chivalric romance**. *The Swordbearer* (1982) is a reaction to **Michael Moorcock**'s Elric stories; *The Tower of Fear* and *Sung in Blood* (1990) are similarly inclined exercises in **sword and sorcery**. He began an extensive occult **detective** series with *Sweet Silver Blues* (1987), whose eighth volume is *Angry Lead Skies* (2002).

COOK, HUGH (1956–). British-born New Zealand writer. His major genre project is a series of **humorous fantasies**, The Chronicles of the Age of Darkness, comprising *The Wizards and the Warriors* (1986; aka *Wizard War*), *The Wordsmiths and the Warguild* (1987; in 2 vols. as *The Questing Hero* and *The Hero's Return*), *The Women and the Warlords* (1987; aka *The Oracle*), *The Walrus and the Warwolf* (1988; aka *Lords of the Sword*), *The Wicked and the Witless* (1989), *The Wishstone and the Wonderworkers* (1990), *The Wazir and the Witch* (1990), *The Werewolf and the Wormlord* (1991), *The Worshippers and the Way* (1992), and *The Witchlord and the Weaponmaster* (1992).

COOK, RICK (1944–). U.S. writer. His fantasies fall into two series. The one comprising *Wizard's Bane* (1989), *The Wizardry Compiled* (1989), *The Wizardry Cursed* (1991), *The Wizardry Consulted* (1995), and *The Wizardry Quested* (1996) transports a computer expert into a **secondary world** where his skills prove to be applicable to the theory of magic. In the other, comprising *Mall Purchase Night* (1993), *The Wiz Biz* (1997), and *Cursed and Consulted: The Continuing Adventures of a Boy and His Dog* (2001), a security guard is caught up in a violent struggle to control a portal to **Faerie**.

COOKE, CATHERINE (1963–). U.S. writer whose relevant works are carefully feminized **Celtic fantasies**, organized into two trilogies. The first comprises *Mask of the Wizard* (1985), *Veil of Shadow* (1987), and

The Hidden Temple (1988), the second *The Winged Assassin* (1987), *Realm of the Gods* (1988), and *The Crimson Goddess* (1989).

COOPER, LOUISE (1952–). British writer. The Tarot fantasy *The Book of Paradox* (1973) was marketed for adults, but most of her subsequent works have been aimed at teenagers. They employ **commodified** formulas but are inventively various. *Lord of No Time* (1977), whose background is an eternal conflict between Order and Chaos, was subsequently expanded as the Time Master trilogy, comprising *The Initiate* (1985), *The Outcast* (1986), and *The Master* (1987), which was then supplemented by the Chaos Gate trilogy, comprising *The Deceiver* (1991), *The Pretender* (1991), and *The Avenger* (1992). The Star Shadow trilogy, comprising *Star Ascendant* (1994), *Eclipse* (1994), and *Moonset* (1995), is a **prequel**. *Daughter of Storms* (1996), *The Dark Caller* (1997), and *Keepers of Light* (1998) are set in the same milieu.

The Indigo sequence, comprising *Nemesis* (1988), *Inferno* (1989), *Infanta* (1989), *Nocturne* (1990), *Troika* (1991), *Avatar* (1991), *Revenant* (1992), and *Aisling* (1993), is a **dark fantasy** about a reluctant but duty-bound demon hunter. Her other dark fantasies include *The King's Demon* (1996), whose amnesiac hero has a **vampire/doppelgänger**; the series comprising *Firespell* (1996, aka *Heart of Fire*), *Blood Dance* (1996, aka *Heart of Stone*), *The Shrouded Mirror* (1996, aka *Heart of Glass*), and *The Hounds of Winter* (1996, aka *Heart of Ice*); *Sacrament of Night* (1997); *Our Lady of the Snow* (1998), with a heroine who sets out to avenge a murdered **goddess**; *Storm Ghost* (1998); and *Demon Crossing* (2002).

Cooper's other **young adult** fantasies include *The Thorn Key* (1988); the **theriomorphic fantasy** *The Sleep of Stone* (1991); *The Summer Witch* (1999); the Mirror Mirror trilogy, comprising *Breaking Through* (1999), *Running Free* (2000), and *Testing Limits* (2001); *Hunter's Moon* (2003); and *Sea Horses* (2003), which began a new series continued in *The Talisman* (2004). Her short fiction is sampled in *The Spiral Garden* (2000).

COOPER, SUSAN (1935–). British-born writer resident in the United States from 1963. She extrapolated the **intrusive fantasy** *Over Sea, Under Stone* (1965) into an elaborate sequence that gradually reveals itself to be an intricate **Celtic fantasy** richly infused with **Arthurian** elements; its young protagonists must aid an immortal **Merlin** as he is drawn into another battle in an eternal war between Light and Dark. The continuation comprises *The Dark Is Rising* (1973), *Greenwitch* (1974), *The Grey King* (1975), and *Silver on the Tree* (1977).

Seaward (1983) is a **portal fantasy** that lets its living protagonist into a peculiar **afterlife**. *The Boggart* (1993) and *The Boggart and the Monster* (1997) are contemporary fantasies, with an impish protagonist who feels out of place in Canada. In *King of Shadows* (1999), a **timeslip** enables a contemporary actor to perform with **Shakespeare** at the Globe. *Green Boy* (2002) is a **hybrid/science fantasy** with an ecological theme. Cooper's work for younger children includes a **recycled** version of *Tam Lin* (1991).

COOVER, ROBERT (1932–). U.S. writer of literary fiction, whose excursions into sophisticated **metafiction** include the **psychological/sports fantasy** *The Universal Baseball Association Inc. J. Henry Waugh, Prop.* (1968) and the **erotic fantasies** "The Babysitter" (in *Pricksongs and Descants*, 1969) and *Spanking the Maid* (1982). The **surreal** novelette *Aesop's Forest* (1986) was published back to back with Brian Swann's *The Plot of the Mice*. *Pinocchio in Venice* (1991) is a heartfelt sequel to Collodi's original in which the aging protagonist reverts to wood. In *John's Wife* (1996), a spell is cast on a small town. *Briar Rose* (1997) is an ironically **sentimental transfiguration**. *Ghost Town* (1998) is a surreal western. *The Adventures of Lucky Pierre* (2002) features a clown-cum–porn star whose life in Cinecity is defined by his movies.

COPPARD, A. E. (1878–1957). British writer. With the exception of his **children's fantasy** *Pink Furniture* (1930), all his work was short fiction. His occasional fantasies are various and frequently enigmatic, the largest fraction being contained in later editions of *Adam and Eve and Pinch Me* (1921; exp. 1922); the title story is a **sentimental fantasy**. "Clorinda Walks in Heaven" is a bittersweet **afterlife fantasy**. "The Elixir of Youth" is a **wish-fulfillment** fantasy with an Irish setting that Coppard was to revisit in "The Gollan" and "Crotty Shrinkwin." "Marching to Zion" is an **allegorical/Christian fantasy**. The bulk of his work in the genre is combined in *Fearful Pleasures* (1946; rev. 1951).

CORELLI, MARIE (1855?–1924). British writer, the most popular in the English language during the 1890s, in spite of the derision heaped upon her by contemporary reviewers. She was a dedicated **lifestyle fantasist**, transforming herself from mere Minnie Mackay (the adoptive and probably natural daughter of poet Charles Mackay) into the psychically and artistically gifted character reflected in the narrator of her first **occult fantasy**, *A Romance of Two Worlds* (1886). The character, like the author, is unable to fulfill her potential until she achieves a crucial existential breakthrough, brought about in the novel by the Chaldean mystic Casimir Heliobas. Heliobas reappeared in *Ardath, The Story of a Dead Self* (1889), working miracles on behalf of a male protagonist similarly recruited to the company of the angels. *The Soul of Lilith* (1892) is a more orthodox **occult fantasy**.

In *The Sorrows of Satan* (1895), the saintly novelist Mavis Clare is so indomitably incorruptible that even **Satan** falls hopelessly in love with her—an unsurpassable masterstroke of **wish-fulfillment**. *Ziska, The Problem of a Wicked Soul* (1897) is a verbose **karmic romance**. *The Strange Visitation of Josiah McNason* (1904) is a Dickensian **Christmas** book. *The Young Diana; An Experiment of the Future* (1918) is a romance of rejuvenation. *The Secret Power* (1921) retreads old ground. Corelli's short fiction includes numerous fantasies, including a feverish account of *The Devil's Motor* (1910) and items collected in *Cameos* (1896) and *The Love of Long Ago, and Other Stories* (1920).

COVILLE, BRUCE (1950–). U.S. writer, prolific in various genres of **children's fiction**. His fantasies include the Magic Shop series, comprising *The Monster's Ring* (1982; aka *Russell Troy, Monster Boy* rev. 2002), *Jeremy Thatcher, Dragon Hatcher* (1991), *Jennifer Murdley's Toad* (1992), *Goblins in the Castle* (1992), *The Skull of Truth* (1997; aka *Charlie Eggleston's Talking Skull*), and *Juliet Dove, The Queen of Love* (2003). Other series include the Unicorn Chronicles, comprising *Into the Land of Unicorns* (1994) and *Song of the Wanderer* (1999), and the Me and Moongobble series, begun with *The Weeping Werewolf* (2004) and *The Evil Elves* (2004), which features educational trips to the Forest of Night in company with an eccentric **wizard**. Coville also recycled **Shakespeare**'s *The Tempest* (1994) and *A Midsummer Night's Dream* (1996) for young readers. *The Prince of Butterflies* (2002) is an ecological parable. *The Monsters of Morely Manor* (2001) is a wide-ranging **hybrid**. Coville has edited numerous **anthologies**, the most relevant being *A Glory of Unicorns* (1998) and *Half-Human* (2001).

CRAIK, MRS. (1826–1887). Married name of British writer Dinah Maria Mulock, most of whose books were initially issued anonymously. She made several notable contributions to the burgeoning field of **children's literature**, including *Alice Learmont: A Fairy Tale* (1852), based in

Scottish folklore; the **anthology** *The Fairy Book* (1863); and the **moralistic fantasies** *Little Sunshine's Holiday* (1871), *The Adventures of a Brownie* (1872), and *The Little Lame Prince* (1875). *Avillion and Other Tales* (1853) includes several fantasies for adults, including the novellas "Avillion," a **visionary fantasy** about the Isles of the Blest, and "The Self-Seer," whose protagonists trade viewpoints with their spirit **doppelgängers**; both novellas were reprinted in *Romantic Tales* (1859).

CRAWFORD, F. MARION (1854–1909). Italian-born U.S. writer active in many genres, including **horror** fiction (refer to HDHL). *Mr Isaacs* (1882) is a marginal **theosophical fantasy**. *The Witch of Prague* (1891) is a more wholehearted **occult fantasy** featuring a **femme fatale**. *With the Immortals* (1888) features an inventor who finds a means of communicating with the dead. *Khaled* (1891) is an **Arabian fantasy**. *Cecilia: A Story of Modern Rome* (1902) is a **wish-fulfillment fantasy** spiced with **karmic romance**.

CRAWSHAY-WILLIAMS, ELIOT (1879–1962). British military man and writer. He followed up the dramas collected in *Five Grand Guignol Plays* (1924) and *More Grand Guignol Plays* (1927) with various novels, including the **timeslip** fantasies *Night in No Time* (1946), *The Wolf from the West: Tracing the Glorious Tragedy of Glyndwr* (1947), and the title story of *The Man Who Met Himself and Other Stories* (1947). The last-named also contains three **visionary fantasies**. *Heaven Takes a Hand* (1949) involves the **Devil** and Socrates in an inquiry as to whether humankind is still worth saving after Hiroshima.

CRESSWELL, HELEN (1934–). British writer, mostly for **children**. Her fantasies for younger children include the poetic *When the Wind Blows* (1966), with an **allegorical** quality that is subtly reproduced in *The Night-Watchmen* (1969), *Up the Pier* (1971), and the rite-of-passage story *The Beachcombers* (1972). *The Bongleweed* (1973), about an exotic plant with a fabulous nature invisible to adults, and the elegiac *The Winter of the Birds* (1975) are similarly inclined. *The Secret World of Polly Flint* (1982), *Moondial* (1987), and *Stonestruck* (1995) are **timeslip** fantasies in which children from the present must lend vital aid to counterparts in the past. *The Return of the Psammead* (1994) is a sequel to an **E. Nesbit** classic.

CROSSLEY-HOLLAND, KEVIN (1941–). British writer for **children**. He **recycled** many legends from **chivalric romance** and **folktales**, including

Havelok the Dane (1964), *King Horn* (1965), and *The Green Children* (1968). *The Callow Pit Coffer* (1969), *The Pedlar of Swaffham* (1971), and *The Wildman* (1976) deal enterprisingly with less familiar materials. His later work in this vein is mostly organized into a series of collections launched by *The Dead Moon* (1982) and extending to *Enchantment: Fairy Tales, Ghost Stories and Tales of Wonder* (2000), *The Nightingale That Shrieked and Other Tales* (2002), *Why the Fish Laughed and Other Tales* (2002), and *Tales from the Old World* (2003).

Crossley-Holland's most original contribution to fantasy literature is a trilogy of **historical fantasies** set at the end of the 12th century. Their hero takes heart from visions of the **Arthurian** past that help him to rise above the awful brutality of the conflicts in which he is engaged; it comprises *The Seeing Stone* (2000), *At the Crossing Places* (2001), and *King of the Middle March* (2003).

CROWLEY, ALEISTER (1875–1947). British occultist who became an exceedingly flamboyant **lifestyle fantasist**. In 1898, he joined the Hermetic Order of the Golden Dawn and soon attempted a takeover, abandoning the resultant splinters in 1908 to form the Argentinum Astrum. The inspiration he drew from literary sources included the establishment of his own **Rabelaisian** Thelema in a Sicilian villa. His early works included many self-published volumes of poetry with mystical and mythological themes, including *Songs of the Spirit* (1898), *Tannhäuser; A Story of All Time* (1902), the verse drama *The Argonauts* (1904), and *Orpheus: A Lyrical Legend* (2 vols. 1905).

Crowley's **occult fantasies** include two volumes of erotica, *White Stains: The Literary Remains of George Archibald Bishop, a Neuropath of the Second Empire* (1898; rep 1973)—whose first edition was allegedly destroyed—and *The Scented Garden of Abdullah the Satirist of Shiraz* (1910; 1991). A series of short stories based on **James Frazer**'s *Golden Bough,* most of which were published in *The International* in 1917–18, was belatedly collected as *Golden Twigs* (1988). *Moonchild* (1929) is a *roman à clef*, including characters based on **W. B. Yeats** and **Arthur Machen**; in these books, two societies of rival magicians quarrel over an experiment to incarnate the eponymous supernatural being. *The Stratagem and Other Stories* (1930) includes the graphic **posthumous fantasy** "The Testament of Magdalen Blair." A series of occult **detective** stories was assembled as *The Scrutinies of Simon Iff* (1987).

Crowley became the primary model for 20th-century literary images of the black magician, appearing in light disguise in W. Somerset

Maugham's *The Magician* (1908), **Edgar Jepson**'s *No. 19* (1910), and various works by **Dion Fortune** and Dennis Wheatley; the image was, however, secondhand, borrowed from **Éliphas Lévi** (whose reincarnation Crowley claimed to be). His literary connections were further complicated when the scholarly fantasist Kenneth Grant "discovered" elaborate parallels between his metaphysical inventions and **H. P. Lovecraft**'s Cthulhu mythos.

CROWLEY, JOHN (1942–). U.S. writer. *The Deep* (1975) and *Engine Summer* (1976) are **hybrids/science fantasies** (refer to *HDSFL*). The magisterial *Little, Big* (1981) is a definitive **contemporary fantasy**, which redefines the relationship between the **primary world** and **Faerie** both geographically—making it a kind of microcosm—and culturally, as a refuge from and counterweight to the potentially apocalyptic spoliation of the world by the forces represented by the Noisy Bridge Rod and Gun Club. The epic **historical fantasy** launched in *Aegypt* (1987)—intended to extend over four volumes, of which the second is *Love and Sleep* (1994) and the third *Daemonomania* (2000)—is equally ambitious, weaving the traditions of Renaissance **magic** and **alchemy** into a **secret history** as complex as *Little, Big*'s. Crowley's short fiction, including items published earlier in *Novelty* (1989) and *Antiquities: Seven Stories* (1993), is fully assembled in *Novelties and Souvenirs* (2004).

CRUMEY, ANDREW (1961–). Scottish writer. *Music, in a Foreign Language* (1994) is a polished exercise in **postmodern/metafiction** set in an alternative world. *Pfitz* (1995) is a similar but more lighthearted endeavor set in the 18th century; its protagonist reappears in "Tales from Rreinnstadt," one of three linked novellas making up *D'Alembert's Principle* (1996), formally exploring the relationship between "Memory, Reason and Imagination." The similarly three-stranded plot of *Mr. Mee* (2000) reconnects the 18th century with the present in accounts of the search for a lost encyclopedia that had a profound effect on Jean-Jacques Rousseau. *Mobius Dick* (2004) is a **surreal** account of multiple **alternative histories**.

CUNNINGHAM, ELIZABETH (1953–). U.S. writer from a family of Episcopalian priests; her fantasies react against this tradition with scrupulous politeness. In *The Return of the Goddess: A Divine Comedy* (1992), the **goddess** is incarnated as a playdough figure in the hands of the priest's wife. *The Wild Mother* (1993) is a contemporary

biblical fantasy exploring the eternal triangle of Adam, Eve, and Lilith. *How to Spin Gold* (1997) **transfigures** Rumpelstiltskin. The **hybrid** Magdalen trilogy launched by *Daughter of the Shining Isles* (2000), to be completed by *Holy Whore* and *The Voice of the Phoenix,* has a **Celtic** heroine.

CURRY, JANE LOUISE (1937–). U.S. writer of **children's fiction**. Her wide-ranging and inventive fantasies include the Abaloc series, comprising *Beneath the Hill* (1967), *The Change-Child* (1969), *The Daybreakers* (1970), *Over the Sea's Edge* (1971), *The Birdstones* (1977), *The Wolves of Aam* (1981), and *The Shadow Dancers* (1983), collectively describing various phases of the 16th-century relocation and gradual adaptation of a community of Welsh elves to America. *The Sleepers* (1968) is an **Arthurian fantasy** in which **Merlin** is freed from his long imprisonment. *Mindy's Mysterious Miniature* (1970; aka *The Housenapper*) and *The Lost Farm* (1974) unravel the mystery of squatters in a doll's house. *The Ice Ghosts Mystery* (1972) is similar in spirit. *Parsley, Sage, Rosemary and Time* (1975), *The Magical Cupboard* (1976), *Moon Window* (1996), and *Dark Shade* (1998) are **timeslip** fantasies. *Poor Tom's Ghost* (1977) and *The Bassumtyte Treasure* (1978) offer variants of conventional stereotypes. *Me, Myself and I: A Tale of Time Travel* (1987) is a zestful account of accumulating paradoxes. *The Christmas Knight* (1993) is a **Christmas fantasy**. *The Egyptian Box* (2002) takes a cautionary approach to the prospect of magical assistance.

CUSACK, LOUISE (1959–). Australian writer. The novella "The Goddess and the Geek" (2000) employs a **chimerical** strategy further developed in the Shadow through Time trilogy comprising *Destiny of the Light* (2001), *Daughter of the Dark* (2002), and *Glimmer in the Maelstrom* (2003). The latter is an **afterlife/quest** fantasy that moves through a baroque series of quasi-**allegorical** settings, including the Earthworld of Ennae, the Airworld of Atheyre, the Fireworld of Haddash, and the Waterworld of Magoria (i.e., Earth) to a climactic confrontation with the Serpent of Death.

CUTTER, LEAH R. (?–). U.S. writer. The **Oriental/historical fantasy** *Paper Mage* (2003) features an original system of **magic** based in the art of origami. *The Caves of Buda* (2004), set in Eastern Europe, draws ingeniously on Romany and **Jewish** folklore, featuring the struggle to maintain a demon in close confinement.

– D –

DAHL, ROALD (1916–1990). British writer best known for **children's fantasies**, although he also wrote numerous ***contes cruels***; TV dramatizations labeled them *Tales of the Unexpected*. The eponymous race featured in his first short story, "The Gremlins" (1942), were redeployed in *Some Time Never: A Fable for Supermen* (1948). His career as a fantasist resumed with *James and the Giant Peach* (1961), an uninhibited **wish-fulfillment fantasy**. The best-selling *Charlie and the Chocolate Factory* (1964), which leavened its wish-fulfillment element with ostentatious moralizing, established him as the most popular children's writer of that era. It was followed by *The Magic Finger* (1966), *Fantastic Mr Fox* (1970), *Charlie and the Great Glass Elevator* (1972), *Danny, the Champion of the World* (1975), *The Wonderful Story of Henry Sugar and Six More* (1977), *The Enormous Crocodile* (1978), *The Twits* (1980), *George's Marvelous Medicine* (1981), *The BFG* (1982), *The Witches* (1983), *The Giraffe and the Pelly and Me* (1985), *Matilda* (1988), *Esio Trot* (1990), and *The Minipins* (1991). The stories are blithely excessive in every respect, including their violence, whose absurd grotesquerie turns their horrific element into humor in the tradition of animated cartoons; the direct appeal to **daydream** extravagance helped make Dahl enormously popular.

DALKEY, KARA (1953–). U.S. writer associated with the group founded by **Emma Bull** and **Will Shetterly**, whose early work was done for their **shared world** enterprise. The couplet comprising *The Curse of Sagamore* (1986) and *The Sword of Sagamore* (1989) is a **humorous/heroic fantasy**. *The Nightingale* (1988) is a **transfiguration** of **Hans Christian Andersen**'s **fairy tale**. *Euryale* (1988) is a **classical fantasy**. The **Oriental fantasy** trilogy comprising *Goa* (1996), *Bijapur* (1997), and *Bhagavati* (1998) is set in 16th-century India. The **historical fantasies** *Little Sister* (1996), *The Heavenward Path* (1998), and *Genpei* (2001) are based on Japanese **myths**. *Steel Rose* (1997) and *Crystal Sage* (1999) are **urban fantasies** set in Pittsburgh. The Water trilogy comprising *Ascension* (2002), *Reunion* (2002), and *Transformation* (2002) is an **Atlantean fantasy** featuring "mermyds."

DALTON, ANNIE (1948–). British writer of **children's fiction**. Her fantasies are mostly **contemporary fantasies** following a template laid down in *Out of the Ordinary* (1988), about unexpected opportunities offered by a summer job. *Night Maze* (1989) is a **dark/alchemical fantasy**. *The Afterdark Princess* (1990) features a mysterious baby-sitter; its sequels are *Dreamsnatcher* (2001), *Midnight Museum* (2001), and *Rules of Magic* (2004). *The Alpha Box* (1991) features sinister magical music. *The Witch Rose* (1991) is a magical flower. *Naming the Dark* (1992) draws material from **Atlantean** and **Arthurian fantasy**. *Swan Sister* (1992) employs a standard **fairy tale** motif.

In the Angels Unlimited series, a dead teenager attends a school for angels where the headmaster is Michael; the protagonist returns thereafter to Earth in different historical periods to carry out various missions, complicated by a rule forbidding manifestation in human form. The series comprises *Winging It* (2001), *Losing the Plot* (2001), *Flying High* (2001), *Calling the Shots*, *Fogging Over* (2002), *Fighting Fit* (2003), *Making Waves* (2003), *Budding Star* (2004), and *Keeping It Real* (2004). The Lilac Peabody series, featuring a minuscule trainee fairy godmother, is similar; it comprises *Lilac Peabody and Sam Sparks, Lilac Peabody and Bella Bright, Lilac Peabody and Charlie Chase,* and *Lilac Peabody and Honeysuckle Hope* (all 2004). Her short fiction is sampled in *The Starlight Princess and Other Princess Stories* (1999).

DALTON, JAMES. British writer, all of whose work was published anonymously. *The Gentleman in Black* (1831) is a **humorous/Faustian fantasy**, as is *The Invisible Gentleman* (1833)—the first three-decker fantasy novel—which anticipates **F. Anstey** in the manner in which the invisible protagonist's exploits continually go awry. The **moralistic** tone of these works is echoed in some of the stories in *The Old Maid's Talisman and Other Strange Tales* (1834) and "The Beauty Draught" (*Blackwood's,* 1840). *Chartley the Fatalist* (1831) and *The Robber* (1832) are **Gothic** parodies. *The Rival Demons* (1836) is a comedy in verse.

DANTE ALIGHIERI (1265–1321). Italian writer who produced one of the key **taproot** texts of modern fantasy in the *Divina Commedia* (written 1307–21), whose three parts—*Inferno, Purgatorio,* and *Paradiso*—offer a comprehensive account of the Christian cosmos. Dante's highly distinctive landscapes—particularly the organization of the Inferno into a series of concentric circles to which different kinds of sinners are assigned, according to the seriousness of their errors—became fundamental to the imagery of Christian eschatology, reducing all rivals to the status of variants and reactions. For this reason, Dantean fantasy is a prolific and highly significant subgenre of **afterlife fantasy**.

Dante's whole scheme is recapitulated in **Harry Blamires**'s trilogy and Santo A. Giampapa's *A Journey in the Otherworld* (1964), but selective **recyclings** are more common; only two components are retained in R. H. Mottram's couplet *The Gentleman of Leisure* (1955) and *To Hell with Crabb Robinson* (1962). Revisited infernos—including those in **John Cowper Powys**'s *Morwyn* (1937), Larry Niven and Jerry Pournelle's *Inferno* (1976), and E. E. Y. Hales's *Chariot of Fire* (1977)—far outweigh revisited Paradisos. Recycled Purgatorios are rare; Lord Holden's *Purgatory Revisited* (1950) is a notable exception. Dantean fantasy is an important medium of **illustration**, its interpreters ranging from Hieronymous Bosch through **William Blake**, Gustave Doré and Robert Rauschenberg to Wayne Barlowe, in *Barlowe's Inferno* (1998).

DARK FANTASY. A term sometimes used as a quasi-euphemistic substitute for "**horror**," although it is more useful as a description of an **ambiguous** subgenre of stories that incorporate elements of horror fiction into one or other of the standard formulas of **commodified fantasy**. Most **sword and sorcery** fiction is dark edged, but **Karl Edward Wagner**'s work in the subgenre is definitively dark. There is also a dark element in many **folktales** that can be redeployed in darkening modern **fairy tales** and **heroic fantasies**, following a pattern foreshadowed in **Robert Browning**'s "Child Roland to the Dark Tower Came."

Because commercially defined horror fiction is almost invariably set in the **primary world**, it is, in effect, a subcategory of **contemporary fantasy**; horror stories set wholly or partly in **secondary worlds**—particularly the ultra-**decadent** fantasies pioneered in ***Weird Tales*** by **Clark Ashton Smith** and other writers of the **Lovecraft** school—are thus more readily classifiable as dark fantasy. The term is also applicable to **intrusive fantasies** that are scrupulous in marginalizing the existential unease generated by magical entities drawn from the standard repertoire of fantasy motifs, as in various works by **Jonathan Carroll** and many diplomatic fantasies for younger readers by such writers as **Anne Bishop**, **Catherine Fisher**, **Margaret Mahy**, and **Bridget Wood**.

DARLINGTON, W. A. (1890–1979). British writer whose fantasies are modeled on those of **F. Anstey**. A series of morale-building sketches written during World War I for *Passing Show* was recast as the best-selling *Alf's Button* (1919), in which a working-class conscript fails to make good use of a uniform button derived from Aladdin's lamp. *Alf's Carpet* (1928) is a sequel to the movie version, which had a markedly different ending. World War II inspired a further sequel, *Alf's New Button* (1940). In *Wishes Limited* (1922), a **fairy**'s attempts at **wish fulfillment** are restricted by trade union rules. In *Egbert* (1924), a barrister is turned into a rhinoceros by an offended **wizard**.

DART-THORNTON, CECILIA (?–). Pseudonym of Australian writer and composer Cecilia Thornton. The Bitterbynde series, comprising *The Ill-Made Mute* (2001), *The Lady of the Sorrows* (2002), and *The Battle of Evernight* (2002), deftly hybridizes **Celtic fantasy** with other **mythical** elements—some of them Australian—taking a rather disenchanted view of the syncretic amalgam and eventually inclining toward an **Odyssean quest** for normality. A linked series, The Crowthistle Chronicles, is launched by *The Iron Tree* (2004).

DAVID, PETER (1956–). U.S. writer for various media—including **comics**—whose early books were bylined "David Peters." His **contemporary fantasy** *Knight Life* (1987) was much expanded for a new edition of 2002, when he added the sequel *One Knight Only* (2003), in which **Arthur** launches a **quest** for the **grail** from the White House. *Sir Apropos of Nothing* (2001) takes a similarly sceptical view of the materials of **chivalric romance**; the **humor** becomes broader and more extravagantly **satirical** in its sequels *The Woad to Wuin* (2002) and *Tong Lashing* (2003). *Fallen Angel* (2004) is an enterprising **graphic novel**.

DAVIDSON, AVRAM (1923–1993). U.S. writer closely associated with ***The Magazine of Fantasy and Science Fiction***, which he edited in 1964. Much of his early work was quirky **contemporary fantasy**, mingled with **sf** (refer to *HDSFL*) in the collections *Or All the Seas with Oysters* (1962), *What Strange Stars and Skies* (1965), and *Strange Seas and Shores* (1971). His work thereafter was more strongly biased toward **historical fantasy**, as exemplified by *The Enquiries of Doctor Esterhazy* (1975; exp. as *The Adventures of Doctor Esterhazy*, 1990) and *The Redward Edward Papers* (1978). *Collected Fantasies* (1982) is an eclectic sampler, while *Everybody Has Somebody in Heaven* (2000) specializes in **Jewish fantasies**. His early novels were less distinctive; *Joyleg* (1962, with Ward Moore) is a comedy about immortality, while *Rogue Dragon* (1965) and *Clash of the Star-Kings* (1966) are **hybrid/science fantasies**.

The ornate proto-**alchemical fantasy** *The Phoenix and the Mirror* (1969) recasts the Roman poet Virgil as Vergil Magus; it was intended to be the first in a nine-part series, but only *Vergil in Averno* (1987) reached print. *Peregrine: Primus* (1971) is a **humorous fantasy** with a fortune-seeking hero who was similarly left bereft of anticipated sequels. *Ursus of Ultima Thule* (1973) and *Marco Polo and the Sleeping Beauty* (1988, with Grania Davis) are more carefully rounded out. *The Boss in the Wall: A Treatise on the House Devil* (1998, with Grania Davis) is a **dark fantasy** about exotic haunters of urban dwellings.

DAVIES, ROBERTSON (1913–95). Canadian writer. Many of his works are lighthearted calls for **re-enchantment** with strong **metafictional** elements. The Salterton Trilogy, comprising *Tempest-Tost* (1951), *Leaven of Malice* (1954), and *A Mixture of Frailties* (1958), employs a special production of **Shakespeare**'s *Tempest* as a transformative device. The Deptford Trilogy, comprising *Fifth Business* (1970), *The Manticore* (1972), and *World of Wonders* (1975), is a **magical** mystery informed by Jungian psychology. The Cornish Trilogy, comprising *The Rebel Angels* (1981), *What's Bred in the Bone* (1985), and *The Lyre of Orpheus* (1988), carries the same cast forward into more explicitly supernatural territory. *High Spirits* (1982) is a collection of **ghost** stories in the **Christmas fantasy** tradition. *Murther & Walking Spirits* (1991) is narrated by a ghost. *The Cunning Man* (1995) features a man of science struggling to reconcile his worldview with the knowledge that he owes his life to a miracle.

DAYDREAM. A consciously formulated fantasy, often indulged to while away spare time or to give expression to frustrated desires. Daydreams are intensely private possessions that most people are reluctant to disclose (although several collections of sexual fantasies have reached print), but their content is presumably reflected in a great deal of **wish-fulfillment fantasy** and fantasies designed to facilitate **escape**. Daydreams may be used constructively to plan actual encounters or to examine ways in which past encounters might have been better handled—a process reflected in small-scale **alternative histories**.

DEAN, PAMELA (1953–). Pseudonym of U.S. writer Pamela Dyer-Bennett. In the trilogy comprising *The Secret Country* (1985), *The Hidden Land* (1986), and *The Whim of the Dragon* (1989), a role-playing **game** intrudes upon the **primary world**. *Tam Lin* (1991) recycles the famous **ballad** in the context of a university. In the **psychological fantasy** *The Dubious Hills* (1994), **wizards** conduct a magical experiment that alters their subjects' perceptions of pain. *Juniper, Gentian and Rosemary* (1998) features three sisters whose life is infused with **magic** by an enigmatic young man.

DEATH. The **symbolic** personification of death is a common stratagem of fantasy art, to the extent that the image of the hooded Grim Reaper carrying his scythe has become a popular scarecrow of **humorous fantasy**, flamboyantly developed in one of the main sequences of **Terry Pratchett**'s Discworld series. Other familiar depictions include the **angel** of death, often called Azrael, and urbane elderly gentlemen. Personable young men, like John Death in **T. F. Powys**'s *Unclay* and female manifestations like Mara in **George MacDonald**'s *Lilith* are also featured, and other idiosyncratic guises are improvised in melancholy fantasies and **horror** stories.

Notable examples of personified Death are featured in Pedro de Alarcón's *The Strange Friend of Tito Gil* (1852; tr. 1890), **Eugene Lee-Hamilton**'s *Lord of the Dark Red Star,* Alberto Casella's play *Death Takes a Holiday* (tr. 1930), **Stephen Vincent Benét**'s "Johnny Pye and the Fool-Killer," L. E. Watkin's *On Borrowed Time* (1937)—in which "Mr. Brink" is temporarily trapped in a magical apple tree—Nik Cohn's *King Death* (1975), and Dan Simmons's "The Great Lover" (1993).

DECADENT FANTASY. The term "decadence" was borrowed from historians of the Roman Empire for application to literary works self-consciously symptomatic of a supposedly parallel phase in 19th-century European culture. Such works often deal with—or are themselves aspects of—neurotic quests for eccentric and extreme sensations capable of combating the dire effects of ennui and spleen. **Charles Baudelaire** was the definitive exponent of "decadent style," and followers of the fin de siècle movement inspired by his example were fascinated by all things abnormal, artificial, morbid, perverse, and exotic; they were inevitably drawn to fantastic themes and bizarre stylistic embellishments, and their work dramatically expanded the ambition, bizarrerie, and grandiloquence of fantastic fiction.

Key figures in the Decadent movement included the poets Paul Verlaine (1844–96) and Stéphane Mallarmé (1842–98), the prose writers Octave Mirbeau (1848–1917), Catulle Mendès (1841–1909), **Jean Lorrain**, Rachilde (1860–1953), **Rémy de Gourmont**, Joris-Karl Huysmans, and **Pierre Louÿs**. Many of these also warrant consideration as **lifestyle fantasists**, the most extravagant French exemplar being the would-be **Rosicrucian** magus Joséphin Péladan (1859–1916). *The Decadent Reader: Fiction, Fantasy, and Perversion from Fin-de-siècle France* (1998), ed. Asti Hustvedt, and two *Dedalus Books of Decadence* (1990 and 1992), ed. Brian Stableford, are useful samplers.

The central document of decadent prose fiction is Huysmans's sarcastic comedy *À rebours* (1884; tr. as *Against the Grain* or *Against Nature*), the "yellow book" that led **Oscar Wilde**'s Dorian Gray to damnation and inspired John Lane's famous periodical. Lane's Keynotes series included several classics of English decadence, but the British movement was nipped in the bud by the fall of its implicit leader, Wilde. Notable short-story writers influenced by its ideals include **Arthur Machen**, **M. P. Shiel**, **Vernon Lee**, **Arthur Ransome**, and R. Murray Gilchrist, the author of *The Stone Dragon and Other Tragic Romances* (1894; exp. as *The Basilisk and Other Tales of Dread* 2003). London's leading lifestyle fantasist was Count Stenbock, the Estonian-born author of *Studies of Death: Romantic Tales* (1894; exp. 1996). John Meade Falkner's *The Lost Stradivarius* (1895) and Shiel's *The Purple Cloud* were the most significant English decadent fantasy novels.

The fugitive spirit of British decadence was carried forward by James Elroy Flecker, **Norman Douglas**, **Lord Berners**, Elinor Wylie's *The Venetian Glass Nephew* (1925), and Ronald Firbank's *Concerning the Eccentricities of Cardinal Pirelli* (1926) and *The Artificial Princess* (1934). Vincent O'Sullivan, whose decadent fantasies are included in *Master of Fallen Years: Complete Supernatural Stories of Vincent O'Sullivan* (1995, ed. **Jessica Amanda Salmonson**) made his home in Europe, although he belonged to a cadre of American "Bohemians" that included **James Huneker**, **Lafcadio Hearn**, Ambrose Bierce, Emma Frances Dawson, and **George Sterling**. The most extravagant American decadent fantasies were, however, produced by the immigrant **George S. Viereck** and **Ben Hecht**; the leading German decadent fantasist, Hanns Heinz Ewers—author of *The Sorcerer's Apprentice* (1907; tr. 1927) and *Alraune* (1911; tr. 1929)—also spent a good deal of time in the United States.

The ultimate examples of exotic decadent prose were, oddly enough produced for the pages of ***Weird Tales*** by Sterling's disciple **Clark Ashton Smith**, whose work in that vein influenced other members of **H. P. Lovecraft**'s circle and many later writers in a similar vein, including **Thomas Ligotti**, **Jessica Amanda Salmonson**, and **Darrell Schweitzer**. An ornately artificial style and a preoccupation with cultural exhaustion are retained in a great many **far-futuristic fantasies** and other texts focused on long-established cities. **Secondary worlds** often present an exaggerated contrast between decadent cities and **Arcadian** landscapes, tacitly viewing civilization in Rousseauesque fashion as a process of corruption. Notable decadent cultures are featured in

Brian Aldiss's *The Malacia Tapestry*, **Sarah Ash**'s *Moths to a Flame,* and **Samuel R. Delany**'s Nevèrÿon series; notable decadent cities include **Fritz Leiber**'s Lankhmar, **M. John Harrison**'s Viriconium, Faren Miller's Xalycis in *The Illusionists* (1991), **Felicity Savage**'s Delta City, and **K. J. Bishop**'s Ashamoil.

DE CAMP, L. SPRAGUE (1907–2000). U.S. writer who set the characteristic tone of the pulp magazine ***Unknown*** with **humorous/chimerical fantasies** applying a distinctively modern rationality to premises borrowed from traditional fantasy. In "None but Lucifer" (1939 with Horace L. Gold), a young American employs modern marketing theory to revitalize the **Devil**'s temptation-and-punishment business. De Camp's long-standing literary partnership with **Fletcher Pratt** began in 1940 with the first of the Harold Shea stories, whose hero is displaced into a series of literary and mythical milieux; the first two novellas, collected in *The Incomplete Enchanter* (1941), visit the worlds of **Nordic** mythology and **Spenser**'s *Faerie Queene,* while *The Castle of Iron* (1941; book 1950) dips into the world of **Ariosto**'s *Orlando Furioso.* The two books were combined as *The Compleat Enchanter* (1975), even though two further novellas had by then been issued in *Wall of Serpents* (1960), which had to be added to the larger omnibus *The Intrepid Enchanter* (1988; aka *The Complete Compleat Enchanter*). The series was further extended by the of **shared world/anthologies** *The Enchanter Reborn* (1992) and *The Exotic Enchanter* (1994), both coedited by **Christopher Stasheff**, to which de Camp contributed *Sir Harold and the Gnome King* (1991) and "Sir Harold of Zodanga."

De Camp and Pratt also collaborated on the **Celtic fantasy** *The Land of Unreason* (1941; book 1942), the **alternative history** fantasy *The Carnelian Cube* (1948), and the **tall stories** collected in *Tales from Gavagan's Bar* (1953; exp. 1978). De Camp's solo fantasies for *Unknown* included the parodic **fairy tale** *The Undesired Princess* (1942; book 1990 with a sequel by David Drake, "The Enchanted Bunny") and *Solomon's Stone* (1942; book 1957), which features an astral plane inhabited by the **dream** projections of earthly men. His subsequent humorous fantasies include those collected in *The Reluctant Shaman* (1970), *The Purple Pterodactyls* (1979), and *Heroes and Hobgoblins* (1981), as well as three volumes written in collaboration with his wife, Catherine Crook de Camp (1907–2000): the novels *The Incorporated Knight* (1987) and *The Pixillated Peeress* (1991), and the collection *Footprints on Sand* (1981).

De Camp was the first posthumous collaborator to extend the career of **Robert E. Howard**'s Conan, completing some fragments for *Tales of Conan* (1955) and revising Bjorn Nyberg's *The Return of Conan* (1957; aka *Conan the Avenger*) before writing many more pastiches in collaboration with **Lin Carter** when the series was reprinted in paperback in the late 1960s. His own **sword and sorcery** stories are more lighthearted; *The Tritonian Ring and Other Pusadian Tales* (1953) collects his early work in that vein, including the 1951 title piece, while the Novaria series comprises *The Goblin Tower* (1968), *The Clocks of Iraz* (1971), *The Unbeheaded King* (1980), and *The Honorable Barbarian* (1989). *The Fallible Fiend,* set in the same quasi-**classical** milieu, is a broader comedy.

De Camp's crucial contribution to the establishment of fantasy as a commercial genre also involved editing a definitive series of showcase anthologies, comprising *Swords and Sorcery* (1963), *The Spell of Seven* (1965), *The Fantastic Swordsmen* (1967), and *Warlocks and Warriors* (1970), their exemplars supported by essays collected in *The Conan Reader* (1968), *Blond Barbarians and Noble Savages* (1975), and *Literary Swordsmen and Sorcerors: The Makers of Heroic Fantasy* (1976). More essays in a similar vein are included with other materials in *Rubber Dinosaurs and Wooden Elephants* (1997). De Camp also wrote *The Miscast Barbarian: A Biography of Robert E. Howard* (1975; exp. as *Dark Valley Destiny: The Life of Robert E. Howard*, 1983, with Catherine Crook de Camp and Jane Whittington Griffin), and *Lovecraft: A Biography* (1976).

DEDALUS. Publishing house specializing in "literary fantasy," founded by Eric Lane, **Robert Irwin** and Geoffrey Smith; its launch package included. Irwin's *The Arabian Nightmare* and Smith's revisionist **vampire** fantasy *The Revenants* (1983, bylined "Geoffrey Farrington"). It went on to reprint a good deal of **decadent** fantasy and some **surreal** fantasy, much of it in translation; it became the English publisher of such writers as Sylvie Germain and **Herbert Rosendorfer** and the discoverer of such native talents as **Andrew Crumey** and David Madsen, author of the **historical fantasy** *Memoirs of a Gnostic Dwarf* (1995) and the **hallucinatory fantasy** *A Box of Dreams* (2003).

Dedalus provided an invaluable account of the historical range and international scope of fantasy literature in a series of showcase **anthologies** including *The Dedalus Book of Austrian Fantasy: The Meyrink Years 1890–1930* (1992; exp. 2003 as *The Dedalus Book of*

Austrian Fantasy: 1890–2000), ed. Mike Mitchell; *The Dedalus Book of German Decadence: Voices of the Abyss* (1994), ed. Ray Furness *The Dedalus Book of Roman Decadence; Emperors of Debauchery* (1994), ed. Geoffrey Farrington; *The Dedalus Book of Portuguese Fantasy* (1995), ed. Eugénio Lisboa and Helder Macedo; *The Dedalus Book of Medieval Literature: The Grin of the Gargoyle* (1995), ed. Brian Murdoch; *The Dedalus Book of Polish Fantasy* (1996), ed. Wiesieck Powaga; *The Dedalus Book of Spanish Fantasy* (1999), ed. Margaret Jull Costa and Annella McDermott; *The Dedalus Book of Greek Fantasy* (2004), ed. David Connolly; and *The Dedalus Occult Reader: The Garden of Hermetic Dreams* (2004), ed. Gary Lachman.

DE HAVEN, TOM (1949–). U.S. writer in various genres. The **humorous fantasy** *Funny Papers* (1985)—categorized by the author as "screwball noir"—was followed up by the marginal *Derby Dugan's Depression Funnies* (1996) and *Dugan Under Ground* (2001). The Chronicles of the King's Tramp trilogy, comprising *Walker of Worlds* (1990), *The End-of-Everything Man* (1991), and *The Last Human* (1992), is an earnest **portal fantasy** in which a **multiverse** is threatened with collapse. *The Orphan's Tent* (1996) is a bizarre mystery involving a vanished rock singer. His short fiction is sampled in *Pixie Meat* (1990).

DEITZ, TOM (1952–). U.S. writer. His work is mostly **contemporary fantasy** set in his native Georgia, whose supernatural aspects are syncretically accumulated in the series comprising *Windmaster's Bane* (1986), *Fireshaper's Doom* (1987), *Darkthunder's Way* (1989), *Sunshaker's War* (1990), *Stoneskin's Revenge* (1991), *Ghostcountry's Wrath* (1995), *Dreamseeker's Road* (1995), *Landslayer's Law* (1997), and *Warstalker's Track* (1999), as well as in the trilogy comprising *Soulsmith* (1991), *Dreambuilder* (1992), and *Wordwright* (1993). *The Gryphon King* (1989) employs elements of **Celtic fantasy** in a similar setting, while the Mexico-set couplet comprising *Above the Lower Sky* (1994) and *Demons in the Green* (1996) is more eclectic. The **intrusive fantasy** series comprising *Bloodwinter* (1999), *Springwar* (2000), *Summerblood* (2001), and *Warautumn* (2002) tracks the consequences of the discovery of a magical gem.

DE LA MARE, WALTER (1873–1956). British writer whose poetry and fiction—especially that written for **children**—routinely employs fantastic motifs. The mildly sinister title piece of *The Listeners* (1912) is one of the most popular children's poems. *Henry Brocken: His Travels and*

Adventures in the Rich, Strange, Scarce-Imaginable Regions of Romance (1904) is a **quest** fantasy with landscapes and characters borrowed from a hectic admixture of literary texts. The **existentialist fantasy** *The Return* (1910), like much of de la Mare's short fiction, edges into the field of **horror** fiction (refer to *HDHL*), but his **ghosts** are not always terrifying, and there are occasional **sentimental fantasies** and oblique pleas for **re-enchantment** in such collections as *The Riddle and Other Stories* (1923), *The Connoisseur and Other Stories* (1926), *Over the Edge* (1930), and *The Wind Blows Over* (1936).

Most of de la Mare's children's stories—the most blatant exception is the classic **animal fantasy** *The Three Mulla-Mulgars* (1910; aka *The Three Royal Monkeys*)—are modeled on **folktales**, but their lighthearted surfaces often conceal murky philosophical depths. The bibliography is inordinately complicated, but the most important collections are *Broomsticks and Other Tales* (1925) and *The Lord Fish* (1933); the versions assembled in *Collected Stories for Children* (1947) are revisions.

DELANY, SAMUEL R. (1942–). U.S. writer and scholar. His novels, from *The Jewels of Aptor* (1962) to *They Fly at Ciron* (1993), played a leading role in the revitalization of hybrid **science fantasy** (refer to *HDSFL*); the **Orphean fantasy** *The Einstein Intersection* (1967) and the **Promethean/grail** romance *Nova* (1968) use classic fantasy motifs to complicate and refine **sf** narratives. Delany's major fantasy series, set in an imaginary **prehistoric** empire, with settings and characters ingeniously that combine **decadent** imagery with barbarian vigor, comprises *Tales of Nevèrÿon* (1979), *Nevèrÿona* (1983), *Flight from Nevèrÿon* (1985), and *The Bridge of Lost Desire* (1987, rev. as *Return to Nevèrÿon,* 1989). The stories are supplemented by various appendices, one of which explains some of the parallels between Nevèrÿon and contemporary New York (the Bridge of Lost Desire being a fantasized version of Brooklyn Bridge). The central thread running through the series is the history of Gorgik the Liberator, a slave who becomes a statesman, but its themes are sexual-political and **metafictional**.

DE LARRABEITI, MICHAEL (1937–). British writer. The unobtrusive race featured in the **children's fantasy** series comprising *The Borribles* (1976), *The Borribles Go for Broke* (1981), and *The Borribles: Across the Dark Metropolis* (1986) presumably derives its name from a fusion of "Borrowers" (refer to **Mary Norton**) with "horrible," and the characters in question are considerably tougher than such relative innocents as **Terry Pratchett**'s Nomes. *Provençal Tales* (1989) **recycles** regional **folktales**.

DE LINT, CHARLES (1951–). Canadian writer. He began publishing short fantasies as chapbooks from his own Triskell Press in 1979, reprinting them as *Triskell Tales* (2000); they included early items in the **Celtic** Cerin Songweaver sequence, which also includes the novel *The Harp of the Grey Rose* (1985). De Lint's other Celtic fantasies include the Angharad series, collected and extended in *Into the Green* (1993). These works reflect a strong interest in **music**; echoes of it infuse all his work.

The Riddle of the Wren (1984) is a conventional **portal fantasy**, but *Moonheart* (1984) and the stories collected in *Spiritwalk* (1992)—which include the 1990 novel *Ghostwood*—broke new ground in the development of the distinctive species of **contemporary fantasy** commonly known as **urban fantasy**, for which de Lint provided the paradigm examples. His cityscapes—initially those of his native Ottawa—overlap a magical realm populated by individuals syncretically drawn from folkloristic traditions that are as varied as the ancestry of modern Canadians. The apparatus was further elaborated in *Mulengro* (1985), *Yarrow* (1986), and *Greenmantle* (1988).

De Lint's Celtic fantasies broadened out their references to British folklore in *Jack the Giant-Killer* (1987), its sequel *Drink Down the Moon* (1990), and *The Wild Wood* (1994). *Wolf Moon* (1988) features a persecuted **werewolf**. *The Little Country* (1991) is a **portal fantasy** in a similar vein, and *Seven Wild Sisters* (2002) also has rural setting, but the bulk of his effort after 1990 was devoted to a long series of urban fantasies set in the imaginary city of Newford; they include the stories in *Dreams Underfoot* (1993), *The Ivory and the Horn* (1995), and *Moonlight and Vines* (1999), as well as some of those in *Waifs and Strays* (2002). The novels in the sequence are *Memory & Dream* (1994), *Trader* (1997), *Someplace to Be Flying* (1998), *Forests of the Heart* (2000), and *The Onion Girl* (2001). The painstaking depiction of a fantasized North America contained in these novels was carefully broadened out in *Spirits in the Wires* (2003) and its sequel *Medicine Road* (2004), which incorporate the Ozarks and Arizona into the same **Faerie**-linked backcloth.

Other short fiction is reprinted in *Tapping the Dream Tree* (2002) and *A Handful of Coppers* (2003). The **horror** novels de Lint initially bylined "Samuel M. Key"—of which the one with most fantasy relevance is *Angel of Darkness* (1990)—were all reprinted under his own name.

DEL REY BOOKS. An imprint of **Ballantine** Books founded in 1977, named after editor in chief Judy-Lynn del Rey. While she took charge of the **sf** line, her husband, Lester, assumed responsibility for a fantasy line markedly different in character from the one **Lin Carter** had instituted in the late 1960s, whose unprofitability had become desperate by 1974. The book that showcased the new line was **Terry Brooks**'s *Sword of Shannara,* which was quickly followed by **Stephen R. Donaldson**'s Chronicles of Thomas Covenant (which had previously been rejected by every commercial publisher in the United States, including Ballantine) and **Piers Anthony**'s *A Spell for Chameleon*. All became best sellers, establishing key templates for the **commodified fantasy** to which Del Rey Books remained steadfastly committed even after Lester del Rey's retirement in 1991.

DELUSIONAL FANTASY. A delusion is an affliction that leads a people to believe that they are other than who they are, or that the world is other than it is. Delusional fantasy is akin to **hallucinatory fantasy**, but delusions may be permanent and are usually deep rooted, thus lending themselves to very different plot development. Whereas **visionary fantasies** often reveal some kind of truth, however elusive, delusional fantasies are intrinsically deceptive and often **horrific**, although they can sometimes be ironically life enhancing. The archetypal example is **Cervantes**'s *Don Quixote*.

Literary representations of spontaneously generated delusions—examples include Gaston Leroux's *The Man with the Black Feather* (1904), H. G. Wells's *Mr Blettsworthy on Rampole Island* (1928), John Knittel's *Nile Gold* (1929), **Ben Hecht**'s *Fantazius Malllare,* **John Gardner**'s *Freddy's Book,* **Robert Irwin**'s *The Limits of Vision,* and Wendy Clarke's *Baudelaire's Desire* (1999)—are not considered to be fantasy fiction by some critics, but **psychological fantasy** of the kind pioneered by **William Gilbert** is interesting precisely because of its borderline situation. Accounts of deliberately induced delusion are more obviously fantastic, although those involving hypnotism—popularized by **George du Maurier**'s *Trilby* and often employed in **humorous fantasy**—are more **ambiguous** than those involving explicit **magic**. Delusion-inducing magic—sometimes called "glamor"—is routinely used by femmes fatales and **wizards** intent on deflecting heroes from their **quests**.

The possibility that reading fantasy with the wrong attitude can generate delusions has haunted **children's fiction** since its inception; Rona

Jaffe's *Mazes and Monsters* (1981) updates the anxiety by applying it to role-playing **games**. *See also* EROTIC FANTASY.

DEMON. A spiritual being, usually possessed of powerful **magic** and often of an evil disposition. In **Christian** thinking, the word became synonymous with **devil**; although the Greek *daimon* and the Latin *daemon* are morally neutral, the English derivative was inevitably tainted by the insistence that all would-be rivals to **God** must be devils in disguise and that all **magic**, especially **witchcraft**, must involve their invocation. The Torah (unlike the folkloristic aspects of the Talmud) was purged by the monotheistic Jews of the demons to which its scriptures may once have referred, but residual Old Testament references to such probable demons as Lilith and Azazel were reconceived by Christians as evidence of agents of the Devil. Islamic folklore similarly retained a demonic hierarchy, headed by Iblis and staffed by **djinn**.

Demons that are not recast as devils are frequently used nevertheless as antagonists—and sometimes as protagonists—in **occult fantasy** and **sword and sorcery** fiction. As modern fantasy writers have taken more interest in anthropological esoterica, the range of demons employed in fantasies has widened considerably.

DETECTIVE FICTION. There is a fundamental incompatibility between the tacit assumptions of detective and fantastic fiction, clearly reflected in a subgenre of detective fiction in which seeming supernatural events are naturalistically resolved, as in **Arthur Conan Doyle**'s *The Hound of the Baskervilles* (1901) and **Eden Phillpotts**'s *Lycanthrope* (1937). Calculated violation of the expectation of a naturalistic resolution—as in John Dickson Carr's *The Burning Court* (1937)—seems to many detective fiction fans to be narrative treason. Many early detectives confronted with **occult** or **psychic** phenomena were passionately zealous in proving them fraudulent.

The first subgenre to resolve this fundamental incompatibility featured "occult detectives" whose mission was not to debunk but to provide **metaphysical** explanations rather than physical ones and exorcisms rather than arrests; much fiction of this type is **horror** fiction, although it intrudes upon the territories of **spiritualist fantasy** and **theosophical fantasy**. Its early protagonists were usually medical men presented with unusual cases, as in the *Blackwood's Magazine* series collected in *Passages from the Diary of a Late Physician* (3 vols. 1838), by Samuel Warren, and the **delusional fantasies** recorded by **William**

Gilbert, but these eventually gave way to freelance consultants like **Algernon Blackwood**'s John Silence, **William Hope Hodgson**'s Carnacki, **Aleister Crowley**'s Simon Iff, **Dion Fortune**'s Dr Taverner, and **Margery Lawrence**'s Miles Pennoyer. The tradition was carried forward into the modern era by **Glen Cook** and Mark Valentine's *In Violet Veils and Other Tales of the Connoisseur* (1999). A few nonspecialist detectives were thrust into frequent contact with fantastic adversaries, most notably **E. Charles Vivian**'s Gees. A significant variant featured "psychic detectives" who solved ordinary crimes by extraordinary means, like J. U. Giesy's astrologically talented "Semi-Dual" and **Sax Rohmer**'s Morris Klaw, who solves crimes by dreaming the solutions.

John Dickson Carr founded a new **hybrid** genre of **timeslip** crime stories in *The Devil in Velvet* (1951), *Fear Is the Same* (1956 as by Carter Dickson), and *Fire, Burn!* (1957), following a precedent set by Bruce Graeme's *Epilogue* (1933), in which timeslipped detectives solve the Dickensian mystery of Edwin Drood, but it remained fugitive. A more spectacular breakthrough was achieved when chimerical texts began to displace hybrids, enabling the establishment of **alternative histories** involving all manner of exotic detectives whose investigation of exotic crimes is methodical and rational within the exotic narrative framework. The boom in this kind of fiction quickly produced such best sellers as **P. N. Elrod** and **Laurel K. Hamilton**; other notable examples include works by **Simon R. Green**, **Rosemary Edghill**, **Tanya Huff**, "Martin Scott" (**Martin Millar**), Lillian Stewart Carl's *Time Enough to Die* (2002) and *Lucifer's Crown* (2004), and Kim Harrison's *Dead Witch Walking* (2004). Such works provide key examples of earnest chimerization, although the subgenre was inevitably infected by humor in such series as Jim Butcher's Dresden Files, extending from *Storm Front* (2000) to *Blood Rites* (2004).

THE DEVIL. When used as a proper noun, the anti-**God** of Christianity, also known as Satan or Lucifer; as a generic noun the term refers to one of his followers from the ranks of the fallen **angels**, to whose company many pagan gods and **demons** were also consigned by **Christian** scholars, the term "demon" thus becoming synonymous with "devil" in that context. In Christian art, the Devil is usually represented as a monstrous figure with a bestial face, horns, a tail, and sometimes cloven feet, borrowed from the Greek god **Pan**.

The Devil is the explicit or implicit adversary of much **horror** fiction (refer to *HDHL*), but his role in fantasy has been complicated by the refinement of **Faustian fantasies** as ingenious contests of wits, the apologetic tradition of **literary satanism**, and the burlesque tradition of **infernal comedies**. He is occasionally featured in **apocalyptic fantasy**, and the Christian reinterpretation that equates him with the serpent in Eden gives him a key role in some **biblical fantasies** as well as many **Christian fantasies**, but his most interesting appearances outside the cited subgenres are in ***contes philosophiques*** that employ him in considerations of the problem of evil (theodicy).

The allegation that the serpent in Eden was actually Satan prefigures his reputation as a master of disguise, exploited in fantasies ranging from **Jacques Cazotte**'s *The Devil in Love* to Arthur Calder-Marshall's *The Fair to Middling* (1959), but his most familiar modern form is an urbane man of the world, as in works ranging from **Marie Corelli**'s *The Sorrows of Satan* to **Stephen King**'s "The Man in Black" (1994). Minor devils are usually weaker carbon copies, although some co-opted demons have distinct identities, notably the amiable Asmodeus featured in Alain René Lesage's *The Devil on Two Sticks* (1707; tr. 1708) and **Edward Bulwer-Lytton**'s *Asmodeus at Large*.

Notable fantasies in which the Devil plays a significant role—although he is often under threat of losing his power and influence to a **thinning** process—include Ferenc Molnar's play *The Devil* (1907; novelization by Joseph O'Brien from Henry W. Savage's English version, 1908), Carl Heinrich's *Orphan of Eternity* (1929), Murray Constantine's *The Devil, Poor Devil!,* Sherard Vines's *Return, Belphegor!* (1932), **Mikhail Bulgakov**'s *The Master and Margarita,* **Robert Nathan**'s *The Innocent Eve,* **Natalie Babbitt**'s two story collections, Jeremy Leven's *Satan* (1982), and **Catherine Webb**'s *Waywalkers*.

DEXTER, SUSAN (1955–). U.S. writer. The series comprising *The Ring of Allaire* (1981), *The Sword of Calandra* (1985), and *The Mountains of Channadran* (1986) is a **humorous** account of the tribulations of a trainee **wizard**. *The Wizard's Shadow* (1993) employs the same **secondary world** but puts more emphasis on **heroic** adventure. The trilogy comprising *The Prince of Ill Luck* (1994), *The Wind-Witch* (1995), and *The True Knight* (1995) reverts to the humorous pattern. *Moonlight* (2001) is another account of the exploits of a young wizard-to-be.

DICKENS, CHARLES (1812–1870). British writer who made a crucial contribution to the evolution of Victorian fantasy by inventing and shaping **Christmas fantasy** and arguing in favor of the necessity of retaining a component of enchantment in **children's literature**. Some anecdotal **humorous/ghost** stories are included in *The Posthumous Papers of the Pickwick Club* (1836–37), including "The Story of the Goblins Who Stole a Sexton," the first of his Christmas stories. The similarly moralistic *A Christmas Carol in Prose* (1843) was followed by *The Chimes* (1844), *The Cricket on the Hearth* (1845), the nonfantastic **allegory** *The Battle of Life* (1846), and *The Haunted Man and the Ghost's Bargain* (1848). *The Chimes* works up a fine pitch of indignation regarding the plight of the poor, and *The Haunted Man* is a profound ***conte philosophique***. His later ghost stories are orthodox **horror** fiction.

A Christmas Carol became a modern myth, extensively recycled and imitated; echoes of it form the core of a small subgenre of "Dickensian fantasy." It was carbon-copied by Tom Gallon's *The Man Who Knew Better* (1902) and **Marie Corelli**'s *Strange Visitation of Josiah McNason;* Connie Willis's "Adaptation" (1994), Bruce Bueno de Mesquita's *The Trial of Ebenezer Scrooge* (2001), and Louis Bayard's *Mr. Timothy* (2003) are notable sequels; Mark Hazard Osmun's *Marley's Ghost* (2000) is a **prequel**.

DICKINSON, PETER (1927–). Zambian-born British writer of wide-ranging **children's fiction**. In the Changes trilogy comprising *The Weathermonger* (1968), *Heartsease* (1969), and *The Devil's Children* (1970), a retreat from civilization is revealed to have been caused by **Merlin**. *Emma Tupper's Diary* (1971) records an encounter with the Loch Ness **monster**. *The Blue Hawk* (1976) is a **historical fantasy** set in Egypt. The mock-**scholarly fantasy** *The Flight of Dragons* (1979) offers a **humorous** account of draconian biology. *Touch and Go* (1997) is a **timeslip** fantasy. *The Lion Tamer's Daughter* (1999) is a **doppelgänger** story. *The Ropemaker* (2001) is a sophisticated **quest** fantasy. *The Tears of the Salamander* (2003) is a historical fantasy set in 19th-century Italy. *Inside Grandad* (2004) features selkies. Dickinson's work for younger children mostly consists of quirky **fairy tales**, including *The Iron Lion* (1972), *Giant Cold* (1984), *A Box of Nothing* (1985), and *Time and the Clockmice, etcetera* (1993). He has also worked in collaboration with his wife, **Robin McKinley**.

DISCH, THOMAS M. (1940–). U.S. writer in various genres (refer to *HDSFL* and *HDHL*). His fantasies include the mock-**children's** stories *The Brave Little Toaster* (1981; book 1986) and *The Brave Little Toaster*

Goes to Mars (1988), which substitute household appliances for the stock characters of Disneyesque **animal fantasy**. The **sf** novel *On Wings of Song* (1979) makes much of the **allegorical** connotations of **flight**. *The M.D.: A Horror Story* (1991) is a **moralistic fantasy** in which a doctor receives a double-edged magical healing gift. *The Silver Pillow* (1988) is a **dark fantasy**. *The Sub: A Study in Witchcraft* (1999) has elements of **theriomorphic/animal fantasy**. His short fiction includes numerous **surreal** fantasies and Swiftian **satires**.

DISKI, JENNY (1947–). British writer whose literary fiction sometimes employs fantasy motifs. *Rainforest* (1987) has a marginal element of **surreal fantasy**. *Like Mother* (1988) is narrated by a brainless child. *Then Again* (1990) is a **timeslip** fantasy. *Monkey's Uncle* (1994) features an intelligent ape. *Only Human: A Comedy* (2000) is an irreverent **biblical fantasy**; *After These Things* (2004) is a sequel. Some satirical **fairy tales** are included in *The Vanishing Princess* (1995).

DISRAELI, BENJAMIN (1804–1881). British statesman and writer. *The Voyage of Captain Popanilla* (1828) and the **classical fantasies** "Ixion in Heaven" (1832–33) and "The Infernal Marriage" (1833–34) are **political satires**. *The Wondrous Tale of Alroy, and the Rise of Iskander* (1833; aka *Alroy*) is a **historical fantasy**.

DJINN. A kind of **demon** featured in **Arabian** fantasy; the word is both singular and plural, but an alternative singular form, *djinni,* is often Anglicized as "genie" in children's fiction. The transition of the Arab world to monotheistic Islam is portrayed in a legend that the djinn were imprisoned in bottles by Suleiman (the biblical Solomon), making them conveniently available for rediscovery in **intrusive fantasies**, especially in echoes of one of the tales in the Arabian Nights that constitute a common formula of **wish-fulfillment fantasy**; examples include Max Adeler's "Mr. Shelmire's Djinn" (1883), **F. Anstey**'s *The Brass Bottle,* and Susan Alice Kerby's *Miss Carter and the Ifrit* (1945).

The **humorous** potential of djinn has been extensively exploited by such writers as **Robert Lynn Asprin**, **Craig Shaw Gardner**, **Elizabeth Scarborough**, and **Tom Holt**, but they are equally useful in **commodified fantasy** as adversaries. In Rachel Caine's Weather Warden series, extending from *Ill Wind* (2003) to *Heat Stroke* (2004), the heroine is eventually resurrected as a djinn. Jonathan Stroud's Bartimaeus series, begun with *The Amulet of Samarkand* (2003) and *Golem's Eye* (2004), features a djinn associated with an apprentice magician.

DONALDSON, STEPHEN R. (1947–). U.S. writer whose first trilogy in the Chronicles of Thomas Covenant—consisting of *Lord Foul's Bane, The Illearth War,* and *The Power That Preserves* (all 1977)—became a spontaneous best seller after being rejected by 47 publishers, demonstrating the absurdity of editorial prejudices against fantasy. Covenant, afflicted by Hanson's disease (leprosy), is translocated into a **secondary world** where history, geography, and metaphysics reflect his plight, thus transmuting his struggle for survival into a mission to save an entire world from the ravages of Lord Foul the Despiser. The second trilogy, comprising *The Wounded Land* (1980), *The One Tree* (1982), and *White Gold Wielder* (1983), undermined its status as **delusional fantasy** by sending a second character into the milieu. *Gilden-Fire* (1981) is a fragment detached from the first trilogy. The series continued in *The Runes of the Earth* (2004).

The **immersive fantasy** title story of the collection *Daughter of Regals and Other Tales* (1984) and the **portal fantasy** couplet Mordant's Need, comprising *The Mirror of Her Dreams* (1986) and *A Man Rides Through* (1987), employ female protagonists well suited to emotionally agonized victim roles. Two of the stories in *Reave the Just and Other Tales* (1998) feature a quasi-**messianic** champion whose willingness to be victimized in others' stead shames them into heroic resistance. Donaldson, a more distinctive writer than **Terry Brooks**, revealed that commodified fantasy need not be restricted to cloning the works of **J. R. R. Tolkien** and **Robert E. Howard**, and that there is more raw anguish in the popular demand for escapism than anyone had dared to imagine.

DONNELLY, MARCUS (?–). U.S. writer. *Prophets for the End of Time* (2000) is a spirited **apocalyptic fantasy** deftly combining satirical humor and sentimentality. *Letters from the Flesh* (2004) is a **religious fantasy** about the conflict between evolutionary theory and creationism, featuring possible alien influences on early Christianity.

DOPPELGÄNGER. A German term, roughly translatable as "walking double," signifying an elaborated shadow or **mirror** image. Such figures are of considerable importance in fantasy literature, often dramatizing the notion that human identity is wrought by an **existential** compromise between reason and emotion, good and evil impulses, or (in Freudian terminology) superego and id. The common ploy of disowning responsibility for regrettable acts by insisting that the actor was "not himself" at the time is easily extrapolated into the **psychological**

fantasy of multiple personality, as in **James Hogg**'s *The Private Memoirs and Confessions of a Justified Sinner,* **Edgar Allan Poe**'s "William Wilson," Claude Houghton's *Neighbours* (1926), and **Nancy Springer**'s *Larque on the Wing*. It is often employed in **moralistic fantasies**, as in **Charles Dickens**'s *The Haunted Man and the Ghost's Bargain,* **Mrs. Craik**'s "The Self-Seer" (1853), **Oscar Wilde's** *The Picture of Dorian Gray,* **James Branch Cabell**'s *There Were Two Pirates,* and **Italo Calvino**'s *The Cloven Viscount*. **Humorous** variants include J. Storer Clouston's *Two's Two* (1916) and William Garrett's *The Man in the Mirror* (1931).

Alter egos often crop up in **alternative histories**, especially those set in **parallel worlds**, as in **Gerald Bullett**'s *Mr. Godly Beside Himself* and **Vernon Knowles**'s "The Shop in the Off-Street" (1935). They also arise in **timeslip** fantasies with an element of **karmic romance**, as in **Edwin Lester Arnold**'s *Lepidus the Centurion* (1901).

Existentialist fantasies involving *doppelgängers* include Henry James's "The Jolly Corner" (1908), Robert Hichens's "The Man in the Mirror" (1950), Elizabeth Sewell's *The Dividing of Time* (1951), Nicholas Royle's *Counterparts* (1993), Alice Thompson's *Justine* (1997), and Peter Straub's *Mr. X.* (1999). Natural *doppelgängers*—identical twins—are featured in many fantasies of coincidental destiny, including **Alexandre Dumas**'s "The Corsican Brothers" (1844), Lois Duncan's *The Stranger with My Face* (1981), and David Ambrose's *Coincidence* (2001).

DOUGLAS, NORMAN (1868–1952). British writer long resident on the island of Capri. His fantasies are wry celebrations of **decadent** mores. *Nerinda* (1901 as by Normyx; separate pub. 1929) is a **delusional/erotic fantasy** about a mermaid. *South Wind* (1917) describes the healthy paganism of the inhabitants of the **Arcadian** island of Nepenthe. The Epicurean parable *They Went* (1920) **transfigures** the legend of Lyonesse. The **classical fantasy** *In the Beginning* (1927) describes the **allegorical** adventures of a lusty demigod in the days before the gods inflicted the curse of morals upon mankind.

DOUGLASS, SARA (1957–). Pseudonym of Australian writer Sara Warnecke. The Wayfarer Redemption **epic fantasy** series, comprising *Battleaxe* (1995; aka *The Wayfarer Redemption*), *Enchanter* (1996), *StarMan* (1996), *Sinner* (1997), *Pilgrim* (1998), and *Crusader* (2000), describes the devastation of the world of Tencendor by **demons**. *Beyond* *the Hanging Wall* (1996) features empathic **healers**. The inventively exotic backcloth of *Threshold* (1997) includes mathematical Magi and the magic of frogs. The Crucible trilogy of **historical fantasies** comprising *The Nameless Day* (2000), *The Wounded Hawk* (2001), and *The Crippled Angel* (2002) describes an **alternative** Wars of the Roses involving Joan of Arc. The Troy Game series launched by *Hades' Daughter* (2002) and *Gods' Concubine* (2004) extends from the fall of Troy and the destruction of Atlantis to the 20th century. *The Betrayal of Arthur* (1998) is a nonfictional analysis of **Arthurian** mythology.

DOYLE, SIR ARTHUR CONAN (1859–1930). British writer in various genres (refer to *HDSFL* and *HDHL*). The 1883 title story of *The Captain of the Polestar and Other Tales* (1890) features a becalmed ship beset by apparitions; the other fantasies include the identity-exchange comedy "The Great Keinplatz Experiment" (1885) and the animate **mummy** story "The Ring of Thoth" (1890). *The Mystery of Cloomber* (1889) is a fantasy of supernatural revenge. *The Parasite* (1894) features a female psychic **vampire**. *Round the Red Lamp* (1894) includes "Lot No. 249" (1892), another account of a hyperactive mummy. *Round the Fire Stories* (1908) includes a cautionary **spiritualist fantasy**, "Playing with Fire" (1900), which acquired an ironic edge when Doyle became a convert; his credulous spiritualist fantasies include *The Land of Mist* (1926) and the title story of *The Maracot Deep and Other Stories* (1929).

DRAGON. A mythical creature usually envisaged as a giant winged reptile capable of breathing fire, although the alternative designation "worm" emphasizes its kinship with flightless giant serpents. The symbolism of dragons differs significantly between cultures, the dragons of **Oriental** mythology being viewed in a kindlier light than the traditional dragons of European mythology, whose primary function was to be slain, either in consequence of their predatory activities—often involving human female sacrifices—or their propensity for accumulating plunderable hoards of gold and gems. Dragon slaying is the ultimate certificate of **heroism** in European legend, including such **Christian** legends as that of St. George. There has, however, been a conspicuous trend in modern fantasy toward their rehabilitation as high-minded creatures blessed with uniquely ancient wisdom.

This rehabilitation began in **children's fantasy**, in some of the items in **Kenneth Grahame**'s *Dream Days,* and **E. Nesbit's** *Book of Dragons*;

further deflation occurred in ironic tales like **Eden Phillpotts**'s *The Lavender Dragon* and Max Beerbohm's *The Dreadful Dragon of Hay Hill* (1928). Although **J. R. R. Tolkien**'s *The Hobbit* revived all the menace of the motif in the vivid depiction of Smaug, his later fantasies capitulated to the trend. An important model of the wondrously wise dragon was provided by **Ursula Le Guin**'s Earthsea series, launched in 1968, a year that also saw the launch of **Anne McCaffrey**'s Pern series, in which dragons enjoy a symbiotic relationship with human riders who employ them in aerial battles in defense of their world; the significance of these exemplars did not become obvious, however, until the launch of the role-playing game *Dungeons and Dragons* in 1974, which made a crucial contribution to draconian charisma, greatly assisted by the attraction of dragons as an item of **illustration**. The new cliché was solidly in place by the time the highly popular series of DragonLance Chronicles **tie-ins**, launched in 1984, placed dragons in the foreground, thanks to work done in the interim by such game-influenced writers as **Raymond E. Feist**.

McCaffrey was following in the footsteps of fellow **sf** writers like **Jack Vance** and **Avram Davidson** in making use of "rationalized" dragons, further analogues of which were developed by **Melanie Rawn** and **Samuel R. Delany**, although the difficulties in making the mythological image plausible were made abundantly clear by **Peter Dickinson**'s tongue-in-cheek *The Flight of Dragons*. Even so, dragon fantasy of the McCaffrey/Rawn variety became an important sector of **commodified fantasy**, whose prominent contributors include **Robin Wayne Bailey**, **Graham Edwards**, **Barbara Hambly**, **Irene Radford**, **Jo Walton**, **Lawrence Watt-Evans**, **Jane Welch**, **Patricia C. Wrede**, Charles Ashton (author of the trilogy launched by *Jet Smoke and Dragon Fire* [1991]), Christopher Rowley (in the series launched by *Bazil Broketail* [1992]), Marjorie B. Kellogg (in the series launched by *The Book of Earth* [1995]), David Cladeer (in *The Dragonslayer's Apprentice* [1997]), Joanne Bertin (in *The Last Dragonlord* [1998]), Jonathan Stroud (in *Buried Fire* [1999]), and Chris Bunch (in the series launched by *Storm of Wings* [2002]).

Interesting variants of dragon fantasy include the **Oriental** dragon fantasies of **Laurence Yep** and **S. P. Somtow**; **R. A. MacAvoy**'s *Tea with the Black Dragon;* Elizabeth Kerner's *Song in the Silence* (1997), in which a **quest** for the land of true dragons reaches an unexpected conclusion, further complicated in *The Lesser Kindred* (2000) and *Redeeming the Lost* (2004); Carol Berg's *Song of the Beast* (2003), in which the dragon riders are villains; and **Lucius Shepard**'s sophisticated account of the dragon Griaule. **Michael Swanwick**'s *The Iron Dragon's Daughter* uses dragon fantasy as a paradigm of the commercial genre. Showcase **anthologies** include *Dragons of Light* (1980) and *Dragons of Darkness* (1981), ed. **Orson Scott Card**, and *The Dragon Quintet* (2003), ed. Marvin Kaye. *Dragons of Fantasy* (2004) by Anne C. Petty is a selective **guide**.

DRAKE, DAVID A. (1945–). U.S. writer best known for **sf** (refer to *HDSFL*). His strong interest in military history informs such works as the **Arthurian fantasy** *The Dragon Lord* (1979) and the stories collected in *Vettius and His Friends* (1989). *The Sea Hag* (1988) is a **far-futuristic** fantasy with **fairy tale** elements. *Old Nathan* (1991) is a **historical fantasy** about a 19th-century American **wizard**. The **sword and sorcery** series comprising *Lord of the Isles* (1997), *Queen of Demons* (1998), *Servant of the Dragon* (1999), *Mistress of the Catacombs* (2001), *Goddess of the Ice Realm* (2003), and *Master of the Cauldron* (2004) is influenced by the work of **Clark Ashton Smith**. Drake has also contributed to several **shared world** projects, including the Thieves World and Hell series.

DRAKE, NATHAN (1766–1836). British scholar whose curious patchwork of essays, poems, and tales *Literary Hours* (3 vols., 1798) includes a notable analysis of the **Gothic** imagination that draws a distinction between the "terrible" and "sportive" strands of Gothic literature—whose central motifs are, respectively, the spectre and the **fairy**. The tales exemplifying his argument include "Henry Fitzowen," culminating in a mission statement by the **fairy** queen.

DREAM. A fantasy arising spontaneously in the mind during sleep. Many dreams are vividly strange, and some—nightmares and "night terrors"—are profoundly disturbing. Diviners have long sought omens and premonitions in dreams, treating their imagery as symbolic, a trend continued into modern **scholarly fantasy** by such psychologists as Sigmund Freud, who worked from the premise that dreams are wish-fulfilment fantasies filtered by a mental censor determined to disguise their sexual content and resentful amorality. In spite of these endeavors, the available evidence lends itself to a variety of contradictory theories. Representations of dreams in literary works always load them with meaning (there would otherwise be no purpose in reporting them), usually drawing upon some preexistent theory, although **hallucinatory fantasies** take them less seriously than do **visionary fantasies**.

Many earnest writers oppressed by the naturalistic conventions of 19th-century fiction felt obliged to present fantastic materials as dreams in order to conserve their irrational plausibility, and the strategem of "excusing" flights of fantasy by writing them off as dreams persisted well into the 20th century in the works of such writers as **John Masefield**, despite its increasing lameness as a method of narrative closure. Such dream fantasies provided a model for **portal fantasies**, the "world" of dreams being a significant prototype of literary **secondary worlds**. Secondary worlds formulated as dreams include the **allegorical** landscape of **John Bunyan**'s *Pilgrim's Progress,* **Branch Cabell**'s trilogy *Smirt*, *Smith,* and *Smire,* and the **Arabian** fantasy milieu of **L. Ron Hubbard**'s *Slaves of Sleep*. The notion that dreams might be more useful portals if they were subject to practiced mental discipline is promoted by such works as **Joseph Shield Nicholson**'s *A Dreamer of Dreams* and **George du Maurier**'s *Peter Ibbetson*.

Many writers attempt to mine dreams for inspiration and to adapt them into fiction; real or pretend opium dreams are featured in the works of **Samuel Taylor Coleridge**, **Charles Baudelaire**, and Claude Farrère. **Surrealists** tend to be particularly fond of the strategy, sometimes applying it with considerable assiduity—as in Dennis Saurat's *Death and the Dreamer* (1946)—but it was also employed by **Lord Dunsany**. Roderick Townley, whose *Night Errands* (1998) is a nonfictional study of how poets use dreams, demonstrated his own use of them in the novels *The Great Good Thing* (2001) and *Into the Labyrinth* (2002). Literary fantasies based on actual dreams include **Robert Louis Stevenson**'s *Strange Case of Dr Jekyll and Mr Hyde* and **Bram Stoker**'s *Dracula*.

DRUID. A chief priest of pre-Roman pagan religion—and hence a central motif of **Celtic fantasy**. Druids are mentioned in a few Roman documents, including Julius Caesar's *Gallic Wars,* and they figure in collections of Welsh legends made long after their extinction. Very little, however, is reliably known about the rites they practiced or the objects of their worship—thus leaving a wide-open field for such **scholarly fantasists** as **Lewis Spence** and such literary accounts as J. W. Brodie-Innes's *Old as the World* (1909), Maurice Leblanc's *Coffin Island* (tr. 1920), **Neil Gunn**'s *Sun Circle,* and **Margaret J. Anderson**'s *The Druid's Gift*. As Celtic fantasy has flourished and diversified so has druidic imagery, as evidenced by exemplary works by Gunn, **Richad Monaco**, **Fay Sampson**, and **Juliet Marillier**. In Sarah Isidore's

Daughters of Bast series (launched 1999), a girl is guided by a cast from her Druid-ruled homeland to a temple of the Egyptian **goddess** Bast. Douglas Niles's Seven Circles trilogy, comprising *Circle at Center* (2000), *Worldfall* (2001), and *The Goddess Worldweaver* (2003), features otherworldly druids.

DRYASDUST. The pseudonym of an unknown British writer whose first venture into fantasy was *Tales of the Wonder Club* (3 vols., 1899–1900); the first two volumes consist of **humorous fantasies** formulated as **tall stories**. *The Wizard's Mantle* (1902) is a similarly humorous account of a cloak of invisibility. These works were reprinted under the byline "M. Y. Halidom," under which name the author went on to publish several **horror** novels, including the **Shakespearean** fantasy *The Poet's Curse* (1911).

DUALISM. The notion that the universe is a battleground of more or less evenly balanced forces of Good and Evil. Within Christendom, it is often associated with Manicheism, a syncretic doctrine founded in third-century Babylonia that fused Judeo-Christian and Buddhist ideas with the dualist tradition of Zoroastrianism, and was early condemned as a heresy—although the Church's increasing preoccupation with the **Devil** subsequently drew its own doctrines in that direction. Variants of dualism recurred in the doctrines of such sects as the 13th-century Albigensian Cathars, who asserted that the universe of matter is a diabolical creation while **God**'s creation is purely spiritual.

Much fantasy literature adopts a tacitly dualistic position, encouraged by the melodramatic potential contained within the thesis as well as its obvious attraction as a solution to the problem of the persistence of evil in a universe ruled by an allegedly omnipotent, omniscient, omnibenevolent **God**—the discourse of theodicy. **John Milton**'s attempted use of *Paradise Lost* to "justify the works of God to men" prompted many literary exercises in theodicy, giving rise to the opposed tradition of **literary satanism** as well as to earnest extended ***contes philosophiques*** like **James Morrow**'s *Blameless in Abaddon,* and **John Cowper Powys**'s *A Glastonbury Romance*, in which the acceptance of Manicheism had been forehadowed.

The Zoroastrian opposition of Ormazd and Ahriman, symbolizing Light and Darkness—**recycled** in Philip K. Dick's *The Cosmic Puppets* (1957) and transfigured in such works as **Patricia McKillip**'s *Ombria in Shadow* and H. L. McCutchen's *LightLand* (2002)—is echoed in so many other Light/Dark oppositions that the adversaries of **commodified fantasy** are often collectively designated as "Dark Lords." **Sword and sorcery** fiction, influenced by the key example of **Michael Moorcock**, routinely substitutes Order and **Chaos** for Light and Darkness. **Stephen R. Donaldson**'s characterization of Lord Foul associates Darkness/Chaos with disease and Light/Order with health, while **Terry Brooks**'s series begun with *Running with the Demon* relabels the opposing forces the Word and the Void. Although chaos attracts some support from writers who fear the sclerotizing effects of too much order, such straightforward substitutions usually make little difference. **Eve Forward**'s *Villains by Necessity* is exceptional in featuring a **quest** to restore balance to a world in which Light has triumphed, although the hero of John C. Wright's *The Last Guardian of Everness* (2004) decides that the agents of Light are best left to sleep while the humans fight the forces of Dark.

Fundamental oppositions between day and night are confused in mythological terms by the role of the **moon**, and similar confusions attend many other oppositions symbolized by pairs of deities, especially when one is male and the other female, as in **Jenny Jones**'s *Fly by Night*. In spite of the example of sexual differentiation, notions of "cooperative dualism"—which see oppositions in terms of complementary partnership, as in Eastern notions of yin and yang—are relatively rare in Western fantasy literature; such oppositions as Ishtar and Nergal in **A. Merritt**'s *The Ship of Ishtar* and Yahweh and Ashtaroth in **Thomas Burnett Swann**'s **biblical fantasies** tend to polarize, although even these male authors tend to equate virtue with the female pole. Such fruitful balances as those implied by **Michael Cobley**'s Earth Mother and Fathertree or **Victoria Strauss**'s Mind and Hand usually come into focus only when they go awry. Alternating distinctions, like the one drawn by F. W. Nietzsche between "Apollinian" and "Dionysian" cultures—and dramatized by **Eden Phillpotts**—are also uncommon in fantasy literature.

DUANE, DIANE E. (1952–). U.S. writer. The trilogy comprising *The Door into Fire* (1979), *The Door into Shadow* (1984), and *The Door into Sunset* (1992) is an early example of feminized **sword and sorcery**. The series comprising *So You Want to Be a Wizard?* (1983), *Deep Wizardry* (1985), *High Wizardry* (1990), *A Wizard Abroad* (1993), *The Wizard's Dilemma* (2001), *A Wizard Alone* (2002), and *The Wizard's Holiday* (2003) is an inventive **humorous fantasy**, which spun off an **animal**

fantasy couplet comprising *The Book of Night with Moon* (1997) and *On Her Majesty's Wizardry Service* (1998, aka *To Visit the Queen*). *Stealing the Elf-King's Roses* (2002) envisages a set of seven **parallel worlds**, only one of which is a setting for workable **magic**. Duane has contributed to various **shared world** enterprises, sometimes in collaboration with her husband, **Peter Morwood**.

DUCORNET, RIKKI (1943–). U.S. writer and artist who used the byline "Erica Ducornet" on her early **children's fiction**, including a version of **Maeterlinck**'s *The Blue Bird* (1970) and the **wish-fulfillment fantasy** *Shazira Shazam and the Devil* (1970 with Guy Ducornet). Her earliest adult novels, retrospectively represented as an "alchemistic quartet" comprising *The Stain* (1984), *Entering Fire* (1986), *The Fountains of Neptune* (1992), and *The Jade Cabinet* (1993), feature ingenious **chimerical** combinations of **fairy tale** and other traditional motifs with vivid **erotic fantasy** in a variety of historical settings. The relatively moderate *Phosphor in Dreamland* (1995), set on the imaginary Caribbean island of Birdland in the 17th century, describes an artist's infatuation with extravaganza. *The Fan Maker's Inquisition* (2000) describes the Marquis de Sade's creation of an imaginary world. *The Word "Desire"* (1977) was the first of several collections whose contents were sampled in *The Complete Butcher's Tales* (1994), which assembles 60 **fabulations**. *Gazelle* (2003) is an **occult fantasy** about a perfumer in 1950s Cairo. *The Monstrous and the Marvelous* (1999) is nonfiction.

DUMAS, ALEXANDRE (1802–1870). French writer whose serial novels—especially *The Three Musketeers* (1843–44) and *The Count of Monte Cristo* (1844–45)—were foundation stones of popular literature. Although neither is fantasy, they both provided significant exemplars for fantasy literature; explicit tribute is paid to them in **commodified fantasies** by **Stephen Brust** and **Joel Rosenberg** and by Arturo Perez-Reverte's literary **occult fantasy** *The Dumas Club* (1993 in Spanish; tr. 1996).

The Corsican Brothers (1844) is a **psychological fantasy** about the bond between a pair of twins conjoined at birth but surgically separated. *Joseph Balsamo* (1846; aka *Memoirs of a Physician*) began a projected series of novels about a quasi-**messianic** sorcerer whose Parisian manifestations were to include the famous lifestyle fantasist Count Cagliostro, but the magical element was progressively minimized during its serialization, and subsequent items in the series were rationalized. *The Woman with the Velvet Necklace* (1851; tr. 1897) uses the German fantasist **E. T. A. Hoffmann** as the central character of an extended version of an **urban legend** previously fictionalized by **Washington Irving**. Serialization of the **epic** novel he intended to be his masterpiece, a wholeheratedly fantastic account of the **Wandering Jew** entitled *Isaac Laquedem,* was interrupted in 1853 by Napoleon III's censors, and he never resumed work on it. *The Wolf-Leader* (1857) is a folkloristic **Faustian fantasy**. Some of Dumas's fantasies for children were translated in *The Phantom White Hare and Other Stories* (1989).

DU MAURIER, GEORGE (1834–1896). British writer and artist. His novels are **sentimental fantasies** with a strong element of **wish fulfillment**. *Peter Ibbetson* (1892) is an unusually extreme **hallucinatory fantasy**. The quasi-autobiographical *Trilby* (1894) remains famous for the sequence featuring the mesmerist Svengali, who turns the tone-deaf heroine into an opera singer. *The Martian* (1897) also has an element of **delusional fantasy**.

DUNCAN, DAVE (1933–). British-born Canadian writer. *A Rose-Red City* (1987) features a supposedly ideal city with a population drawn from different historical eras. The **portal fantasy** trilogy comprising *The Reluctant Swordsman* (1988), *The Coming of Wisdom* (1988), and *The Destiny of the Sword* (1988) is stereotypical **sword and sorcery**. Two four-volume sequences set in the lavishly populated land of Pandemia—the first comprising *Magic Casement* (1990), *Faery Lands Forlorn* (1991), *Perilous Seas* (1991), and *Emperor and Clown* (1991), and the second *The Cutting Edge* (1992), *Upland Outlaws* (1993), *The Stricken Field* (1992), and *The Living God* (1994)—are more enterprising in their **recycling** of the familiar materials of **commodified fantasy**, the element of wit being conspicuously sharpened.

The Reaver Road (1992) and *The Hunter's Haunt* (1995) have elements of **Arabian fantasy**. *The Cursed* (1995) features a great plague. The Great Game trilogy of **historical fantasies**, comprising *Past Imperative* (1996), *Present Tense* (1996), and *Future Indefinite* (1997), makes elaborate use of **portals** linking **alternative worlds** in the run-up to World War I. Having reverted briefly to stereotyped sword and sorcery in a trilogy bylined "Ken Hood," comprising *Demon Sword* (1995), *Demon Rider* (1997), and *Demon Knight* (1998), Duncan settled into his own distinctive brand of lighthearted **military fantasy** in a series whose main sequence, Tales of the King's Blades, comprises *The Gilded Chain* (1998), *Lord of the Fire Lands* (1999), *Paragon Lost* (2002), *Impossible Odds* (2003), and *The Jaguar Knights* (2004). The spin-off King's Daggers series comprises *Sir Stalwart* (1999), *The Crooked House* (2000), and *Silvercloak* (2001); *Sky of Swords* (2000) is a **prequel**.

DUNSANY, LORD (1878–1957). Irish writer who played a vital role in devising and defining the kinds of **secondary world** that were to become central to modern genre fantasy, contriving a bridge between the writers who influenced him—including contributors to the **Celtic revival** and the **Decadent** movement as well as **George MacDonald** and **William Morris**—and the ***Weird Tales*** writers who were introduced to his method by **H. P. Lovecraft**'s pastiches. The vignettes in *The Gods of Pegana* (1905) invented a mythos for a secondary world that was elaborated in the more ambitious *Time and the Gods* (1906) before flowering into gaudy maturity in the title story of *The Sword of Welleran and Other Stories* (1908), which—together with "The Fortress Unvanquishable Save for Sacnoth"—pioneered the transformation of traditional **chivalric romance** into vigorous **sword and sorcery** fiction.

The stories in *A Dreamer's Tales* (1910) and *The Book of Wonder* (1912) became more languidly self-indulgent in their irony, while those in *Fifty-one Tales* (1915; aka *The Food of Death*) are slight. The stories in *Tales of Wonder* (1916; aka *The Last Book of Wonder*) and *Tales of Three Hemispheres* (1919) occasionally recapture the spirit of the earlier collections. This material is sampled in numerous collections; almost all of it is reprinted in the omnibuses *The Hashish Man and Other Stories* (1996) and *The Complete Pegana* (1998). Dunsany also wrote a number of plays set in similar milieux, beginning with *King Argimenes and the Unknown Warrior* (1910), which was reprinted with others in *Five Plays* (1914). *Plays of Gods and Men* (1917), *If* (1921), *Plays of Near and Far* (1922), and *Alexander and Three Small Plays* (1926) also include significant elements of fantasy.

Dunsany's first novel, *The Chronicles of Rodriguez* (1922; aka *Don Rodriguez of Shadow Valley*), is only marginally fantastic, but *The King of Elfland's Daughter* (1924) is a dramatic extended plea for **re-enchantment** typical in its attitude and method of the postwar period. *The Charwoman's Shadow* (1926) is an impressive **immersive fantasy** and *The Blessing of Pan* (1927) a thoughtful **intrusive fantasy** in the same vein. Few of his subsequent works took fantasy as seriously; most of his relevant short-story collections are collections of **tall stories** narrated by a clubman; the series comprises *The Travel Tales of Mr Joseph Jorkens* (1931), *Mr Jorkens Remembers Africa* (1934), *Jorkens Has a Large Whiskey* (1940), *The Fourth Book of Jorkens* (1948), and *Jorkens Borrows Another Whiskey* (1954). Alcoholic inspiration also figures large in *My Talks with Dean Spanley* (1936), whose soft-focus adventures in **animal fantasy** are echoed in the title story of *The Man Who Ate the Phoenix* (1948) and *The Strange Journeys of Colonel Polders* (1950).

Lin Carter paid tribute to Dunsany's historical centrality by sampling his work extensively in the **Ballantine Adult Fantasy** collections *At the Edge of the World* (1970), *Beyond the Fields We Know* (1972), and *Over the Hills and Far Away* (1974). Everett Bleiler also edited a sampler, *Gods, Men and Ghosts* (1972). *In the Land of Time and Other Fantasy Tales* (2004), ed. S. T. Joshi, includes two previously uncollected items.

DURGIN, DORANNA (1960–). U.S. writer and wildlife **illustrator**. *Dun Lady's Jess* (1994) features a magical horse changed into a woman; *Changespell* (1997) and *Changespell Legacy* (2002) are sequels, and *Barrenlands* (1998) is a **prequel**. The couplet comprising *Touched by Magic* (1996) and *Wolf Justice* (1998) is more action oriented, as are *Wolverine's Daughter* (2000) and *Seer's Blood* (2001). *A Feral Darkness* (2001) is a **portal fantasy** of the **Celtic** type, whose heroine accidentally starts a plague.

– E –

EAGER, EDWARD (1911–1964). U.S. writer whose **children's fantasies**—*Red Head* (1951), *Mouse Manor* (1952), *Half Magic* (1954), *Knight's Castle* (1956), *Magic by the Lake* (1957), *The Time Garden* (1958), *Magic or Not?* (1959), *The Well-Wishers* (1960), and *Seven Day Magic* (1962)—are strongly influenced by **E. Nesbit**'s cautionary **wish-fulfillment fantasies**.

ECO, UMBERTO (1932–). Italian scholar whose best-selling historical novel *The Name of the Rose* (1980; tr. 1983) launched a secondary career that continued in the monumental account of a **secret history,** *Foucault's Pendulum* (1988; tr. 1989), and the baroque, postmodernist **metafiction** *The Island of the Day Before* (1994; tr, 1995). The inventive protagonist of *Baudolino* (2000; tr. 2002) is the creator of Prester John and the elaborator of many other fancies. *See also* TRAVELER'S TALES.

EDDINGS, DAVID (1931–). U.S. writer. The Belgariad **commodified fantasy** series comprising *Pawn of Prophecy* (1982), *Queen of Sorcery* (1982), *Magician's Gambit* (1983), *Castle of Wizardry* (1984), and *Enchanter's End-Game* (1984) became a best seller and was supplemented by a second quintet, the Malloreon, comprising *Guardians of the West* (1987), *King of the Murgos* (1988), *Demon Lord of Karanda* (1988), *Sorceress of Darshiva* (1989), and *The Seeress of Kell* (1991). The Elenium trilogy comprising *The Diamond Throne* (1989), *The Ruby Knight* (1990), and *The Sapphire Rose* (1991) lightened the tone with elements borrowed from **Cervantes** and **Perrault**; it was followed by a carbon copy comprising *Domes of Fire* (1992), *The Shining Ones* (1993), and *The Hidden City* (1994).

Eddings acknowledged the long-term involvement of his wife Leigh in his projects by adding her name to his byline when he returned to the world of the Belgariad in the **prequel** couplet *Belgarath the Sorceror* (1995) and *Polgara the Sorceress* (1997), as well as in the "nonfictional" accessory *The Rivan Codex* (1998). *The Redemption of Althalus* (2000) is a **picaresque fantasy**. The Dreamers quartet was launched with *The Elder Gods* (2003) and *The Treasured One* (2004).

EDDISON, ERIC RUCKER. (1882–1945). British civil servant whose contribution to the post–World War I glut of pleas for **re-enchantment** was the remarkable **heroic fantasy** *The Worm Ouroboros* (1922), in which rival populations inhabiting the planet Mercury go to war in the enthusiastic spirit of the **Nordic** sagas, on which Eddison was an expert (the final scene of his historical novel *Styrbiorn the Strong* [1926] is set in Valhalla, and he translated *Egil's Saga* [1930]). He returned to fantasy of a different kind in a series begun with *Mistress of Mistresses: A Vision of Zimiamvia* (1935), an eccentric **afterlife fantasy** that is broadly **Arcadian**, although feuds are pursued as zestfully as **erotic** adventures. It was followed by *A Fish Dinner in Memison* (1941), which includes a highly unorthodox account of the creation of the Earth, but a third volume, *The Mezentian Gate* (1958), was never completed. Ballantine reprinted all Eddison's fantasies in the wake of **J. R. R. Tolkien**'s *Lord of the Rings,* on the basis of a conspicuous kinship between the author's interests and the extraordinarily self-indulgence of their private world-building.

EDENIC FANTASY. Narrowly defined, Edenic fantasy is a subcategory of **biblical fantasy**, but the notion of a primal garden has a mythical resonance that extends beyond the story of Adam and Eve, linked to the classical notions of **Arcadia**. It lies behind such nostalgic fantasies as W. H. Hudson's *Green Mansions* (1904) and the title novel of Gerald Warre Cornish's *Beneath the Surface and Other Stories* (1918). Edenic **satires** include **Mark Twain**'s *Extracts from Adam's Diary* and **John Erskine**'s *Adam and Eve;* more meditative exercises include **Rémy de Gourmont**'s *Lilith*, **Gerald Bullett**'s *Eden River,* Horace Horsnell's *The Cool of Evening* (1942), Anne Chamberlin's *Leaving Eden* (1999), and Elsie V. Aidinoff's *The Garden* (2004). Fruit from one or other of the trees of knowledge occasionally crops up in **intrusive fantasies**, as in **David Lindsay**'s *The Violet Apple*.

EDGERTON, TERESA (1949–). U.S. writer. The trilogy comprising *Child of Saturn* (1989), *The Moon in Hiding* (1989), and *The Work of the Sun* (1990) is a modified **Celtic fantasy**, as is the related one comprising *The Castle of the Silver Wheel* (1993), *The Grail and the Ring* (1995), and *The Moon and the Thorn* (1995). The couplet comprising *Goblin Moon* (1991) and *The Gnome's Engine* (1991) employs a more idiosyncratic **alternative historical** setting, as does *The Queen's Necklace* (2001).

EDGHILL, ROSEMARY (1956–). U.S. writer in various genres who published her early work as "eluki bes shahar." Her Bast series (1994–96) of mysteries features a Wiccan detective; her wholehearted fantasies include the Twelve Treasures series comprising *The Sword of Maiden's Tears* (1994), *The Cup of Morning Shadows* (1995), and *The Cloak of Night and Daggers* (1997); the **timeslip** romance *Met by Moonlight* (1998); and the **satire** *The Warslayer* (2002), in which a TV actress is recruited by otherworldly **wizards** in search of a hero. The Childeric the Shatterer series, begun with *Vengeance of Masks* (2003), is also tongue in cheek. Her short fiction is sampled in *Paying the Piper at the Gates of Dawn* (2003). She has worked on **shared world** enterprises with **Andre Norton**, **Marion Zimmer Bradley**, and **Mercedes Lackey**.

EDWARDS, GRAHAM (1965–). British writer. The trilogy comprising *Dragoncharm* (1995), *Dragonstorm* (1996), and *Dragonsflame* (1997) is **commodified dragon** fantasy. The Stone trilogy, comprising *Stone & Sky* (1999), *Stone & Sea* (2000), and *Stone & Sun* (2001), features a vast enclosure where history is "stored," and from which mythical creatures emerge through cracks in its vertical wall; a Victorian naturalist who goes through such a crack eventually gains access to the **multiverse**.

ELBOZ, STEPHEN (1956–). British writer in various genres. *The House of Rats* (1991) is a **dark fantasy** in which a well-regulated house goes to pot when its master vanishes; the **Gothic** fantasy *The Byzantium Bazaar* (1996) is similarly replete with images of decay. The heroine of *The Games-Board Map* (1993) is trapped in a secondary world compounded out of various games. *Ghostlands* (1996) features a vicar's wife who is a **witch**. In *Temmi and the Flying Bears* (1998), a baby bear with a broken wing is rescued from a witch-queen's castle; *Temmi and the Frost Dragon* (2002) is a sequel. In the **historical fantasy** series comprising *A Handful of Magic* (2000), *A Land without Magic* (2001), *A Wild Kind of Magic* (2001), and *An Ocean of Magic* (2003), English magic is threatened by the advancement of 19th-century science.

ELF. A term that entered English from Saxon and **Nordic** sources, in which it signified a kind of dwarf. It then merged with Celtic notions of mischievous "little people," such as brownies and leprechauns. In Anglo-Norman writings, Saxon/Celtic elves were further merged with French images of *fées* (**fairies**). By the time literary works like **Johann Ludwig Tieck**'s *The Elves,* **Charles Nodier**'s *Trilby,* and **James Hogg**'s *The Brownie of Bodsbeck* were produced, these various terms were hardly distinguishable, although subsequent folklorists like **Thomas Keightley** and **K. M. Briggs** made heroic efforts to do so. "Elfland" became a popular literary synonym for **Faerie** in a British context, its popularity boosted by **W. B. Yeats**'s reference to "the Horns of Elfland" and **Lord Dunsany**'s *The King of Elfland's Daughter*. Such re-ennobling exercises prepared the way for **J. R. R. Tolkien** to populate his works with a superior race of tall, aristicratic, and slightly ethereal elves who became prototypical of many similar races in genre fantasy and role-playing **games**. Not all American elves fit this stereotype; alternative images are developed in **Jane Louise Curry**'s accounts of relocated Welsh elves and in such works as Jan Carr's *The Elf of Union Square* (2004).

ELIADE, MIRCEA (1907–1986). Rumanian scholar long resident in the United States, a prolific writer on religion, mythology, and **occult** science. These interests inform and permeate his ***contes philosophiques*** and **metaphysical fantasies**, some of which are translated in *Two Tales* *of the Occult* (1940; tr. 1970; aka *Two Strange Tales*), *Fantastic Tales* (1948–52; tr. 1969), *Tales of the Sacred and the Supernatural* (1962–76; tr. 1981), and *Youth without Youth and Other Novellas* (1976–80; tr. 1988). They add marginal substance to the novels *The Forbidden Forest* (1955; tr. 1978) and *The Old Man and the Bureaucrats* (1968; tr. 1979). Much of his work in this vein remains untranslated, but he is a figure of central importance in the evolution of 20th-century literary fantasy, comparable to **Herman Hesse** and **Italo Calvino.**

ELLIOTT, KATE (1958–). Name adopted by U.S. writer Alis A. Rasmussen, who wrote the **portal fantasy** *The Labyrinth Gate* (1988) and the feminized **planetary romance** trilogy comprising *A Passage of Stars, Revolution's Shore,* and *The Price of Ransom* (all 1990) under her own name. She achieved greater success with the **commodified** Crown of Stars series, comprising *King's Dragon* (1997), *Prince of Dogs* (1998), *The Burning Stone* (1999), *Child of Flame* (2000), and *The Gathering Storm* (2002), in which seemingly extinct **elves** play a significant posthumous role in the fortunes of a **secondary world**.

ELLISON, HARLAN (1934–). U.S. short-story writer in various genres (refer to *HDSFL* and *HDHL*). Most of the stories in his earlier collections, including *Ellison Wonderland* (1962), *Paingod and Other Delusions* (1967), and *I Have No Mouth and I Must Scream* (1967), employ the trappings of **sf**, but those in *Deathbird Stories: A Pantheon of Modern Gods* (1975), *Strange Wine* (1978), and *Shatterday* (1980) mostly discard that apparatus in favor of straightforward **fabulation**. His work varies from poignant ***contes cruels*** like "Pretty Maggy Moneyeyes" (1967) through intense **psychological fantasies** like "Shatterday" (1975) to **sentimental fantasies** like "One Life, Furnished in Early Poverty" (1970) and "Paladin of the Lost Hour" (1985). *The Essential Ellison* (1987) is a capacious sampler.

ELROD, P. N. (?–). U.S. writer who pioneered **hybrid/vampire detective** fiction in the Vampire Files series, comprising *Bloodlist* (1990), *Lifeblood* (1990), *Bloodcircle* (1990), *Art in the Blood* (1991), *Fire in the Blood* (1991), *Blood on the Water* (1992), *A Chill in the Blood* (1998), *The Dark Sleep* (1999), *Lady Crymsyn* (2000), and *Cold Streets* (2003). The Strahd series of historical vampire fantasies comprises *The Memoirs of a Vampire* (1993) and *The War against Azalin* (1998). The Barrett series, comprising *Red Death* (1993), *Death and the Maiden* (1994), *Death Masque* (1995), and *Dance of Death* (1996), is similar to the Vampire Files. The Ethical Vampires series, written in collaboration with Nigel Bennett and comprising *Keeper of the King* (1996), *His Father's Son* (2001), and *Siege Perilous* (2004), has an **Arthurian/grail/quest**. *Quincey Morris, Vampire* (2001) is a sequel to **Bram Stoker**'s *Dracula*. In *The Adventures of Myhr* (2003), a catman and a **wizard** wander the **multiverse**.

EMERSON, RU (1944–). U.S. writer. *The Princess of Flames* (1986) and the trilogy comprising *To the Haunted Mountains* (1987), *In the Caves of Exile* (1988), and *On the Seas of Destiny* (1989) are tales of dispossession and recovery, the first leavened with Tarot fantasy and the second employing a cat as narrator. *Spellbound* (1990) is a **historical fantasy** subversively **transfiguring** classic fairy tales. The Night Threads series, comprising *The Calling of the Three* (1990), *The Two in Hiding* (1991), *One Land, One Duke* (1992), *The Craft of Light* (1993), *The Art of the Sword* (1994), and *the Sword of Power* (1996), is a **portal fantasy** featuring an unusual variety of **magic**. She wrote *The Sword and the Lion* (1993), a historical fantasy about the displacement of **goddess** worship by triumphant patriarchy, as "Roberta Cray."

ENCHANTMENT. A term derived from the Old French *enchanter,* a version of the Latin *incantare* (literally "sing against"), meaning to assault, delude, or render captive by means of magic. It is closely related to the Old French *faerie,* in which the actors of enchantment are elusive and perhaps imaginary supernatural beings. The term is frequently used in the critical literature to describe the effect of fairy tales on the reader, as in Bruno Bettelheim's study of *The Uses of Enchantment: The Meaning and Importance of Fairy Tales*. In **J. R. R. Tolkien**'s seminal essay "On Fairy-stories," enchantment is the psychological process that induces the secondary belief necessary to the sustenance of **secondary worlds**. Apologists for fantasy often argue that a measure of this kind of enchantment is necessary to mental health and routinely prescribe **re-enchantment** as an antidote to the dispiriting effects of disenchantment. The seductive aspect of enchantment is conserved in much **erotic fantasy**, although its traditional association with the luring away of children is preserved in tales ranging from **Hans Christian Andersen**'s "The Snow Queen" to Kate Thompson's *The Beguilers* (2001). *See also* FAIRY.

ENDE, MICHAEL (1929–1995). German writer whose father was the **surrealist** painter Edgar Ende. His first **children's fantasy** was translated as *Jim Button and Luke the Engine Driver* (1960; tr. 1963), but *Momo* (1973; tr. 1974, initially as *The Grey Gentlemen*) is a very different and far more sophisticated **allegory** about a time bank, counting the **existential** cost of maturation. The best-selling *The Neverending Story* (1979; tr. 1981) sets out a detailed exemplary argument for the necessity of **enchantment** while remaining conscious of its hazards. *Mirror in the Mirror* (1984; tr. 1986), based on a sequence of lithographs by his father, is a surreal **classical fantasy**. In *Ophelia's Shadow Theater* (1988; tr. 1989), a prompter in a theater collects shadows and teaches them to perform. Ende returned to **metafictional** children's fantasy of a more relaxed kind in *The Night of Wishes; or, The Satanarchaeolidealcohellish Notion Potion* (1989; tr. 1992), in which Beelzebub and Tyrannia Vampirella concoct a punch that might allow them to reach their quota of evil by the New Year's Eve deadline.

EPIC FANTASY. An epic is a long narrative poem, usually based in **mythology** and featuring legendary **heroes**. Epics were the first works of fantasy literature; even such early examples as the Sumerian epic of Gilgamesh, **Homer**'s *Iliad* and *Odyssey,* and the Hindu *Ramayana* are unmistakably literary constructions, albeit mingled with pseudohistorical material. Wholly artificial constructions like **Ariosto**'s *Orlando Furioso* and **Edmund Spenser**'s *Faerie Queene* were produced long before Elias Lonnrot synthesized the *Kalevala* (1835) as the Finnish national epic and Henry Wadsworth Longfellow borrowed its rhythmic method to fake the Native American epic *Hiawatha* (1855). The tradition of epic poetry, further sustained by Christian fantasists like **John Milton** and **Romantic** poets like **Percy Shelley**, continued to produce fantasies in abundance in the 19th and 20th centuries, including **Andrew Lang**'s *Helen of Troy,* **Gerhart Hauptmann**'s *Till Eulenspiegel,* **John Cowper Powys**'s *Lucifer,* **John Gardner**'s *Jason and Medeia,* and Robert E. Kauffmann's *The Mask of Ollock* (2002).

Many epic poems are key **taproot texts** of modern fantasy, but there is a particular link between the epic tradition and **commodified fantasy**, in that **J. R. R. Tolkien**'s lifelong dalliance in Middle-earth was conceived as an attempt to synthesize the epic that Old (i.e., pre–Norman Conquest) England never had; insofar as *The Lord of the Rings* is spun off from *The Silmarillion,* the primary model of commodified fantasy retains and exemplifies many of the pretensions as well as the narrative formula of the epic. This makes the notion of "epic fantasy" more than a mere advertising slogan, although its frequent use as such has reduced its critical utility somewhat. Epic fantasies are multivolume works—usually insistent **immersive fantasies**, although some retain **portal fantasy** frames—that routinely extend far beyond their initial trilogies; they gradually build up detailed historical and geographical images of **secondary worlds**, within which elaborate hero myths are constructed.

Although most epic fantasies are strictly commodified, the format readily lends itself to greater ambition, as seen in the works of such practitioners as **Guy Gavriel Kay**, **Tad Williams**, **George R. R. Martin**, **Steven Erikson**, and Terry McGarry's Eiden Myr series, begun with *Illumination* (2001) and *The Binder's Road* (2003). From the viewpoint of most readers, it provides the core of the modern genre, constituted by the works of **Terry Brooks**, **Stephen R. Donaldson**, **Katherine Kurtz**, **David Eddings**, **Robert Jordan**, **Robin Hobb**, **Terry Goodkind**, and **Kate Elliott**. The success of these works prompted commercial publishers to commission hundreds more in the late 1990s, resulting in a glut. Examples include Laura Resnick's trilogy, comprising *In Legend Born* (1998), *The White Dragon* (2003), and *The Destroyer Goddess* (2004); Marcus Herniman's Arrandin trilogy, comprising *The Siege of Arrandin* (1999), *The Treason of Dortrean* (2001), and *The Fall of Lautun* (2003); John Marco's Tyrants and Kings trilogy, comprising *The Jackal of Nar* (1999), *The Grand Design* (2000), and *The Saints of the Sword* (2001); Ricardo Pinto's Stone Dance of the Chameleon couplet, comprising *The Chosen* (1999) and *The Standing Dead* (2002); and R. Scott Bakker's Prince of Nothing trilogy, launched by *The Darkness That Comes Before* (2003).

ERCKMANN-CHATRIAN. The collaborative signature adopted by Émile Erckmann (1822–99) and Alexandre Chatrian (1826–90), French-speaking natives of Alsace. Much of their fiction reflects the marginal status of their homeland, especially the partly recycled **folktales** and offbeat **horror** stories (refer to *HDHL*) first collected as *Contes fantastiques* (1860) and *Contes du bord du Rhin* (1862). After the successful theatrical production in 1867 of a melodrama of supernatural revenge known in English as *The Polish Jew* or (in Henry Irving's adaptation) *The Bells,* they restricted themselves to historical fiction. The bibliography of Erckmann-Chatrian's fantasies is inordinately complex, but most can be found in a series of translations issued by Ward Lock in the 1870s, including *Popular Tales and Romances* (1872), *Confessions of a Clarinet Player* (1874), *The Man-Wolf and Other Stories* (1876), *The Wild Huntsman and Other Stories* (1877),

Stories of the Rhine (1877), and *The Polish Jew and Other Stories* (1880). An 1873 novelization of *The Bells* bears their byline but is not by them. *The Best Tales of Terror of Erckmann-Chatrian* (1981), ed. Hugh Lamb, is a useful sampler.

ERICKSON, STEVE (1950–). U.S. writer whose **postmodern/metafictions** employ fantastic devices to distort landscapes and time schemes in the attempt to find a mythical essence within the perceived realities of the 20th-century United States. *Days between Stations* (1985), *Rubicon Beach* (1986), *Tours of the Black Clock* (1989), *Arc d'X* (1993), *Amnesiascope* (1996), *American Nomad* (1997), and *The Sea Came In at Midnight* (1999) feature **alternative histories** stocked with exotic characters and images.

ERIKSON, STEVEN (1959–). Canadian writer born Steven Rune Lundin, under which name he published his first book in 1991. His **epic fantasy** series The Malazan Book of the Fallen, begun with *Gardens of the Moon* (1999), *Deadhouse Gates* (2000), *Memories of Ice* (2001), *House of Chains* (2002), and *Midnight Tides* (2004), offers an unusually detailed account of its **secondary world**. *Blood Follows* (2002) is a linked novella. *The Healthy Dead* (2004) and *Fishin' with Grandma Matchie* (2004) are offbeat **dark fantasies**.

EROTIC FANTASY. In common parlance, erotic fantasies are **daydreams** constructed as part and parcel of sexual experience, whose **commodified** literary extensions form the subgenre of pornography. However exaggerated they may be, the vast majority are necessarily naturalistic; ideals of sexual attractiveness do, however, test the boundaries of actuality, with the result that the most perfect partners imaginable tend to become supernaturalized in various ways. For the extreme Romantic—**Théophile Gautier** is a cardinal example—no merely human partner could ever live up to the standard set by daydream ambition. Furthermore, sexual passion is routinely conceived and represented as if it were a kind of supernatural force, irresistible in its most powerful manifestations and in its more durable versions, providing a kind of magical glue binding couples together; "love potions" are a chief stock in trade of **witches**. It is arguable that the idea of love promoted and celebrated by modern genre romance is sufficiently supernaturalized to make the entire genre's status **ambiguous**, if not **hybrid**—in which case its recent extension into **paranormal romance** is readily understandable.

For these reasons, there is a substantial sector of fantasy literature that consists of projections of the erotic impulse; this strain extends across several subgenres and often stretches their limits. Sexual attraction is a powerful force generating literary **timeslips** and summoning the **ghosts** of **sentimental fantasy**, as well as motivating **quests** (a cliché mercilessly satirized in **Cervantes**'s definitive **delusional fantasy** *Don Quixote*). It is hardly surprising, therefore, that Aphrodite—the Greek goddess of love and beauty, called Venus by the Romans—is one of the two GrecoRoman deities whose importance extends far beyond **classical fantasy**, the other being **Pan**, who functions to some extent as a male equivalent.

Aphrodite's symbolic presence dominates such ***contes philosophiques*** as **Pierre Louÿs**'s *Aphrodite,* **John Erskine**'s *Venus the Lonely Goddess,* **George S. Viereck**'s *Gloria,* and Daniel Evan Weiss's *Honk If You Love Aphrodite* (1999). Her co-option into **chivalric romance**, via the legend of the German knight Tannhaüser, inspired such works as **Ludwig Tieck**'s "The Faithful Eckhart," **Max Adeler**'s "Mr Skinner's Night in the Underworld," **Aubrey Beardsley**'s *Under the Hill,* and **Vernon Lee**'s "The Gods and Ritter Tanhuser" (1913). A legend of similar provenance reported in Richard Burton's *Anatomy of Melancholy* (1621), in which a ring is unwisely placed on the finger of her statue, has been recycled in Prosper Mérimée's "The Venus of Ille" (1837), **F. Anstey**'s *The Tinted Venus,* and **Anthony Burgess**'s *The Eve of St. Venus*. Although Aphrodite's son and accomplice Eros, called Cupid or Amor by the Romans, was the source of the term "erotic," he is less widely reflected in literature than in art, where he is often represented as a cherubic bowman firing arrows of desire.

The fascination Aphrodite holds for male authors is further reflected in the immense significance in Romantic literature of the **femme fatale**, whose powers of sexual attraction are so great that her pursuers become utterly careless of their own well-being, often perishing as a result—a notion reflected in classical legends of sirens, blood-drinking lamias, and sorceresses like Circe. The archetypal femmes fatales of Judeo-**Christian** myth and legend are Lilith—Adam's first wife, allegedly expelled from **Eden** for refusing to submit to his mastery—and Salome, the daughter of Herodias who pleased Herod with her dancing and claimed the head of John the Baptist as her reward. An extravagant analysis of the significance of femmes fatales in the context of **romanticism** can be found in Mario Praz's *The Romantic Agony* (1933), which has chapters devoted to "The Beauty of the Medusa" and "La Belle Dame sans Merci." Gautier's "Clarimonde" (1836) and "One of Cleopatra's Nights" (1838) take it for granted that the intensity of the erotic experience provided by a femme fatale would compensate for its brevity; the luxurious exoticism of Gautier's erotic fantasies was fervently echoed in the work of **Gérard de Nerval** but was treated more cynically by **Charles Baudelaire** and the **decadent** fantasists who came after him, as in Catulle Mendès's series tr. as *Lila and Colette and the Isles of Love* (1885; tr. 1931).

The femmes fatales of the decadent imagination tend to be more deceptive than their Romantic forebears, as well as more cruel; key French examples include Barbey d'Aurevilly's *Les Diaboliques* (1874), Villiers de l'Isle Adam's *L'Ève Future,* and Octave Mirbeau's *Torture Garden* (1899). Their extreme equivalents in English literature tend to be sinister figures of menace, as in **Matthew Gregory Lewis**'s *The Monk*, J. Sheridan le Fanu's "Carmilla" (1872), **Arthur Machen**'s "The Great God Pan," and **Arthur Conan Doyle**'s *The Parasite;* sincere masochistic appreciation can, however, be found in such poems as **John Keats**'s "La Belle Dame sans Merci" and Algernon Swinburne's "Dolores" and "Faustine" (both 1866), as well as Vernon Lee's lubricious "Amour Dure," **Rider Haggard**'s awestricken *She,* and Max Beerbohm's sarcastic *Zuleika Dobson* (1911). Such American examples as **Edgar Allan Poe**'s "Morella" and "Ligeia," **Nathaniel Hawthorne**'s "Rappaccini's Daughter," and Fitz-James O'Brien's "The Diamond Lens" (1858) are mostly anemic, although Robert W. Chambers, in "The Demoiselle d'Ys" (1896), and **A. Merritt**, in *Dwellers in the Mirage,* tried to breathe new life into Gautieresque romanticism. The ***Weird Tales*** writers **C. L. Moore** and **Clark Ashton Smith** tried to sustain it, even while satirists like **James Branch Cabell** and **John Erskine** were cultivating a determinedly sceptical kind of sophistication that became the dominant voice of 20th-century erotic fantasy.

The most obvious male counterpart of the femme fatale is Don Juan, whose legend was first recorded in the early 17th century and was dramatized by Molière in 1665 before Mozart turned it into the opera *Don Giovanni* (1787). The account of the rake being dragged off to hell by an outraged statue is, however, merely the anxious underside of male fantasy. The equivalent female fantasy was very rarely found in supernaturalized versions in the 19th century, although Emily Brontë's Heathcliff came close. For most of the 20th century, the prevalent assumption of genre romance was that the only explicit supernaturalization required in female erotic fantasy involved building bridges to the lost world of Romance, especially to figures based on the popular image of **Lord Byron**. Such figures were, however, largely confined by female writers to the genre of historical fiction until the advent of paranormal romance.

Notable modern attempts to put more fantasy into erotic fantasy, in various ways, include Hélène Cixous's *The Third Body* (1970; tr. 1999), Seamus Cullen's *Astra and Flondrix* (1976), **Angela Carter**'s *The Infernal Desire Machines of Dr. Hoffmann,* **Storm Constantine**'s *Hermetech,* Francisco Rebolledo's *Rasero* (1993; tr. 1995), Nicholson Baker's *The Fermata* (1994), Ann Arensberg's *Incubus* (1999), **Francesca Lia Block**'s *Nymph,* Christopher Moore's *The Lust Lizard of Melancholy Cove* (1999), **Jacqueline Carey**'s *Kushiel's Dart,* **Geoff Ryman**'s *Lust,* and Jennifer Stevenson's *Trash Sex Magic* (2004).

ERSKINE, BARBARA (1944–). Byline used by British writer Barbara Hope-Lewis, a significant pioneer of **paranormal romance**. *Lady of Hay* (1986), *Kingdom of Shadows* (1988), *Midnight Is a Lonely Place* (1994), *House of Echoes* (1996), and *On the Edge of Darkness* (1998) all feature **timeslips** or other transtemporal exchanges of passionate experience, as do some of the stories in *Encounters* (1990) and *Distant Voices* (1996). *Child of the Phoenix* (1992) is a **historical fantasy**. *Whispers in the Sand* (2000) describes an Egyptian journey attended by a ghostly ancestor; two sequel novellas are included with other materials in *Sands of Time* (2003). *Hiding from the Light* (2002) also features subtler echoes of the past.

ERSKINE, JOHN (1879–1951). U.S. writer whose early essay "Magic and Wonder in Literature" was reprinted in *The Moral Obligation to Be Intelligent and Other Essays* (1915). Most of his works **recycle** myths and legends—usually purged of their supernatural components—for **satirical** purposes. *The Private Life of Helen of Troy* (1925) employs **classical** materials, *Galahad* (1926) those of **chivalric romance**. The **Edenic fantasy** *Adam and Eve* (1927) contrasts Lilith and Eve as ideals of femininity, the pusillanimity of Adam's choice echoing in the **Odyssean fantasy** *Penelope's Man* (1927). The stories in *Cinderella's Daughter and Other Sequels and Consequences* (1930) **transfigure** the classic **fairy tales**. *Uncle Sam* (1930) deals with myths of a more modern stripe, while *Solomon, my Son!* (1935) is more wide ranging. *Venus, the Lonely Goddess* (1949) is atypically **sentimental**.

ESCAPISM. Escape is one of the three fundamental functions of fantasy identified by **J. R. R. Tolkien**'s essay "On Fairy-stories," which defends the notion of escapism against the pejorative connotations frequently attached to it. Tolkien denies that literary escapism is a kind of desertion reflective of cowardice or laziness, although he refrains from using the analogy of a holiday taken for purposes of refreshment. Many critics who condemn fantasy as escapist fare do not, in any case, think that a temporary escape from the burdens of social responsibility is an inherently bad thing; their argument is that there are much healthier **secondary worlds** to escape to than are found in **fairy tales** or genre fantasies.

Countering the latter argument requires a more robust apologetic strategy, like the one employed by Edmund Burke's *A Philosophical Enquiry into the Origin of Our Ideas of the Sublime and Beautiful* (1757), which emphasizes the contribution ambitious fantasy might make to the escaper's mental flexibility and imaginative reach. Burke's argument seems irrelevant to the stereotyped formulas of **fairy tales** and **commodified fantasies**, whose familiarity does not breed contempt and more readily invites consideration as affirmative ritual. Tolkien's notion of **eucatastrophe** and Bruno Bettelheim's analysis of *The Uses of Enchantment,* both of which stress repetitive affirmation rather than imaginative flexibility, tacitly surrender this point.

Literary fantasies couched as celebrations or critiques of escapism include **Joseph Shield Nicholson**'s *A Dreamer of Dreams,* **George du Maurier**'s *Peter Ibbetson,* **Arthur Machen**'s *The Hill of Dreams,* **Vernon Knowles**'s *The Ladder,* Maude Meagher's *Fantastic Traveller* (1931), **James Thurber**'s "The Secret Life of Walter Mitty," **Jonathan Carroll**'s *Bones of the Moon,* and Christopher Fowler's *Calabash* (2000). The most outspoken apologies for escapism tend to focus on protagonists in extreme circumstances, such as Jack London's strait-jacketed prisoner in *The Star Rover* (1915) or Majgull Axelsson's paraplegic girl in *April Witch* (1997; tr. 2002). James Hilton's *Lost Horizon* (1933) made the Tibetan lamasery of Shangri-La—a precious quasi-**Arcadian** refuge from a sick world—a potent symbol of escape.

EUCATASTROPHE. A term coined by **J. R. R. Tolkien** in his seminal essay "On Fairy-stories," where it is opposed to Tragedy in an argument asserting that the uplifting effect of **fairy tales** is a vital aspect of their social and psychological function. It refers to the final "turn" of a story that gives rise to "a piercing glimpse of joy, and heart's desire, that for a moment passes outside the frame, rends indeed the very web of story."

The term has become a significant element of the genre's critical discourse in spite of its rather awkward coinage ("good disaster" is suspiciously oxymoronic) and the fact that it adds little to the commonplace notion of a "happy ending."

EXISTENTIALIST FANTASY. The philosophical tradition of existentialism, founded by Søren Kierkegaard and carried forward by Martin Heidegger and Jean-Paul Sartre, attempts to define and evaluate the fundamental conditions of human identity and agency. The project arguably began in literary works, and it has remained closely associated with literary exemplification, particularly with endeavors in **psychological fantasy** that tend toward ***contes philosophiques***.

Heidegger's assertion that the most fundamental aspect of the human condition is *angst* resulting from awareness of death can easily be extrapolated into a partial explanation of some of the classic themes of fantasy, including **wish-fulfillment fantasies** of **immortality** and various forms of **afterlife**, the personalization of **Death**, and the compensatory construction of **secondary worlds**. John Clute's suggestion that **bondage** is central to the development of fantasy literature argues that testing the limits and exploring the perversities of "free will" has always been an important spur to literary fantasization and that the most important function of **children's fantasy** may be the construction of parables of maturation mapping the route from childhood to adulthood in terms of the acquisition of personal responsibility and Sartrean "authenticity." Notable existentialist fantasies include **Franz Kafka**'s *Metamorphosis,* **Herman Hesse**'s *Steppenwolf,* and **Richard Grant**'s *Kaspian Lost*.

Some **animal fantasies** are thought experiments in exotic existentialism, and many fantasies dealing with **ghosts**, **vampires**, and other traditional paraphernalia of **horror** fiction are experiments of a similar kind. **Raymond Briggs**'s parodic *Fungus the Bogeyman* takes this kind of "adversarial existentialism" to a ludicrous extreme.

– F –

FABLE. A short prose fiction formulated to express and exemplify a useful truth or moral precept, often employing animals as representations of human character traits. The term is closely related to the French *fabliau,* which usually relates to items of vulgar and cynical narrative verse. The fables credited to Aesop are among the earliest recorded prose fantasies, although they were first written down—and perhaps composed—much later than the sixth century BC in which Aesop supposedly lived. Other early examples include those attributed to Pilpay, first recorded in Sanskrit. Translation into Arabic in the eighth century assisted the furtherance of a native tradition; they were first translated into English in 1570. The 17th-century French writer Jean de la Fontaine produced new versions of Aesop's and Pilpay's fables and also composed many others, mostly in verse, in collections published between 1668 and 1694. His example was followed by many 18th-century writers, including the Britons John Gay and Robert Dodsley. The subgenre was introduced into **children's** literature at an early stage, the first British collection thus adapted being William Godwin's *Fables Ancient and Modern* (1805). The fable attracted academic study and criticism from folklorists, in such works as Thomas Newbigging's *Fables and Fabulists, Ancient and Modern* (1895). Notable 20th-century fabulists include **T. F. Powys**, **Italo Calvino**, **James Thurber**, and Jacquetta Hawkes in *Fables* (1953).

FABULATION. In common parlance, any fanciful composition is describable as a fabulation, but in the critical lexicon the term's use usually follows the meaning attached to it by Robert Scholes in *The Fabulators* (1967; revised as *Fabulation and Metafiction,* 1979). Scholes defines it as "ethically constrained fantasy" or "didactic romance," distinguishing it from "pure romance" by virtue of its acute consciousness of its own artifice. The distinction alleviates the need for the kind of "willing suspension of disbelief" suggested by **Samuel Taylor Coleridge**; readers of fabulations never commit any kind of belief to the narratives they read, reveling instead in their manifest artificiality.

As Scholes observed, the narrative techniques of fabulation made a spectacular comeback in late 20th-century American literature, which seemed remarkable partly because early 20th-century Anglo-American literature had purged itself of fabulation to a far greater extent than most European traditions (or their Latin American extensions), thus giving such work an appearance of novelty. Theorists hastened to explain the renaissance of American fabulation in terms of a **postmodern** phase in which fiction could no longer legitimately pretend to be "about" the world and must therefore be concerned with the **metafictional** processes of its own making.

Although many critics would condemn **commodified fantasy** in its entirety to the realms of "pure romance," thus reserving "fabulation" to work produced by more prestigious literateurs, there was always a strong element of fabulation in the kinds of fantasy produced for pulp magazines and for the consumption of **children**. It is arguable that all fantasy fiction is fabulation and that what delineates fantasy fiction from myth making, legend mongering, allegedly divine revelation, and other forms of constructive delusion is precisely the shared awareness that it *is* fantasy. Notable practitioners of fabulation include **Slavomir Mrozek**, **John Barth**, **Donald Barthelme**, **R. A. Lafferty**, **Angela Carter**, **Rikki Ducornet**, **Harlan Ellison**, **Kelly Link**, **Alasdair Gray**, and **Steven Millhauser**. *Conjunctions 39: The New Wave Fabulists* (2002), a special issue of the journal guest-edited by Peter Straub, is a showcase **anthology**.

FAERIE. An Old French term signifying **enchantment** by supernatural beings living more or less invisibly in close proximity with humankind—and, by extension, the **parallel world** that those beings inhabit. The beings themselves thus became the faery or **fairy** folk, whose nature and variety depended on idiosyncratic local tradition. In modern fantasy fiction, Faerie is usually used to refer to the world of Faerie, the primary model for all **secondary worlds**; writers for adults generally prefer the name to the rather childish "Fairyland," although "Elfland" retains sufficient gravitas to maintain rivalry. The vagueness of Faerie's boundaries—often involving its separation by portals—reflects the common assumption that a **magic** spell is required to facilitate its perception and that once it has been perceived another will be required to restore perception of the **primary world**, often at some cost in terms of time.

Although Faerie is the backcloth of all **fairy tales**, it has a special significance in literary accounts that suggest that it is moving further away or that its connections with the primary world are being severed—the cardinal example of **thinning**. The notion that Britain's Faerie had suffered such a severance—evoked by **Walter Besant** in "Titania's Farewell" and **Andrew Lang** in *That Very Mab*—paved the way for heroic expeditions thereto in stories pleading for **re-enchantment** after World War I, including **Gerald Bullett**'s *Mr Godly Beside Himself*, **Lord Dunsany**'s *The King of Elfland's Daughter*, and **Hope Mirrlees**'s *Lud-in-the-Mist*. The latter two conserve a sense of Faerie as an **Arcadian** realm, and it is often employed as such. Subsequent accounts of

Faerie often maintain this sense of exilic severance, whose counterpart is found in numerous American fantasies in which an immigrant Faerie seems ill fitted to its new location, as in **Raymond E. Feist**'s *Faerie Tale,* **Rick Cook**'s *Mall Purchase Night,* and John M. Ford's *The Last Hot Time* (2000). European versions like that in **Sylvia Townsend Warner**'s *The Kingdoms of Elfin* seem more comfortably situated even when they have undergone sweeping changes or belong to the darker end of the spectrum, like the version in **Garry Kilworth**'s *The Knights of Liöfwende*.

FAIRY. An anglicization of the French **faerie**, which absorbed and largely displaced the Anglo-Saxon **elf** in English parlance after the Norman conquest. The term first became common in the 13th century, although folktales involving such beings had already been recorded by chroniclers such as Walter Map, Giraldus Cambrensis, and Gervase of Tilbury. The Celtic mythology of the mound-dwelling Sidhe was readily accommodated within an already confused framework that included a host of ill-diferentiated entities; labels that survived alongside fairy and elf itself include **goblin**, pixie, brownie, and gnome, causing considerable problems for such taxonomically inclined folklorists as **Thomas Keightley**.

Fairies imported into English literature in the Elizabethan era, most notably by **Edmund Spenser**'s *Faerie Queene* and **William Shakespeare**'s *A Midsummer Night's Dream,* made much of the notion of a fairy court, which had been foreshadowed by the representation of the fairy king Oberon in the **chivalric romance** *Huon of Bordeaux* (c1220). Such courts became part of the fashionable apparatus of 18th-century fairy literature in France in the wake of **Madame d'Aulnoy**'s satires. Antoine Galland's translations of Arabian folklore encouraged the conflation of European fairies and Middle Eastern peris; the resultant **hybrid** tradition extended into the 19th century in the works of **Charles Nodier**, the founding father of French Romanticism, by which time the German Romantic movement had revived a powerful interest in Teutonic fairy mythology among such writers as J. K. Musaeus and **Ludwig Tieck**.

Fairies returned in force to British Romantic poetry in such works as Percy Shelley's "Queen Mab" and then became a popular subject for 19th-century British painters, partly because nude fairies were more acceptable to the censorious Victorian consciousness than nude women—a loophole exploited by theatrical "fairy pageants" that featured elaborate tableaux of nude female children. Artists like Richard Dadd, however, found a sinister side of fairy life, reflected in such poems as Christina Rossetti's **erotic fantasy** "Goblin Market" and such satires as John Hunter Duvar's *Annals of the Court of Oberon* (1895). A more innocent and **sentimental** view was preserved in children's fiction, notably in Jean Ingelow's landmark text *Mopsa the Fairy* (1869), in which a boy tries to return a lost company of fairies to their homeland. Victorian fairies took on a literary life of their own; they play a major role in **re-enchanted** images of the 19th century in such modern stories as Holly Black and Tony DiTerlizzi's Spiderwick Chronicles, advertised as "Vintage Victorian fantasy" and launched with *The Field Guide* (2003) and *The Seeing Stone* (2003).

Victorian fairy art and its associated tales reflected ineradicable confusions as to how large fairies were and whether or not they possessed wings—confusions that persist to the present day. Similar confusions as to what kinds of magic fairies were likely to perform were created by writers and translators for children, who often substituted "bad fairies" for **witches** on the absurd assumption that it might somehow be protective—a move wryly reflected in Arthur Thrush's *The Capture of Nina Carroll* (1924), in which fairies and witches are at odds. The net result of these moves was to rob the term "fairy" of its last vestiges of specific significance, although that is not entirely out of keeping with its original coinage. Modern fairies are usually friendly—in contrast to goblins—but can still play an adversarial role, as in **Anne Bishop**'s Tir Alainn trilogy and **Nancy Springer**'s *Fair Peril*. They have occasionally made technological progress, as in **Eoin Colfer**'s Artemis Fowl series and **Tad Williams**'s *War of the Flowers,* or developed punkish sensibilities, as in works by **Francesca Lia Block** and **Martin Millar**.

FAIRY TALES. As **J. R. R. Tolkien**'s essay "On Fairy-stories" points out, relatively few so-called fairy tales actually feature **fairies**. The term, which came into common parlance in the mid-18th-century, was borrowed from the French *contes des fées* to describe **folktales** that had been adapted for use as **children's fiction**. A similar distinction was drawn by the Brothers Grimm when they titled their collection of *Kinder- und Hausmärchen,* in contrast to **J. K. Musäus**'s *Volksmärchen* and the category of *kunstmärchen* [**art fairy tales**]. When **Hans Christian Andersen**'s works were marketed in Britain they were sometimes labeled *Household Tales* in imitation of Grimm's terminology, but "fairy tales" eventually became standardized, especially in respect of a group of a dozen tales that remain familiar to almost everyone in the West—the last vestiges of a common oral culture.

The earliest printed versions of two such tales—"Beauty and the Beast" and "Puss-in-Boots"—appeared in Gianfrancesco Straparola's *Le piacevoli notti* [Nights of Entertainiment] (1550–53); both were reproduced, along with the first printed versions of "Cinderella," "Snow White," and "Rapunzel," in Giambattista Basile's *Pentamerone* (1634). These Italian versions differ considerably from the versions of the same tales offered by **Perrault** and the **Grimms**, who further extended the basic stock to include "Sleeping Beauty," "The Frog Prince," "Rumpelstiltskin," and "Jack and the Beanstalk."

Attempts to account for the endurance and fascination of themes inherited by fairy tales from folk tales—attempts aided by such taxonomists as Edwin Hartland and Vladimir Propp—have varied quite markedly. Maureen Duffy's *The Erotic World of Faery* (1972) and Bruno Bettelheim's *The Uses of Enchantment* (1976) employ Freudian theory to argue that fairy tales are disguised **erotic fantasies** and ought to continue to offer covert psychoanalytic counseling. Jack Zipes's *Fairy Tales and the Art of Subversion* (1983) prefers the thesis that they were spontaneous expressions of class resentment, until the likes of the Brothers Grimm subverted their meanings by grafting on bourgeois homilies.

Although the first novel-length fairy tales were composed in the early 19th century by **Charles Nodier** and Sara Coleridge, the fairy tale remained firmly wedded to the short-story format as its 19th-century exponents proliferated, notable composers including **E. H. Knatchbull-Hugessen**, **Frank R. Stockton**, **Oscar Wilde**, **E. Nesbit**, **Laurence Housman**, **Netta Syrett**, **Bram Stoker**, and **Maurice Baring**. The form has retained its importance even in the inhospitable economic climate of the modern adult marketplace, in **anthologies** edited by Ellen Datlow and **Terri Windling**. Around a core of brief children's tales, however, the 20th century has seen the proliferation of an ever-expanding halo of novel-length works, within which most wholly original fiction of the fairy tale variety now thrives, its progress spearheaded by such innovative and sophisticated works as **John Crowley**'s *Little, Big,* Peg Kerr's *The Wild Swans* (1999), and Jean Ferris's *Once Upon a Marigold* (2002).

Fairy tales must have been subject to routine **transfiguration** while they were **recycled** as folktales, but in recent times transfigured fairy tales have become astonishingly profligate, reflecting the fact that there are very few referents available for literary use with which so many potential readers are familiar. The familiar tales are often transfigured on a wholesale basis, as in collections by such writers as **John Erskine**, **Osbert Sitwell**, **Angela Carter**, **Tanith Lee**, **Vivian Vande Velde**, and **Francesca Lia Block**; such individual items as Frank White's *The Dryads and Other Tales* (1936), Caryl Brahms and S. J. Simon's *Titania Had a Mother* (1944), and Rebecca Lickiss's *Never After* (2002); and series of novels by such writers as **Donna Jo Napoli**, **Sophie Masson**, **Gregory Maguire**, **Mercedes Lackey**, and Adèle Geras. Such exercises sometimes adopt a calculatedly cynical viewpoint, as in *The Fairies Return* (Peter Davies, 1934), *Twice upon a Time* (1999, ed. Denise Little and Martin H. Greenberg)—which favors the villains' viewpoints—Mitzi Sereto's *Erotic Fairy Tales* (2001), and Richard Park's *The Ogre's Wife: Fairy Tales for Grownups* (2002).

Notable transfigurations of individual tales include **Eleanor Farjeon**'s *The Glass Slipper;* **Donald Barthelme**'s *Snow White;* **Robert Coover**'s *Briar Rose;* D. J. MacHale's *East of the Sun, West of the Moon* (1992); **Leon Garfield**'s *The Wedding Ghost;* **Robin McKinley**'s two versions of *Sleeping Beauty;* Gregory Maguire's *Confessions of an Ugly Stepsister* (1999); the second novella in Gioia Timpanelli's *Sometimes the Soul* (2000); **Elizabeth Cunningham**'s *How to Spin Gold;* Gary D. Schmidt's *Straw into Gold* (2001); Cameron Dokey's *Beauty Sleep* (2002); E. D. Baker's *The Frog Princess* (2002); Gregory Frost's *Fitcher's Brides* (2002); Shannon Hale's *The Goose Girl* (2003); and Edith Pattou's *East* (2003). Generic transfigurations like Alice Thomas Ellis's *Fairy Tale* (1996) are also commonplace.

Showcase anthologies of fairy tales are very numerous; those of historical interest include examples by **Jack Zipes** and **Marina Warner**, as well as *The Queen's Mirror: Fairy Tales by German Women 1780–1900* (2001), ed. Shawn C. Jarvis and Jeannine Blackwell. Heidi Anne Heiner's *SurLaLune* website (established 1998) is an invaluable archive.

FALLON, JENNIFER (1959–). Pseudonym of Australian writer Jennifer Ryan. Her fantasies—set in the **secondary world** of Medalon, ruled by the oppressive Sisters of the Blade—have elements of **political fantasy** contained within intricate plotlines. The Demon Child trilogy comprises *Medalon, Treason Keep,* and *Harshimi* (all 2000), the Second Sons trilogy *The Lion of Senet* (2002), *Eye of the Labyrinth* (2003), and *Lord of the Shadows* (2004). The Hythrun Chronicles, a **prequel**, was launched with *Wolfblade* (2004).

FANTASTIC ADVENTURES. U.S. pulp magazine launched as a companion to *Amazing Stories* in 1939, under the editorship of Ray Palmer, who was succeeded in 1950 by Howard Browne. Unlike *Astounding*'s companion ***Unknown***, which was founded a few months afterward, it was initially a **science fiction** magazine, but it soon began to experiment with *Unknown*-style **humorous fantasies** by **Nelson S. Bond**, **Robert Bloch**, and William P. McGivern, as well as pastiches of **Edgar Rice Burroughs**'s Tarzan stories. When *Unknown* was sacrificed to wartime economies, *FA* featured more work of that kind, although sf continued to take priority; it published pastiches of **Thorne Smith** by Bloch and Charles F. Myers and adventure fantasies by "Geoff St. Reynard" (Robert W. Krepps), as well as later works by *Unknown* regulars **L. Sprague de Camp**, **Theodore Sturgeon**, **Fritz Leiber**, and **L. Ron Hubbard**.

When *Fantastic Adventures* folded in 1953 it had already been replaced by the digest *Fantastic,* launched in 1952, whose early issues featured "slick" fantasy of the varieties favored by *The Magazine of Fantasy & Science Fiction*. When Paul Fairman succeeded Browne as editor in 1955, however, it became a clone of *Amazing* until it was taken over in 1958 by Cele Goldsmith. Goldsmith's *Fantastic Stories of the Imagination* played a key role in laying the groundwork for genre fantasy; she provided a home for **Fritz Leiber**'s **sword and sorcery** series and featured work in the same subgenre by **John Jakes** and **Roger Zelazny**. Leiber and Zelazny were also given a much freer rein to improvise avant-garde work, as were other new recruits like **Ursula Le Guin** and **Thomas M. Disch**. The title was sold in 1965, mostly using reprints until Ted White took over the editorship from 1968 until 1979 and again made its pages available for experiments in sword and sorcery (including **Robert E. Howard** pastiches by Sprague de Camp and **Lin Carter**), although he still mingled such work with sf. *FA* was merged with *Amazing* in 1980, but the title was resurrected in 2002 by Edward J. McFadden.

FANTASTIQUE. A French word frequently used as a generic description in place of the Anglo-American **horror**, although the range of texts so differentiated is significantly different. The import of Tzvetan Todorov's *Introduction à la littérature fantastique* (1970; tr. 1973 as *The Fantastic: A Structural Approach to a Literary Genre*) is confused by translation, because there is no real equivalent in English parlance for the fine distinctions Todorov draws between *fantastique* (tr. as "fantastic"), *inconnu* (tr. as "uncanny"), and *merveilleux* (tr. as "marvelous"). For Todorov, the essence of *fantastique* is the hesitation between psychological and supernatural interpretations of exotic phenomena, and a character's subsequent indecision as to whether he or the world has suffered a breakdown.

It is arguable that some such indecision is essential to the differentiation of the sensation of horror from that of terror, but if so it also has considerable relevance to the fantasy genre, because horror is not the only conceivable psychological reaction to that kind of hesitation. In the tradition of fantasy fiction that extends from the sophisticated **fairy** romances of 18th-century France through the works of **Lewis Carroll** and **F. Anstey** to the comedies of **L. Sprague de Camp** and **Fletcher Pratt**, the characters react with amusement rather than horror to confrontation with the inexplicable, and their behavioral response is pragmatic rather than paranoid. Such pragmatic reactions—easily granted to imaginatively adaptable children like Alice—are the basis of the **chimerical** effect whose narrative energy much fantasy exploits.

FANTASYLAND. Diana Wynne Jones's *The Tough Guide to Fantasyland* (1996) is a **satirical** tourist **guide** to the kind of stereotyped **secondary world** employed by modern genre fantasy. The term was also adopted (independently) by John Clute as a description of the stereotyped "basic venue" of **commodified/epic fantasy**. It is a direct descendant of the similarly generalized backcloth employed in literary **fairy tales**, whose evocation is signified by the phrase "once upon a time." The device is useful because the set of expectations it places in the reader's mind—usually enabled in genre fantasy, as Jones and Clute both point out, by the inclusion of a prefatory map—provides a useful background against which the idiosyncratic variations of particular secondary worlds show up as variations. In the absence of some such set of preliminary assumptions, the writer's world-building labor would be much more onerous.

FAR-FUTURISTIC FANTASY. A subgenre spanning **fantasy** and **sf** (refer to *HDSFL*), including a great many **hybrid** texts based on the premise that magical entities and forces hypothetically removed from the Earth's past by a **thinning** process will enjoy a spectacular resurgence in the senile world's "second childhood," perhaps as a residue of no-longer-understood technologies that have outlasted their makers. **Clark Ashton Smith**'s tales of Zothique provided a cardinal example, perfectly adapted to the extremism of his stylistic **decadence**, although an earlier precedent had been set by **William Hope Hodgson** in *The Night Land*. **Jack Vance**'s Dying Earth updated the milieu. Other significant contributors to the subgenre within the fantasy genre include **Michael Shea**; Oliver Johnson, in the Lightbringer trilogy, comprising *The Forging of the Shadows* (1996), *The Nations of the Night* (1998), and *The Last Star at Dawn* (1999); and Christopher Rowley's trilogy set after the apparent extinction of Man the Cruel, comprising *The Ancient Enemy* (2000), *The Shast War* (2001), and *Doom's Break* (2002).

FARJEON, ELEANOR (1881–1965). British writer from a literary family who began writing for the family magazine, then called *Farjeon's Fortnightly,* while it was edited by her brother Herbert in 1899–1901. *Pan-Worship and Other Poems* (1908) is solidly in the tradition of **decadent/Arcadian fantasy**. *The Soul of Kol Nikon* (1914) is a bleak account of a changeling's futile attempt to acquire a soul, its desperation leading to a typical postwar plea for **re-enchantment** in *Gypsy and Ginger* (1920). The ornately stylized *Martin Pippin in the Apple Orchard* (1921) features a kind of English nature-spirit akin to Shakespeare's Puck, part satyr as well as part **fairy**; the tales the spirit tells were not intended for children but were widely interpreted as such. The character reappeared in *Martin Pippin in the Daisy Field* (1937), which was in fact aimed at the children's market, as were the similar compendia *Faithful Jenny Dove and Other Tales* (1925), *Kaleidoscope* (1928), *The Old Nurse's Stocking-Basket* (1931), and *Jim at the Corner* (1934).

The Fair of St. James (1932) and *Humming Bird* (1936) retained a conscientiously adult and rather gnomic sophistication. The **erotic fantasy** *Ariadne and the Bull* (1945) **transfigures** various **classical** materials. Farjeon's full-length children's fantasies *The Silver Curlew* (1953) and *The Glass Slipper* (1955) both originated as plays, the latter written in collaboration with Herbert in 1946.

FARMER, PENELOPE (1939–). British writer, mostly for children. The fantasy series comprising *The Summer Birds* (1962) begins with a carefully moderated **transfiguration** of **J. M. Barrie**'s *Peter Pan*; its sequels are the **dream** fantasy *Emma in Winter* (1966) and the **timeslip** fantasy *Charlotte Sometimes* (1966). *The Magic Stone* (1964) is a magically complicated family drama. *A Castle of Bone* (1972) features a cupboard that can turn back time and functions as a **portal** to a personalized **secondary world**. *William and Mary* (1974) features a portal that can grant access to pictures and poems. *Year King* (1977) carries forward themes trailed by **James Frazer** in *A Castle of Bone*. *Eve: Her Story* (1985) is a **feminized/Edenic fantasy** for adults. *Glasshouses* (1988) is an **occult fantasy**. *Thicker than Water* (1989) is a **ghost story**.

FAUSTIAN FANTASY. Stories in which humans make pacts with the **Devil**. The earliest to be recorded is a medieval cautionary tale about a bishop named Theophilus, but the subgenre is named for a scholar at the university of Heidelberg in the early 16th century who was said to have traded his soul for earthly knowledge. The printed version of the legend by Johann Spies appeared in 1587 and was promptly borrowed by Christopher Marlowe for *The Tragical History of Dr. Faustus* (c1592; pub. 1604). By then, the notion of diabolical pacts had been adopted by theologians into the slanders used to justify the persecution of heretics; **witches** were assumed to have made such pacts. Although the subgenre extends into **horror** fiction, many Faustian fantasies are much lighter in tone, often focusing on the exact wording of the contract defining the pact in order to set up ingenious narrative twists when settlement falls due. The most famous transfigurations of Faust's story is **J. W. Goethe**'s, the basis of several operas; modern ones include Thomas Mann's metaphorical *Doctor Faustus* (1947; tr. 1948), Robert Nye's *Faust* (1980), and **Michael Swanwick**'s *Jack Faust*.

Many 19th-century Faustian fantasies portray the Devil and his agents as sly, urbane con men who achieve their victories by subtle trickery, as in Adalbert von Chamisso's *Peter Schlemihl* (1814; tr. 1824; aka *The Shadowless Man*), **Eden Phillpotts**'s *A Deal with the Devil,* and Austin Fryers's *The Devil and the Inventor* (1900). The tables are often turned, though, as in **James Dalton**'s *The Gentleman in Black* or **Walter Herries Pollock**'s "An Episode in the Life of Mr Latimer" (1883).

Twentieth-century examples were forced by the pressure of **melodramatic inflation** to become increasingly ingenious, no matter which side they took; notable examples include Max Beerbohm's "Enoch Soames" (in *Seven Men*, 1919), **Stephen Vincent Benét**'s "The Devil and Daniel Webster," **Sylvis Townsend Warner**'s *Lolly Willowes,* **T. F. Powys**'s "The Two Thieves," **Mervyn Wall**'s Fursey stories, Bertrand Russell's "Satan in the Suburbs" (1953), Patrick Ravignant's *An Edge of Darkness* (1963; tr. from French 1965), Jorge de Sena's *The Wondrous Physician* (1966; tr. from Portuguese 1986), **Leon Garfield**'s *The Ghost Downstairs,* Josephine Leslie's *The Devil and Mrs Devine* (1975),

William Hjortsberg's *Fallen Angel* (1978), John Updike's *The Witches of Eastwick* (1984), **Paula Volksky**'s *The White Tribunal*, Kim Wilkins's *The Infernal* (1999), and Andy Duncan's "Beluthahatchie" (1997). *Deals with the Devil* (1958), ed. Basil Davenport, is a showcase **anthology**.

FEIST, RAYMOND E. (1945–). U.S. writer whose early novels drew on his experience designing fantasy role-playing **games**. The plot of the **epic** *Magician* (1982; rev. 1992) is as carefully orchestrated as any games master's design, but the series extrapolated from it adopted a spirit more closely akin to swashbuckling Ruritanian romance. The role played by magic became increasing peripheral and arbitrary as the couplet comprising *Silverthorn* (1985) and *A Darkness at Sethanon* (1986) gave way to the couplet comprising *Prince of the Blood* (1989) and *The King's Buccaneer* (1989), and to the series comprising *Shadow of a Dark Queen* (1994), *Rise of a Merchant Prince* (1995), *Rage of a Demon King* (1997), and *Shards of a Broken Crown* (1998). A linked series written in collaboration with **Janny Wurts** comprises *Daughter of the Empire* (1987), *Servant of the Empire* (1989), and *Mistress of the Empire* (1989). The game-based Krondor series comprising *The Betrayal* (1998), *The Assassins* (2000), and *Tear of the Gods* (2000) returned to basics, as did the Legends of the Riftwar **shared world** series, comprising *Honoured Enemy* (2001, with William R. Forschen), *Murder in LaMut* (2002, with Josel Rosenberg), and *Jimmy the Hand* (2003, with Steve Stirling). *Faerie Tale* (1988) is a **dark fantasy** juxtaposing **Faerie** with contemporary America. The Conclave of Shadows trilogy, comprising *Talon of the Silver Hawk* (2002), *King of Foxes* (2003), and *Exile's Return* (2004), developed a new milieu.

FEMINIZED FANTASY. Sarah Lefanu's study of feminist **sf** *In the Chinks of the World Machine* (1988; aka *Feminism and Science Fiction*) draws a careful distinction between feminist and "feminized" fiction. While the former examines sexual-political power structures and their underlying logic with conscientious scepticism, the latter extols the virtues of femininity, valuing empathy more highly than technical competence, patient diplomacy more highly than aggressive violence, and intuition (especially when magically aided) more highly than rationality. Although it is reasonably appropriate to subsume sf of both kinds under the "feminist" heading, there is a far better case for subsuming **fantasy** that modifies traditional sex roles under the other label. There is a good deal of bone fide feminist fantasy—a great many **fairy tales** have been rewritten with exactly this ideological purpose in mind, as illustrated by **Angela Carter** and **Jack Zipes**—but it is far outweighed by feminized fantasy.

To some extent, the generic difference of balance is a logical corollary of the **recycling** process that generates so much fantasy fiction, which finds it much easier to change the viewpoint of the relevant **taproot texts** than alter their content. It is a relatively straightforward task to retell **Arthurian** legends from a female viewpoint that gives more moral credit to **Morgan le Fay** and Guinevere than male versions routinely do, but providing a feminist revision would subject the conventions of **chivalric romance** to a massive overhaul. Future and extraterrestrial settings, by contrast, have no such burden of expectation attached to them. Even in hypothetical **alternative historical** settings, like those employed in **sword and sorcery** fiction, **amazon** swordswomen can hardly avoid being rare exceptions to the rule, while female aristocrats championing the ideals of femininity—especially their magical extensions—blend in with no trouble at all. **Marion Zimmer Bradley**, whose feminized Arthurian fantasy *Mists of Avalon* became one of the 20th-century's best-selling books, put the main emphasis of her series of *Sword and Sorceress* anthologies where it seemed to belong, not on the swordplay but on the specifically feminine varieties of magic advertised by **Jules Michelet**'s classic **scholarly fantasy** *La sorcière*, especially that of **healers**.

Feminized fantasy is perfectly hospitable to the serious consideration of sexual stereotyping, as in the work of **P. C. Hodgell**, **Rachel Ingalls**, **Nancy Springer**, **Tamora Pierce**, Nancy Kress's *The Prince of Morning Bells* (1981), Lynn Flewelling's series begun with *The Bone Doll's Twin* (2001), and Sarah Micklem's *Firethorn* (2004). A more assertive kind of feminism is, however, evident in the works of **Phyllis Ann Karr**, **Elizabeth Lynn**, **Jessica Amanda Salmonson**, Kate Muir's *Suffragette City* (1999), and Cass Dalglish's *Nin* (2000).

FERAL CHILDREN. Thought experiments investigating what might become of a child denied normal processes of education and "civilization" are common in fantasy, often featuring lost infants suckled and reared by animals; notable examples include Ronald Ross's *The Child of Ocean* (1889), **Rudyard Kipling**'s Mowgli stories, **Edgar Rice Burroughs**'s tales of Tarzan, Nicholas Luard's *Kala* (1990), and Jill Paton Walsh's *Knowledge of Angels* (1994). A showcase **anthology** is *Mother*

Was a Lovely Beast (1974), edited by Philip José Farmer, whose own attempts to "update" the myth of Tarzan rarely question the racist assumptions assailed in Neville Farki's *The Death of Tarzana Clayton* (1985).

FÉVAL, PAUL (1816–1887). French writer. Many of his early works were based on Breton folklore, but the fantasies among them mostly remained unreprinted. The serial novels he began to write in 1843 made a crucial contribution to the literary development of **secret histories**, many of those featuring complex criminal conspiracies ultimately being bound together into a more or less coherent sequence spanning the centuries. His reluctance to produce wholehearted fantasies caused such novels as *The Vampire Countess* (1856; tr. 2003) to become bizarrely contorted as they struggled to retain their **ambiguity**—an absurdity acknowledged and extrapolated in the Gallandesque and conscientiously **metafictional** *Knightshade* (1860; tr. 2001), *The Wandering Jew's Daughter* (1864; tr. 2004), and the flamboyant *Vampire City* (1875; tr. 1999), whose protagonist is the English **Gothic** novelist Ann Radcliffe.

FFORDE, JASPER (1961–). British writer. *The Eyre Affair* (2001) is a **chimerical** account of an **alternative history** in which the Crimean War has been going on for 131 years when supervillain Acheron Hades kidnaps Jane Eyre as Surrealists and Modernists brawl in the street. In the sequels *Lost in a Good Book* (2002), *The Well of Lost Plots* (2003), and *Something Rotten* (2004), the **humor** grows broader but remains conscientiously literary.

FINNEY, CHARLES G. (1905–1984). U.S. writer. His most notable work is the phantasmagoric **erotic fantasy** *The Circus of Dr Lao* (1935), about a traveling show with exhibits that transform the life of a small town in Arizona where the inhabitants are unready for **re-enchantment** on such a generous scale; its method is echoed in **Ray Bradbury**'s *Something Wicked This Way Comes,* Arthur Calder-Marshall's *The Fair to Middling* (1959), and Tom Reamy's *Blind Voices* (1978). In Finney's **Oriental fantasy** *The Unholy City* (1937), a resident of the same small town visits the surreal civilization of Heilar-Wey; the novella *The Magician out of Manchuria* (1968) is similar in spirit. *The Ghosts of Manacle* (1964) includes a few fantasy stories.

FINNEY, JACK (1911–1995). U.S. writer in various genres (refer to *HDSFL* and *HDHL*). *The Woodrow Wilson Dime* (1968) and *Marion's Wall* (1973) are comedies in the vein of **Thorne Smith**, but the latter has an elegiac element that transforms it into a **sentimental fantasy** more akin to his **escapist/timeslip fantasy** *Time and Again* (1970), whose belated sequel was *From Time to Time* (1995). The short fiction collected in *The Third Level* (1957; aka *The Clock of Time*) and *I Love Galesburg in the Springtime* (1963) includes numerous lighthearted fantasies; those involving timeslips are reassembled in *About Time* (1986).

FISHER, CATHERINE (?–). British writer of **dark**-edged **children's fiction**, often set in her native Wales and drawing upon **Celtic** materials. *The Conjuror's Game* (1990) features a sinister **healer**. *Fintan's Tower* (1991) is a **quest** fantasy. *The Candle Man* (1994) features an attempt to lift a curse. The Snow-Walker trilogy, comprising *The Snow-Walker's Son* (1994), *The Empty Hand* (1995), and *The Soul Thieves* (1996), is a **picaresque fantasy** set in an icy **secondary world**. *Belin's Hill* (1997) is a thriller in which bad **dreams** intensify in the wake of an accident. The Book of the Crow series, comprising *The Relic Master* (1999), *The Interrex* (1999), *Flain's Coronet* (2000), and *The Margrave* (2001), is a melodramatic quest fantasy. *Darkwater Hall* (2000) is a **timeslip** fantasy with an element of **Faustian fantasy**. In *The Lammas Field* (1999), magical **music** draws the protagonist into a **secondary world**. *Corbenic* (2002) features a contemporary **quest** for the Holy **Grail.** The series begun with *The Oracle* (2003; aka *The Oracle Betrayed*) and *The Archon* (2004) hybridizes elements of Greek and Egyptian mythology. Her short fiction is sampled in *The Hare and Other Stories* (1994).

FISHER, JUDE (?–). Pseudonym of British writer Jane Johnson, who also wrote, in collaboration with **M. John Harrison**, as "**Gabriel King**." As "Fisher," she produced the **epic** Fool's Gold trilogy, launched with *Sorcery Rising* (2002) and *Wild Magic* (2003), to be concluded with *The Rose of the World*.

FLAUBERT, GUSTAVE (1821–1880). French writer. Much of the juvenilia reprinted in his *Oeuvres complètes* (1885; exp. 1922) is fantasy, including "Rève d'enfer" (written 1837), "The Dance of Death" (written 1838), and the drama "Smarh" (written 1839), a pioneering exercise in **literary satanism**. The last-named paved the way for a phantasmagoric account of *Le Tentation de Saint Antoine* (written 1848–49; published as *La Première* *tentation de Saint Antoine*, 1908; tr. as *The First Temptation of St. Anthony*, 1910), which he was persuaded not to publish for fear of giving offense. He modified it in 1856, but the version he eventually published in 1874 (tr. as *The Temptation of St. Anthony*, 1895) was even more carefully revised. The collection *Three Tales* (1877; tr. 1903) includes two **Christian fantasies**, one of them a **transfiguration** of the story of Salome.

FLIGHT. Dreams of flying are common, and **myth**, legend, and folklore all feature an abundance of devices facilitating flight, including such staples as winged horses and magic carpets. **Angels** and **fairies** are frequently equipped with wings, whose possession is so often envied by humans that **classical** legend includes the cautionary fable of Icarus, whose pride in his artificial wings preceded a fatal fall.

Winged humans enjoy more positive experiences in such **sentimental fantasies** as **Barry Pain**'s *Going Home* and Nathalia Crane's *An Alien from Heaven* (1929). The women whose wings are clipped in Inez Haynes Gillmore's *Angel Island* (1914) embody a different symbolism. Some characters who discover that they can fly without the need of wings are content with self-indulgent **wish-fulfillment fantasies**, as described in Eric Knight's tales of *The Flying Yorkshireman* and Michael Harrison's *Higher Things* (1945), but some of those so blessed fall prey to **messianic** pretensions, as in Neil Bell's "The Facts about Benjamin Crede" (1935) and **Ronald Fraser**'s *The Flying Draper*.

Notable fantasies of flight of more recent vintage, and considerably greater variety, include **Grace Chetwin**'s *Child of the Air,* **Thomas M. Disch**'s *On Wings of Song,* **Angela Carter**'s *Nights at the Circus,* **William Mayne**'s *Antar and the Eagles,* Rita Murphy's *Night Flying* (2000), Laurel Winter's *Growing Wings* (2000), Phyllis Shalant's *When Pirates Came to Brooklyn* (2002), and Lia Nirgad's *As High as the Scooter Can Fly* (2002). A more discreet elevation is featured in Tom Robbins's *Fierce Invalids Home from Hot Climates* (2000).

FLINT, KENNETH C. (?–). U.S. writer specializing in **Celtic fantasy**. *A Storm upon Ulster* (1981; aka *The Hound of Culain*) and its prequel *Isle of Destiny* (1988) **recycle** the legend of Cuchulain without emphasizing its supernatural aspects, but the trilogy comprising *Riders of the Sidhe* (1984), *Champions of the Sidhe* (1984), and *Master of the Sidhe* (1985) features the Tuatha Dé Danaan, the ancient pantheon whose members were reduced to mere **fairy** folk after Christianization. The trilogy comprising *Challenge of the Clans* (1986), *Storm Shield* (1986), and *The*

Dark Druid (1987) **recycles** the legends of Finn Mac Cumhail. *Isle of Destiny* (1988) is a **historical fantasy**, while *Cromm* (1990), *Legends Reborn* (1992), and *The Darkening Flood* (1995) are **intrusive fantasies**. *Most Ancient Song* (1991) and *The Enchanted Isles* (1991) appeared under the byline "Casey Flynn."

THE FLYING DUTCHMAN. A legend dating from the 18th century. Captain Vanderdecken, frustrated in his attempts to round the Cape of Good Hope by adverse weather, utters a curse that renders his entrapment permanent: a classic instance of **bondage**. It fascinated many later writers, although its **transfiguration** by **William Austin** predated any straightforward **recycling**. Notable versions include **Captain Marryat**'s *The Phantom Ship,* **Richard Wagner**'s opera (1843), W. Clark Russell's *The Death Ship* (1888), **Tom Holt**'s *Flying Dutch,* and **Brian Jacques**'s *Castaways of the Flying Dutchman*.

FOLKTALES. Stories preserved in oral tradition that command less respect than **myths** or **legends**, by virtue of foregrounding the tribulations of common mortals rather than **gods** or **heroes**. They are usually set in an imaginary past ("once upon a time") when supernatural beings were routinely involved in human affairs, although their antiquity is unmeasurable. Folktales continue to be produced in the form of anecdotal "urban legends," but their study is handicapped by the fact that the act of recording them fundamentally alters their nature.

A few folktales were recorded in classical times, and many more were written down in the Renaissance, but only when vernacular languages began to generate literatures of their own, independently of church Latin, were European folktales reproduced in print *as stories;* precisely for that reason, the folktale-based stories reproduced in Gianfrancesco Straparola's *Le piacevoli notti* (1550–53; usually tr. as *Nights*) and Giambattista Basile's *Pentamerone* (1634–36) are probably as carefully rewrought as those in **Charles Perrault**'s moralizing collection of 1691, which began the transformation of folktales into **fairy tales** for the education and edification of children. This transformation was made in opposition to religious suspicion of Europe's pagan heritage, which led to many folktales being revised; the Church's persecution of **witches** had sought support in folktales reproduced as "evidence" in such documents as Jacob Sprenger and Heinrich Kramer's infamous *Malleus Maleficarum* (1486). Folktales dealing with **ghosts**, **werewolves**, and **vampires** were routinely co-opted as testimony into a long rear-guard action fought against sceptics critical of the Church's witch hunting; their produce included such works as Francesco Maria Guazzo's *Compendium Maleficarum* (1608), Joseph Glanvill's *Saducismus Triumphatus* (1681), and Dom Augustine Calmet's highly influential *Dissertation sur les apparitions des anges, des démons et des esprits* (1746; tr. as *The Phantom World*). "True" ghost stories became a genre in their own right and still represent the most prolific genre of new folktales.

When Johann Musäus and the Grimm brothers set out to record German *märchen,* the idea that such tales preserved something of the authentic *volksgeist* of German-speaking people was popular among German **Romantics**, but they knew that their efforts were belated. Attempts to build comprehensive collections of regional folktales in the British isles—including T. Crofton Croker's *The Fairy Legends and Traditions of the South of Ireland* (1825), Mrs. Bray's *Traditions, Legends and Superstitions of Devonshire* (1838), Robert Hunt's *Popular Romances of the West of England; or, The Drolls, Traditions and Superstitions of Old Cornwall* (1865), and work done by **W. B. Yeats** and the family of **Arthur Quiller-Couch**—also began too late to sustain any serious claim of "authenticity," although it is not obvious that oft-repeated tales can reasonably be said to have "true" versions preserving hypothetical "originals." While some folktales are obviously more synthetic than others—Richard M. Dorson mounted a vitriolic attack on "fakelore" in the *American Mercury* in 1950, further elaborated in *Folklore and Fakelore* (1976)—there is no recoverable purity in any of them.

Folklorists have struggled to explain the patterns revealed by thematic categorization since **Thomas Keightley**'s diffusionist theories and Edwin Sidney Hartland's proto-psychological analyses—in *The Science of Fairy Tales,* 1870—fell into disrepute. Antti Arne's analysis of *The Types of the Folktale* (1910; tr. 1961) and Vladimir Propp's *Morphology of the Folktale* (1920s; tr. 1968) mapped out basic patterns; their work was carried forward by others, including Stith Thompson—who edited a six-volume *Motif Index of Folk Literature* (1955)—in *The Folk Tale* (1946) and Graham Anderson in *Fairytale in the Ancient World* (2000). The folktales collected by anthropologists from Native American, African, Polynesian, and many other cultures are likely to be the last surviving relics of tribal societies, whose ways of life were obliterated by the 20th-century globalization of Western culture.

FORD, JEFFREY (1955–). U.S. writer. *Vanitas* (1988) is a **dark fantasy** set in the Carnival of the Dead. The trilogy comprising *The Physiog-*

nomy (1997), *Memoranda* (1999), and *The Beyond* (2001) features an exponent of an exotic **occult** science who is eventually forced into a Dantean wilderness when the city in which he lives is destroyed. *The Portrait of Mrs. Charbuque* (2002) is a **historical fantasy**, set in late 19th-century New York, in which a painter accepts a commission to paint a portrait without seeing his subject. His short fiction is sampled in *The Fantasy Writer's Assistant and Other Stories* (2002).

FORSTER, E. M. (1879–1970). British writer. His early work, collected in *The Celestial Omnibus and Other Stories* (1911) and *The Eternal Moment and Other Stories* (1928), is mostly fantasy—including **classical fantasies**, **allegories**, and **afterlife fantasies**—and the lectures collected in *Aspects of the Novel* (1927) include one on the specific problems of writing fantasy fiction.

FORSYTHE, KATE (1966–). Australian writer of **Celtic fantasy**. The series comprising *The Witches of Eileanan* (1998), *The Pool of Two Moons* (1998), *The Cursed Tower* (2000), *The Forbidden Land* (2001), *The Skull of the World* (2001), and *The Fathomless Caves* (2002), following the tribulations of a young witch, was planned as a trilogy but was expanded to **epic** dimensions. The Rhiannon's Ride trilogy, begun with *The Tower of Ravens* (2004), employs the same milieu.

FORTUNE, DION (1890–1946). British **lifestyle fantasist**; born Violet Firth. She joined the Order of the Golden Dawn in 1919 and the Theosophical Society in 1923 before founding her own Fraternity of the Inner Light in 1927. She wrote a good deal of **scholarly fantasy** about various **occult** traditions. *The Secrets of Dr Taverner* (1926) collects an **occult detective** series. *The Demon Lover* (1927), *The Winged Bull* (1935), and *The Goat-Foot God* (1936) are accounts of exotic spiritual redemption akin to the works of **Marie Corelli** but far less orthodox, featuring male magicians modeled on **Aleister Crowley**. *Sea Priestess* (1938) and its sequel *Moon Magic* (1956) feature a syncretic **goddess** whose modern worshippers include a reincarnation of **Morgan le Fay**.

FORWARD, EVE (1972–). U.S. writer and artist whose full name is Eve Forward-Rollins. In *Villains by Necessity* (1995), miscellaneous villains set out to restore balance to a world in which Light has triumphed. The equally enterprising *Animist* (2000) features "animism" as an academic discipline, in which graduates are paired with empathetic animals that help them evade magicians bent on exterminating their science.

FOSTER, ALAN DEAN (1946–). U.S. writer best known for **sf** (refer to *HDSFL*). His principal fantasy series is a lighthearted **portal fantasy** in which the Earth-reared protagonist becomes a hero in a **secondary world**; the series comprises *Spellsinger at the Gate* (1983; 2-volume version as *Spellsinger* and *The Hour of the Gate*), *The Day of the Dissonance* (1984), *The Moment of the Magician* (1984), *The Paths of the Perambulator* (1985), *The Time of the Transference* (1986), *Son of Spellsinger* (1993), and *Chorus Skating* (1994). *Maori* (1988) is a **historical fantasy** set in 19th-century New Zealand. *To the Vanishing Point* (1998) is a **hybrid/science fantasy** featuring a bizarre **parallel world**. The Journeys of the Catechist series, set in a fantasized Africa, comprises *Carnivores of Light and Darkness* (1998), *Into the Thinking Kingdoms* (1999), and *A Triumph of Souls* (2000). *Mad Amos* (1996) collects a series of fantasies set in the Old West. In *Kingdoms of Light* (2001), a dead **wizard**'s pets become human in order to save the world from **goblins**. Some short fantasies are included in *Metrognome and Other Stories* (1990).

FOUQUÉ, FRIEDRICH, BARON DE LA MOTTE (1777–1843). German writer whose central involvement in the Romantic movement inspired several landmark fantasies. He revived the tradition of **chivalric romance** in the play *Sigurd* (1808) and the novella translated as *Aslauga's Knights* (1810; tr. 1827). *Undine* (1811; tr. 1818) is a classic **art fairy tale** in which the foundling daughter of an elemental king falls in love with a knight who turns out to be faithless, with tragic consequences. *The Magic Ring* (1813; tr. 1825) is the first modern **quest** fantasy, a prototype for generic **heroic fantasy**. *Sintram and His Companions* (1815; tr. 1820) is an **allegory** based on an engraving by Albrecht Dürer. The best known of Fouqué's short works is the often-imitated Faustian **wish-fulfillment fantasy** "The Bottle-Imp" (1814; tr. 1823), which probably recycles a **folktale**.

FOX, GARDNER F. (1911–1986). U.S. writer best known for **comic** books. His novels include the **hybrid/science-fantasy** couplet *Warrior of Llarn* (1964) and *Thief of Llarn* (1966), and also two **sword and sorcery** series imitative of **Robert E. Howard**. The first comprises *Kothar: Barbarian Swordsman* (1969), *Kothar of the Magic Sword!* (1969), *Kothar and the Demon Queen* (1969), *Kothar and the Conjurer's Curse* (1970), and *Kothar and the Wizard Slayer* (1970), and the second, *Kyrik: Warlock Warrior* (1975), *Kyrik Fights the Demon World* (1975), *Kyrik and the Wizard's Sword* (1976), and *Kyrik and the Lost Queen*

(1976). Fox wrote the **portal fantasy** *The Druid Stone* (1965) as "Simon Majors." Some of the historical novels he wrote as "Jefferson Cooper" have elements of **biblical fantasy**.

FOX, KAREN (?–). U.S. writer whose **paranormal** "Fae Romances" are unusually various and enterprising. The hero of *Prince of Charming* (2000) is trapped in a portrait by an evil spell. In *Buttercup's Baby* (2001) a **fairy** from Titania's court visits the modern world. *Grand Design* (2001), is a **timeslip** fantasy. *Cupid's Melody* (2003) involves **reincarnation**. *Impractical Magic* (2003) is a wry **feminized fantasy**.

FRANCE, ANATOLE (1844–1924). Pseudonym of French writer Anatole-François Thibault. "The Honey-Bee" (1889; tr. 1909; aka *Bee* and *The Kingdom of the Dwarfs*) is a moralistic novella in the tradition of **Charles Nodier**'s *Trilby,* in which the eponymous princess is abducted by the dwarf king. *Thaïs* (1890; tr. 1901) is a sceptical **Christian fantasy** reminiscent of **Gustave Flaubert**'s *The Temptation of St. Anthony* (1874), in which Anthony's disciple Paphnuce saves the soul of the eponymous courtesan but lives to regret it.

The attacks on the life-denying asceticism of Christian orthodoxy featured in *Tales from a Mother-of-Pearl Casket* (1892; tr. 1896, aka *Mother of Pearl*) are relatively lighthearted, but those in *The Well of Santa Clara* (1895; tr. 1903, aka *The Well of St. Clare*) are more robust, especially "Saint Satyr," which explains how the tomb of a mistakenly beatified satyr became a refuge for the last remnants of **Arcadian** glory, and *The Human Tragedy* (separate pub. 1917), in which a saintly monk imprisoned by medieval churchmen discovers that his only friend is the **Devil**. This long-drawn-out adventure in **literary satanism** eventually culminated in the subgenre's masterpiece, *The Revolt of the Angels* (1914), in which a guardian **angel** converted to Epicurean free thought organizes a new revolution against the tyranny of heaven.

The first story in *Crainquebille, Putois, Riquet and Other Profitable Tales* (1904; tr. 1924) is a **humorous fantasy** about an artifact of the imagination ironically brought to life. In the **satire** *Penguin Island* (1908; tr. 1909), a company of penguins mistakenly baptized by a myopic saint recapitulate the history of France. *The Seven Wives of Bluebeard and Other Marvellous Tales* (1909; tr, 1920) features satires modeled on legends and **folktales**.

FRASER, RONALD (1888–1974). British writer. His fantasies express the hope that certain spiritually blessed human beings might contrive a bountiful transcendence of the human condition, while recognizing that such epiphanies would inevitably alienate them from their loved ones. In the mildly satirical *The Flying Draper* (1924), the **Oriental fantasy** *Landscape with Figures* (1925) and the striking botanical fantasia *Flower Phantoms* (1926), the theme is treated lightheartedly, but it became more earnest in the **metaphysical fantasies** *Miss Lucifer* (1939) and *The Fiery Gate* (1943) before reverting to **humorous** development in *Beetle's Career* (1951) and the series of ***contes philosophiques*** comprising *A Visit from Venus* (1958), *Jupiter in the Chair* (1958), *Trout's Testament* (1960), and *The City of the Sun* (1961). *A Work of Imagination: The Pen, the Brush, the Well* (1974) re-embraced a more serious mysticism.

FRAZER, JAMES (1854–1941). British anthropologist. He wrote one **classical fantasy**, "The Quest of the Gorgon's Head" (in *Sir Roger de Coverley and Other Literary Pieces,* 1920); his vast importance in modern fantasy fiction derives from his massive **scholarly fantasy** *The Golden Bough* (2 vols., 1890; exp. in 3 vols., 1900; further exp. in 12 vols., 1911–15), which replaced August Comte's "law" of the three stages of explanation (religion, metaphysics, and science) with a supposedly universal scheme of cultural evolution in which magical beliefs—interpreted as a practical pseudoscience based in mistaken laws—were replaced by religious systems that progressed from primitive fertility cults to monotheism before giving way to science.

Although it was never taken seriously by anthropologists, who were sceptical of Frazer's armchair speculations and syncretic interpretations, it had an enormous influence on literary men, including such pioneers of Modernism as T. S. Eliot, Ezra Pound, and D. H. Lawrence, as well as fantasists like **Aleister Crowley**, Henry Treece, **Naomi Mitchison**, and Robert Graves. It was a great inspiration to subsequent **scholarly fantasists**: **Margaret Murray** reinterpreted the entire history of European **witch** hunting as an assault on the relics of Frazerian cults; Graves linked it to **goddess** worship, in *The White Goddess;* and **Jessie Weston** greatly expanded the analogical use Frazer made of the **allegory** contained in **Chrétien de Troyes**'s *Conte du graal*. Assisted by these elaborations, *The Golden Bough* became a key **taproot text** of genre fantasy, echoed in a great many **historical** and **prehistoric fantasies** by such writers as **Helen Beauclerk** and Naomi Mitchison, including some **Arthurian fantasies**, and works offering quasi-theoretical accounts of **magic**. Notable examples include **Aleister Crowley**'s *Golden Twigs*,

John Fowles's Gravesian *Mantissa* (1982), **Penelope Farmer**'s *Year King*, and **Lindsay Clarke**'s *Alice's Masque*.

FRENCH FANTASY. The origins of French vernacular literature lie in the "courtly **romances**" of the 12th century, which dutifully reflected the chivalric delusions of the aristocratic patrons, who paid for their preservation in manuscript. In the 13th century, verse romances were supplemented, and eventually supplanted, by prose. The recording of **folktales** by chroniclers began in the same period, although it was not until the late 17th century that their substance was **transfigured** by **Madame d'Aulnoy** and **Charles Perrault**. Their influence at court facilitated the extrapolation of an 18th-century genre of **erotic** and **satirical** *fantaisies* featuring fairies and other supernatural beings, especially borrowings from **Antoine Galland**'s enormously popular *Arabian Nights;* notable examples include such works as Augustin-Paradis de Moncrif's *The Adventures of Zeloide and Amanzarifdine* (1715; tr. 1929), Claude-Prosper Crébillon *fils' The Sofa* (1740; tr. 1741), Jean-Galli de Bibiena's *The Fairy Doll* (1744; tr. 1925), **Jacques Cazotte**'s *The Devil in Love,* and **Anthony Hamilton**'s precursors to **Voltaire**'s ***contes philosophiques***.

Charles Nodier, who identified an emergent French school of Gothic fiction as *"l'école frénétique"* [frenetic school], and Théophile Gautier were the leading fantastists of the French Romantic movement, while **Honoré de Balzac** moved on from early frenetic novels to the "philosophical studies" element of his human comedy. The frequent **ambiguity** of freneticism—which eschewed explicit fantasy in the work of such influential practitioners as Victor Hugo and Jules Janin—paved the way for the development of a distinctively French genre of the ***fantastique***. This tendency to ambiguity accompanied the frenetic school as it was imported into the popular fiction by Eugéne Sue, Frédéric Soulié, **Alexandre Dumas**, and **Paul Féval** that reached unprecedentedly vast audiences as newspaper serials. Shorter fiction remained more hospitable to explicit fantasy, however, in the works of such writers as **Erckmann-Chatrian**.

In the mid-19th century, **Charles Baudelaire** interpreted the decline of the Romantic worldview as a reflection of a more general **decadence**, reflected in such literary ornamentation as elaborate **symbolism**—a trend carried forward by Villiers de l'Isle Adam, Catulle Mendès, **Marcel Schwob**, **Rémy de Gourmont**, **Pierre Louÿs**, **Jean Lorrain**, and **Maurice Maeterlinck**. Jules Laforgue's *Moral Tales* (1887; tr. 1928), which transfigured erotic fantasies drawn from **myth**, legend, and literature in a flamboyantly parodic fashion, provided a bridge to the **surrealism** of **Alfred Jarry** and **Guillaume Apollinaire**, while Jules Lemaître, whose short fiction is sampled in *Serenus and Other Stories* (1886; tr.1920) and *On the Margins of Old Books* (1905; tr. 1929), carried forward a trend in playful **metafiction**. Baudelaire and **Gustave Flaubert** also instituted a rich tradition of French **literary satanism**, whose ambitions flourished in the work of **Anatole France**.

Surrealism encouraged the cultivation of a kind of ambiguity more confused, and hence more flexible, than that of *fantastique* horror fiction, which was carried forward into the **existentialist** era by such writers as Raymond Roussel, in *Locus Solus* (1914; tr. 1970); Julien Gracq, author of the influential **allegory** *The Castle of Argol* (1938; tr. 1951); Maurice Sandoz, author of *Fantastic Memories* (1944; tr. 1957); and Maurice Druon, author of the **fairy tale** *Tistou of the Green Thumbs* (1957; tr. 1958) and the **classical fantasy** *The Memoirs of Zeus* (tr. 1964). This ambiguity extended into the work of Jean Cocteau, Boris Vian, **Marcel Aymé**, and **Michel Tournier**. It became perfectly possible for phantasmagorical works like Michel Bernanos's possibly **posthumous fantasy** *The Other Side of the Mountain* (1967; tr. 1968) to retain a crucial ambiguity that defies definite classification.

Although the horrific aspects of the *fantastique* thrived in the second half of the 20th century—as outlined in Marcel Schneider's *Histoire de la Littérature Fantastique en France* (1964) and Jean-Baptiste Baronian's *Panorama de la Littérature Fantastique de la Langue Française* (1978) and showcased by such editors as Alain Doremieux, Daniel Conrad, and Benoit Domis—French *fantaisie* only began to revive in the popular marketplace when the sudden explosion of American genre fantasy provided a new set of exemplars. The greatest resurgence of interest was in **historical fantasy**, often with a domestic setting but including such conscientious exotica as **Christian Jacq**'s accounts of ancient Egypt.

By 1990, French popular fantasy and French literary fantasy had begun a process of cross-fertilization that promised a considerable increase in variety and ambition. Notable recent examples that have been translated include Marc Behm's *Afraid to Death* (1991; tr. 2000), Jacqueline Harpman's *Orlanda* (1996; tr. 1999), Marie Darrieussecq's *My Phantom Husband* (1998; tr. 1999), Daniel Arsand's *The Land of Darkness* (1998; tr. 2001), Erik L'Homme's *Quadehar the Sorcerer*

(2002; tr. 2003), Flavia Bujor's *The Prophecy of the Gems* (2002; tr. 2004; aka *The Prophecy of the Stones*), and Hervé Jubert's *Dance of the Assassins* (2002; tr. 2004). Significant genre writers who have not yet been translated include Michel Pagel, Pierre Grimbert, Rachel Tanner, Xavier Mauméjean, Fabrice Anfosso, Michel Robert, Jean-Louis Fetjaine, Mathieu Gaborit, and Léa Silhol. New magazines wholly or partly devoted to fantasy fiction include *Faeries* (founded 2000) and *Asphodale* (founded 2002).

FRIESNER, ESTHER M. (1951–). U.S. writer. The **Arabian fantasy** series comprising *Mustapha and His Wise Dog* (1985), *Spells of Mortal Weaving* (1986), *The Witchwood Cradle* (1987), and *The Water King's Laughter* (1989) is lightheartedly stereotypical, but her work became more distinctive as she developed a more extravagant kind of **humorous fantasy** in the **urban fantasy** trilogy *New York by Knight* (1986), *Elf Defence* (1988), and *Sphynxes Wild* (1989). The comedy became gradually more extravagant in three further trilogies, one comprising *Here be Demons* (1988), *Demon Blues* (1989), and *Hooray for Hellywood* (1999); one *Gnome Man's Land* (1991), *Harpy High* (1991), and *Unicorn U* (1992); and the third *Majyk by Accident* (1993), *Majyk by Hook or Crook* (1994), and *Majyk by Design* (1994).

Friesner's other works include the **quest** fantasies *Harlot's Ruse* (1986) and *The Silver Mountain* (1986); the **alternative history** fantasies *Druid's Blood* (1988), *Yesterday We Saw Mermaids* (1991), *Child of the Eagle* (1996), and the couplet comprising *The Psalms of Herod* (1995) and *The Sword of Mary* (1996); and the **wish-fulfillment fantasy** *The Wishing Season* (1993; exp. 1996). She collaborated with **Lawrence Watt-Evans** on *Split Heirs* (1993) and **Robert Asprin** on *E.godz* (2003). Her short fiction is sampled in *Up the Wall and Other Stories* (2000) and *Death and the Librarian and Other Stories* (2002). Her anthologies of humorous fantasy include *Alien Pregnant by Elvis* (1994; with Martin H. Greenberg); *Blood Muse* (1995; with Greenberg), featuring "**vampires** in the Arts"; and the series comprising *Chicks in Chainmail* (1995), *Did You Say Chicks?* (1998), *Chicks 'n' Chained Males* (1999), *The Chick Is in the Mail* (2000), and *Turn the Other Chick* (2004), which refuse to take **amazons** seriously.

FRITH, NIGEL (1941–). British writer whose fantasies **recycle** myths from various sources; the **Hindu** myth–based *The Legend of Krishna* (1975; aka *Krishna*) and the **Nordic** *The Spear of Mistletoe* (1977; aka

Asgard) do so straightforwardly, but the trilogy comprising *Jormundgand* (1986), *Dragon* (1987), and *Olympiad* (1988) is more syncretically and **transfiguratively** ambitious. *Snow* (1993) is a **contemporary/ghost story**.

FUNKE, CORNELIA (1958–). German writer for **children**. *The Thief Lord* (2000; tr. 2002) makes marginal use of a time-shifting carousel. In the more ambitious *Inkheart* (2003), which follows in the footsteps of **Michael Ende**'s *The Neverending Story,* characters come to life as the protagonist reads a book aloud—including the villainous Capricorn. In *The Dragon Rider* (2004), the young **dragon** Firedrake is warned that humans are planning to destroy his homeland and seeks refuge beyond the Rim of Heaven.

FUREY, MAGGIE (1955–). British writer. The series comprising *Aurian* (1994), *Harp of Winds* (1994), *The Sword of Flame* (1995), and *Dhiammara* (1997) is a **feminized/epic fantasy** whose heroine makes gradual progress toward self-actualization as an **immortal** wielder of **magic.** The Shadowleague series, comprising *The Heart of Myrial* (1998), *The Spirit of the Stone* (2001), and *The Eye of Eternity* (2002; aka *Echo of Eternity*), is set in a world divided by Curtain Walls.

– G –

GAARDER, JOSTEIN (1952–). Norwegian philosopher and writer of challenging **sentimental fantasies** for **children**. *The Frog Castle* (1988; tr. 1999) is a **transfiguration/fairy tale** *The Solitaire Mystery* (1990; tr. 1996) is an elaborate **quest** fantasy involving symbolic playing cards. *Sophie's World* (1991; tr. 1994) is an ambitious exercise in didacticism that embeds a synoptic history of philosophy within a **metafiction** stocked with characters from legend and literature; it became an international best seller. In *Through a Glass Darkly* (1993; tr. 1996), a terminally ill girl discusses her prospects with an **angel**. In *The Christmas Mystery* (1992; tr. 1996), the story revealed by an Advent calendar prompts a **timeslip** to Bethlehem. *Maya* (1999; tr. 2000) is a complex metafictional mystery in which the Joker steps out of a deck of cards. In *The Ringmaster's Daughter* (2001; tr. 2002), a boy with a rich imagination grows up to be a ghostwriter and hoaxer. In *The Orange Girl* (2003; tr. 2004), a posthumous letter describes a curious quest.

GABALDON, DIANA (1952–). U.S. writer of historical fiction who edged into fantasy in a best-selling **timeslip** romance series pairing an 18th-century Scotsman with a 20th-century wife: *Outlander* (1991; aka *Cross Stitch*), *Dragonfly in Amber* (1992), *Voyager* (1993), *The Drums of Autumn* (1996), and *The Fiery Cross* (2001). The last-named expands its scope to take in the American War of Independence. *The Outlandish Companion* (1999) is a **guide**.

GAIMAN, NEIL (1960–). British writer whose early work was in the **comic**-book medium, very successful in the **graphic novel** format. He worked on *Violent Cases* (1987) and *Outrageous Tales of the Old Testament* (1987) before redesigning two old superheroes, *Black Orchid* (1988–89) and *The Sandman* (1989–96; reprinted in 10 vols.); the 75 issues of the latter project converted the eponymous character into the personalization of **Dream**, supplementing him with a set of **allegorical** siblings (Destiny, Destruction, Despair, Desire, Delirium, and **Death**) whose exploits extended into text in the anthology *The Sandman: Book of Dreams* (1996) and the **Oriental fantasy** novella *The Dream Hunters* (1999) and further graphic novels like *The Sandman: Endless Nights* (2003).

Gaiman wrote an **apocalyptic fantasy** in collaboration with **Terry Pratchett**, *Good Omens: The Nice and Accurate Prophecies of Agnes Nutter, Witch* (1990), and some short fiction—including items collected in *Angels & Visitations: A Miscellany* (1993; exp. 1998 as *Smoke and Mirrors*)—before switching his major effort into the text medium. *Neverwhere* (1996), the novelization of a TV serial, became a U.S. best seller, preparing the way for *Stardust* (1998), a sophisticated **fairy tale** fantasy cast in the archaic mold of **Hope Mirrlees** and **Lord Dunsany**. *American Gods* (2001) cleverly elaborates the notion that **gods** are created and sustained by worship. The **dark/portal fantasy** *Coraline* (2002) takes its heroine to the world of her "other mother" (the wicked stepmother of fairy tales). *Snow Glass Apples* (2002) is a play based on a Snow White **transfiguration**. Further short fiction is collected in *Adventures in the Dream Trade* (2002). *The Wolves in the Walls* (2003) is a scary picture book.

GALLAND, ANTOINE (1646–1715). French Islamist who collected manuscripts while a member of a French diplomatic mission to the Levant in 1670–75. In 1692, he became assistant to Barthélemy d'Herbelot on the *Bilbliothèque orientale,* an encyclopedia of Islamic culture, and brought it to completion in 1697, two years after d'Herbelot's death. Its samples of folklore were praised by **Charles Perrault** and became a useful source for fanciful literateurs. Galland followed it up with a translation of the tale of Sinbad the Sailor (1701), which he subsequently integrated into his translation (12 vols., 1704–16) of a collection known in English as *The Arabian Nights* or *The Thousand and One Nights*. This phenomenally successful and highly influential work became the source book for the subgenre of **Arabian fantasy**.

Galland's collection (sometimes augmented and routinely **transfigured** by other hands) was translated into other languages long before any translations were made directly from Arabic. Because several of the tales in Galland—including those of Aladdin and Ali Baba—appear to have no prior manuscript sources, he is suspected of having made them up. Most of the pastiches that followed in some profusion are entirely fake; they include François Pétis la Croix's collection of Persian tales (1712; tr. 1714) and three collections by Thomas-Simon Gueulette—*Chinese Tales* (1725), *Tartarian Tales* (1730; tr. 1759; aka *The Thousand and One Quarters of an Hour*), and *Mogul Tales* (1736). The author of *The Tales of the Genii* (1765), an untraveled clergyman named James Ridley, poses as "Charles Morell," British ambassador to the Mogul empire. Galland's model was more freely adapted in Jan Potocki's sprawling *Manuscript Found in Saragossa* (partial pub. 1813–14 in French; 1847 in Polish; full English tr. 1995), **Captain Marryat**'s *The Pacha of Many Tales*, **Paul Féval**'s *Knightshade,* and **Robert Irwin**'s *The Arabian Nightmare*.

GAMES. Many games involve an element of **psychological fantasy**; the "let's pretend" element of collective play is often formalized in rule-bound games, including card games and board games, and such games are often **transfigured** in fantasy fiction, as in **Lewis Carroll**'s Alice books and **Dahlov Ipcar**'s *The Warlock of Night*. A reverse transfiguration was achieved in the 1970s, when the apparatus of literary fantasy was adapted into Gary Gygax's hugely successful role-playing game (RPG) *Dungeons and Dragons* (launched 1974; advanced version 1978). *D&D* is formulated as a **quest** undertaken by a company of characters—each of which is managed and developed by a player—following an obstacle course devised by a "dungeon master" whose negotiation is arbitrated by dice. The apparatus provided for dungeon masters was plundered wholesale from **sword and sorcery** fiction and the works of **J. R. R. Tolkien**, compounded into a syncretic mass whose substance was rapidly reexported into the **fantasyland** of **commodified fantasy**. The range of literary plunder was broadened by rival game designers, notably Chaosium, which followed up the **Michael Moorcock**–influenced *RuneQuest* (launched 1978) with scenarios adapted from the work of **H. P. Lovecraft** (*Call of Cthulhu,* 1981) and the **Arthurian** RPG *Pendragon* (1984).

The boom in RPGs prompted the development of books that were, in effect, game scenarios, in which the reader-as-character negotiated a way through a maze of options in the hope of discovering a satisfactory conclusion. *The Warlock of Firetop Mountain* (1982), by Steve Jackson and Ian Livingstone, launched a highly successful and much-imitated Fighting Fantasy series in Britain, the profits being ploughed into Games Workshop, a company with early products that included the RPG *Warhammer* (launched 1986). By this time, the owners of *D&D* had launched a best-selling series of **tie-in** novels reexporting their game scenarios into the text medium, a campaign spearheaded by **Margaret Weis** and Tracy Hickman's DragonLance Chronicles (launched 1984). A career path opened up for writers who had begun their careers as game designers or specialist tie-in writers to diversify their exploits in commodified fantasy; those who followed it include **Raymond E. Feist**, **R. A. Salvatore**, Rose Estes, Ed Greenwood, **Michael A. Stackpole**, and **Thomas Harlan**.

Jackson and Livingstone eventually sold Games Workshop to Citadel Miniatures, a company that made plastic models used to represent characters. In order to enhance their core business, that company switched most of its effort from RPGs to war games, which required whole armies of figures; *Warhammer Fantasy Battle* displaced the RPG and was supplemented by the futuristic *Warhammer 40,000* as Games Workshop globalized its operations. U.S. companies discovered another merchandising route when they devised RPGs that used customized playing cards instead of dice as arbiters of success; early examples included *Amber* (based on **Roger Zelazny**'s series) and *Everway*, but the first great success of this new form was White Wolf's *Vampire: The Masquerade* (1991). It was followed by *Magic: The Gathering* (1993); the commercial triumph of that game—boosted by the ploy of producing some of the vital playing cards in such small quantities that they become valuable collectors' items—eventually allowed its producers, Wizards of the Coast, to take over TSR, the owners of *D&D,* which had had a meteoric career. U.S.-produced products of this kind were, however, outdone in marketing terms by a Japanese import, the child-oriented *Pokémon* cards; Wizards of the Coast were taken over in their turn—by Hasbro—in 1999.

Computers were first used as venues for fantasy-based games in 1977, when the Tolkien-based *Adventure* was created, played as a text dialogue; by the early 1980s, there was an expanding genre of "interactive fiction." Graphic representations were added in 1984 to *The Hobbit*. A theory of interactive narrative developed by Brenda Laurel in 1985 proposed a system of plot generation based on Aristotle's *Poetics*. In the meantime, rapid progress was being made in iconic computer games that involved shooting space invaders, asteroids, and other miscellaneous adversaries, promising an eventual fusion. The first commercial computer-based RPG was *Ultima* (launched 1980), but its evolving series was overtaken in 1988 by *Heroes of the Lance* and *Pools of Radiance,* which borrowed the scenarios of TSR's two best-selling tie-in series. These were, however, individual adventure games; collective play on the nascent Internet required the development of "Multi-user dungeons" (MUDs); these were developed on an amateur basis during the 1980s for use in connection with *Ultima On-Line*.

Shooting games began a rapid evolution toward action-adventure excursions in ever more elaborate **virtual realities**, their scenarios benefiting from successive generations of new special effects. The arrival of the mouse in the late 1980s killed off text-based interactive fictions and prompted the rapid evolution of graphic versions. The most significant fantasy example was *Myst* (1993), with an introduction describing it as a "book" that the player was "entering"—**immersive fantasy** in a new form. As game consoles marketed by Sega and Nintendo evolved rapidly in the early 1990s, the imagery of fantasy was exploited by such shooting games as *Doom* (1993), designed by a former RPG player. By 1999, development budgets, such as for *Final Fantasy VII,* were exceeding those of Hollywood movies.

MUD-assisted clones of *Ultima On-Line*—including *Neverwriter* and *Lords of Empyria*—made steady progress in the 1990s, eventually spawning *Everquest* (released 1999), with a fantasyworld, Norrath, that expanded rapidly. By 2004, *Everquest* was held on multiple servers, each one capable of hosting up to 3,000 simultaneous players. Sony reported that the game had 450,000 subscribers in 2004—greater than the annual sales of any but the best-selling books—while the global leader among such online RPGs, the South Korea–based *Lineage,* had more than a million. As with immersive fantasy books, the plotlines developed in online RPGs were initially formularistic in the extreme, but *Everquest2* and *Lineage2,* both launched in 2004, explored the potential for greater flexibility. In the meantime, cyberspatial "game spaces" have become increasing popular as locations for **secondary worlds**, assisting the growth of **hybrid/science fantasy** in which a science-fictional frame holds a magical scenario; notable examples include **Tad Williams**'s Otherworld series, **Will Shetterley**'s *The Tangled Lands,* and **Vivian Vande Velde**'s *User Unfriendly*.

GARCIA MÁRQUEZ, GABRIEL (1928–). Colombian writer who became famous as the popularizer of **magic realism**, leading the way into the Anglo-American market for many other Latin American writers. His first publication in 1947 was a **posthumous fantasy**, but much of his early work was naturalistic; the intrusion of fantastic materials is traceable in the omnibus *Collected Stories* (1984), and the subsequent collection translated as *Strange Pilgrims* (1992; tr. 1993) is heavily biased toward fantasy themes, especially **afterlife fantasy**. The novel translated as *One Hundred Years of Solitude* (1967; tr. 1970) is set in the town of Macondo, first introduced in the naturalistic "Leaf Storm" (1952; tr. 1979), where the history of the exemplary locale is seamlessly confused with all manner of fantastic intrusions, which perform various **allegorical** and **satirical** functions in assisting the story of the town and its inhabitants to become a politically judgmental account of Colombia and its people. *The Autumn of the Patriarch* (1975; tr. 1976), *Love in the Time of Cholera* (1985; tr. 1988), and *The General in his Labyrinth* (1989; tr. 1990) are more restrained, but their narrative methods are similar. In *Of Love and Other Demons* (1994; tr. 1995) a young priest is seduced by an exotic girl.

GARDNER, CRAIG SHAW (1949–). U.S. writer most of whose work is **humorous fantasy**. The series comprising *A Malady of Magicks* (1986), *A Multitude of Monsters* (1986), *A Night in the Netherhells* (1987), *A Difficulty with Dwarves* (1987), *An Excess of Enchantments* (1988), and *A Disagreement with Death* (1989) converts stereotypical genre materials into pun-laden pantomime comedy. The trilogy comprising *Slaves of the Volcano God* (1989), *Bride of the Slime Monster* (1990), and *Revenge of the Fluffy Bunnies* (1991) is more enterprising in its conversion of concatenations of movie clichés into **secondary**

worlds. *The Other Sinbad* (1991), *A Bad Day for Ali Baba* (1991), and *Scheherazade's Night Out* (1992, aka *The Last Arabian Night*) employ the background of **Arabian fantasy** for the same kind of slapstick, but Gardner appeared to tire of it thereafter; *Raven Walking* (1994; aka *Dragon Sleeping*), *Dragon Waking* (1995), and *Dragon Burning* (1996) are straightforward accounts of displaced humans working out their issues in a stereotyped **secondary world**. As "Peter Garrison," he wrote the **chimerical** series comprising *The Changeling War* (1999), *The Sorcerer's Gun* (1999), and *The Magic Dead* (2000).

GARDNER, JOHN (1933–1982). U.S. scholar—not to be confused with the British thriller writer of the same name—whose academic work included studies of **Arthurian** romance and a translation of the **epic** of Gilgamesh. His early fiction recycled the legends of Beowulf, in *Grendel* (1971), and *Jason and Medeia* (1973) in an **epic** poem. The stories collected in *The King's Indian* (1974) are mostly **fabulations**, and *In the Suicide Mountains* (1977) incorporates similar materials. *Freddy's Book* (1980) is a complex **delusional fantasy** whose protagonist uses fantasy imagery in self-therapy; *Mickelsson's Ghosts* (1982) and the incomplete *Shadows* (in *Stillness and Shadows*, 1986) are similar but **darker**.

GARFIELD, LEON (1921–1996). British writer best known for vivid historical fiction set in the 18th century, marketed for **children**. The title novella of *Mr Corbett's Ghost and Other Stories* (1968) is a phantasmagoric **Christmas fantasy**. *The Ghost Downstairs* (1972) is a graphic **Faustian fantasy**. *The Wedding Ghost* (1985) is a stylish **sentimental fantasy** ingeniously transfiguring a **fairy tale**. *Empty Sleeve* (1988) is also a **ghost** story. Garfield **recycled** two **classical fantasies**, *The God beneath the Sea* (1970) and *The Golden Shadow* (1973), both in collaboration with Edward Blishen; his *Shakespeare Stories* (1985) includes prose versions of *The Tempest* and *A Midsummer Night's Dream*.

GARNER, ALAN (1934–). British writer best known for **children's fantasies**. The couplet comprising *The Weirdstone of Brisingamen* (1960) and *The Moon of Gomrath* (1963) feature increasingly insistent intrusions of apparatus from Celtic, Arthurian, and other mythical and legendary sources into the landscapes surrounding Alderley Edge in Cheshire, which cannot in the end be confined. *Elidor* (1965) is an elaborate **portal fantasy** in which sacred objects recovered from a **secondary world** cause havoc until they can be used to redeem the version of

Faerie, whose key they hold. *The Owl Service* (1967) **recycles** a Celtic legend in a present-day setting with remarkable intensity, and the same theme of **bondage** by eternal recurrence recurs in *Red Shift* (1973). His work changed direction thereafter, although he published numerous collections of straightforwardly recycled **fairy tales** and eventually revisited his old territory, albeit tentatively, in the **historical fantasies** *Strandloper* (1996) and *The Well of the Wind* (1998). The mystery *Thursbitch* (2003) has **visionary** and fabular elements.

GARNETT, RICHARD (1835–1906). British writer and scholar. His delicately **humorous** and **decadent** fantasies were collected in *The Twilight of the Gods* (1888; exp. 1903); they recruit motifs eclectically from various mythologies, many of them sarcastic **Christian fantasies** with sensibility that extends into **literary satanism** in "The Demon Pope," "The Bell of St. Euschemon," and "Alexander the Ratcatcher." The title story, which tracks the career of Prometheus after his liberation, is an archetypal account of **thinning**, and the other **classical fantasies** included are similarly elegiac in spite of their caustic wit.

GASKELL, JANE (1941–). British writer. *Strange Evil* (1957), written when she was 14, is a **portal fantasy** featuring an unusual version of **Faerie**. *King's Daughter* (1958), about an exile from Atlantis, prepared the way for a trilogy of **Atlantean fantasies** comprising *The Serpent* (1966; 2-vol. version as *The Serpent* and *The Dragon*), *Atlan* (1966), and *The City* (1966), to which *Some Summer Lands* (1977) was a belated sequel. *The Shiny Narrow Grin* (1964) is an early revisionist **vampire** novel. *Sun Bubble* (1990) has some marginal fantastic content.

GAUTIER, THÉOPHILE (1811–1872). French writer, a leading figure in the Romantic movement. Many of his works—including the lush **erotic fantasy** *Mademoiselle de Maupin* (1835), the blithely **decadent** *Fortunio* (1837), the historical extravaganzas "One of Cleopatra's Nights" (1838) and "King Candaules" (1844), and the mock-**chivalric romance** *Captain Fracasse* (1863)—are self-consciously exotic but sparing in their use of explicit supernaturalism. The two shorter items were included with other classic erotic fantasies—the **vampire** story "Clarimonde" (1836), the **timeslip** fantasy "Arria Marcella" (1852), the humorous **ghost story** "Omphale" (1834), and the **hallucinatory fantasy** "The Mummy's Foot" (1840)—in **Lafcadio Hearn**'s collection *One of Cleopatra's Nights and Other Fantastic Romances* (1882) in advance of their appearance in F. C. Sumichrast's 24-volume translation of *The Works of Théophile Gautier* (1900–1903).

Gautier's other fantasies include the **doppelgänger** story "The Duplicated Knight" (1840); the **identity-exchange** story *Avatar* (1856); *Jettatura* (1857), about a man cursed with the evil eye; *Spirite* (1866), a **sentimental fantasy** in which love transcends death; and the playful "Mademoiselle Dafné" (1866). Although Gautier represented the zenith of French **romanticism**, he was also the first to recognize its obsolescence; his memorial introduction to the third edition of **Charles Baudelaire**'s *Les Fleurs du Mal* echoed the regretful note of his own fantasies, whose **wish-fulfillment** aspect was consistently bittersweet. His most often reprinted tales are frequently retitled, including all the items in *My Fantoms* (tr. by Richard Holmes, 1976). The formula of his erotic fantasies continued to recur in such pastiches as Pierre Bessand-Massenet's *Amorous Ghost* (1955, 1957).

GEARY, PATRICIA (1951–). U.S. writer. *Living in Ether* (1982) is a **contemporary fantasy** set in California. *Strange Toys* (1987) is an account of a magically complicated sibling relationship. The sensitive heroine of *The Other Canyon* (2002) exercises her talent on a Native American artifact.

GEMMELL, DAVID (1948–). British writer specializing in action-adventure fantasy, whose work echoes the fierce narrative drive and resolute masculinity of **Robert E. Howard**. The Drenai series, comprising *Legend* (1984; aka *Against the Horde*), *The King beyond the Gate* (1985), *Waylander* (1986), *Quest for Lost Heroes* (1990), *Waylander II: In the Realm of the Wolf* (1992), the collection *The First Chronicles of Druss the Legend* (1993), *The Legend of Deathwalker* (1996), *Winter Warriors* (1997), and *Hero in the Shadows* (2000), is set in a disintegrating quasi-medieval empire. A new Druss the Legend series began with *White Wolf* (2003) and *Swords of Night and Day* (2004).

A more loosely knit sequence includes a post-holocaust trilogy, comprising *Wolf in Shadow* (1987; aka *The Jerusalem Man*), *The Last Guardian* (1989), and *Bloodstone* (1994); a quasi-**Arthurian** couplet, comprising *Ghost King* (1988) and *The Last Sword of Power* (1988); and two **historical fantasies** set in ancient Greece, *Lion of Macedon* (1991) and *Dark Prince* (1991). *Ironhand's Daughter* (1995) and *The Hawk Eternal* (1995) are **portal fantasies** with female heroes. The Rigante series comprises *Sword in the Storm* (1998), *Midnight Falcon* (1999), *Ravenheart* (2001), and *Stormrider* (2002).

Gemmell's other works include *Knights of Dark Renown* (1989), about a company of displaced medieval knights; *The Lost Crown* (1989), featuring a child warlock and a conceited owl; *Morning Star* (1992), which **transfigures** the legend of Robin Hood; the **heroic fantasy** *Dark Moon* (1996); and the **planetary romance** *Echoes of the Great Song* (1997). He wrote *White Knight, Black Swan* (1993) as "Ross Harding."

GENTLE, MARY (1956–). British writer. *A Hawk in Silver* (1977; rev. 1985) is a **contemporary fantasy** in which survivors of **Atlantis** are manifest as **fairy** folk. Some of her later work is a **hybrid/science fantasy**, but the sequence comprising *Rats and Gargoyles* (1990), *The Architecture of Desire* (1991), and the lead story in the collection *Left to His Own Devices* (1994)—to which two of the stories in the earlier *Scholars and Soldiers* (1989) are also related—offers a complex account of a **god**-governed city in a **secondary world** ruled by rats, the apparatus eventually leaking into the **primary world**; *White Crow* (2003) is an omnibus. *Grunts!* (1992) is a satire of **commodified fantasy** seen from the viewpoint of mercenary orcs unaware that they have signed up on the side of Evil. *Ash: A Secret History* (2000; in the United States 1999–2000 in 4 vols., *A Secret History, Carthage Ascendant, The Wild Machines,* and *Lost Burgundy*) is an elaborate **historical fantasy** about the exploits of a female warrior in 15th-century Burgundy. The book *1610: A Sundial in a Grave* (2003) is similar in kind, as is the novella *Under the Penitence* (2004). More short fiction is collected in *Cartomancy* (2004).

GERMAN FANTASY. German fantasy is rooted in such extensions of French chivalric romance as Wolfram von Eschenbach's *Parzifal* (c1210), which co-opted the legend of Prester John into the story of the **grail** and gave **Chrétien de Troye**'s hero a son named Lohengrin. The tradition was revived by the Romantic movement, whose Gothic component—at its most extreme in the *schauerroman* ["horrid novel"]—was considerably darker than the English Gothic novels and French *romans frénétiques* it helped to inspire.

Although the *schauerroman* is the foundation stone on which modern **horror fiction** is built, many German examples retain enough of the substance of **chivalric romance** to give them a **chimerical** quality carried over into the *kuntsmärchen* [**art fairy tales**] of **J. K. Musäus**, **Ludwig Tieck**, Clemens Brentano, the **Baron de la Motte Fouqué**, **Wilhelm Hauff**, and Adalbert von Chamisso; Johann Apel's often-recycled Faustian fantasy about a magic bullet, "Der Freischutz" (1810), is an archetypal example. The **delusional fantasies** of **E. T. A. Hoffmann** also edge from **ambiguity** toward chimerical status. The German Romantics and the linguistic theorist **Jacob Grimm** seemed perfectly happy to accept the inference that if *märchen* really did embody the German *volksgeist,* there must be an element of violent perversity therein—a notion that persisted long afterward in such cultural products as Nazi mysticism.

Romanticism faded away in the 1820s, but collections of old and new *märchen* continued to appear in the work of such writers as Ludwig Bechstein and the Freiherr von Ungern-Sternberg, supplemented by the **Christian fantasies** of Gottfried Keller (1819–90). The most remarkable extensions of German fantasy in this period were in the theater and concert hall, initially in the work of **Richard Wagner** and later that of Richard Strauss, whose chief librettist Hugo von Hoffmannstahl continued the tradition of **art fairy tales** in *Four Stories* (1905; tr. 1968) and wrote nonmusical fantasy plays along with **Gerhardt Hauptmann**.

The literary fantasy written in the late 19th century by such writers as Oscar Panizza and Karl Strobl retained a strong component of horror, carried forward into the 20th century by the **surreal** fantasies of Alfred Kubin and **Leo Perutz**; the **historical fantasies** of Paul Busson, notably *The Man Who Was Born Again* (1921; tr. 1927) and *The Fire Spirits* (1923; tr. 1929); the **occult** fantasies of **Gustav Meyrink**; and the **decadent** fantasies of Hanns Heinz Ewers. Exceptions to the rule included Manfred Kyber's **animal fables**.

Hoffmanstahl, Meyrink, and Perutz helped to build a distinctively Austrian school of German-language fiction, showcased in *The Dedalus Book of Austrian Fantasy: The Meyrink Years 1890–1930* (1993; exp. as *The Dedalus Book of Austrian Fantasy 1890–2000*), ed. Mike Mitchell; it suffered even greater disruption by the realism-favoring Nazis than did the domestic tradition, but it survived; its subsequent contributors included Alexander Lernet-Holenia, author of *The Resurrection of Maltravers* (1936; tr. 1988) and *Count Luna: Two Tales of the Real and Unreal* (1955; tr. 1956), and Christoph Ransmayr, author of *The Last World* (1988; tr. 1990) and *The Dog King* (1997).

German fantastic fiction was slow to recover after World War II, although significant exemplars were provided by Günter Grass, whose first quasi-**allegorical** novel, *The Tin Drum* (1959; tr. 1962), is centered on a mute boy who refuses to grow up. As in other European nations, fantasy made a greater impact in **children's fiction** before 1980, in the work of such writers as **Michael Ende**—a success carried forward into the work of **Cornelia Funke**—but the critical success of **Herbert Rosendorfer** and the commercial success of **Hans Bemmann** created influential precedents thereafter. Other notable works originated in German include Gert Hoffman's *Balzac's Horse and Other Stories* (1988), Reinhardt Jung's *Dreaming in Black and White* (1996; tr. 2000), and Eugen Egner's *Androids from Milk* (1999; tr. 2001).

GHOST. The visible relic of a dead person, usually insubstantial and often elusive. Accounts of revenant spirits are common elements of folklore in many cultures; such restless spirits are often featured as demanders of justice or bringers of warnings, with the result that the great majority of such stories carry a frisson of **horror**; this allowed the ghost story to become a central subgenre of horror fiction (refer to *HDHL*) from the Gothic novel onward. Some spirits, however, return to offer reassurance that death is not the end for those who are loved and lost, so the idea has a consolatory aspect that allows accounts of ghostly visitations to form a substantial part of the subgenre of **sentimental fantasy**, as reflected in such works as **Théophile Gautier**'s *Spirite* and **Robert Nathan**'s *So Love Returns*.

There is also a strong tradition of **humorous** ghost stories, pioneered by **R. H. Barham** and **Charles Dickens**; the latter gave such a significant role to ghosts in *A Christmas Carol* that **Christmas fantasy** became almost synonymous with "Christmas ghost stories"—an association that took on an earnest aspect when Christmas magazine supplements attained their heyday as the fashionability of **spiritualist fantasy** peaked. The advent of psychical research societies in the late 19th century generated a good deal of **metaphysical fantasy** in which ghosts are speculatively explained, as in the **occult detective** subgenre and such recherché works as Mary Harriott Norris's *The Veil* (1907).

The importance of ghosts in horror fiction is **satirically** reflected in a good deal of humorous fantasy and ensures that ghostly apparitions are a common symptom of **delusional fantasy**. There is a sense in which all **afterlife fantasies** are ghost stories, although **posthumous fantasies** are more easily interpreted as exercises in ghostly **existential fantasy**, especially those in which spirits are becalmed on Earth because they cannot "progress" to the next phase in their destiny.

Until the boom in **children's**/horror stories began in the 1980s, the roles of ghosts in children's fantasy were usually calculated to deemphasize, if not to dispel, their fearful aspect, so children's ghost stories are closely linked with **timeslip** fantasies, their apparitions functioning primarily as transtemporal bridges. Ghosts in children's fiction often play mentoring roles, offering educational glimpses into the past, as in works by **Penelope Lively** and **Eva Ibbotson**; many are enlivening presences, as in Nancy Atherton's series begun with *Aunt Dimity's Death* (1992).

Literary fiction makes considerable use of ghosts whose function is **symbolic** even when their manifestations are by no means **ambiguous**; characters who are writers are particularly prone to be pestered by ghosts, as in Brian Moore's *Fergus* (1970) and *The Mangan Heritage* (1979) and Marcel Möring's *In Babylon* (1997 in Dutch; tr. 1999). Other recent examples of haunted literary fiction include Josephine Boyle's *The Spirit of the Family* (2000), Sarah Blake's *Grange House* (2000), Sean Desmond's *Adam's Fall* (2000), Jessica Adams's *I'm a Believer* (2002), Susie Maloney's *The Dwelling* (2003), and John Harwood's *The Ghost Writer* (2004).

GIANT. An unnaturally large human being. Giants appear in many **myth** systems, being particularly prominent in **Nordic** mythology, although the Titans of **classical** mythology were presumably also giants and even Genesis refers back to a time when "there were giants in the Earth." They are standard adversaries of **folktales**; according to such folklorists as Robert Hunt, they have a particular significance in British folklore, dutifully reflected in the work of such pioneers of British fantasy as **John Sterling**. They also feature in **chivalric romance** as stern challenges for heroic knights, although the ones **Cervantes**'s Don Quixote took on turned out to be windmills. Notable examples from early fantasy literature include **Rabelais**'s Gargantua and Pantagruel and the inhabitants of Brobdingnag in **Jonathan Swift**'s *Gulliver's Travels*.

The British tradition of giant fantasy was carried into the 20th century by **Eric Linklater** in *A Spell for Old Bones*, **John Cowper Powys** and Andrew Sinclair in the trilogy of **satires** comprising *Gog* (1967), *Magog* (1972), and *King Ludd* (1988), but most 20th-century giants are relatively modest in size, like those in Hilary Mantel's *The Giant O'Brien* (1998) and Harvey Jacobs' *American Goliath* (1997). Some, however, go to the opposite extreme; the Rabelaisian aspects of Joe Orton's *Head to Toe* (1971) and **Jane Gaskell**'s "Caves" (1984) question the suggestion that size doesn't matter in a calculatedly gross fashion.

GILBERT, WILLIAM (1804–1890). British medical man and writer, the father of **W. S. Gilbert**. He was a pioneer of psychiatry, extrapolating his work in that field in two anonymously issued collections of hypothetical case studies in **delusional fantasy**, *Shirley Hall Asylum; or, The Memoirs of a Monomaniac* (1863) and *Doctor Austin's Guests* (1866). *The Magic Mirror, a Round of Tales for Young and Old* (1866) is a compendium of cautionary **wish-fulfillment fantasies**. *The Wizard of the Mountain* (1867) similarly mingles elements of horror and humor in its **moralistic fantasies**, which are far more generous with punishments than rewards; "The Innominato's Confession" explains this imbalance by arguing that the idea of **magic** is essentially diabolical, tempting rebellion against divine providence. *The Washerwoman's Foundling* (1867) and *The Seven-Leagued Boots* (1869) are **fairy tales** of a similar ilk.

GILBERT, WILLIAM S. (1836–1911). British humorist. His two collections of *Bab Ballads* (1867–73) adapted the tradition of nonsense poetry pioneered by **Edward Lear** and **Lewis Carroll** for adult readers. His early work for the **theater** was mostly **humorous fantasy**, including *The Palace of Truth* (1871), *The Wicked World* (1873), and *Topsyturvydom* (1974); the last title was sometimes used as a quasi-generic term when the subversive spirit of these early works was carried forward into the light operas he wrote in collaboration with composer Arthur Sullivan. These include *Iolanthe, or the Peer and the Peri* (1882), in which the House of Lords and the ruling hierarchy of **Faerie** trade places, and *Ruddigore; or, The Witch's Curse* (1887), about a line of baronets condemned to commit a sin a day or perish. Gilbert's prose fiction was sampled in *Foggerty's Fairy and Other Tales* (1890; exp. as *The Lost Stories of W. S. Gilbert*, ed. Peter Haining, 1982).

GILMAN, GREER (1951–). U.S. writer. *Moonwise* (1991) is a highly sophisticated **quest** fantasy couched in an extraordinarily rich and complex language and set against the background of the conflict between two lunar **goddesses**, the side effects of which include the cycle of the seasons. The similarly stylized "Jack Daw's Pack" (2000) is equally complex in its redeployment of mythical materials, here incarnate as symbolic playing cards. Jack Daw is an upstart **god** whose ambitions are also featured in "A Crowd of Bone" (2003), the second item of a projected three-part mosaic.

GOBLIN. No clear division can be drawn between goblins (or hobgoblins) and other **fairy** subspecies, many of which play malevolent or mischievous roles in various **folktales**, but literary goblins are usually situated at the malign end of the spectrum, whether in **humorous fantasies** like **Charles Dickens**'s "The Story of the Goblins Who Stole a Sexton" or darker moralistic fantasies like **Christina Rossetti**'s "Goblin Market" and **George MacDonald**'s *The Princess and the Goblin*. The makers of the evil mirror in **Hans Christian Andersen**'s "The Snow Queen" are usually—but not invariably—called goblins in translations, licensing such transfigurative exercises as **C. J. Cherryh**'s *The Goblin Mirror*. Other notable modern deployments of goblins include **Alan Dean Foster**'s *Kingdoms of Light,* Hilari Bell's *The Goblin Wood* (2003), a revenge fantasy in which a human renegade sides with goblins, and Clare B. Dunkle's trilogy begun with *The Hollow Kingdom* (2003), in which a goblin king catches 19th-century human trespassers and involves them in his conflict with the **elves**.

GOD. When used as a generic noun, a superhuman entity employed as an object of worship; as a proper noun, the supreme being of monotheistic religions, signified in the Judeo-Christian tradition by the tetragrammaton expandable as Yahweh and Jehovah, and called Allah by Muslims. The appointment of the *one* God required all others to be rendered obsolete or demonized, but the gods of the **classical** pantheon—and, to a lesser extent, those of the **Nordic** pantheon—retain considerable narrative utility as symbols of various aspects of nature and human propensity, so they remain significant figures even beyond the limits of fantasy literature.

Reverence demands that God maintain a dignified absence from most **Christian fantasies**, where He is more often represented by **angels**, but He often appears in unflattering roles in antireligious **satires**—especially mocking **apocalyptic fantasies**—and exercises in **literary satanism**. Notable **religious fantasies** that attempt His description in order to explore or explain his mysterious ways include **G. K. Chesterton**'s *The Man Who Was Thursday*, Robert Munson Grey's *I, Yahweh* (1937), several **allegories** by **T. F. Powys**, and **James Morrow**'s *Towing Jehovah*. The Greco-Roman all-father is diplomatically substituted in such works as **Percy Shelley**'s *Prometheus Unbound,* Benjamin Disraeli's "Ixion in Heaven," and Maurice Druon's *The Memoirs of Zeus* (1963).

The gods of tribes who lost out in the relentless march of Western progress and colonial adventurism are almost invariably represented in fiction as mere idols; even when they maintain an an active supernatural presence, it is usually **demonic** and often in the process of **thinning**, in accordance with a principle—reflected in such works as **Richard Garnett**'s "The Twilight of the Gods," **Laurence Housman**'s *Gods and Their Makers,* and **Neil Gaiman**'s *American Gods*—holding that gods decline as the number and faith of their worshippers dwindle. Gods who refuse to fade away politely under such circumstances inevitably become problematic, as in **Felicity Savage**'s *Humility Garden*.

GODDESS. A female god. Modern neopagans and the **scholarly fantasies** associated with their renaissance routinely claim (despite a dearth of plausible evidence) that worship of the male gods who were ultimately fused into *the* God displaced an older and much more widespread form of monotheistic worship devoted to *the* Goddess, who was known by different names in different cultures—including Gaia, Isis, Innana, Astarte, Ishtar, and Parvati—but always played the same Earth Mother role. She is allegedly reproduced in weaker guise in many goddesses of later provenance, having been fragmented in the **classical** pantheon and elsewhere, and is more feebly echoed in queens of **Faerie** and other femmes fatales. **Feminized fantasy** very often adopts a version of this scholarly fantasy into its background; **Robert Graves**'s *The White Goddess* is an often-used **taproot text** and goddess worship has been integrated into modern **lifestyle fantasy/witchcraft** by such practitioners as "Starhawk."

Notable examples of goddess fantasy include **David Lindsay**'s *Devil's Tor,* various works by **Dion Fortune**, **Marion Zimmer Bradley**'s *The Forest House,* **Greer Gilman**'s *Moonwise,* **Louise Cooper**'s *Our Lady of the Snow,* **Elizabeth Hand**'s *Waking the Moon,* and Brenda Gates Smith's *Secrets of the Ancient Goddess* (1999), Karen Michalson's *Enemy Glory* (2001) and *Hecate's Glory* (2003)—in which a young trainee **wizard** becomes a reluctant acolyte of the goddess of evil—**Elizabeth Cunningham**'s *The Return of the Goddess,* **Freda Warrington**'s *The Court of the Midnight King,* **Nalo Hopkinson**'s *The Salt Roads,* and Anne Harris's *Inventing Memory* (2004). *See also* EROTIC FANTASY.

GOETHE, JOHANN WOLFGANG VON (1749–1832). German writer, a central figure of German literature and its **Romantic** movement. He wrote **ballads** based in folklore and began work on a definitive dramatic version of *Faust* in 1773, although its two parts did not see publication until 1808 and 1832. The seven tales collected in *Unterhaltungen deutscher Ausgewanderten* [Conversations with the German Emigrants] (1795) include two **ghost** stories and the classic **art fairy tale** *Das Märchen* (tr. as "Goethe's Fairy Tale"). The story translated as "The New Melusina" (1817) is a **transfigured** folktale. *See also* FAUSTIAN FANTASY.

GOGOL, NIKOLAI (1809–1852). Russian writer. His early stories, cast in the form of **folktales**, were collected in volumes translated as *Evenings on a Farm near Dikanka* (1831–32) and *Mirgorod* (1835). His later works were **satirical fabulations**, the most famous being "The Nose" (1836), a pioneering exercise in absurdism in which the eponymous feature is detached from its natural setting in order to take up an independent existence as a civil servant, and "The Overcoat" (1842), which tells of a clerk's death-defying determination to acquire that garment. The most comprehensive sampler of his work is *The Collected Tales and Plays of Nikolai Gogol* (1964).

GOLDMAN, WILLIAM (1931–). U.S. writer best known as a movie scriptwriter. His affectionate **metafictional** satire *The Princess Bride: S. Morgenstern's Classic Tale of True Love and High Adventure, the "Good Parts" Version* (1971) masquerades as an abridgement of a book from which the author's grandfather read to him in his childhood, carefully omitting all the boring bits. *The Silent Gondoliers: A Fable by S. Morgenstern* (1983) is a slim sequel. *Magic* (1976) is a **delusional fantasy** about a ventriloquist whose dummy becomes his **doppelgänger**.

GOLDSTEIN, LISA (1953–). U.S. writer. *The Red Magician* (1982) is a **historical fantasy** set in a Jewish village in Eastern Europe before World War II. *The Dream Years* (1985) is a **timeslip** fantasy featuring the Paris of the **Surrealist** movement. *Tourists* (1989) is a surreal fantasy set in an imaginary Middle Eastern country. *Strange Devices of the Sun and Moon* (1993) is set in a version of 16th-century London intimately linked to **Faerie**. In *Summer King, Winter Fool* (1994), the conflict of personified seasons is mirrored in the lives of human characters. The heroine of *Walking the Labyrinth* (1996) discovers magical family secrets. *Dark Cities Underground* (1999) is a **dark/portal fantasy**. *The Alchemist's Door* (2002) is a historical fantasy featuring John Dee and Rabbi Loew. Goldstein's short fiction collections *Daily Voices* (1989) and *Travelers in Magic* (1994) mingle fantasy and **sf**. She wrote *Daughter of Exile* (2004) as Isabel Glass.

GOLEM. In Jewish legend, a humanoid creature molded out of clay and animated by a spell written on paper and placed in its mouth. The 16th-century rabbi Judah Loew was said to have created one to defend the Jews of the Prague ghetto against a pogrom. Literary **recyclings** of the story include Shulamith Ish-Kishor's *The Master of Miracle* (1971) and **Isaac Bashevis Singer**'s *The Golem*. Other golem stories of note include **Gustav Meyrink**'s *The Golem,* **Sean Stewart**'s *Resurrection Man,* **Cynthia Ozick**'s *The Puttermesser Papers,* **Michael Chabon**'s *The Amazing Adventures of Kavalier and Clay,* Thane Rosenbaum's *The Golems of Gotham* (2002), and Frances Sherwood's *The Book of Splendor* (2002).

GOODKIND, TERRY (1948–). U.S. writer. The Sword of Truth sequence, comprising *Wizard's First Rule* (1994), *Stone of Tears* (1995), *Blood of the Fold* (1996), *Temple of the Winds* (1997), *Soul of the Fire* (1999), *Faith of the Fallen* (2000), *The Pillars of Creation* (2001), and *Naked Empire* (2003), plus the novella *Debt of Bones* (1998; rev. 2001), is a **commodified**, **epic fantasy** of a violent and atypically cynical stripe.

GOREY, EDWARD (1925–2000). U.S. illustrator. The many brief picture books he began issuing in 1953 resemble orthodox **children's** books in their format but incorporate a strong element of **surreal** black **humor**. Most of the early volumes were gathered into the omnibuses *Amphigorey* (1972), *Amphigorey Too* (1975), and *Amphigorey Also* (1983). Gorey's works—especially those in which the text is rendered in verse—continue the nonsense tradition founded by **Edward Lear** (some of whose works he illustrated for new editions) and **Lewis Carroll**, but delight in gruesome and macabre twists. His last books were *The Haunted Tea-Cosy: A Dispirited and Distasteful Diversion for Christmas* (1998) and *The Headless Bust: A Melancholy Meditation on the False Millennium* (1999).

GOTHIC FANTASY. A term imported as a category description, by analogy with Gothic architecture, to describe the **horror** novels that enjoyed a hectic fad in Britain at the end of the 18th century (refer to *HDHL*). The fact that almost all of them were set in the past distinguishes them from the bulk of modern horror fiction, linking them to the tradition of **chivalric romance**. **Nathan Drake** pointed out that there was a "sportive" element to the Gothic imagination as well as a sinister one, incorporating **fairy** lore. Some so-called Gothic novels, most conspicuously **William Beckford**'s *Vathek,* are more appropriately considered as fantasies.

Once the fad was over, familiarity had robbed many of the images prolifically deployed by the Gothic novelists of their power to frighten readers, and they were frequently deployed with comedic intent or as mere grotesquerie, thus facilitating the proliferation of a self-conscious and tongue-in-cheek kind of Gothic fantasy, elements of which can be seen in **humorous ghost** stories—notably **Charles Dickens**'s **Christmas fantasy** *A Christmas Carol*—and archly **decadent fantasies** by writers like **Richard Garnett** and **Vernon Lee**. By 1900, however, new life had been breathed into the old images by more artful writers of **intrusive** horror stories, and an uneasy balance was struck between ghosts that still had the power to strike terror and those that had lost the knack, with considerable scope for tonal **ambiguity**.

The grotesque element of Gothic fantasy was made sophisticated in the 20th century by ornately mannered and calculatedly archaic **moral fantasies** like those offered by Isak Dinesen (Karen Blixen) as *Seven Gothic Tales* (1934) and Ghislain de Diesbach in *The Toys of Princes* (1960 in French; tr. 1962). American Gothic had always seemed out of place, even in the days of Charles Brockden Brown, **Nathaniel Hawthorne**, and **Edgar Allan Poe**, and this encouraged 20th-century cultivation of its grotesque element, especially in "Southern Gothic" fictions used to highlight contrasts between the progressive impetus of the North (symbolized by New York) and the atavistic archaism of the South (symbolized by New Orleans). Much American Gothic material is nonsupernatural, but its fantasy component is evident in such writers as Mary Elizabeth Counselman and some works by Joyce Carol Oates, notably in *Bellefleur* (1980), *A Bloodsmoor Romance* (1982), and *Mysteries of Winterthurn* (1984). Other modern examples include Joe R. Lansdale's *Freezer Burn* (1999) and Tom Piccirilli's *A Choir of Ill Children* (2003), but the most spectacular development in the subgenre has come about because of its extraordinary hospitability to vampires, as displayed by **Anne Rice** and Stephen Gresham's *In the Blood* (2001). As with decadent English Gothic, the fad quickly gave rise to parody, in such works as Charlaine Harris's series begun with *Dead until Dark* (2001) and Andrew Fox's series begun with *Fat White Vampire Blues* (2003).

The introduction to the showcase **anthology** *The New Gothic* (1991), ed. Patrick McGrath and Bradford Morrow, points out that the old Gothic was largely defined by its "furniture"; the stories in it—including works by **Angela Carter** and **Robert Coover**—demonstrate that such furniture has a very different aesthetic value when it is transplanted to modern literary dwellings.

GOUDGE, ELIZABETH (1900–1984). British writer. Fantasy is very evident in her work for **children**, which she began to publish in *The Fairies' Baby and Other Stories* (1919). In *Smoky-House* (1940), **fairies** assist the protagonists to combat smugglers. *The Little White Horse* (1946) and *Linnets and Valerians* (1964) are enterprising accounts of the lifting of family curses. *The Valley of Song* (1951) is an **Arcadian fantasy** in which a family feud is healed by benevolent **witchcraft**. Goudge's work for adults occasionally reflects her sincere belief in witchcraft and **ghosts**, although she usually employed her extensive knowledge of legend and superstition in a carefully noncommittal fashion.

GOURMONT, RÉMY DE (1858–1915). French writer. He was a major figure in the **Decadent** movement and the leading literary critic of his day. Several fantasies are included in *Studies in Fascination* (1892; tr. in the omnibus *The Angels of Perversity*, 1992), and there are others scattered in his later collections. His play *Lilith* (1892; tr. 1946) is a forthright exercise in **literary satanism**, and the novel translated as *A Night in the Luxembourg* (1906; tr. 1912) is a **sentimental/hallucinatory fantasy**. Some of his whimsical philosophical essays about the vagaries of the sexual impulse represent themselves as letters from *Mr Antiphilos, Satyr* (1913; tr. 1922).

GRAHAME, KENNETH (1859–1932). British writer. Like **J. M. Barrie**, he came to regard childhood as an ideal state of being, conflating its rose-tinted memory with nostalgia for a lost paradise. This confusion is amply displayed in the collections of conscientiously artificial **children's** stories *The Golden Age* (1895) and *Dream Days* (1898). The sensibility was perfected in the classic **animal fantasy** *The Wind in the Willows* (1908), which includes an incongruous item of **Arcadian fantasy** in the chapter titled "Piper at the Gates of Dawn." The novel's curiously elastic and somewhat paradoxical pattern of anthropomorphization owes something to the example of earlier writers, including **Beatrix Potter**, but it is highly distinctive. **William Horwood** has written sequels.

GRAIL. A symbolic vessel featured in the **allegorical** episode of **Chrétien de Troyes**'s **Arthurian fantasy** tracking Perceval's ambition to become a knight. It is glimpsed in the castle of the wounded Fisher

King (Jesus) and is therefore identified with the cup from which Christ drank at the Last Supper, which was supposedly used by Joseph of Arimathea to collect his blood at the crucifixion—thus being the "original" communion chalice. The notion that questing for the ever-elusive grail was a key mission of Arthur's knights was elaborated in a 13th-century manuscript by a Cistercian monk, translated as *The Quest of the Holy Grail,* the climactic vision in which is credited to Galahad. The incorporation of Chrétien's story into Welsh documents encouraged an alternative interpretation wherein the image was derived from **Celtic** mythology, perhaps from a cauldron used in pagan religious rites—a version that figures largely in such **scholarly fantasies** as **Jessie Weston**'s. The Christian version has similarly become a key component of the **secret histories** developed by rival schools of scholarly fantasy.

The story of the grail continues to be **recycled** in works by **Richard Monaco**, **Lindsay Clarke**, and Nancy McKenzie's *Grail Prince* (2002), **transfigured** in such interpretative historical fantasies as Bernard Cornwell's trilogy, comprising *Harlequin* (2000; aka *The Archer's Tale*), *Vagabond* (2002), and *Heretic* (2003), and redeployed in works by **Arthur Machen**, **Charles Williams**'s *War in Heaven*, Gerald Heard's "The Cup" (1947), **James Blaylock**'s *The Paper Grail,* and Pamela Smith Hill's *The Last Grail Keeper* (2001).

GRANT, JOHN (1949–). Pseudonym of British writer Paul Barnett, active in various genres. His major fantasy novels are *Albion* (1991), about a society in which people lack long-term memory, and *The World* (1992), which relocates that milieu within a complex **multiverse** in need of renewal. His short fiction is sampled in *Take No Prisoners* (2004). With **John Clute**, he coedited *The Encyclopedia of Fantasy* (1997).

GRANT, RICHARD (1952–). U.S. writer. His early work forms a loose sequence that comprises *Saraband of Lost Time* (1985), *Rumors of Spring* (1987), *View from the Oldest House* (1989), and *Through the Heart* (1992): a **hybrid** post-holocaust **science fantasy** in which the fantasy elements are predominant—most conspicuously in the second, which involves a spiritual **quest** in an **Arcadian** landscape. *Tex and Molly in the Afterlife* (1996) is a witty and stylish **contemporary** and **posthumous fantasy**. *In the Land of Winter* (1997) features a modern **witch** who falls victim to a modern witch hunt when her daughter is taken into the care of social workers. *Kaspian Lost* (1999) is an **exis-**

tentialist fantasy in which a boy tries to reconstruct fragmentary memories of a confusing interval of his life.

GRAPHIC NOVEL. A term coined in the 1980s to describe ambitious **comic**-strip projects. Collections of comic-book issues far outnumbered long stories written specifically for the format, but they aspired nevertheless to the kind of seriousness attached to the more ambitious French *bandes dessinées*. Translations of Hergé's *Adventures of Tintin* and René Goscinny's *Asterix the Gaul* provided formal models, while other translations from the French showcased more sophisticated artwork. Translations of Japanese *manga* also became a significant influence in the early 1990s.

Fantasy elements were peripheral to the Asterix series but central to the humorous **Arabian fantasy** of Goscinny's other major project *Iznogoud* (1962–94). The legacy of **chivalric romance** was evident in France in such series as François Bourgeon's *Les Compagnons du crépuscule* [Companions of the Twilight] (1984–90), and more diverse French legends were dramatized in graphic novels by Didier Comès. American graphic novels inevitably drew their primary material from superhero comics, but the more adventurous writers to work in the medium—especially **Neil Gaiman**, in *Sandman* reprints and *Harlequin Valentine* (2002)—soon began to broaden the format's scope.

Notable examples of graphic novel fantasy include Alan Moore and Kevin O'Neill's The League of Extraordinary Gentlemen series (launched 2000) and Carla Speed McNeill's Finder series (launched 1999). William Messner-Loebs and Sam Kieth's **historical fantasy** *Epicurus the Sage* (2003) features the exploits of the great philosopher. Micah Harris and Michael Gaydos's *Heaven's War* (2004) describes a mystical confrontation between **Aleister Crowley** and the **Inklings**. Stephen Weiner's *Faster than a Speeding Bullet: The Rise of the Graphic Novel* (2003) is a compact history of the format.

GRAY, ALASDAIR (1934–). Scottish artist and writer. Much of his self-illustrated fantasy consists of distinctive **fabulations** scattered within the collections *Unlikely Stories, Mostly* (1983), *Lean Tales* (1985 with James Kelman and Agnes Owens), *Ten Tall Tales and True* (1993), *Mavis Belfrage: A Romantic Novel, with Five Shorter Tales* (1996), and *The Ends of Our Tethers* (2003). His novels are mostly naturalistic or **sf**, but *Lanark: A Life in Four Parts* (1981) is a highly distinctive **epic/Odyssean/afterlife fantasy** of an stripe set in the infernal realm of

Unthank. *1982 Janine* (1984) has elements of **erotic** and **metaphysical fantasy**.

GRAY, NICHOLAS STUART (1922–1981). Scottish actor/director and writer, whose work for the **theater** included numerous **fairy tale** adaptations, including *Beauty and the Beast* (1950), *The Marvellous Story of Puss-in-Boots* (1954), and several adaptations of **Hans Christian Andersen**, notably *The Tinder-Box* (1951) and *The Imperial Nightingale* (1956). His fiction **transfigures** similar materials. *Over the Hills in Fabylon* (1954) is a generalized celebration of **enchantment**, but *Down in the Cellar* (1961) has a **darker** edge. *The Seventh Swan* (play and book, 1962), *The Stone Cage* (1963), *The Sorcerer's Apprentice* (1965), and *The Further Adventures of Puss-in-Boots* (1971) are further fairy tale **transfigurations**. *Grimbold's Other World* is an **animal fantasy**. *The Apple-Stone* (1965) uses a template established by **E. Nesbit**. Gray's short fiction is collected in *Mainly in Moonlight* (1965).

GREEN, ROGER LANCELYN (1918–1987). British writer. *Tellers of Tales* (1946; exp. 1953, 1956, 1965, and 1969), a collection of biographies and bibliographies of children's writers—especially fantasists—was an important historical survey; he followed it up with more detailed accounts of several key writers, including **Andrew Lang**, **Lewis Carroll**, and **J. M. Barrie**, and also wrote two biographies of **C. S. Lewis**. His anthologies of fantasy include the notable showcases *Modern Fairy Stories* (1955) and *Fairy Stories* (1958), the latter concentrating on Victorian material. Most of his fiction **recycles** myths and legends, but *From the World's End* (1948) is an enterprising **visionary fantasy**, and *The Land beyond the North* (1958) brings the **classical** Argonauts to Britain.

GREEN, SHARON (1942–). U.S. writer who wrote numerous **planetary romances** in the sadomasochistic vein of John Norman before developing more elaborate fantasy backcloths and less obsessive adventures in *The Rebel Prince* (1987), *Lady Blade, Lord Fighter* (1987), and two couplets, one comprising *The Far Side of Forever* (1987) and *Hellbound Magic* (1989) and the other *Mists of the Ages* (1988) and *Dawn Song* (1990). The trilogy comprising *Silver Princess, Golden Knight* (1993), *Dark Mirror, Dark Dreams* (1994), and *Wind Whispers, Shadow Shouts* (1995) is a **portal fantasy** featuring a masochistic female **theriomorph**. *Enchanting* (1994) is a **paranormal romance**. *The Hidden Realms* (1993) is an account of soul stealing. *Game's End* (1996), the Blending series (comprising *Convergence* [1996], *Competitions* [1997], *Challenges* [1998], *Betrayals* [1999], and *Prophecy* [1999]), and the Blending Enthroned trilogy (comprising *Intrigues* [2000], *Deceptions* [2001], and *Destiny* [2002]), are hectic **sword and sorcery** adventures.

GREEN, SIMON R. (1955–). British writer, also of **sf**. The series comprising *Hawk & Fisher* (1990; aka *No Haven for the Guilty*), *Winner Takes All* (1991; aka *Devil Take the Hindmost*), *The God Killer* (1991), *Wolf in the Fold* (1991; aka *Vengeance for a Lonely Man*), *Guard against Dishonor* (1991), and *The Bones of Haven* (1992; aka *Two Kings in Haven*) is hard-boiled **detective** fiction set in a **secondary world**. The trilogy comprising *Blue Moon Rising* (1991), *Blood and Honour* (1992), and *Down among the Dead Men* (1993) is a **quest** fantasy that was fused with the earlier series by *Beyond the Blue Moon* (2000). *Shadows Fall* (1994) is a **hybrid/science fantasy**. The **chimerical** *Drinking Midnight Wine* (2001) juxtaposes the real world of Veritie with a syncretic realm of Mysterie. The series launched with *Something from the Nightside* (2003), *Agents of Light and Darkness* (2003), and *Nightingale's Lament* (2004) is hard-boiled detective fiction in which a part of London is permanently becalmed at 3 A.M.

GREEN, TERENCE M. (1947–). Canadian writer whose early work, collected in *The Woman Who Is the Midnight Wind* (1987), is mostly **sf**. The **timeslip** story *Children of the Rainbow* (1992) prepared the way for the more elaborate exploration of family history carried out in *Shadow of Ashland* (1996) and *St. Patrick's Bed* (2001), the latter featuring **ghosts**; *A Witness to Life* (1999) is a **prequel** to *The Shadow of Ashland,* whose narrative is an atypical example of **time reversal**.

GRIMM, BROTHERS. German folklorists Jacob Ludwig Grimm (1785–1863) and Wilhelm Karl Grimm (1786–1859), who were closely involved with the German Romantic movement; Jacob was a pioneer in the scientific study of the German language and its associated folklore, to whose preservation both brothers became strongly committed. Their collection of *Kinder- und Hausmárchen* ["Children's and Household Tales"] (1812–15 in 3 vols.) was a landmark in the history of fantasy fiction.

Later scholars, including Heinz Rölleke, John S. Ellis, and **Jack Zipes**—who prepared a definitive 241-item collection of *The Complete Fairy Tales of the Brothers Grimm* (1987)—criticized the brothers' reliance on middle-class informants and their tendency to rewrite tales to emphasize their **moralistic** aspect and to remove "offensive" material, but the Grimms' versions of "Hansel and Gretel," "Rumpelstiltskin," "The Twelve Dancing Princesses," "The Little Tailor," "Briar Rose," "Snow White and Rose Red," and many others were important contributions to the bedrock of modern **fairy tales**.

The Grimms' tales are **darker** than those adopted into literary form by French writers a century before—their "Ashputtle" is much harsher than **Perrault**'s "Cendrillon"—and this endeared them to modern writers ambitious to exploit the horrific potential of revisionist folktales; such writers delight in puns like **Tanith Lee**'s *Red as Blood; or, Tales from the Sisters Grimmer* (1983). The dubious antiquity of some of the Grimms' tales is proclaimed by their inclusion of a version of "Little Red Riding Hood," which Perrault probably originated, so the darker elements may have more to do with the license granted to German child-care givers to indulge in moral terrorism—graphically illustrated by Heinrich Hoffmann's *Struwwelpeter*—than any deep-seated *volksgeist*.

GRIMWOOD, KEN (1945–2003). U.S. writer whose first venture into fantasy was the **timeslip** romance *Breakthrough* (1976). *Replay* (1986) is a more complicated **existential fantasy**, in which the protagonist attempts to exploit the opportunities provided by a series of timeslips that return his mature consciousness to his younger body, generating a sequence of personal **alternative histories**. *Into the Deep* (1995) is a **science fantasy** parable.

GRUNDY, STEPHAN (1967–). U.S. writer. His **epic fantasy** *Rhinegold* (1994) **recycles** the **Nordic** legends on which **Richard Wagner** based the Ring cycle, carefully **thinning** out the supernatural elements as the story progresses. *Attila's Treasure* (1996) is set in the same milieu. *Gilgamesh* (1999) recycles the Sumerian epic.

GUIDE. Guidebooks to **classical** and other **mythologies** and **Arthurian** and other legends provided models for guides to the imaginary universes of fantasy literature, which became significant in respect of **epic fantasy**. **Ballantine**'s publication of Robert Foster's *The Complete Guide to Middle-earth* (1978; expanded from a 1971 version) provided a key model for other such exercises, including guides to **Robert Jordan**'s *Wheel of Time* series and Gene Wolfe's *Book of the New Sun*. The A-to-Z format of Alberto Manguel and Gianni Guadalupi's *Dictionary of Imaginary Places* (1980; rev. 1987), which takes in **L. Frank Baum**'s Oz, **Ursula Le Guin**'s Earthsea, **Tove Jansson**'s Moominland, **Sylvia**

Townsend Warner's *Kingdoms of Elfin,* Paul Féval's *Vampire City,* and many others, as well as Middle-earth, is mimicked in **Diana Wynne Jones**'s **satirical** *Tough Guide to Fantasyland.*

GUNN, NEIL M. (1891–1973). Scottish writer whose works—including the stories in *Hidden Doors* (1929) and the novels *Second Sight* (1940), *The Silver Darlings* (1941), *The Silver Bough* (1948), and *The Well at the World's End* (1951)—often contain elements of **visionary fantasy** and echoes of legendary exploits. *Sun Circle* (1933) borrows from a **Frazerian/scholarly fantasy** as to its depiction of **druidic** ritual and religion. *Young Art and Old Hector* (1942) includes several exemplary **folktales**, and its sequel *The Green Isle of the Great Deep* (1944) is a wholehearted **afterlife fantasy** in which the condition of the land of the dead mirrors the historical predicament of the Highlands. *The Other Landscape* (1954) forsakes the imagery of **Celtic** folklore for the ideology of Eastern mysticism.

GYPSY. A corruption of "Egyptian," also spelled "gipsy," applied to an ethnic group also known as Roma (or Romany), Bohemians, and Zingari (or Zincali). Gypsies arrived in Europe in the 14th century as wanderers; the range of names applied to them signifies the widespread confusion as to their origins. As pagan outsiders with an arcane language (based on Sanskrit), they were routinely credited with magical abilities, decribed in some detail by **Charles Godfrey Leland**. Gypsy fortune-tellers became a literary cliché, and a sojourn with the gypsies became a staple element of the personal histories concocted by modern **lifestyle fantasists**. Notable fantasies giving significant roles to gypsies include "The Gypsy Christ" by William Sharp (**Fiona MacLeod**), **Charles Williams**'s *The Greater Trumps,* **John Crowley**'s *Aegypt,* and Eliza-Beth Gilligan's Gypsy Silk series, launched with *Magic's Silken Snare* (2003). Romany folklore has only recently become available as a resource; **Leah R. Cutter**'s *The Caves of Buda* is one of the few novels that draws upon it.

– H –

HAGGARD, SIR H. RIDER (1856–1925). British writer who followed up his classic boys' book *King Solomon's Mines* (1885) with the widely imitated *She: A History of Adventure* (1886), which founded the subgenre of **karmic romance** and established a new model of the femme fatale in Ayesha, alias She-Who-Must-Be-Obeyed; she was featured in three sequels, *Ayesha; or, The Return of She* (1905), *She and Allan* (1920), and *Wisdom's Daughter* (1923). The hero's triangular relationship with the femme fatale and her mundane rival was echoed in many other stories, including two **timeslip** fantasies featuring Allan Quatermain from *King Solomon's Mines*, *The Ancient Allan* (1920), and *Allan and the Ice-Gods* (1927); other Haggard heroes who suffered in similar fashion include Odysseus in *The World's Desire* (1890, with **Andrew Lang**) and the Viking protagonists of *Eric Brighteyes* (1891) and *The Wanderer's Necklace* (1914).

Haggard's other fantasies include *Stella Fregelius: A Tale of Three Destinies* (1903), the 1905 title novella of *Smith and the Pharaohs and Other Tales* (1920), and the anti-hunting **allegory** *The Mahatma and the Hare: A Dream Story* (1911). There are fantasy elements in several of his **lost race** stories, including *The Ghost Kings* (1908; aka *The Lady of the Heavens*), *The Yellow God* (1909), *Queen Sheba's Ring* (1910), and *When the World Shook* (1919). His occult beliefs were hardened by the death of his son in World War I, but the consequent dogmatic defensiveness did not work to the advantage of such **occult** romances as *Love Eternal* (1918). Revisitations of Haggard's *She* include **Richard Monaco**'s *Journey to the Flame* and **Peter Tremayne**'s *The Vengeance of She*; a further Haggard sequel by another hand is Mildred Downey Broxon's *Eric Brighteyes 2: A Witch's Welcome* (1979, as by "Sigfridur Skaldaspilir").

HALLUCINATORY FANTASY. A subdivision of **visionary fantasy** in which the implication of revelation carried by more pretentious kinds of vision is much reduced and in which the **dream** experience is temporary and clearly confined (unlike the stubborn confusions of **delusional fantasy**). The literary device of justifying a fantastic narrative by revealing it as a dream is so elementary and intrinsically anticlimactic that it fell into disrepute in the 20th century, although it had earlier been fundamental to such subgenres as **allegory**. The suspicion that life itself might be a kind of dream and we mere figments of it is broached in such fantasies as **Lewis Carroll**'s *Through the Looking Glass*. The notion that a dreamer might become lost in a hallucinatory wilderness where all apparent awakenings are mere renewals, featured in Jan Potocki's *The Saragossa Manuscript*, is dubbed *The Arabian Nightmare* by **Robert Irwin**.

In the 19th century, when the opium-solution laudanum was the only available painkiller, its hallucinogenic effects influenced the literary works of **E. T. A. Hoffmann**, **Samuel Coleridge**, **Théophile Gautier**, and others, while **Jean Lorrain** reconfigured hallucinations induced by drinking ether and synthesized hallucinations supposedly induced by hashish, in much the same way that some modern fantasists have tried to model trips induced by the fungal alkaloids psilocybin and muscarine, the plant derivatives peyotl and ayahuasca, or laboratory-purified LSD. As **Charles Baudelaire** pointed out in his study of *Artificial Paradises,* however, the aftereffects of such drugs are not at all conducive to literary endeavor.

Showcase **anthologies** of hallucinatory fantasy include *The Night Fantastic* (1991), ed. **Poul** and **Karen Anderson**; *Strange Dreams* (1993), ed. **Stephen R. Donaldson**; and *Perchance to Dream* (2000), ed. Denise Little.

HAMBLY, BARBARA (1951–). U.S. writer. The Darwath series, comprising *The Time of the Dark* (1982), *The Walls of Air* (1983), *The Armies of Daylight* (1983), *Mother of Winter* (1996), and *Icefalcon's Quest* (1998), uses a Californian **portal** to introduce its protagonists into a commodified **fantasyland** that quickly outgrew its formulaic origins. The enterprising trilogy comprising *The Ladies of Mandrigyn* (1984), *The Witches of Wenshar* (1987), and *The Dark Hand of Magic* (1990) features the travails of a **wizard** bereft of educational institutions that might teach him to control and develop his powers. The sequence comprising *The Silent Tower* (1986), *The Silicon Mage* (1988), *Dog Wizard* (1993), and *Stranger at the Wedding* (1994, aka *Sorcerer's Ward*) is a convoluted **chimerical/science fantasy** that links California to a **secondary world** more securely and more ingeniously than does the Darwath series.

The series comprising *Dragonsbane* (1986), *Dragonshadow* (1999), *Knight of the Demon Queen* (2000), and *Dragonstar* (2002) offers a **humorous** slant on draconian confrontation. *Those Who Hunt the Night* (1988; aka *Immortal Blood*) and its sequel *Travelling with the Dead* (1995) are revisionist **vampire** stories. The couplet comprising *The Rainbow Abyss* (1991) and *The Magicians of Night* (1992) is an ironic **Odyssean fantasy**. *Bride of the Rat God* (1994) is a **historical fantasy** set in 1920s Hollywood. *Stranger at the Wedding* (1994; aka *Sorcerer's Ward*) features a female wizard's return home. *Magic Time* (2001, with Marc Scot Zicree) is an **apocalyptic/urban fantasy**. *Sisters of the*

Raven (2002) is an ironic account of men losing magical power as women gain it in a quasi-**Arabian** setting.

HAMILTON, COUNT ANTHONY (1646–1720). British writer removed to France in childhood when his parents went into exile with King Charles II. His fantasy stories were all published posthumously, the humorous **Arabian fantasy** *The Four Facardins,* the similarly extravagant **Oriental fantasy** "Story of May-Flower," and the extravagant **Faustian fantasy** "The Enchanter Faustus" in 1730, and the incomplete "Zeneyda"—which introduces various mythical entities, including **fairies**, to contemporary Paris—in 1731. These were reprinted, with the **chimerical** "The Ram," in 1749, in a collection that included completions of *The Four Facardins* (which had probably been intended as a fragmentary text) and "Zeneyda" by M. de Levis; its English translation, *Fairy Tales and Romances* (1844), added a rival continuation of *The Four Facardins* by **M. G. Lewis**, who had arranged its earlier publication as an individual item.

HAMILTON, LAUREL K. (1963–). U.S. writer. She followed up the revenge fantasy *Nightseer* (1992) with a highly successful series of **detective** thrillers set in an **alternative history** in which the United States has granted civil rights to vampires and **werewolves**; the heroine is a "fey princess." It comprises *Guilty Pleasures* (1993), *The Laughing Corpse* (1994), *Circus of the Damned* (1995), *The Lunatic Cafe* (1996), *Bloody Bones* (1996), *The Killing Dance* (1997), *Burnt Offerings* (1998), *Blue Moon* (1999), *Obsidian Butterfly* (2000), *Narcissus in Chains* (2001), *Cerulean Sins* (2003), and *Incubus Dreams* (2004). A parallel series began with *A Kiss of Shadows* (2000), *A Caress of Twilight* (2002), and *Seduced by Moonlight* (2004).

HAND, ELIZABETH (1957–). U.S. writer whose early works were **hybrid/science fantasies** (refer to *HDSFL*). *Waking the Moon* (1994) is an elaborate **contemporary fantasy** about the reawakening of the long-dormant **Goddess**. *Glimmering* (1997) is a millennial **science fantasy**. *Black Light* (1999) is a **contemporary fantasy** set in a New York state artists' community that had been featured earlier in some of the stories set in *Last Summer at Mars Hill* (1998). *Chip Crockett's Christmas Carol* (2000) is a transfigurative **Dickensian/fantasy** reprinted with three other novellas in *Bibliomancy* (2003). *Mortal Love* (2004) is a **historical fantasy** about a **muse**; it takes much inspiration from Victorian **fairy** painting and its **Shakespearean** influences.

HARD FANTASY. A term used in several different ways to construct analogies with hard **science fiction** (refer to *HDSFL*). The first tentative suggestion, made in the late 1980s by writers of **historical fantasy**, was that it might be used to refer to texts that are scrupulously faithful to historical and anthropological data save for the fantasizing device of assuming that the magical and mythical beliefs held by the cultures portrayed have an element of truth in them, as in the work of **Christian Jacq**. A 1994 essay by **Michael Swanwick** subtitled "A Cruise through the Hard Fantasy Archipelago in Search of the Lonely and the Rum . . ." wondered whether it was possible to unite a considerable number of the best fantasy texts in such a way that they might form a fundamental organizing structure similar to that provided for genre sf by hard sf; he concluded that the "hardness" of the fantasy genre is more akin to an archipelago of islands than a literary continent, because fantasy texts refuse to accept the logical bonds that tie hard sf texts together, thus being fundamentally resistant to assembly within the kind of common enterprise that unites hard sf texts in celebration of the mechanics of progress.

In the Clute/Grant *Encyclopedia of Fantasy* (1997), by contrast, Gary Westfahl used the term to describe the kind of fantasy—popularized by ***Unknown***—in which **magic** is regarded as "an almost scientific force of Nature . . . subject to the same sorts of rules and principles." Paradigm examples include Randall Garrett's Lord Darcy series (1967–81), set in a **secondary world** where **James Frazer**'s "laws of magic" are indeed laws of nature. This is probably the most useful application, given the recent proliferation of **hybrid** and **chimerical** works playing with such notions, including notable series by **L. E. Modesitt**, **J. Gregory Keyes**, and **Rick Cook**, Lyndon Hardy's trilogy begun with *Master of the Five Magics* (1980), **Andrew Crumey**'s philosophical fantasies, **Felicity Savage**'s *Ever,* **Sara Douglass**'s *Threshold,* **Ian Irvine**'s *Geomancer,* and **Eve Forward**'s *Animist*.

HARLAN, THOMAS (1964–). U.S. game designer and writer. His Oath of Empire series is an **epic/alternative history** featuring a world without Christianity where sorcery thrives, and monotheism is popularized by Mohammed of Mekkah. It comprises *The Shadow of Ararat* (1999), *The Gate of Fire* (2000), *The Storm of Heaven* (2001), and *Dark Lord* (2002).

HARMAN, ANDREW (1964–). British writer specializing in slapstick **humorous fantasy**, exemplified by *The Sorcerer's Appendix* (1993),

The Frogs of War (1994), *The Tome Tunnel* (1994), *Fahrenheit 666* (1995), *101 Damnations* (1995), *The Scrying Game* (1996), *The Deity Dozen* (1996), *A Midsummer Night's Gene* (1997), and *Beyond Belief* (1998). *It Came from on High* (1998) is **chimerical/science fantasy**. In *The Suburban Salamander Incident* (2000), Titania and her "feyrie court" are holed up beneath a golf course. In *Talonspotting* (2001), an experiment in animal therapy goes awry.

HARRIS, DEBORAH TURNER (1951–). U.S. writer. The trilogy comprising *The Burning Stone* (1986), *The Gauntlet of Malice* (1987), and *Spiral of Fire* (1987) is set in a fantasized version of medieval Scotland, as is the trilogy comprising *Caledon of the Mists* (1994), *The Queen of Ashes* (1995), and *The City of Exile* (1997). She collaborated with **Katherine Kurtz** on the **occult fantasy** sequence comprising *The Adept* (1991), *The Lodge of the Lynx* (1992), *The Templar Treasure* (1993), *Dagger Magic* (1995), and *Death of an Adept* (1996), and on the **historical fantasies** *The Temple and the Stone* (1998) and *The Temple and the Crown* (2001).

HARRIS, JOEL CHANDLER (1848–1908). U.S. journalist whose ventures into **children's fantasy** include a long series of **animal fantasies** bylined "Uncle Remus," featuring the long battle of wits between Brer Rabbit and Brer Fox, based in Negro folklore. They began to appear in periodicals in 1879 and in book form in 1881, the most comprehensive omnibus being *The Complete Tales of Uncle Remus* (1955).

HARRIS, MacDONALD (1921–1993). Pseudonym of U.S. writer Donald William Heiney. A muted fantasy element emerges by slow degrees in the literary novels *Bull Fire* (1973) and *Pandora's Gallery* (1979); *Herma* (1981), featuring an opera singer who can change sex at will, is more extravagant. *Screenplay* (1982) is a **timeslip** fantasy. *Tenth* (1984) is a **metafiction** with elements of **Faustian fantasy**. *The Little People* (1986) is a **delusional fantasy** involving **Faerie**. *Glowstone* (1987) is an ornate **historical fantasy**. His short fiction is sampled in *Cathay Stories and Other Fictions* (1988).

HARRIS, WILSON (1921–). Guyana-born writer resident in the United Kingdom from 1959. The sequence comprising *Palace of the Peacock* (1960), *The Far Journey of Oudin* (1961), *The Whole Armour* (1962), and *The Secret Ladder* (1964), with the associated *Heartland* (1964), treats the history of his homeland in a manner similar to the way in which **Gabriel Garcia Márquez** treated the history of Colombia in his definitive exercises in **magical realism**. The sequence comprising *The Eye of the Scarecrow* (1965), *The Waiting Room* (1967), *Tumatumari* (1968), and *Ascent to Onai* (1970) is a further elaboration of the theme, as are *Black Marsden* (1972), *Companions of the Day and Night* (1975), and *The Angel at the Gate* (1982). *The Sleepers of Roraima* (1970) and *The Age of the Rainmakers* (1971) recycle native American folklore. *Da Silva's Cultivated Wilderness and Genesis of the Clowns* (1977) is an omnibus of two novellas; *The Tree of the Sun* (1978) carries forward the story of the painter Da Silva, launching a long meditation on the role of the artist that extends to *The Mask of the Beggar* (2003).

The trilogy comprising *Carnival* (1985), *The Infinite Rehearsal* (1987), and *The Four Banks of the River of Space* (1990) extends from **Dantean fantasy** into **Odyssean allegory**. In *Resurrection at Sorrow Hill* (1993), inmates of an asylum re-create historical figures and **transfigured** history in the process; *Jonestown* (1996) uses similar invocations to draw comparisons between pre-Columbian and post-Columbian perspectives. In *The Dark Jester* (2001), an artist-cum-trickster engages in philosophical dialogue with the Dreamer, echoing a confrontation between the conquistador Pizarro and the Incan emperor Atahualpa.

HARRISON, M. JOHN (1945–). British writer in several genres (refer to *HDSFL*). Much of his fantasy is gathered into a loosely knit series set in the definitively **decadent** city of Viriconium, including *The Pastel City* (1971), *A Storm of Wings* (1980), *In Viriconium* (1982; aka *The Floating Gods*), and the stories collected in *Viriconium Nights* (1984; U.S. and British versions differ). The **psychological fantasy** *The Course of the Heart* (1992) picks up themes from the later volumes while examining the troublesome relationship between the **primary world** and a constructed **secondary world**. His collaborative work as "**Gabriel King**" is markedly different in kind. Some fantasies are included in the collection *Travelling Arrangements* (2000).

HAUFF, WILHELM (1802–1827). German writer associated with the **Romantic** movement whose **art fairy tales**, mostly cast as **Arabian fantasy**, were gathered into three volumes of *Märchenalamanache* (1826–28). Various translated samplers entitled *Tales* or *Fairy Tales* are less well known than an omnibus combining Hauff's *The Giant's Heart* with Adalbert von Chamisso's *The Shadowless Man* (1814). Hauff's untranslated satirical novels, heavily influenced by **E. T. A. Hoffmann**, include *Memoiren des Satan* ["Satan's Memoirs"] (1825–26) and *Phantasien im Bremer Ratskeller* ["Apparitions in the Bremer Inn"] (1827).

HAUPTMANN, GERHART (1862–1946). German writer best known as a playwright. One act of the play translated as *Hannele: A Dream Poem* (1893; tr. 1894) is couched as a delusional **afterlife fantasy**, but *The Sunken Bell* (1896; tr. 1898) is a more wholehearted **hallucinatory moralistic fantasy** based in Teutonic folklore. *And Pippa Dances* (1906; tr. 1907) is similarly hallucinatory, but *The Bow of Odysseus* (1914; tr. 1917) **recycles** the myth in meditative fashion. The novel translated as *The Fool in Christ, Emanuel Quint* (1910; tr. 1911) is a **Christian fantasy**. *Phantom* (1923; tr. 1923) is a delusional fantasy. *The Island of the Great Mother* (1924; tr. 1925) is an exotic robinsonade. In the verse **epic** *Till Eulenspiegel* (1928), the borrowed hero undertakes far-ranging explorations of European myth and legend.

HAWTHORNE, JULIAN (1846–1934). U.S. writer, the son of **Nathaniel Hawthorne**. He was long resident in London, often retitling and rewriting his works for separate British and U.S. publication. Much of his short fiction is **horror** (refer to *HDHL*), but the **visionary fantasy** "The New Endymion" (1879) transfigures a Greek **myth**, and the four items collected in *Yellow-Cap* (1880), including the **allegory** "Calladon," are **art fairy tales**. *Archibald Malmaison* (1879) is a **psychological fantasy**. He cobbled together an **alchemical fantasy**, *Doctor Grimshawe's Secret* (1882), from miscellaneous documents left behind by his father, which had earlier been organized by other hands into the rather different *Septimius* (1872) and *The Dolliver Romance* (1876). *The Professor's Sister* (1888; aka *The Spectre of the Camera*) is a fantasy of suspended animation. His work for the pulp magazines included a series of **spiritualist fantasies** comprising "Absolute Evil" (1918), "Fires Rekindled" (1919), and "Sara was Judith?" (1920). His daughter Hildegarde wrote a few **sentimental/ghost stories**, assembled by **Jessica Amanda Salmonson** in *Faded Garden: The Collected Ghost Stories of Hildegarde Hawthorne* (1985).

HAWTHORNE, NATHANIEL (1804–1864). U.S. writer, one of the central figures of 19th-century American literature. Most of his fantasies embody the conviction summed up in the title of *Twice-Told Tales* (1837; exp. in 2 vols., 1842) that human lives inevitably fall into long-established patterns formulated by **myth**, history, and ancestry. Many shade into **horror** fiction and a few into **sf**. His classic **allegories** and **moral fantasies** include "Young Goodman Brown" (1935), in which an injunction disobeyed leads to unwelcome revelations; "The Hall of Fantasy" (1843), about a "stock exchange" of fanciful ideas; the enigmatic "Ethan Brand" (1850), about a **quest** for the unpardonable sin; "The Snow Image" (1851), in which parental refusal of credulity injures childhood imagination; and "Feathertop" (1852), about a scarecrow who can pass for human as long as he does not catch sight of his image in a mirror. *A Wonder-Book for Boys and Girls* (1852) and *Tanglewood Tales for Girls and Boys* (1852) recycle **classical** myths.

Hawthorne's **Gothic**-tinted novels (refer to *HDHL*) relegate fantastic elements to **ambiguous** margins, as in *The Scarlet Letter* (1850). At his death, he left several incomplete drafts of an **alchemical fantasy** about the quest for the elixir of life, different compounds of which were published as *Septimius* (1872), *The Dolliver Romance* (1876), and *Doctor Grimshawe's Secret* (1882), the last-named constructed by his son **Julian Hawthorne**.

HAYDON, ELIZABETH (?–). Pseudonymous U.S. writer. The Symphony of Ages trilogy, comprising *Rhapsody: Child of Blood* (1999), *Prophecy: Child of Earth* (2000), and *Destiny: Child of the Sky* (2001), is an **epic** fantasy featuring magical **music**. The series continues in *Requiem for the Sun* (2002) and *Elegy for a Lost Star* (2004).

HEALER. Magical **secondary worlds** rarely play host to scientifically trained physicians, medical care usually being the responsibility of herbalists and gifted individuals who bring about cures by psychic effort or the grace of the **Goddess**; similar figures often crop up in fantasies set in the **primary world**, where they are routinely persecuted as **witches**, although they usually fare better in **contemporary fantasies** like **Elizabeth Scarborough**'s *The Healer's War*.

Healers are popular heroes of nonviolent **feminized** fantasy, particularly tales of difficult apprenticeship. Notable **secondary world** fantasies featuring healers include series by **Nick O'Donohoe** and **Judith Merkle Riley**, **Alice Hoffman**'s *Green Angel*, **Nancy Willard**'s *Things Invisible to See*, **Sherryl Jordan**'s *Secret Sacrament*, **Sara Douglass**'s *Beyond the Hanging Wall*, and Victoria Hanley's *The Seer and the Sword* (2001).

HEARN, LAFCADIO (1850–1904). Greek-born U.S. writer resident in Japan from 1891. The lapidary style he honed in his 1882 translations of

Théophile Gautier's *nouvelles* and the early prose-poetry posthumously assembled in *Fantasies* (1914) was well suited to the **Oriental fantasies** in *Some Chinese Ghosts* (1887). His later works in that vein, including those collected in *Kwaidan: Stories and Studies of Strange Things* (1904), benefit from his intimate association with their cultural context; a few others are included in *In Ghostly Japan* (1899), *Shadowings* (1900), *The Romance of the Milky Way and Other Studies and Stories* (1905), and *Karma and Other Stories* (1921); much of this work is reprinted in *The Selected Writings of Lafcadio Hearn* (1949).

HECHT, BEN (1893–1964). U.S. writer best known as a playwright and screenwriter. A **decadent** sensibility held in check in his commercial work gained expression in the blithely excessive **delusional fantasy** *Fantazius Mallare: A Mysterious Oath* (1922) and its phantasmagoric sequel *The Kingdom of Evil: A Continuation of the Journal of Fantazius Mallare* (1924). The stories in *A Book of Miracles* (1939), most of which were reprinted in *The Collected Short Stories of Ben Hecht* (1945), include the **humorous fantasy** "The Heavenly Choir," the **theriomorphic satire** "The Adventures of Professor Emmett," and two striking **religious fantasies**, "Death of Eleazer" and "Remember Thy Creator," the latter being an intense exercise in **literary satanism**. The **sentimental fantasy** *Miracle in the Rain* (1943) presumably originated as a treatment for the movie it eventually became.

HEINLEIN, ROBERT A. (1907–1988). U.S. writer, a central figure in the evolution of **sf** (refer to *HDSFL*). His early fantasies, mostly written for ***Unknown***, include "The Devil Makes the Law" (1940; reprinted with a new title in *Waldo and Magic Inc*, 1950), which describes an **alternative history** in which workable magic is regulated by law; the solipsistic fantasy "They" (1941); "Waldo" (1942), in which a high-tech future is disturbed by anarchic **magic**; and the offbeat **hybrid** *The Unpleasant Profession of Jonathan Hoag* (1942; book 1959). All of these are collected in *The Fantasies of Robert A. Heinlein* (1999). He returned to the genre in the robust **heroic fantasy** *Glory Road* (1963). *Job: A Comedy of Justice* (1983) is a **satirical/afterlife fantasy**.

HELPRIN, MARK (1947–). U.S. writer. *Winter's Tale* (1983), a spectacular **urban fantasy** with **messianic** elements in which New York becomes symbolic of a 20th-century civilization in need of **re-enchantment** and repair, is akin to **John Crowley**s *Little, Big* in its outlook and literary method. The trilogy comprising *Swan Lake* (1989), *A City in Winter*

(1996), and *The Veil of Snows* (1997) is a children's **quest** fantasy, whose first element **recycles** the story of the famous ballet. The early short fiction in *A Dove in the East and Other Stories* (1975) occasionally employs marginal fantastic devices.

HEROIC FANTASY An alternative term routinely used by critics who thought **sword and sorcery** sounded too downmarket while fantasy was struggling to assert its independence as a commercial genre. It had the advantage of a wider range of reference, being more readily applicable to **J. R. R. Tolkien**'s *Lord of the Rings* and such **children's fantasies** as **Lloyd Alexander**'s Chronicles of Prydain, thus embracing all the overlapping fields specified by the other terms bandied about in the same era for the same reason: **high fantasy**, **quest** fantasy, and **epic fantasy**. Because the commercial genre eventually expanded to cover an even wider territory, "heroic fantasy" remains useful mainly as a description of those texts in which the primary focus is replication or calculated variation of the recipe for hero myths detailed by **Joseph Campbell**.

The heroes of **classical mythology** have analogues in every culture, thus licensing Campbell's insistence that the hero is an elementary archetype. The earliest proto-English **epic** poem *Beowulf,* probably first recorded in the early eighth century, is a significant **taproot text**, as are two imaginary histories of Britain written around 1135 to provide English Norman barons with appropriate accounts of their new heritage, Geoffrey of Monmouth's *History of the Kings of Britain* and Geffrei Gaimar's *History of the English,* which recorded (and almost certainly invented) the seeds of the medieval hero myths of King Arthur and Havelok the Dane. The manufacturers of **chivalric romance** elaborated these exemplars and added many more; the Anglo-Norman *Romance of Horn* (c1170, credited to a cleric named Thomas) pioneered a much-imitated template in which an unjustly dispossessed aristocrat undergoes various errant exploits before returning to reclaim his birthright; Horn's story was recycled in **ballads** and tales, but the formula far outlasted the name. The enormously popular *Amadis of Gaul*—its earliest surviving version is a Spanish manuscript from the beginning of the 16th century—was altered and expanded by many of its recyclers, providing a key template and inspiring numerous sequels, including *Palmerin of England* (tr. 1596).

Arthurian fantasy provides a key venue for modern heroic fantasies; other notable examples include **Poul Anderson**'s *Three Hearts and Three Lions,* **Robert A. Heinlein**'s *Glory Road,* the works of **P. C.**

Hodgell, **Lawrence Watt-Evans**'s *Touched by the Gods,* Kim Hunter's trilogy comprising *Knight's Dawn* (2001), *Wizard's Funeral* (2002), and *The Scabbard's Song* (2003), and **Gene Wolfe**'s *The Knight*. "Antiheroic fantasies" like **Peter David**'s *Sir Apropos of Nothing* are variants rather than contradictions.

HESSE, HERMAN (1877–1962). German-born writer who became a Swiss citizen. His early work, from 1900 on, included numerous **art fairy tales**, translations of which are collected in *Strange News from Another Star* (1972) and *Pictor's Metamorphoses* (1982), most of whose contents are reproduced in *The Fairy Tales of Herman Hesse* (1995), ed. **Jack Zipes**. His later work includes several exotic **existentialist fantasies** yearning for some kind of transcendence of the human condition: *Demian* (1919; tr. 1965) and *Siddhartha* (1922; tr. 1954) explore relatively orthodox paths, but the painstakingly **allegorical** *Steppenwolf* (1927; tr. 1929) is more ambitious.

HIGH FANTASY. A term used by **Lloyd Alexander** in a 1971 essay on "High Fantasy and Heroic Romance" and subsequently developed by **Kenneth J. Zahorski** and Robert H. Boyer in an attempt to develop a terminology with which to deal with genre materials. In Zahorski and Boyer's taxonomy, high fantasy consists entirely of fiction set in secondary worlds, while the "low fantasy" with which it is immediately contrasted consists of fiction set in the primary world, into which magical objects and entities are introduced piecemeal (i.e., **intrusive fantasies**). Not all **immersive fantasies** qualify as high fantasy, however; the category as defined by Zahorski and Boyer excludes **humorous fantasy**, **animal fantasy**, "**myth** fantasy" (of the **recycled** variety), **fairy tales**, **gothic fantasy**, **science fantasy**, and **sword and sorcery**. The term never thrived, partly because it was difficult to establish dividing lines between high fantasy and some of these other subgenres, and partly because of the difficulty of accommodating **portal fantasies** to the scheme.

HINDU MYTHOLOGY. Despite the popularity of "Eastern mysticism" in the 19th-century occult revival, especially in connection with **Madame Blavatsky** and her followers, only a few of the ideas contained in the Vedic sacred writings are frequently echoed in Western fantasy literature, usually fused with notions drawn from other religious traditions. Fantasies of **reincarnation** tend to borrow more heavily from Buddhist ideas—thus qualifying as **karmic romances**—but Hindu notions of transmigration are also reflected there, often without distinction. Richard Francis Burton, who translated **Antoine Galland**'s *Arabian Nights* into English, produced a similar exercise of his own using a Hindu source, in *Vikram and the Vampire* (1870).

The motif from Hindu myth that crops up most frequently in fantasy is the notion of an avatar, one of a series of incarnations of a god; it is adapted to apply to all deities in **Edgar Jepson**'s *The Horned Shepherd* and *The Avatars: A Futurist Fantasy* (1933) by "A.E." (George W. Russell) but applied narrowly in Sonia Singh's *Goddess for Hire* (2004), which features a Californian avatar of Kali. The folkloristic notion of the world as Brahma's dream—which would be ended if he awoke—is sometimes cited in **hallucinatory fantasies**. The broadest range of such motifs is found in the works of **F. W. Bain**, although Ashok K. Banker's series begun with *Prince of Ayodha* (2003) and *Siege of Mithila* (2003) promises to be comprehensive. Notable Western stories based in Hindu myth include various works by **Nigel Frith** and **Tanith Lee**, **Paula Volsky**'s *The Gates of Twilight,* and Suzanne Fisher Staples' *Shiva's Fire* (2000), but the cultural background is used more innovatively in Chitra Banerjee Divakaruni's *The Mistress of Spices* (1997), about a magic-dealing grocery store, and *The Conch Bearer* (2003), which features a magical seashell. Siddharth Dhanvant Shangvi's *The Last Song of Dusk* (2004) is an example of Indian **magic realism**.

HISTORICAL FANTASY. A term applied to fantasies in which the actual history of the primary world is conscientiously reproduced, save for limited infusions of working magic located within a **secret history**—but no clear boundary separates such carefully disciplined works from **alternative histories**, or from stories set in "histories" that are themselves fantastic. The Clute/Grant *Encyclopedia* calls the latter "lands-of-fable"; the worlds of **Arthurian** and **Arabian fantasy** are notable examples. Historical fantasies dovetail neatly with the notion that the world used to be more magical than it is now, having been subject over the centuries to a **thinning** process. Fantastic devices are routinely used to contain and organize panoramic views of human history, as in **Charles Godfrey Leland**'s *Flaxius,* **Katharine Burdekin**'s *The Rebel Passion,* and Virginia Woolf's *Orlando* (1928).

Historical fantasies tend to cluster in particular periods and locations; those of conspicuous recent fashionability include renaissance Italy, as in **R. A. MacAvoy**'s *Damiano* and **Midori Snyder**'s *The Innamorati,* and 19th-century England, especially London. Such works usually draw their inspiration from other literary works, many London examples echoing Regency romances or Dickensian eccentricities, as in Jeffrey E. Barlough's Western Lights series launched by *Dark Sleeper* (2000) and *The House in the High Wood* (2001), Libba Bray's *A Great and Terrible Beauty* (2003), and **Susannah Clarke**'s *Jonathan Strange and Mr. Norrell*. The history of France has a particular resonance because of its association with **chivalric romance**, as reflected in C. Dale Brittain's *Count Scar* (1997) and L. Warren Douglas's series begun with *The Sacred Pool* (2000). The subgenre is frequently employed for revisionist exercises like Ann Chamberlin's feminist Joan of Arc Tapestries (1999–2001).

HOBAN, RUSSELL (1925–). U.S. writer and **illustrator**. His picture books for younger **children** include numerous **animal fantasies**; the more enterprising examples include *The Mole Family's Christmas* (1969) and *The Dancing Tigers* (1979). His work for older children, including *The Mouse and His Child* (1967), *The Sea-Thing Child* (1972), and *The Trokeville Way* (1996), is mildly **allegorical** and deftly **sentimental**. His adult novels are usually more discreet in their deployment of fantasy motifs, as in the **quest** fantasy *The Lion of Boaz-Jachin and Jachin-Boaz* (1973), the **delusional fantasy** *Kleinzeit* (1974), and the dark **historical fantasy** *Pilgermann* (1983), but *The Medusa Frequency* (1987) is a **hallucinatory/metafiction** with elements of **Orphean fantasy**. Similar themes are echoed in *Angelica's Grotto* (1999) and *Amaryllis Night and Day* (2001). In *Her Name Was Lola* (2004), a writer loses his memory when a girlfriend casts a spell on him. Some of the stories in *The Moment under the Moment* (1992) are fantasy.

HOBB, ROBIN. Pseudonym employed by **Megan Lindholm** on an elaborately detailed **epic fantasy** series made up of three trilogies. The first comprises *Assassin's Apprentice* (1995), *Royal Assassin* (1996), and *Assassin's Quest* (1997); the second *Ship of Magic* (1998), *Mad Ship* (1999), and *Ship of Destiny* (2000); and the third *Fool's Errand* (2001), *Golden Fool* (2003), and *Fool's Fate* (2003).

HODGELL, P. C. (1951–). U.S. writer. The sequence comprising *God Stalk* (1982), *Dark of the Moon* (1985), *Seeker's Mask* (1994), and various items of short fiction—including those in *Blood & Ivory* (1994; exp. 2002 as *Blood & Ivory: A Tapestry*)—is a detailed account of the career of a female hero, which questions the norms of **feminized fantasy** and masculine **heroic fantasy**.

HODGSON, WILLIAM HOPE (1877–1918). British writer, most of whose work lies in the borders of **horror** and **sf** (refer to *HDSFL* and *HDHL*). His importance to the fantasy genre derives from his use of **parallel worlds** in *The House on the Borderland* (1908) to model the division of the human psyche, and his provision in *The Night Land* (1912) of a crucial exemplar of **far-futuristic fantasy** that is **decadent** in style, **sentimental** in substance, **hallucinatory** in method, and spectacularly phantasmagoric in its decor. *William Hope Hodgson's Night Lands,* volume 1: *Eternal Love* (2003), ed. Andy W. Robertson, is a derivative anthology.

HOFFMAN, ALICE (1952–). U.S. writer of great versatility. The elements of fantasy in her work are usually muted, as in *Illumination Night* (1987), which features a modest **giant**, and *Second Nature* (1994), about a mysterious stranger. They are more extravagantly developed in *Practical Magic* (1995), an account of domestic **witchcraft**; *The River King* (2000), an exotic murder mystery with fugitive **ghosts**; and *Aquamarine* (2001), which features a mermaid. In *Indigo* (2002), characters with webbed fingers search for their origins. Characters in *Green Angel* (2003) and *The Probable Future* (2003) possess healing gifts. *Blackbird House* (2004) collects twelve linked stories about a haunted house.

HOFFMAN, NINA KIRIKI (1955–). U.S. writer. *Child of an Ancient City* (1992, with **Tad Williams**) is an **Arabian fantasy**. *The Unmasking* (1992) is a dark-edged **moralistic fantasy**. The **contemporary fantasy** sequence comprising *The Thread That Binds the Bones* (1993), the stories combined with it in *Common Threads* (1995), *A Red Heart of Memories* (1999), and *Past the Size of Dreaming* (2001) features a family of magically talented individuals struggling to maintain their secret situation in a changing world; *A Stir of Bones* (2003) is a **prequel**, and *The Silent Strength of Stones* (1995) is set in the same milieu. *A Fistful of Sky* (2002) features an adolescent **witch**. A few fantasies are mingled with other materials in the collections *Legacy of Fire* (1990), *Courting Disasters and Other Strange Affinities* (1991), *Common Threads* (1995), and *Time Travelers, Ghosts, and Other Visitors* (2003).

HOFFMANN, E. T. A. (1776–1822). German writer and composer, a central figure in the **Romantic** movement. He made a crucial contribution to the evolution of psychological **horror** fiction (refer to *HDHL*), much of his pioneering work taking the form of vivid **hallucinatory fantasies** drawing on the inspiration of *märchen* collected by **Musäus** and the

Grimm brothers. Hoffmann preferred to describe them as "stories in the manner of Jakob Callot" (Callot was a pioneering caricaturist); "The Golden Pot" (1814; tr. 1827) is a cardinal example. His **art fairy tales** include "Nutcracker and the King of the Mice" (1816), the untranslated "Klein Zaches gennant Zinnober" (1819), "Princess Bambiilla" (1820), and "The King's Bride" (1821). *The Life and Opinions of Kater Murr* (1820–21; tr. 1969) is a parodic *bildungsroman* with a cat for protagonist.

HOGG, JAMES (1770–1835). Scottish writer caricatured by *Blackwood's* contributor Christopher North (John Wilson) as "the Ettrick Shepherd," whose nickname was frequently attached to posthumous collections of his work. The most comprehensive is *Tales and Sketches of the Ettrick Shepherd* (6 vols., 1837). His many tales based in Scottish folklore include three novellas collected in *The Brownie of Bodsbeck* (1818); the title story is a **historical fantasy**, and "The Hunt of Eildon" is a **theriomorphic fantasy** whose protagonists end up in **Faerie**. *The Private Memoirs and Confessions of a Justified Sinner* (1824) is often categorized as a late **Gothic** novel (refer to *HDHL*) but is better regarded as an intense **psychological fantasy** and a key example of the **doppelgänger** motif.

HOLDSTOCK, ROBERT (1948–). British writer whose early work was mostly **sf** and **horror** (refer to *HDHL*); some commodified **sword and sorcery** was bylined "Richard Kirk" and "Chris Carlsen." The series comprising *Mythago Wood* (1984), *Lavondyss* (1988), the title piece of *The Bone Forest* (1991), *The Hollowing* (1993), the stories in *Merlin's Wood* (1994), and *Gate of Ivory, Gate of Horn* (1997, aka *Gate of Ivory*) is about a magical wood where archetypes of the collective unconscious of British and Breton folklore—including **Arthur**, Robin Hood, the Green Man, and the Wild Hunt—are systematically manifest. *The Fetch* (1991, aka *Unknown Regions*), "The Ragthorn" (1991 with Garry Kilworth), and *Ancient Echoes* (1996) are further **dark fantasies** based in a similar **metaphysical** system. The Merlin Codex series begun with *Celtika* (2001) and *The Iron Grail* (2002) is a **hybrid** of **Celtic** and **classical** forms.

HOLLAND, TOM (1947–). British writer whose works include several **dark/historical fantasies**. The couplet comprising *The Vampyre: Being the True Pilgrimage of George Gordon Sixth Lord Byron* (1995, aka *Lord of the Dead*) and *Supping with Panthers* (1987, aka *Slave of my*

Thirst) is revisionist **vampire** fiction. *Deliver Us from Evil* (1997) is similarly set in the 19th century. In *The Sleeper in the Sands* (1998), the discovery of Tutankhamen's tomb reveals the truth behind conventional **Arabian fantasy**.

HOLT, TOM (1961–). British writer who produced a long sequence of **humorous fantasies** deftly **recycling** and chimerically combining **mythical** motifs, borrowing most copiously from **Nordic**, **classical**, and **Arabian** sources: *Expecting Someone Taller* (1987), *Who's Afraid of Beowulf?* (1988), *Flying Dutch* (1991), *Ye Gods!* (1992), *Overtime* (1991), *Here Comes the Sun* (1993), *Grailblazers* (1994), *Faust among Equals* (1994), *Odds and Gods* (1995), *Djinn Rummy* (1996), *My Hero* (1996), *Paint Your Dragon* (1996), *Open Sesame* (1997), *Wish You Were Here* (1998), *Only Human* (1999), *Snow White and the Seven Samurai* (2000), *Valhalla* (2000), *Nothing but Blue Skies* (2001), *Falling Sideways* (2002), *Little People* (2002), *A Song for Nero* (2003), *The Portable Door* (2003), and *In Your Dreams* (2004).

HOMER. The byline attached to two **epic** poems, probably dating from the eighth century B.C., the literary genius of which was loudly proclaimed as classical civilization came into flower, and which were to become foundation stones of modern literature. Legend represents Homer as a blind peripatetic singer, but that is an exercise in **symbolism** akin to the poet's own appeal to the **Muse**. The *Iliad,* which describes the duel between Achilles and Hector during the siege of Troy, can pass for history embellished with **allegorical** intrusions by the gods of the **classical** pantheon, but the *Odyssey,* which describes Odysseus's attempts to get home after the end of that siege, is manifestly a fantastic compilation of **travelers' tales**; it serves as a model for the subgenre of **Odyssean fantasies.** The Sumerian epic of Gilgamesh is older, and the Indian historical epic the *Ramayana* is of comparable antiquity, but neither circulated so widely in written form or gave rise to so rich a supplementary literature.

HOPKINSON, NALO (1961–). Jamaican-born writer resident in Canada since 1977. Most of her work is **chimerical/science fantasy** (refer to *HDSFL*). *Brown Girl in the Ring* (1998) and *Midnight Robber* (2000) invoke the **mythical** elements of voodoo in exotic settings. *The Salt Roads* (2003) is a complex **historical fantasy** about the advent of a **goddess**; its characters include **Charles Baudelaire**. The varied collection *Skin Folk* (2001) includes several fantasies based in Afro-Caribbean folklore. She edited the anthologies *Whispers from the Cotton Tree Root: Caribbean Fabulist Fiction* (2000) and *Mojo: Conjure Stories* (2003).

HORROR. A term used as a genre label in the commercial arena; unlike other genre labels, it refers to the intended effect of the work rather than thematic content. Supernatural horror fiction is more obviously a subcategory of fantasy than of **sf**, with which it is often combined in the critical and bibliographical literature under the blanket term "supernatural fiction." Further confusion is added by critics who use "**dark fantasy**" or "**Gothic fiction**" as preferred synonyms for "horror fiction" because the latter seems to imply crude sensationalism.

The advent of genre fantasy occasioned determined attempts to draw fundamental distinctions between fantasy and horror fiction, although even the most dignified **high fantasy** is not entirely purged of elements of horror. Most commercial horror fiction is a subspecies of **contemporary fantasy**, and the largest remainder is a subspecies of **historical fantasy**, but there are good reasons for separating out the two for special critical consideration, because the relationship between their fantasy elements and naturalistic ones is distinctive. The sense of horror communicated by such exotic fantasies as **William Beckford**'s *Vathek* or **Edgar Allan Poe**'s "The Masque of the Red Death"—which echoes in a great deal of **decadent fantasy**—is more aesthetic than visceral or existential, and it makes more sense to consider such texts as "dark fantasies" than as supernaturalized thrillers. Horror fiction derives its generic status from the contrast between disturbing intrusions and "normality," whereas fantasy is primarily conceived in terms of **secondary worlds**, leakage therefrom being on the margins of the genre rather than at the core.

HORWOOD, WILLIAM (1944–). British writer best known for **animal fantasies**. The sequence comprising *Duncton Wood* (1980), *Duncton Quest* (1988), *Duncton Found* (1989), *Duncton Tales* (1991), *Duncton Rising* (1992), and *Duncton Stone* (1993) features moles; *The Book of Silence* (1992) collects related short stories. *The Stonor Eagles* (1982) and *Callanish* (1984) involve eagles; the Wolves of Time sequence comprising *Journeys to the Heartland* (1995) and *Seekers at the Wulfrock* (1997) features wolves on a world-saving **quest**. *Skallagrigg* (1987) is a **messianic fantasy**. *The Willows in Winter* (1993), *Toad Triumphant* (1995), *The Willows and Beyond* (1996), and *The Willows at Christmas* (1998) are sequels to **Kenneth Grahame**'s *Wind in the Willows*.

HOUSMAN, CLEMENCE (1861–1955). British artist and writer. She illustrated some of the fantasies written by her brother **Laurence Housman**. Her allegorical **erotic fantasy** *The Were-wolf* (1896) was one of the most striking products of the short-lived English **Decadent** movement. *The Unknown Sea* (1898) similarly features an enigmatic femme fatale. The **Arthurian fantasy** *The Life of Sir Aglovale de Valis* (1905) is a mildly Quixotic homage to **chivalric romance**.

HOUSMAN, LAURENCE (1865–1959). British writer whose early work included numerous **fairy tales**, original items being collected in *A Farm in Fairyland* (1894), *The House of Joy* (1895), *The Field of Clover* (1898), and *The Blue Moon* (1904)—whose contents were recombined in *Moonshine and Clover* (1922) and *A Doorway in Fairyland* (1922)—while *What-O'Clock Tales* (1932) offered more straightforward **recyclings**. *All-Fellows: Seven Legends of Lower Redemption* (1896) and *The Cloak of Friendship* (1905)—also reprinted in an omnibus edition in 1923—are plaintive **Christian fantasies** cast in the form of legends. *Gods and Their Makers* (1897) is an offbeat **metaphysical fantasy** exploring the relationship between humans and their deities.

Housman's later works are lighter in tone, including numerous **satires** and **fabulations**; some were added as makeweights in *Gods and Their Makers and Other Stories* (1920); more are mingled with other materials in *Odd Pairs* (1925), *What Next?* (1938), *Strange Ends and Discoveries* (1948), and *The Kind and the Foolish* (1952). Several of his plays have fantasy elements, including *Prunella; or, Love in a Dutch Garden* (1904 with Harley Granville-Barker), *Alice in Ganderland* (1911), *The Return of Alcestis* (1916), and *The Death of Orpheus* (1921).

HOWARD, ROBERT E. (1906–1936). U.S. writer for the pulp magazines, prolific in several genres. He provided the guiding examples for the **sword and sorcery** subgenre in a sequence written for ***Weird Tales***, begun with "The Shadow Kingdom" (1929), in which the hero, Kull, has fought his way to a throne in a forgotten prehistoric era loosely based in **theosophical/scholarly fantasy**. Kull—whose adventures were showcased in *King Kull* (1967), edited and augmented by **Lin Carter** before the originals were collected in *Robert E. Howard's Kull* (1985)—was soon replaced by an equally ambitious barbarian from Cimmeria (probably Ireland) named Conan, whose recapitulation of Kull's rise to kingship was chronicled in 17 stories published between 1932 and 1936.

Howard's Conan stories were supplemented by previously unpublished stories revised by **L. Sprague de Camp** when they were reprinted in a series of volumes comprising *Conan the Conqueror* (1950; aka, with text restored, as *Hour of the Dragon*), *The Sword of Conan* (1952), *King Conan* (1953), *The Coming of Conan* (1953), *Conan the Barbarian* (1954), and *Tales of Conan* (1955). De Camp also revised a novel written by a fan, Bjorn Nyberg, issued as an addendum to the series as *The Return of Conan* (1957; aka *Conan the Avenger*). In 1966–71, Carter and de Camp organized a paperback reprint series in 11 volumes, further padded by revisions of Howard fragments and pastiches; they added a further six volumes of pastiches in 1977–80, launching a sequence carried forward for another two decades by numerous other hands, including **Robert Jordan** and Roland J. Green, dramatically enhancing the hero's cult following.

Howard's other fantasies include a series of **sword and sorcery** stories featuring a British barbarian opposed to Roman conquest, *Bran Mak Morn* (1969; abr. as *Worms of the Earth*), and various oddments assembled in *The Gods of Bal-Sagoth* (1979). It was, however, Conan who became the paradigm example of the ultramasculine barbarian whose reserves of strength, courage, and sheer willpower are adequate to any situation, including assaults by sorcerous magic; he represents a power fantasy whose lack of inhibition exceeds that of the more decorous heroes of **Edgar Rice Burroughs**, and who enjoyed a setting more appropriate than the metropolitan arenas inhabited by early **comic**-book superheroes.

HUBBARD, L. RON (1911–1986). U.S. writer for the pulp magazines, very prolific from 1932 to 1941. He wrote westerns before being instructed to offer his services to John W. Campbell, the editor of **sf** magazine *Astounding Stories*—who used him sparingly until the founding of ***Unknown*** provided a much more suitable arena for his abilities, extravagantly displayed in the **escapist** fantasy "The Ultimate Adventure" (1939), the **Arabian fantasies** *Slaves of Sleep* (1939; book 1948) and "The Case of the Friendly Corpse" (1941), the **posthumous fantasy** *Death's Deputy* (1940; book 1948), and the **Thorne Smith** homage *Triton* (1940 as "The Indigestible Triton"; exp. 1949). *Typewriter in the Sky* (1940), a **humorous fantasy** in which the hero is trapped in a hack writer's story, struggling to avoid the fate reserved in such fiction for villains, was combined in a 1951 book with the strongly contrasted **psychological fantasy** *Fear* (1940). *Fear*'s representation of a man tormented by repressed guilt in terms of "demons" laid the groundwork for the cult-founding **scholarly fantasy** *Dianetics* (1950), whose antipathy to contemporary psychiatric medicine is reflected in *Masters of Sleep* (1950) and which became the founding document of a remarkably successful **lifestyle fantasy**.

HUDSON, W. H. (1841–1922). Argentine-born British naturalist and writer. There is a strong element of **Arcadian fantasy** in his mystical Utopian novel *A Crystal Age* (1887) and the best-selling *Green Mansions* (1904), whose success cleared the way for belated publication of his allegorical **children's fantasy** *A Little Boy Lost* (1905).

HUFF, TANYA (1957–). Canadian writer. The couplet comprising *Child of the Grove* (1988) and *The Last Wizard* (1989) is a **feminized/quest** fantasy. *Gate of Darkness, Circle of Light* (1989) is an **urban fantasy** set in Toronto. The sequence *Blood Price* (1991), *Blood Trail* (1992), *Blood Lines* (1993), *Blood Pact* (1993), and *Blood Debt* (1997) comprises **detective** stories in which the heroine is assisted by a **vampire**; it resumed in *Smoke and Shadows* (2004). *The Fire's Stone* and the series comprising *Sing the Four Quarters* (1994), *Fifth Quarter* (1995), *No Quarter* (1996), and *The Quartered Sea* (1999) are elaborate **quest** fantasies, the final two items featuring awkward **identity exchanges**. In the series comprising *Summon the Keeper* (1998), *The Second Summoning* (2001), and *Long Hot Summoning* (2003), a boardinghouse is host to a **portal** to hell. Huff's short fiction is sampled in *What Ho, Magic!* (1999), *Stealing Magic* (1999), and *Relative Magic* (2003).

HUGHES, MONICA (1925–2003). British-born Canadian **children's** writer, best known for westerns and **sf** (refer to *HDSFL*). In *Where Have You Been, Billy Boy?* (1995), a **timeslip** is precipitated by a carousel. *Castle Tourmandyne* (1995) features a magical Victorian dollhouse. In *The Seven Magpies* (1996), World War II evacuees tamper with ancient magic. *The Story Box* (1998), set on an island where fiction is banned and dreams are suppressed, is a heartfelt **moralistic fantasy**.

HUGHES, TED (1930–1998). British poet who branched out into **children's fantasy** in the Kiplingesque *How the Whale Became and Other Stories* (1963); further fantasies of origination are featured in *Tales of the Early World* (1988) and *The Dreamfighter and Other Creation Tales* (1995). *The Iron Man* (1968; aka *the Iron Giant*) is a fervent **moralistic fantasy** with a sequel, *The Iron Woman* (1993), which tackles different **political** issues. The **animal fantasies** *What Is the Truth?* (1984) and *Ffangs the Vampire Bat and the Kiss of Truth* (1986) are equally moralistic but more lighthearted. His plays for children, collected in *The Coming of the King and Other Plays* (1970; exp. as *The Tiger's Bones and Other Plays for Children* 1973), include **transfigurations** of Beauty and the Beast and the story of **Orpheus**. His **scholarly fantasy** *Shakespeare and the Goddess of Complete Being* (1992) reinterprets the bard's work in the context of modern theories of the primal **Goddess**.

HUMOROUS FANTASY. The supplementation of trilogies of Greek tragedies with comic relief in the form of "satyr plays" launched the subversive traditions of **satire** and parody, carried forward by Aristophanes, **Lucian**, and **Apuleius**. There is also an important element of humor in Aesopian **fables**. The revival of humorous fantasy after the Renaissance was slow, but once there were models to be mocked it was only a matter of time before writers like **Rabelais** and **Cervantes** obliged. Eighteenth-century **French fantasy** was steeped in condescending wit, although the advent of the Romantic movement set such irreverence firmly aside for a while.

Modern Anglo-American humorous fantasy is rooted in parodic **ghost stories**, the **Christmas fantasy** tradition launched by **Charles Dickens** and the grotesque comedies of **Edgar Allan Poe**. **Douglas Jerrold**'s *A Man Made of Money* demonstrated the literary potential of literalized puns. As Victorian attitudes hardened, they called forth anarchic opposition in the form of the "nonsense" promoted by **Edward Lear**, **Lewis Carroll**, and **W. S. Gilbert**, and the subversive **intrusive fantasies** of **F. Anstey**. As Victorianism began to decay, its absurdity was widely celebrated—although the inevitable backlash ruined **Oscar Wilde**—and the Edwardian era became much more hospitable to the stylishly urbane wit of such writers as Max Beerbohm and **Ernest Bramah**.

Anstey's work was paralleled by American humorists like **Frank Stockton** and **John Kendrick Bangs**, but it was not until American attitudes hardened in the era of the Volstead Act that the way was opened for a defiant championship of the potential of alcohol as an agent of **reenchantment** by **Thorne Smith**, while **James Branch Cabell**, **George S. Viereck**, and others fought the prudishness that had taken new heart from Prohibition. Although the relevant repressions abated, the comedies they had inspired became foundation stones of rich traditions in both Britain and the United States, carried forward by such writers as **John Collier**, **T. H. White**, **James Thurber**, and the suppliers of ***Unknown***.

Because fantasy was long considered an annex to the **sf** genre in the commercial marketplace, and there was a widespread editorial belief that humorous sf was difficult to sell, comic fantasy led a slightly fugitive existence in the 1960s; the initial dominance of the nascent commercial genre by **high fantasy** did not immediately encourage experimentation. Once key exemplars had been put in place by **Terry Pratchett** and **Piers Anthony**, however, humorous fantasy was quickly **commodified** by such writers as **Craig Shaw Gardner**, **Robert Asprin**, **Esther Friesner**, C. Dale Brittain—whose Wizards of Yurt series extended from *A Bad Spell in Yurt* (1991) to *Is This Apocalypse Necessary?* (2000)—and New Zealander **Hugh Cook**. A British boom led by **Terry Pratchett** and **Tom Holt** included the works of **Andrew Harman** and **Robert Rankin**, **Martin Millar**'s pseudonymous Thraxas series, Colin Webber's *Merlin and the Last Trump* (1993) and *Ribwash* (1994), James Bibby's Ronan series (1995–98) and *Shapestone* (2000), Peter Chippindale's *Laptop of the Gods: A Millennium Fable* (1998), Gordon Houghton's *The Apprentice* (1999), Matthew Thomas's *Before & After* (1999), and Debi Gliori's trilogy comprising *Pure Dead Magic* (2001), *Pure Dead Wicked* (2002), and *Pure Dead Brilliant* (2003).

Showcase **anthologies** of humorous fantasy include *Smart Dragons, Foolish Elves* (1991) and *Betcha Can't Read Just One* (1993), ed. **Alan Dean Foster**, and two "Mammoth" anthologies edited by **Mike Ashley**.

HUNEKER, JAMES (1860–1921). U.S. writer best known as a **music** critic. The short fiction collected in *Melomaniacs* (1902), strongly influenced by the French **Decadent** movement, includes several fantasies celebrating the **visionary** effects of music. A few more are in *Visionaries* (1905). The stories appended to the essay collection *Bedouins* (1920) include two exercises in **literary satanism**, "The Supreme Sin" and "The Vision Malefic."

HYBRID TEXTS. Texts in which elements drawn from different sources are combined in such a way as to harmonize their content. Hybridization of other types of fantasy with **sf** entails providing speculative "rational explanations" for motifs that would be seen as magical or supernatural in other contexts. Another kind of hybridization widely practiced within the field of fantasy is a process of syncretic amalgamation founded in the view that rival **myth** systems are merely different interpretations of the same underlying metaphysical reality. **Theosophical** syncretism, **Joseph Campbell**'s argument that all hero myths are versions of the same "monomyth," and the claim that all **goddesses** are more or less distanced representations of Mother Earth are its most familiar manifestations. Syncretic hybridization has a significant effect on the processes of **recycling** and **transfiguration**, not only on the way such work is carried out but on the way its produce is seen by critics and writers. *See also* SCIENCE FANTASY.

– I –

IBBOTSON, EVA (1925–). Pseudonym of British writer Maria Wiesner, whose **children's fiction** includes several lively fantasies involving **ghosts** or **witches**, notably *The Great Ghost Rescue* (1975), *Which Witch?* (1979), *A Company of Swans* (1985), *The Haunting of Hiram* (1987; aka *The Haunting of Granite Falls*), *Not Just a Witch* (1989), *The Secret of Platform 13* (1994), and *Dial-a-Ghost* (1996). The protagonists of *Island of the Aunts* (1999) are kidnapped to a magical island. *The Worm and the Toffee-Nosed Princess* (1983) collects shorter fantasies.

IDENTITY EXCHANGE. One of the functions of human consciousness, which makes social life—and, as a side effect, literature—possible is the ability to identify with others by placing ourselves imaginatively "in their shoes." Literalizing extrapolations of this faculty inevitably crop up routinely in fantasy fiction. Although the term implies a mutual exchange, it may also be applied to cases of displacement whereby a single personality exchanges one body for another; some such device is often invoked in **timeslip** fantasies and accounts of **doppelgängers**.

Accounts of identity exchange that aspire to **existentialist** depth include **John Sterling**'s *The Onyx Ring,* Théophile Gautier's "Avatar," **Walter Besant**'s *The Doubts of Dives,* Ignatius Donnelly's *Doctor Huguet* (1891), Robert Hichens's *Flames* (1897), Horace Newte's *The Ealing Miracle* (1911), **Charles de Lint's** *Trader,* **Seabury Quinn**'s *Alien Flesh,* and Laurel Marian Doud's *This Body* (1998). **Mrs. Craik**'s "The Self-Seer," **Gerald Bullett**'s *Mr Godly beside Himself*, **Frank Baker**'s *Sweet Chariot* (1942), and Gill Alderman's *Lilith's Castle* (1999), which involve exchanges with otherworldly **doppelgängers**, are similarly philosophical. The alternative **humorous** tradition, spearheaded by Robert MacNish's **Faustian fantasy** "The Metempsychosis" (1826 as by "A Modern Pythagorean"), was popularized by **F. Anstey**'s *Vice Versa;* variations of the cautionary theme of the latter include **Arthur Conan Doyle**'s "The Great Keinplatz Experiment," **R. Andom**'s "The Strange Adventure of Roger Wilkins," **Thorne Smith**'s *Turnabout,* P. G. Wodehouse's *Laughing Gas* (1936), Angus MacLeod's *The Body's Guest* (1958), and George McBeth's **erotic fantasy** *The Transformation* (1975).

The piratical element of **Théophile Gautier**'s *Avatar* is echoed in such thrillers as T. W. Speight's *The Strange Experiences of Mr Verschoyle* (1901), **Barry Pain**'s *An Exchange of Souls,* **Seabury Quinn**'s *Alien Flesh,* and **Tim Powers**'s *The Anubis Gates*. Accounts of posthumous identity hijacking include Elleston Trevor's *The Immortal Error* (1946) and J. Russell Warren's *This Mortal Coil* (1947).

ILLUSTRATION. The illustration of fantasy literature, which became increasingly important in the 19th century, had a long tradition of fantastic art to draw upon, much of which was and is a significant influence upon the literary imagination. Much **classical myth** imagery survives in sculpture and much Egyptian material in tomb paintings. Early painters in oils whose imagery remains a significant stimulant include Hieronymus Bosch, Matthias Grünewald, and Pieter Brueghel. The romantic imagination—especially its **Gothic** offshoot—was primed by Salvator Rosa and Henry Fuseli; later 19th-century fantasy took some inspiration from the allegedly insane John Martin and the Bedlamite Richard Dadd. The latter was one of many Victorian artists swept up by a vogue for painting fairies; other major contributors included Joseph Noel Paton and John Anster Fitzgerald. The first important fantasist to fuse text and illustration into a coherent whole was **William Blake**.

Illustration became a vital generic support for texts in the marketing of **children's fantasy**, a significant precedent being set by William Mulready's illustration of William Roscoe's *The Butterfly's Ball and the Grasshopper's Feast* (1807). George Cruikshank was one of the first artists to **recycle** a **fairy tale** to fit it to his own illustrations, while John Tenniel was the first to form a "symbiotic" relationship with a particular writer, **Lewis Carroll**. Many fantasy classics were re-released in the 19th century in lavishly illustrated editions; those which proved particularly attractive to artists include **Dante**'s *Divine Comedy* and **Milton**'s *Paradise Lost,* both of which brought heroic efforts from Gustave Doré, the most prolific fantasy illustrator of his era.

For much of the century, there was a wide technological gulf separating the artistic possibilities open to oil painters and those available to engravers of illustrations, although hand coloration was not out of the question for such expensive projects as Richard Doyle's *In Fairyland* (1870). New techniques permitted photographic reproduction to become commonplace in the 1860s, and a further revolution took place at the end of the 1880s as a new era of color illustration began. The techniques thus condemned to obsolescence, however, had produced abundant work that had a beauty unique to their methods, which had brought monochromatic work to various peaks of achievement in the pre-Raphaelite produce of **William Morris**'s Kelmscott Press, **Aubrey Beardsley**'s illustration of *Le Morte d'Arthur,* and **Laurence Housman**'s decorative work. The new color illustrators also produced line drawings—color plates usually supplied only a small fraction of the illustrative material for most books—but it was usually their work in color that attracted most attention and defined their achievements.

The most celebrated fantasy illustrators of the late 19th century include Arthur Rackham, Charles Robinson, Edmund Dulac, Willy Pogany, Kay Nielsen, and Harry Clarke. Those who produced some of their own texts included **Howard Pyle**, William Heath Robinson, and Jean de Bosschère—a tradition carried forward into the 20th century by **Dr. Seuss**, **Maurice Sendak**, and **Edward Gorey**. Early 20th-century writers whose work benefited from distinctive illustration included **Lord Dunsany** (by Sidney H. Sime), **Ben Hecht** (by Wallace Smith), and various writers reprinted by the Bodley Head in sumptuous series that matched **James Branch Cabell** and **Anatole France** with Frank Papé and **Richard Garnett** with Henry Keen.

Several 19th- and 20th-century movements that gave rise to a good deal of literary fantasy also embraced artistic endeavors. The French **Decadent** movement was illustrated and inspired by Gustave Moreau, Odilon Redon, and Felicien Rops, while its Belgian offshoot was greatly encouraged by Jean Delville and Fernand Khnopff. **Surrealism**'s visual component, developed by such painters as Max Ernst and Salvador Dali, had an even more intimate feedback relationship with its literary arm. On the other hand, illustrators working in the commercial arena for the pulp magazines also found their most extravagant opportunities in the fantasy arena, where Virgil Finlay and **Hannes Bok** did their finest work.

The role played by illustrators in assisting the emergence of commodified fantasy in the 1970s was considerable, the belated success of **Robert E. Howard**'s **sword and sorcery** stories being closely associated with their illustration by such artists as Frank Frazetta and Boris Vallejo. Fairy painting made a dramatic comeback in the work of Brian Froud, whose *Faeries* (1978) launched an influential series; Richard and Wendy Pini, in the *ElfQuest* comic series (launched 1978); Roland and Claudine Sabatier, in *The Great Encyclopedia of Fairies* (1996; tr. 1999, with text by Pierre Dubois); and Suza Scalora, in *The Fairies* (1999). This boom was accompanied by similar booms in artwork depicting unicorns and dragons. Modern children's fantasy still provides a vital arena for lavish illustration, exemplified by key works by such writers as **Jane Yolen** and **Nancy Willard**.

"Fantasy Art" rapidly became a medium in its own right within and alongside genre fantasy, promoted by **Ballantine**'s serial of heavily illustrated *Ariel* anthologies (4 vols., 1976–78) and has continued to exist in symbiotic relationship with it; its significant contributors often contribute to **graphic novels** as well as producing cover art for books, record sleeves, and independent paintings; significant contributors to the medium include Roger Dean, Stephen Fabian, Rodney Matthews, Don Maitz, Bob Eggleton, and Greg and Tim Hildebrandt. Its accomplishments are chronicled and celebrated in an annual showcase edited by Cathy and Arnie Fenner, *Spectrum: The Best in Contemporary Fantastic Art* (launched 1994). Literary projects prompted by fantasy art include Naomi Mitchison's *Beyond the Limit,* based on drawings by **Wyndham Lewis**, texts written by **Michael Ende** to accompany paintings by his father, **Harlan Ellison**'s *Mind Fields* (1994, written to accompany paintings by Jacek Yerka), and a series of novellas based on Brian Froud's paintings that include **Patricia McKillip**'s *Something Rich and Strange*.

Contemporary writers/illustrators who have produced texts inseparable from their illustrations include **Tove Jansson**, **Dahlov Ipcar**, **Russell Hoban**, **Alasdair Gray**, Patrick Woodroffe—in *Pentateuch* (1980; rev. 1987 as *The Second Earth: The Pentateuch Retold*; originally issued with a double album of progressive rock **music** by Dave Greenslade), *The Adventures of Tinker, the Hole-Eating Duck* (1979), *Mickey's New Home* (1985), and *The Dorbott of Vacuo; or, How to Live With the Fluxus Quo* (1987)—and Shaun Tan, in *The Lost Thing* (2000) and *The Red Tree* (2001). Other notable illustration-based items include **Paul**

Stewart and Chris Riddell's Deepwoods series, Nick Bantock's eccentric **afterlife fantasy** *The Museum of Purgatory* (1999), and Ernest Drake's *Dragonology* (2003). Fantasy art is showcased online by such sites as Elfwood (launched 1996) and artpromote's Fantasy Art Gallery.

IMMERSIVE FANTASY. A term employed in Farah Mendlesohn's "Toward a Taxonomy of Fantasy" (2001), in company with **intrusive fantasy** and **portal fantasy**, to contrive a fundamental trisection of the field of fantasy literature. Immersive fantasies are those set entirely within **secondary worlds**, and in which the protagonists belong to those worlds. The most important consequence of immersion, Mendlesohn points out, is that viewpoint characters must accept the fantastic entities with which they are surrounded as aspects of their normality, however exceptional particular encounters may be. This tends to diminish the "sense of wonder" ordinarily associated with fantastic manifestations in intrusive or portal fantasies, by requiring the reader to share the character's assumed acceptance—an act of imaginative reconstruction enabled by the process **J. R. R. Tolkien** calls "**enchantment**," leading to the establishment of what he calls **secondary belief**. The distinctive characteristics and effects of "**high fantasy**" are side effects of the immersive process.

IMMORTALITY. The most awkward attribute of human consciousness, according to **existentialist** philosophers, is an awareness of the inevitability of death. Corollaries of this awareness include angst (death anxiety) and all manner of psychological avoidance strategies, which inevitably generate psychological and literary fantasies of immortality, including various kinds of **afterlife fantasies** and such fervent **wish-fulfillment fantasies** as **Oscar Wilde**'s *The Picture of Dorian Gray*. Immunity to death by natural causes is routinely attributed to **gods**, **angels**, **demons**, and other spiritual beings, who are often imagined to be able to gift such immunity to human beings. The notion that humans might discover a magical means of acquiring longevity for themselves was a central element of **alchemical fantasy** before **sf** (refer to *HDSFL*) provided a plethora of imaginable methods of defying aging and disease.

Given its psychological foundations, it is not surprising that many fantasies go to great lengths to construct arguments to the effect that human immortality would be a curse rather than a blessing, ruined by the ennui of endless repetition—a thesis exemplified in the legends of the

Wandering Jew and the **Flying Dutchman**. Most traditional tales of immortality gained are cautionary, often—like the myth of Tithonus, recapitulated in **Jonathan Swift**'s Struldbruggs, in which longevity is not accompanied by immunity from aging—involving an unanticipated sting; much fantasy literature reemphasizes the argument in a manner reminiscent of Aesop's parable of the fox and the grapes. Notable examples include Mary Shelley's "The Mortal Immortal" (1834), W. Harrison Ainsworth's *Auriol* (1850), **Eugene Lee-Hamilton**'s *The Romance of the Fountain,* George Allan England's "The Elixir of Hate" (1911), Claude Farrére's *The House of the Secret* (1923), **Natalie Babbitt**'s *Tuck Everlasting,* John Boyne's *The Thief of Time* (2001), and Pete Hamill's *Forever* (2003).

The suggestion that boredom, alienation, and the continual loss of loved ones might be prices well worth paying for the reward of eternal life is relatively rare, although it is acknowledged in **Eden Phillpotts**'s *The Girl and the Faun* and loudly trumpeted by George Bernard Shaw's *Back to Methuselah* (1921) and by **George S. Viereck** and Paul Eldridge in *My First Two Thousand Years*. The frustration of demands for immortality is one of the key challenges to the ingenuity of **Faustian fantasy**. The kind of conditional immortality featured in **vampire** stories is easier to balance in terms of costs and benefits, as is the often-interrupted kind featured in **karmic romances** where protagonists are held in **bondage**.

The advent of genre fantasy renewed literary fascination with the idea of longevity as a key reward of magical expertise and a useful endpoint for **quests**, as in **Fletcher Pratt**'s *The Well of the Unicorn*, **Tanith Lee**'s *The Birthgrave,* and **Tim Powers**'s *On Stranger Tides* (1987)—to the extent that **Diana Wynne Jones**'s *Tough Guide to Fantasyland* sarcastically deduces the rule that "the longer a person marinades her/himself in Magic, the longer she/he lives." Jones provided her own reappraisal of the role of the accursed wanderer in *The Homeward Bounders* (1981). The ultimate extrapolation of the existential plight of immortals buoyed up by hope in spite of being plagued by ennui is **Michael Moorcock**'s "Dancers at the End of Time" sequence.

The elixir of life and the fountain of youth are the most popular fantasy motifs associated with immortality; another is Gilgamesh's pearl of immortality, as featured in Brenda W. Clough's *How Like a God* (1997) and *The Doors of Death and Life* (2000). Longevity is frequently used as a facilitating device in panoramic **historical fantasies**, as in **Frank**

Stockton's *The Vizier of the Three-Horned Alexander,* **Charles Godfrey Leland**'s *Flaxius,* Cutcliffe Hyne's *Abbs: His Story through Many Ages* (1929), **Virginia Woolf**'s *Orlando,* and **Thomas Berger**'s *Little Big Man*.

INFERNAL COMEDY. Hell was invented by theologians as a kind of ultimate deterrent for the purposes of psychological terrorism. Although it retains that function in much **horror** fiction, **afterlife fantasy** has mobilized a good deal of resistance, often by conflating the **Dantean** inferno of **Christian fantasy** with the gloomy but relatively hospitable **underworld** of **classical mythology** and drawing narrative energy from the **chimerical** combinations of damned individuals that might be contrived there.

The tradition of infernal comedy was pioneered by **John Kendrick Bangs**'s *A Houseboat on the Styx* and carried forward by Edgar C. Blum's *Satan's Realm* (1899), Robert B. Vale's *Efficiency in Hades* (1923), **Frederick Arnold Kummer**'s *Ladies in Hades,* **John Collier**'s *The Devil and All,* and Marmaduke Dixey's *Hell's Bells* (1936), although it fell into disuse after World War II, when images of the afterlife became more inventively various. Infernal comedies routinely suppose that the Inferno is not far from Paradise in geographical terms, and not so very different as a habitation; there is, therefore, a parallel subgenre of "paradisal comedies," whose notable examples include **Mark Twain**'s *Extracts from Captain Stormfield's Visit to Heaven* and Alan Griffiths' *Strange News from Heaven* (1934).

INGALLS, RACHEL (1940–). U.S. writer resident in Britain since 1965. There are elements of **religious allegory** in her early fiction, including *Theft* (1970) and some of the stories in *Mediterranean Cruise* (1973; rev. as *The Man Who Was Left Behind and Other Stories;* combined with the previous item as *Something to Write Home About,* 1988). *Mrs. Caliban* (1982) and *Binstead's Safari* (1983) are **erotic fantasies** with a sexual political agenda; the former is combined with the similar contents of *Three of a Kind* (1985; aka *I See a Long Journey*) and *The End of Tragedy* (1987) in *Mrs. Caliban and Other Stories* (1993). *Black Diamond* (1992; abridged as *Be My Guest: Two Novellas*) and *The Pearlkillers* (1986) include further items in the same distinctive vein.

THE INKLINGS. A discussion group that first met in **C. S. Lewis**'s rooms in Magdalen College, Oxford, in the 1930s, subsequently moving to a local pub. **J. R. R. Tolkien** and Owen Barfield were key members, and **Charles Williams** joined in 1939; it slowly faded away after Williams's death in 1945 and had ceased to exist by 1950, but Tolkien's slowly expanding text of *The Lord of the Rings* and its associated materials had by then been subject to intensive collective scrutiny. Barfield, the author of *Poetic Diction: A Study in Meaning* (1928)—which advanced theoretical arguments regarding the intimate involvement of myth in the evolution of language—had an important influence on his fellow members' uses of **taproot texts** and theories of fantasy.

INSTAURATION FANTASY. A term used by John Clute in the *Encyclopedia of Fantasy* to refer to fantasies of large-scale renewal and restoration—**re-enchantment** writ large. Some such wholesale transformation is often the aim, if not always the outcome, of the **quests** undertaken in the **messianic** variants of **heroic fantasy**.

THE INTERNATIONAL ASSOCIATION FOR THE FANTASTIC IN THE ARTS (IAFA). An organization formed in 1982 to maintain an annual International Conference on the Fantastic in the Arts (ICFA), which had been inaugurated in 1980 under the sponsorship of Margaret Gaines Swann, the mother of **Thomas Burnett Swann**, as a memorial to her son. IAFA continued the tradition of inviting professional guests, including artists as well as writers, in order to maintain a more eclectic input than the general run of academic conferences. In 1985, the organization introduced an annual William L. Crawford Memorial Award, sponsored by **Andre Norton**, for the best debut fantasy novel; it added a Distinguished Scholarship Award in 1986 and created its own *Journal of the Fantastic in the Arts* in 1988.

INTRUSIVE FANTASY A category defined by Farah Mendlesohn in "Toward a Taxonomy of Fantasy" (2001), where it forms part of a basic trisection of the field with **immersive fantasy** and **portal fantasy**, although it is also associated with the splinter category of **liminal fantasy**. Intrusive fantasies are those set in the primary world, in which context the introduction of a magical object or supernatural being is disruptive—a "bringer of chaos," whose effect on the viewpoint character is one of amazement or **horror**. Intrusive fantasies almost invariably follow normalizing story arcs: the story begins with the advent of the intrusion and is oriented toward its eventual exorcism.

Mendlesohn points out that intrusive fantasy differs from **portal fantasies**—where portals are initially manifest as intrusions—in that its protagonists, and hence its readers, "are never expected to become accustomed to the fantastic"; this difference reemphasizes the normalizing tendencies of its story arcs, because amazement is a wasting asset. Thus, while the protagonists of **portal fantasy** sequences like **L. Frank Baum**'s Oz series eventually find their fantasy worlds becoming immersive, intrusive fantasies tend to discard familiarized protagonists in favor of new ones, thus resisting extrapolation into **series**; series can, however, be generated by using particular locations as prolific generators of intrusions, as in the cases of **Robert Holdstock**'s *Mythago Wood* and **Lucy Boston**'s Green Knowe.

INVISIBILITY. Because the burdensome obligations of social life are policed by countless observing eyes, or at least by the possibility of observation, there is a delicious imaginative liberation to be found in **daydreams** of becoming invisible, which are presumably commonplace. Caps and rings that make their wearers invisible are common motifs in folklore. As with tales of **immortality**, many literary fantasies are cautionary tales exploring the downside of the possibility. **James Dalton**'s *Invisible Gentleman* gets no joy from his **Faustian** bargain, while Charles Wentworth Lisle's *The Ring of Gyges* (1886) dwells on the cynicism and paranoia that would result from the ability to penetrate the poses and hypocrisies of one's fellows.

Other notable thought experiments in this vein include **A. E. Coppard's** "The Gollan," Christopher Priest's *The Glamour* (1984), and **Thomas Berger**'s *Being Invisible;* it is a key theme in **J. R. R. Tolkien**'s *The Hobbit* and *The Lord of the Rings*. The glee undermined in cautionary tales by embarrassment is rarely given full rein, although Jorge de Sena's *The Wondrous Physician* (1979) is more self-indulgent than most. Paranoid fantasies of being observed by invisible entities are common in **horror** fiction, although some—like Guy de Maupassant's "The Horla" (1887)—are important examples of **psychological fantasy**, as are fantasies in which invisibility is a metaphor for inconsequentiality, including Charles Beaumont's "The Vanishing American" (1955) and Robert M. Coates's "The Man Who Vanished" (1957).

IPCAR, DAHLOV (1917–2003). U.S. **illustrator** and writer whose **children**'s picture books include several **animal fantasies**. Her fantasies for older children are unusually sophisticated. *The Warlock of Night* (1969) uses a chess game to symbolize the rivalry of night and day. *The Queen of Spells* (1973) is a sentimental **recycling** of **Tam Lin**. *A Dark Horn Blowing* (1978) also draws on **ballads** in its account of a young woman abducted into **Faerie**. Her short fiction is sampled in *The Nightmare and Her Foal and Other Stories* (1990).

IRVINE, ALEXANDER C. (1969–). U.S. writer. *A Scattering of Jades* (2002) is a **historical fantasy** mythologizing America. *One King, One Soldier* (2004) features an **alternative history** in which the rival candidates contending for the position of a **Jessie Weston**-esque Fisher King include **decadent** poet Arthur Rimbaud. *Rossetti Song* (2002) and *Unintended Consequences* (2003) mingle short fantasies with other materials.

IRVINE, IAN (1950–). Australian writer. In the View from the Mirror quartet, comprising *A Shadow on the Glass* (1998), *The Tower on the Rift* (1998), *Dark Is the Moon* (1999), and *The Way between Worlds* (1999), a deceitful **mirror** with a long memory becomes the object of a **quest**. The Well of Echoes series, set in the same milieu and comprising *Geomancer* (2001), *Tetrarch* (2002), *Alchymist* (2003), *Scrutator* (2003), and *Chimaera* (2004), is a **hybrid/science fantasy** in which the forbidden art of geomancy must be recovered to combat crystalline "clankers."

IRVING, WASHINGTON (1783–1859). U.S. writer long resident in Europe, an important pioneer of the short-story form. His satirical essay offering *A History of New York* (1809, bylined Diedrich Knickerbocker) is a manifest **scholarly fantasy**. His serial miscellany *The Sketch Book of Geoffrey Crayon* (7 vols., 1819–20; omnibus 1820) included three Americanized **folktales** drawn from German sources, including "Rip van Winkle" and "The Legend of Sleepy Hollow." He recycled others in *Tales of a Traveller* (1824 as by Geoffrey Crayon), including the **Faustian fantasy** "The Devil and Tom Walker," but treated the Spanish legends retold in *The Alhambra* (1832) more reverently. His work had a considerable influence on **Edgar Allan Poe** and **Nathaniel Hawthorne**, and his adaptive strategy was copied by others, notably **William Austin**.

IRWIN, MARGARET (1889–1967). British writer best known for historical fiction. Two of her novels added significant pleas for **reenchantment** to the British flood that followed the end of World War I. *Still She Wished for Company* (1924; aka *Who Will Remember?*) is a bittersweet **timeslip** romance. *These Mortals* (1925) tells the story of a girl reared in the isolation of her father's magical palace, whose romantic illusions about the world of men are rudely shattered by exposure to its hypocrisies and delusions. Two more timeslip stories are among the fantasies in *Madame Fears the Dark: Seven Stories and a Play* (1935; rev. as *Bloodstock and Other Stories*, 1953).

IRWIN, ROBERT (1946–). British scholar and writer. His expertise in Islamic studies enabled him to compile a definitive account of the history of *The Arabian Nights* (1994) and greatly assisted the composition of his own **Arabian fantasy** *The Arabian Nightmare* (1983), a **hallucinatory fantasy** in which the protagonist becomes lost in a labyrinthine web of interlocking **dreams** and tales. *The Limits of Vision* (1986) is a **humorous/delusional fantasy** in which a housewife mounts a heroic crusade against Mucor, the Dark Lord of dirt. *Exquisite Corpse* (1995) is a subtler **delusional fantasy** set against the background of the **Surrealist** movement. *Prayer-Cushions of the Flesh* (1997) is an **erotic fantasy** of the harem. *Satan Wants Me* (1999) is a convoluted **occult fantasy**.

ITALIAN FANTASY. Italian Renaissance writers produced some important **taproot texts** employed by modern fantasy, most notably **Dante**'s *Divine Comedy,* various **folktales** recorded by Gianfrancesco Straparola and Giambattista Basile, and **Ariosto**'s *Orlando Furioso*. Another important source was the the 15th-century Commedia dell'arte, which initially consisted of wandering troupes of actors who improvised **humorous** plays using stock characters that became increasingly stereotyped as the figures of the harlequinade—including the clown Pierrot, the comic cavalier Scaramouche, and the clever servant and practical joker Harlequin; the tradition was continually reinvented and remodeled, most famously by the 18th-century Venetian playwright Carlo Gozzi—who imported a strong element of fantasy—eventually being transmuted into modern pantomimes and puppet shows.

The Italian **Romantic** movement was a pale shadow of its northern relatives and laid little groundwork for the development of a fantasy tradition. A few fugitive works by Giacomo Leopardi and others were its principal legacy, to which belated additions were made by I. U. Tarchetti, whose work is sampled in *Fantastic Tales* (1992). The work of **recycling** the legacy of Italian folktales was left to the late 19th-century ventures of "Carlo Collodi" (Carlo Lorenzini), author of *Pinocchio* (1883), to Emma Perodi, and to the more sustained 20th-century labors of **Italo Calvino**. Italy was, however, more significantly affected by the **Decadent** and **Surrealist** movements; as in Germany, such work came to be regarded with some suspicion by the fascist political elite, but such opposition proved a spur rather than a blanket, assisting the motivation of such writers as Tommaso Landolfi, whose short fiction is eclectically sampled in *Words in Commotion and Other Stories* (1982; abridged tr. 1986), Dino Buzzati, Primo Levi, and Calvino.

Calvino's towering example helped to increase interest in fantastic materials, preparing the way for the further experiments in literary fantasy—including Anna Maria Ortese's *The Iguana* (1965; tr. 1987) and Alessandro Boffa's *You're an Animal, Viskovitz!* (1998; tr. 2002), and the tentative formation of a commercial genre with domestic exponents who include Valerio Evangelisti, author of a series of novels featuring the inquisitor Nicholas Eymerich (launched 1994) and the Magus trilogy, featuring **Nostradamus** (1999). *See also* FAIRY TALES.

– J –

JACQ, CHRISTIAN (1947–). French Egyptologist, author of a long series of **historical fantasies** whose first sequence comprises *The Son of Light* (tr. 1997), *The Temple of a Million Years* (tr. 1997, aka *The Eternal Temple*), *The Battle of Kadesh* (tr. 1998), *The Lady of Abu Simbel* (1996; tr. 1998), and *Under the Western Acacia* (1996; tr. 1999). *The Black Pharaoh* (1999; tr. 1999), set 500 years later, serves as a bridge to a second sequence, comprising *Nefer the Silent* (2000), *The Wise Woman* (2000), *Paneb the Ardent* (2000; tr. 2001), and *The Place of Truth* (2001). A further sequence comprises *The Empire of Darkness* (2001; tr. 2002), *The War of the Crowns* (2002; tr. 2003), and *The Flaming Sword* (2002; tr. 2003).

JACQUES, BRIAN (1939–). British writer. Most of his work belongs to a successful sequence of **animal fantasies** featuring the mice of Redwall Abbey, comprising *Redwall* (1986), *Mossflower* (1988), *Mattimeo* (1989), *Mariel of Redwall* (1991), *Salamandastron* (1992), *Martin the Warrior* (1993), *The Bellmaker* (1995), *Outcast of Redwall* (1995), *The Pearls of Lutra* (1996), *The Long Patrol* (1997), *Marlfox* (1998), *The Legend of Luke* (1999), *Lord Brocktree* (2000), *Taggerung* (2001), *Triss* (2002), *Loamhedge* (2003), and a variety of merchandising spinoffs. *Castaways of the Flying Dutchman* (2001) and *The Angel's Command* (2003) follow the adventures of a boy and a dog washed away from the deck of the accursed ship. His short fiction is sampled in *Seven Strange and Ghostly Tales* (1991) and *The Ribbajack and Other Curious Yarns* (2004).

JAKES, JOHN W. (1932–). U.S. writer best known for historical fiction and **sf** (refer to *HDSFL*). Most of his fantasy is **sword and sorcery** imitative of **Robert E. Howard**, including a series collected as *Brak the Barbarian* (1968), *Brak the Barbarian versus The Sorceress* (1969), *Brak the Barbarian versus The Mark of the Demons* (1969), *Brak: When the Idols Walked* (1978), and *The Fortunes of Brak* (1980). *The Last Magicians* (1969) is in a similar vein. *Mention My Name in Atlantis* (1972) is a parody of the subgenre's clichés. The historical romance *Veils of Salome* (1962, initially bylined "Jay Scotland") recycles a classic item of **erotic fantasy**.

JANSSON, TOVE (1914–2001). Swedish-speaking Finnish writer and **illustrator**. Her fantasy series, launched in 1945, deals witha highly distinctive **secondary world** constructed by the unhuman inhabitants of the Moomin Valley construct, which she developed in **comic** strips and stage plays as well as books. Although they are in the tradition of **Lewis Carroll**, whose translations Jansson illustrated, along with **Tolkien**'s *The Hobbit,* their particular blend of **humor**, **sentimentality**, and lyricism—with darker intrusions—is distinctive. The English translations are *Finn Family Moonmintroll* (1950; aka *The Happy Moomins*), *Comet in Moominland* (1951), *The Exploits of Moominpapa* (1952), *Moominland Midwinter* (1958), *Moominsummer Madness* (1961), *Tales from Moomin Valley* (1963), *Moominpapa at Sea* (1966), and *Moominvalley in November* (1971). The characters were subsequently licensed for use by other writers.

JARRY, ALFRED (1873–1907). French writer, an important pioneer of **surrealism**. The work he did in association with his invention of "pataphysics"—a paradoxical science dealing with the exceptions excluded by natural laws—is a kind of anti-**sf** (refer to *HDSFL*), and much of his other work, including the plays of the Ubu cycle, is **Gothically** grotesque. There are significant elements of **hallucinatory fantasy** in the novel translated as *Days and Nights* (1897; tr. 1989), and of **erotic fantasy** in *Visits of Love* (1898; tr. 1993) and the historical novel *Messalina* (1900; tr. 1985). The drama *Caesar Antichrist* (1895; tr. 1992) is a hectic **apocalyptic fantasy** and "The Other Alcestis" (1896; tr. 1989) a vivid **biblical fantasy**.

JARVIS, ROBIN (1964–). British writer. The **animal fantasy** series comprising *The Dark Portal* (1989), *The Crystal Prison* (1989), *The Final Reckoning* (1990), *The Alchymist's Cat* (1991), *The Oaken Throne*

(1993), and *Thomas* (1995) might be regarded as **urban-fantasy** equivalents of **Brian Jacques**'s Redwall series, featuring tough and streetwise metropolitan mice instead of **Grahame**-esque country mice. The trilogy comprising *The Whitby Witches* (1991), *A Warlock in Whitby* (1992), and *The Whitby Child* (1994) is **dark fantasy**; a similar trilogy of "Tales from the Wyrd Museum" comprises *The Woven Path* (1995), *Raven's Knot* (1996), and *The Fatal Strand* (1998). The series launched by *Thorn Ogres of Hagwood* (1999); and *Dark Waters of Hagwood* (2004) is a **theriomorphic fantasy** featuring "werlings." The Intrigues of the Reflected Realm series, launched with *Deathscent* (2001), is an **alternative history** in which Elizabeth I has been enthroned for 178 years and England's native fauna is drastically depleted.

JEFFERIES, MIKE (1943–). British **illustrator** and writer. The **commodified fantasy** series, comprising *The Road to Underfall* (1986), *Palace of Kings* (1987), *Shadowlight* (1988), *The Knights of Cawdor* (1995), *Citadel of Shadows* (1996), and *The Siege of Candlebane Hall* (1998), is stereotyped, as is the feminized couplet *Glitterspike Hall* (1989) and *Hall of Whispers* (1990). *Shadows in the Watchgate* (1991) and *Stone Angels* (1993) are **dark fantasies** of unfortunate animation. *Hidden Echoes* (1992) is a **portal fantasy** in which the protagonist is a fantasy writer. The protagonists of *Children of the Flame* (1994) combat the effects of an ancient curse; *The Ghosts of Candleford* (1999) is similar.

JEPSON, EDGAR (1863–1938). British writer. He was on the fringes of the English Decadent movement; **A. E. Waite**'s *Horlick's Magazine* published his heretical **Christian fantasy** *The Horned Shepherd* (1904). Similar echoes of **James Frazer** in **scholarly fantasy** recur in two items improvised from the relics of aborted novels, "Marsh Horny" and "The Resurgent Mysteries," in *Captain Sentimental and Other Stories* (1911), both of which deal with the supposed survival of pagan cults in Victorian Britain—a thesis that became central to the scholarly fantasies of **Margaret Murray** and the **lifestyle fantasies** of Gerald Gardner, from which modern witchcraft took its inspiration. *The Mystery of the Myrtles* (1909) and *No. 19* (1910; aka *The Garden at Number 19*) are **occult fantasies** inspired by the impostures of **Aleister Crowley**, the latter featuring a conjuration of Pan that Crowley went on to attempt. *The Moon Gods* (1930) is a **lost race** novel in which a Carthaginian society is borrowed from **Gustave Flaubert**'s *Salammbô*.

JEROME, JEROME K. (1859–1927). British writer. *Told after Supper* (1891) is a collection of parodic **Christmas/ghost stories**. The title story of *The Passing of the Third Floor Back* (1907) features an enigmatic lodger in a boardinghouse who revitalizes the lives of his neighbors; the other fantasies include the ironic **Faustian fantasy** "The Soul of Nicholas Snyders, or the Miser of Zandam" and the **wish-fulfillment fantasy** "His Time Over Again." *Malvina of Brittany* (1916) includes the tongue-in-cheek title story about a stray from **Faerie** and the **theosophist fantasy** "The Lesson."

JERROLD, DOUGLAS (1803–1857). British humorist associated with *Punch,* long before **F. Anstey** joined the staff, whose work included some significant precursors of Ansteyan fantasy. *The Chronicles of Clovernook* (1846) includes some **tall tales** reminiscent of the work of **R. H. Barham**. *A Man Made of Money* (1848–49) is a graphic **wish-fulfillment fantasy** with moral echoes of **Honoré de Balzac**'s *The Magic Skin*.

JEWISH FANTASY. The preservation in writing of Jewish **folktales** began in the Talmud, and the cultural coherency of the Jewish tradition may well have allowed orally transmitted tales to be conserved with unusual care. A new phase of recording began with such Yiddish texts as *The Mayse-Book* (1602), some of whose inclusions are sampled in Joachim Neugroschel's showcase **anthology** *The Great Works of Jewish Fantasy and the Occult* (1976), which also features Yudl Rosenberg's version of "The Golem" (1909) and Ber Horovitz's version of "The Dybbuk." Neugroschel also edited *The Dybbuk and the Yiddish Imagination: A Haunted Reader* (2000), collecting materials related to that motif, but the **golem** is a much more common motif.

The Israel Folktale Archives, established in the late 1950s by Dov Noy, has amassed a considerable collection, samples of which are **recycled** in English in a series of collections by Howard Schwartz: *Elijah's Violin and Other Jewish Folktales* (1983), *Miriam's Tambourine: Jewish Folktales from Around the World* (1988), and *Lilith's Cave: Jewish Tales of the Supernatural* (1991). Similar anthologies have been compiled by **Josepha Sherman**. Such materials are routinely referenced and **transfigured** in the works of modern writers, often reproducing a darkly ironic humor acquired by the tales during their transmission through the era of the Diaspora. Notable examples can be found in the work of many U.S. writers, including **Ben Hecht**, **Avram Davidson**, **Cynthia Ozick**,

Lisa Goldstein, Bernard Malamud's collections *The Magic Barrel* (1958) and *Idiots First* (1963) and his **religious fantasy** *God's Grace* (1982), Kate Bernheimer's *The Complete Tales of Ketzia Gold* (2002), and d. g. k. goldberg's eclectically **chimerical** *Skating on the Edge* (2001). Examples from elsewhere include Brazilian Moacyr Scliar's *The Centaur in the Garden* (1980; tr. 1984) and Zimbabwe-born South African Patricia Schonstein's *A Time of Angels* (2003) and *The Apothecary's Daughter* (2004). A sampler of modern Jewish fantasy is *With Signs & Wonders: An International Anthology of Jewish Fabulist Fiction* (2001), ed. Daniel M. Jaffe.

JONES, DIANA WYNNE (1934–). British writer who found her metier in **young adult** fantasy, often drawing disparate ideas into unusual **chimerical** combinations with remarkable effect. *Wilkins' Tooth* (1973; aka *Witch's Business*), *The Ogre Downstairs* (1974), *Dogsbody* (1975), and *Eight Days of Luke* (1975) are **humorous fantasies**. The Dalemark series, comprising *Cart and Cwidder* (1975), *Drowned Ammet* (1977), *The Spellcoats* (1979), and *The Crown of Dalemark* (1973), is relatively conventional **immersive fantasy**, but the Chrestomanci series, featuring a **multiverse**-roaming troubleshooting **wizard** who assists various adolescents to come to terms with burgeoning magical powers—comprising *Charmed Life* (1977), *The Magicians of Caprona* (1980), *Witch Week* (1982), and *The Lives of Christopher Chant* (1988), plus the short pieces in *Mixed Magics* (2000)—is much more distinctive. A multiverse of **alternative histories** is also featured in the **messianic/Odyssean fantasy** *The Homeward Bounders* (1981).

The Time of the Ghost (1981) is an **existential/ghost story**, wherein the protagonist's **quest** to determine her identity is echoed in various ways in *Fire and Hemlock* (1984), which **transfigures** the tale of **Tam Lin**; the intricate **timeslip** fantasies *Archer's Goon* (1984) and *A Tale of Time City* (1987); and the reversed **portal fantasy** *Howl's Moving Castle* (1986) and its sequel *Castle in the Air* (1990). *Hexwood* (1993) is a **science fantasy**. *Black Maria* (1991; aka *Aunt Maria*) is a **feminist** comedy with a satirical aspect echoed in *Wild Robert* (1991), in which a ghost is horrified by the state of the modern world, and *A Sudden Wild Magic* (1992). The protagonist of *Deep Secret* (1997), who has the taxing responsibility of ensuring that his civilization does not collapse, experiences a similar distress; *The Merlin Conspiracy* (2003) is a sequel.

Jones's impatience with the cliches of contemporary genre fantasy led her to compile the merciless *Tough Guide to Fantasyland* (1996), with a parodic spirit that was extrapolated in *The Dark Lord of Derkholm* (1998) and its sequel *Year of the Griffin* (2000). Her shorter fiction is collected in several overlapping collections: *Warlock at the Wheel and Other Stories* (1984), *Stopping for a Spell* (1989), *Everard's Ride* (1995), *Minor Arcana* (1996), *Believing Is Seeing* (1999), and *Unexpected Magic* (2004).

JONES, GWYNETH (1952–). British writer best known under her own name for **sf** (refer to *HDSFL*), although she published *Water in the Air* (1977) and *Dear Hill* (1980) under that name before beginning to sign some of her **children's fiction** "Ann Halam"; she reverted to her own name for the **ghost story** *King Death's Garden* (1986). As "Halam," she wrote the **intrusive fantasies** *Ally, Ally Aster* (1981) and *The Alder Tree* (1982) before turning to **immersive fantasy** in the **far-futuristic** Inland trilogy comprising *The Daymaker* (1987), *Transformations* (1988), and *The Skybreaker* (1990). Much of her subsequent work for teenagers was **horror fiction** or sf, but she began a series of **hybrid/science fantasies** featuring magical **music** for adults under her own name, with *Bold as Love* (2001), *Castles Made of Sand* (2002), and *Midnight Lamp* (2003).

JONES, JENNY (1954–). British writer. The trilogy comprising *Fly by Night* (1990, aka *Flight Over Fire*), *The Edge of Vengeance* (1991), and *Lies and Flames* (1992) is a **chimerical/science fantasy** in which worshippers of the **moon/goddess** battle patriarchal sun worshippers. In *The Webbed Hand* (1994), monstrous Fireflies plot the destruction of an imaginary kingdom. In *Firefly Dreams* (1995), aquamancers battle pyromancers. *The Blue Manor* (1995) is a **metafiction** involving the sinister infection of a novel by the locale in which it is being penned. *The House of Birds* (1996) makes much of the imagery of **flight**. *The Carver* (1997) and *Where the Children Cry* (1998) are **dark fantasies**. *Shadowsong* (2000) echoes legends of **Orpheus**.

JONES, J. V. (1963–). British writer resident in the United States from 1980. The setting of the **epic fantasy** trilogy comprising *The Baker's Boy* (1995), *A Man Betrayed* (1996), and *Master and Fool* (1996) is also used as a backcloth in the Sword of Shadows series, comprising *A Cavern of Black Ice* (1999), *A Fortress of Grey Ice* (2002), and *A Sword from*

Red Ice (1004). *The Barbed Coil* (1997) is an elaborate **portal fantasy** featuring a world in which patterns have magical power.

JORDAN, ROBERT (1948–). Pseudonym of U.S. writer James Oliver Rigney, Jr., who wrote seven novels featuring **Robert E. Howard**'s Conan series in 1982–84 before beginning the **epic** Wheel of Time sequence comprising *The Eye of the World* (1990), *The Great Hunt* (1990), *The Dragon Reborn* (1991), *The Shadow Rising* (1992), *The Fires of Heaven* (1993), *Lord of Chaos* (1994), *A Crown of Swords* (1996), *The Path of Daggers* (1998), *Winter's Heart* (2000), and *Crossroads of Twilight* (2003), with one volume to come. The series set out to take **quest** fantasy to a new extreme, drawing motifs from numerous legendary and literary sources in order to fuse them into an unprecedentedly all-inclusive whole. *New Spring* (1998; exp. 2003) is a prequel. *The World of Robert Jordan's The Wheel of Time* (1997, with Teresa Patterson) is a **guide**.

JORDAN, SHERRYL (1949–). New Zealand **illustrator**, who moved on from picture books to novels examining the plights of outsiders and outcasts in a variety of settings. *Rocco* (1990, aka *A Time of Darkness*) is a **timeslip** fantasy. *The Juniper Game* (1991) features an otherworldly visitor. *The Wednesday Wizard* (1991) is a **timeslip** fantasy, as are *Denzil's Dilemma* (1992) and *Denzil's Great Bear Burglary* (1997), wherein the protagonist is displaced from the Middle Ages to the present. In *Winter of Fire* (1993), a magically gifted girl sides with the Quelled against the aristocratic Chosen. *Tanith* (1994; aka *Wolf-Woman*) features a **feral child** in a primitive society. *Sign of the Lion* (1995) is the story of a magical child pledged to a mysterious woman before her difficult birth. *Secret Sacrament* (1996) tracks the tribulations of a **healer**. The heroine of *The Raging Quiet* (1999) is accused of witchcraft when she opens communication with a deaf boy. *The Hunting of the Last Dragon* (2002) tells the story of the last dragon hunt in medieval England.

JUSTER, NORTON (1929–). U.S. writer. His first novel, *The Phantom Tollbooth* (1962), became a classic **children's fantasy** in the same exuberant vein as **James Thurber**'s stories; its hero passes through the eponymous **portal** into an **allegorical** landscape, where he must help to end the war between Dictionopolis and Digitopolis and reunite the realm of Wisdom. His picture books *The Dot and the Line* (1963) and *Alberic the Wise and Other Journeys* (1965) are didactic **fabulations** of a similar kind, as is *AS: A Surfeit of Similes* (1989).

– K –

KAFKA, FRANZ (1883–1924). Czech writer who wrote in German; his distinctively surreal **dark fantasies** present a quasi-**allegorical/existentialist** dramatization of 20th-century anxieties about alienation. The protagonist of the **theriomorphic fantasy** novella translated as *Metamorphosis* (1915; tr. 1937) does not thrive as a giant bug. The protagonist of *The Trial* (written 1914–15; published 1925; tr. 1937) is trapped in an inexorably frustrating legal process. The protagonist of the unfinished *The Castle* (1926; tr. 1930) cannot persuade the authorities to recognize his identity. Several ***contes philosophiques*** are assembled in *The Great Wall of China and Other Pieces* (1931; tr. 1933). Derivatives of his works include Marc Estrin's *Insect Dreams: The Half Life of Gregor Samsa* (2002).

KARMIC ROMANCE. A story embracing a version of the Buddhist thesis that every living being is heir to the accumulated effects of morally weighted actions carried out during previous incarnations, often presenting images of moral evolution frustrated by some kind of **bondage**. Karmic romance became a popular subgenre at the end of the 19th century under the influence of the **occult** revival, especially as reflected in **H. Rider Haggard**'s *She* and the works of **Edwin Lester Arnold**, **Mrs. Campbell Praed**, and **Lily Adams Beck**. Notable examples include A. P. Sinnett's *Karma* (1885), Hume Nisbet's *Valdmer the Viking* (1893), **Marie Corelli**'s *Ziska,* Fergus Hume's *A Son of Perdition* (1912), Mary Bligh Bond's *Avernus* (1924), Roy Devereux's *When They Came Back* (1938), Warwick Deeping's *I Live Again* (1942), and Francis Ashton's *Alas, That Great City* (1948). Thanks to **theosophical** intrusions, sequences of incarnation are often traced back to **Atlantis**, as in Marjorie Livingston's trilogy comprising *Island Sonata* (1944), *Muted Strings* (1946), and *Delphic Echo* (1948). Similar patterns recur in many fantasies that have shed the vestiges of Buddhist terminology, especially **timeslip** fantasies; examples include works by **Moyra Caldecott** and **Helen Cresswell**'s *Moondial*.

KARR, PHYLLIS ANN (1944–). U.S. writer and **Arthurian** scholar, the author of a massive *The King Arthur Companion* (1983; exp. 1997 as *The Arthurian Companion*; rev. 2001). She redeployed such materials in the mystery novel *The Idylls of the Queen* (1982), the humorous *The Follies of Sir Harald* (2002), and several items of short fiction. She began a series of quasi-**Arcadian/immersive fantasies** featuring Torin the Toymaker in 1974; its only novel is *At Amberleaf Fair* (1986). *Frostflower and Thorn* (1980) and *Frostflower and Windbourne* (1982) are **feminist fantasies**. *Wildraith's Last Battle* (1982) is a **sword and sorcery** novel.

KAY, GUY GAVRIEL (1954–). Canadian writer who helped **J. R. R. Tolkien**'s son prepare *The Silmarillion* for posthumous publication before embarking on his own **epic/portal fantasy** trilogy, The Fionavar Tapestry, comprising *The Summer Tree* (1985), *The Wandering Fire* (1986), and *The Darkest Road* (1986). The quasi-Platonic **metaphysical** frame that orchestrates events in the **secondary world** is highly distinctive and remarkably comprehensive. *Tigana* (1990) is a further development of one of the series' principal narrative threads, the replacement of matrilineal and matriarchal institutions by patriarchal ones. *A Song for Arbonne* (1992) examines the role played by troubadours in the making of **romance**. *The Lions of Al-Rassan* (1995) is an elaborate **historical fantasy** set in a version of Spain that reproduces the cultural milieu of actual medieval troubadours. The Sarantium Mosaic, comprising *Sailing to Sarantium* (1998) and *Lord of Emperors* (2000), makes similar use of an **alternative** Byzantium. *The Last Light of the Sun* (2004) focuses on the Cyngaels, the secondary world's equivalent of Celts, and continues Kay's preoccupation with building elaborate plot structures in which humble individuals play vital roles. *Beyond This Dark House* (2003) is a collection of **poetry**.

KAYE, MARVIN (1938–). U.S. writer in various genres. Some of his early work—including the heroic fantasies *The Masters of Solitude* (1978) and *Wintermind* (1984)—were written in collaboration with Parke Godwin. *The Incredible Umbrella* (1979) and its sequel *The Amorous Umbrella* (1981) are **humorous fantasies** modeled on ***Unknown*** fantasies by **L. Sprague de Camp** and **Fletcher Pratt**, the first featuring an **alternate world** based on the works of **W. S. Gilbert**. The stories in *The Possession of Immanuel Wolf and Other Improbable Tales* (1981) are similar in spirit. *A Cold Blue Light* (1983 with Godwin) and its solo sequel *Ghosts of Night and Morning* (1987) are **detective** stories of an **occult** variety. *Fantastique* (1992) is a **transfiguration** of Hector Berlioz's *Symphonie Fantastique* (1830). The relationship between **music** and fantasy is further explored in the novellas assembled in Kaye's anthology *The Vampire Sextette* (2001);

The Dragon Quintet (2003) and *The Fair Folk* (2004) similarly consist of thematically organized novellas.

KEARNEY, PAUL (1967–). Northern Ireland–born writer resident in Denmark before returning to Britain in 1998. The writer protagonist of *The Way to Babylon* (1992) is unblocked by a sojourn in the **secondary world** of his earlier books. The **portal fantasies** *A Different Kingdom* (1993) and *Riding the Unicorn* (1994) describe similar **quests** for **re-enchantment**. The Monarchies of God series, comprising *Hawkwood's Voyage* (1995), *The Heretic Kings* (1996), *The Iron Wars* (1999), *The Second Empire* (2000), and *Ships from the West* (2002), is set in an **alternative history** and features a pioneering voyage across the Great Western Ocean to a magical New World, whose agents eventually return to transform the Old. *The Sea Beggars: The Mark of Ran* (2004) features a similarly **epic** journey in a dying world.

KEATS, JOHN (1795–1821). British poet who made prolific use of **classical mythology** in his deeply **romantic** poetry, as in *Endymion* (1818); its companion pieces "Hyperion" and "The Fall of Hyperion" were left incomplete at his death (all of them are **transfigured** in a **science-fantasy** series by Dan Simmons). *Poems* (1820) features the similarly inclined "Lamia," drawn—via Richard Burton's *Anatomy of Melancholy*—from the same anecdotal source as **Théophile Gautier**'s "Clarimonde," and exhibiting the same inversion of sympathy. Burton may also have provided the inspiration for the **erotic fantasies** "The Eve of St. Agnes" and "La Belle Dame Sans Merci," both of which draw on the mythology of **Faerie**; the imagery of the latter poem—augmenting that of its own source, **Tam Lin**—has been highly influential in modern fantasy.

KEIGHTLEY, THOMAS (1789–1872). British folklorist. *Fairy Mythology* (1828; rev. 1850; aka *The World Guide to Gnomes, Fairies, Elves and Other Little People*) is a massive syncretic survey of myths and legends relating to the supernatural beings routinely gathered together as **fairy** folk, and of their literary representations. It was written in association with the theoretically inclined *Tales and Popular Fictions: Their Resemblance and Transmission from Country to Country* (1834), which attempts to track and explain the diffusion and evolution of the fundamental beliefs and images. The former was sampled in **John Sterling**'s *Athenaeum*, for which Keightley also wrote essays on **John Milton** and **classical mythology**. Although its underlying thesis is a **scholarly fan-**

tasy, Keightley's work was a very useful compendium of lore for late 19th-century writers, and its echoes still resound in almost all modern fantasy dealing with **Faerie**.

KELLER, DAVID H. (1880–1966). U.S. writer best known for **sf** (refer to *HDSFL* and *HDHL*), although the hobbyist writing he did before his recruitment to the pulps was strongly influenced by **James Branch Cabell**. His equivalent of the biography of the life of Manuel was an imaginary history of the Hubler family, whose hypothetical ancestry was rooted in the French Hubelaires. Items from this patchwork appeared (long after being written) as *The Sign of the Burning Hart: A Tale of Arcadia* (1938) and two flirtatious exercises in **literary satanism**, *The Devil and the Doctor* (1940) and *The Homunculus* (1949). One item of a series of 15 short stories following a Cornish branch of the family appeared in ***Weird Tales*** in 1929, and 10 more were reprinted in 1969–71. Keller wrote several **erotic fantasies** inspired by his interest in Freudian psychology, notably "The Golden Bough" (1935) and *The Eternal Conflict* (1939 in French; 1949).

KENNEALY-MORRISON, PATRICIA (1946–). U.S. writer who signed herself Patricia Kennealy until 1994, when she appended the name of Doors singer Jim Morrison. Her major contribution to the genre is a hybrid **science-fantasy** series **recycling** elements of **Celtic** Arthuriana in a **planetary romance** framework; it comprises *The Copper Crown* (1985), *The Throne of Scone* (1986), *The Silver Branch* (1988), *The Hawk's Gray Feather* (1990), *The Oak above the Kings* (1994), *The Hedge of Mist* (1996), *Blackmantle* (1997), and the **prequel** *Deer's Cry* (1998).

KERR, KATHARINE (1944–). U.S. writer. Most of her genre work belongs to a sequence set in the pseudo-**Celtic** kingdom of Deverry; its apparatus is augmented by motifs drawn from many other sources, including **karmic romance**, as well as the stereotypical elements of **commodified/epic fantasy**. It comprises *Daggerspell* (1986), *Darkspell* (1987), *The Bristling Wood* (1989; aka *Dawnspell*), *The Dragon Revenant* (1990; aka *Dragonspell: The Southern Sea*), *A Time of Exile* (1991), *A Time of Omens* (1992), *A Time of War* (1993; aka *Days of Blood and Fire*), *A Time of Justice* (1994; aka *Days of Air and Darkness*), *The Red Wyvern* (1997), *The Black Raven* (1999), *The Fire Dragon* (2000), and *The Gold Falcon* (2004). She coedited the theme anthologies *Enchanted Forests* (1995) and *The Shimmering Door* (1996; aka *Sorceries*).

KEYES, J. GREGORY (1963–). U.S. writer who sometimes shortens his signature to "Greg Keyes." The couplet comprising *The Waterborn* (1996) and *The Blackgod* (1997) is stereotypical **commodified fantasy**, but the sequence of **science fantasies** comprising *Newton's Cannon* (1998), *A Calculus of Angels* (1999), *Empire of Unreason* (2000), and *The Shadows of God* (2001) is an enterprising **alchemical fantasy** set in **alternative history**. The Kingdoms of Thorn and Bone series, launched with *The Briar King* (2003) and *The Charnel Prince* (2004), is a **messianic fantasy** with an alternative-history setting.

KILWORTH, GARRY (1941–). British writer whose early work was mostly **sf** (refer to *HDSFL*). His many **animal fantasies** include *Hunter's Moon* (1989; aka *The Foxes of First Dark*), *Midnight's Sun: A Story of Wolves* (1990), *Frost Dancers: A Story of Hares* (1992), and *House of Tribes* (1995), in which the protagonists are mice. A trilogy more explicitly aimed at **children**, featuring The Welkin Weasels, comprises *Thunder Oak* (1997), *Castle Storm* (1998), and *Windjammer Run* (1999); he returned to that milieu in *Gaslight Geezers* (2001), *Vampire Vole* (2002), and *Heastward Ho!* (2003). Kilworth's other children's fantasies include *The Wizard of Woodworld* (1987), *The Rain Ghost* (1989), the collection *Dark Hills, Hollow Clocks* (1990), *The Drowners* (1991), *Billy Pink's Private Detective Agency* (1993), the **timeslip** fantasy *The Phantom Piper* (1994), *The Raiders* (1996), *The Gargoyle* (1997), and *Nightdancer* (2002).

In the **Shakespearean** fantasy *A Midsummer's Nightmare* (1996) the **fairy** court decamps from Sherwood to the New Forest. The Navigator Kings trilogy, comprising *The Roof of Voyaging* (1996), *The Princely Flower* (1997), and *Land-of-Mists* (1998), is based in Polynesian **myth**. The couplet comprising *Angel* (1993) and *Archangel* (1995) is a melodramatic **dark fantasy**. *Shadow-Hawk* (1999) is based on legends of Borneo. The Knights of Liöfwende trilogy, comprising *Spiggot's Quest* (2002), *Mallmoc's Castle* (2003), and *Boggart and Fen* (2004), features a **portal** to a dark version of **Faerie**. Kilworth's shorter adult fantasies include "The Ragthorn" (1991 with Robert Holdstock) and the **surreal** title story of *Hogfoot Right and Bird-Hands* (1993).

KING, GABRIEL. Collaborative pseudonym of **M. John Harrison** and Jane Johnson, employed for a trilogy of sophisticated **animal fantasies** comprising *The Wild Road* (1997), *The Golden Cat* (1998), and *The Knot Garden* (2000). *See also* JUDE FISHER.

KING, STEPHEN (1947–). U.S. writer best known for his best-selling **horror** fiction (refer to *HDHL*). There are elements of fantasy in the futuristic Dark Tower sequence—inspired by an image from **Robert Browning**—begun with *The Gunslinger* (1982) and continued in *The Drawing of the Three* (1987), *The Waste Lands* (1991), *Wizard and Glass* (1997), *Wolves of the Calla* (2003), and *Song of Susannah* (2004), with *The Dark Tower* to come; Robin Furth's *Stephen King's The Dark Tower: A Concordance,* volume 1 (2003), is a **guide**. The **quest** fantasy King wrote with Peter Straub, *The Talisman* (1984)—to which *Black House* (2001) is a sequel—and his solo novel *The Eyes of the Dragon* (1985), aimed at younger readers, are more wholehearted fantasies. *Insomnia* (1994) has elements of **metaphysical fantasy**. *The Girl Who Loved Tom Gordon* (1999) is an account of healthy psychological fantasizing.

KINGSLEY, CHARLES (1819–1875). British clergyman and writer who recycled three **classical** myths in *The Heroes* (1856) before producing the **moralistic/children's fantasy** *The Water Babies* (1863), in which a chimney sweep's boy becomes a water sprite in order to undertake a redemptive **quest** that might qualify him for a more authentic **afterlife**. Kingsley's friend **George MacDonald** employed its example to prompt yet another cleric, **Lewis Carroll**, to produce *Alice's Adventures in Wonderland,* but the result was not quite what he intended. Charles's brother Henry (1830–76) was more faithful to his exemplar when he produced the **allegorical** *The Boy in Grey* (1871).

KING-SMITH, DICK (1922–). British writer. Most of his **children's fantasies** are aimed at younger readers, but his more elaborate **animal fantasies** include *The Fox Busters* (1978), *The Sheep-Pig* (1983; aka *Babe: The Gallant Pig*)—which made his name when it was filmed—*Noah's Brother* (1986), *The Schoolmouse* (1994), and *Godhanger* (1996). *The Merman* (1997) features a rare male of the species. *The Crowstarver* (1998) features a foundling child who has an uncanny rapport with animals. *The Roundhill* (2000) is a **ghost** story featuring the model for **Lewis Carroll**'s Alice.

KINSELLA, W. P. (1935–). Canadian writer whose relevant work is all **sports fantasy**. The title story of *Shoeless Joe Jackson Comes to Iowa* (1980) was expanded as *Shoeless Joe* (1982), a **sentimental fantasy** in which baseball is employed to symbolize the American psyche in need of **re-enchantment**. *The Iowa Baseball Confederacy* (1986) is a **time-slip** fantasy in the same vein; more baseball fantasies are included in *The Thrill of the Grass* (1984) and *The Further Adventures of Slugger McBatt* (1988). Some of Kinsella's other collections include **tall stories** and **fabulations**. He edited the **anthology** *Baseball Fantastic* (2000).

KIPLING, RUDYARD (1865–1936). British writer whose childhood years in India prompted him to produce numerous exotic short stories. Those for adults are usually tinged with **horror**, like those in *The Phantom Rickshaw and Other Tales* (1888), which include the **hallucinatory** fantasy of the afterlife "The Strange Ride of Morrowby Jukes" (1885), although those in *Many Inventions* (1893) and *The Day's Work* (1898) are more varied. The novella *They* (1905) is a wholehearted sentimental **ghost story**.

Kipling's work for **children** is unusually vivid; the **animal fantasies** in *The Jungle Book* (1894) and *The Second Jungle Book* (1895) include an influential series about the **feral child** Mowgli, who receives a valuable education in the Law of the Jungle from his mentors. *Just So Stories for Little Children* (1902) is a classic collection of absurd confections in which didacticism is blithely parodic. *Puck of Pook's Hill* (1906) and *Rewards and Fairies* (1910) employ a fantasy story as a frame for a series of stories describing a **thinning** process that eventually renders British history thoroughly mundane, save for **astrological** illusions. *Debits and Credits* (1926) includes several notable fantasies, including the **Arabian fantasy** "The Enemies to Each Other," and the **satirical** afterlife fantasy "On the Gate." An eclectic sampler is *Kipling's Fantasy* (1992).

KNATCHBULL-HUGESSEN, E. H. (1829–1893). British statesman, whose elevation to the peerage in 1880 encouraged the reprinting under his new title (Lord Brabourne) of selections from several volumes of **fairy tales** he had produced as **Christmas fantasies** in *Stories for My Children* (1869), *Crackers for Christmas* (1870), *Moonshine* (1871), *Tales for Teatime* (1872), *Queer Folk* (1873, dated 1874), *River Legends* (1874), *Whispers from Fairy-Land* (1874), *Higgledy-Piggledy* (1875), *Uncle Joe's Stories* (1878), and *Other Stories* (1879). He went on to add *The Mountain Sprite's Kingdom and Other Stories* (1880), *Ferdinand's Adventure* (1882), *Friends and Foes from Fairyland* (1885), and *The Magic Oak-Tree and Prince Filderkin* (1894). His work offers a cardinal example of the application of censorious Victorian sensibility to **folktale** materials.

KNOWLES, VERNON (1899–1968). Australian writer long resident in Britain. Four of the nine calculatedly quaint and mannered items in *The Street of Queer Houses and Other Stories* (1924) were reprinted, with 11 new items, in *The Street of Queer Houses and Other Tales* (1925). *Here and Otherwhere* (1926) contains more items in the same vein, including the **wish-fulfillment fantasy** "The Shop in the Off-Street." *Silver Nutmegs* (1927) includes a novella wryly celebrating the **escapist** impulse, separately reprinted as *The Ladder* (1929). Eight stories selected from the latter collections were reprinted, along with four new stories, in *Two and Two Make Five* (1935).

KOTZWINKLE, WILLIAM (1938–). U.S. writer. His **children's fantasies** include *Elephant Boy: A Story of the Stone Age* (1970), *The Supreme, Superb, Exalted, and Delightful, One and Only Magic Building* (1973), *Dream of Dark Harbor* (1979), *The Ants Who Took Away Time* (1978), and the parodic **animal fantasies** collected in *Trouble in Bugland: A Collection of Inspector Mantis Mysteries* (1983). *Doctor Rat* (1976) successfully crossed over into the adult market, where his teasing **fabulations** became more wholehearted by degrees. Although *Fata Morgana* (1977) and *Herr Nightingale and the Satin Woman* (1978) are content with peripheral **surrealism**, *The Exile* (1987)—a **timeslip/identity exchange** fantasy—is far more explicit. *The Bear Went Over the Mountain* (1996) is an offbeat **animal fantasy**. Some of the short fiction featured in *Elephant Bangs Train* (1971) is fantasy; *Jewel of the Moon* (1985), *Hearts of Wood and Other Timeless Tales* (1985), *The Hot Jazz Trio* (1989), and *Tales from the Empty Notebook* (1995) are entirely composed of fantasy stories.

KUMMER, FREDERICK ARNOLD (1873–1943). U.S. writer best known for detective fiction. *The Second Coming: A Vision* (1916, with Henry P. Janes) is an earnest **Christian fantasy**; it contrasts strongly with the **infernal comedies** *Ladies in Hades: A Story of Hell's Smart Set* (1928) and *Gentlemen in Hades: The Story of a Damned Debutante* (1930), which **satirize** the mores of the Roaring Twenties in a manner akin to the works of **Thorne Smith**.

KURIMOTO, KAORU (?–). Japanese writer. Her Guin Saga, intended to consist of 100 books (95 were complete in 2004, plus 19 in a spinoff series) began translation in *The Leopard Mask* (1979; tr. 2003), *Warrior in the Wilderness* (1979; tr. 2003), and *The Battle of Nospherus* (1980; tr. 2003). It is a distinctive example of Japanese **heroic fantasy**, also displayed in a three-volume graphic novel adaptation of *The Sword of Paros* by Yumiko Igarashi. Her untranslated work also includes material in the spirit of **H. P. Lovecraft**.

KURTZ, KATHERINE (1944–). U.S. writer. She was the first writer to publish original work in the **Ballantine Adult Fantasy Series**, establishing the Deryni series—which adds other elements to a quasi-historical **Celtic** base—as one of the foundation stones of the nascent **commodified** genre. The first trilogy, comprising *Deryni Rising* (1970), *Deryni Checkmate* (1972), and *High Deryni* (1973), pioneered what was to become a familiar pattern when it was followed by a **prequel** trilogy comprising *Camber of Culdi* (1976), *Saint Camber* (1978), and *Camber the Heretic* (1981), which was then followed by two fill-in trilogies, one comprising *The Bishop's Heir* (1984), *The King's Justice* (1985), and *The Quest for Saint Camber* (1986), and another (set earlier in the timeline) comprising *The Harrowing of Gwynedd* (1989), *King Javan's Year* (1992), and *The Bastard Prince* (1994). The series continued in *King Kelson's Bride* (2000) and *In the King's Service* (2003). *The Deryni Archives* (1986; exp. 2002 as *Deryni Tales*) adds a miscellany of short fiction, while *Deryni Magic: A Grimoire* (1990) is a **scholarly fantasy** explaining the theory and practice of the **magic** featured in the series.

Lammas Night (1983) is a **dark/historical fantasy** whose inclinations were extended in *Two Crowns for America* (1996) and in novels written in collaboration with **Deborah Turner Harris**. In *St. Patrick's Gargoyle* (2001), gargoyles are eccentric guardian **angels**. She edited two anthologies of **Templar** fantasy: *Crusade of Fire: Mystical Tales of the Knights Templar* (1997) and *On Crusade: More Tales of the Knights Templar* (1998).

KUSHNER, ELLEN (1955–). U.S. writer who coedited an anthology with **Terri Windling** before publishing "The Unicorn Masque" in Windling's first *Elsewhere* anthology and becoming involved with Windling's Endicott Studio project. *Swordspoint* (1987) is set in a **secondary world** that has already been subject to rigorous **thinning**; *The Fall of Kings* (2002, with Delia Sherman) carries the same milieu forward. *Thomas the Rhymer* (1990) is an elaborate **transfiguration** of the **ballad** in which **Faerie** is reconfigured as "Ballad-Land." Kushner wrote and narrated *The Golden Dreydl: A Klezmer Nutcracker* (2000), a Chanukah-celebrating performance piece for the Shirim Klezmer Orchestra's adaptation of Tchaikovsky's *Nutcracker Suite*.

KUTTNER, HENRY (1915–1958). U.S. writer best known for **sf** (refer to *HDSFL*). He was briefly associated with the **Lovecraft** circle, and much of his early fiction was **sword and sorcery** in the vein of **Robert E. Howard**, including two brief series featuring *Elak of Atlantis* (1938–41; book 1985) and *Prince Raynor* (1939; book 1987). He wrote **humorous fantasies** for ***Unknown,*** including "The Misguided Halo" (1939) and "Compliments of the Author" (1942). Before marrying **C. L. Moore** in 1940, Kuttner collaborated with her on "Quest of the Starstone" (1937), which contrived a meeting between her two key characters, Jirel of Joiry and Northwest Smith; they produced numerous exotic melodramas in the manner of **A. Merritt**, all cast as **science fantasy**.

– L –

LACKEY, MERCEDES (1950–). U.S. writer. She is the most prolific producer of **commodified fantasy**, the central thread of her work being a long sequence of novels set in the **secondary world** of Valdemar, including several trilogies: *Arrows of the Queen* (1987), *Arrow's Flight* (1987), and *Arrow's Fall* (1988); *Magic's Pawn* (1989), *Magic's Promise* (1990), and *Magic's Price* (1990); *Winds of Fate* (1991), *Winds of Change* (1992), and *Winds of Fury* (1993); *Storm Warning* (1994), *Storm Rising* (1995), and *Storm Breaking* (1996); *The Black Gryphon* (1994), *The White Gryphon* (1995), and *The Silver Gryphon* (1996); and *Owlflight* (1997), *Owlsight* (1998), and *Owlknight* (1999). The last two trilogies were written in collaboration with her husband, Larry Dixon. Other Valdemar-set books are the novels *The Oathbound* (1988), *Oathbreakers* (1989), *Brightly Burning* (2000), and *Take a Thief* (2001), the **anthologies** *Swords of Ice and Other Tales of Valdemar* (1996) and *Sun in Glory* (2003), and the collection *Oathblood* (1998). The series beginning with *Exile's Honor* (2002) and *Exile's Valor* (2003) is a **prequel** to the first trilogy. The **guide** *The Valdemar Companion* (2001), ed. John Helfers and Denise Little, includes an original novella. The opening of the Valdemar setting to other writers reflected Lackey's increasing involvement in collaborative and **shared-world** projects; two novels combined as *Bedlam's Bard* (1992) were co-credited to Ellen Guon, while *Beyond World's End* (2001), *Spirits White as Lightning* (2001), and *Mad Maudlin* (2003) were co-credited to **Rosemary Edghill**.

The Bardic Voices series, four of which—*The Lark and the Wren* (1992), *The Robin and the Kestrel* (1993), *The Eagle and the Nightingales* (1995), and *Four and Twenty Blackbirds* (1997)—Lackey wrote solo, also became a shared-world endeavor with *A Cast of Corbies* (1994 with Josepha Sherman). Others include novels featuring an elvish Road Racing Association, variously co-credited to Dixon, Mark Shepherd, and **Holly Lisle**. Lackey has also contributed to collaborative projects with **Marion Zimmer Bradley**, **C. J. Cherryh**, **Andre Norton**, **Piers Anthony**, and **Anne McCaffrey**. *The Shadow of the Lion* (2002 with Eric Flint and Dave Freer), a massive **alternative-history fantasy** mostly set in 16th-century Venice, continues in *This Rough Magic* (2003). *The Outstretched Shadow* (2003 with James Mallory) launched the Obsidian trilogy. *This Scepter'd Isle* (2004 with Roberta Gellis) is a **historical fantasy** about the early life of Elizabeth I.

Lackey's other solo work includes several **occult detective** stories, notably *Sacred Ground* (1994), and the **historical fantasy** *The Fire Rose* (1995). *Firebird* (1996), based on the Russian fairy tale that inspired Stravinsky's ballet, was followed by *The Black Swan* (1999), based on Tchaikovsky's *Swan Lake*. *The River's Gift* (1999) is in the same vein. *The Serpent's Shadow* (2001) is a **transfiguration** of Snow White set in 1909 London with an Anglo-Indian heroine; *The Gates of Sleep* (2002) transfigures Sleeping Beauty in Victorian England. *Joust* (2003) and *Alta* (2004) feature dragons and their riders. *The Fairy Godmother* (2004) is a paranormal romance. Lackey's short fiction is sampled in *Fiddler Fair* (1998) and *Werehunter* (1999). Her anthologies include *Flights of Fantasy* (1999), featuring birds of prey.

LAFFERTY, R. A. (1914–2002). U.S. writer best known for **sf** (refer to *HDSFL*), although his **surreal** and **chimerical/fabulations**, of spiritual evolution invariably include motifs drawn from **myth** and folklore. Fantasy elements predominate in the sequence begun by *The Devil Is Dead* (1971), which continued in *Archipelago* (1979) and *More than Melchisedech* (3 vols., 1992), *Serpent's Egg* (1987), and *Sindbad: The 13th Voyage* (1989). The short-story collections following *Through Elegant Eyes* (1983) and *Ringing Changes* (1984), most of which were produced as pamphlets by **small presses**, also feature enigmatically whimsical material that defies ready classification.

LAGERLÖF, SELMA (1858–1940). Swedish writer. Much of her work—including the episodic *Gösta Berling's Saga* (1891; tr. 1898)—

describes conflicts between pietistic ideas of Christian virtue and codes of conduct based in pagan tradition. Many of her short works are **sentimental** exercises in **Christian fantasy**, examples of which are included in *Invisible Links* (1894–98; tr. 1899), *From a Swedish Homestead* (1899; tr. 1901), and *Christ Legends and Other Stories* (1904; tr. 1908), although "The Legend of the Christmas Rose" is in *The Girl from the Marsh Croft* (1904; tr. 1910). *Herr Arne's Hoard* (1904; 1923; aka *The Treasure*) is an account of divine vengeance visited on three Scottish soldiers. *The Wonderful Adventures of Nils* (1906; tr. 1907) and *The Further Adventures of Nils* (1907; tr. 1911) are **theriomorphic/children's fantasies** commissioned to aid in the teaching of geography. *Thy Soul Shall Bear Witness!* (1912; tr. 1921) is a **hallucinatory fantasy** based on a legend asserting that the last man to die on New Year's Eve must drive Death's cart during the coming year. *Lilicrona's Home* (1911; tr. 1913) tells the story of an unfortunate pastor's daughter whose wicked stepmother might be a dispossessed water sprite. *The General's Ring* (1925; tr. 1928; aka *The Lowenskold Ring*) is a **historical fantasy** about a curse.

LANG, ANDREW (1844–1912). Scottish writer and pioneer of anthropology. He followed an edition of *Perrault's Fairy Tales* (1888) with a notable series of **anthologies** launched with *The Blue Fairy Book* (1890) and followed by volumes in *Red* (1890), *Green* (1892), *Yellow* (1894), *Grey* (1900), *Violet* (1901), *Crimson* (1903), *Brown* (1904), *Orange* (1907), *Olive* (1907), and *Lilac* (1910); he also produced two volumes of recycled **animal fantasies** (1896–99) and a volume of *Arabian Nights Entertainments* (1898). He wrote a new text to fit one of the picture sequences in Richard Doyle's *In Fairyland* (1869), *The Princess Nobody* (1884), and a dark-edged account of a child abducted into **Faerie**, *The Gold of Fairnilee* (1888), before achieving greater commercial success with two **humorous/children's fantasies**, *Prince Prigio* (1889) and *Prince Ricardo of Pantouflia* (1893). The stories in *Tales of a Fairy Court* (1906) are in a similarly light vein.

Lang's works for adults includes a verse epic *Helen of Troy* (1882) and a **satirical** account of the return to England of an exiled **fairy** queen, *"That Very Mab"* (1885, with May Kendall). The title piece of *In the Wrong Paradise and Other Stories* (1886) is a satirical **afterlife fantasy**. In collaboration with **Walter Herries Pollock**, he parodied **H. Rider Haggard**'s *She* in *He, by the Author of It* (1887) but went on to collaborate with Haggard on the earnest **Odyssean fantasy** *The*

World's Desire (1890). He discovered and published Robert Kirk's seemingly credulous account of *The Secret Commonwealth of Elves, Fauns and Fairies* (written 1691) in 1893.

LATIN AMERICAN FANTASY. Latin American fantasy grew out of a syncretic process that mingled European literary and religious traditions with native **myth** and folklore. Such links began to be forged in the 19th century in the works of such Argentine writers as Juana Manuela Gorriti and Eduardo Ladislao Holmberg; they began to spread to other nations in the early 20th century—to Peru in the works of Clemente Palma, Uruguay in the works of Horace Quiroga and Feliberto Hernandez, Brazil in the works of Jorge Amado, Mexico in the works of Juan José Arreola, and Guatemala in the works of Miguel Angel Asturias.

These native traditions came into full flower in the 1940s, when the Argentinian **Jorge Luis Borges**, his associate Adolfo Bioy Casares, and their countryman Julio Cortazar produced much of their seminal work. They were followed by the Colombian **Gabriel Garcia Márquez**, the Peruvian Mario Vargas Llosa, the Mexicans Carlos Fuentes and Juan Rulfo, the Cuban Alejo Carpentier, the Argentinian Enrique Anderson Imbert, and the Brazilian Paulo Coelho. The purportedly distinctive manner of their use of the fantastic came to be characterized as **magic realism**.

LAWHEAD, STEPHEN R. (1950–). U.S. writer long resident in Britain. The **religious fantasy** trilogy comprising *In the Hall of the Dragon King* (1982), *The Warlords of Nin* (1983), and *The Sword and the Flame* (1984) disguises its **Christian** affiliations more carefully than do later works; the **Arthurian** series comprising *Taliesin* (1987), *Merlin* (1988), *Arthur* (1989), *Pendragon* (1994), *Grail* (1997), and *Avalon: The Return of King Arthur* (1999) is more explicit. The **portal fantasy** trilogy comprising *The Paradise War* (1991), *The Silver Hand* (1992), and *The Endless Knot* (1993) deals with other **Celtic fantasy** materials in a similar fashion. *Byzantium* (1996) is a **historical fantasy** about a journey to the eponymous city. The Celtic Crusades trilogy, comprising *The Iron Lance* (1998), *The Black Rood* (2000), and *The Mystic Rose* (2001), features a search for the true cross, inevitably involving **Templars**. *City of Dreams* (2003) is set in an **alternative history** in which Jesus is belatedly incarnated in Pennsylvania.

LAWRENCE, ANN (1942–87). British writer. *Tom Ass; or, The Second Gift* (1972) is a **transfiguration** of **Apuleius**. *The Half-Brothers* (1973), set in **Faerie**, similarly hovers uneasily between adult and **children's fantasy**; the **portal fantasy** *The Conjuror's Box* (1974) explicitly chooses the latter direction but retains a conscientious thematic sophistication. *The Good Little Devil* (1978) is an enterprising **Christian fantasy**. *The Hawk of May* (1980) and *Merlin the Wizard* (1986) are **Arthurian fantasies**. *Beyond the Firelight* (1983) and *Tales from Perrault* (1988) **recycle** familiar materials, the former consisting of **Arabian fantasies**. *Summer's End: Stories of Ghostly Lovers* (1987) anticipated the rise of **paranormal romance**.

LAWRENCE, LOUISE (1943–). Pseudonym of British writer Elizabeth Wintle Holden. Most of her work is **sf** (refer to *HDSFL*), but the couplet comprising *The Wyndcliffe* (1974) and *Sing and Scatter Daisies* (1977) is a **sentimental fantasy** about a young woman's love affair with a **ghost**. In *Cat Call* (1980), the magic of an ancient cat cult is invoked against the children of a quiet village. *The Earth Witch* (1981) is a **paranormal romance** told from the male viewpoint. *The Dram Road* (1983) is a ghost story. The trilogy comprising *Journey through Llandor* (1995), *The Road to Irriyan* (1996), and *The Shadow of Mordican* (1997) is a stereotypical **portal fantasy**.

LAWRENCE, MARGERY (1889–1969). British writer in several genres, much of whose work in marked by sincere belief, and a strong interest, in the **occult**, especially **ghostly** manifestations. The stories assembled in *Nights of the Round Table* (1926), *The Terraces of Night* (1932), *The Floating Cafe and Other Stories* (1936), and *Strange Caravan* (1941) mingle **horror** and fantasy. Those in *Number Seven, Queer Street* (1945) and *Master of Shadows* (1959) comprise a series of **occult detective** stories. *The Bridge of Wonder* (1939), *The Rent in the Veil* (1951), *The Tomorrow of Yesterday* (1966), and *A Residence Afresh* (1969) are all **spiritualist fantasies**, the third combined with **Atlantean fantasy**.

LEAR, EDWARD (1812–1888). British artist and poet, great pioneer of the limerick form and of the literary "nonsense" further developed by **Lewis Carroll** and **W. S. Gilbert**. The items initially published in *The Book of Nonsense* (1846), *Nonsense Songs, Stories, Botany and Alphabets* (1871), *More Nonsense Pictures, Rhymes, Botany, etc.* (1872), and *Laughable Lyrics* (1876) were recombined in many subsequent selections; the most notable fantasy items are "The Owl and the Pussycat," "The Jumblies," "The Dong with the Luminous Nose," and "The Pobble Who Has No Toes."

LEE, TANITH (1947–). British writer whose earliest works were **children's fantasies**, including *The Dragon Hoard* (1971), *Companions on the Road* (1975), and *The Winter Players* (1976), although she soon diversified into **feminized/sword and sorcery** for adults in the breezily **erotic** *The Birthgrave* (1975), which was supplemented by the sequels *Vazkor, Son of Vazkor* (1978; aka *Shadowfire*), and *Quest for the White Witch* (1978). A similar trilogy comprises *The Storm Lord* (1976), *Anackire* (1983), and *The White Serpent* (1988). Her work for younger readers continued with *The Castle of Dark* (1978) and its sequel *Prince on a White Horse* (1982); *Shon the Taken* (1979); the trilogy comprising *Black Unicorn* (1991), *Gold Unicorn* (1994), and *Red Unicorn* (1997); and the series comprising *Law of the Wolf Tower* (2000; aka *Wolf Tower*), *Wolf Star Rise* (2000), *Queen of the Wolves* (2001; aka *Wolf Queen*), and *Wolf Wing* (2002).

In the meantime, Lee's adult fiction ranged more widely, including excursions into **sf** (refer to *HDSFL*) and **horror** (refer to *HDHL*), an element of which was imported into the Flat Earth series, comprising *Night's Master* (1978), *Death's Master* (1979), *Delusion's Master* (1981), *Delirium's Mistress* (1986), and *Night's Sorceries* (1987), as well as *Volkhavaar* (1977) and *Day by Night* (1980). Much of her subsequent fiction, including the **science fantasy** *Sabella* (1980), *The Blood of Roses* (1990), and the trilogy comprising *Dark Dance* (1992), *Personal Darkness* (1993), and *Darkness, I* (1994), involved unorthodox **vampires** or—as in *Lycanthia* (1981) and *Heart-Beast* (1992)—**werewolves**. Its eroticism became increasingly heated and stylized, particularly in an episodic series set in the Paris-inspired city of Paradys, comprising *The Book of the Damned* (1988), *The Book of the Beast* (1988), *The Book of the Dead* (1991), and *The Book of the Mad* (1993).

Sung in Shadow (1983) is a **Shakespearean** fantasy. *Madame Two Swords* is a **historical fantasy** set in revolutionary France, while *A Heroine of the World* (1989) is set in an **alternative** Russia. She made use of Hindu mythology in the mosaic *Tamastara; or, The Indian Nights* (1984) and *Elephantasm* (1993), and of Near Eastern mythology in *Vivia* (1995). *Reigning Cats and Dogs* (1995) is a **dark fantasy** set in quasi-Dickensian London; *When the Lights Go Out* (1996) is similarly dark. The Secret Books of Venus series, set in an alternative 18th-century Italy, comprises *Faces under Water* (1998), *Saint Fire* (1999), *A Bed of Earth* (2002), and the **far-futuristic** *Venus Preserved* (2003). *White as Snow* (2000) is a transfiguration of Snow White. In *Mortal*

Suns (2003), an aged seer recalls her youth in a fantastic court. *Piratica* (2004) is an alternative history in which the heroine is determined to follow in her mother's unorthodox footsteps. *Cast a Bright Shadow* (2004) launched the Lionwolf trilogy.

Lee's short fiction is collected in *Unsilent Night* (1981), *Cyrion* (1982), *Red as Blood; or, Tales from the Sisters Grimmer* (1983), *The Gorgon and Other Beastly Tales* (1985), *Dreams of Dark and Light* (1986), *Forests of the Night* (1989), *Women as Demons* (1989), and *Nightshades* (1993).

LEE, VERNON (1856–1935). Pseudonym of British writer Violet Paget, born in France and long resident in Italy. She was the half-sister of **Eugene Lee-Hamilton**, as whose lectrice she served during his long incapacitation by neurasthenia. She followed a series of *Studies of the Eighteenth Century in Italy* (1880) with a collection of *Tuscan Fairy Tales* (1888). "A Culture-Ghost; or, Winthrop's Adventure" (written 1874; published 1881) appeared shortly after her literary manifesto for such endeavours, "Faustus and Helena: Notes on the Supernatural in Art" (1880), which proposed that the supernatural can retain its proper power over the imagination only if it is allowed to remain obscure, ambiguous, and paradoxical.

The landmark collection *Hauntings* (1890) included the vivid **erotic fantasies** "Amour Dure" and "Dionea" alongside more orthodox **ghost** stories (refer to *HDHL*). A further **erotic fantasy**, "The Virgin of the Seven Daggers" (1889), remained unreprinted until it appeared in *For Maurice: Five Unlikely Stories* (1927), although the anti-romantic "Prince Alberic and the Snake Lady" (1896) was reprinted in *Pope Jacynth and Other Fantastic Tales* (1904) alongside several **satirical** Christian **legends**. Her other fantasies include *The Prince of the Hundred Soups: A Puppet Show in Narrative* (1883), *The Legend of Madame Krasinska* (1890), the fictionalized essay "A Seeker of Pagan Perfection, Being the Life of Domenico Neroni, Pictor Sacrilegus" (1891), and two other items in *For Maurice,* most notably the **humorous/classical fantasy** "The Gods and Ritter Tanhûser" (1913). The most comprehensive sampler of her work is the Ash-Tree Press omnibus *Hauntings: The Supernatural Stories* (2002).

LEE-HAMILTON, EUGENE (1845–1907). British writer long resident in continental Europe and North America, the half-brother of **Vernon Lee**. *The Lord of the Dark Red Star* (1903) is a graphic **historical fantasy** with

Faustian elements. *The Romance of the Fountain* (1905) is a cautionary tale of **immortality**.

LEGEND. No clear boundary separates the term "legend" from "myth" or "**folktale**," but legends occupy an intermediate status, focusing on real or imaginary historical individuals of some importance rather than **gods** or common folk. The most considerable overlap concerns tales of legendary heroes, stories that are often promoted to the rank of "hero myths." **Christian fantasy** makes much of the legends of the saints, and **Arthurian fantasy** is similarly based in legendary lore.

LE GUIN, URSULA K. (1929–). U.S. writer best known for **sf** (refer to *HDSFL*), although she made her debut with the **sentimental fantasy** "April in Paris" (1962). The trilogy comprising *A Wizard of Earthsea* (1968), *The Tombs of Atuan* (1971), and *The Farthest Shore* (1972)—to which she later appended *Tehanu: The Last Book of Earthsea* (1990), *Tales from Earthsea* (2001), and *The Other Wind* (2001)—is a sophisticated and highly influential **immersive fantasy** initially marketed for **children**, which demonstrated the scope that genre fantasy might contain for **allegorical** exploration of processes of maturation and self-development. The extent to which the Earthsea series was theoretically informed is made manifest in the essays collected in *The Language of the Night* (1979; rev. 1989); its several crucial contributions to the development of genre theory include "From Elfland to Poughkeepsie" (1973). More items in the same vein are included in *Dancing at the Edge of the World* (1989).

The mosaic *Orsinian Tales* (1976) and the related novel *Malafrena* (1979) offer accounts of a nonsupernatural **secondary world**. *The Beginning Place* (1980; aka *Threshold*) is a **portal fantasy** dramatizing problems of adolescence; *Gifts* (2004) was also marketed for **young adults**. The title story of *Buffalo Gals and Other Animal Presences* (1987) is a delicately crafted **animal fantasy**, and there are fantasy elements in some of the stories in *Unlocking the Air and Other Stories* (1996). The series begun with *Catwings* (1988) consists of children's **animal fantasies** featuring flying cats; *Solomon Leviathan's Nine Hundred and Thirty-first Trip around the World* (1983), *Fire and Stone* (1989), *A Ride on the Red Mare's Back* (1992). and *Fish Soup* (1992) are in a similar vein.

LEIBER, FRITZ (1910–1992). U.S. writer. In the mid-1930s, he wrote "Adept's Gambit" (first published in *Night's Black Agents*, 1947), a stylish **picaresque/heroic fantasy** pairing the barbarian Fafhrd with the slight but clever Gray Mouser; more conventional **sword and sorcery** stories featuring the same characters—moved from their original historical setting to the **decadent** city of Lankhmar in the **secondary world** of Nehwon—began to appear in ***Unknown*** in 1939. The series ultimately became crucial to the evolution of the subgenre, demonstrating that it had far greater scope, in terms of wit and sophistication, than had interested **Robert E. Howard**. It was a vital influence on later recruits to the genre, including **L. Sprague de Camp** and **Michael Moorcock**. A then-definitive five-volume edition, in order of the series' internal chronology, comprises *Swords and Deviltry* (1970), *Swords against Death* (1957 as *Two Sought Adventure*; rev. 1970), *Swords in the Mist* (1968), *Swords against Wizardry* (1968; includes one collaboration with Harry Otto Fischer), and *The Swords of Lankhmar* (1968). Later additions were *Swords and Ice Magic* (1977) and *The Knight and Knave of Swords* (1988).

Leiber's other work for *Unknown* included the ***conte philosophique*** "Smoke Ghost" (1941), which laid the ideative foundations for **urban fantasy**; another significant item in the same vein, *Conjure Wife* (1943; book 1953), casually proposes that rationalism is a male prerogative and that all women are **witches**. An **existentialist fantasy** intended for *Unknown* appeared in an abridged version as "You're All Alone" (1950) and in a mutilated 1953 book version before the text was restored as *The Sinful Ones* (1980). *The Green Millennium* (1953) is a light-hearted **contemporary fantasy**. Leiber's short fantasies are mingled with **sf** and **horror** stories (refer to *HDSFL* and *HDHL*) in numerous collections, notably *The Secret Songs* (1968), *Night Monsters* (1969; exp. 1974), and *The Ghost Light* (1991). His **animal fantasies** are collected in *Kreativity for Kats and Other Feline Fantasies* (1990) and *Gummitch and Friends* (1992). *Our Lady of Darkness* (1977) is a summation and extrapolation of Leiber's cultivation of a distinctive kind of urban fantasy.

LELAND, CHARLES GODFREY (1824–1903). U.S. writer whose casual misrepresentation of some of his poetry as translations of Italian pagan ritual, as *Gypsy Sorcery and Fortune Telling* (1891) had earlier done, in *Aradia: The Gospel of the Witches* (1899) made a significant contribution to subsequent **scholarly fantasies.** *Johnnykins and the Goblins* (1876) is a **moralistic fantasy**. The mosaic *Flaxius: Leaves from the Life of an Immortal* (1902) is a far-ranging **historical fantasy**.

LÉVI ÉLIPHAS (1810–1875). Pseudonym of French **scholarly** and **lifestyle fantasist** Alphonse Louis Constant, whose *The Doctrine and Ritual of Transcendental Magic* (1854–56; tr. 1896) became the principal source book of all subsequent practical handbooks of "high magic," including those used by the "Rosicrucian lodges" of late 19th-century Paris, and those penned by **A. E. Waite** (Lévi's English translator) and **Aleister Crowley**. *The History of Magic* (1859; tr. 1913) provided the earlier book with appropriately elaborate, but largely imaginary, historical foundations; its success probably prompted **Jules Michelet** to dash off *La sorcière*.

LEWIS, C. S. (1898–1963). British writer, much of whose fantastic fiction consists of idiosyncratic exercises in **Christian** apologetics. *The Pilgrim's Regress* (1933; rev. 1943) tells the story of his own conversion. He placed **sf** (refer to *HDSFL*) at the service of **religious fantasy** in *Out of the Silent Planet* (1938) and *Perelandra* (1943; aka *Voyage to Venus*), although *That Hideous Strength* (1945)—heavily influenced by **Charles Williams**—completed the trilogy by veering into **metaphysical fantasy** involving **Merlin**; an uncompleted fourth volume, published as the title piece of *The Dark Tower and Other Stories* (1977) offers horrific visions of a **parallel world**. *The Screwtape Letters* (1942) takes the form of letters written by a worldly-wise **devil** to his callow nephew. *The Great Divorce* (1945) is an enterprising **afterlife fantasy**. *Till We Have Faces: A Myth Retold* (1956), is a poignant **classical fantasy** recycling the tale of Cupid and Psyche.

Lewis's phenomenally successful **children's fantasy** series the Chronicles of Narnia, comprising *The Lion, the Witch and the Wardrobe* (1950), *Prince Caspian* (1951), *The Voyage of the Dawn Treader* (1952), *The Silver Chair* (1953), *The Horse and his Boy* (1954), *The Magician's Nephew* (1955), and *The Last Battle* (1956), conceals its message artfully. Some juvenilia were assembled in *Boxen: The Imaginary World of the Young C. S. Lewis* (1985), edited by Walter Hooper. Lewis's contributions to the **Inklings**' discussions of the significance and literary utility of mythical and fantastic materials are reflected in *An Experiment in Criticism* (1961) and *Of Other Worlds: Essays and Stories* (1966).

LEWIS, MATTHEW GREGORY (1775–1818). British writer best known as the author of the lurid **Gothic** horror novel *The Monk; a Romance* (1796) (refer to *HDHL*). He was a prolific writer of stage melodramas, some of which—including *One o'Clock! or, The Knight and the*

Wood Daemon (1811)—are fantasies, as are "Amorassan; or, The Spirit of the Frozen Ocean" and a few other items in *Romantic Tales* (4 vols., 1808; abridged in one vol. 1838), most of which are adaptations of works by other hands. Lewis's translation of **Anthony Hamilton**'s *The Four Facardins* included his own extensive continuation as well as a translation of one by M. de Levis. The first volume of his collection of **ballads** *Tales of Wonder* (2 vols., 1801)—which includes some original compositions—was reprinted by Henry Morley in *Tales of Terror and Wonder* (1887) with a collection of parodies that had been falsely advertised as Lewis's work. The anthology was influential, largely by virtue of including translations of **J. W. Goethe**'s "The Erl-King," Gottfried Bürger's "Leonora" and "The Wild Huntsmen," and early works by **Walter Scott**.

LEWIS, WYNDHAM (1882–1957). U.S.-born British writer and critic. With Ezra Pound, he edited *Blast, the Review of the Great English Vortex* (1914–15), where he published his exemplary Vorticist drama *The Enemy of the Stars* (book 1932), a fantastic extravaganza in which Hanp—symbolic of violent and dull-witted Mankind—battles Arghol, the wise and rational spirit of intellectualism. The enterprising and highly idiosyncratic **Dantean fantasy** *The Childermass* (1928) launched a project collectively titled *The Human Age;* it was never completed, although two further parts—*Monstre Gai* and *Malign Fiesta*—were appended to it when it was reprinted in a two-volume edition of 1955, along with a synoptic account of the unwritten fourth section, *The Trial of Man*. His artwork inspired **Naomi Mitchison**'s **hallucinatory fantasy** *Beyond the Limit*.

LIFESTYLE FANTASY. All "lifestyles" act out psychological fantasies, but most are thoroughly naturalistic. The term is employed here to describe those lifestyles that embrace and enact some kind of magic, mysticism, or calculated madness. As with **scholarly fantasy**, it is impossible to make distinctions between lifestyle fantasists who are sincere believers and those who are merely poseurs; the term does not discriminate between devout satanists and playactors whose black masses are purely theatrical affairs, nor between practitioners of **alchemy**, **astrology**, or **witchcraft** who are mere confidence tricksters and those who have absolute faith in the authenticity of their practices.

A significant English model was the Friars of St. Francis of Wycombe, established by Sir Francis Dashwood in 1752 at Medmenham Abbey, although the Hell-Fire Club, whose name it inherited in popular gossip, was actually an earlier social gathering that met at the George and Vulture Inn in London—an establishment with another claim to fame, its appearance in **Charles Dickens**'s *Pickwick Papers*. The rituals of such societies lent impetus to the **Gothic** revival in literature and exercised a powerful influence on the most conspicuous lifestyle fantasists of the 19th century, who laid the foundations of the occult revival. The **Byronic** pose, which remained enormously fashionable long after **Edward Bulwer-Lytton** claimed to have killed it off by championing a brighter form of dandyism, extended into lifestyle fantasy in its more extreme versions, echoing in the impostures of such **decadent** diabolists as Count Stenbock. Other 19th-century lifestyle fantasists who provided considerable fodder for literary fantasists included mesmerists, spiritualists, cheiromancers, theosophists, and Rosicrucians. Many prominent lifestyle fantasists—including **Éliphas Lévi**, **Madame Blavatsky**, **Aleister Crowley**, and **Dion Fortune**—also wrote scholarly fantasies and dabbled in literary fantasies, helping to secure a positive feedback loop of influences.

Writers whose fiction expresses and exaggerates the yearnings of their lifestyle fantasies include **Marie Corelli** and "Baron Corvo," although **L. Ron Hubbard** gave up fantasy writing when he discovered that marketable **lifestyle fantasies** were far more profitable. The lifestyle fantasy that has had the most conspicuous influence on modern fantasy fiction is the neopaganism that colonized imaginative territory carved out by the scholarly fantasies of **Jules Michelet**, **James Frazer**, and **Margaret Murray**; their **transfigured** history of witch persecution—enriched with a substantial slice of **fairy** mythology—has been fed back into literary fantasy on a prodigious scale.

LIGOTTI, THOMAS (1953–). U.S. writer. His early short fiction, collected in *Songs of a Dead Dreamer* (1986; exp. 1989), extrapolated the **decadent** aspect of **Lovecraftian** fiction in a **surreal** mode influenced by German expressionism (refer to *HDHL*). *Grimscribe: His Life and Works* (1991) and *Noctuary* (1994) carried forward the project, while *The Agonizing Resurrection of Victor Frankenstein & Other Gothic Tales* (1994) offered **metafictional** extrapolations of classic texts. *The Nightmare Factory* (1996) is an eclectic collection. *My Work Is Not Yet Done* (2002) assembles "Three Tales of Corporate Horror," whose title novella is a scathing **Gothic** satire.

LIMINAL FANTASY. A category initially defined by Farah Mendlesohn in "Toward a Taxonomy of Fantasy" (2001) as "estranged fantasy"; the substitute term has the advantage of avoiding too much confusion with the notion of "cognitive estrangement," developed by Darko Suvin and regarded by him—but not by fantasy theorists—as the sole prerogative of **sf** and the basis of its essential superiority to fantasy.

Liminal fantasy is perhaps best seen as a splinter category of **intrusive fantasy** in which fantastic or magical devices are not perceived by the characters as "disruptive of expectation" but as something ordinary and expectable, thus undermining the "sense of wonder" in a manner akin to **immersive fantasies**—the fundamental effect, if not the calculated strategy, of **magical realism**. Effectively, liminal fantasies are immersive fantasies set in the primary world; Mendlesohn regards the category as "the most demanding" of the four types detailed in her article, because "it depends for its effectiveness on the understanding and subversion of our expectations of the fantastic." The ability to deploy narrative strategies of this degree of sophistication is central to the evolution of **postmodern/fabulation**.

LINDHOLM, MEGAN (1952–). U.S. writer. The trilogy comprising *Harpy's Flight* (1983), *The Windsingers* (1984), and *The Limbreth Gate* (1984) is a stereotypical **commodified fantasy**, to which *Luck of the Wheels* (1989) was subsequently appended. *The Wizard of the Pigeons* (1986) and *Gypsy* (1992, with **Steven Brust**) are more enterprising **urban fantasies**. The couplet comprising *The Reindeer People* (1988) and *The Wolf's Brother* (1988) is a **prehistoric fantasy**. *Cloven Hooves* (1991) is a dark **contemporary fantasy**. Lindholm relaunched her career under the pseudonym "**Robin Hobb**."

LINDSAY, DAVID (1878–1945). British writer. His first novel, *A Voyage to Arcturus* (1920), is a complex and robust **allegorical** fantasy in which the hero encounters many strange beings and undergoes a series of painful metamorphoses while struggling to comprehend the creative force of Shaping and its crucial relationship to the symbolic figures of Crystalman and Surtur. *The Haunted Woman* (1922) is a **metaphysical/timeslip** fantasy; its protagonist achieves brief intervals of liberation from the burden of repression and constraint to which civilization has subjected human consciousness. *Sphinx* (1923) attempts to embed metaphysical imagery of the same sort within a conventional domestic drama embellished by **hallucinatory fantasy**. *The Violet Apple,* written immediately afterward but not published until 1975, makes similar use of **biblical fantasy**. In *Devil's Tor* (1932), a threatened apocalyptic return of the primal **goddess** frames a syncretic mythos revising some of the metaphysical notions detailed in *A Voyage to Arcturus,* but the fuller elaboration of his revised thesis that he intended to set out in *The Witch* (1975) was never completed.

LINDSKOLD, JANE (1962–). U.S. writer. *Brother to Dragons, Companion to Owls* (1994) is an **ambiguous/science fantasy** in which a mad girl who talks to inanimate objects goes on the run. *Pipes of Orpheus* (1995), in which Orpheus is an accursed wanderer, explains the fate of the children of Hamelin. *When the Gods Are Silent* (1997) is an account of rapid **thinning** and the consequent **quest** to bring magic back. *Changer* (1998) is a recklessly syncretic **contemporary/theriomorphic fantasy** with **Arthurian** elements; *Legends Walking* (1999) is a sequel. *Lord Demon* (1999 with Roger Zelazny) is a contemporary **Oriental fantasy** featuring an exiled **demon**. The theriomorphic fantasy series comprising *Through Wolf's Eyes* (2001), *Wolf's Head, Wolf's Heart* (2002), *The Dragon of Despair* (2003), and *Wolf Captured* (2004) is set in a **secondary world**. *The Buried Pyramid* (2004) is an Egyptian fantasy adventure.

LINK, KELLY (1969–). U.S. writer and **small press** publisher. The wide-ranging **fabulations** collected in *Stranger Things Happen* (2001) are uncommonly inventive and stylish. With her husband, Gavin Grant, Link runs the Small Beer Press, which issued the eccentrically eclectic magazine *Lady Churchill's Rosebud Wristlet* (launched 1997) from its sixth issue. The couple took over from **Terri Windling** as editors of the fantasy section of *The Year's Best Fantasy and Horror* in 2003. Link edited the notable showcase **anthology** *Trampoline* (2003).

LINKLATER, ERIC (1899–1974). Scottish writer. His play *The Devil's in the News* (1929), a **spiritualist fantasy** in which the spirits of real and fictitious individuals are invoked, laid the groundwork for a series of dramatic dialogues broadcast by the BBC during World War II in which historical figures from different eras debate philosophical issues. They are reprinted in *The Cornerstones: A Conversation in Elysium* (1941), *The Raft and Socrates Asks Why* (1942), *The Great Ship and Rabelais Replies* (1944), and *Crisis in Heaven: An Elysian Comedy* (1944).

The fantasy stories mingled with others in *God Likes Them Plain* (1935), *Sealskin Trousers* (1947), and *A Sociable Plover* (1957) include satirical **fairy tales**, irreverent **Christian fantasies** and **humorous classical fantasies**. *The Impregnable Women* (1938) transfigures Aristophanes' *Lysistrata,* while *A Spell for Old Bones* (1949) is a political **allegory** featuring clumsy giants of ancient Scotland. *The Wind on the Moon* (1944) is a frivolous **children's** story with elements of **animal fantasy**; *The Pirates in the Deep Green Sea* (1949) is a more wholehearted fantasy of undersea adventures. *Husband of Delilah* (1962) is a **biblical fantasy**, more fanciful than Linklater's earlier account of *Judas* (1939). *A Terrible Freedom* (1966) is a **dark/hallucinatory fantasy**.

LISLE, HOLLY (1960–). U.S. writer who frequently participates in **shared world** enterprises, including work done in association with **Marion Zimmer Bradley**. The trilogy comprising *Fire in the Mist* (1992), *Bones of the Past* (1993), and *Mind of the Magic* (1995) is **feminized/commodified fantasy**. *Minerva Wakes* (1994) and *Mall, Mayhem and Magic* (1995, with Chris Guin) are **contemporary fantasies**. In the **humorous** trilogy comprising *Sympathy for the Devil* (1996), *The Devil & Dan Cooley* (1996 with Walter Spence), and *Hell on High* (1997 with Ted Nolan), the denizens of hell return to Earth, eventually opening a theme park. The series comprising *Curse of the Black Heron* (1998), *Thunder of the Captains* (1996 with Aaron Alliston), and *Wrath of the Princes* (1997 with Alliston) is a Bardic fantasy. The Secret Texts series, comprising *Diplomacy of Wolves* (1998), *Vengeance of Dragons* (1999), and *Courage of Falcons* (2000), is **theriomorphic fantasy**; *Vincalis the Agitator* (2002) is a **prequel**. The World Gates trilogy of contemporary fantasies comprises *Memory of Fire* (2002), *Wreck of Heaven* (2003), and *Gods Old and Dark* (2004).

LITERARY SATANISM. William Blake's observation that **John Milton** had been "of the devil's party without knowing it" when he scrutinized Satan's character and motivation in *Paradise Lost* was expanded by **Percy Shelley** into an ardent championship of the **Devil**'s heroic rebellion against divine tyranny. Shelley cast his own adversarial **epic** as a **Promethean fantasy**, but later fantasists who took it upon themselves to attack **God**'s moral entitlement to dictate the terms of human existence frequently used the Devil and various other fallen **angels** to lead the charge. **Gustave Flaubert**'s *Temptation of St. Anthony* was beaten into print by **Charles Baudelaire**'s hymn to Satan in *Les Fleurs du Mal,* which was amplified by **Jules Michelet** into a four-act ritual "Communion of Revolt" in his

scholarly fantasy *La sorcière* before **Anatole France** brought explicit literary satanism to the peak of its achievement in *The Human Tragedy* and *The Revolt of the Angels*.

Notable 20th-century additions to the sceptical tradition of literary satanism include Jonathan Daniels's *Clash of Angels* (1930); the parodic *The Memoirs of Satan* (1932), by William Gerhardi and Brian Lunn; **Mikhail Bulgakov**'s *The Master and Margarita;* **David H. Keller**'s *The Devil and the Doctor;* Raoul Fauré's *Mister St. John* (1947); Alan Sillitoe's cycle of poems *Snow on the North Face of Lucifer* (1979); **Nancy Springer**'s *Metal Angel;* Jeremy Leven's *Satan: His Psychotherapy and Cure by the Unfortunate Dr. Kassler, J.S.P.S.* (1982); Ed Marguand's *The Devil's Mischief* (1996); and Glen Duncan's *I, Lucifer* (2002).

Sympathy for the Devil's minions—which is usually less combative than outright literary satanism—echoes in such modern texts as **John Collier**'s *The Devil and All,* **C. S. Lewis**'s *Screwtape Letters,* and is carried to an extreme in Miranda Seymour's *The Reluctant Devil* (1990). A wry note of sympathy is also sounded in some **Christian fantasies**, including **Marie Corelli**'s *The Sorrows of Satan* and Alfred Noyes's *The Devil Takes a Holiday* (1955).

LIVELY, PENELOPE (1933–). British writer born in Cairo. Her work for adults is naturalistic, but most of her **children's** books are fantasy. In *The Wild Hunt of Hagworthy* (1971; aka *Wild Hunt of the Ghost Hounds*), an ancient ritual revived by a country vicar unleashes powerful **ghostly** forces. *Whispering Knights* (1971) similarly features an accidental summoning, with echoes of **Arthurian fantasy**. *The Driftway* (1972) is a less melodramatic account of history come to life, as is *The Ghost of Thomas Kempe* (1973), in which a revenant Elizabethan **wizard** is frustrated by the unfamiliarity of modern life. *The House in Norham Gardens* (1974) explores a more profound cultural divide between modern England and ghostly tribesmen from New Guinea. *A Stitch in Time* (1976) evokes more extensive temporal vistas. *The Voyage of QV66* (1978) is an **animal fantasy** set in the aftermath of a new Deluge. *Treasures of Time* (1979), *The Revenge of Samuel Stokes* (1981), and *Uninvited Ghosts and Other Stories* (1984) revisited old ground. The collection *Beyond the Blue Mountains* (1997) includes some fantasies.

LLYWELYN, MORGAN (1937–). U.S.-born Irish writer. Her historical novels set in Ireland initially used legendary material as decor, but *The*

Horse Goddess (1982) moved decisively into the field of **Celtic fantasy**. The earlier sections of *The Elementals* (1993) describe the postdiluvian settlement of Ireland, while *Bard: The Odyssey of the Irish* (1984) offers an account of the origins of Irish **fairy** mythology. *The Isles of the Blest* (1989) features a journey into **Faerie**. *Red Branch* (1989; aka *On Raven's Wing*) allows the legend of Cuchulainn to retain its supernatural elements, although *Finn MacCool* (1994) does not, *Druids* (1991) having already negotiated the series back to desupernaturalized territory. The Arcana couplet, written in collaboration with Michael Scott, comprising *Silverhand* (1995) and *Silverlight* (1997), is orthodox **heroic fantasy**. *The Earth Is Made of Stardust* (2000) samples her short fiction.

***LOCUS*.** U.S. periodical founded in 1968 as a fanzine; by 1976, when editor Charles N. Brown devoted himself to it full-time, it was the trade journal of the **sf** field (refer to *HDSFL*); it also kept track of the overlapping fields of fantasy and **horror** fiction, thus bearing witness to the inexorable rise of **commodified fantasy**. The near-definitive record of fantastic fiction published in the United States and United Kingdom that it has maintained since the early 1980s, cumulatively collated on the Locus On-Line website, is invaluable to scholars with interests located anywhere on the fantasy spectrum.

LOFTING, HUGH (1886–1947). British writer resident in the United States after 1919. His major contribution to the genre is a long **children's** series chronicling the adventures of Dr. Dolittle, who can communicate with **animals**. It comprises *The Story of Dr Dolittle* (1920), *The Voyages of Dr Dolittle* (1922), *Dr Dolittle's Post Office* (1923), *Dr Dolittle's Circus* (1924), *Dr Dolittle's Zoo* (1925), *Dr Dolittle's Caravan* (1926), *Dr Dolittle's Garden* (1927), *Dr Dolittle in the Moon* (1928), *Dr Dolittle's Return* (1933), *Dr Dolittle and the Secret Lake* (1948), *Dr Dolittle and the Green Canary* (1950), and *Dr Dolittle's Puddleby Adventures* (1952). *The Twilight of Magic* (1930) is an elegiac quasi-**historical fantasy**.

LOGSTON, ANNE (1962–). U.S. writer. The trilogy comprising *Shadow* (1991), *Shadow Dance* (1992), and *Shadow Hunt* (1992) is a **picaresque fantasy** featuring a larcenous female elf; *Greendaughter* (1993) and *Wild Blood* (1995) are **prequels**, *Dagger's Edge* (1994) and *Daggers's Point* (1995) sequels. *Firewalk* and *Waterdance* (1999) are **paranormal romances**. The Crystal Keep series, launched by *Guardian's Key* (1996) and *Exile* (1999), is set in a citadel with a surfeit of doors, a resident Oracle, and an all-powerful Guardian.

LONDON, JACK (1876–1916). U.S. writer whose short fiction made a considerable contribution to the development of **sf** (refer to *HDSFL*); some of his **prehistoric fantasies**—*Before Adam* (1906)—employ **reincarnation** as a narrative device. He wrote several offbeat **ghost stories**, including "The Eternity of Forms" (1911). *The Star Rover* (1915; aka *The Jacket*) is a **visionary/escapist fantasy** about serial reincarnation. *Hearts of Three* (1918) novelized an unproduced film script written in collaboration with scenarist Charles William Goddard, which features a **lost race** and drug-induced visions.

LORRAIN, JEAN (1855–1906). Pseudonym of French writer Paul-Alexandre-Martin Duval, one of the most enthusiastic participants in the **Decadent** movement. His **poesque** fantasies include the title piece of *Sonyeuse* (1891) and the psychic vampirism story "The Egregore" (1887), but his most distinctive work is a sequence of **hallucinatory fantasies** based on his experiences using ether as a stimulant; most are collected in *Nightmares of an Ether-Drinker* (2002), alongside a few **occult fantasies** and dark-edged **fairy tales**, including "The Princess of the Red Lilies" (1894). His archetypal decadent novel *Monsieur de Phocas* (1901; tr. 1994) also features some graphic hallucinatory sequences.

LOST RACE. An exotic society newly discovered or rediscovered by modern explorers. Such societies figure in many naturalistic adventure stories, including almost all of those bordering on **sf** or utopian fantasy. The lost races most relevant to fantasy preserve some kind of working magic; the eternal flame in **Rider Haggard**'s *She* is a cardinal example. **Edgar Rice Burroughs** and **E. Charles Vivian** made particularly prolific use of the motif; other examples from the pulps include *The Seal of John Solomon* (1915; book 1924), by Alan Hawkwood (H. Bedford-Jones), and **Francis Stevens**'s *The Citadel of Fear*. Relics of **Atlantis** often feature in lost race stories, including Frank Aubrey's *A Queen of Atlantis* (1898) and Pierre Benoît's *Atlantida* (1919). Exotic lost races often inhabit **underworlds**, like the ones featured in James de Mille's *Strange Manuscript Found in a Copper Cylinder* (1888), Joyce Preston Muddock's *The Sunless City* (1905), and John Beynon's *The Secret People* (1935).

LOUŸS, PIERRE (1870–1925). French writer. *Aphrodite* (1895; tr. 1900) is a feverish **erotic fantasy** set in ancient Alexandria. *The Adventures of King Pausole* (1901; tr. 1926) is a **Rabelaisian** comedy set in the imaginary kingdom of Tryphême. Six prose-poems with motifs drawn from **classical mythology** were collected as *The Twilight of the Nymphs* (1893–95; 1925; tr. 1928); his other short stories, collected as *Sanguines* (1903; tr. 1932), include several ironic fantasies. All are reprinted in *The Collected Works of Pierre Louÿs* (1932).

LOVECRAFT, H. P. (1890–1937). U.S. writer whose work is equally significant as **sf** (refer to *HDSFL*), **horror** (refer to *HDHL*), and fantasy. The United Amateur Press Association, which he joined in 1914, put him in contact with **Clark Ashton Smith**, Frank Belknap Long, and others, with whom he formed a postal neo-Romantic *cénacle* dedicated to the production and promotion of supernatural fiction adapted to a rationalistic era. He turned down the editorship of ***Weird Tales*** in 1924 but exerted a considerable influence on many of its key contributors by means of voluminous correspondence; his early disciples included Donald Wandrei, **Robert Bloch**, **Henry Kuttner**, and **Fritz Leiber**. Wandrei and August Derleth founded Arkham House to reprint Lovecraft's work in *The Outsider and Others* (1939), providing a haven for many other writers of weird fiction.

Most of Lovecraft's pure fantasy stories, which are heavily influenced by the works of **Lord Dunsany**, are reprinted in *Dagon and Other Macabre Tales* (1965; corrected 1986); they include "The Cats of Ulthar" (written 1920; 1926), "The Other Gods" (written 1921; 1938), "The Doom That Came to Sarnath" (written 1919; 1938), and "The Quest of Iranon" (written 1921; 1939). The longest of them, the **hallucinatory fantasy** *The Dream-Quest of Unknown Kadath* (written c1924; 1943), was reprinted along with the related stories "The Silver Key" (1929) and "Through the Gates of the Silver Key" (1934, with E. Hoffman Price) in *At the Mountains of Madness and Other Novels* (1964; corrected 1985).

Lovecraftian fantasy is an astonishingly prolific subgenre; his fantasy is most conspicuously influential in the works of **Brian Lumley** and **Darrell Schweitzer**. Lovecraft features as a character in Richard Lupoff's *Lovecraft's Book* (1985) and in David Barbour and Richard Raleigh's *Shadows Bend* (2000), in which he and **Robert E. Howard** are en route to a meeting with Clark Ashton Smith. Lovecraftian fiction has been subject to the same **chimerical** trends as other subgenres, producing such exotic confrontations as P. H. Cannon's H. P. Lovecraft/ P. G. Wodehouse cross *Scream for Jeeves* (1994); *Shadows over Baker Street* (2003), ed. Michael Reaves and John Pelan, starring Sherlock Holmes; Nick Mamatas's *Move Under Ground* (2004), featuring beat writers Jack Kerouac and William Burroughs; and Thomas Wheeler's *The Arcanum* (2004), featuring **Arthur Conan Doyle**.

LOW FANTASY. The logical concomitant of **high fantasy**, defined by **Kenneth J. Zahorski** and Robert H. Boyer as the set of stories featuring "nonrational happenings that are without causality or rationality because they occur in the rational world where such things are not supposed to occur." The consequence of this disjunction is usually **humorous** or **horrific**, as opposed to the **enchantment** of high fantasy. Low fantasy corresponds roughly to Farah Mendlesohn's category of **intrusive fantasy**, although it presumably takes aboard some of the **portal fantasies** for which the Zahorski/Boyer schema makes no comfortable accommodation.

LUCIAN. Greek satirist, often called Lucian of Samosata, active in the second century A.D. He wrote numerous tongue-in-cheek dialogues involving **gods**, **ghosts**, and courtesans, and a sequence of anecdotal **tall stories** describing the philosophical explorations of Menippus, whose **quest** for enlightenment takes him as far afield as the **underworld**, Olympus, and the **Moon**. Lucian's *True History* also uses the Moon as a destination for the ultimate **traveler's tale**. He wrote an earlier version of the story used by **Apuleius** as the basis for *The Golden Ass* but may have **recycled** it himself.

LUCKETT, DAVE (1951–). Australian writer of **humorous fantasies** for **children**. *The Adventures of Addam* (1995) and *The Best Batsman in the World* (1996) are archetypal **wish-fulfillment fantasies**; *The Last Eleven* (1997) is also a **sports fantasy**. *The Wizard and Me* (1996) is a **contemporary fantasy**. In the Tenebran trilogy, comprising *A Dark Winter* (1998), *A Dark Journey* (1999), and *A Dark Victory* (1999), the Order lands must be defended against the armies of Dark. In the series comprising *Rhianna and the Wild Magic* (2000; aka *The Girl, the Dragon, and the Wild Magic*), *Rhianna and the Dogs of Iron* (2002; aka *The Girl, the Apprentice and the Dogs of Iron*), and *Rhianna and the Castle of Avalon* (2002; aka *The Girl, the Queen, and the Castle*), wild magic continually gets loose, upsetting a carefully ordered **secondary world**. *The*

Truth about Magic (2004), in which a **wizard** from the Department of Wishes arrives in the village of Widdershins, launched a new series.

LUMLEY, BRIAN (1937–). British writer best known for **horror** fiction (refer to *HDHL*), much of it in the tradition of **H. P. Lovecraft**'s Cthulhu mythos. He also extrapolated the background of Lovecraft's **hallucinatory fantasy** *The Dream-Quest of Unknown Kadath* in a series of **sword and sorcery** stories comprising *Hero of Dreams* (1986), *Ship of Dreams* (1986), *Mad Moon of Dreams* (1987), *Elysia: the Coming of Cthulhu* (1989), and the items collected in *Iced on Aran and Other Dreamquests* (1990). Three volumes of Tales from the Primal Land—*The House of Cthulhu and Other Tales of the Primal Land* (1984), *Never a Backward Glance* (1991, aka *Tarra Khash: Hrossak!*), and *Sorcery in Shad* (1993)—pay similar homage to the Hyperborean fantasies of **Clark Ashton Smith**. A trilogy spun off from Lumley's Necroscope series of horror novels, featuring a **secondary world** populated by vampires and comprising *Blood Brothers* (1992), *The Last Aerie* (1993), and *Bloodwars* (1994), is also of fantasy relevance, as are the stories in *Harry Keogh: Necroscope and Other Weird Heroes!* (2003).

LYNN, ELIZABETH A. (1946–). U.S. writer also active in **sf** (refer to *HDSFL*). The Chronicles of Tornor trilogy, comprising *Watchtower* (1979), *The Dancers of Arun* (1979), and *The Northern Girl* (1980), embodies a discourse on sexual politics. *The Silver Horse* (1984) is a **children's fantasy**. *Tales from a Vanished Country* (1990) features a higher proportion of fantasy stories than does *The Woman Who Loved the Moon and Other Stories* (1981). The series begun with *Dragon's Winter* (1998) and *Dragon's Treasure* (2003) features a world cursed by magical glaciation.

– M –

MABINOGION. A term coined by Lady Charlotte Guest as a title for her collection of translations taken from the 14th-century *White Book of Rhydderch* and the 15th-century *Red Book of Hergest,* issued in 1838–49 (*mabinogi* means "tales"). Some are adapted from French **romances**, and others include **Arthurian** references that probably arrived by the same Anglo-Norman route; some folklorists insist that the French material must have been derived from hypothetical **Celtic** sources, but the fact that literary products original to **Chrétien de Troyes** are included make that unlikely. The four "branches" of Welsh mythology that open the collection are a fragmentary record of Welsh legend and myth; they underlie a good deal of Celtic fantasy, being straightforwardly **recycled** by such writers as **Kenneth Morris** and **Evangeline Walton**, and echoing in such **contemporary fantasies** as **Alan Garner**'s *The Owl Service* and **Jenny Nimmo**'s *The Snow Spider*.

MACAVOY, R. A. (1949–). U.S. writer. *Tea with the Black Dragon* (1983) is a **contemporary fantasy** featuring an unusual **dragon**; *Twisting the Rope* (1986) is a sequel. The trilogy comprising *Damiano* (1983), *Damiano's Lute* (1984), and *Raphael* (1984), set in an **alternative** Renaissance Italy, features a team of adventurers composed of a **witch**, an **angel**, and a gifted dog. *The Book of Kells* (1985) is a **Celtic/timeslip** fantasy. *The Grey Horse* (1987) is a **historical fantasy** set in 19th-century Ireland. The trilogy comprising *Lens of the World* (1990), *King of the Dead* (1991), and *The Winter of the Wolf* (1993; aka *The Belly of the Wolf*) tells a life story set in a **secondary world** devoid of **commodified fantasy**'s stereotypical trappings.

MacDONALD, GEORGE (1824–1905). Scottish writer whose brief experience as a clergyman precipitated a crisis of faith that affected all of his literary work. His first **art fairy tale**, *Phantastes: A Faerie Romance for Men and Women* (1858), marks a significant explicit transformation of **visionary fantasy** into **portal fantasy**; its hero, Anodos ("upward path"), enjoys an educative progress akin to but very different from that of **John Bunyan**'s pilgrim. *The Portent: A Story of the Inner Vision of the Highlanders, Commonly Called the Second Sight* (1864) is a **psychological fantasy** tending toward **horror**.

Although the stories inserted into the text of the novel *Adela Cathcart* (1864) were extracted and supplemented for marketing as **children's fantasies** as *Dealings with the Fairies* (1867), the **allegorical** elements of such stories as "The Golden Key" and "The Shadows" are highly sophisticated—more so than the similar elements in **Hans Christian Andersen**'s most ambitious works. "The Light Princess," on the other hand, is a **humorous fantasy** with a straightforward moral. *At the Back of the North Wind* (1871) is an archetypally Victorian children's story in which a poor boy's release from wretchedness through fantasy can only be a prelude to death. *The Princess and the Goblin* (1872) is a more upbeat melodrama with **heroic fantasy** elements; its sequel *The Princess* *and Curdie* (1883) is considerably darker in its narrative development. In parallel with these novels MacDonald continued to add short stories and novellas to a repertoire whose elements were recombined in numerous selections; *Works of Fancy and Imagination* (10 vols., 1871) was comprehensive at the time, gathering in such notable allegorical pieces as "The Carasoyn"; a more focused sampler is *The Fairy Tales of George MacDonald* (5 vols., 1904).

The Wise Woman: A Parable (1875; aka *The Lost Princess*) is a substantial **art fairy tale**. The historical novel *Thomas Wingfold, Curate* (1876) includes interpolated "Passages from the Autobiography of the Wandering Jew." The title story of *The Gifts of the Child Christ* (1882) is a notable **Christian fantasy**, and "The History of Photogen and Nycteris" (aka "The Day Boy and the Night Girl") is another allegory. MacDonald returned wholeheartedly to allegorical portal fantasy for adults in *Lilith* (1895), whose **Edenic fantasy** elements are carefully confused with other materials; its symbolism remains stubbornly obscure, and the story's conclusion is more abandonment than completion, but it seemed a highly significant exemplar to the **Inklings**. **Lin Carter** reprinted a good deal of MacDonald's work in the **Ballantine Adult Fantasy Series**—including the three-novella collection *Evenor* (1972)—thus establishing him as a key ancestor of genre fantasy.

George MacDonald's son Greville MacDonald (1856–1944) wrote the Cornish fairy story *Billy Barnicoat* (1925) and a **Christian fantasy** recycling the legend of St. George, *The Wonderful Goatskin* (1944).

MACHEN, ARTHUR (1863–1947). Welsh writer briefly associated with the Order of the Golden Dawn by virtue of his friendship with **A. E. Waite**, with whom he wrote the exceedingly esoteric *The House of the Hidden Light* (1904 in a 3-copy edition; 2003). The reprint was issued by the specialist Tartarus Press; its many volumes of Machen's works include the sampler *Ritual and Other Stories* (1992), containing numerous fantasies from 1889–91, and *Ornaments in Jade* (1997), restoring a text first issued in 1936 but containing similar lapidary items written in the early 1890s, by which time Machen had already published a **Celtic** parody of **Chaucer**'s *Canterbury Tales, The Chronicle of Clemendy* (1888). His own theory of fantasy literature—which makes much of an "ecstasy" that is a more exaggerated version of **Tolkien**'s **enchantment**—was set out in *Hieroglyphics* (1902).

Machen's most successful contributions to the English **Decadent** movement were the novellas *The Great God Pan and the Inmost Light*

(1894) and the mosaic *The Three Impostors; or, the Transmutations* (1895). Because "The Great God Pan" (1890) is a graphic **horror** story, Machen's primary reputation has always been in that field (refer to *HDHL*), but most of these items are equally significant as fantasy, especially the aborted novel "The White People" (1899), which describes subtle and sinister intrusions from a distinctively Celtic dimension of **Faerie**, whose effects are seen in several other works reprinted with it in the early sampler *The House of Souls* (1906) and the title stories of *The Shining Pyramid* (1924; the 1923 U.S. collection of the same title is a sampler) and *The Children of the Pool and Other Stories* (1936). He was already working in the 1890s on two quasi-autobiographical **psychological fantasies** belatedly published as *The Hill of Dreams* (1907) and *The Secret Glory* (1922), both of which celebrate the escapist power of the imagination with a then-unparalleled intensity; spinoff from the later **grail** romance included *The Great Return* (1915) and "The Secret of the Sangraal" (1925).

Machen continued to produce fantasies during World War I, when such seeming indulgence became rare; he precipitated an accidental *cause célèbre* when "The Bowmen" (1914) was willfully misinterpreted as a record of actual apparitions observed during the retreat from Mons, giving rise to the legend of "the **Angels** of Mons." He tried unavailingly to set the record straight in *The Bowmen and Other Legends of the War* (1915), but his example inspired a minor subgenre, whose other examples include the stories collected in Charles L. Warr's *The Unseen Host* (1916) and some of the material in E. B. Osborn's *The Maid with Wings* (1917). His most notable postwar fantasy was the **alchemical fantasy** *The Green Round* (1933); his later short fiction was collected in *The Cosy Room and Other Stories* (1936).

MacLEOD, FIONA (1855–1905). Pseudonym of Scottish writer William Sharp, whose work under his own byline included the **Christian fantasy** title piece of *The Gypsy Christ and Other Tales* (1895). He maintained the existence of his alter ego fervently from 1893 to1896, in which years "she" produced numerous novels, stories, poems, and essays, becoming a leading contributor to the **Celtic** revival by inventing folklore on a scale not seen since the days of James Macpherson's Ossian, in the stories collected in *The Sin-Eater and Other Tales* (1894) and *The Washer at the Ford and Other Legendary Moralities* (1896). The **allegorical** novels *Pharais* (1894) and *The Mountain Lovers* (1895) prepared the way for the wholeheartedly fantastic *Green Fire* (1896), a bizarre **metaphysical fantasy** with a strong element of **Arcadian fantasy** that was further developed in the mystical pieces assembled in *The Dominion of Dreams* (1899) and *Where the Forest Murmurs* (1906). The short stories were re-sorted into a three-volume set of *Spiritual Tales*, *Barbaric Tales*, and *Tragic Romances* in 1895, and a seven-volume *Complete Works* was issued posthumously in 1910–12.

MAETERLINCK, MAURICE (1862–1949). Belgian dramatist who made a crucial contribution to the **Decadent** movement. His earliest fantasies were the **Poesque**, "Onirologie" (1889), and the play *Princess Maleine* (1889; tr. 1894), the first of many symbolist dramas describing the gradual unfolding of a tragic scheme at the behest of malign fate; three shorter items in this vein were advertised as "plays for marionettes," but not because they were intended for puppet shows.

Maeterlinck's most important fantasy plays include the mock-**chivalric romances** translated as *Pelleas and Melisanda* (1892; tr. 1894) and *Aglavaine and Selysette* (1896; tr. 1897) and several **fairy tale** romances: *The Seven Princesses* (1891; tr. 1894); *Sister Beatrice and Ardiane & Barbe Bleue* (1901); *Joyzelle* (1903); the famous **allegory** *The Blue Bird* (1909), which is by far his most optimistic work; and its sequel *The Betrothal* (1918). *The Blue Bird*'s translator, Alexander Texeira de Mattos, did a prose version of the sequel as *Tyltyl* (1920; aka *The Bluebird Chooses* in the United States). *The Miracle of Saint Anthony* (1918) and *The Power of the Dead* (1923) are **Christian fantasies**.

Maeterlinck's contemplative fatalism is abundantly expressed in many essays, some of which qualify as **scholarly fantasies**; they include studies of the existential plight of bees and ants, accounts of paranormal phenomena, and attempts to extrapolate metaphysical systems from astronomical discoveries. A 23-volume set of his works was issued in the United States in 1915–21.

MAGAZINES. Fantasy has always been marginal in the fiction marketplace, subject to such editorial prejudice that would-be pioneers like **John Sterling** and **Edward Bulwer-Lytton** had to become editors themselves to make homes for their work. **Charles Dickens** as editor maintained the space for **Christmas fantasies** opened up by the author's own early Christmas books, and **A. E. Waite** had to use the absurd medium of *Horlick's Magazine* to continue his championship of **Decadent** fantasy in 1904, when the *Yellow Book* and *The Savoy* had vanished. The British magazine that contributed most to the development of fantasy literature was, however, *Punch*, whose employees included (at different times) **Douglas Jerrold**, **F. Anstey**, and **A. A. Milne**.

Some of the most important foundation stones of **commodified fantasy** were laid in the U.S. pulp magazines, where **Edgar Rice Burroughs** and **A. Merritt** became influential exemplars; the contribution made by Frank Munsey's pulps was so significant that two magazines, *Famous Fantastic Mysteries* (1939–51) and *Fantastic Novels* (1940–51), were founded to reprint material therefrom, although both went on to reprint a wider range of material. The subgenre of **sword and sorcery**, a significant product of "the unique magazine" ***Weird Tales***, was taken up by some fantasy magazines founded as companions to **sf** magazines (refer to *HDSFL*), including ***Unknown*** and ***Fantastic Adventures***' successor *Fantastic*. *Imagination*'s companion *Imaginative Tales* (founded 1954) initially specialized in **humorous fantasy** in the tradition of **Thorne Smith**, although it soon abandoned the strategy.

The association between sf and fantasy was important because the sf magazines provided their readers with a primary education in the then-arcane art of reading **immersive fantasies** that dispensed with the introductory apparatus of **portal fantasies** (which Burroughs, Merritt, and their imitators had had to retain). The intimacy of the continued association between sf and sword and sorcery fiction in the marketplace—which is not reflected in the history of **intrusive fantasies** in spite of the key examples published in *Unknown*—reflects the fact that they require similar reading skills, of a kind that remained esoteric until the 1960s.

While sf's "idea as hero" stories adapted quite well to the more restrictive format of the "digest" magazines that replaced the pulps, and while various kinds of whimsical fantasy clung to a subsidiary niche in *The Magazine of Fantasy and Science Fiction,* sword and sorcery stories and **quest** fantasies required more space for expansion. The British magazine *Science-Fantasy* provided a venue for **Michael Moorcock**'s early experiments in that subgenre, as well as a refuge for **Thomas Burnett Swann**'s **classical fantasies**. It was not until paperback books replaced magazines as the chief medium of popular fiction, however, that the various forms of **commodified fantasy** found the abundant narrative space they required. At that point, the eventual economic victory of genre fantasy over sf may have become inevitable, although it was not widely anticipated. ***Realms of Fantasy*** could never hope to be as crucial to its genre's development as the sf magazines had been to theirs, although it now seems as likely a candidate as any to be the last surviving fiction magazine in the commercial arena.

MAGIC. The definitive element of a fantasy story, according to **Lin Carter**, is that it assumes and displays the workability of magic. A magical event is one that occurs outside the normal working of cause and effect, by virtue either of the intervention of some supernatural agency or the accomplishment of some kind of formulaic spell. The term is routinely extended to embrace techniques of divination, which threaten to undermine the pattern of cause and effect by facilitating avoidance of its impending effects. The idea is closely related to that of superstition, which describes rules of procedure intended to secure good luck and avoid bad luck (whose supernatural extrapolations include curses); such rules are the psychological spinoff of a built-in tendency to search for patterns in experience, which inevitably takes aboard imaginary as well as real examples; it is conceivable that all magical ideas may be explicable in these terms.

Belief in magic was once thought by sophisticated philosophers to be the prerogative of primitive minds or peoples, and it was widely anticipated that the attainment of the Age of Reason and its subsequent Age of Enlightenment would lead to the extinction of magical belief in the civilized world. This assumption proved utterly mistaken; belief in the workability of magic is probably more widespread now than it has ever been before. Ironically, the most resistant enclave of stern scepticism is to be found among practitioners of stage magic, in which seemingly impossible accomplishments are simulated by ingenious trickery or sleight of hand. The remarkable sophistication of such trickery demonstrates the difficulty of judging the limits of practicality; charlatans desirous of persuading people that they have magical abilities have considerable deceptive resources available to them. It was also widely thought, once upon a time, that participation in fantasy literature implied or required belief in magic, but theorists have convincingly insisted, since the days of Edmund Burke and **Samuel Taylor Coleridge**, that the opposite is true: that fantasy's literary effects depend on the fact that its producers and consumers—including young listeners—are fully conscious of the nature of the exercise.

The idea of magic has been strongly affected in Western civilization by the development of monotheistic religions that have taken a monopolistic view of violations of cause and effect, reserving benevolent effects to **God** (redefining them as "miracles") while condemning all other magical endeavors to the category of "sorcery," inherently **demonic** no matter what its intentions might be—an argument supported by the fantasies of **William Gilbert**. Although many medieval Christian scholars took a keen interest in **alchemy**, **astrology**, and various forms of ritual magic, the persecution of lay practitioners became increasingly urgent during the great **witch** hunt of the 16th and 17th centuries, resulting in the development of an ideological "resistance movement"; its defensive tactics were incorporated into a tradition of **scholarly fantasies** that now serve fantasy literature as **taproot texts**.

Fantasy literature **recycles** all the kinds of magic anyone ever believed in and all the **scholarly fantasies** reinterpreting its nature. Different magical systems are often seen in conflict, such conflicts sometimes being underlaid by a fundamental contrast between ritualized and academicized magic, on the one hand, and "wild magic" on the other, whose resistance to those kinds of discipline is wryly celebrated by such writers as **Alan Garner** and **Dave Luckett**. Innovative accounts of magical systems—sometimes embracing their **metaphysical** bases as well as their practical application—can be found in the works of **Clive Barker**, **Leah R. Cutter**, **Ru Emerson**, and **J. V. Jones**.

MAGIC REALISM. A term transplanted from art criticism in the 1920s, initially to refer to the poetry of the Chilean Pablo Neruda; it was widely used in the latter half of the 20th century to characterize the works of other **Latin American** writers—most significantly and definitively **Gabriel Garcia Márquez**—and its use gradually became far more promiscuous, expanding its scope to take in all literary fantasy of a vaguely **surreal** nature.

When narrowly defined, the term usually refers to works that adopt a viewpoint in which everyday experience is routinely confused by events and entities reflecting culturally approved magical beliefs, which do not appear as **intrusive** "bringers of chaos"—however extraordinary or troublesome they may be—but as recognizable aspects of the tribulations of life. A magic realist text does not hybridize magical and rationally sanctioned beliefs in the manner of credulous **occult fantasy** or hybrid **science fantasy** but rather seems to deny or break down the very category of **magic**; for this reason, it is closely related to the category of **liminal fantasy**, identified by Farah Mendlesohn.

This narrative technique is by no means new, but its application in Latin American texts does have a particular vigor and resonance. Its roots are detectable in stories by the Brazilian writer Machado de Assis, sampled in *The Devil's Church* (1882–1905; tr. 1977) and in Massimo Bontempelli's *The Boy with Two Mothers* (1929; tr. in *Separations*, 2000). Other paradigmatic examples include Jorge Amado's *Dona Flor and Her Two Husbands* (1966; tr. 1969), Julio Cortazar's *62: A Model Kit* (1968; tr. 1972), and José Saramago's *Blindness* (1997).

MAGUIRE, GREGORY (1955–). U.S. writer. *The Lightning Timer* (1978), *The Daughter of the Moon* (1980), and *Lights on the Lake* (1981) are children's **contemporary fantasies** set in the town of Canaan Lake. *The Dream Stealer* (1983) transfigures a Russian folktale. His **prequel** to **L. Frank Baum**'s Oz series *Wicked: The Life and Times of the Wicked Witch of the West* (1995) was adapted into a Broadway musical; it was followed by two other **transfigurations** for adults: *Confessions of an Ugly Stepsister* (1999), based on Cinderella, and *Mirror Mirror* (2003), a **historical fantasy** based on Snow White. *Lost* (2001) is a delusional **ghost story**. His later work for children includes the **humorous** Hamlet Chronicles, comprising *Seven Spiders Spinning* (1994), *Six Haunted Hairdos* (1997), *Five Alien Elves* (1999), *Four Stupid Cupids* (2000), *Three Rotten Eggs* (2002), and *A Couple of April Fools* (2004), in which school holidays bring forth various otherworldly visitors. *Leaping Beauty and Other Animal Fairy Tales* (2004) features more transfigurations.

MAHY, MARGARET (1936–). New Zealand writer. Many of her stories for younger readers—of which the first was *The Dragon of an Ordinary Family* (1969)—are inventive fantasies; the most enterprising include those collected in *Mahy Magic* (1986; aka *The Boy Who Bounced and Other Magic Tales*) and *The Girl with the Green Ear: Stories about Magic in Nature* (1992), and the **metafictional** novella *A Villain's Night Out* (1999). Her work for **young adults** ranges across a wide spectrum; including the thematically linked **dark fantasies** *The Haunting* (1982), *The Changeover: A Supernatural Romance* (1984), *The Tricksters* (1986), *Dangerous Spaces* (1991), and *Alchemy* (2002), in which supernaturally talented teenagers discover that they are heirs to various peculiar "curses" reflecting aspects of family dysfunction. *Shick Forest and Other Stories* (2004) samples her short fiction for older readers.

MANN, THOMAS (1875–1955). German writer whose use of **symbolism** imports fantastic imagery into the margins of some of his major works, notably "Death in Venice" (1913; tr. 1925) and *The Magic Mountain* (1924; tr. 1927). "Mario and the Magician" (1930) is a political **allegory**. The trilogy begun with *Joseph and His Brothers* (1933; tr. 1934; omnibus 1960) is a **metafictional/biblical fantasy**. *The Transposed Heads* (1940; tr. 1941) is an outright **Oriental fantasy** transfiguring an Indian legend. *Doctor Faustus* (1947; tr. 1948) is a sophisticated **Faustian fantasy**. *The Holy Sinner* (1951) features a terminal **theriomorphic** transformation.

***MÄRCHEN*.** A German word, identical in the singular and the plural, signifying "tale" or "tales." It is often used as a contraction of *volksmärchen* ("**folktale**") or, thanks to the **Brothers Grimm**, *kindermärchen* ("**children's** tale"). It has been widely adopted into English in the parlance of fantasy criticism by academics anxious to avoid the childish connotations of "**fairy tales**." The portmanteau term *kunstmärchen* is also widespread in critical parlance; it is here translated as **art fairy tale**.

MARIE DE FRANCE. The signature attached to a series of Breton lays (narrative poems) and a number of fables written between 1160 and 1178, probably by an Anglo-Norman noblewoman associated with Henry II's court. The 12 lays are fantasized love stories, whose importance in the development of fantasy fiction—apart from being the work of the first significant female contributor to that tradition—is the range of their transfigurations, embracing the **classical** and contemporary **Arthurian** romance, sometimes in a spirit of hybridization. The most significant precedent was set by *Sir Orfeo,* which **transfigures** the story of **Orpheus** as a **chivalric romance**, although *Bisclavret*—which features a sympathetic werewolf—is generally regarded as her masterpiece. Modern transfigurations of Marie's lays include works by **Gillian Bradshaw** and **Sophie Masson**.

MARILLIER, JULIET (?–). New Zealand writer resident in Australia. The Sevenwaters trilogy, comprising *Daughter of the Forest* (1999), *Son of the Shadows* (2000), and *Child of the Prophecy* (2001), is a sophisticated **epic/Celtic fantasy** in which **druids** are threatened by the advent of Christianity; the series exhibits a strong ecological consciousness, using the "fair folk" as censorious commentators on human folly. The Saga of the Light Isles series, launched by *Wolfskin* (2002) and *Foxmask* (2004), is set in the Orkneys, where the natives' harmonious way of life is disrupted and spoiled by **Nordic** invaders.

MARKS, LAURIE J. (1957–). U.S. writer. The trilogy comprising *Delan the Mislaid* (1989), *The Moonbane Mage* (1990), and *Ara's Field* (1991) makes interesting use of a quasi-**angelic** race in transfiguring and extrapolating **Hans Christian Andersen**'s fable of "The Ugly Duckling." *The Watcher's Mask* (1992) and *Dancing Jack* (1993) draw on the same psychological wellspring. The Elemental Logic series launched by *Fire Logic* (2002) and *Earth Logic* (2004) is set in a world in which personality is determined by mixtures of elemental influences.

MARRYAT, CAPTAIN (1792–1848). British writer best known for **children's fiction** and naval romances. *The Pacha of Many Tales* (1835) sets a series of blithely **picaresque** adventures in a framework borrowed from **Antoine Galland**'s *Arabian Nights;* the fantastic items include **tall stories** improvised by the sailor Huckaback, a more ingenious liar than Sinbad. *Snarleyvow; or, The Dog Fiend* (1837) is a desupernaturalized parody of **Gothic** romance. *The Phantom Ship* (1839) is a graphic **recycling** of the legend of the **Flying Dutchman** in which a notable **werewolf** story is interpolated.

MARTIN, GEORGE R. R. (1948–). U.S. writer whose early work was mostly **sf** (refer to *HDSFL*). Much of his short fantasy, including "The Ice Dragon" (1980) and "Remembering Melody" (1981), is ardently **sentimental**. *Fevre Dream* (1982) is a **historical fantasy** featuring southern **Gothic** vampires. *The Armageddon Rag* (1983) is a thriller that teases the reader with an exotic apocalyptic threat. Martin supervised a successful **shared world** scenario that subjected the **comic** book mythology of superheroes to mildly cynical analysis, *Wild Cards* (13 vols., 1987–95), before moving into the center ground of genre fantasy with the **epic** Song of Fire and Ice trilogy, comprising *A Game of Thrones* (1996), *A Clash of Kings* (1998), and *A Storm of Swords* (2000). *A Feast for Crows* (2004) began a further endeavor in the same vein.

MARTIN, GRAHAM DUNSTAN (1932–). Scottish writer. *Giftwish* (1980) and *Catchfire* (1981) are immersive **children's fantasies**, much lighter in tone than *Soul Master* (1984), an adult novel deploying similar materials in the service of a dark **political allegory**. His later works are mostly **sf** (refer to *HDSFL*), although the ambiguous **science fantasy** *Half a Glass of Moonshine* (1988) involves an enigmatic **ghost**. *An Inquiry into the Purposes of Speculative Fiction: Fantasy and Truth* (2003) explores the psychological roots of folkloristic and literary fantasy.

MARTINE-BARNES, ADRIENNE (1942–). U.S. writer who uses her maiden name, Adrienne Martinez, on nonfantasy works. *The Dragon Rises* (1983) elaborates the premise that King **Arthur** and Count Dracula are aspects of the same archetype. The series comprising *The Fire Sword* (1984), *The Crystal Sword* (1988), *The Rainbow Sword* (1989), and *The Sea Sword* (1989) is a wide-ranging **historical fantasy**, with elements of **Celtic fantasy** that were more explicitly developed in a trilogy she wrote with **Diana Paxson**, comprising *Master of Earth and Water* (1993), *The Shield between the Worlds* (1994), and *Sword of Fire and Shadow* (1995).

MASEFIELD, JOHN (1878–1967). British poet. Some of his verse is based in beast **fables** and **fairy tales**, and his plays include the **Arthurian fantasy** *Tristan and Isolt* (1923; book 1927) and several **Christian fantasies**. His most substantial contributions to the genre are **children's fantasies**; the tentative imaginary adventures featured in *A Book of Discoveries* (1910) paved the way for more substantial accounts of *The Midnight Folk* (1927) and *The Box of Delights* (1935), both starring the laconic orphan Kay Harker; the latter story is a masterpiece of eccentricity with a central plot—involving the kidnapping of a Cathedral choir—that is elaborately decorated with fantasy motifs.

MASSON, SOPHIE (1959–). Australian writer born in Indonesia to French parents of Breton descent. Her early fiction was naturalistic, but *The Gifting* (1996) and its sequel *Red City* (1998) mix Roman history and **Celtic** legend in their accounts of a **decadent** city. Many of her subsequent works are enterprising **transfigurations** of **fairy tales**. The StarMaker series comprises *Carabas* (1996; aka *Serafin*), based on Puss-in-Boots; *Malkin* (1998; aka *Cold Iron*), which adds **Shakespearean** elements to Tattercoats; and *Clementine* (1999), based on Sleeping Beauty. The Lay Lines series of neo-**chivalric romances** takes its inspiration from **Marie de France**; it comprises *The Lady of the Pool* (1998), *The Lady of the Flowers* (1999), and *The Stone of Oakenfast*, the last-named being original to the omnibus *Forest of Dreams* (2001). *The Green Prince* (2000) is based on a French fairy tale; *The Firebird* (2001) on a Russian tale.

Masson's work became more adventurously innovative with *The Hand of Glory* (2002), an **alternative history** of Australia with supernatural elements, and *The Tempestuous Voyage of Hopewell Shakespeare* (2003), a **contemporary fantasy** contriving a **chimerical** fusion of elements drawn from Shakespeare and **Robert Louis Stevenson**. *In Hollow Lands* (2004) is a Breton fantasy set in the 14th century, about children abducted by korrigans (Breton **fairies**). *Snow, Fire, Sword* (2004) blends Indonesian and **Arabic myths**. She also edited an anthology of **Arthuriana**, *The Road to Camelot* (2002).

MATHESON, RICHARD (1926–). U.S. writer in various genres (refer to *HDHL*). His early **spiritualist fantasy** *Come Fygures, Come Shadows* (2003) and the **Arabian fantasy** *Abu and the Seven Marvels* (2004) were written long before publication, when the market was inhospitable to such experiments. *Bid Time Return* (1975; aka *Somewhere in Time*) is a **sentimental/timeslip** romance with a passionate insistence on the supernatural power of love that was more elaborately developed in the **afterlife fantasy** *What Dreams May Come* (1978), symptomatic of a developing credulity incompatible with the writing of further fantasy fiction.

MATSON, NORMAN (1893–1965). U.S. writer. *Flecker's Magic* (1926), chosen as an exemplar by **E. M. Forster** for the lecture on fantasy reprinted in *Aspects of the Novel,* is an account of an American art student in Paris who comes into possession of a **magic** ring that he refuses to use. *Doctor Fogg* (1929), in which Flecker reappears in a minor role, is a **science fantasy** that similarly advances the moral that mundanity is always preferable to fantasy. Given this conviction, Matson was an odd choice to complete a fragmentary **erotic fantasy** left behind when **Thorne Smith** died, but *The Passionate Witch* (1941) spawned the movie *I Married a Witch* (1942) and the TV show *Bewitched,* both of which restored a little of Smith's anarchic humor. Matson's sequel, *Bats in the Belfry* (1943), stubbornly persisted in arguing that good wives ought not to be **witches**.

MAYNE, WILLIAM (1928–). British writer of **children's fiction**, whose fantasies make few concessions to their readers' supposedly tender age. His complex **timeslip** fantasy *Earthfasts* (1966) was belatedly converted into a trilogy by the addition of *Cradlefasts* (1995) and *Candlefasts* (2000). *Over the Hills and Far Away* (!968; aka *The Hill Road*) employs a timeslip to bring problems of adolescence into a heightened and more elaborate focus, in a manner further refined in the **hallucinatory fantasy** *A Game of Dark* (1971). Mayne's education in a cathedral choir school—reflected in many of his works—supplies the background to the **dark fantasies** *It* (1977) and *Cuddy* (1996), while his fascination with bleak landscapes is reflected in two of the novellas in *All the King's Men* (1982). In *Antar and the Eagles* (1989), whose infant hero is kidnapped by eagles, is a notable allegory of **flight**. Folklore is **recycled** in a 1984 series for younger readers collected in *The Book of Hob Stories* (1991) and *Hob and the Goblins* (1993); the *The Blemyah Stories* (1987) features an imaginary being of a similar ilk. *The Worm in the Well* (2002) **recycles** the legend of the Lambton Worm as an effective **heroic fantasy**.

McCAFFREY, ANNE (1926–). U.S. writer whose **hybrid/science fantasies** are almost all represented as **sf** (refer to *HDSFL*), although the **dragons** featured in the Pern series of **planetary romances** provided the key exemplar of dragon fantasy. The early novellas in the Pern series, combined into *Dragonflight* (1968), appeared in *Analog* before commodified fantasy was established as a genre, and *Dragonquest* (1971) also retains a science-fictional gloss, but the **children's** spinoff trilogy comprising *Dragonsong* (1976), *Dragonsinger* (1977), and *Dragondrums* (1979) emphasize the fantasy element, as did the best-selling *The White Dragon* (1978). The subsequent novels in the series—*Moreta, Dragonlady of Pern* (1983), *Nerilka's Story* (1986), *Dragonsdawn* (1988), *The Renegades of Pern* (1989), *All the Weyrs of Pern* (1991), *The Chronicles of Pern: First Fall* (1993), *The Dolphin's Bell* (1993), *The Dolphins of Pern* (1994), *Red Star Rising* (1996; aka *Dragonseye*), *The MasterHarper of Pern* (1998), *The Skies of Pern* (2001), and *Dragon's Kin* (2003, with Todd McCaffrey)—form a near-definitive **epic fantasy** that has been highly influential as a model. *The People of Pern* (1988) and *The Dragonlover's Guide to Pern* (1989, with **Jody Lynn Nye**) are **guides**.

McCaffrey's labeled fantasies are for **children**; they include a series begun in 1985 with *The Girl Who Heard Dragons* (collection 1995), which became the basis of a **shared world** series by **Elizabeth Scarborough**; the Unicorn Girl **shared world** series (1997–99); *An Exchange of Gifts* (1995), in which a runaway princess and a poor boy must hide their magical talents; *Nobody Noticed the Cat* (1996), about a talented cat; and *If Wishes Were Horses* (1998), about a **healer**. She edited the anthology *Alchemy & Academe* (1970).

McCAUGHREAN, GERALDINE (1951–). British writer. She produced straightforwardly **recycled** versions of *One Thousand and One Arabian Nights* (1982), *Greek Myths* (1993), *Roman Myths* (2001), and *Myths* *and Legends of the World* (4 vols. 1996–99) for **children**. The mosaic *A Pack of Lies* (1988) features the exotic pitches of a supernatural salesperson. *The Maypole* (1990) and *Fires' Astonishment* (1990) extrapolate the substance of two **ballads**. *The Stones Are Hatching* (1999) features dangerous progeny of a "Worm." *It's Not the End of the World* (2004) is a **biblical fantasy** about the Deluge. *See also* DRAGON.

McKENNA, JULIET E. (1965–). British writer. The series comprising *The Thief's Gamble* (1999), *The Swordsman's Oath* (1999), *The Gambler's Fortune* (2000), *The Warrior's Bond* (2001), and *The Assassin's Edge* (2002) is a **picaresque fantasy** with much swashbuckling. The Aldabreshin Compass series, begun with *Southern Fire* (2003) and *Northern Storm* (2004), features a society steadfastly opposed to **magic**. *Turns and Chances* (2004) is a novella set in the same milieu.

McKIERNAN, DENNIS L. (1932–). U.S. writer. The three-decker novel comprising *The Dark Tide* (1984), *Shadows of Doom* (1984), and *The Darkest Day* (1984), set in Mithgar, pays homage to **J. R. R. Tolkien**, similarly redeploying elements of Nordic **mythology**; *Trek to Kraggen-Cor* (1986) and *The Brega Path* (1986) constitute a sequel. *Dragondoom* (1990) and *The Eye of the Hunter* (1992) concentrate on sociopolitical aspects of the scenario; *Voyage of the Fox Rider* (1993) and *The Dragonstone* (1996) broaden the argument toward a general discussion of theodicy. Early short fiction from the series is assembled in *Tales of Mithgar* (1994); it is continued in the Hell's Crucible couplet *Into the Forge* (1997) and *Into the Fire* (1998), then in the novel *Silver Wolf, Black Falcon* (2000) and the stories collected in *Red Slippers* (2004). The unrelated **metaphysical fantasy** *Caverns of Socrates* (1995) employs a computer **game** as a launchpad. *Once upon a Winter's Night* (2001) **transfigures** the **fairy tale** "East of the Sun, West of the Moon."

McKILLIP, PATRICIA A. (1948–). U.S. writer. Her first published works were the **children's fantasies** *The House on Parchment Street* (1973), a **ghost** story, and *The Throme of the Erril of Sherill* (1973; reissued 1982 with "The Harrowing of the Dragon of Hairsbreath"), a **humorous fantasy** in the tradition of **James Thurber**. *The Forgotten Beasts of Eld* (1974 but written earlier), a **moralistic fantasy** about the sentimental education of an enchantress, made a significant crossover into the adult market as genre fantasy began to take off.

The trilogy comprising *The Riddle Master of Hed* (1976), *Heir of Sea and Fire* (1977), and *Harpist in the Wind* (1979) is a more orthodox

feminized/heroic fantasy. *Stepping from the Shadows* (1982) is a naturalistic novel about the making of a fantasy writer; McKillip then digressed into **sf** (refer to *HDSFL*) before returning to wholehearted fantasy with a sequence of distinctive and exceptionally stylish works that placed her at the cutting edge of the burgeoning commercial genre and a figure of central importance within it. *The Changeling Sea* (1988) is aimed at younger readers, but *The Sorceress and the Cygnet* (1991) brought a meditative sophistication and a seasoning of comedy to an unusual **quest** fantasy; the adventures and philosophical inquiries continued in *The Cygnet and the Firebird* (1993). *Something Rich and Strange* (1994), issued in a series based on **illustrations** by Brian Froud, is an exquisitely detailed romance in which a female artist and her halfhearted lover are separately seduced by sea sprites.

In *The Book of Atrix Wolfe* (1995), a fugitive magician hides among wolves while searching for the lost daughter of the Queen of the Wood. *Winter Rose* (1996) juxtaposes Victorian England and a **parallel world** of **Faerie**. *Song for the Basilisk* (1998), which features a royal child who finds a new destiny after surviving a massacre, brought a new sophistication to **bardic fantasy**. *The Tower at Stony Wood* (2000) is an equally sophisticated neo-**chivalric romance**. *Ombria in Shadow* (2002) is a **fairy tale** romance of fabulous city and its dark counterpart. *In the Forests of Serre* (2003) is a **dark** and complex story including **transfigurations** of Russian folklore. *Alphabet of Thorn* (2004) continues the development of themes broached in its immediate predecessors; one of its heroines—a translator working in a library who revitalizes an item of ancient folklore and weaves its contents into the texture of the present—might be regarded as a reflection of the author at work.

McKINLEY, ROBIN (1952–). U.S. writer resident in Britain since 1992. *Beauty* (1978) is an unusually enterprising **recycling** of a classic **fairy tale**. Others are included, alongside pastiches, in *The Door in the Hedge* (1981), while *Deerskin* (1993) restores adult material censored from **Charles Perrault**'s "Donkeyskin"; *Rose Daughter* (1997) and *Spindle's End* (2000) revisit the theme of *Beauty* on behalf of younger readers. The series comprising *The Blue Sword* (1982), its **prequel** *The Hero and the Crown* (1985), and several items in *A Knot in the Grain and Other Stories* (1994) is a **heroic fantasy** set in the imaginary kingdom of Damar. In *The Stone Fey* (1998), a young woman develops a relationship with an elusive mountain creature. *Sunshine* (2003) is a striking futuristic fantasy in which all supernatural species except vampires are accepted following the Voodoo Wars. McKinley and her husband, **Peter Dickinson**, each contributed three stories to *Water: Tales of Elemental Spirits* (2002, aka *Elementals: Water*). She edited a notable showcase **anthology**, *Imaginary Lands* (1985).

MELODRAMATIC INFLATION. The necessity of continually increasing the magnitude of the threats that a hero is required to overcome in a sequential plot or a **series** of books. Because fantasies featuring protagonists and antagonists equipped with magical or superhuman powers have no intrinsic limits, melodramatic inflation routinely places entire worlds—or even **multiverses**—in jeopardy. The black magicians with whom the protagonists of **heroic fantasy** are faced in the early phases of their careers tend to be replaced in short order by **demons**, and then by dark **gods**, whose summary dispatch often comes to seem ludicrously artificial, frequently forcing the retirement of series heroes because no greater challenges remain for them to overcome. **Immersive fantasy** trilogies often build to an **apocalyptic** "final battle" at the end of the third volume, in which the settlement of moral order is so extreme that authors of sequel trilogies are driven to great lengths to invent new and nastier antagonists; many writers, understandably, settle for writing **prequels**, which may then serve as starting points for fill-in exercises.

MERFOLK. Chimerical sea creatures human above the waist and fish below. They tend to be confused with sirens, routinely featuring in modern fantasy as seductive singers. The key exemplar provided by **Hans Christian Andersen**'s "The Little Mermaid" echoes in many other texts, most notably **Oscar Wilde**'s carefully reconfigured "The Fisherman and his Soul"; **H. G. Wells**'s *The Sea Lady* and **Norman Douglas**'s *Nerinda* are sceptical reactions. Many mid-20th-century modern fantasies featuring mermaids employed their **erotic** potential to **humorous** ends—including Norman Walker's *Loona, A Strange Tail* (1931); *Peabody's Mermaid* (1946), by Guy and Constance Jones; and **Robert Bloch**'s "Mr Margate's Mermaid"—but **Theodore Sturgeon**'s "A Touch of Strange" (1958) and **Ray Bradbury**'s "The Shoreline at Sunset" (1959) carefully conserved their **sentimental** aspect.

Poul Anderson's *The Merman's Children* restored the gravity of the folkloristic tradition in a striking account of the inexorable **thinning** of **Faerie**; Alida Van Gores' *Mermaid's Song* (1989) is similarly inclined. Other notable mermaid stories include Julia Blackburn's *The Leper's*

Companions (1999), Alan Temperley's *Huntress of the Sea* (1999), **Alice Hoffman**'s *Aquamarine*, **Donna Jo Napoli**'s *Sirena*, and Carol Ann Sima's *The Mermaid That Came between Them* (2002). Variants are usually modest, like the "mermyds" of **Kara Dalkey**'s Water series; **Tod Robbins**'s "The Whimpus" is more adventurous. Fake mermaids—sometimes known as "Jenny Hanivers"—have long been a stock in trade of taxidermists and curio sellers; **Jane Yolen**'s "The Malaysian Mer" (1982) features an unusually lively example. *Mermaids!* (1985), ed. Gardner Dozois and Jack Dann, is a showcase **anthology**.

MERLIN. The legendary king's magical advisor becomes the central figure in much **Arthurian fantasy** that puts the emphasis on **magic** rather than **chivalric heroism**, and he is particularly prominent in **Celtic** variants. He is the prototype of the **wizards** of modern fantasy, his brand of magic sometimes being opposed to that of **Morgan le Fay**. As with Arthur, legend suggests that Merlin never died—instead, being imprisoned in a tree—thus being ever ready to return when the time is ripe, as he does in works by **C. S. Lewis**, **Susan Cooper**, **Peter Dickinson**, **Jane Louise Curry**, Robert Newman's *Merlin's Mistake* (1970), and Colin Webber's **humorous** *Merlin and the Last Trump* (1993).

Notable transfigurations of Merlin's life story are wrought by **Mary Stewart**, **Jane Yolen**, and **T. A. Barron**, and in Robert Nye's *Merlin* (1978) and J. Robert King's *Mad Merlin* (2000). Other notable literary portraits of Merlin can be found in **John Cowper Powys**'s *Porius*, Alvaro Cunqueiro's *Merlin and Company* (1955 in Spanish; tr. 1996), and **Ann Lawrence**'s *Merlin the Wizard*.

MERRITT, A. (1884–1943). U.S. writer whose lush pulp fantasies took escapism to exotic extremes unexplored by **Edgar Rice Burroughs** but never found a satisfactory terminus. "Through the Dragon Glass" (1917) and "The People of the Pit" (1918) were practice runs for the classic **portal fantasy** "The Moon Pool" (1918), which features a carefully guarded magical doorway through which—it is implied—all the treasures of the human imagination lie. Unable to live up to that prospectus, the sequel (combined with the original in the book version) seemed distinctly lame; the further sequel *The Metal Monster* (1920; rev. 1927 as "The Metal Emperor"; book 1946) probably took a wrong turn in moving toward **sf** (refer to *HDSFL*). The novella "The Face in the Abyss" (1923) was more appropriately supplemented by "The Snake Mother"

(1930), but the combination of the two as *The Face in the Abyss* (1931) reduced the impact of the former item considerably.

The **hallucinatory fantasy** *The Ship of Ishtar* (1924; book 1926) foreshadowed **sword and sorcery** fiction in co-opting its protagonist to play the hero in an eternal struggle between Ishtar and Nergal. Its pessimistic conclusion is echoed in the **sentimental fantasy** "The Woman of the Wood" (1926). Merritt used a **lost race** framework in *Dwellers in the Mirage* (1932), which modeled its protagonist's **Haggard**-esque emotional conflicts too honestly for its initial editor, who substituted a false happy ending (Merritt's conclusion was revealed in a 1941 reprint). *Burn, Witch, Burn!* (1933) is a thriller featuring murderous dolls animated by a **witch**; its sequel *Creep, Shadow!* (1934) invokes an ancient curse relating to the destruction of the drowned land of Ys.

Merritt left a number of fragmentary works, two of which—*The Fox Woman and the Blue Pagoda* (1946) and *The Black Wheel* (1947)—were fleshed out by his disciple **Hannes Bok**. The former was reprinted in *The Fox Woman and Other Stories* (1949); a few others appear, along with poetry and a biography of the author, in *A. Merritt: Reflections in the Moon Pool* (1985), ed. by Sam Moskowitz.

MESMERISM. A therapeutic system—the forerunner of modern hypnotism—invented by Franz Mesmer (1734–1815). It allegedly involved the transmission between individuals of a kind of life force called "animal magnetism." It was adopted as a staple device by such contemporary writers as **E. T. A. Hoffmann** and was subsequently recruited to add plausibility to **visionary fantasies** by **Edgar Allan Poe** and **Marie Corelli**; it was also routinely employed in tales of **identity exchange** and psychic **vampirism**, and used to invoke memories of **reincarnation** in such works as **Mrs. Campbell Praed**'s *Nyria* and the later adventures of **Rider Haggard**'s Allan Quatermain. The literary image of the mesmerist was redefined by the exemplar of Svengali in **George du Maurier**'s *Trilby,* whose peers are featured in numerous **occult fantasies**, but late 20th-century versions became more modest and more benign under the influence of hypnotism's popularity as a therapeutic technique and the increasing fashionability of "past-life regression."

MESSIANIC FANTASY. In the Old Testament, the messiah is the prophesied deliverer of the Jews from historical misfortune; Christianity is founded on the proposition that Jesus was he and will return to supervise the **apocalypse** before instituting his reparative 1,000-year reign.

The term is applied by analogy to any deliverer whose advent or return is widely anticipated and quasi-apocalyptic in its significance. Folklore often attaches a messianic glamor to legendary heroes like King **Arthur** and Frederick Barbarossa, and **heroic fantasy** often features their like; one of the subgenre's favorite themes is the displacement into a **secondary world** of a discontented inhabitant of the **primary world** in order to play a messianic role, as in **Stephen R. Donaldson**'s Thomas Covenant series.

Disguised **Christian fantasies** often use symbolic substitutes, like **C. S. Lewis**'s Aslan and **G. P. Taylor**'s Raphah. A significant variant features messianic protagonists whose reemergence is ironically unwelcome—examples include **Edgar Jepson**'s *The Horned Shepherd*, Damon Knight's *The Man in the Tree* (1983), Theodore Sturgeon's *Godbody* (1986), and **James Morrow**'s *Only Begotten Daughter*—although such accounts are quite distinct from accounts of evil messiahs, known in Christian parlance as "antichrists." Another variant features **quests** to find and protect children unlucky enough to be heirs to messianic destinies, as in Rebecca Neason's *The Thirteenth Scroll* (2001) and *The Truest Power* (2002). Other notable messianic fantasies include **Elizabeth Goudge**'s *The Little White Horse,* **Fay Sampson**'s *Them,* **Jane Yolen**'s *Sister Light, Sister Dark,* and **David Zindell**'s Ea cycle.

METAFICTION. A term that became fashionable in the 1980s as a description of one of the central strands of **postmodern** fiction, consisting of **fabulations** whose core subject matter is the process of literary creativity; in *Fabulation and Metafiction* (1979), Robert Scholes defines it succinctly as "experimental fabulation." Metafiction's exceedingly acute consciousness of its own fictionality often involves the redeployment of material from other texts in order to lay bare or explore their hidden subtexts, so it routinely involves complex exercises in **recycling** and **transfiguration**; its history extends back at least as far as **Paul Féval**'s *Knightshade*.

The Clute/Grant *Encyclopedia* uses the term **recursive fantasy** to refer to fantasies in which protagonists enter **secondary worlds** based on previously existing fictions—**Walter de la Mare**'s *Henry Brocken,* **John Myers Myers**'s *Silverlock,* and **Stephen King**'s Dark Tower series are conspicuous examples—adding a second meaning in which a similar effect is obtained by reference to fictions that have no existence outside the text that refers to them, such as **Michael Ende**'s *The Neverending Story* and **Jonathan Carroll**'s *The Land of Laughs*. Another notable subset of metafictions features writers whose creations get out of control in various ways, as in **Flann O'Brien**'s *At Swim-Two-Birds*, Michael Joyce's *Peregrine Pieram* (1936), and **Cornelia Funke**'s *Inkheart*.

Conscious postmodern sophistication has resulted in a dramatic increase in the number and variety of metafictions; habitual practitioners include **Steven Millhauser**, **Jostein Gaarder**, and **Jasper Fforde**. Playful examples of extraordinary literary convolution include **Michael Bishop**'s *Who Made Stevie Crye?*, **Umberto Eco**'s *The Island of the Day Before,* Rebecca Lickiss's *Eccentric Circles* (2001), and Roderick Townley's *The Great Good Thing* (2001). Jeremy Dronfield's *The Alchemist's Apprentice* (2001) features a book whose nonexistence is partly a result of its having enchanted millions. In Marius Brill's *Making Love: A Conspiracy of the Heart* (2003), a book falls in love with its reader. Thomas Wharton's *Salamander* (2001) is about the attempted creation of an infinite book.

METAPHYSICAL FANTASY. Fiction attempting to define or devise a realm of existence that lies outside the scope of sensory perception, usually in order to assist speculative explanations to reach beyond what is observable and measurable. All **myth**-based and **religious fantasies** have a metaphysical component, because the provision of such metaphysical explanations is one of the primary functions of myth and religion, but the term is reserved here to those fantasies that attempt originality in defining new metaphysical systems.

Some **occult fantasy**, including most **alchemical fantasy**, is metaphysical in its implications, and texts that attempt to define the relationship between the primary world and **Faerie** often have recourse to metaphysical speculation, as do other **hybrid texts** attempting to reconcile the products of rival worldviews. Writers whose work is primarily dedicated to metaphysical speculation include **Algernon Blackwood**, **David Lindsay**, **Mircea Eliade**, and **Ronald Fraser**; other notable examples include **Fiona MacLeod**'s *Green Fire,* G. Ware Cornish's *Beneath the Surface* (1918), **Charles Williams**'s *The Place of the Lion,* Herbert Read's *The Green Child* (1935), E. H. Visiak's *The Shadow* (1936), Jules Romains's *Tussles with Time* (1951; tr. from French 1952), and Daniel Quinn's *The Holy* (2002). Designers of **secondary worlds** in genre fantasy rarely pay much attention to their metaphysical frames, the chief exceptions being **Guy Gavriel Kay** and writers giving serious consideration to the notion of the **multiverse**.

MEYRINK, GUSTAVE (1868–1932). Austrian writer. His early short fiction is sampled in translation in *The Opal and Other Stories* (1903–1907; tr. 1994), but later collections, including *Goldmachergeschichten* ["Stories about Alchemists"] (1925), remain untranslated. His first novel, *The Golem* (1915; abridged tr. 1928; restored text tr. 1977), is a **dark/hallucinatory fantasy**. *The Green Face* (1916; tr. 1992) and *Walpurgisnacht* (1917; tr. 1993) move portentously toward potentially redemptive **apocalypses** with fantastic harbingers that are deeply enigmatic. The **occult fantasy** *The White Dominican* (1921; tr. 1994) concentrates more intently on the individual fate of its protagonist, as does the complex **alchemical fantasy** *The Angel of the West Window* (1927; tr. 1991).

MICHELET, JULES (1798–1874). French historian, of whom it was said that no other ever cared less for accuracy. Always in need of money to support himself while he compiled his ambitious narrative history of France, he was inspired by the success of Éliphas Lévi to dash off the popular potboiler *La Sorcière* ["The Female Witch"] (1862; tr. as *The Witch of the Middle Ages* and *Satanism and Witchcraft*). Its second part is a series of journalistic accounts of famous sorcery trials, but its long lyrical prologue is a deliberate **scholarly fantasy** approvingly representing the **witches** of France as a **feminized** underground movement of social protest against the tyranny of church and state. Supplemented by the works of **Charles Godfrey Leland** and **Margaret Murray**, it became a key element in the ideological apparatus of modern paganism, witchcraft, and **goddess** worship; it is a vital, if largely unacknowledged, **taproot text** of genre fantasy.

MIDDLETON, HAYDN (1955–). British writer. The couplet comprising *The People in the Picture* (1987) and *The Collapsing Castle* (1990) are **contemporary fantasies** whose supernatural elements are based in **Celtic fantasy**. *Son of Two Worlds* (1987) straightforwardly **recycles** a tale from the ***Mabinogion***. The trilogy comprising *The King's Evil* (1995), *The Queen's Captives* (1996), and *The Knight's Vengeance* (1997) is an **Arthurian fantasy** foregrounding Mordred. *Grimm's Last Fairytale* (1999) is an account of the last days of the famous folklorist.

MIÉVILLE, CHINA (1972–). British writer. *King Rat* (1998) is a graphic **contemporary fantasy** based on the story of the Pied Piper. *Perdido Street Station* (2000) is a complex **immersive fantasy** in which **hybridization** of disparate materials coalesces into a graphic image of the **decadent** city of New Crobuzon. *The Scar* (2002) is an **Odyssean**

fantasy set in the same **secondary world** of Bas Lag. *Iron Council* (2004) returns to New Crobuzon for an account of rebellion and a legendary nation on wheels. *The Tain* (2002) is a novella in which London is threatened by invasion from the world within **mirrors**. Miéville placed his work within the context of a vague movement, careless of traditional generic boundaries, which he dubbed "The New Weird" in *Locus* 515 (2003), naming **Steve Cockayne** and Steph Swanston—author of *The Year of Our War* (2004)—as other key examples.

MILES, ROSALIND (1943–). British writer. Her fantasies are **feminized** Arthuriana boldly exhibiting a "New Age" sensibility. The Guenevere series comprises *Queen of the Summer Country* (1999), *The Knight of the Sacred Lake* (2000), and *Child of the Holy Grail* (2000). The Isolde series comprises *Isolde: Queen of the Western Isle* (2002), *The Maid of White Hands* (2003), and *The Lady of the Sea* (2004).

MILITARY FANTASY. Armies are common features of **heroic fantasy**, but their military organization is subject to careful consideration in only a small minority of stories. Matters of training and tactics first came into focus in **timeslip** stories in the wake of **Mark Twain**'s *Connecticut Yankee in King Arthur's Court*, but the emergence of a manifest subgenre of military fantasy was not clearly evident until the advent of an obvious subgenre of military sf (refer to *HDSFL*), many of whose practitioners took a keen interest in the history of military organization, especially in the Roman Empire. The reflection of such interests can be seen in the fantasies of **David Drake**, **Glen Cook**, **David Gemmell**, **Dave Duncan**, and **James Barclay**, and in such military **sf** spinoff as Elizabeth Moon's Deed of Paksenarion series, begun with *Sheepfarmer's Daughter* (1988). The influence of military sf was combined with the influence of fantasy war-gaming, which generated work by such writers as **Michael A. Stackpole** as well as **tie-in** projects.

The technofetishism of military sf has its equivalent in fantasy in a fascination for medieval arms and armor, especially swords. Striking examples include K. J. Parker's Fencer trilogy, comprising *Colours in the Steel* (1998), *The Belly of the Bow* (1999), and *The Proof House* (2000), and Richard Brown's Golden Armour series, comprising *The Helmet* (2000), *The Shield* (2000), and *The Spurs* (2000). The corrupting armor in John Marco's *The Devil's Armor* (2003) adds an ironic twist reminiscent of such avid magical weapons as **Michael Moorcock**'s Stormbringer. *See also* GAMES.

MILLAR, MARTIN (?–). Scottish writer, His work under his own byline includes *The Good Fairies of New York* (1992), in which punk **fairies** are air-freighted to New York after getting drunk; *Lux and Alby Sign On and Save the Universe* (1999), in which the fairies in question join up with characters from earlier novels, with **apocalyptic** consequences; and *Suzy, Led Zeppelin and Me* (2002), in which Jimi Hendrix, Janis Joplin, and Hank Williams take a zeppelin trip from heaven to see a 1972 Led Zeppelin concert. The **hybrid** Thraxas series, bylined "Martin Scott"—comprising *Thraxas* (1999), *Thraxas and the Warrior Monks* (1999), *Thraxas at the Races* (1999), *Thraxas and the Elvish Isles* (2000), *Thraxas and the Sorcerers* (2001), *Thraxas and the Dance of Death* (2002), *Thraxas at War* (2003), and *Thraxas under Siege* (2003)—is also **humorous**, featuring the exploits of a private investigator in a magical city.

MILLHAUSER, STEVEN (1943–). U.S. writer who dabbles extensively in **metafiction**. *From the Realms of Morpheus* (1986) is a complex **underworld** fantasy with concerns that overlap with those of the short fiction in *In the Penny Arcade* (1986). *The Barnum Museum* (1990) allows access to various fantasy worlds, including that of the board **game** Cluedo, "The Eighth Voyage of Sinbad," and (**Lewis Carroll**'s) "Alice, Falling." Two of the novellas in *Little Kingdoms* (1993) describe intimate relationships between artists and the worlds contained in their works, while the third, "The Princess, the Dwarf and the Dungeon," is an **art fairy tale**. *Martin Dressler: The Tale of an American Dreamer* (1997) is a **fabulatory** *bildungsroman* in which a focus on the American Dream is retained by the phantasmagoric *Enchanted Night* (2000) and some of the stories in *The Knife Thrower and Other Stories* (1999). The three novellas in *The King in the Tree* (2004) include **transfigurations** of the stories of Tristan and Don Juan.

MILNE, A. A. (1882–1956). British writer associated with *Punch,* whose idiosyncratic vein of **humor** fed the **fairy tale** extravaganza *Once on a Time* (1917) and echoes in the classic fantasy world Milne built around toy **animals** owned by his son Christopher Robin Milne, elaborated in *Winnie-the-Pooh* (1926) and *The House at Pooh Corner* (1928). Subsequent works inspired by this endeavor include a fine collection of parodic essays in literary criticism by Frederick Crews, *The Pooh Perplex* (1963). More children's fantasies are collected in *Prince Rabbit and the Princess Who Could Not Laugh* (1926). Milne's plays include the allegorical **fairy tale** *The Ivory Door* (1928) and a dramatization of **Kenneth Grahame**'s *Wind in the Willows*, *Toad of Toad Hall* (1929).

MILTON, JOHN (1608–1674). British poet of vast influence, particularly by virtue of his authorship of the **epic** *Paradise Lost* (1667; rev. 1674); its version of Lucifer's rebellion, the subsequent war in heaven, and the **Devil**'s temptation of Adam and Eve became definitive, eclipsing the verse drama to which it was a counterblast—Justus van den Vondel's anti-Puritan *Lucifer* (1654)—in the eyes of many subsequent writers who used it as a **taproot text**. Its influence has not always reflected Milton's intentions, given that he is credited with the inspiration of the tradition of **literary satanism** and is extensively quoted in such examples thereof as **Philip Pullman**'s *His Dark Materials*.

Milton's other works of fantasy relevance include a masque that came to be known as *Comus* (1634), after the character of an imaginary **classical** deity—the offspring of Bacchus and Circe—who seduces travelers into drinking a **theriomorphic** liquor; the **Christian fantasy** poem *Paradise Regained* (1671); and a **biblical fantasy** play modeled on the Greek tragedy *Samson Agonistes* (1671). (These works also echo Vondel's endeavors in such satires as "The Passing of Orpheus" and "Rivalry of Apollo and Pan," and the biblical fantasies "Adam in Exile" and "Noah.")

MINIATURIZATION. Stories in which humans are reduced in size, thus being enabled to see the world, especially its insect life, from a different viewpoint. Many didactic tales of this kind present themselves as **sf** (refer to *HDSFL*) despite obvious logical difficulties, but their deployment in fantasy is complicated by various myths of preexistent "little people." The notion that **fairies** are miniature human beings, with or without insectile wings, takes some warrant from the supposition that **elves** were a species of dwarfs, but it only became commonplace through the agency of Victorian fairy art, which routinely made fairies comparable in size to insects—a notion that exerted an enormous influence on the development of **children's fantasy**. Such representations dovetail neatly with didactic stories in which human protagonists are miniaturized; **Charles Kingsley**'s The Water Babies is a notable **hybrid**, and the notion of **Faerie** as a miniature world within our own is elaborately sophisticated in **John Crowley**'s *Little, Big.*

The Lilliputians described in Jonathan Swift's *Gulliver's Travels* (1726) were extensively copied and are **recycled** in such works as **T. H.**

White's *Mistress Masham's Repose* and Willis Hall's *The Return of the Antelope* (1985). Many other kinds of little people continue to thrive in fantasy, including **Mary Norton**'s *The Borrowers* and **Terry Pratchett**'s *Truckers.* Miniaturization sometimes enables protagonists to enter the world of their playthings, as in **F. Anstey**'s *Only Toys,* and there is an interesting subset of fantasy stories featuring dollhouses, which includes **Jane Louise Curry**'s *Mindy's Mysterious Miniature,* **Monica Hughes**'s *Castle Tourmandyne,* several works by **Kathryn Reiss**, and **Nancy Willard**'s *Uncle Terrible.*

MIRRLEES, HOPE (1887–1978). British writer. Her early **immersive fantasy** *Lud-in-the-Mist* (1926), which makes much of the notion of "forbidden fruit," as deployed in **Christina Rossetti**'s *Goblin Market,* was a late but highly significant addition to post–World War I pleas for **re-enchantment**. It was reprinted by **Lin Carter** in the **Ballantine Adult Fantasy Series**, subsequently exerting considerable influence on **James P. Blaylock** and **Neil Gaiman**.

MIRRORS. Reflection has long seemed a quasi-**magical** property, and mirrors routinely feature as magical devices in **fairy tales**, the most famous being the one featured in the oft-**recycled** tale of Snow White and that featured in the opening sequence of **Hans Christian Andersen**'s "The Snow Queen." Literary mirrors often reveal more than they should, accommodating phantom intruders in such tales as one interpolated in **George MacDonald**'s *Phantastes.* They may also serve as **portals**, as in **Lewis Carroll**'s *Through the Looking Glass,* or as generators of doppelgängers, as in William Garrett's *The Man in the Mirror* (1931) and **Peter Dickinson**'s *The Lion-Tamer's Daughter.*

Notable 20th-century fantasies in which mirrors play a crucial role include **Avram Davidson**'s *The Phoenix and the Mirror* (1966), **Louise Cooper**'s Mirror Mirror trilogy, **Ian Irvine**'s *A Shadow on the Glass,* and China Miéville's *The Tain. Mirrors* (2001), ed. Wendy Cooling, is a showcase **anthology**.

MITCHISON, NAOMI (1897–1999). Scottish writer in various genres, primarily noted for novels set in the distant past, which often foreground magical beliefs and practices derived from **Frazerian/scholarly fantasy**, as in *The Corn King* and the *Spring Queen* (1931), the 18th-century-set *The Bull Calves* (1947)—with a protagonist who becomes a **witch**—and *Early in Orcadia* (1987). Fantasy elements are more conspicuous in *Beyond the Limit* (1935), a **hallucinatory fantasy**

intimately linked to **Wyndham Lewis**'s **illustrations**; the **timeslip** fantasy *The Big House* (1950); *Travel Light* (1952), based in **Nordic** mythology; and *To the Chapel Perilous* (1955), a **satirical/chivalric romance**.

MODESITT, L. E., JR. (1943–). U.S. writer also known for **sf** (refer to *HDSFL*). The series comprising *The Magic of Recluce* (1991), *The Towers of the Sunset* (1992), *The Magic Engineer* (1994), *The Order War* (1995), *The Death of Chaos* (1995), *The Fall of Angels* (1996), *The Chaos Balance* (1997), *The White Order* (1998), *Colors of Chaos* (1999), *Magi'i of Cyador* (2000), *Scion of Cyador* (2000), and *Wellspring of Chaos* (2004) features rival followers of Order and **Chaos** attempting to find new ways of exploiting the elaborate rules governing their **magic**, against the background of an evolving technology. *Of Tangible Ghosts* (1994) is set in an **alternative history** in which the living and dead maintain routine communications. In the Spellsong Cycle series, comprising *The Soprano Sorceress* (1997), *The Spellsong War* (1998), *Darksong Rising* (1999), *The Shadow Sorceress* (2001), and *Shadowsinger* (2002), a **portal** gives access to a world where **music** is magical. The **secondary world** featured in Corean Chronicles, comprising *Legacies* (2002), *Darknesses* (2003), and *Scepters* (2004), has **Arcadian** elements.

MOLLOY, MICHAEL (1940–). British journalist who became editor of the *Daily Mirror* in 1974 and editor in chief of the Mirror Group in 1984. His **children's fiction** includes a lighthearted fantasy adventure trilogy comprising *The Witch Trade* (2001), *The Time Witches* (2001), and *The Wild West Witches* (2004), in which castaways are drawn into a **quest** in a **secondary world**. *The House on Falling Star Hill* (2004) is a **portal fantasy**.

MONACO, RICHARD (1940–). U.S. scholar and writer. The sequence comprising *Parsival; or, A Knight's Tale* (1977), *The Grail War* (1979), *The Final Quest* (1980) and *Blood and Dreams* (1985) offers a sceptical account of the **grail** quest. *Runes* (1984) and *Broken Stone* (1985) are **historical fantasies** in which Romans contest with **druids**. *Journey to the Flame* (1985) is a **metafictional** recycling of **Rider Haggard**'s *She*.

MONSTERS. Creatures, including humans, whose nature or appearance induces a combination of fear and revulsion, sometimes confused with pity. Whereas **horror** fiction, virtually by definition, uses monsters as generators of terror (refer to *HDHL*), fantasy routinely challenges, undermines, or defuses their horrific aspects, as is very evident in fantasy deployments of **dragons**, **vampires**, **giants**, and **werewolves**, and in **Raymond Briggs**'s parodic assault on the archetypal monster of parental terrorism in *Fungus the Bogeyman.* Even the standardized adversaries of **commodified fantasy** rarely lack apologists for long; trolls are stoutly defended by **John Vornholt** and orcs by **Stan Nicholls**.

Monsters continue to be used as antagonists in celebratory **heroic fantasy**, in which capacity they are required to seem terrible, but daylit combat offers a perspective quite different from that of night-obscured stalking, sometimes allowing them to borrow a little of their opponents' glamor. **Joseph Campbell**'s contention that the monsters a hero meets on his road of trials are symbolic projections of his unconscious fears and desires is reflected in such accounts of dragon slaying as **William Mayne**'s *The Worm in the Well,* such freak-show fantasies as **Charles G. Finney**'s *The Circus of Dr. Lao,* and such **psychological** melodramas as E. H. Visiak's sea-monster story *Medusa* (1929).

Mythical monsters have long been catalogued in exotic bestiaries; a useful modern sampler is Joseph Nigg's **anthology** *The Book of Fabulous Beasts* (1999).

THE MOON. The fundamental **dualism** of light and darkness, which symbolize good and evil in so many fantasies, is confused by the cyclical role of the moon in ameliorating the darkness of certain nights. Quasi-dualistic oppositions between deities associated with the sun, who are usually male, and deities associated with the moon, who are frequently female, tend to be complex in both myth and literature, also reflecting the moon's relationship with tides. The firm association between the moon and various female deities of **classical** mythology ensures that images of the **goddess** in modern literary fantasy are almost invariably imbued with lunar imagery, as in significant works by **Greer Gilman** and **Elizabeth Hand**.

The primary link between the moon and female nature is the approximately lunar pattern of the menstrual cycle, which secures a link between moon goddesses and **erotic fantasy** exemplified in such stories as **Barry Pain**'s "The Moon-Slave" (1901) and **James Branch Cabell**'s "The Music from behind the Moon" (1926). The moon is also linked in folklore to madness ("lunacy"), nonsense ("moonshine"), unlikelihood ("once in a blue moon"), and unattainability ("crying for the moon"). Its specific link with lycanthropy is of particular importance in fantasy literature, and a generalized transformative power is reflected in such works as **Steven Millhauser**'s *Enchanted Night.*

Some classical writers wondered whether the moon might be the habitation of the souls of the dead, with the result that it sometimes figures in **afterlife fantasies**; in **John Cowper Powys**'s "The Mountains of the Moon" it plays host to the astral bodies of earthly dreamers. **Children's fantasies** sometimes literalize the fanciful allegation that it is made of green cheese or employ the Man in the Moon (whose face or figure is supposedly discernible in its surface markings) as a character. In **Ariosto**'s *Orlando Furioso*, everything wasted on Earth, including misspent time, broken vows, and unanswered prayers, is stored on the moon—a notion recalled or **recycled** by numerous later writers. Another significant literary precedent was set by **Aleister Crowley**'s *Moonchild,* whose central figure is echoed in various **occult fantasies**.

MOORCOCK, MICHAEL (1939–). British writer and editor. In the latter capacity, he was primarily associated with the new wave **sf** (refer to *HDSFL*) of New Worlds, but a key project of his early writing career was a **sword and sorcery** series that helped to revive, revitalize, and sophisticate that subgenre. His earliest experiments were reprinted in *Sojan* (1977), but the first to reach a considerable audience—in the magazine *Science-Fantasy,* where "The Dreaming City" appeared in 1961—were stories featuring the albino hero Elric of Melniboné, whose possession and use of the bloodthirsty sword Stormbringer places him at the focal point of a crucial contest in a long war between Order and **Chaos**.

The Elric stories collected in *The Stealer of Souls* (1963) and *Stormbringer* (1965) were revised and reedited more than once as the series expanded. A then-comprehensive version reissued by DAW Books in the 1970s was quickly supplemented by additional titles, but the series had become further complicated by its relocation in a broader context in which Elric became a version of an archetypal hero whose incarnations were elaborately distributed through an infinitely repetitive **multiverse**. "The Eternal Champion" (*Science-Fantasy,* 1962) gave birth to a similar series; other series produced at high speed—including the Runestaff series, featuring *Dorian Hawkmoon* (1967–69), and its spinoff Count Brass series (1973–75), and two series featuring Prince Corum (1971 and 1973–74)—were eventually bound up with it in a vast series of omnibuses uniting almost all Moorcock's genre-relevant work as *The Tale of the Eternal Champion* (1992–93).

Volume 1 of *The Tale of the Eternal Champion* features Von Bek, whose adventures were first chronicled in the 1980s. Volume 2 is The Eternal Champion series, volume 3 Hawkmoon, and volume 4 Corum, whose second series of adventures is volume 10, *The Prince of the Silver Hand.* Elric's adventures are distributed in volume 8, *Elric of Melniboné,* and volume 12, *Stormbringer,* while volume 14 features Count Brass. Most of the remaining volumes collect sf or **science-fantasy** stories, the most important of the latter being the **decadent** and **far-futuristic** fantasy sequence collected in volumes 7 and 11, *The Dancers at the End of Time* (originally 1972–76) and *Legends from the End of Time* (originally 1976). A few more fantasies are, however, included in the miscellany offered in volume 13 under the title *Earl Aubec and Other Stories.*

The fantasies Moorcock did not include in this series of omnibuses include a trilogy of **Edgar Rice Burroughs** pastiches he produced in 1965; *Gloriana, or the Unfulfill'd Queen* (1978), a **historical fantasy** set in an **alternative** Elizabethan England; and the **surreal urban fantasy** couplet *Mother London* (1988) and *King of the City* (2000). His subsequent work in the genre includes a continuation of the Von Bek series, comprising *Blood: A Southern Fantasy* (1995), *Fabulous Harbours* (1995), and *The War amongst the Angels* (1996), and some of the stories in *Lunching with the Anti-Christ* (1995). He collaborated with **Storm Constantine** on *Silverheart* (2000) and began a new Elric series with *The Dreamthief's Daughter* (2000) and *The Skrayling Tree* (2003). *Wizardry and Wild Romance: A Study of Epic Fantasy* (1987) offers an idiosyncratic account of the nature of the fantasy genre and the methodology of fantasy writing.

MOORE, C. L. (1911–1987). U.S. writer. Before her marriage to **Henry Kuttner**, she wrote two influential series for ***Weird Tales:*** the Northwest Smith sequence pioneered the **hybrid/science fantasy** (refer to *HDSFL*), while the Jirel of Joiry sequence was the first **sword and sorcery** series to feature a female hero. "Black God's Kiss" (1934), which launched the latter series, is a remarkable **erotic fantasy** with symbolism and feverish purple prose that impressed **A. Merritt**, although he opined that Moore was bound to lose the relevant narrative energy once she was married (and presumably later thought the prediction amply justified). The series is reprinted in *Jirel of Joiry* (1969; aka *Black God's Shadow*), although a story in which the two heroes meet, "The Quest of the Starstone" (1937 with Kuttner), was not included. Most of Moore's subsequent work was couched as science fantasy or **sf** (refer to *HDSFL*), but "Fruit of Knowledge" (1940) is an **Edenic fantasy** and "Daemon" (1946) a **sentimental fantasy**. Among the items she and Kuttner subsequently identified as collaborations, the **portal fantasies** with the most abundant fantasy content are probably mostly her work, especially the Merritt pastiche *The Dark World* (1946; book 1965) and the **myth**-based fantasies "Lands of the Earthquake" (1947) and *The Mask of Circe* (1948; book 1975).

MÓR, CAISEAL (1961–). Australian writer and musician; his expertise on the harp informs the historical **Celtic fantasy** trilogy comprising *The Circle and the Cross* (1995), *The Song of the Earth* (1996), and *The Water of Life* (1997); the trilogy comprising *The Meeting of the Waters* (2000), *The King of Sleep* (2000), and *The Raven Game* (2002) is a **prequel**. *Carolan's Concerto* (1999) also features **magical music**. *The Well of Yearning* (2004) launched a new trilogy.

MORALISTIC FANTASY. All worlds within texts have an intrinsic moral order, in that the author has the power to determine which characters will be rewarded or punished; what is meant by a "happy ending" is that virtue has been rewarded, according to the ideals of "poetic justice." The primary work of the human imagination throughout history has been its resistance to the apparent lack of moral order in the real world; the bulk of fantasy literature's "raw materials" must have arisen as means of pretending that moral accounts left achingly unsettled on Earth will be paid in full in the **afterlife** or in the wake of the **apocalypse**. All fantasy literature is therefore moralistic—but some items are more moralistic than others.

Fables are designed to exemplify their morals, and such subgenres as **religious fantasy** and **chivalric romance** are also essentially moralistic; such narrative techniques as **satire** and **allegory** similarly have a moral component built in. The fantasies in which the moralistic aspect tends to stand out as a deliberate imposition are those in which fundamental materials are drawn from other traditions, which therefore have to be **transfigured** in order to emphasize a moral message; the cardinal example is **Charles Perrault**'s adaptation of **folktales** into **fairy tales**; the strategy was carried forward by such disciples as Madame de Genlis's *Tales of the Castle* (1784; tr. 1806) and **Anatole France**'s *Bee*. **Humorous fantasy** was similarly adapted by such 19th-century writers as **James Dalton** and **Charles Dickens**.

Much fantastic apparatus has arisen from priestly and parental terrorism—the use of imaginary threats in persuading people to be cooperative. The most obvious literary produce of such crusades is to be found in **horror** fiction, but the tactics of parental terrorism—and opposition thereto—have had a profound effect on the evolution of **children's fantasy**, starkly demonstrated by Heinrich Hoffmann's graphic *Struwwelpeter* (1845) and Carlo Collodi's *Pinocchio* (1883), whose hapless wooden hero has a hard time acquiring the moral sensibility that will qualify him as a human being. Lene Kaaberbol's series begun with *The Shamer's Daughter* (2000; tr. from Danish 2002), in which the heroine can extract confessions with her censorious gaze, is slightly more subtle.

MORGAN LE FAY. An enchantress in **Arthurian** legend, whose Anglo-Norman name identifies her as a **fairy**, although Malory represents her as Arthur's half-sister; in **William Morris**'s *Earthly Paradise* she becomes the posthumous wife of another legendary hero, Ogier the Dane. Modern fantasy often represents her as **Merlin**'s rival, and she is a key character in much **feminized** fantasy; the heroine of **Dion Fortune**'s *Sea Priestess* (1938) and *Moon Magic* (1956) is her **reincarnation**, and she plays important roles in Arthurian **transfigurations** by such writers as **Marion Zimmer Bradley**, **Vera Chapman**, **Fay Sampson**, and **Nancy Springer**. Her role is also reassessed by such male writers as J. Robert King, in *Le Morte d'Avalon* (2003).

Celtic Arthuriana occasionally links Morgan le Fay to the Morrigan, a spell-casting Irish war **goddess** who serves as a femme fatale in the legend of Cuchulainn, but the Morrigan's roles in such novels as **Alan Garner**'s *The Weirdstone of Brisingamen* and Pat O'Shea's *The Hounds of the Morrigan* (1985) are usually quite distinct, and the similarity of the names is almost certainly coincidental.

MORLEY, CHRISTOPHER (1890–1957). U.S. writer. *Where the Blue Begins* (1922) is an offbeat **animal fantasy**. *Thunder on the Left* (1925) is a poignant **wish-fulfillment fantasy** in which a child's desire to understand the mysteries of adulthood precipitates a **timeslip** with an effect that can only be tragically disenchanting. The brief **sentimental fantasy** *The Arrow* (1927) tends to an opposite extreme. *The Trojan Horse* (1957) is a **satirical/classical fantasy**.

MORRIS, GERALD (?–). U.S. writer whose vocation as a Baptist pastor of the Living Water Christian Fellowship colors the **moralistic** component of his series of **Arthurian fantasies**, featuring Gawain's squire Terence. It comprises *The Squire's Tale* (1998), *The Squire, His Knight, and His Lady* (1999), *The Savage Damsel and the Dwarf* (2000), *Parsifal's Page* (2001), *The Ballad of Sir Dinadin* (2003), and *The Princess, the Crone, and the Dung-Cart Knight* (2004).

MORRIS, JANET E. (1946–). U.S. writer. Her novels of the late 1970s and early 1980s were couched as **science fantasy** (refer to *HDSFL*), although they were biased in their ambience toward the newly emergent fantasy genre, to which she committed herself wholeheartedly in a seven-volume sequence extending from *Beyond Sanctuary* (1985) to *Storm Seed* (1990, with Chris Morris) spun off from the Thieves' World **shared world** series; the later volumes were written in collaboration with her husband, Chris. She then went on to develop an enterprising shared-world enterprise in collaboration with **C. J. Cherryh**, launched with the anthology *Heroes in Hell* (1986); the series cleverly adapted the backcloth of **Dantean fantasy** as a stage for violent adventures with ironic echoes of **infernal comedy**. The last of its anthologies was *Prophets in Hell* (1989); her more substantial contributions included *The Gates of Hell* (1986, with Cherryh), *The Little Helliad* (1988, with Chris Morris), and *Explorers in Hell* (1989, with **David A. Drake**).

MORRIS, KENNETH (1879–1937). Welsh-born writer who spent the greater part of his adult life in a Californian community run by an offshoot of the **Theosophical** Society; most of his fiction—in which championship of the **metaphysical** principles of his faith is muted—was written for the organization's publications, under various pseudonyms. A few **mythologically** syncretic **moralistic** fantasies, reminiscent of the work of **Richard Garnett**, were reprinted in *The Secret Mountain and Other Tales* (1926); a more comprehensive collection was assembled by Douglas A. Anderson as *The Dragon Path* (1995). The **Celtic fantasies** *The Fates of the Princes of Dyved* (1914) and *Book of the Three Dragons* (1930) begin as straightforward recyclings of the ***Mabinogion*** but diverge from the originals as their narrative momentum builds; the latter appears to be incomplete. *The Chalchiuhite Dragon* (1992) is a mythological fantasy set in pre-Columbian America.

MORRIS, WILLIAM (1834–1896). British writer and artist, a member of the Pre-Raphaelite Brotherhood. His outrage against the poor quality of mass-produced goods in the wake of the Industrial Revolution led him to campaign for socialism and for the conservation and further sophistication of traditional craftsmanship—to which end he designed wallpaper, fabrics, and furniture and founded the Kelmscott Press to publish fine books.

His early contributions to the *Oxford and Cambridge Magazine* included several neo-**chivalric romances**, the most significant being the **allegorical** novella "The Hollow Land" (1856), a **portal fantasy** featuring an **Arcadian** earthly paradise symbolic of the dreams of Art. Similar milieux and themes dominate his poetry, including Arthuriana in *The Defence of Guinevere and Other Poems* (1858) and the sequence of **epics** *The Life and Death of Jason* (1867), *The Earthly Paradise* (1868–70), and *Sigurd the Volsung and the Fall of the Niblungs* (1876), which moved from **classical** to Nordic **taproot texts**, mingling the two in the intermediate title. After publishing the politically inspired **visionary fantasy** *A Dream of John Ball* (1888; initially combined with *A King's Lesson*) he mingled verse with prose in *The House of the Wolfings* (1889), a mannered but realistic depiction of medieval life in which fantastic elements are marginal.

The Roots of the Mountains (1890) makes even less use of fantastic intrusions, but its setting is detached from actual **historical** trappings, preparing the way for the development of the magically infused setting of *The Story of the Glittering Plain; or, The Land of Living Men* (1890), which elaborates and reassesses the theme of "The Hollow Land." It was followed by a sequence of similar **quest** fantasies, three of which were reprinted by **Lin Carter** as significant ancestral texts of "adult fantasy." In Carter's view, Morris took up the cause that **George MacDonald** had pioneered in *Phantastes* and prepared the way for its further development by **J. R. R. Tolkien.** *The Wood beyond the World* (1894) introduces an element of **erotic fantasy** into the formula, but Morris found such material difficult and moved it away from the center of the more elaborate prose epic *The Well at the World's End* (1896), in which a flexible employment of imaginary geography is much closer in spirit to that of genre fantasy than to the formalized allegorical representations of **Bunyan**'s *Pilgrim's Progress*. Between the two, he published the orthodox chivalric romance *Child Christopher and Goldilind the Fair* (1895). *The Water of the Wondrous Isles* (1897) is closer in spirit to **Odyssean fantasy** in the uncertain trajectory of its heroine's wanderings. The similarly posthumous *The Sundering Flood* (1897) returned to the quasi-historical settings of his earlier novels.

The Kelmscott Press inspired the foundation of several other private presses, notably one operated by David Nutt, which published a good deal of Arthuriana and such chivalric romances as E. Hamilton Moore's *The Story of Etain and Otinel* (1905).

MORROW, JAMES (1947–). U.S. writer. His early **sf** (refer to *HDSFL*) deploys motifs more commonly associated with fantasy; *The Wine of Violence* (1981) is a **moralistic fantasy** featuring a fluid that soaks up aggression, and *The Continent of Lies* (1984) is an **Orphean fantasy** about **dream** control. In *This Is the Way the World Ends* (1986), the spectral "unadmitted"—who lost the opportunity to be born because of an apocalyptic nuclear war—puts those responsible on trial. Morrow moved decisively into the field of **Christian fantasy** in *Only Begotten Daughter* (1990), a scathingly **satirical** account of a new incarnation. *City of Truth* (1991) is a **fabular** account of the city of Veritas, where truthfulness is compulsory, and its perverse but comforting opposite Satirev. In *Towing Jehovah* (1994), **God** commits suicide, but the **angels** and the Vatican attempt a cover-up. In the sequel *Blameless in Abaddon* (1996), charges are laid against the divine corpse in the Court of Human Rights, where problems of theodicy are hotly debated. In *The Eternal Footman* (1999), the blasting of God's skull into orbit prompts a plague of death anxiety and an attempt to formulate a new, more up-to-date religion. The corrosive scepticism of these works is further reflected in the sarcastic series that provides the title sequence of *Bible Stories for Adults* (1996); further items are in *The Cat's Pajamas and Other Stories* (2004). The journal *Paradoxa* dedicated a special issue (vol. 5, no. 12) to Morrow's works in 1999.

MORWOOD, PETER (1956–). Pseudonym of British writer Robert Peter Smith. The series comprising *The Horse Lord* (1983), *The Demon Lord* (1984), *The Dragon Lord* (1986), and *The Warlord's Domain* (1989) draws on Japanese mythology but offers stereotyped genre adventures rather than **Oriental fantasy**; a later version of the setting is featured in *Greylady* (1993) and *Widowmaker* (1989). The trilogy comprising *Prince Ivan* (1990), *Firebird* (1992), and *The Golden Horde* (1993) is a **historical fantasy** set in Russia. Morwood has also written **tie-ins** and contributions to **shared world** projects in collaboration with his wife, **Diane Duane**.

MROZEK, SLAVOMIR (1930–). Polish writer best known as a playwright, some of his absurdist dramas being translated in *Six Plays*

(1967) and *The Emigrants* (1974). In the latter, the characters create their own version of reality. Mrozek's short fiction—including numerous satirical **fabulations**—is sampled in *The Elephant* (1957; tr. 1962) and *The Ugupu Bird* (1959–65; tr. 1968).

MULTIVERSE. A vast array of **parallel worlds**; infinite versions inevitably contain all possible universes. Although the "many worlds interpretation" of quantum-mechanical uncertainties gives a gloss of scientific respectability to the notion—supporting its prolific use in **sf** (refer to *HDSFL*) as a frame for **alternative histories**—the term was popularized by **Michael Moorcock**, who used it to establish conceptual and metaphorical links between the highly various worlds described within his texts. Moorcock's multiverse thus became an inherently **chimerical** superstructure hospitable to all kinds of fantasy, including elaborate exercises in **metafiction** like those undertaken in **L. Sprague de Camp** and **Fletcher Pratt**'s Harold Shea series.

The term had previously been used in the **metaphysical fantasies** of **John Cowper Powys**, and its use in fantasy tends to be more mystical than scientific, regarding the cosmic elements as experimental exercises in creation rather than accidental products of quantum fluctuation—an attitude dramatically clarified in such works as **Diane Wynne Jones**'s *The Homeward Bounders* and **Ian Watson**'s *Queenmagic, Kingmagic*. Other writers who have made significant use of multiverses include **C. J. Cherryh**, **Tom de Haven**, **John Grant**, **Michael Scott Rohan**, and **James Stoddard**.

MUMMY. A corpse subjected to some kind of preservative process before interment; the archetypal examples are those entombed in ancient Egypt. Mummies provide a graphic imaginative link between present and past, and the notion that some of them might be revivable is commonly encountered in fantasy. In Jane Webb's *The Mummy! A Tale of the Twenty-second Century* (1827), the revived mummy of Cheops is a sinister presence, but the theme is treated lightheartedly in such 19th-century tales as **Edgar Allan Poe**'s "Some Words with a Mummy" and **Théophile Gautier**'s "The Mummy's Foot." The **occult** revival prompted more earnest treatments, often with an element of **erotic fantasy**—including Edgar Lee's *Pharaoh's Daughter* (1889), Theo Douglas's *Iras: A Mystery* (1896), and Clive Holland's *An Egyptian Coquette* (1898)—and licensed the use of mummies in such thrillers as **Arthur Conan Doyle**'s "The Ring of Thoth" and "Lot No. 249," Guy

Boothby's *Pharos the Egyptian* (1899), **Bram Stoker**'s *The Jewel of Seven Stars,* George Griffith's *The Mummy and Miss Nitocris* (1906), **Algernon Blackwood**'s "The Nemesis of Fire" (1908), and **Sax Rohmer**'s *The Brood of the Witch-Queen*. The casting of John Knittel's *Nile Gold* (1929) and **Eliot Crawshay-Williams**'s "Nofrit" as **hallucinatory fantasies** reflects a decline in plausibility, but the motif was revived again in **Anne Rice**'s *The Mummy; or, Rameses the Damned* (1989).

MUNDY, TALBOT (1879–1940). Pseudonym of British-born writer William Lancaster Gribbon, resident in the United States from 1909. His work for the pulp **magazines**—primarily *Adventure*—is mostly set in the Far East; after *King of the Khyber Rifles* (1916), some of its more exotic inclusions took on elements of **theosophical fantasy**, most notably a loosely knit series featuring the exotic exploits of a U.S. secret agent. It comprises "Moses and Mrs Aintree" (1922), *The Mystery of Khufu's Tomb* (1922; book 1933), *The Nine Unknown* (1923; book 1924), *The Devil's Guard* (1926; aka *Ramsden*), and *Jimgrim* (1931). Other works with significant fantastic elements include *Om: The Secret of Abhor Valley* (1924), *Black Light* (1930), *Full Moon* (1935; aka *There Was a Door*), and *Old Ugly Face* (1940). Mundy also wrote a series of **historical fantasies**, comprising *Queen Cleopatra* (1929, *Tros of Samothrace* (1934; 4-vol. edition 1967; 3-vol. edition 1976), and *The Purple Pirate* (1935), whose tone and manner are similar to the work of **Robert E. Howard**.

MUNN, H. WARNER (1903–1981). U.S. writer peripherally associated with the **Lovecraft** circle. He contributed a series of **theriomorphic fantasies** to ***Weird Tales*** (1928–31), collected as *The Werewolf of Ponkert* (1958) and further expanded in *Tales of the Werewolf Clan* (2 vols., 1979). *King of the World's Edge* (1939; book 1966) is an enterprising **Arthurian fantasy** with a sequel belatedly published as *The Ship from Atlantis* (1967; combined with its predecessor as *Merlin's Godson*, 1976); their theme was further extrapolated in the epic **historical fantasy** *Merlin's Ring* (1974), and Munn also wrote a prequel, *The Lost Legion* (1980). His uncollected short fiction—much of it produced as gift books for private circulation—includes numerous fantasies illustrating his scholarly interest in folklore and **occultism**.

MURRAY, MARGARET (1863–1963). British scholar. Her work as an Egyptologist remains academically respectable, but her highly fanciful

scholarly fantasy *The Witch Cult in Western Europe* (1921) set the florid speculations of **Jules Michelet** in a theoretical framework derived from **James Frazer** to produce a vivid account of **witches** secretly maintaining pagan fertility cults against the hostility of the church. This notion was summarized in an article, "Witchcraft," that she contributed to the *Encyclopaedia Britannica* (editions from 1929 to 1968) and expanded in *The God of the Witches* (1931). *The Divine King in England* (1952) extended it to the proposition that the English royal family was, throughout the Middle Ages, the mainstay of the British witch cult, involved in periodic ritual murder.

Murray's ideas were taken up by Gerald Gardner, who "rediscovered" pagan "covens" of the kind she described and dedicated himself to their "preservation," thus launching the most successful modern **lifestyle fantasy**, reflected and elaborated in a great deal of modern fantasy fiction. Literary works explicitly based on Murray's thesis include *The Last Devil* (1927), by Signe Toksvig, and *Melusine; or, Devil Take Her* (1936), by Charlotte Haldane; "wiccan" fantasies by such writers as **Gael Baudino** and **Diana L. Paxson**, and such works as **Freda Warrington**'s *Dark Cathedral,* are a little further removed.

MUSÄUS, JOHANN KARL (1735–1787). German scholar and writer. His pioneering collection of *Volksmärchen der Deutschen* (5 vols., 1782–87; partly tr. as *Popular Tales of the Germans,* 1791) was the first major collection of national folklore; it prompted the **Brothers Grimm** to attempt a more comprehensive survey and inspired literary works by such pillars of German **romanticism** as **Ludwig Tieck** and the **Baron de la Motte Fouqué**. Musäus's fiction, sampled in Thomas Carlyle's showcase anthology of *German Romance* (1827), includes "Libussa" (1782), about the gifted offspring of a woodsman and a dryad, and "Dumb Love" (1782; aka "The Spectre Barber"), an unusual account of posthumous punishment.

MUSE. A source of literary inspiration, usually personified as a woman. Homer appeals to one for assistance in remembering his lines, but subsequent classical writers divided the labor between nine daughters of Mnemosyne (memory) fathered by Zeus. From the Renaissance on, muses were routinely represented by writers as demanding mistresses, vampiric in their effect—a notion graphically extrapolated in **Tim Powers**'s *The Stress of Her Regard*. Many writers have looked to actual individuals to fill the role; **Robert Graves** waxed eloquent on the subject, linking his various muses to his idiosyncratic but influential idea of the **goddess**; "real" muses feature in such literary fantasies as **Elizabeth Hand**'s *Mortal Love,* but symbolic ones—as in **John Barth**'s *The Book of Ten Nights and a Night*—remain more common.

MUSIC. Fantastic literature has a close relationship with music, which extends from **ballads** through operas (the list of operas with fantastic librettos occupies 24 pages of the Clute/Grant *Encyclopedia*) to modern "folk music" and such genres as "Gothic rock." As with sexual passion, the psychological effects of music are often represented as a quasi-magical phenomenon, as reflected in the mythical significance of **Orpheus**'s lyre and **Pan**'s pipes, or even an instrument of divine revelation, as in **James Huneker**'s more extreme studies of melomania and **Zoran Zivkovic**'s *Seven Touches of Music*. It is partly for these reasons that composers are routinely drawn to fantastic themes, while music is routinely used in fantastic fiction as a magical agent. The establishment of **bardic fantasy** as a subgenre of **commodified heroic fantasy** was entirely natural.

Composers whose works have had a considerable influence on literary fantasy include **Richard Wagner**, Wolfgang Amadeus Mozart (whose *The Magic Flute* is transfigured in **Marion Zimmer Bradley**'s *Night's Daughter* and Cameron Dokey's *Sunlight and Shadow,* 2004), and Hector Berlioz, whose *Symphonie Fantastique* is transfigured by **Marvin Kaye**. Other transfigurations of classical musical can be found in the work of **Mercedes Lackey**.

Magical music frequently figures as an agent of temptation and transportation, as in **transfigurations** of the folktale of the Pied Piper by **Robert Browning** and others, and **Ludwig Tieck**'s version of the Tannhaüser myth. It is sometimes gifted with redemptive or **healing** powers, as in **Alan Garner**'s *Elidor,* where the salvation of the **secondary world** is accomplished by a **unicorn**'s sacrificial song. Writers of fantasy who are also accomplished musicians—the combination is remarkably common—routinely make such uses of magical music in their work; notable examples include **Charles de Lint**, **Paul Brandon**, **Vera Nazarian**, and **Caiseal Mór**.

Modern musicians who have dabbled in literary fantasy in addition to their lyrics are numerous; examples include Mortiis, in *Secrets of my Kingdom* (2001); Karen Michalson of Point of Ares, whose *Enemy Glory* (2001) is named after the band's first album (1996); and Luke Sutherland, veteran of several bands, whose quasi-autobiographical

Venus as a Boy (2004) features an Orkney-born boy who can generate such sexual ecstasy in others that they see **angels**. These musicians are not as numerous, however, as those who have produced concept albums with themes drawn from fantasy literature; notable examples of the latter include Rick Wakeman's *Myths and Legends of King Arthur and the Knights of the Round Table* (1975), Dave Greenslade's *Pentateuch of the Cosmogony* (1980 with text and **illustration** by Patrick Woodroffe), Hawkwind's **Michael Moorcock**–based *Chronicles of the Black Sword* (1985), Fields of the Nephilim's *Elizium* (1990), Inkubus Sukkubus's *Heartbeat of the Earth* (1995), The Garden of Delight's *Scheoul* (1996), Faith and the Muse's *Annwyn, beneath the Waves* (1996), and Ataraxia's *Lost Atlantis* (1999).

Notable works in which magical music plays a central role include **E. T. A. Hoffmann**'s "Ritter Gluck," F. W. Bourdillon's *Nephelé* (1896), J. Meade Falkner's *The Lost Stradivarius,* **James Branch Cabell**'s "The Music from behind the Moon," Patricia Lynch's *Brogeen Follows the Magic Tune* (1952), Nancy Kress's *The White Pipes* (1985), **Grace Chetwin**'s *The Chimes of Alfaylen,* Greg Bear's *Songs of Earth and Power* (1994), **Sarah Ash**'s *Songspinners,* **China Miéville**'s *King Rat,* Geoff Nicholson's *Flesh Guitar* (1998), **Elizabeth Scarborough**'s *Phantom Banjo,* **Jane Lindskold**'s *Pipes of Orpheus,* **Gwyneth Jones**'s series begun with *Bold as Love,* Naomi Kritzer's *Fires of the Faithful* (2002) and *Turning the Storm* (2003), and numerous works by **Gael Baudino**, **L. E. Modesitt**, and **Elizabeth Haydon**. Fantasy novels with accessory CDs include Laura Esquivel's *The Law of Love* (1995; tr. 1996). *See also* EROTIC FANTASY.

MYERS, JOHN MYERS (1906–1988). U.S. writer. *Silverlock* (1949) is a **metafictional** romp through the "Commonwealth" of literature. *The Moon's Fire-Eating Daughter* (1981) is a companion piece of sorts, contriving encounters with creators rather than their creations.

MYTH. A term derived from the Greek word for "story," thus licensing the commonplace meaning of something once believed but now recognized as fiction; in specialized definitions employed by anthropologists and folklorists, by contrast, myths are sacred narratives concerning the interaction of the human and divine worlds. No clear boundary separates myths from legends and **folk tales**, but the term tends to be reserved for stories that deal with the creation and divine administration of the world rather than matters of imaginary history featuring **heroic** or charismatic individuals (legends) or fancies that were never afforded any kind of reverent awe (folktales).

The myths of different cultures—particularly the **classical** and **Nordic** mythologies—provide the bedrock of a large fraction of modern fantasy. One of the earliest "encyclopedias" of mythology, whose compilation encouraged the syncretic amalgamation so evident in literary recycling and transfiguration, was Giovanni Boccaccio's *De genealogia deorum gentilium* [On the Genealogy of the Gods and the Gentiles] (1350–74). **Hindu** mythology and various **Oriental** mythologies have also given rise to substantial subgenres of fantasy literatures. Persian mythology has given rise to a few examples, notably Hilari Bell's Book of Sohrab series launched with *Flame* (2003). The fastest-growing areas are, however, African mythology—especially in its Afro-Caribbean variants, as exemplified by the work of **Nalo Hopkinson**—and Native American mythology. As the 20th century ended, the latter category enjoyed a considerable boom, variously reflected in such works as Win Blevins's *Ravenshadow* (1999), Norma Johnson's *Feather in the Wind* (2001), Eden Robinson's *Monkey Beach* (2000), Morrie Ruvinsky's *Dream Keeper* (2000), Gerald Vizenor's *Chancers* (2000), Nancy Wood's *Thunderwoman: A Mythic Tale of the Pueblos* (1999), and Marly Youmans's *The Curse of the Raven Mocker* (2003).

MYTHOPOEIC FANTASY. Mythopoeisis is the process by which **myths** are made; the core of mythopoeic fantasy consists of the output of writers who see their endeavors as a matter of manufacturing myths, although the label is routinely applied to writers engaged in the constructive remaking of myths. The term was popularized by the **Inklings**, whose use of it prompted Glen H. Goodknight to found in 1967 a Mythopoeic Society devoted to their works. The society began holding annual conferences (Mythcons) in 1970, broadening the scope of its interests to accommodate a wider constituency; the Mythopoeic Fantasy Awards for fiction and scholarship were instituted in 1971. Both awards were divided in 1992, the former into adult and **children's** categories and the latter into "Inklings Studies" and "Myth and Fantasy Studies."

– N –

NAPOLI, DONNA JO (1948–). U.S. writer for **children** and **young adults**. The trilogy comprising *The Prince of the Pond* (1992), *Jimmy, the Pickpocket of the Palace* (1995), and *Gracie, the Pixie in the Puddle*

(2004), which **transfigures** and dramatically extrapolates the **fairy tale** of the Frog Prince, set a pattern for many more unusually enterprising transfigurations. *The Magic Circle* (1993) is based on Hansel and Gretel. *Zel* (1996) undermines the motif in which the heroine encounters a handsome prince. *Spinners* (1999, with Richard Tchen) transfigures Rumpelstiltskin, *Crazy Jack* (1999) Jack and the Beanstalk, *Beast* (2000) Beauty and the Beast (from the Beast's viewpoint), and *Breath* (2003) the Pied Piper.

Napoli's other fantasies include two **classical fantasies**—*Sirena* (1998), featuring sirens, and *The Great God Pan* (2003), in which Pan is involved in the beginning of the Trojan War. *Song of the Magdalene* (1996) is a marginal **Christian fantasy**. In the Angelwings series (16 vols. 1999–2001) for younger readers, apprentice angels must work hard to earn their wings.

NATHAN, ROBERT (1894–1985). U.S. writer. His deftly polished and mock-naive literary style was perfectly adapted to fabular material, and elements of fantasy often crept into the margins of his early depictions of American rural life. However, it was not until he followed the **biblical fantasy** *Jonah* (1925; aka *Son of Amitai*) with the wholehearted **Christian fantasy** *The Bishop's Wife* (1928) that fantasy motifs—in the latter case an **angel**—became central to many of his works. The afterlife fantasy *There Is Another Heaven* (1929) contrasts the ideals of Judaism and Christianity, while *Road of Ages* (1935) imagines a new Diaspora. *The Innocent Eve* (1951) and *Heaven and Hell and the Megas Factor* (1975) carried such meditations into polite exercises in **literary satanism**, while further exploratory expeditions in euthanasia are featured in *The River Journey* (1949) and *The Train in the Meadow* (1953).

Nathan broke new ground in the classic **sentimental/timeslip** fantasy *Portrait of Jennie* (1940), which foreshadowed a sequence of **erotic fantasies** in which supernatural bridges built by the power of love usually prove heartrendingly fragile. The others include the plaintively **humorous** *The Married Look* (1950) and *The Rancho of the Little Loves* (1956), and the earnestly elegiac *So Love Returns* (1958), *The Wilderness-Stone* (1960), and *Mia* (1970). Similar issues are less directly addressed in *But Gently Day* (1943), the **Faustian fantasy** *The Devil in Love* (1963), and the mock-**Arthurian fantasies** *The Fair* (1964) and *The Elixir* (1971). His later works became increasingly nostalgic; the mock-**chivalric romance** *Sir Henry* (1955) and *The Mallot Diaries* (1965), in which a population of gentle Neanderthals inhabit a secret enclave, may be ironic reflections of his perception of his own situation. Nathan stands alongside **James Branch Cabell** as one of the leading American fantasists of the mid-20th century; his influence on the work of **Peter S. Beagle** was profound.

NAZARIAN, VERA (1966–). Armenian-Russian writer, artist, and musician who moved to Lebanon 1975 and became a U.S. citizen in 1999. *Dreams of the Compass Rose* (2002) is a remarkable collage of **dream** fantasies displaying an ancient alternate world, categorized by the author as "mythic **high fantasy**." *Lords of the Rainbow* (2003) is an "**epic** fantasy romance" in which color—here perceived as a series of personified avatars—is removed from the world. *The Clock King and the Queen of the Hourglass* (2004) is a painstaking **allegory**.

NERVAL, GÉRARD DE (1808–1855). Pseudonym of French poet Gérard Labrunie, whose work bridged the **Romantic** and Symbolist movements. His prose includes a collection of **Hoffmanesque** tales, *La main de gloire* (1832) and an **alchemical fantasy** written in collaboration with **Alexandre Dumas**, *L'alchimiste* (1839); the most celebrated are the **hallucinatory/erotic fantasies** contained in *Daughters of Fire* (1854; tr. 1922). A further item of the same kind, *Aurelia* (1855), is translated with other items in *Selected Writings* (1958). "The Tale of the Caliph Hakim" and "The Tale of the Queen of the Morning and Soliman the Prince of the Genii" are **Arabian fantasies** appended to the travelogue *Journey to the Orient* (1851; tr. 1972).

NESBIT, E. (1858–1924). British writer who initiated a new phase in **children's fiction** with her accounts of the adventures of the Bastable family, alongside which she wrote humorous **fairy tales** collected in *The Book of Dragons* (1899) and *Nine Unlikely Tales* (1901); the two strands of her work were brought together in a trilogy of **Ansteyan** novels in the comprising *Five Children and It* (1902), *The Phoenix and the Carpet* (1904), and *the Story of the Amulet* (1906). *The Enchanted Castle* (1907), *The Magic City* (1910), and *Wet Magic* (1913) carried the process of evolution farther into hectic **portal fantasies** with an infusion of nonsense à la **Lewis Caroll**, while *The House of Arden* (1908) and *Harding's Luck* (1909) employed **timeslips** as a means of dramatizing the principles of the author's staunch Fabian socialism. Her later collections include *The Magic World* (1912). Nesbit's work for adult readers occasionally employs fantastic elements, usually to generate **horror** (refer to *HDHL*), although *Dormant* (1911; aka *Rose Royal*) is a **hybrid/science fantasy** about suspended animation.

NEWCOMB, ROBERT (?–). U.S. writer. His **commodified/epic fantasy** Chronicles of Blood and Stone, comprising *The Fifth Sorceress* (2002), *The Gates of Dawn* (2003), *The Scrolls of the Ancients* (2004), depicts the kingdom of Eutracia in the aftermath of devastating war, the order restored by immortal **wizards** coming under renewed threat.

NEWMAN, KIM (1959–). British writer and film critic. His work is blithely chimerical, combining elements of **sf** (refer to *HDSFL*), **horror** (refer to *HDHL*), and fantasy. Fantasy elements are conspicuous in the **apocalyptic fantasy** *Jago* (1991) and the **Faustian fantasy** *The Quorum* (1994) but are displayed to more spectacular effect in the **metafictional/alternative history** sequence launched with *Anno Dracula* (1992), in which vampirism becomes firmly established in Western civilization after the Count (having survived the destruction visited upon him by **Bram Stoker**) marries Queen Victoria. Later volumes include *The Bloody Red Baron* (1995) and *Judgment of Tears: Anno Dracula 1959* (1998; aka *Dracula Cha Cha Cha*). The **vampire** heroine of the series is carried forward from a series of game **tie-in** novels bylined "Jack Yeovil," whose unusually inventive fantasy inclusions are *Drachenfels* (1989), *Beasts in Velvet* (1991), and *Genevieve Undead* (1993). In *Life's Lottery: A Choose-Your-Own-Adventure Book* (1999), the reader decides which of numerous alternative lives the hero has to endure. Newman's short fiction is collected in *The Original Dr Shade and Other Stories* (1994), *Famous Monsters* (1995), *Seven Stars* (2000), and *Unforgivable Stories* (2000).

NICHOLLS, STAN (?–). British writer. The Nightshade Chronicles, comprising *The Book of Shadows* (1996), *The Shadow of a Sorcerer* (1997), and *A Gathering of Shadows* (1998), pit a one-armed hero against a sorcerer. The trilogy comprising *Bodyguard of Lightning* (1999), *The Legion of Thunder* (1999), and *Warriors of the Tempest* (2000) represent orcs as the victims of prejudice and a bad press. The trilogy begun with *Quicksilver Rising* (2003) and *Quicksilver Zenith* (2004) features an accursed wanderer caught between rival empires.

NICHOLSON, JOSEPH SHIELD (1850–1927). British writer who published three anonymous fantasy novels. *Thoth* (1888) describes a technologically advanced but decadent **lost race** coexistent with Periclean Athens. *A Dreamer of Dreams* (1889) is a **moralistic/Faustian fantasy**. *Toxar* (1890) is a striking **wish-fulfillment fantasy** in which an empathically gifted slave tells his masters what they want to know in order that warped ambition might lead them to destruction.

NICHOLSON, WILLIAM (1948–). British writer best known as a screenwriter. In the trilogy of **children's fantasies** comprising *The Wind Singer* (2000), *Slaves of the Mastery* (2001), and *Firesong* (2002), refugees from the highly regulated city of Amaranth venture into the surrounding wilderness in search of a solution to its mysterious afflictions but find their mission frustratingly difficult.

NIMMO, JENNY (1944–). British writer of **children's fiction**, much of which employs magical animals as agents or catalysts of change. *The Bronze Trumpeter* (1974) is a **timeslip** fantasy featuring the cast of the *commedia dell'arte*. The **portal fantasy** trilogy comprising *The Snow Spider* (1986), *Emlyn's Moon* (1987; aka *Orchard of the Crescent Moon*), and *The Chestnut Soldier* (1989) makes enterprising use of imagery derived from the ***Mabinogion***. *Griffin's Castle* (1994) has wild beasts summoned from a stone wall. In *Ultramarine* (1991) and its sequel *Rainbow and Mr Zed* (1992), a mysterious man from the sea explains the heroine's unusual ancestry. *The Rinaldi Ring* (1999) features a ghost girl from World War I. *Milo's Wolves* (2001) and *The Night of the Unicorn* (2003) revisit Nimmo's favorite theme. The series begun with *Midnight for Charlie Bone* (2002), *The Time Twister* (2003; aka *Charlie Bone and the Time Twister*), and *The Blue Boa* (2004; aka *Charlie Bone and the Invisible Boy*) is a **J. K. Rowling**–influenced account of the exploits of a boy who can hear the thoughts of people in photographs at a special academy.

NIX, GARTH (1963–). Australian writer. *The Ragwitch* (1991) is a dark **Orphean fantasy**. *Sabriel* (1995) describes the problematic traffic passing through a wall separating a nonmagical region of an imaginary continent from territories where aberrant **afterlives** may be generated. The sequel couplet *Lirael: Daughter of the Clayr* (2001) and *Abhorsen* (2003) begins 14 years later. The series comprising *The Seventh Tower: The Fall* (2000), *Castle* (2000), *Aenir* (2000), *Above the Veil* (2001), *Into Battle* (2001), and *The Violet Keystone* (2001) tracks the exploits of a boy who falls out of a tower and has to learn the secrets of the **dark**

world outside. In the Keys to the Kingdom series, launched with *Mister Monday* (2003), *Grim Tuesday* (2003), and *Drowned Wednesday* (2004), the will defining the inheritance of a magical kingdom is torn into seven pieces.

NODIER, CHARLES (1780–1844). French writer who became the guiding light of the French **Romantic** movement, hosting its first *cénacle*. He helped the director of the Porte-Saint-Martin **theater**, Jean-Toussaint Merle, improvise dramas based on a number of **Gothic** romances, including an 1820 version of John Polidori's *The Vampyre*—in which steamboat pioneer Achille de Jouffroy also had a hand—and *Le Monstre et le Magicien* (1826), adapted from Mary Shelley's *Frankenstein*. Nodier's prose fantasies include the **hallucinatory fantasy** *Smarra* (1821; tr. 1993) and the **art fairy tales** *Trilby* (1822; tr. 1895) and *La fée aux miettes* [The Crumb-Fairy] (1832).

NONSENSE. The production of nonsense as a calculated literary art form was popularized by the **humorous** verse of **Edward Lear** and taken up by **Lewis Carroll**, although earlier precedents can be found—notably **Jacques Cazotte**'s *A Thousand and One Follies* and Horace Walpole's bizarre *Hieroglyphic Tales* (1785). The 19th-century tradition founded by Lear and Carroll was extended by **W. S. Gilbert**, **F. Anstey**, James F. Sullivan, and **Rudyard Kipling** (in his *Just So Stories*) but became less obvious in the 20th century, despite **G. K. Chesterton**'s championship in "A Defence of Nonsense" (1901) and **Oscar Wilde**'s lament for "The Decay of Lying." The main reason for this retreat was the collapse of Victorian rigidity, but nonsense retained a muted presence within British extensions of **surrealism**. Such eccentricities as **John Cowper Powys**'s "suckfist gibberish" and J. L. Synge's mathematical fantasia *Kandelman's Krim* (1957) maintained a presence until nonsense made a more robust comeback in the work of such writers as **Terry Pratchett** and **Jeff Noon**.

In the United States, Prohibition and its associated prudery provided a rigid moral stance ripe for nonsensical assault in the works of such writers as **Thorne Smith**; and the tradition was carried forward by the likes of **James Thurber** before infecting modern **humorous fantasy**; notable examples of modern American nonsense can be found in the works of **Edward Gorey** and **Daniel M. Pinkwater**. Examples from other languages pose problems for translators, but a nonsensical spirit is evident in the works of **Tove Jansson**.

The kind of "sense" from which nonsense dissents is ideological—which is to say that it tries to pass itself off as something that is "naturally true" although it is, in fact, mere pretense—and the assaults of nonsense are akin to those of **satire**, although they attack the roots rather than the branches of the relevant ideological formations. In its ultimate developments, in such Pratchett novels as *Hogfather* and *The Thief of Time,* the careful extrapolation of "nonsensical" premises is a powerful and thoroughly rational form of scepticism that has the additional advantage of being very witty.

NOON, JEFF (1957–). British writer whose hectic **surrealist** fictions make abundant use of imagery drawn from **sf** (refer to *HDSFL*), although they became more assertively **chimerical** after *Nymphomation* (1997) and *Automated Alice* (1996), following a method explained in *Cobralingus* (2000). *Pixel Juice* (1998) assembles 50 short pieces into a kaleidoscopic mosaic.

NORDIC FANTASY. Fantasies based in northern European mythology. The most substantial mythical network involves a population of **gods** known as the Aesir—including Odin, Thor, Loki, and Baldur—in a long war with invading Vanir, which also involves the dwarfs of Alfheim (from whose name the word **elf** is derived) and the **giants** of Jotunheim. The ultimate climax of the war is the battle of Ragnarok—described in the 10th-century Icelandic poem *Völuspá*—which completes the *götterdämmerung* ["twilight of the gods"]. The 10th-century records are much elaborated in an account of the Norse gods interpolated in a manual for Icelandic poets, now known as the *Prose Edda,* compiled by Snorri Sturluson in the early 13th century. The near-contemporary Teutonic *Niebelunglied* and Scandinavian *Volsunga Saga* complete the set of key **taproot texts**. Other northern European myths and legends that have survived, thanks to early literary **recyclings**, include the hero myth of Beowulf and a Finnish cycle belatedly incorporated into the *Kalevala*.

The Icelandic cycle was a vital source for **William Morris** and provided raw materials extensively **transfigured** by **J. R. R. Tolkien**, while the Teutonic cycle was revitalized and reinterpreted by German **romanticism**, including the operatic interpretations of **Richard Wagner**. Icelandic sagas provided useful models for **heroic fantasy**, employed in **Rider Haggard**'s *Eric Brighteyes* and **E. R. Eddison**'s *The Worm Ouroboros*. Henrik Ibsen's dramatic poem *Peer Gynt* (1867) borrows many of its allegorical figures from Scandinavian **folktales**. Modern writers who have made notable use of Nordic materials include **Poul Anderson**, **Stephan Grundy**, **Nigel Frith**, **Dennis McKiernan**, **Mickey Zucker Reichert**, and **Elizabeth H. Boyer**. Bernard King's trilogy *Starkadder* (1985), *Vargr-Moon* (1986), and *Death-Blinder* (1988) is one of the more graphic transfigurations of Nordic mythology's violent imagery, while Patricia Elliott's *The Ice Boy* (2002) finds a kinder face in recycling the hopeful myth of Baldur; **Lois Tilton**'s celebration of Loki in *Written in Venom* is an offbeat exercise in **literary satanism**.

NORTON, ANDRE (1912–2005). U.S. writer who began writing fantasies in the 1930s; the two novellas making up *Garan the Eternal* (1972) date from that era. She recycled medieval romances for **children** in *Rogue Reynard* (1947) and *Huon of the Horn* (1951) before turning to **sf** (refer to *HDSFL*). When her work became popular she moved back toward fantasy in such **hybrid** creations as *Witch World* (1963), about a **parallel world** where magical powers are cosmetically rationalized; the series extending from it eventually became a **shared world**. Norton's solo contributions are *Web of the Witch World* (1964), *Year of the Unicorn* (1965), *Three against the Witch World* (1965), *Warlock of the Witch World* (1967), *Sorceress of the Witch World* (1968), *The Crystal Gryphon* (1972), *Spell of the Witch World* (1972), *The Jargoon Pard* (1974), *Trey of Swords* (1977), *Zarsthor's Bane* (1978), *Lore of the Witch World* (1980), *Gryphon in Glory* (1981), *Horn Crown* (1981), *'Ware Hawk* (1983), *The Gate of the Cat* (1987), and *The Wardling of Witch World* (1996), the last-named being part of a Secrets of the Witch World series, mostly written by others.

Norton dispensed with hybridizing devices in a series displacing child characters into a variety of historical and imaginary settings, comprising *Steel Magic* (1965; aka *Gray Magic*), *Octagon Magic* (1967), *Fur Magic* (1968), *Dragon Magic* (1972), *Lavender-Green Magic* (1974), and *Red Hart Magic* (1976). A similar pattern recurs in *Here Abide Monsters* (1973). The poignant **quest** fantasy *The Hand of Llyr* (1994) is more ambitious, as are *Mirror of Destiny* (1995), in which a war between humanity and the inhabitants of **Faerie** is narrowly averted, and *The Monster's Legacy* (1996), in which an apprentice embroiderer flees to mountains formerly guarded by a magical beast. *Wind in the Stone* (1999) is an **Orphean fantasy**.

Norton wrote *Black Trillium* with **Julian May** and **Marion Zimmer Bradley**, her own sequel being *Golden Trillium* (1993). Her other collaborative endeavors outside the Witch World sequence include novels written with Phyllis Miller and **Mercedes Lackey**, the **alternative history** fantasy *The Shadow of Albion* (1999 with **Rosemary Edghill**), and a sequence including *To the King a Daughter* (2000, *Knight or Knave* [2001]) and *A Crown Disowned* (2002) written with Sasha Miller. Norton's fondness for cats is expressed in many of her works, especially *Mark of the Cat* (1994) and five *Catfantastic* anthologies (1989–99). Her short fiction is collected in *The Many Worlds of Andre Norton* (1974; aka *the Book of Andre Norton*), *High Sorcery* (1970), *Perilous Dreams* (1976), *Moon Mirror* (1988), *Grand Master's Choice* (1989), and *Wizards' Worlds* (1989).

NORTON, MARY (1903–1992). British writer best known for a popular series of **children's fantasies** featuring diminutive scavengers, comprising *The Borrowers* (1952), *The Borrowers Afield* (1955), *The Borrowers Afloat* (1959), *The Borrowers Aloft* (1961), the brief *Poor Stainless* (1966; book 1971, aka *The Last Borrowers' Story*), and *The Borrowers Avenged* (1982). She had earlier written *The Magic Bed-Knob* (1943) and its sequel *Bonfires and Broomsticks* (1947), which are better known under their omnibus title *Bedknob and Broomsticks* (1957). In the **portal fantasy** *Are All the Giants Dead?* (1975), the sceptical protagonist discovers the world to which **fairy tale** characters have retired.

NOSTRADAMUS (1503–1566). French **lifestyle fantasist** who published a volume of 353 oracular quatrains in 1555, subsequently extending the catalogue to 1,040, each one allegedly referring—with calculated ambiguity, obliquity, and obfuscation—to a single year of future history. The flexibility of their meaning has allowed serial rereadings of his works to be fitted to the expanding historical record—every manufactured hit increasing his reputation—resulting in a growing number of cameo appearances in **historical fantasies**, such as the one in **James Morrow**'s *This Is the Way the World Ends*. He is central to the screenplay-based *Nostradamus* (1996), by Knut Boeser, but peripheral to **Judith Merkle Riley**'s *The Master of All Desires*. Modern **scholarly fantasies** devoted to his work are very numerous; David Ovason's *Secrets of Nostradamus* (1997) is one of the more ingenious.

NOYES, ALFRED (1880–1958). British poet who tried to keep the flickering flame of **romanticism** alight in the 20th century. He compiled *The Magic Casement: An Anthology of Fairy Verse* (1908) and produced an early study of ***William Morris*** (1908). There are some fantasies in the short-story collections *Walking Shadows* (1918) and *The Hidden Player* (1924). *The Secret of Pooduck Island* (1943) is a **children's fantasy**. *The Devil Takes a Holiday* (1955) is an ambivalent exercise in **literary satanism**.

NYE, JODY LYNN (1957–). U.S. writer. In *The Magic Touch* (1996), a high school graduate is accepted into the Fairy Godmothers' Union as a trainee and discovers talent for making wishes come true. The transition from school to the "real" world is also modeled in two series of **humorous fantasies**, one comprising *Mythology 101* (1990), *Mythology Abroad* (1991), *Higher Mythology* (1993), and *Advanced Mythology* (1999), the other *Waking in Dreamland* (1998), *School of Light* (1999), and *The Grand Tour* (2000). She has also written several **tie-ins** and worked in collaboration with **Robert Lynn Asprin**.

– O –

O'BRIEN, FLANN (1911–1966). Pseudonym of Irish writer Brian O'Nolan, who wrote irreverent polemical journalism as "Myles na Gopaleen." His first novel, *At Swim-Two-Birds* (1939), is a marvelously complicated **metafiction** with intrusions of **Celtic fantasy**. *The Third Policeman* (written 1939–40; pub. 1967) is a **surreal** and sarcastic **posthumous fantasy**. *The Dalkey Archive* (1964) transplants some of its text into an absurdist fantasy about a mad scientist whose mastery of time threatens to precipitate the apocalypse.

OCCULT FANTASY. Occult means "hidden"; occult fantasy involves **quests** to uncover or recover the kinds of concealed knowledge to which **scholarly fantasists** throughout history have claimed to have access, including the secrets of **alchemy**, **Rosicrucianism**, the **Jewish** Cabala, and various other aspects of a loosely knit "hermetic tradition" said to have descended from the legendary Hermes Trismegistus. There was considerable interest in occult matters among Renaissance scholars, whose activities laid the groundwork for a further "occult revival" following the corrosions of the Age of Reason and the Age of Enlightenment. That new celebration began with the **Gothic** boom and **romanticism**, gathering pace throughout the 19th century; this revival was assisted as well as reflected by the depiction of Gothic villains equipped with occult knowledge—often won by **Faustian** means—in the earnest occult fantasies of such writers as **Edward Bulwer-Lytton** and **Honoré de Balzac**, and such thrillers as Hume Nisbet's *The Great Secret* (1895), *The Master of the Magicians* (1890, by Elizabeth Stuart Phelps and Herbert D. Ward), and **F. Marion Crawford**'s *The Witch of Prague*.

By the end of the century, the best-selling works of **Marie Corelli** were the tip of a huge conglomerate iceberg, whose components included **spiritualist** and **theosophical fantasy**. Literary fantasies fed gluttonously on a boom in scholarly fantasies, as did such lifestyle fantasists as the members of the Order of the Golden Dawn, who included—mostly on a temporary basis—**Arthur Machen**, **W. B. Yeats**, **A. E. Waite**, **Aleister Crowley**, and **Dion Fortune** as well as the **surrealist** painter Ithell Colquhoun, who chronicled its history in *The Sword of Wisdom: MacGregor Mathers and the Golden Dawn* (1975). The omnivorously syncretic spirit of such organizations, reflected in such works as **John Symonds**'s *The Guardian of the Threshold,* was continued by such hybridizers as Kenneth Grant, who found significant inspirational parallels between the work of Crowley and **H. P. Lovecraft**, lending a new dimension to Lovecraftian fiction, as reflected in some of the novels of the prolific scholarly fantasist Colin Wilson, notably *The Philosopher's Stone* (1969).

An inextricable confusion of overt and covert fantasy continues in such **ambiguous** occult fantasies as David Ovason's *The Zelator: The Secret Journals of Mark Hedsel* (1999), difficulties shrewdly observed by such convoluted **metafictions** as **Peter Ackroyd**'s *The House of Doctor Dee* and **Robert Irwin**'s *Satan Wants Me*. The late 20th-century boom in **secret history** novels contributed to a new resurgence of occult fantasy in such works as Arturo Perez-Reverte's *The Dumas Club* (1993; tr. 1996) and Steven Kotler's *The Angle Quickest for Flight* (1999).

ODOEVSKY, VLADIMIR (1804–1869). Russian writer who imported the seeds of German **romanticism** into his homeland, where they fell on stony ground. He published two collections of stories, one translated as *Russian Nights* (1833; tr. 1965) and the second (1844) sampled in *The Salamander and Other Gothic Tales* (1992). The latter's most significant inclusions are the striking **alchemical fantasies** "The Sylph" (1837), "The Cosmorama" (1839), and "The Salamander" (1841).

O'DONOHOE, NICK (1952–). U.S. writer. His fantasies include the Crossroads series, comprising *The Magic and the Healing* (1994),

Under the Healing Sign (1995), and *The Healing of Crossroads* (1996), in which **healers** venture into the only **secondary world** in which **unicorns** and other magical creatures can thrive—which inevitably comes under threat as traffic increases. The enterprising **humorous fantasy** *The Gnomewrench in the Dwarfworks* (1999) features an **underworld** of dwarves recruited by the Allies during World War II; *The Gnomewrench in the Peopleworks* (2000) is a sequel.

ODYSSEAN FANTASY. By virtue of his starring role in **Homer**'s **epics**, Odysseus (Ulysses, in Roman texts) became an archetype of ingenious and long-suffering heroism and one of the key symbolic figures of fantasy literature. The subgenre of Odyssean fantasy extends from straightforward **recyclings** and **transfigurations** to embrace all stories of wanderers who must overcome awkward obstacles in order to return home—as stranded protagonists of **portal fantasy** often have to do. The margins of the subgenre broaden to accommodate all stories of much-tried wanderers whose objectives involve some kind of **quest** for personal "completion." Other characters from the *Odyssey* who recur with some frequency in modern fantasy include the **monstrous** cyclops, the lotus eaters, and the enchantress Circe.

Notable transfigurations of the *Odyssey,* or incidents therefrom, include James Joyce's *Ulysses* (1922), **Eden Phillpotts**'s "Circe's Island," **John Erskine**'s *Penelope's Man,* Ernst Schnabel's *The Voyage Home* (1958), and Daniel Evan Weiss's *Honk If You Love Aphrodite* (2000). Sequels by other hands include François Fénélon's *Telemachus* (1699), *The World's Desire* by **H. Rider Haggard** and **Andrew Lang**, **John Cowper Powys**'s *Atlantis,* and Nikos Kazantzakis's *The Odyssey: A Modern Sequel* (1938; tr. 1958). Odyssean fantasies of a broader stripe include **L. Frank Baum**'s *The Wonderful Wizard of Oz,* **Barbara Hambly**'s *The Rainbow Abyss,* **Diana Wynne Jones**'s *The Homeward Bounders,* **Isabel Allende**'s *City of the Beasts,* **Paul Stewart**'s Edge Chronicles, and D. J. MacHale's Bobby Pendragon series, launched with *The Merchant of Death* (2002).

OFFUTT, ANDREW J. (1934–). U.S. writer. His early work was mostly **sf**, but the **planetary romances** *Messenger of Zhuvastou* and *Ardor on Aros* (both 1973) moved decisively into fantasy, pastiching, and parodying the excesses of **Edgar Rice Burroughs** and **Robert E. Howard**. Further exercises in the same **hybrid** vein include *Chieftain of Andor* (1976, aka *Clansman of Andor*), *My Lord Barbarian* (1977), *King*

Dragon (1980), *Deathknight* (1990), and *The Shadow of Sorcery* (1993). *Sword of the Gael* (1975) launched a series featuring one of Howard's less famous heroes, but the Conan parody *The Black Sorcerer of the Black Castle* (1976) was followed by several contributions to the ever-extending Conan series. With Richard K. Lyon, Offutt wrote a **sword and sorcery** trilogy comprising *Demon in the Mirror* (1978), *Eyes of Sarsis* (1980), and *War of the Spider* (1981); the solo trilogy comprising *The Iron Lords* (1979), *Shadows Out of Hell* (1980) and *The Lady of the Snowmist* (1983) is similar. He also edited a series of sword and sorcery **anthologies**, *Swords against Darkness* (5 vols., 1977–79).

ONIONS, OLIVER (1873–1961). British writer. Most of his short fantasies are **horror** stories (refer to *HDHL*), but his novels include the **time reversal** story *The Tower of Oblivion* (1921); *A Certain Man* (1931), about a man who acquires a magical suit of clothes; the **Gothic fantasy** *The Hand of Kornelius Voyt* (1939); and *A Shilling to Spend* (1965), about a self-perpetuating coin. His wife, Berta Ruck (1878–1978), wrote the cautionary **wish-fulfillment** fantasy *The Immortal Girl* (1925).

ORIENTAL FANTASY. A fantasy set in the Far East. "The Orient" used to include North Africa, especially for French writers, but **Arabian fantasy** is here considered a separate category, Oriental fantasy being restricted to Asia; **Hindu mythology** is also isolated as a subcategory. Important **taproot texts** for Oriental fantasy include the Indian epics the *Ramayana* (c500 BC) and the *Mahabharata* (c400 BC–AD 400) and Wu Che'ng-en's 16th-century **epic** *Journey to the West,* or *Monkey* (tr. 1942). Japanese mythology was popularized in the West by **Lafcadio Hearn**, who **recycled** some material from late 18th-century tales by Akinari Ueda, sampled in *Tales of Rain and Moon* (1974). Accounts of real and fictitious journeys to the Orient—the latter ranging from *The Marvellous Adventures of Sir John Maundeville* (c1355) to Gérard de Nerval's *Journey to the Orient* and Eça de Queiroz's *The Mandarin* (1880; tr. from Portuguese 1993)—provided a flow of inspiration for Oriental fantasy.

Notable contributors to the subgenre include **Ernest Bramah**, **Lily Adams Beck**, **Sax Rohmer**, **Talbot Mundy**, **Frank Owen**, **E. Hoffman Price**, **Charles G. Finney**, **Kara Dalkey**, **Jessica Amanda Salmonson**, and **Eric van Lustbader**; other notable works include **Margarite Yourcenar**'s *Oriental Tales*, Richard Lupoff's *Sword of the*

Demon (1977); Graham Diamond's *Samarkand* (1980), *Samarkand Dawn* (1981), and *Cinnabar* (1985); Barry Hughart's *Bridge of Birds* (1984), *The Story of the Stone* (1988), and *Eight Skilled Gentlemen* (1991); Stephen Marley's *Spirit Mirror* (1988), *Mortal Mask* (1991), and *Shadow Sisters* (1993); Kij Johnson's *The Fox Woman* (2000) and *Fudoki* (2003); Lian Hearn's *Across the Nightingale Floor* (2002), *Grass for his Pillow* (2003), and *Brilliance of the Moon* (2004); and **Leah R. Cutter**'s *Paper Mage*.

Notable Oriental fantasies by writers of Oriental descent include various items by **S. P. Somtow** and **Laurence Yep**, M. Lucie Chin's *The Fairy of Ku-She* (1988), Larissa Lai's *When Fox Is a Thousand* (1995), Kenji Nakagami's *Snakelust* (1999), Alvin Lu's *The Hell Screens* (2000), Atiq Rahimi's *Earth and Ashes* (1999; tr. 2002), and Hiromi Goto's *The Kappa Child* (2001).

ORPHEAN FANTASY. According to legend, Orpheus was a Thracian minstrel, the son of the **muse** Calliope, whose **music** upon the lyre was said to charm wild beasts. He traveled with the Argonauts, drowning out in one incident the song of the sirens. A good deal of modern fantasy invokes his name as a symbol of the quasi-**magical** power of music, but the subgenre of Orphean fantasy is primarily derived from his journey into the **underworld** in search of his wife Eurydice; Orpheus won her a reprieve but lost it again by breaching an ambiguous injunction. The subgenre takes in any similar **quest** to recover a loved one, including parents, siblings, children, or close friends. An early **recycling** of the story is **Marie de France**'s *Sir Orfeo,* which **transfigures** it as a **chivalric romance**. Other notable transfigurations include Jean Cocteau's play *Orphée* (1927), Constantine Fitzgibbon's *The Golden Age* (1975), **Russell Hoban**'s *The Medusa Frequency,* **Francesca Lia Block**'s *Ecstasia,* and Chet Williamson's *Second Chance* (2002). Notable examples of the broader genre include John Gordon's *The Edge of the World* (1983), Edith Pattou's *Hero's Song* (1991), and *Fire Arrow* (1997), **Salman Rushdie**'s *The Ground beneath Her Feet,* and **Chris Wooding**'s *Poison*.

OWEN, FRANK (1893–1968). U.S. writer who also used the pseudonym "Roswell Williams." His **oriental** novels *The House Mother* (1929), *Rare Earth* (1931), and *The Scarlet Hill* (1941) have only fugitive elements of fantasy, but the lapidary short stories in *The Wind That Tramps the World* (1929) and *The Purple Sea* (1930) are far more explicit. Those in *Della Wu, Chinese Courtezan and Other Oriental Love Tales* (1931) and *A Husband for Kutani* (1938) are longer and less fantastic, but the latter includes the notable **alchemical fantasy** "Doctor Shen Fu." *The Porcelain Magician* (1948) is an eclectic sampler. Owen also wrote several collections of **children's fantasies** with his wife Ethel, including *Coat Tales from the Pockets of the Happy Giant* (1927), *The Dream Hills of Happy Country* (1928), *Windblown Stories* (1930), and *The Blue Highway* (1932). Ethel Owen's solo works in a similar vein include *The Pumpkin People* (1927) and *Hallowe'en Tales & Games* (1928).

OZICK, CYNTHIA (1928–). U.S. writer. Her short fiction includes numerous items of **Jewish fantasy**, some of which are collected in *The Pagan Rabbi and Other Stories* (1971). Items of a similar ilk are mingled with other materials, in *Bloodshed and Three Novellas* (1976) and *Levitation: Five Fictions* (1982). In *The Puttermesser Papers* (1997), a woman constructs a **golem**.

– P –

PAIN, BARRY (1864–1928). British writer best known as a **humorist**. Most of his collections contain some whimsical fantasies, the most notable items including "The Celestial Grocery" in *In a Canadian Canoe* (1891), "The Glass of Supreme Moments" in *Stories and Interludes* (1891), the **erotic fantasy** "The Moon-Slave" in *Stories in the Dark* (1901), and "The Tree of Death" in *Short Stories of Today and Yesterday* (1928). *The One Before* (1902) is an **Ansteyan** comedy tracking the chaos caused by a ring that causes everyone who puts it on to take on the personalities of its previous wearer. *An Exchange of Souls* (1911) is a **hybrid/science fantasy** about an experiment in personality transfer. The title novella of *The New Gulliver and Other Stories* (1913) is a grotesque **satire**. The allegorical *Going Home: Being the Fantastic Romance of the Girl with Angel Eyes and the Man Who Had Wings* (1921) is an unusual **sentimental fantasy**.

PAN. The god of **Arcadia**. He became a frequent presence in late 19th-century English literature by virtue of his identification with both the seductive and frightening aspects of "nature," which made him a convenient symbolic adversary of civilization and progress. His utility was further increased by the appropriation of his physical appearance into Christian images of the **Devil**, making him a key figure of disguised **literary**

satanism. He became a key figure in the iconography of the Aesthetic movement; hymns of praise dedicated to him include **Oscar Wilde**'s "Pan" (1881) and **Edgar Jepson**'s *The Horned Shepherd,* while Henry Nevinson's *The Plea of Pan* (1901) and **Eden Phillpotts**'s *Pan and the Twins* offered more cautious endorsements. His invocation became a central pillar of the **lifestyle fantasies** of **Aleister Crowley** and **Dion Fortune**. His sinister aspects are conserved in such stories as **Arthur Machen**'s "The Great God Pan," E. F. Benson's *The Angel of Pain* (1905), Alice and Claude Askew's *The Devil and the Crusader* (1909), Stephen McKenna's *The Oldest God* (1926), and **Lord Dunsany**'s *The Blessing of Pan*. More recent manifestations—including **Tom Robbins**'s *Jitterbug Perfume* and **Donna Jo Napoli**'s *The Great God Pan*—continue to make much of his ambiguity.

Pan's associates, the satyrs (fauns, in Roman terminology), are routinely confused with the drunken Sileni similarly associated with Dionysus, whose singular incarnation Silenus became the central figure of the "satyr plays" ancestral to the tradition of **satire**. European writers like **Anatole France**, **Rémy de Gourmont**, Théo Varlet, Ruben Dario, and Fernando Pessoa used them in the way that British writers used Pan (1888–1935); British representations, like **Arthur Ransome**'s "The Ageing Faun" (1912) and Oswald Couldrey's "The Inquisitive Satyr" (1914) tend to diminish them to ineffectual cuteness; **Norman Douglas**'s *In the Beginning* is more respectful. Their female counterparts in Arcadia, the nymphs, are less well represented, although dryads—nymphs associated with groves or individual trees—crop up in such **sentimental fantasies** as Justin McCarthy's *The Dryad* (1905), **A. Merritt**'s "The Woman of the Wood" (1926), and E. V. de Fontmell's *Forbidden Marches* (1929).

PAOLINI, CHRISTOPHER (1984–). U.S. wunderkind whose novel *Eragon* (2003; book 2004)—the first part of the Inheritance trilogy—was self-published on his alagaesia.com website before being extensively publicized by a commercial publisher. Its youthful hero finds a mysterious stone, which draws him into an **epic** adventure with **dragons**, **elves**, and various monsters; he eventually finds his vocation as a dragon rider.

PARALLEL WORLD. A world situated "alongside" our own. The most obvious **mythical** examples are **Faerie** and the classical **underworld**. Movement between the **primary world** and parallel **secondary worlds** forms the basis of most modern **portal fantasies**. The notion was complicated in the 19th century by pseudoscientific notions of an "astral plane" and the mathematical jargon of "dimensions," the latter allowing its adoption into **sf** (refer to *HDSFL*)—which soon took aboard the idea of an infinite **multiverse** of parallel worlds.

PARANORMAL ROMANCE. A nascent subgenre of generic romantic fiction that began a spectacular period of growth in the 1990s, inspired by the success of **timeslip** romances by such writers as **Barbara Erskine**. Extreme **sentimental fantasies** had long embodied the conviction that love can defy the laws of nature—a conviction maintained even by such sceptical analyses of the mythology of modern romance as **Margaret Irwin**'s *These Mortals*—but commodified romantic fiction remained stubbornly naturalistic until the 1980s, with occasional rare (and bizarre) exceptions like H. M. E. Clamp's *Rebel Angels* (c1936). Even the poplar U.S. subgenre of "Gothic romances" rarely admitted supernatural materials, in spite of the example set by **tie-ins** to the successful supernatural TV soap opera *Dark Shadows*.

A significant threshold was crossed when the prominent genre writer **Nora Roberts** published the timeslip romance trilogy begun with *Time Was* (1989). Several of her peers, including Madeline Baker, began to produce timeslip romances on a regular basis—Baker's, begun with *Whisper in the Wind* (1991), brought western settings into the **hybrid** mix. Romance publishers issued several **Christmas fantasy** anthologies in the early 1990s, including *A Christmas Kiss* (Zebra, 1992) and *Angel Christmas* (Topaz, 1995), testing the market further with such hybrid anthologies as *Dreamscape* (Harlequin, 1993), *Enchanted Crossings* (Love Spell, 1994), *Love Potion* (Jove, 1995), *Timeswept Brides* (Jove, 1996), and *Bewitched* (Jove, 1997).

Madeline Baker attached the byline "Amanda Ashley" to a long series of **vampire** romances, begun with *Embrace the Night* (1995). Another writer of vampire romances, Maggie Shayne, began a similar series featuring **witches** with *Eternity* (1998). One popular subgenre ripe for such crossovers was the Regency romance, which was supernaturalized in such novels as Sandra Heath's *Marigold's Marriages* (1999) and Barbara Metzger's *Miss Treadwell's Talent* (1999) and *The Painted Lady* (2001). The range continued to broaden in such anthologies as *Faery Magic* (Zebra, 1998), *Haunting Hearts* (Jove, 1998), and *Once upon a Rose* (2001). Zebra's *Once upon a Waltz* (2001), featuring Regency fantasies, was quickly followed by Kensington's *His Eternal Kiss* (2002), featuring Regency vampires. *Out of This World* (Jove, 2001) took in

Roberts's **sf** byline "J. D. Robb" and **Laurel K. Hamilton**. By this time, the Romance Writers of America had a Paranormal Special Interest chapter and introduced a "Paranormal" category into its annual awards, thus securing the nascent subgenre's name.

Most paranormal romances retained **intrusive** and **portal fantasy** frameworks to begin with, but the secondary worlds of **immersive fantasy** offered such perfect venues for rags-to-riches romance that almost all **commodified fantasies** included romance subplots. When Tor and the Harlequin imprint Silhouette launched labeled paranormal romance lines in 2004, they dramatically increased the scope for the introduction of immersive generic romances. Silhouette tested the possibility in two anthologies trailing the new line in 2003; the authors in *Charmed Destinies* included **Mercedes Lackey** and sf writer Catherine Asaro, while *When Darkness Falls* featured **Tanith Lee**. Asaro went to write *The Charmed Sphere* (2004) and edit a further showcase **anthology** of generic **hybrids,** *Irresistible Forces* (2004).

Other writers who have made notable contributions to the subgenre include **Caroline Stevermer**, **Anne Logston**, **Karen Fox**, and **Kristine Kathryn Rusch** (as Katherine Grayson). Notable Regency hybrids include Karen Harbaugh's trilogy *Cupid's Mistake* (1997), *Cupid's Darts* (1998), and *Cupid's Kiss* (1999). Vampire romances include Mary Janice Davidson's *Undead and Unwed* (2004) and Katie MacAlister's *Sex and the Single Vampire* (2004). Timeslip romances include R. Garcia y Robertson's *Knight Errant* (2001) and *Lady Ribyn* (2003). Garthia Anderson's *Spellbound in Seattle* (2003) is an **alternative history** romance. Julie Kenner's *Aphrodite's Kiss* (2001), *Aphrodite's Passion* (2002), *Aphrodite's Secret* (2003), and *Aphrodite's Flame* (2004) are fantasized mystery romances.

The fantasization of commodified romantic fiction inevitably brought the mythology of romantic love into sharper focus; exaggerating its ideological assumptions could not help but call them into question. Inevitably, the boom in paranormal romance immediately called forth such cynical responses as d. g. k. goldberg's . . . *Doomed to Repeat It* (2002).

PAXSON, DIANA L. (1943–). U.S. writer. The series comprising *Lady of Light* (1983), *Lady of Darkness* (1983), *Silverhair the Wanderer* (1986), *The Earthstone* (1987), *The Sea Star* (1988), *The Wind Crystal* (1990), and *The Jewel of Fire* (1992) is set in California in the wake of a catastrophe that has paved the way for a magical renaissance.

Brisingamen (1984) and *The Paradise Tree* (1987) are **contemporary fantasies** set in the same milieu. The **Celtic fantasy** *White Mare, Red Stallion* (1986) and the **Arthurian fantasy** *The White Raven* (1988) were followed by a trilogy of a similar ilk **recycling** the legend of Finn MacCool, written with **Adrienne Martine-Barnes**: *Master of Earth and Water* (1993), *The Shield between the Worlds* (1994), and *Sword of Fire and Shadow* (1995).

The Serpent's Tooth (1991) is a **Shakespearean** fantasy. The trilogy comprising *The Wolf and the Raven* (1993), *The Dragons of the Rhine* (1995), and *The Lord of Horses* is a **Nordic fantasy** recycling the *Nibelunglied*. The Hallowed Isle series, comprising *The Book of the Sword* (1999), *The Book of the Spear* (1999), *The Book of the Cauldron* (1999), and *The Book of the Stone* (2000) is another Arthurian fantasy. Paxson continued **Marion Zimmer Bradley**'s Avalon series in *Priestess of Avalon* (2000) and *Ancestors of Avalon* (2004); she took over Bradley's anthology series *Sword and Sorceress* from volume 21 (2004).

PEAKE, MERVYN (1911–1968). British writer and artist. The trilogy comprising *Titus Groan* (1946), *Gormenghast* (1950), and *Titus Alone* (1959; rev. 1970) is an archetypal example of modern **Gothic** grotesquerie (refer to *HDHL*). The associated novella *Boy in Darkness* (1976) is a formal **allegory** with elements of **animal fantasy**. *Mr Pye* (1953) is a lighthearted **religious fantasy** in which the hero is afflicted with angelic and diabolical stigmata as his moral condition changes. A few more fantasies, including poetry and items designed for children, are reprinted in *Peake's Progress: Selected Writings and Drawings* (1978; rev. 1981), edited by his widow, Maeve Gilmore.

PEARCE, PHILIPPA (1920–). British writer. Her work for younger **children** includes some marginal fantasies and **recycled** tales, but her crucial contribution to fantasy literature is the classic **timeslip** fantasy *Tom's Midnight Garden* (1958), in which the protagonist meets a girl from Victorian times in a ghostly garden and embarks upon a problematic but enlightening relationship. *The Way to Sattin Shore* (1983) is also a timeslip fantasy. The stories in *The Shadow-Cage and Other Tales of the Supernatural* (1977) and *Who's Afraid? and Other Strange Stories* (1986) tend toward **horror** fiction; they are reprinted with other material in the omnibus *Familiar and Haunting* (2002).

PENNICOTT, JOSEPHINE (?–). Australian writer and artist. The **dark/portal fantasy** trilogy comprising *Circle of Nine* (2001), *Bride of the*

Stone (2002), and *A Fire in the Shell* (2003) features an unusual **secondary world** whose **goddesses** are in conflict with fallen **angels**.

PERRAULT, CHARLES (1628–1703). French civil servant. He dabbled in verse **fabulation** before publishing his classic collection of moralistic adaptations of folktales *Histoires ou contes de temps passés* (1697; tr. under various titles, most famously *Tales of Mother Goose*). Its success, following that of **Madame d'Aulnoy**, prompted a flood of similar adaptations and new tales in the same vein. Perrault's versions of "The Sleeping Beauty," "Little Red Riding Hood" (which he seems to have invented), "Bluebeard," "Cinderella," "Puss-in-Boots," and "Hop o'my Thumb" became standard, and his notion that traditional tales might profitably be rewritten to provide educative tools for the "civilization" of children helped to shape the culture of modern childhood. **Angela Carter**'s *The Fairy Tales of Charles Perrault* (1977) is one of many modern versions. Little Red Riding Hood became one of the most frequently transfigured **fairy tales**, testifying to Perrault's skill as a synthesist (although those that take the wolf's side testify to his limitations as a moralist); notable examples include Anthony Schmidt's *Darkest Desire* (1998), Manlio Argueta's *Little Red Riding Hood* (tr. from Spanish 1998), and Debbie Viguié's *Scarlet Moon* (2004).

PERUTZ, LEO (1884–1957). Austrian writer exiled in 1938, settling in Israel. He was one of the most prolific and versatile fantasists of the early 20th century. The novel translated as *From Nine to Nine* (1918; tr. 1926) is a **posthumous fantasy**. *The Marquis de Bolibar* (1920; tr. 1926, aka *The Marquis of Bolivar*) is a **historical fantasy** featuring the **Wandering Jew**. *The Master of the Day of Judgment* (1923; tr. 1939) is a **moralistic/visionary fantasy**; *The Virgin's Brand* (1933; tr. 1934) is a companion piece reversing the hallucinogenic effect. *Saint Peter's Snow* (1933; 1990) features a plot by the German government to use drugs for social control; it was immediately banned by the Nazis. In *Turlupin* (1923; tr. 1996), an aristocrat's fate is magically bound up with a mango tree. *By Night under the Stone Bridge* (1953; tr. 1989) is a historical fantasy set in medieval Prague. *Leonardo's Judas* (1957; tr. 1989) is a **religious fantasy** picking up themes from the untranslated *Die Geburt des Antichrist* (1921).

PHILLPOTTS, EDEN (1862–1960). British writer. His early work was mostly humorous, including items collected in *Fancy Free* (1901) and

Transit of the Red Dragon (1903). *A Deal with the Devil* (1895) is a **Faustian fantasy** in the manner of **F. Anstey**. *My Laughing Philosopher* (1896) records imaginary conversations between the protagonist and a bronze bust, foreshadowing the Epicurean sensibility that Phillpotts subsequently extrapolated in a long series of fabular **classical fantasies**.

The Girl and the Faun (1916) is a poignant **Arcadian fantasy**. *Evander* (1919) is a rare extrapolation of Nietzschean **dualism**. *Pan and the Twins* (1922) extrapolates a similar ideological conflict, more lightheartedly than **Anatole France**'s championship of satyrs against Christians. In *The Treasures of Typhon* (1924), a halfhearted Epicurean undertakes a **quest** for a magical plant. *Circe's Island* (1925) is an amalgam of **Odyssean** and **Orphean fantasy**. In *The Miniature* (1926), the classical gods deliver a harsh verdict on the philosophical evolution of humankind—a theme carried forward in *The Owl of Athene* (1936), where they decide to subject the species to an acid test. *Arachne* (1927) **recycles** the eponymous legend but contrives a better moral. *Alycone* (1930) chronicles the misadventures of an inept poet.

The Lavender Dragon (1923) is a **moralistic fantasy** in which a benevolent dragon steals lonely humans to populate a utopia. *The Apes* (1927) is an ironic **allegory** of evolution. *The Flint Heart* (1910) and *Golden Island* (1938) are **children's fantasies**.

PHOENIX. A fabulous bird; it reproduced by a process of self-renewal involving the consumption of its old body by fire, thus giving it an important symbolism carried from **classical** sources into **alchemical** philosophy and then into such ***contes philosophiques*** as **Voltaire**'s "The Princess of Babylon." It features in such modern fantasies as **E. Nesbit**'s *The Phoenix and the Carpet,* which inspired Edward Ormondroyd's *David and the Phoenix* (1957); the **Ballantine Adult Fantasy Series** volume *Double Phoenix* (1971), which combined **Roger Lancelyn Green**'s *From the World's End* (1948); Edmund Cooper's "The Firebird"; and **Cherith Baldry**'s trilogy begun with *The Book of the Phoenix.*

PICARESQUE FANTASY. "Picaresque" is the term given to a genre of fiction originated in Spain that followed the exploits of rogues and thieves with mock-ironic sympathy. It has analogues in **Arabian fantasy** in the spirit of **Antoine Gallande**, exaggerated in such pastiches as **Captain Marryat**'s *The Pacha of Many Tales*. The strategy never died out, but it became morally problematic as respect for law and government increased. In **secondary worlds**, however, it is easy to represent ruling classes and their law-enforcement agencies as totally corrupt and thus make "criminals" heroic. The strategy is common in Arabian fantasy and was imported into **sword and sorcery** fiction by **Fritz Leiber**, **Jack Vance**, and **Michael Shea**.

Picaresque fantasy's popularity was boosted by the commercial success of the *Thieves' World* **shared world** series, which echoes in the work of such writers as **Anne Logston** and **Juliet E. McKenna** and in Megan Whalen Turner's *The Thief* (1996), Lynn Flewelling's Nightrunners series (1996–99), Beth Hilgartner's *A Business of Ferrets* (2000), and *Parliament of Owls* (2002), **Eve Forward**'s *Villains by Necessity,* and Mindy L. Klasky's Glasswright series (2000–2003). As **Diana Wynne Jones**'s *Tough Guide to Fantasyland* points out, the thieves of **commodified fantasy** are usually organized into guilds like those in **Trudi Canavan**'s Black Magician trilogy; the assassin's guild is a prominent feature of **Terry Pratchett**'s Discworld series.

PIERCE, MEREDITH ANN (1958–). U.S. writer for **young adults**. *The Darkangel* (1982) is a vivid **psychological fantasy** featuring a seductive **vampire**; *A Gathering of Gargoyles* (1984) and *The Pearl of the Soul of the World* (1990) are sequels. The Firebringer trilogy, comprising *Birth of the Firebringer* (1985), *Dark Moon* (1992), and *The Son of Summer Stars* (1996), features a **unicorn** prince involved in a similarly striking conflict between Good and Evil. *The Woman Who Loved Reindeer* (1985) is a **messianic fantasy**. *Where the Wild Geese Go* (1988) and *Treasure at the Heart of the Tanglewood* (2001) are **quest** fantasies featuring misfit children. Her short fiction is sampled in *Waters Luminous and Deep* (2004).

PIERCE, TAMORA (1954–). U.S. writer for **young adults**. In the series comprising *Alanna: The First Adventure* (1983), *In the Hand of the Goddess* (1984), *The Woman Who Rides Like a Man* (1986, aka *The Girl Who Rides Like a Man*), and *Lioness Rampant* (1988), young protagonists of opposite sexes trade places in order to seek their preferred vocations. Two further series set in the same **secondary world**—one comprising *Wild Magic* (1992), *Wolf-Speaker* (1994), *The Emperor Mage* (1994), and *Realm of the Gods* (1996), the other *First Test* (1999), *Page* (2000), *Squire* (2001), and *Lady Knight* (2002)—similarly offer feminized adventures in **magic**. *Trickster's Choice* (2003) launched a further series in the same milieu.

The Circle of Magic quartet, comprising *Sandry's Book* (1997, aka *The Magic in the Weaving*), *Tris's Book* (1998, aka *The Power in the Storm*), *Daja's Book* (1998), and *Briar's Book* (1999), tracks the education of four magically talented children—a theme continued in The Circle Opens series, comprising *Magic Steps* (2000), *Street Magic* (2001), *Cold Fire* (2002), *Shatterglass* (2003), and *Trickster's Queen* (2004).

PINKWATER, DANIEL M. (1941–). U.S. writer of **children's fiction**, much of it cast as **hybrid** or **chimerical/science fantasy**, almost all of which is characterized by a distinctive **humor** that retains echoes of the British **nonsense** tradition. Notable examples include *Wizard Crystal* (1973), *Magic Camera* (1974), *I Was a Second Grade Werewolf* (1983), *Devil in the Drain* (1984), *Lizard Music* (1988), *Borgel* (1990), and *Wempires* (1991). A novel for adults, *The Afterlife Diet* (1995), is a **satirical/afterlife fantasy**.

PLANETARY ROMANCE. A term that has replaced **interplanetary romance** in the parlance of **sf** criticism (refer to *HDSFL*) as a categorization of exotic adventure stories in the tradition pioneered by **Edgar Rice Burroughs**. The subgenre is host to a large number of exercises in hybrid **science fantasy**. It provided light cosmetic disguise for exercises in **sword and sorcery** when genre fantasy was not yet established as a viable marketing category, being used in that fashion by such writers as Leigh Brackett, **Lin Carter**, and **Andrew J. Offutt**, following a precedent set by **Edwin Lester Arnold** even before Burroughs popularized the form. The use of planetary romance for **fabulations** of a more sophisticated kind was pioneered by **Ray Bradbury**, also following precedents set by such writers as **E. R. Eddison**. Extraterrestrial settings continue to be employed for some such exercises, including Rosemary Kirstein's *The Steerswoman* (1989) and its sequels, and Anselm Audley's Aquasilva trilogy, comprising *Heresy* (2001), *Inquisition* (2002), and *Crusade* (2003).

POE, EDGAR ALLAN (1809–1849). U.S. writer, a key figure in the evolution of modern short fiction and a pioneer of several subsequently commercialized genres, most notably detective fiction, **sf** (refer to *HDSFL*), and psychological **horror** fiction (refer to *HDHL*). His importance in the development of fantasy outside the last two categories is less obvious, but his intense interest in matters of abnormal psychology and his development of a distinctively **decadent** style were highly influential. His **humorous fantasies** about the **Devil**'s work, including "Bon Bon" (1832), "The Duc de l'Omellette" (1832), "The Devil in the Belfry" (1839), and "Never Bet the Devil Your Head" (1841), are his purest genre products, but the exotic **erotic fantasies** "Berenice" (1835), "Morella" (1835), and "Ligeia" (1838); the quintessential decadent fantasies "The Fall of the House of Usher" (1839) and "The Masque of the Red Death" (1842); the **doppelgänger** story "William Wilson" (1840); and the intense narrative poem "The Raven" (1845) all provided exemplars of the greatest importance. The title of his first collection, *Tales of the Grotesque and Arabesque* (2 vols., 1840), was chosen to signify their attempt to establish a new post-Romantic ambience, which reached its philosophical and stylistic extremes in such studies as "The Imp of the Perverse" (1845) and "The Domain of Arnhem" (1847).

POETRY. **Myth** and **legend** have always been key sources of poetic inspiration and imagery; by virtue of its origins in such forms as the **epic**, the popular **ballad**, and **Marie de France**'s lays, fantasy has always been exemplified in poetic forms. Such subgenres as the **fable** and the **chivalric romance** evolved from poetry into prose and retained sturdy connections into the 20th century. Folklore has also been a significant source of poetic imagery, warranting such collections as **A. E. Waite**'s *Elfin Music;* **Charles Perrault**'s pioneering collection of **fairy tales** included some verse items; and "nursery rhymes" evolved alongside other aspects of **children's fantasy**, laying groundwork for the verse elements of **nonsense**. Folk **music** is still a thriving genre, its imagery—especially in respect of **Celtic** sources—still richly permeated by fantasy.

The poetry of the **Romantic** movement was heavily impregnated with fantasy motifs, as exemplified by **M. G. Lewis**'s *Tales of Wonder;* such motifs were especially evident in Britain in the works of **Walter Scott**, **Lord Byron**, **Percy Shelley**, and **John Keats**, and they were carried forward into the work of the pre-Raphaelites and **Algernon Swinburne**—taking a sidestep into the nonsense of **Edward Lear**—and thence to such reactionary Romantics as **W. B. Yeats**, **William Hope Hodgson**, and **Alfred Noyes**. In France, such imagery was carried from the works of **Charles Nodier**, **Théophile Gautier**, and Charles Leconte de Lisle into the symbolist works of **Charles Baudelaire**, **Gérard de Nerval**, and Stéphane Mallarmé; there were also parallel developments in Germany. Narrative poems within this tradition that made highly influential contributions to the evolution of fantasy literature include

Scott's *Lay of the Last Minstrel*, **Samuel Taylor Coleridge**'s *Rime of the Ancient Mariner,* **Christina Rossetti**'s *Goblin Market,* and Arthuriana by Alfred Lord Tennyson, **Charles Williams**, and many others.

The evolution of significant subgenres of popular fantasy in ***Weird Tales*** was closely associated with poetic activity; **H. P. Lovecraft** and **Robert E. Howard** both write neo-Romantic poetry, while **Clark Ashton Smith** was primarily a poet, working in a decadent tradition established by such West Coast Bohemians as Ambrose Bierce, Edward Markham, and **George Sterling**. Sterling's "A Wine of Wizardry" was sufficiently significant as a "manifesto" for literary fantasy that **Lin Carter** reprinted it in one of his showcase anthologies (along with **Oscar Wilde**'s "The Sphinx").

The 20th-century decline in the status of poetry relative to that of prose has reduced the influence of poetry within the context of fantasy literature, but its produce remains prolific, even in such demanding genres as the epic. Writers who conceive of themselves as poets who write prose "on the side" often prefer to deal in fantasy, whether for adults—like **Sir Arthur Quiller-Couch**, **George Mackay Brown**, and **Peter Redgrove**—or for children, like **Walter de la Mare**, Randall Jarrell, **John Masefield**, **Ted Hughes**, and **Nancy Willard**.

POLDER. A term derived from Dutch meaning a tract of land reclaimed from the sea and protected from reinundation by dikes. It is employed in the Clute/Grant *Encyclopedia* to refer to an artificially maintained enclave isolated—usually by magic—from the world at large. Many such enclaves are microcosmic **secondary worlds** hidden within the **primary** one, connected to it by some kind of **portal**; polders of this kind are often **Arcadian** tracts insulated against the march of progress and its **thinning** effect. Secondary worlds often have polders of their own, including ordered enclaves protected from corrosive **Chaos**.

POLITICAL FANTASY. A subgenre whose **utopian** mode is mostly extrapolated into modern **sf** (refer to *HDSFL*), and with **satirical** examples often categorized as sf even when they employ narrative spaces more usually associated with fantasy. The association of modern fantasy with quasi-medieval settings derived from **fairy tales** and **chivalric romances** has standardized feudal social systems to the extent that the politics of fantasy often seems ultraconservative, thus robbing it of the authority to make any meaningful comment on modern sociopolitical systems or to indulge in any kind of socially progressive thought experiment. Critics who assume that the "escapist" aspect of fantasy involves an intellectually treasonous disengagement with political thought and action—including sf admirers like Darko Suvin—tend to consider this conservatism final proof of the essential worthlessness of the entire genre, in spite of the extravagant use of fantasy in political satire and the writings of such political activists as **Benjamin Disraeli** and **Upton Sinclair**.

Fantasy's seeming commitment to the ideals of monarchy and aristocracy is, however, superficial; the order of hierarchical privilege retained by many genre fantasies tends to be chimerically founded on a distinctively modern regard for human and civil rights. The good kings of genre fantasy tend to carry out their functions in a presidential manner and tend to hold more liberal views than the majority of actual U.S. presidents, let alone actual kings. One consequence of this is that although there are relatively few modern fantasies that qualify as political fantasies in the sense that they exemplify alternative systems of government, there are a great many with feudal templates that serve as battlegrounds—or at least playgrounds—for discussion of the kinds of responsibilities that ought to go hand in hand with the exercise of power and the possession of privilege.

Revolutions in **Faerie** are rare—although they do occur, as in **Gerald Bullett**'s *Mr Godly beside Himself*—but that does not necessarily mean that the rhetoric of **fairy tales** is irredeemably committed to nostalgia for an obsolete political order. Indeed, the complaints made by such historians as **Jack Zipes** and **Marina Warner**, and the crusades mounted by such writers as **Angela Carter** and **Donna Jo Napoli** to subvert the sexual politics of traditional tales, take it for granted that such tales can and ought to be formulated in such a way as to champion oppositional positions. Assaults on the nostalgic conservatism of **J. R. R. Tolkien** and **C. S. Lewis** mounted by such writers as **Dennis McKiernan**, **Philip Pullman**, and **China Miéville** similarly assume that it is a disposable and problematic feature of the genre.

POLLACK, RACHEL (1945–). U.S. writer. *Unquenchable Fire* (1988) and its sequel *Temporary Agency* (1994) are set in an **alternative** world where magical practices are regulated by guilds. *Godmother Night* (1996) is an ambitious **fairy tale/transfiguration**. Her short fiction is collected in *Burning Sky* (1998). Pollack coedited *Tarot Tales* (1989) with Caitlin Matthews.

POLLOCK, WALTER HERRIES (1850–1926). British writer, mostly in a **humorous** vein. With his mother, Lady Julia Pollock, and W. K. Clifford, he compiled *The Little People and Other Tales* (1874). With **Walter Besant**, he wrote the Ansteyan novella "Sir Jocelyn's Cap" (1884–85; reprinted in *King Zub*, 1897), and with **Andrew Lang**, he produced the **Rider Haggard** parody *He* (1887). His collaborations with the U.S. writer J. Brander Matthews included the comic fantasy "Edged Tools" (1886). He wrote *The Were-Wolf: A Romantic Play in One Act* (1898) with Lilian Moubrey. His solo works include a novella about a family curse, "Lilith" (1874–75), which was reprinted as the first item in *The Picture's Secret: A Story, to Which Is Added an Episode in the Life of Mr Latimer* (1883), along with a **Faustian fantasy**. Both items were reprinted again in *A Nine Men's Morrice: Stories Collected and Recollected* (1889), the second being reseparated into two constituent parts. "The Phantasmatograph" (1899) is a hybrid **science fantasy** about a camera that can record thoughts and fantasies.

PORTAL FANTASY. A story in which transitions occur between the **primary world** and a **secondary** one. The portal may be purely symbolic—like the gates of ivory and horn that serve as fabular entrances to worlds of **visionary fantasy**—but material ones evolved as a means of avoiding the necessity for long voyages to **lost lands** and became vital facilitating devices once the Earth's surface had run out of terra incognita. Tunnels and **mirrors** are among the most common portal devices. Portal fantasy was adopted by Farah Mendlesohn as a fundamental category in "Toward a Taxonomy of Fantasy" (2001); its narrative strategy is intermediate between those of **intrusive** and **immersive fantasy**, remaining convenient because it allows the reader to view a fantasy world from a more or less familiar viewpoint rather than exercising the much more considerable act of identification required by immersion. A reader's experience of a secondary world is significantly different if it is presented in a portal fantasy rather than an immersive fantasy.

Mendlesohn initially defined portal fantasies rather narrowly, excluding portals that "leak," but wisely relented; such a move sets aside many accounts of **Faerie** and many **contemporary fantasies** where boundaries between the mundane and the fantastic are ill defined. Portal fantasies are usually accounts of educative, and sometimes **allegorical**, **quests**. Early examples include **George MacDonald**'s *Phantastes,*

William Morris's "The Hollow Land," Mrs. Molesworth's *The Cuckoo Clock* (1877), Somerset Maugham's "The Choice of Amyntas" (1899), and **L. Frank Baum**'s *The Wonderful Wizard of Oz*. It was imported to pulp fiction by **A. Merritt** but proved equally useful to such writers as **James Branch Cabell**, and it was repopularized in **children's fiction** by **C. S. Lewis**, whose use of a wardrobe as a portal to Narnia has become a paradigm example of the device. **Norton Juster**'s *Magic Tollbooth* is another cardinal example.

Unlike intrusive fantasies, which present mysteries to be "unpicked" or adversaries to be exorcized, portal fantasies typically present obstacle courses to be "navigated," sometimes becoming more rather than less mysterious in the process. This pattern is not only typical of fantasies that move into **parallel worlds** but also of the great majority of **timeslip** fantasies. The compass of the fundamental story arc is, however, always pointed homeward, whereas characters in an **immersive fantasy** must find a destiny of their own within their own framework of normality.

POSTHUMOUS FANTASY. A term used by some critics to describe all stories in which the protagonists experience some kind of life after death, but more narrowly defined in the Clute/Grant *Encyclopedia* to refer to stories with protagonists who are slow to realize that they are dead and that they have embarked upon a journey into the unknown. Posthumous fantasies are typically set in a version of the **primary world**, albeit one that may undergo a gradual metamorphosis, while **afterlife fantasies** are set in some kind of **secondary world**. A significant precedent was set by Ambrose Bierce's "An Occurrence at Owl Creek Bridge" (1891), which employs its protagonist's belated awareness of his death as a "twist in the tail" ending—a device repeated as frequently as the growth of unfamiliar audiences will allow. The device has been standardized in the notion that **ghosts** are existentially becalmed, being unable to "move on" to a secondary afterlife until they can tear themselves away from earthly concerns.

Notable examples of posthumous fantasy include Sutton Vane's *Outward Bound* (play 1923; novel 1929), Rebecca West's *Harriet Hume* (1929), Michael Maurice's *Marooned* (1932), Claude Houghton's *Julian Grant Loses His Way* (1933), James Gould Cozzens's *Castaway* (1934), **Charles Williams**'s *All Hallow's Eve,* G. W. Stonier's *Memoirs of a Ghost* (1947), **Flann O'Brien**'s *The Third Policeman,* William Golding's *Pincher Martin* (1956), **Gene Wolfe**'s *Peace,* **Richard Grant**'s

Tex and Molly in the Afterlife, and Joseph Skibell's *A Blessing on the Moon* (1997). There is an interesting subcategory of stories that invite interpretation as posthumous fantasies although no explicit discovery is ever made; it includes Ruthven Todd's *The Lost Traveller* (1943) and Michel Bernanos's *The Other Side of the Mountain* (1967; tr. 1968). Another interesting subcategory consists of stories with protagonists who remain on Earth as servants of **Death**, including **Selma Lagerlöf**'s *Thy Soul Shall Bear Witness!,* **L. Ron Hubbard**'s *Death's Deputy,* and Gordon Houghton's *Damned If You Do* (2000).

POSTMODERNISM. A term that overspilled literary critical theory in the 1980s, ambitious to embrace every aspect of contemporary culture. "Modernism" in this view is with the extent to which the world is "knowable" within the limits of our instruments of discovery. Postmodernism transforms such questions by challenging the basic assumption that the world is sufficiently definite and stable to be known whatever instruments might be brought to the task, thus assuming that all cultural artifacts are best understood as constituting an ideologically guided system of convenient delusions.

The related concept of "postmodernity" suggests that modern culture has entered a distinctive stage in which simulations have lost contact with any allegedly represented reality, referring only to one another—the literary reflection of this being the increasing popularity and incipient dominance of **metafiction**. Modern fantasy writers, seen from this viewpoint, are all participants in the same linguistic games of pastiche and transfiguration, and some are very conscious of the fact; it is the latter group who are most susceptible to consideration as "postmodern fantasy writers." They include **Paul Auster**, **John Barth**, **Andrew Crumey**, **Steve Erickson**, and **Steven Millhauser**. Other notable examples of conspicuously postmodern fantasy include Matthew Remski's *Silver* (1998) and Jack O'Connell's *Word Made Flesh* (1999).

POTTER, BEATRIX (1866–1943). British writer and illustrator who produced a classic series of **moralistic/animal fantasies** for **children**, stories that exhibit a distinctive pattern of calculated anthropomorphization. The most notable inclusions are *The Tale of Peter Rabbit* (1901), *The Tailor of Gloucester* (1903), *The Tale of Squirrel Nutkin* (1903), *The Tale of Benjamin Bunny* (1904), *The Tale of Two Bad Mice* (1904), *The Tale of Mrs Tiggy-Winkle* (1905), *The Tale of Mr Jeremy Fisher* (1906), *The Tale of Tom Kitten* (1907), *The Tale of Jemima*

Puddle-Duck (1908), *The Tale of the Flopsy Bunnies* (1909), *The Tale of Mrs Tittlemouse* (1910), *The Tale of Mr Tod* (1912), and *The Tale of Pigling Bland* (1913). Similar animal characters provided the personnel of *The Fairy Caravan* (1929), a traveling circus joined by a runaway guinea pig. *Sister Anne* (1932) **recycles** Bluebeard, and *Wag-by-Wall* (1944) **transfigures** a Scottish folktale.

POWERS, TIM (1952–). U.S. writer whose early work was mostly **sf** (refer to *HDSFL*). *The Drawing of the Dark* (1979) is a **historical fantasy** featuring a reincarnate hero who was once King **Arthur**. The **timeslip** fantasy *The Anubis Gates* (1983) broke new ground in pioneering a new kind of **hybrid/science fantasy**, bringing modernity into collision with the **Romantic** movement (here represented by **Lord Byron** and **Samuel Taylor Coleridge**). The method was echoed in the swashbuckling pirate romance *On Stranger Tides* (1987) before *The Stress of her Regard* (1989) returned to the Romantic era, here employing **John Keats** and **Percy Shelley** as key characters in a highly inventive **erotic fantasy**. *Last Call* (1992) imported the argument of **Jessie Weston**'s **scholarly fantasy** into contemporary Las Vegas; *Earthquake Weather* (1997) carried its themes forward while simultaneously providing a sequel to the Los Angeles–set **theosophist fantasy** *Expiration Date* (1995). *Declare* (2000) is a spy thriller-cum-conspiracy theory novel in which investigators discover fallen **angels** at work. *Night Moves and Other Stories* (2001) includes two collaborations with **James Blaylock**; one more (with solo stories by both authors) is in *The Devils in the Details* (2003).

POWYS, JOHN COWPER (1872–1963). British writer who used his fiction to popularize idiosyncratically **dualist** metaphysical theories formulated in opposition to his clergyman father's orthodoxy. An early version is set out in an **epic** poem initially titled "The Death of God" (written 1906; pub. as *Lucifer* 1956)—a striking example of **literary satanism**—while a later one is outlined in some detail in *A Glastonbury Romance* (1932), whose climax is a hymn to the mother **goddess** Cybele.

Morwyn; or, The Vengeance of God (1937) is a tirade against vivisection, involving an expedition to a **Dantean/underworld** where Taliesin guides the protagonist to the place where **Merlin** sleeps alongside various forgotten deities. **Celtic** imagery, often syncretized with other mythological materials, crops up repeatedly in other novels of the period, notably the Arthurian **transfiguration** *Porius* (1951) and *The Brazen Head* (1956), an **alchemical fantasy** based on a popular legend. *Atlantis* (1954) is a sequel to **Homer**'s *Odyssey;* Powys subsequently transfigured the *Iliad* in the **scholarly fantasy** *Homer and the Aether* (1959).

The reckless animism of Powys's early surreal **fabulation** *The Owl, the Duck and—Miss Rowe! Miss Rowe!* (1930) was recovered in a series of highly exotic novellas with which Powys concluded his career. The most lucid is "The Mountains of the Moon," in which the **Moon** is inhabited by the astral bodies of earthly dreamers; it was published with *Up and Out: A Mystery Tale* (1957), an **apocalyptic fantasy** in which survivors of the world's explosion—including the monstrous Org and his inamorata Asm—float through the cosmos encountering various philosophers, deities, and personified ideas. The Earthbound *All or Nothing* (1960) develops the author's fascination with **giants**. *You and Me* (1975) revisits the Moon. In *Real Wraiths* (1976), four ghosts encounter various representatives of the underworld. *Two and Two* (1976) sends the magician Wat Kums on a cosmic journey mounted on a titan's back. The final items in the series, collected in *Three Fantasies* (1985), dissolve into a kind of **nonsense** the author called "suckfist gibberish."

POWYS, THEODORE FRANCIS (1875–1953). British writer. Like his elder brother, **John Cowper Powys**, he found his father's theology difficult to reconcile with his experience of the world, but his response was not so extreme. His **religious fantasies**, which are among the most powerful and adventurous modern **Christian fantasies**, describe educative visits paid to a group of Dorset villages by various exemplary individuals. Tinker Jar (Yahveh) appears as an avenger in the title novella of *The Left Leg* (1923), while the mute fisherman of *Mockery Gap* (1925) discreetly illuminates the lives of a few innocents. *The Market Bell,* which was written at about the same time but remained unpublished until 1991, is a muted **Faustian fantasy** in which the eponymous prophetic bell plays the key symbolic role. *Mr Weston's Good Wine* (1927) is a more forthright **allegory** in which a fatherly deity comes to Folly Down as a seller of symbolic wines. *Fables* (1929, aka *No Painted Plumage*) consists of surreal dialogues, some of them between humans and natural forces, others featuring nonhuman creatures and inanimate objects; a projected second volume never materialized.

In "Christ in a Cupboard" (1930), reprinted in *The White Paternoster and Other Stories* (1930), Jesus visits a virtuous family but is sent away when his charity imperils their wealth; by the time they finally have need of him, he has metamorphosed into the **Devil**. In "The Key of the Field" (1930), Jar becomes a squire who lets a field to a good man and rescues him from subsequent misfortune by letting him into his beautiful garden, while "The Only Penitent" (1931) features a querulous vicar who hears Jar's confession that he is responsible for "every terror in the earth" but grants him absolution because he is also the author of **death**; both were reprinted in *Bottle's Path and Other Stories* (1946) and the sampler *God's Eyes a-Twinkle* (1947). In *Unclay* (1931), the innocent John Death loses a warrant and must stand idly by while his intended "victims" suffer at the hands of a sadistic farmer. In the **Faustian** title novella of *The Two Thieves* (1932), a man steals deadly sins in liquid form from the Devil, becoming rich and powerful until Tinker Jar comes to steal them back again. Another Mr. Weston story was belatedly issued as the first item in *Two Stories: Come and Dine and Tadnol* (1967); posthumously published stories featuring Jar include "The Scapegoat" (1978) and "No Wine" (1979).

PRAED, MRS. CAMPBELL (1851–1935). Australian-born writer, born Rosa Murray-Prior. She went to England when she married in the late 1880s; once there, she developed a keen interest in the fashionable **occultism** of the day and incorporated its themes into some of her novels. *Affinities: A Romance of Today* (1885), which describes the psychic domination of a young woman by a **decadent** poet, also features a female occultist modeled on **Madame Blavatsky**. Blavatsky's ideas provided the basis for the sensational **spiritualist fantasy** *The Brother of the Shadow: A Mystery of Today* (1886), and the personality-displacement stories *The Soul of Countess Adrian* (1891) and *The Insane Root: A Romance of a Strange Country* (1902). *"As a Watch in the Night": A Drama of Waking and Dreaming in Five Acts* (1901) is a more orthodox **theosophical fantasy**. *Nyria* (1904) is an early case study in "past life regression." *The Body of His Desire: A Romance of the Soul* (1912) describes the temptation of an Anglican clergyman by a supernatural femme fatale. The psychically talented heroine of *The Mystery Woman* (1913) helps to avert a world war.

PRANTERA, AMANDA (1942–). British-born writer long resident in Italy. *The Cabalist* (1985) is a **dark/contemporary fantasy** set in Venice. *Conversations with Lord Byron on Perversion, 163 Years after his Lordship's Death* (1987) is a computerized **spiritualist fantasy**. The

historical fantasy *The Kingdom of Fanes* (1995) follows the misfortunes of a princess whose postmarital experiences reflect several popular **fairy tales**. In *Don Giovanna* (2000), an amateur production recapitulates and **transfigures** Mozart's opera. *Spoiler* (2003) is a **Gothic** thriller featuring arcane prophecies of the Antichrist.

PRATCHETT, TERRY (1948–). British writer whose **humorous fantasies** were initially issued by a small press because conventional editorial wisdom at the time considered the subgenre commercially inviable; when the paperback editions became spectacular best sellers, the precedent brought about a sea of change in the marketplace. His first publication, the **Faustian fantasy** "The Hades Business" (1963), had been written while he was at school. *The Carpet People* (1971; rev. 1992) is a **children's fantasy** set in the microcosm of a carpet. Two **sf** novels (refer to *HDSFL*) subsequently helped set the scene and tone for the **chimerical** Discworld **series**, in which multitudinous tropes of myth, legend, folklore, and literary fantasy are wryly subverted, either deconstructed by injections of common sense or bizarrely reconstructed by ingenious logical extrapolations. As the series progressed, the comedy became darker and the plotting more robust, many of the later items being neatly crafted thrillers with a mordant humor that serves to intensify rather than alleviate the dramatic tension.

The main sequence of the Discworld novels comprises *The Colour of Magic* (1983), *The Light Fantastic* (1986), *Equal Rites* (1987), *Mort* (1987), *Sourcery* (1988), *Wyrd Sisters* (1988), *Pyramids* (1989), *Guards! Guards!* (1989), *Moving Pictures* (1990), *Reaper Man* (1991), *Witches Abroad* (1991), *Small Gods* (1992), *Lords and Ladies* (1992), *Men at Arms* (1993), *Soul Music* (1994), *Interesting Times* (1994), *Maskerade* (1995), *Feet of Clay* (1996), *Hogfather* (1996), *Jingo* (1997), *The Last Continent* (1998), *Carpe Jugulum* (1998), *The Fifth Elephant* (1999), *The Truth* (2000), *Thief of Time*. (2001), *Night Watch* (2002), *Monstrous Regiment* (2003), and *Going Postal* (2004). Subsidiary to the main sequence are *Eric* (1990, with Josh Kirby), *The Last Hero* (2001, with Paul Kidby), *The Amazing Maurice and His Educated Rodents* (2001), *The Wee Free Men* (2003), and *A Hat Full of Sky* (2004), which are more explicitly marketed as **children's fantasies** (the whole project has an immense following among teenagers). There are also various spinoff volumes, including graphic novels and screenplay scripts. The main sequence contains four major subseries; one features the hapless **wizard** Rincewind and his colleagues in the Unseen

University, the second a company of **witches** headed by the redoubtable Granny Weatherwax, the third the exploits of the Discworld's personalized **Death**, and the fourth the city of Ankh-Morpork's makeshift police force, the Watch. None of these sequences is segmental; all of them make significant progress as the history of the Discworld moves forward and the metaphysical backcloth becomes ever more detailed.

Pratchett's other works include the hybrid **science-fantasy** trilogy comprising *Truckers* (1989), *Diggers* (1990), and *Wings* (1990), the **apocalyptic fantasy** *Good Omens: The Nice and Accurate Prophecies of Agnes Nutter, Witch* (1990, with **Neil Gaiman**), and a trilogy of **contemporary fantasies** for children begun with the sf novel *Only You Can Save Mankind* (1992), which moved into chimerical territory in *Johnny and the Dead* (1993) and *Johnny and the Bomb* (1996).

PRATT, FLETCHER (1897–1956). U.S. writer who wrote a good deal of **sf** (refer to *HDSFL*) and nonfiction before teaming up with **L. Sprague de Camp** to write **humorous fantasies** for ***Unknown***. They include the Harold Shea series, featuring a series of **parallel worlds** playing host to various mythologies and literary fantasies, where the heroes pit their 20th-century wits against the naive **magic** of the indigenes. The **Nordic fantasy** "The Roaring Trumpet" and the **Spenserian** fantasy "The Mathematics of Magic" (both 1940) were reprinted as *The Incomplete Enchanter* (1941). *The Castle of Iron* (1941; exp. 1950) features the world of **Ariosto**'s *Orlando Furioso,* whose similarity to Spenser's causes some confusion. "The Wall of Serpents" (1953), featuring the world of the *Kalevala,* and the **Celtic fantasy** "The Green Magician" (1954) were reprinted as *The Wall of Serpents* (1960, aka *The Enchanter Completed*). The first two volumes were misleadingly reissued as *The Compleat Enchanter* in a 1975 omnibus, to which the third was added to make up *The Intrepid Enchanter* (1988, aka *The Complete Compleat Enchanter*); more items were subsequently added by de Camp and others. Pratt also collaborated with de Camp on *The Land of Unreason* (1941; exp. 1942), in which an American tourist in Britain is carried off as a changeling by drunken leprechauns; *The Carnelian Cube* (1948), which features a further series of **alternative worlds**; and the **tall tales** collected in *Tales from Gavagan's Bar* (1953; exp. 1978).

Pratt's solo works include two earnest **immersive fantasies** that attempted to rescue that kind of work from the action-adventure slant it had taken on in the **sword and sorcery** fiction of **Robert E. Howard** and his successors. *The Well of the Unicorn* (1948, initially bylined "George U. Fletcher"), which borrows its setting from **Lord Dunsany**, is a bildungsroman in which magic plays a marginal and largely symbolic role. *The Blue Star* (1952 in *Witches Three,* separate edition 1969) is even more realistic in its narrative method and **political fantasy** elements, but Pratt was forced to publish it himself and was persuaded that there was no point in making further attempts; he did not live to see the boom in **heroic fantasy** that brought his works back into print.

PREHISTORIC FANTASY. Most literary accounts of prehistoric life attempt a naturalism that entitles them to be considered **sf** (refer to *HDSFL*), even if the means of their recovery involves a frame of **visionary fantasy** assisted by notions of "race memory" or **reincarnation**. Prehistoric fantasies in which humankind's ancestors are credited with modest psychic powers are classifiable as a **hybrid/science fantasy**. There is, however, a significant residue of prehistoric fantasy that features working **magic**, most of which is extrapolated from Frazerian or theosophical **scholarly fantasy**; much **sword and sorcery** fiction is set in imaginary prehistorical periods, as are **Atlantean fantasies** and some **biblical fantasies**. An interesting subcategory consists of stories in which prehistoric events are juxtaposed or interwoven with much later events in order to display some kind of eternal recurrence; examples include Henri Barbusse's *Chains* (1925), **Gerald Bullett**'s *Marden Fee,* and **Alan Garner**'s *Red Shift*. Fantasies that feature blithely imaginary prehistories include **Norman Douglas**'s *In the Beginning* and some of the items in **Italo Calvino**'s *Cosmicomics* and *T zero*.

PREQUEL. An addition to a **series** set before the first-published item. The supplementation of series with prequels is particularly important in **immersive fantasy**, not only because increasing the detail of secondary worlds often involves filling in their history but because stories set in **secondary worlds** often attain quasi-apocalyptic climaxes that restricts the scope for further development in the direction of the future.

PRICE, E. HOFFMAN (1898–1988). U.S. writer best known for **horror** fiction (refer to *HDHL*), although much of the pulp **magazine** work sampled in *Strange Gateways* (1967) and *Far Lands, Other Days* (1975) has strong elements of **Oriental fantasy** and sincerely based **theosophical fantasy**. His association with **H. P. Lovecraft**'s circle—he collaborated with Lovecraft on "Through the Gates of the Silver Key" (1934)—is reflected in a **decadent** stylistic gloss that he reapplied to his favorite themes in *The Devil Wives of Li-Fong* (1979) and *The Jade Enchantress* (1982), which also have elements of **astrological fantasy**.

PRICE, SUSAN (1955–). British writer of **dark** fantasies for **young adults** who made her debut with *The Devil's Piper* (1973). The Ghost World trilogy comprising *Ghost Drum* (1987), *Ghost Song* (1992), and *Ghost Dance* (1993) features shamanistic **magic**. In *Foiling the Dragon* (1994), a poet is kidnapped on behalf of a dragon king. In the couplet comprising *Elfgift* (1995) and *Elfking* (1996), a half-breed heir triumphs over opposition but has to defend his position. *The Sterkarm Handshake* (1999) is a **historical fantasy** set in the 16th century in which borderers battle elves from the 21st century; *A Sterkarm Kiss* (2004) is a sequel. In *The Bearwood Witch* (2001), a girl with exotic ambitions teams up with a witch. *The Wolf-Sisters* (2001) and *The Wolf's Footprint* (2003) are historical **theriomorphic fantasies**. In *The King's Head* (2002), a disembodied head found on a battlefield becomes a storyteller. Price's short fiction is collected in *Hauntings* (1995), *Nightcomers* (1997), and *Ghosts and Lies* (1998).

PRIESTLEY, J. B. (1894–1984). British writer. Many of the fantastic devices he used—including the **timeslips** he incorporated into his "time plays" *Dangerous Corner* (1932), *Time and the Conways* (1937), and *I Have Been Here Before* (1937)—are on the margins of **sf** (refer to *HDSFL*), although *Johnson over Jordan* (1939) is an **afterlife fantasy** and *An Inspector Calls* (1945) is a straightforward **moralistic fantasy**. The novel *Albert Comes Through* (1933) is a satirical **hallucinatory fantasy**. *The Thirty-first of June* (1961) is a **portal fantasy** for **children**. The short stories collected in *The Other Place* (1953) are mostly fantasies.

PRIMARY WORLD. A term derived as a logical consequence of the widespread use of the term **secondary world** to describe fantastic milieux. It is particularly relevant to **portal fantasies**, in which the story arc usually takes the protagonist from an ostensibly "real" world into a manifestly fantastic one and back again.

PROMETHEAN FANTASY. In classical mythology, Prometheus (the name means "forethought") was a Titan who might have been the progenitor of the human race, perhaps by molding the originals of the species out of clay. At any rate, he became the champion of humankind, persuading Zeus to accept partial animal sacrifices instead of whole ones (leaving the meat to be eaten) and then stealing the fire of the gods for human use; as punishment, the gods chained him up and dispatched an eagle on a daily basis to rip out his constantly regenerated liver. The first story is reflected in Mary Shelley's decision to call Victor Frankenstein "The Modern Prometheus," but the theft of divine fire is more widely reflected in literature, and its metaphorical transfigurations constitute the exemplary core of the subgenre of Promethean fantasy, which is particularly significant in **sf** (refer to *HDSFL*). **Percy Shelley** appointed Prometheus as the hero of his pioneering exercise in disguised **literary satanism** *Prometheus Unbound,* and he is the central figure of **John Sterling**'s "Cydon," **Richard Garnett**'s "The Twilight of the Gods," and **Karel Capek**'s "The Punishment of Prometheus." John Updike's allegory *The Centaur* (1963) refers to his exotic tutelage. Other notable examples include **Diana Wynne Jones**'s *The Homeward Bounders* and Peter Verhelst's *Tonguecat* (1999 in German; tr. 2003).

PROPHECY. An account of future events rendered by an oracle or a divinely inspired individual. In religion, a prophecy functions as both promise and threat; it is a reassuring declaration that the obvious moral inequities of the present will one day be set right—usually by a rain of destruction from which only the righteous will be saved—and a warning to the effect that the wicked had better repent before the day arrives. The notion is paradoxical, in that its authority is tacitly based on a theory of inevitable destiny while its usefulness depends on the ability to act in such a way as to avoid disastrous outcomes; the fact that prophecies come true only if they are ignored is ironically observed in the legend of the Trojan princess Cassandra. A further complication is featured in the **myth** of Oedipus, whose father's reaction to the prophecy that Oedipus would kill him sets off a chain of events leading to the prophecy's fulfillment. The most reliable oracles—the one at Delphi being the best-known **classical** example—tend to cloak their utterances in such a way that their meaning is perceptible only after the fact, thus avoiding the possibility of negation while conserving a reputation for accuracy. **Lifestyle fantasists** with prophetic pretensions—most notably **Nostradamus**—tend to follow suit.

Prophecies of various kinds play a leading role in fantasy. The prophetic reputation of actual **dreams** is recklessly overinflated, but literary dreams have a much better record. The same is true of literary oracles and all methods of divination; if workable **magic** is taken as *the* definitive feature of fantasy fiction, accurate divination is its first corollary.

The hand of fate is a powerful operator in most **secondary worlds**, working tirelessly to make sure that prophecies are fulfilled no matter what their recipients may do to avoid that fulfillment—although the attempts in question may be a significant generator of narrative suspense, and the manner of the final delivery may provide striking demonstrations of authorial ingenuity. Such narrative forms as the ***conte cruel*** thrive on the irony of prophecies fulfilled, although modern ***contes philosophiques*** often argue against the tyranny of fate and **existentialist fantasies** insist on the freedom of human choice, even within the most ferociously constrained circumstances.

Subgenres in which prophecy is a central motif include **astrological fantasies** and such parallel endeavors as Tarot fantasies, and many **apocalyptic fantasies**. Notable examples including the vagaries of the Cassandra and Oedipus effects include **John Buchan**'s *The Gap in the Curtain* and **Marion Zimmer Bradley**'s *The Firebrand*.

PSEUDONYM. A name adopted for the purpose of publication. Pseudonyms are of particular significance in fantasy literature; some of its authors—most notably **Homer** and Thomas Malory—are probably as imaginary as their products. Fantasy often requires the invention of hypothetical narrators such as **François Rabelais**'s Alcofrybas Nasier—who intrudes metafictionally into his own narrative—and **Jonathan Swift**'s Lemuel Gulliver. An element of imposture is necessary to such projects as the **Gallandesque** *Tales of the Genii* composed by an obscure English clergyman named James Ridley, who passed them off as translations by an ambassador to the Mogul Empire, Charles Morell. Horace Walpole used two layers of deception when he issued the **moralistic/Gothic** fantasy *The Castle of Otranto* as a translation by "William Marshal" of an Italian manuscript by "Onuphrio Muralto."

The practice of using pseudonyms has been greatly encouraged in modern times by pressure put on writers active in different commodified genres to use different names in order to avoid confusing reader expectations—thus Martin Millar writes fantasies as "Martin Scott," **Stephen R. Donaldson** wrote mysteries as "Reed Stephens," and **Nora Roberts** writes **sf** as J. D. Robb. Computerized stock control also leads bookstore chains like Barnes and Noble to order exactly as many copies of a writer's latest book as the last actually sold, thus locking many bylines into a downward spiral that greatly encourages relabeling, after the fashion of **Kate Elliott**, **Robin Hobb**, and **Michelle West**.

PSYCHOLOGICAL FANTASY. Fantasy is a psychological phenomenon as well as a literary one, but fiction that deals with "fantasies" in the psychological sense is not usually considered part of fantasy literature—although there is an interesting marginal subset of texts focused on the politics of **escapism**. The point at which the ability to escape into private fantasy becomes supernaturalized is sometimes unclear, especially in accounts of fantasies produced by such mental aberrations as schizophrenia, paranoia, and multiple-personality disorder. Such subgenres as **hallucinatory fantasy**, **delusional fantasy**, and **wish-fulfillment fantasy** present numerous **ambiguous** cases. Wherever **philosophical** speculation and analysis begin to complicate or displace the **horror** aspects of such ambiguous texts, they tend toward the fantasy genre.

Most philosophical and psychological models of the human mind tend to imagine it as fundamentally divided between "higher" powers of reason and "lower" impulses and appetites, the two being forever in conflict. A tendency to conceive of the "lower" elements as supernatural forces beyond conscious control, that the will is sometimes impotent to suppress, is one of the primary motivating forces of **mythopoesis** and hence of literary fantasizing; its effects can easily be seen in such subgenres as **erotic fantasy** and in the development of such motifs as the **doppelgänger**. Fantasies that consciously address or carefully allegorize questions of this sort lie at the core of the subgenre of psychological fantasy.

The extrapolation of psychology into various schools of psychoanalysis is one of the most pervasive modern schools of **scholarly fantasy**. While the theories of Sigmund Freud feed the subgenre of erotic fantasy in such works as **David H. Keller**'s *The Eternal Conflict,* the ideas of Carl Jung have offered much more widespread inspiration, particularly the notion of a collective unconscious inhabited by "archetypes," whose symptomatic images allegedly play a major role in shaping the motifs of **myth**, **legend**, folklore, **dreams**, and fantasy fiction. Jung's list of archetypal images include the Mother, the Spirit, and the Trickster; folklorists, literary theorists, and anthropologists—notably **Joseph Campbell**—routinely place stereotypes like the Divine Child, the Unwilling Hero, the Wise Old Man, and the Enchanted Prince in this context.

A straightforward dramatization of Jung's ideas can be found in Keller's "The Abyss," but many modern writers of fantastic fiction use and modify Jungian schemes to organize and "explain" the patterns of their fantastic devices; notable examples include **Robert Holdstock**'s *Mythago Wood* series and **Charles De Lint**'s *The Wild Wood* (1994). Other notable psychological fantasies include **Nancy Springer**'s *Larque on the Wing,* S. Andrew Swann's *God's Dice* (1997, in which a psychologist dreams of a fantasy world that anchors his various **alternative** selves), Helmut Krausser's *The Great Bagarozy* (1997 in German; tr. 1999), and Andrew Cartmell's *The Wise* (1999).

PULLMAN, PHILIP (1946–). British writer. His **Orphean fantasy** *Galatea* (1978) was marketed for adults, but his subsequent work was redirected at the **children's** market. *Count Karlstein, or The Ride of the Demon Huntsman* (1982) was the first of many to deploy elements of **horror** fiction. *The Firework-Maker's Daughter* (1995) is an **Oriental fantasy** featuring an encounter with a **goddess**. *Clockwork* (1996) is a **Faustian fantasy**. He broke significant new ground in the best-selling series collectively known as *His Dark Materials,* launched with *Northern Lights* (1995, aka *The Golden Compass*), a striking **immersive fantasy** set in an **alternative world** where individuals' souls are manifest as animal "daemons" whose shape fluctuates as their characters are formed in childhood but eventually settle into revealing stasis. *The Subtle Knife* (1997) places that world alongside ours in a **multiverse** where forces are gathering for a replay of the war described in **John Milton**'s *Paradise Lost,* while *The Amber Spyglass* (2000) extrapolates the trilogy into an exercise in **literary satanism** more wholehearted and melodramatic—though less explicit—than any previously launched into the adult market. *Lyra's Oxford* (2003) is a spinoff novella. *I Was a Rat! . . . or The Scarlet Slipper* (1999) reexamines the story of Cinderella from an unorthodox angle.

PYLE, HOWARD (1853–1911). U.S. **illustrator** and writer, most of whose work was for **children**, although *A Modern Aladdin* (1892) is an adult fantasy set in Paris. He **recycled** many traditional tales, including the series of Malory adaptations comprising *The Story of King Arthur and His Knights* (1903), *The Story of the Champions of the Round Table* (1905), *The Story of Sir Launcelot and His Companions* (1907), and *The Story of the Grail and the Passing of Arthur* (1911). His original works include the collections *The Wonder Clock* (1887) and *Twilight-Land* (1894); the latter's ostensible narrators include Faustus and Sindbad. *Otto and the Silver Hand* (1888) and *Men of Iron* (1994) are not fantasies but are of note because of their determined subversion of the illusions of **chivalric romance**. *The Garden behind the Moon* (1895) is an **allegorical/sentimental fantasy** based in Pyle's Swedenborgian beliefs.

– Q –

QUEST. A term that conflates two obsolete meanings, one which refers to hunting, especially with dogs, and the other to a search for the truth (as in "inquest"). A quest thus becomes a search for a particular objective, whose attainment will involve some kind of revelation—a double meaning ideally suited to fantasy literature, where objects of search tend to be symbolic as well as material. *Chrétien de Troyes*'s **grail** is the cardinal exemplar; others include the well at the world's end, the fountain of youth, fallen stars, and the philosopher's stone. Because a quest is an intrinsically heroic enterprise, all quest fantasies are—or must eventually turn into—**heroic fantasies**, although not all heroic fantasies are quest fantasies.

There is a sense in which quest fantasies proceed in the opposite direction to **Odyssean fantasies**, although the two subgenres are often fused—in the fashion reflected in the subtitle of **J. R. R. Tolkien**'s *The Hobbit: or, There and Back Again*—and heroic questors are required by **Joseph Campbell**'s monomythical formula to bring some token of their success home, even when they operate in **immersive** rather than **portal fantasies**.

Quest fantasy lends itself readily to minimal plotting and is easily stretchable to enormous length. The rapid multiplication of **commodified epic** fantasies in which characters wander around hypothetical landscapes collecting magical objects prompted Nick Lowe to coin the term "plot coupons" for such items, by analogy with marketing enterprises in which consumers collect coupons until they have a set that is redeemable for some kind of "gift"—usually, in commodified fantasy, the salvation of the world. Examples of quest fantasy are very numerous; the most extreme include works by **Paul Kearney**, **Paula Volsky**'s *The Luck of Relian Kru,* and Paulo Coelho's *The Alchemist* (1988; tr. 1989).

QUILLER-COUCH, SIR ARTHUR (1863–1944). British writer, primarily a poet, who often signed himself "Q." His father and grandfather were both enthusiastic collectors of the **folk tales** of Cornwall, which provided material for most of his **ghost stories** and **humorous fantasies**, which in turn are mingled with other materials in the collections *Noughts and Crosses* (1891), *"I Saw Three Ships" and Other Winter's Tales* (1892), *Wandering Ghosts* (1895), *Old Fires and Profitable Ghosts* (1900), *The Laird's Luck* (1901), *The White Wolf and Other Fireside Tales* (1902), *Two Sides of the Face* (1903), and *Shakespeare's Christmas* (1905). *Castle Dor* (1962, posthumously completed by Daphne du Maurier) features a magically inspired reenactment of the tale of Tristan and Isolde.

QUINN, SEABURY (1889–1969). U.S. writer. He was a prolific contributor to ***Weird Tales***, which featured his extensive series of **occult/detective** stories featuring Jules de Grandin, most of which are also **horror** stories (refer to *HDHL*). More central to the fantasy genre are his sentimental **Christmas fantasy** *Roads* (1938; rev. book 1948) and *Alien Flesh* (1977), an **erotic fantasy** featuring an **identity exchange**.

– R –

RABELAIS, FRANÇOIS (1494–1553). French scholar whose groundbreaking series of satirical fantasies featuring the **giant** Gargantua, his son Pantagruel, and the latter's companion Panurge, first published between 1532 and 1564, was gathered together into an omnibus usually known in translation as *Gargantua and Pantagruel*. The characters' absurd adventures provide scathing commentaries on contemporary society as well as a great deal of grotesquerie for its own sake; influenced by **Lucian**, they had an equal influence on **Jonathan Swift** and **Voltaire**, becoming crucial to the entire traditions of **satirical fantasy** and the ***conte philosophique***, as well as the tradition of **erotic fantasy**. The adjective "Rabelaisian" is routinely applied to exuberantly reckless bawdiness.

Panurge has affinities with such ingenious servants as Arlequino in the *commedia dell'arte,* although his voyage of discovery in search of advice as to whether or not to marry is a spectacular parody of **Romantic** quests. Suspicions of atheism, which led to the author's persecution and thus to the increasing pessimism of the later texts, were unjustified, although the key motif of the defiantly irreligious monastery of Thélème (Thelema) became a powerful symbol of resistance to moral tyranny, its motto "do as thou wilt" gladly adopted by **Aleister Crowley**. Rabelais's influence echoes resonantly in the works of such writers as **Pierre Louÿs** and **Marcel Aymé**; Francis Watson's *Trinc!* (1932) is a modern extension of the series.

RADFORD, IRENE (1950–). U.S. writer. The Dragon Nimbus series, comprising *The Glass Dragon* (1994), *The Perfect Princess* (1995), *The Loneliest Magician* (1996), and *The Wizard's Treasure* (2000), is an account of corrosive **thinning**. The **prequel** trilogy *The Dragon's Touchstone* (1997), *The Last Battlemage* (1997), and *The Renegade Dragon* (1999) finds the **dragons** nearer to their heyday. The Merlin's Descendants series, comprising *Guardian of the Balance* (1999), *Guardian of the Trust* (2000), *Guardian of the Vision* (2001), and *Guardian of the Promise* (2003), is an interesting extrapolation of **Arthurian fantasy**, which ultimately reaches the Elizabethan era.

RANKIN, ROBERT (1949–). British **humorist** who imports all manner of **chimerical** fantastic materials into mundane settings in order to generate bizarre situations and hectic action. The tone of his works was set by the trilogy comprising *The Antipope* (1981), *The Brentford Triangle* (1982), and *East of Ealing* (1984) but became much more extravagant when the series was extended by *The Sprouts of Wrath* (1988). *Nostradamus Ate My Hamster* (1996), *The Brentford Chainstore Massacre* (1997), *Sprout Mask Replica* (1997), *Sex and Drugs and Sausage Rolls* (1999), and *Web Site Story* (2001) share the same setting. The trilogy comprising *Armageddon: The Musical* (1990), *They Came and Ate Us* (1991), and *The Suburban Book of the Dead* (1992) juxtaposes a time-tripping Elvis Presley with B-movie **sf** motifs.

The trilogy comprising *The Book of Ultimate Truths* (1993), *Raiders of the Lost Car Park* (1994), and *The Greatest Show off Earth* (1994) draws inspiration from such sources as *Fortean Times* and the *Weekly World News,* as does *The Most Amazing Man Who Ever Lived* (1995). *The Garden of Unearthly Delights* (1995), in which Earth enters a zone of noncausality where magic works and technology doesn't, is closer to the core of genre fantasy. *A Dog Called Demolition* (1996) is the story of the world's first "surreal killer." *The Dance of the Voodoo Handbag* (1998) introduced private eye Laszlo Woodbine, also featured in *Waiting for Godalming* (2000) and *The Fandom of the Operator* (2001). In *The Hollow Chocolate Bunnies of the Apocalypse* (2002), nursery rhyme characters are murdered in Toy City. *The Witches of Chiswick* (2003) are more down to earth than their equivalents in Eastwick.

RANSOME, ARTHUR (1884–1967). British writer best known for the best-selling **children's fiction** he wrote in the 1930s and 1940s, which totally eclipsed his earlier career as a **decadent fantasist**. A few **fairy tales** not aimed at children are included in the collection *The Stone Lady* (1905); the **sentimental fantasies** in *The Hoofmarks of the Faun* (1911) are even more mature. *The Elixir of Life* (1915) is a **dark fantasy**.

RASPE, RUDOLF ERIC (1737–1794). German scholar and swindler who translated James Macpherson's fake Celtic **epics** before producing an account of *Baron Münchhausen's Narrative of His Marvellous Travels and Campaigns in Russia* (1785), which became a paradigm example of **tall story**–telling and caused considerable embarrassment to the actual baron. Later English editions took aboard extensions of the narrative by several other hands, far wordier than the laconic originals. Raspe also used Münchhausen as the narrator of his **Gothic fantasy** *Koenigsmark the Robber; or, The Terror of Bohemia* (1790; tr. 1801).

RATIONALIZED FANTASY. The Clute/Grant *Encyclopedia* uses this term in three ways. The first refers to works in which magic is strictly rule bound, usually by Frazerian laws, and is similar to the same book's definition of **hard fantasy**. The second refers to the much larger category of stories that appear to be fantasy until a de-supernaturalizing explanation is provided in the climax—a formula that almost acquired generic status in the "weird menace" pulps. The third refers to hybrid **science fantasies** in which familiar fantasy motifs are provided with pseudoscientific explanations. A fourth meaning often encountered in reviews and commentaries is equivalent to the description of "de-supernaturalized fantasy" used in these pages; it refers to **historical** fictions that focus intently on the substance of **myth** and **legend**, employing viewpoint characters who take belief in magic and the supernatural for granted but refrain from featuring any occurrences that a rationalist reader would construe as magical or supernatural. **Arthurian** and **classical fantasy** both have substantial fringes of this kind.

RAWN, MELANIE (1953–). U.S. writer. Her early works deployed **dragons** similar to those deployed in **Anne McCaffrey**'s **planetary romances**. In her first trilogy, comprising *Dragon Prince* (1988), *The Star Scroll* (1989), and *Sunrunner's Fire* (1990), dragons are initially regarded as pests—and hence as the legitimate targets of murderous knight-errantry—but its hero's discovery that dragon eggs can be **alchemically** converted into gold brings about a new relationship between the species. The story continued in the Dragon Star trilogy, comprising *Stronghold* (1990), *The Dragon Token* (1991), and *Skybowl* (1993). The Exiles series, comprising *The Ruins of Ambrai* (1994), *The Mageborn Traitor* (1997), and *The Captal's Tower* (2004), is a tale of persecution set in a world of reversed sex roles. *The Golden Key,* a collaborative project with **Jennifer Roberson** and **Kate Elliott**, is set in an alternative medieval Spain, featuring magically talented members of an artists' guild.

REALMS OF FANTASY. Bimonthly U.S. magazine launched in 1994, under the editorship of Shawna MacCarthy, as a companion to *Science Fiction Age*. It survived the latter magazine's demise to establish itself as the chief U.S. market for short fantasies of all kinds. Its Folkroots department examines the sources of modern fantasy, while its Gallery section showcases fantasy **illustration**.

RECURSIVE FANTASY. The Clute/Grant *Encyclopedia* gives two definitions of "recursive fantasy," the first referring to fantasies in which protagonists enter **secondary worlds** based on previously existing fictions, the second to **metafictions** that depict "tangled reality levels" without reference to actual preexistent works. Both kinds of fantasy are discussed here as subsets of **metafiction**.

RECYCLING. One of the key features of literary fantasies based on **myths**, legends, and **folk tales** is that they continue the process of serial transmission that presumably carried the stories across the centuries before they were first written down; they are regarded as "common property" available for retelling and reshaping. No clear boundary can be drawn between "straightforward" retellings, which carefully conserve the main features of the story, and more adventurous ones that incorporate elements of reinterpretation, make inquiries into puzzles of motivation and logic, introduce new materials, and draw out new morals. This spectrum extends into radical **transfigurations**, which place the stories in different cultural contexts, reverse roles, offer satirical subversions, and so on. The license to recycle traditional materials in which no one has any definable intellectual property rights is often tacitly assumed to apply to all literary products that resemble myths, legends, or folktales; this is part of the process by which influential works join the population of **taproot texts**.

Notable recyclers of traditional material—usually but not invariably writing for **children**—include **Howard Pyle**, **Padraic Colum**, **Kevin**

Crossley-Holland, Randy Lee Eickhoff, **Morgan Llewelyn**, **Michael Scott**, and **Geraldine McCaughrean**.

REDGROVE, PETER (1932–2003). British writer, best known as a poet. His first novels, written in collaboration with his wife, Penelope Shuttle—*The Terrors of Dr Treviles* (1974) and *The Glass Cottage* (1976)—are complex fabulations employing **metaphysical** contexts reminiscent of those framing works by **John Cowper Powys**. His solo novels are **ambiguous/science fantasies** (refer to *HDSFL*) with **occult** and **erotic** elements. *The One Who Set Out to Study Fear* (1989) **recycles** tales from the **Brothers Grimm** in a **surreal** manner.

REED, JEREMY (1951–). British writer in the **surrealist** tradition. After the marginal **occult fantasy** *Black Rock* (1987), his prose works began to pay explicit homage to the **French** literary tradition, by using its heroes as characters—**Charles Baudelaire** (as viewed by his mistress) in *Red Eclipse* (1989), Isidore Ducasse in *Isidore: A Novel about the Comte de Lautréamont* (1991), and the timeslipping "divine Marquis" in *When the Whip Comes Down: A Novel about de Sade* (1992). *Chasing Black Rainbows: A Novel about Antonin Artaud* (1994) and *Diamond Nebula* (1994) deemphasize fantasy elements as they move into the present and future. *Dorian* (1997) is a sequel to **Oscar Wilde**'s *The Picture of Dorian Gray*. *Boy Caesar* (2004) is an account of **reincarnation**.

RE-ENCHANTMENT. However the term is construed, the permanent loss or neglect of **enchantment** is generally considered to be a bad thing. A single-minded and narrowly focused concentration on brute reality may sometimes be necessary, even over extended periods, but few people—at least among literary folk—would recommend it as a way of life. A good deal of fantasy literature takes a polemical view of the necessity of re-enchantment after any such period of disenchanting concentration, routinely proposing a determined reinvestment in some kind of **magic**, often symbolized by **Faerie**.

The arguments for re-enchantment deployed in the 19th century, by such writers as **Charles Dickens** and **Lewis Carroll**, protested against campaigns to make factual and moral education the principal focus of **children's literature**. In the aftermath of World War I, a considerable number of unusually heartfelt pleas of this kind were produced in Britain; notable examples include **Stella Benson**'s *Living Alone,* **Gerald Bullett**'s *Mr Godly beside Himself,* **Hope Mirrlees**'s *Lud-in-the-Mist,*

Lord Dunsany's *The King of Elfland's Daughter,* and **Margaret Irwin**'s *These Mortals*. The phenomenon was less obvious in the United States, which had been less affected by the privations of the war, but something similar can be observed in the postwar works of **James Branch Cabell** and **Thorne Smith**.

World War II does not seem to have had a similarly widespread effect—although *The Lord of the Rings* was completed in its aftermath—perhaps because the **science-fictional** myth of the Space Age took off so spectacularly in that period. There is, however, nothing halfhearted about the pleas for re-enchantment embodied in such modern examples as Paul Gallico's *The Man Who Was Magic* (1967), **Michaela Roessner**'s *Walkabout Woman,* **Midori Snyder**'s Oran trilogy, and **Monica Hughes**'s *The Story Box*.

REES, CELIA (1949–). British writer who diversified from thrillers into teenage **horror** fiction—including *Blood Sinister* (1996), the **Templar** fantasy *Ghost Chamber* (1997), and *The Soul Taker* (1997)—before producing the more relaxed *H.A.U.N.T.S.* series, comprising *H Is for Haunting* (1998), *A Is for Apparition* (1998), *U Is for Unbeliever* (1998), *N Is for Nightmare* (1998), *T Is for Terror* (1999), and *S Is for Shudder* (1998)—repackaged in three volumes as *City of Shadows, A Trap in Time,* and *The Host Rides Out* and in the omnibus *A Trap in Time*—which features a boy with second sight. Rees then ventured into **historical fantasy** in *The Cunning Man* (2000) and a series launched with *Witch Child* (2001) and *Sorceress* (2002), in which an English girl is dispatched to the American colonies when she shows signs of being a **witch**.

REICHERT, MICKEY ZUCKER (1962–). U.S. writer. The series launched by *Godslayer* (1987) drafts an American soldier into a war rooted in **Nordic fantasy**; his story was continued in *Shadow Climber* (1988), *Dragonrank Master* (1989), *Shadow's Realm* (1990), and *By Chaos Cursed* (1991) before the trilogy comprising *The Last of the Renshai* (1992), *The Western Wizard* (1992), and *Child of Thunder* (1993) moved the whole milieu on to a larger stage, further employed in the trilogy comprising *Beyond Ragnarok* (1995), *Prince of Demons* (1996), and *The Children of Wrath* (1998). *The Legend of Nightfall* (1993) features a powerful mage trapped in an assistant role. *Spirit Fox* (1998, with Jennifer Wingert) features a young woman invested with an **animal** spirit. *Flightless Falcon* (2000) is a **picaresque fantasy**. *The Beasts of*

Barakhai (2001) and *The Lost Dragons of Barakhai* (2002) are **theriomorphic/portal fantasies**.

REINCARNATION. The notion that some undying essence within a living being is serially reincarnated is common to several mythologies, some of which also assert that the sequence might move "upward" toward some kind of perfection or "downward" toward degradation, according to the moral quality of each individual incarnation; the latter notion is the central assumption of the subgenre of **karmic romance**. The idea of reincarnation is also a staple of **spiritualist** and **theosophical fantasy**. The most popular sources of reincarnated souls, in **lifestyle fantasy** as well as fantasy literature, are **Atlantis** and ancient Egypt, the latter owing its prominence to the iconic significance of **mummies**.

Apart from karmic romances, the most common use of serial human reincarnation in fantasy is to facilitate large-scale **historical** surveys, like the one carried out in **Jack London**'s *The Star Rover,* but the notion may also be used to construct intense **psychological fantasies** like Paul Busson's *The Man Who Was Born Again* (1921) and Frank de Felitta's *Audrey Rose* (1976). Stories featuring the reincarnation of humans as animals tend to take a much broader view of karmic penalty, if they invoke it at all; notable examples include **W. H. Hudson**'s "Marta Riquelme" (1902), Robert Hichens's "The Black Spaniel" (1905), L. P. Jacks's "The Professor's Mare," **Ben Hecht**'s "The Adventures of Professor Emmett," and James Herbert's *Fluke* (1977). Reincarnation on other worlds than Earth was a particular fascination of the 19th-century French spiritualist and **sf** writer Camille Flammarion, whose popularization of the notion prompted such variants as Mortimer Collins's *Transmigration* (1874).

Contes philosophiques considering various aspects of the notion include **Rudyard Kipling**'s "The Finest Story in the World" (1893), **M. P. Shiel**'s "Tulsah," and Sydney Fowler Wright's "The Choice" (1929). Notable recent examples include Laura Esquivel's *The Law of Love* (1995 in French; English tr. 1997), David Ambrose's *A Memory of Demons* (2003) and Jeremy Reed's *Boy Caesar* (2004).

REISS, KATHRYN (1957–). U.S. writer for **young adults**. In *Time Windows* (1991), a dollhouse offers a window to the past. *Dreadful Sorry* (1993) and *Rest in Peace* (1997) are **ghost** stories, the second involving **dreams**. *Pale Phoenix* (1994), *PaperQuake* (1998), and *Paint by Magic* (2002) are **timeslip** fantasies. The series comprising *Dollhouse of the*

Dead (1997), *The Headless Bride* (1997), and *Sweet Miss Honeywell's Revenge* (2004) feature a haunted dollhouse.

RELIGIOUS FANTASY. Religious fantasy is an awkward category, because religions embody items of belief that seem obviously fantastic to nonbelievers but are accepted as matters of faith by adherents. Thus, fiction featuring active interventions in human affairs by Jesus or guardian angels is routinely produced by Christians as inspirational literature, intended to be consumed as a more accurate record of the real world than any mundanely naturalistic fiction. On the other hand, there is a good deal of lore contained within any religious system that is usually seen as allegorical, metaphorical, or straightforwardly fanciful; an insistence on the absolute literal truth of every word of Scripture is often seen as bizarre and rationally unsustainable even within the ranks of the devout. There is, therefore, no reason why Christians cannot accept the existence and utility of a subgenre of **Christian fantasy**, just as Jews routinely accept the validity of **Jewish fantasy**, although followers of Islam often find the idea of **Arabian fantasy** problematic in relation to the Quran—as evidenced by the response to **Salman Rushdie**'s *The Satanic Verses*.

Much religious fantasy is actually anti-religious fantasy of a **satirical** stripe, but successful works of that kind often call forth responses; George Bernard Shaw's account of *The Adventures of the Black Girl in Her Search for God* (1932) spawned numerous replies in kind, including the title piece of Brigid Brophy's *The Adventures of God in His Search for the Black Girl* (1973). Many sincere believers—including clerics—have used calculated **fabulations** as a means of exploring the implications of their doubts and beliefs. By the same token, nonbelievers in a particular religion may well find its lexicon of ideas useful in establishing hypothetical situations that explore general issues in theology or metaphysics in a sensitive fashion.

Religious fantasy does not, therefore, necessarily demean religion, although the flexibility of mind required to participate in fantasy, as a writer or a reader, may well be corrosive of the rigidity of mind required to sustain unyielding faith. Arch-dogmatists are always likely to disapprove of it, although that has never inhibited writers like **C. S. Lewis** and **Harry Blamires** and does not prevent the production of such works as Barbara Timberlake Russell's *The Taker's Stone* (1999) and **G. P. Taylor**'s *Shadowmancer*.

RICE, ANNE (1941–). U.S. writer. She became the best-selling member of a group of writers who redeemed the idea and image of the **vampire** from its use as an icon of **horror** fiction (refer to *HDHL*). The series comprising *Interview with the Vampire* (1976), *The Vampire Lestat* (1985), *The Queen of the Damned* (1988), *The Tale of the Body Thief* (1992), and *Memnoch the Devil* (1995) retains an element of horror but subordinates it to flamboyant **erotic fantasy**, intense **existentialist fantasy,** and far-ranging **historical fantasy**, climaxing in the last-named volume with a Miltonian exercise in theodicy that reexamines its own qualifications as **literary satanism**. *Pandora* (1998), *The Vampire Armand* (1998), *Vittorio the Vampire* (1999), and *Blood and Gold: The Vampire Marius* (2001) are adjuncts to the series. *The Mummy; or, Rameses the Damned* (1989) and *Servant of the Bones* (1996) vary the formula by employing less versatile revenants. The **timeslip** fantasy *Violin* (1997) also features supernatural predation.

The image of the **witch** is subject to a similarly thoroughgoing makeover in Rice's trilogy comprising *The Witching Hour* (1990), *Lasher* (1993), and *Taltos* (1994); *Merrick* (2000) and *Blood Canticle* (2003) combine her series by introducing witches to vampires. She also extrapolated a familiar **fairy tale** motif into explicit pornography in a trilogy bylined "A. N. Roquelaure," comprising *The Claiming of Sleeping Beauty* (1983), *Beauty's Punishment* (1984), and *Beauty's Release* (1985).

RILEY, JUDITH MERKLE (1942–). U.S. writer of **historical fantasies**. *A Vision of Light* (1989), set in 14th-century England, features a healing gift; *In Pursuit of the Green Lion* (1999) is a sequel, but the third volume in the series, [The Water-Devil], has only been published in German. In *The Oracle Glass* (1994), set in 17th-century France, a girl is trained as a seer by La Voisin, a leading figure in one of the most notorious French sorcery trials. *The Serpent Garden* (1996) features Henry VIII. In *The Master of All Desires* (1999), Catherine de Medici goes in search of the head of Menander the Undying, which formerly enabled **Nostradamus** to obtain advice from Anael, the Spirit of History.

ROBBINS, TOD (1888–1949). British writer resident in the United States during and after World War I, when he wrote fiction for the pulp magazines, much of it non-supernatural **horror** fiction (refer to *HDHL*). His fantasies include "The Whimpus" (1919), a tongue-in-cheek account of a nasty **mermaid**, and "Toys of Fate" (1921; aka "Toys"), an **allegory**

in which a shopkeeper unwisely sells a model of his village to Mr. Fate. The title story of *Who Wants a Green Bottle? and Other Uneasy Tales* (1926)—which had earlier appeared in *Silent, White and Beautiful and Other Stories* (1920)—is a phantasmagoria based in Scottish folklore. "Wild Wullie the Waster" is a quieter story in a similar vein; two tales based in Irish folklore, "A Bit of a Banshee" and "A Son of Shaemas O'Shea," are broader comedies.

ROBBINS, TOM (1936–). U.S. writer whose novels present a fantasized version of contemporary America. In the marginal *Another Roadside Attraction* (1971), the **mummy** of Jesus is the object of various **quests**. *Jitterbug Perfume* (1984), which features **Pan**, is more wholeheartedly fantastic than the similarly **erotic** *Even Cowgirls Get the Blues* (1976) and *Still Life with Woodpecker* (1980). *Skinny Legs and All* (1990) is also flamboyant in spinning off fantasy materials from its central erotic theme. *Fierce Invalids Home from Hot Climates* (2000) features a shaman-enlightened CIA agent whose feet can no longer touch the ground. *Villa Incognito* (2003) features the Japanese trickster figure Tanuki.

ROBERSON, JENNIFER (1953–). U.S. writer in various genres. The Cheysuli series, comprising *Shapechangers* (1984), *The Song of Homana* (1985), *Legacy of the Sword* (1986), *Track of the White Wolf* (1987), *A Pride of Princes* (1988), *Daughter of the Lion* (1989), *Flight of the Raven* (1990), and *A Tapestry of Lions* (1992), is **theriomorphic fantasy**. The series comprising *Sword-Dancer* (1986), *Sword-Singer* (1988), *Sword-Maker* (1989), *Sword-Breaker* (1991), *Sword-Born* (1998), and *Sword-Sworn* (1999) is feminized **sword and sorcery** fiction.

ROBERTS, KATHERINE (1962–). British **children's** writer. The Echorium sequence, comprising *Song Quest* (1999), *The Crystal Mask* (2001), and *Dark Quetzal* (2003), features magical **music**. The heroine of *Spellfall* (2000) fights to save the soultrees of Earthaven. The Seven Fabulous Wonders series, begun with *The Great Pyramid Robbery* (2001), *The Babylon Game* (2002), *The Amazon Temple Quest* (2003), *The Mausoleum Murder* (2004), and *The Olympic Conspiracy* (2004), features **historical fantasy** adventures.

ROBERTS, KEITH (1935–2000). British writer best known for **sf** (refer to *HDSFL*), although his first published story (1965) launched the series collected in *Anita* (1970; exp. 1990), about a teenage **witch**. In the mosaic *Pavane* (1968), an apparent **alternative history** of England turns out to be a post-holocaust replay masterminded by **fairies**; a similar **chimerical** amalgam is featured in the futuristic series collected in *Kaeti and Company* (1986), *Kaeti's Apocalypse* (1986), and *Kaeti on Tour* (1992). *Gráinne* (1987) is a **contemporary fantasy** with strong echoes of **Celtic fantasy**. A few fantasies are mingled with sf stories in his collections, most prominently in *The Passing of the Dragons* (1977), *Ladies from Hell* (1979), and *Winterwood and Other Hauntings* (1989).

ROBERTS, NORA (1950–). U.S. writer, very prolific in the field of genre romance, who also writes **sf** as "J. D. Robb." She began diversifying into romance/suspense crossovers before edging into fantasy in the Hornblower brothers **timeslip** series, comprising *Time Was* (1989), *Times Change* (1990), and *Time and Again* (2002). The Three Sisters Island trilogy, comprising *Dance upon the Air* (2001), *Heaven and Earth* (2001), and *Face the Fire* (2002), features an ancient curse. The trilogy comprising *Key of Light* (2003), *Key of Knowledge* (2003), and *Key of Valor* (2004) describes a **quest** for the keys to the souls of **goddesses**. Her collections of novellas include *A Little Magic* (2002) and *A Little Fate* (2004), both featuring **Celtic** romantic fantasies. Her best-selling status gave her a pivotal influence in moving forward the cause of **paranormal romance**.

ROBERTS, TANSY RAYNER (1978–). Australian writer. The **humorous fantasy** series comprising *Splashdance Silver* (1998), *Liquid Gold* (1999), and various short stories, featuring Delta Void, is set in the world of Mocklore. She coedited *AustrAlien Absurdities* (2002) with Chuck McKenzie and is a member of the collective that publishes *Andromeda Spaceways Inflight Magazine* (launched 2002).

ROESSNER, MICHAELA (1950–). U.S. writer. *Walkabout Woman* (1988) is a plea for **re-enchantment** describing the **quest** of an Australian aborigine woman to renew the dreamtime. *Vanishing Point* (1993) features a more elaborate quest involving **alternative** worlds. The couplet comprising *The Stars Dispose* (1997) and *The Stars Compel* (1999) is a **historical/astrological fantasy** set in Renaissance Florence and Rome.

ROHAN, MICHAEL SCOTT (1951–). British writer, who wrote **sf** before switching to fantasy in *The Ice King* (1986, with Allan Scott as

"Michael Scot"; aka *Burial Rites*), a **contemporary fantasy** with **Nordic** intrusions. The background of the Winter of the World trilogy, comprising *The Anvil of Ice* (1986), *The Forge in the Forest* (1987), and *The Hammer of the Sun* (1988), resembles that of Nordic fantasy without making explicit use of it; the series continues in *The Castle of the Winds* (1998), *The Singer and the Sea* (1999), and *Shadow of the Seer* (2001).

The trilogy comprising *Chase the Morning* (1990), *The Gates of Noon* (1992), and *Cloud Castles* (1993) establishes the **primary world** at the core of a **multiversal** array of historical and legendary **alternatives**, whose intersections direct the protagonist through various **chimerical** encounters, the third including **Arthurian** materials; the series continues in *Maxie's Demon* (1997). *A Spell of Empire: The Horns of Tartarus* (1992 with Scott) is a **picaresque fantasy** set in an alternative Europe where a northern Nibelung Empire confronts a southern Tyrrhennian Empire. *The Lord of Middle Air* (1994) is a **historical fantasy** set in the 13th century, featuring a venture into **Faerie** by the reputed wizard Michael Scot (whom Rohan, like **Sir Walter Scott**, claims as an ancestor). *Shaman* (2001) is a revenge fantasy.

ROHMER, SAX (1883–1959). Pseudonym of British writer Arthur Sarsfield Ward, a prolific writer of popular thrillers, most notably the long series featuring the charismatic villain Fu Manchu. His fantasies are usually **horror** stories (refer to *HDHL*) with marginal **sf** elements, but he frequently drew on the legacy of **Arabian fantasy** and Egyptian mythology, most notably in *The Quest of the Sacred Slipper* (1914), *Brood of the Witch Queen* (1918), and some of the stories in *Tales of Secret Egypt* (1918), *The Haunting of Low Fennel* (1920), and *Tales of East and West* (1932). A few of the exotic **detective** stories in *The Dream Detective* (1920) and some items in *The Wrath of Fu Manchu and Other Stories* (1973) are also fantasies. The series comprising *Nude in Mink* (1950, aka *Sins of Sumuru*), *Sumuru* (1951, aka *Slaves of Sumuru*), *The Fire Goddess* (1952, aka *Virgin in Flames*), *Return of Sumuru* (1954, aka *Sand and Satin*), and *Sinister Madonna* (1956) has fugitive elements of **erotic fantasy**. *The Romance of Sorcery* (1914) is a **scholarly fantasy** culled from **Éliphas Lévi** and **Jules Michelet**.

ROMANCE. The Old French term *romanz* signified the vernacular; originally used in the phrase *roman courtois,* the prefix *roman* was adopted into the description of many other genres, including the *roman d'aventure* and the *roman d'antiquité*; after a somewhat convoluted etymological journey it ended up as the French word for "novel." It made its way into English via Anglo-Norman and was retained in such phrases as **chivalric romance**.

Romance became popular as a critical term in the 18th century, when such works as Richard Hurd's *Letters on Chivalry and Romance* (1762) examined chivalric romance as a product of feudal society and construed its supernatural elements allegorically. "Realism" and "romance" were frequently used thereafter as paired opposites, and it was in that context that **romanticism** became the definitive term of a movement. Romance was almost always regarded as the more "primitive" element of the pair and realism the more "advanced"; Clara Reeve's suggestion in *The Progress of Romance* (1785) that romance not only had a future but was capable of further evolution was unusual, but the fact that the argument was presented as a dialogue allowed unsympathetic readers to side with the spokesman of convention if they wished.

The implications of the English word have shifted as dramatically and confusingly as those of its French counterpart. Ironically, it has reverted in common parlance to something more closely akin to its origin, being commonly applied to matters of courtship; the commodified genre of "romance" consists of stereotyped love stories whose fantastic nature was obscured by their exclusion of obvious supernatural intrusions until the development in the 1990s of **paranormal romance**. The term's use in fantasy criticism, however, often remains deliberately archaic.

ROMANTICISM. A movement in the arts and philosophy with reverberations that profoundly affected intellectual, social, and political life from the late 18th to the mid-19th century. It was originally conceived, in Germany, as the dialectical antithesis of classicism in the field of aesthetics, implying a retreat from formal constraint in order to allow the imagination freer play; as it spread, however, it came to be seen as a rebellion against the ideas, rewards, and supposed lessons of the Enlightenment, challenging the intellectual hegemony of science and reason, as well as the social hegemony of tradition. Extreme romanticism championed subjectivity against the supposed excesses of objectivity, and rhyme against the supposed excesses of reason, although its correlation with a dramatic resurgence of interest in the supernatural, folklore, **mythology**, and the elements of **chivalric romance** was essentially academic, conducted in a spirit of conscientious fabulation. It was not until romanticism became **decadent** that it became unrepentantly fantastic, although French romanticism was entangled from its inception with the cult of "sensibility" established by Jean-Jacques Rousseau and its apparent glorification of the "noble savage."

Leading German Romantics included **Johann Wolfgang von Goethe**, "Novalis," Friedrich Schiller, **Ludwig Tieck**, **Johann Musäus**, and **Friedrich de la Motte Fouqué**. English romanticism, foreshadowed by James Macpherson's invention of Ossian and by the "graveyard poetry" of Edward Young, was theorized by **Nathan Drake**, **Samuel Taylor Coleridge,** and **William Blake**; **Percy Shelley**, **Lord Byron**, and **John Keats** were among its most significant converts. The central figures of the French movement included **Charles Nodier**, Victor Hugo, **Théophile Gautier**, and—his adoption permitted because America had no movement of its own to speak of—**Edgar Allan Poe**. (The unique character of American fantastic literature is partly due to the fact that imported Romantic ideas seemed irrelevant to a nation with an expanding frontier that was determinedly obliterating a world strongly akin to the one whose allegedly tragic loss European Romanticism was lamenting).

The historical novel and its **Gothic** spinoff were key products of romanticism, as were collections and imitations of **fairy tales**. Although the Romantic movements went into a long decline after 1848, their influence was not discarded; they were the parents of decadence and **symbolism** and the grandparents of **surrealism** and expressionism. Romanticism was a component of the development of individualism, insisting that man is not *entirely* a political animal and that the world of private experience provides a haven where anyone may enjoy a precious freedom from the tyranny of social regulation. Fantasy, in the psychological sense, is the mechanism that exercises this freedom, and fantasy literature is a key instrument in its exercise.

ROSENBERG, JOEL (1954–). U.S. writer. The series comprising *The Sleeping Dragon* (1983), *The Sword and the Chain* (1984), *The Silver Crown* (1985), *The Heir Apparent* (1987), *The Warrior Lives* (1989), *The Road to Ehvenor* (1991), and *The Road Home* (1995) begins as a **portal fantasy** in which role-playing **gamers** are drawn into their gameworld, but it is gradually transfigured into a stereotypical **immersive fantasy** series. The setting is **reycled** in *Not Exactly the Three Musketeers* (1999), a parody of **Alexandre Dumas** that was followed by *Not Quite Scaramouche* (2000) and *Not Really the Prisoner of Zenda*

(2003). *Legacy* (2004) and *To Home and Ehvenor* (2004) reverted to the original schema. *D'Shai* (1991) and *The Hour of the Octopus* (1994) are fantasy/mystery **hybrids**. The Keeper of the Hidden Ways trilogy, comprising *The Fire Duke* (1995), *The Silver Stone* (1996), and *The Crimson Sky* (1998), is a **contemporary** fantasy blending **Celtic** and **Nordic** materials. *Paladins* (2004) is set in an **alternative** 17th century, in an England where Mordred defeated **Arthur** and founded a dynasty.

ROSENDORFER, HERBERT (1934–). German writer. The novel translated as *The Architect of Ruins* (1969; tr. 1992) is an elaborate **metafictional/visionary fantasy**. In *Letters Back to Ancient China* (1983; tr. 1997), a displaced 10th-century mandarin reports his impressions of the modern world. *Stephanie; or, A Previous Existence* (1987; tr. 1995) is also a **timeslip** fantasy.

ROSICRUCIAN FANTASY. The notion of a secret doctrine known to members of a long-estabished Brotherhood of the Rosy Cross was popularized by three pamphlets, one of which—generally known as the *Fama Fraternitus* (1614; tr. 1652)—is a brief biography of the magician Christian Rosenkreutz, while the second, *Confessio Frateritas* (1615), fills in the historical background of his magical initiation, providing a key source of inspiration for the **scholarly fantasies** of Éliphas Lévi and many others. The third, signed by the philosopher Johann Valentin Andreae (who also wrote the Utopian romance *Christianopolis,* 1619; tr. 1916), was translated as *The Heretick Romance; or, the Chymical Wedding* (1616; tr. 1690); it is an archetypal **alchemical romance**.

The three documents exerted a powerful influence on **lifestyle fantasists**, renewed when the brotherhood was given literary publicity by **Edward Bulwer-Lytton**'s *Zanoni,* which gave rise to a plethora of Rosicrucian lodges in late 19th-century Paris and inspired the founding of the Order of the Golden Dawn. **A. E. Waite**'s *The Real History of the Rosicrucians* (1887) summarized the imaginary history of such lifestyle fantasies. Specific Rosicrucian imagery continues to crop up in such works as **Lindsay Clarke**'s *The Chymical Wedding,* although it has mostly been absorbed into the syncretic amalgam of creeds underlying modern **occult fantasy**.

ROSSETTI, CHRISTINA (1830–1894). British poet, sister of the pre-Raphaelite poet and painter Dante Gabriel Rossetti. Strikingly atypical of her work is the long poem *Goblin Market* (1862), which poses as a moralistic **fairy tale** although its account of the redemption by sisterly love of a girl unwise enough to consume "forbidden fruit" is easily decodable as a fervent **erotic fantasy**. Her other long fantasy poem, *The Prince's Progress* (1875), is an account of an errant prince whose impatient bride-to-be dies of frustration when he is delayed too long on the road. Her prose tales, including "The Story of Nick" (1857), "Hero" (1865), and the long **hallucinatory fantasy** that opens the collection *Speaking Likenesses* (1874) are equally moralistic, although their sternness similarly seems to overlie deep anxieties.

ROWLING, J. K. (1965–). British writer. The series she began with *Harry Potter and the Philosopher's Stone* (1997, aka *Harry Potter and the Sorcerer's Stone*) and extended in *Harry Potter and the Chamber of Secrets* (1998), *Harry Potter and the Prisoner of Azkaban* (1999), *Harry Potter and the Goblet of Fire* (2000), and *Harry Potter and the Order of the Phoenix* (2003), with two books still to come, became the best-selling books of their era throughout Europe and the United States. The series blends the traditional British boarding-school story with the American high-school **horror** story—in which metaphorical modeling of the hormonal dramas of adolescents had evolved from crude B movies like *I Was a Teenage Werewolf* (1957), through **Stephen King**'s *Carrie* (1976), to the 1990s TV series *Buffy the Vampire-Slayer*—and embeds the amalgam in an archetypal **heroic fantasy** cast (unusual, for a **children's fantasy**) as an expansive **series**.

In the mundane sphere, Harry Potter is the despised and abused ward of the revolting Dursley family, but at school he is an apprentice **wizard** marked for greatness, having turned the tables on the vile Lord Voldemort—the slayer of his parents—while still in his cradle. He and Voldemort are now engaged in a desperate race against time; while Harry learns to use his gradually maturing **magic**, Voldemort slowly regains his power and influence, losing a series of preliminary skirmishes while apparently preparing to precipitate a magical Armageddon that only Harry can prevent. Two volumes of "nonfictional" spinoff are *Fantastic Beasts and Where to Find Them by Newt Scamander* (2001) and *Quidditch through the Ages by Kennilworthy Whisp* (2001).

The astonishing commercial success of the Harry Potter series inevitably sparked a boom in magical school stories, ranging from the imitative series comprising *The Magickers* (2001), *The Curse of Arkady* (2002), and *The Dragon Guard* (2003), by "Emily Drake" (Rhondi Vilott Salsitz), and **Jenny Nimmo**'s Charlie Bone series to E. Rose

Sabin's conscientiously cynical *A School for Sorcery* (2002) and its **prequel** *A Perilous Power* (2004).

RUSCH, KRISTINE KATHYRN (1960–). U.S. writer and editor active in various genres (refer to *HDSFL*). With her husband, Dean Wesley Smith, she founded the innovative small press Pulphouse, and she edited ***The Magazine of Fantasy and Science Fiction*** from 1991 to 1998. *The White Mists of Power* (1991) is a **bardic fantasy**. *The Gallery of His Dreams* (1991) is a **sentimental/timeslip** fantasy. The young heroine of *Heart Readers* (1993) must apply her empathic talent to the salvation of a kingdom. In the Fey series, comprising *Sacrifice* (1995), *Changeling* (1996), *Rival* (1997), *The Resistance* (1998), and *Victory* (1998), islanders seek refuge in an invisible fortress before turning the tables on invaders. The Black Throne series, set in the same milieu, comprises *The Black Queen* (1999) and *The Black King* (2000). In *Fantasy Life* (2003), a family in Oregon protects mythical sea creatures. Rusch used the byline "Katherine Grayson" on a number of "paranormal romances," including *Utterly Charming* (2000), *Thoroughly Kissed* (2001), *Completely Smitten* (2002), *Simply Irresistible* (2003), and *Absolutely Captivated* (2004).

RUSHDIE, SALMAN (1947–). Indian-born writer resident in Britain from 1961 until he relocated to the United States after spending years in hiding because of a *fatwa* issued against him by Iran's Ayatollah Khomeini on the basis of false rumors that the vivid **religious fantasy** *The Satanic Verses* (1988) was blasphemous. *Grimus* (1975) is an elaborate **Orphean fantasy**. In *Midnight's Children* (1980), 1,001 children born at the moment of India's independence obtain magical talents; similar marginal fantasy elements with a **magical realism** ambience are employed in *Shame* (1983) and *The Moor's Last Sigh* (1995). *Haroun and the Sea of Stories* (1990) is a children's **portal fantasy** in which the young hero must retrieve the power of story for purposes of **re-enchantment**. *The Ground beneath Her Feet* (1999) is another **Orphean fantasy**. The collection *East, West* (1994) includes a few fantasies.

RUSSELL, SEAN (1952–). Canadian writer. In *The Initiate Brother* (1991) and *Gatherer of Clouds* (1992), a mystically gifted mock-**Oriental** monk plays a **messianic** role. In *World without End* (1995) and *Sea without a Shore* (1996), an ocean voyage at the dawn of an Age of Enlightenment terminates on an unexpected island. In the River into Darkness couplet comprising *Beneath the Vaulted Hills* (1997) and *The*

Compass of the Soul (1998), the last great mage has all but eradicated **magic** when he meets opposition. The Swan's War series, comprising *The One Kingdom* (2001), *The Isle of Battle* (2002), and *The Shadow Roads* (2004), is an **epic** fantasy.

RUSSIAN FANTASY. The integration of Russian folklore into literature by such writers as **Nikolai Gogol**, **Vladimir Odoevsky**, and **Ivan Turgenev** was considerably more phantasmagoric and philosophically complicated than the parallel patterns in Western Europe. Further examples can be found in the work of Fedor Sologub, sampled in *The Sweet-Scented Name and Other Fairy Tales, Fables and Stories* (tr. 1915). Although the Russian Revolution suppressed such materials—including the work of **Mikhail Bulgakov**—in the name of "socialist realism," it continually crept back into examples of Russian **sf** (refer to *HDSFL*) and burst forth again after the collapse of communism in works by such writers as Yuri Buida, author of *The Zero Train* (1993; tr. 2001) and *The Prussian Bride* (1998; abr. tr. 2002), and Victor Pelevin, whose works range from *The Life of Insects* (tr. 1996) to *Homo Zapiens* (tr. 2002). **Commodified fantasy** rapidly became established, encouraging Russia's Annual SF Writers' Congress to institute a "sword award," whose winners include Yuri Braider, Nikolai Chadovich, Andrei Lazarchuk, Mikhail Uspensky, and Evegny Lukin.

RYMAN, GEOFF (1951–). Canadian-born writer, resident in Britain since 1973. *The Warrior Who Carried Life* (1985) is an innovative **quest** fantasy climaxing in **Eden**. *The Unconquered Country* (1984; book 1986) is a **surreal/hybrid/science fantasy**. *"Was . . ."* (1992, aka *Was*) is a marginal **sentimental fantasy** drawing heavily on the imagery of **L. Frank Baum**'s *The Wonderful Wizard of Oz* and the history of the movie version starring Judy Garland. *Lust* (2001) is an **erotic fantasy**.

– S –

SABERHAGEN, FRED (1930–). U.S. writer best known for **sf** (refer to *HDSFL*). The Empire of the East trilogy, comprising *The Broken Lands* (1968), *The Black Mountains* (1971), and *Changeling Earth* (1973, aka *Ardneh's World*), is a **hybrid/science fantasy**, but the sequel trilogy comprising the Books of Swords (1983–84) reflects its origins as a **game** scenario. The Books of Lost Swords series, comprising *Woundhealer's Story* (1986), *Sightblinder's Story* (1987), *Stonecutter's Story* (1988), *Farslayer's Story* (1989), *Coinspinner's Story* (1989), *Mindsword's Story* (1990), *Wayfinder's Story* (1992), and *Shieldbreaker's Story* (1994), is similarly **commodified**.

The Dracula Tape (1975) helped prepare the way for revisionist **vampire** fiction, casting the count as an altruist whose motives were disastrously misconstrued by Stoker's superstitious protagonists; *The Holmes-Dracula File* (1978) continued the **metafictional** theme; some of the later volumes in the series are **hybrid** thrillers, but Holmes and Dracula got together again in *Seance for a Vampire* (1994). *A Sharpness in the Neck* (1996) invokes Robespierre, Napoleon, and the Marquis de Sade.

The Black Throne (1990, with **Roger Zelazny**) features **Edgar Allan Poe**. *Merlin's Bones* (1995) is a far-ranging **Arthurian fantasy**. *Dancing Bears* (1996) is a **theriomorphic fantasy**. The Book of Gods series, begun with *The Face of Apollo* (1998), *Ariadne's Web* (1999), *The Arms of Hercules* (2000), *God of the Golden Fleece* (2001), and *Gods of Fire and Thunder* (2002), began as **classical fantasy** but extended into **Nordic fantasy**.

SALMONSON, JESSICA AMANDA (1950–). U.S. editor and writer whose earliest publications were in the **small press** publication *The Literary Magazine of Fantasy and Terror* (1973), which she (then he) edited as Amos Salmonson. Her **anthology series** *Amazons!* (2 vols., 1979–82) and *Heroic Visions* (2 vols., 1983–86) are wholly or partly dedicated to **sword and sorcery** stories with female heroes; her own works in that vein include an **Oriental fantasy** trilogy, comprising *Tomoe Gozen* (1981; aka *The Disfavored Hero*), *The Golden Naginata* (1982) and *Thousand Shrine Warrior* (1984), and *The Swordswoman* (1982). *Ou Lu Khen and the Beautiful Madwoman* (1985) is a further Oriental fantasy.

Salmonson's short fantasies, many of a **decadent** stripe, are mingled with **horror** stories in *A Silver Thread of Madness* (1989), *John Collier and Fredric Brown Went Quarrelling through My Head* (1989), *The Eleventh Jaguarundi* (1995), and *The Dark Tales* (2002). *The Mysterious Doom and Other Ghostly Tales of the Pacific Northwest* (1992) **recycles** local folklore. A series of **occult/detective** stories is collected in *Harmless Ghosts: The Penelope Penniweather Stories* (1990) and *Phantom Waters* (1995). *Mr Monkey and Other Sumerian Fables* (1995) recycles the oldest known examples of **fables**.

A strong scholarly interest in 19th-century **ghost** stories, especially those by female writers—reflected in the anthologies *Tales of Moonlight* (1983), *The Haunted Wherry and Other Rare Ghost Stories* (1985), *What Did Miss Darrington See? An Anthology of Feminist Supernatural Fiction* (1989), and *Tales of Moonlight II* (1989)—led Salmonson to compile collections of the supernatural fiction of such writers as Hildegarde Hawthorne, Anna Nicholas, and Sarah Orne Jewett, much of which tends to the **sentimental** rather than the horrific.

SALVATORE, R. A. (1959–). U.S. writer, mostly of **game/tie-in** fantasies developing *Dungeons and Dragons* scenarios. Works not tied to such enterprises include the Chronicles of Ynis Aiellke, comprising *Echoes of the Fourth Magic* (1990), *The Witch's Daughter* (1991), and *Bastion of Darkness* (2000); the Spearwielder's Tale trilogy, comprising *The Woods out Back* (1993), *The Dragon's Dagger* (1994), and *Dragonslayer's Return* (1995); the **picaresque** Crimson Shadow trilogy, comprising *The Sword of Bedwyr* (1995), *Luthien's Gamble* (1996), and *The Dragon King* (1996); and the **dark fantasy** Demon Wars trilogies, the first comprising *The Demon Awakens* (1997), *The Demon Spirit* (1998), and *The Demon Apostle* (1999), and the second *Mortalis* (2000), *Transcendence* (2002), and *Immortalis* (2003). Other Demon Wars novels include *Ascendance* (2001) and the **prequel** series launched by *The Highwayman* (2004).

SAMPSON, FAY (1935–). British writer. Her **children's fiction** includes several fantasies, notably *The Chains of Sleep* (1981) and the Pangur Bán **animal fantasy** series comprising the stories in *Pangur Bán: The White Cat* (1983) and the novels *Finnglas of the Horses* (1985), *Finnglas and the Stones of Choosing* (1986), *Shape Shifter: The Naming of Pangur Bán* (1988), *The Serpent of Senargad* (1989), and *The White Horse is Running* (1990). *Them* (2003) is a **messianic fantasy**.

Sampson's work for adults includes a series of **feminized/Arthurian fantasies** featuring **Morgan le Fay**, collectively entitled *Daughter of Tintagel,* comprising *Wise Woman's Telling* (1989), *White Nun's Telling* (1989), *Blacksmith's Telling* (1990), *Taliesin's Telling* (1991), and *Herself* (1992). *Star Dancer* (1993) is a **historical fantasy** based on Sumerian mythology, featuring the **goddess** Inanna. In *The Silent Fort* (2003), **druids** resist the Roman invasion of Devon. *The Island Pilgrimage* (2004) is a love story with elements of **religious fantasy**.

SAND, GEORGE (1804–1876). Pseudonym of French writer Aurore Dupin, baronne Dudevant. *The Devil's Pool* (1846; tr. 1847) is an **ambiguous** account of peasant life and superstition. *The Naiad* (1857; tr. 1892) is a **delusional** fantasy cast as a legal case study. The **allegorical** aspirations of the Jules Verne–inspired **hallucinatory fantasy** *Journey within the Crystal* (1865; tr. 1992) also infected the stories she was prompted to write for her grandchildren, *Tales of a Grandmother* (1872–76; abr. tr. 1930); these include the quasi-autobiographical novella "The Castle of Pictordu," the allegory of **flight** "Wings of Courage," a heartfelt story of a frog princess ("Queen Coax"), and an account of the destruction of "The Giant Yéous."

SATIRE. A literary work criticizing collective or individual vices by holding them up to ridicule, usually by means of incongruous exaggeration. The term is derived from the "satyr plays" of Greek drama, which provided tragedy with its comedic complement and counterweight. The genre was soon taken up by poets and prose writers; in the latter medium, it often took the form of fantastic voyages culminating in images of exotic societies, as exemplified by **Lucian**, **François Rabelais**, **Jonathan Swift**, and many others. The artifice of satire was crucial to the development of self-conscious **fabulation**, beginning with the earliest **fables**; **animal fantasy** continues to boast such modern exemplars of the satirical fable as **George Orwell**'s *Animal Farm*. **Visionary fantasy** was also used for satirical purposes from an early stage.

Portal fantasies became a significant medium of satire when the supply of terra incognita ran out, although much satire was also relocated in the narrative spaces of **sf**. **Intrusive fantasy** of the kind associated with **F. Anstey** has considerable scope for satire, exploited by many modern fabulators; key examples include **Thomas Berger** and **James Morrow**. Satire remains very evident in various fields of **religious fantasy**, especially **infernal comedy**. **Erotic fantasy** is also a fertile field for satire; mythological and legendary symbolizations of the erotic impulse are used satirically in the works of such writers as **John Erskine** and **George S. Viereck**.

SAVAGE, FELICITY (1975–). Irish-born writer resident in the United States. The Garden of Salt couplet, comprising *Humility Garden* (1995) and *Delta City* (1996), is a **decadent fantasy** featuring a rebellion against the rule of manifest **gods**. The three-decker novel *Ever,* whose individual volumes are *The War in the Waste* (1997), *The Daemon in the*

Machine (1998), and *A Trickster in the Ashes* (1998), is set in an **alternative** world in which **demonic** power has been domesticated and ingeniously exploited.

SCARBOROUGH, ELIZABETH (1947–). U.S. writer. The series comprising *Song of Sorcery* (1982), *The Unicorn Creed* (1983), *Bronwyn's Bane* (1983), and *The Christening Quest* (1985) offers **humorous** versions of **commodified** formulas, as do the **Arabian fantasy** *The Harem of Aman Akbar; or, The Djinn Decanted* (1984), *The Drastic Dragon of Draco, Texas* (1986), and *The Goldcamp Vampire; or, the Sanguinary Sourdough* (1987). The Vietnam-set *The Healer's War* (1988), by contrast, is an intense drama in which fantastic elements offer amelioration of the depths of desperation; a similar spirit is evident in *Nothing Sacred* (1991) and *Last Refuge* (1992), in which a Far Eastern refuge from the world's troubles becomes a base for social renewal.

Scarborough's adventures in comic fantasy continued in the trilogy comprising *Phantom Banjo* (1991), *Picking the Ballad's Bones* (1991), and *Strum Again?* (1992), in which the world-saving potential of folk **music** makes its practitioners the target of demonic attack. The heroine of the series comprising *The Godmother* (1994), *The Godmother's Apprentice* (1995), and *The Godmother's Web* (1998) is a magically talented social worker who finds that old **fairy tale** motifs still crop up with distressing regularity. *The Lady in the Loch* (1998) is a **hybrid** mystery featuring **Walter Scott**. Scarborough's short fiction is sampled in *Scarborough Fair and Other Stories* (2003).

SCHEHERAZADE. The ostensible narrator of **Antoine Galland**'s *Arabian Nights,* whose life depends on her storytelling expertise; the name is also rendered Shahrazad. She became an archetypal figure, her skill elaborately celebrated by many sympathetic writers, ranging from **Paul Féval** to **John Barth** and **Isabel Allende**. Her plight is reexamined in Barth's "Dunyazadiad" and Githa Hariharan's *When Dreams Travel* (1999), and her story is further extrapolated in Anthony O'Neill's *Scheherazade* (2001) and Cameron Dokey's *The Storyteller's Daughter* (2002).

SCHOLARLY FANTASY. The history of imaginative fiction cannot be adequately explained without taking note of the influential loop connecting literary fantasies with **lifestyle fantasies** and **scholarly fantasies**, a loop through which material circulates very freely; an innovation in any one field routinely infects the others. The problems of defining fantasy literature and lifestyle fantasy are eased by the stratagem of identifying the operation of some kind of magic within a literary text and by the pretense of being able to work some kind of magic in a fantasized lifestyle, but scholarly fantasies are more various. Not all histories of magical beliefs are scholarly fantasies, although such materials are uncommonly amenable to fantastic extrapolation; on the other hand, it is by no means impossible to construct very fanciful hypotheses to "explain" perfectly mundane materials.

Any work presented as nonfiction may legitimately be called a scholarly fantasy if it can be objectively demonstrated that the case made therein far exceeds the warrant of available evidence, especially if it employs fanciful "secondary elaboration" in an attempt to nullify countervailing evidence and logical contradiction. There are, inevitably, accidental elements of scholarly fantasy in many early works of scholarship whose authors were forced to depend on unreliable hearsay—including such historians as Herodotus and such natural historians as Pliny—or adventurous speculation, after the fashion of medical theorists and cosmological theorists. The most notable deliberate scholarly fantasy in **classical** literature is Plato's invention of **Atlantis**, which was probably not intended to deceive, although subsequent propagandistic exercises—Geoffrey of Monmouth's *History of the Kings of Britain* is a particularly significant example—probably were; at any rate, scholarly fantasies rapidly became sophisticated in the artistry of deception.

Whatever their followers may claim, and however sincere their practitioners might be, all treatises on **alchemy**, **astrology**, **reincarnation**, **spiritualism**, **theosophy**, and ritual **magic** are scholarly fantasies. In terms of the history of fantasy literature, however, such texts are of less significance than historical studies that produce fanciful hypotheses to "explain" the history of magical beliefs and the persecution of **witches** in unduly credulous terms, whether (like **Éliphas Lévi**) they accept the workability of magic or merely (like **James Frazer** and **Margaret Murray**) offer recklessly fabricated accounts of the magical beliefs supposedly held by their subjects.

Scholarly fantasies are bound to emerge from the human sciences in some profusion, because the understanding at which those sciences aim involves trying to see things as other social actors see (or, in history, saw) them. Such acts of imaginative identification are intrinsically difficult to test, and such evidence as the past leaves behind usually fits several different accounts of what the relevant actors might have thought they were doing. When interpretations of the past have to come to terms with the fantasies entertained by the people of the past, attempts to sort out what was actually believed, to what extent, and on what grounds become extremely difficult; such attempts risk infection not only by the fantasies of the objects of study but by fantasies born of earlier attempts to understand them. In consequence, scholarly fantasies once thought extinct or obsolete sometimes make spectacular comebacks, often in **transfigured** forms. This is one reason why belief in magic and divination seems to be more widespread now than ever before—and why both accidental and calculated scholarly fantasies are more widespread now than they have ever been before.

Fantasy literature inevitably makes avid use of scholarly fantasies whenever such borrowing is convenient or aesthetically appealing; even the most candid **fabulation** requires the cultivation of narrative plausibility. Thus, **Celtic fantasy** draws extensively on the fantasies of **Lewis Spence**, **Arthurian** and **grail** quest fantasy on the fantasies of **Jessie Weston**, and **goddess** fantasy on the post-Frazerian fantasies of Robert Graves. **Taproot texts** are not merely treasure houses ripe for plunder but sources of authority, and antiquity lends such authority even to the wildest allegations that fabricated antiquity is a valuable asset. Obvious and frankly preposterous inventions can not only be excused by the pretence that they are ancient but invested with a precious glamor. Literary poseurs are, however, less prone to the danger of falling prey to their own rhetoric than are scholarly fantasists; many scholarly fantasists—like most lifestyle fantasists—appear to be failed literateurs, for whom nonfictional representation of their ideas was a fall-back position.

SCHWEITZER, DARRELL (1952–). U.S. editor and writer, very active in the **small press** field. He has been associated with various revivals of ***Weird Tales*** since 1977; his own work is solidly set in **Lovecraftian** tradition, although his scholarly interests extend farther back to such writers as **Lord Dunsany**. The story series collected in *We Are All Legends* (1981) is an elegiac **heroic fantasy**. *The White Isle* (1975; exp. book 1989) is an **Orphean fantasy**. *The Shattered Goddess* (1982) is a **far-futuristic fantasy**. *The Mask of the Sorcerer* (1991; exp. book 1995) is set in a **prehistoric** milieu. Short stories employing equally various settings are mingled with other materials in *Tom O'Bedlam's Night Out and Other Strange Excursions* (1985), *Refugees from an Imaginary Country* (1999), and *The Great World and the Small: More*

Tales of the Ominous and Magical (2001). *Transients and Other Disquieting Stories* (1993) is more inclined toward **horror**.

SCHWOB, MARCEL (1867–1905). French writer. He was one of the most versatile contributors to the French **Decadent** movement; his friendship with **Oscar Wilde**—he helped **Pierre Louÿs** to polish the final draft of *Salomé*—assisted the movement's exportation to Britain. His works include two collections of tales inspired by **Charles Baudelaire**'s translations of **Edgar Allan Poe**, translations from which are sampled in *The King in the Golden Mask and Other Stories* (1982).

SCIENCE FANTASY. A term used in several different ways, most frequently to refer to a **hybrid** tradition of pulp fiction extending from the works of **Edgar Rice Burroughs** and **A. Merritt**, which borrowed notions from the vocabulary of **sf** (refer to *HDSFL*) to add plausibility to exotic exercises in uninhibited escapism. Although the primary form of such fiction is the **planetary romance**, the jargon of **parallel worlds** gave a significant boost to hybrid **portal fantasies**, and the use of **far-futuristic fantasy** by **Clark Ashton Smith** opened up another useful arena. While sf retained its dominant position in the paperback marketplace, there was considerable pressure on writers of **immersive fantasy** to use tokenistic science-fictional frames. That pressure evaporated after 1980. Many writers continued to employ various kinds of **hybridization** for purely aesthetic reasons, but a more enduring legacy was the kind of **chimerical** science fantasy pioneered by ***Unknown***, which enjoyed a considerable resurgence once genre fantasy was firmly established in its commercial niche. The chimerical combinations favored by writers who dabbled in **fabulation** further enhanced the modern dominance of chimerical science fantasy over hybrid forms.

SCIENCE FICTION. A kind of fantasy that mimics the method of science in extrapolating rationally plausible consequences from empirically licensed premises. This method is particularly useful for the generation of hypothetical technologies and for constructing plausible images of the near future; consequently, almost all fantasies featuring imaginary machines or set in the future are generally reckoned to be sf, even if their claims to rational plausibility are derisory. Although a good deal of sf is **intrusive**, featuring newly developed hypothetical technologies or alien invasions, and while many sf stories employ **portals** of various kinds to transport their protagonists into the future or alien worlds, it was sf writers who were forced by the nature of their concerns to develop the narrative techniques appropriate to **immersive fantasy**.

Because it was the pulp sf magazines that trained their audience in the esoteric skills required in reading immersive fantasy, pulp experiments in other kinds of immersive fantasy—most notably **sword and sorcery** fiction—shared a substantial fraction of the same audience, and the relevant subgenres remained closely associated until the assumption of economic hegemony by paperback books facilitated their fission. This close association encouraged the growth and development of various kinds of **science fantasy**, and it also ensured that when **commodified fantasy** emerged in the 1970s it would be displayed in the same display space as sf in bookshops. The competition for shelf space thus instituted was always certain to be won by commodified fantasy, partly because its raw materials are more universally accessible but mainly because it is amenable to the tight formularizarion required to secure predictability of effect, while sf is not.

Writers of "hard sf" who dabble in pure fantasy—notably **Robert A. Heinlein**, **Poul Anderson**, Greg Bear, in *Songs of Earth and Power* (1994), and Lois McMaster Bujold, in *The Curse of Chalion* (2001) and *Paladin of Souls* (2003)—inevitably bring a sensibility to the task quite distinct from that of writers of science fantasy whose work sheds its hybrid elements, like **Andre Norton**, **Marion Zimmer Bradley**, Julian May—in the Boreal Moon series (launched 2003)—and Sean McMullen, in the Moonworlds saga (launched 2003). Several recent debutants in the field of commodified fantasy have been sf writers **pseudonymously** repackaging themselves; notable examples include "David Farland" (Dave Wolverton), author of the Runelords series (1998–2003); "Valery Leith" (Tricia Sullivan), author of the Everien trilogy, comprising *The Company of Glass* (1999), *The Riddled Night* (2000), and *The Way of the Rose* (2001); and "S. L. Farrell" (Stephen Leigh), author of the Cloudmages series (launched 2003).

SCOTT, MICHAEL (1943–). Irish writer. His early works **recycled/ Celtic** legends and **folk tales** in *The Song of the Children of Lir* (1983) and *Irish Folk and Fairy Tales* (3 vols., 1984). The trilogy comprising *A Bright Enchantment, A Golden Dream,* and *A Silver Wish* (all 1985), the couplet comprising *The Last of the Fianna* (1987) and *The Quest of the Sons* (1988), and *Navigator: The Voyage of Saint Brendan* (1988, with Gloria Gaghan) are less straightforward in their recycling. The **bardic fantasy** trilogy comprising *Magician's Law* (1987), *Demon's Law*

(1988), and *Death's Law* (1989) embeds similar materials in an elegiac **historical fantasy** of **thinning**. The De Danann Tales comprise *Windlord* (1991) and *Earthlord* (1991). Scott's subsequent work maintained its melodramatic pitch by transplanting similar raw materials into **horror** fiction; fantasy elements are most conspicuous in *Banshee* (1990) and *Reflection* (1992). He collaborated with Morgan Llywelyn on the Arcana series and various other projects.

SCOTT, SIR WALTER (1771–1832). Scottish writer. He compiled an important **anthology** of **ballads**, *Minstrelsy of the Scottish Border* (1802), and his own **Romantic** poetry makes copious use of Scottish **legends** and **fairy** lore. "The Lay of the Last Minstrel" (1805) helped define an image of the **wizard**—as a learned practitioner of various medieval arts, including **astrology** and **alchemy**—that echoes resonantly in modern fantasy literature. The publishing company Scott founded played a major role in popularizing similar materials in verse and prose. A few of his historical novels draw on Scottish legendry without becoming wholeheartedly fantastic, most notably *The Bride of Lammermoor* (1819) and *The Monastery* (1820). *Redgauntlet* (1824) includes the often-reprinted "Wandering Willie's Tale," about a dangerous excursion to the world of the dead (refer to *HDHL*).

SECONDARY WORLD. A term coined by **J. R. R. Tolkien** in "On Fairy-stories" (1947) to describe the kind of location in which **fairy tales** generally take place, the imaginative entry into which by the reader involves the process of **enchantment**. It proved such a useful term that its range of reference was broadened to take in other kinds of fantastic locations—especially the spaces that lie on the other side of **portals**—as it became one of the basic terms of critical discourse in relation to fantasy literature. The means by which **secondary worlds** can be linked to the **primary world** are many and various; although there are only three fundamental dimensions of potential displacement—backward in time, forward in time, and "sideways" into a **lost** or **parallel world**—their use is complicated by more elaborate narrative strategies. With the exception of **far-futuristic fantasies**, futuristic scenarios are usually surrendered to **sf**, but the past and parallel worlds are each stocked with several subspecies of imaginary locations.

The idea that lands once existed that have vanished from the Earth's surface, usually by inundation, is central to **Atlantean fantasy** and its analogues. The hypothetical continent of Lemuria, invented by zoologists attempting to understand similarities between the ecosystems of Madagascar and India when continental drift was still regarded as a **scholarly fantasy**, was integrated into **theosophical fantasy**, along with the sub-Arctic realm of Hyperborea popularized by Pliny the Elder, and spread therefrom into other subgenres, notably **sword and sorcery** fiction. Some later **scholarly fantasists** moved Lemuria from the Indian Ocean to the Pacific, a new variant being popularized in *The Lost Continent of Mu* (1926) by James Churchward. Other lost continents of scholarly fantasy include John Newbrough's Pan and **Lewis Spence**'s Antillia, but these are of negligible relevance to fantasy fiction; the drowned land of Lyonesse or Ys is more commonly encountered.

Other lands reported in **traveler's tales** that remained plausible secondary-world settings until the early 20th century include the **biblical** Ophir, the South American lands of Eldorado and Cibola (the "seven cities" from which the Aztecs allegedly sprung), and the kingdom of Prester John—although what literary travelers usually find in such places is not so much the worldly wealth they seek as a reconnection with a quasi-**Arcadian** way of life. No clear boundary separates mundane geographical fancies from overtly supernatural locations like the Isles of the Blessed, the **Arthurian** Avalon, Cokaygne, St. Brendan's Isle, and the **Celtic** Tir-nan-Og, which are often syncretically combined by writers interested in their strategic modification. Historical inventions such as **James Branch Cabell**'s Poictesme or **Clark Ashton Smith**'s Averoigne are only slightly easier to sustain than contemporary ones like Anthony Hope's Ruritania and **T. F. Powys**'s Folly Down.

"Sideways" movements long preceded the sophistication of the idea of displacement in a fourth (or fifth) dimension, although the precise topographical relationship between the everyday world and such parallels as **Faerie** and various **underworlds** was never easy to define. The dreams of **visionary** and **hallucinatory fantasy** were the principal means of access to imaginary locations in the 19th century, thus linking those subgenres to the evolution of portal fantasy. Visionary access continued in use throughout the 20th century, in spite of the increased plausibility of dimensional portals, because it provided a ready means of "personalizing" imaginary locations to fit their content to the problems and ambitions of individual protagonists. Another convenient strategy of sideways movement is **miniaturization**, which allows imaginary locations to be packed away in the interstices of the primary world. **Science fantasies** routinely use extraterrestrial Earth-clones, thus establishing the subgenre of **planetary romances**. The rapid proliferation of computer **games** has greatly encouraged the location of secondary worlds in cyberspace.

The secondary worlds of **immersive fantasy** often refuse to specify any definite temporal or spatial relationship to the primary world, although their replication of the physical conditions of Earth's surface tacitly implies that they can be considered as alternatives within a generous **multiverse**. Worlds within texts may, however, be credited with an entirely independent existence, any resemblances to our own being merely fortuitous.

SECRET HISTORY. A pattern of events imagined to be taking place "behind the scenes" of recorded history without disturbing it. Historical fiction makes much of such unrecorded events, and supernaturalized versions form the core of **historical fantasy**. Texts that allege that the recorded version of events is deeply mistaken or calculatedly deceptive edge into **alternative history**.

Secret histories involving workable magic, the actual existence of **vampires**, or the reality of **Faerie** are assisted in their plausibility by the assumption that some kind of **thinning** process has removed such supernatural apparatus from the modern world. Many secret histories, however, propose that supernatural devices have been deliberately concealed rather than thinned out, reserved for the esoteric use of secret societies. The latter notion is fundamental to much **occult fantasy**, especially **Rosicrucian fantasy**.

The notion that secret societies and conspiracies have played a major role in determining social progress while carefully removing all trace of themselves from the historical record is fundamental to a subgenre of thriller fiction pioneered by **Paul Féval**, which has recently enjoyed a spectacular revitalization in such best sellers as **Umberto Eco**'s *Foucault's Pendulum* and Dan Brown's *The Da Vinci Code* (2003). The **Templars** usually play a leading role in the secret histories mapped out in contemporary thrillers, but not in those constructed by such elaborate **historical fantasies** as **Mary Gentle**'s *Ash: A Secret History*.

SEDGWICK, MARCUS (1968–). British writer. *The Dark Horse* (2001) is a **prehistoric fantasy** with **Nordic** elements. *Witch Hill* (2001) features disturbing **dreams** of a **witch**. *The Book of Dead Days* (2003) is an unconventional **Faustian fantasy** involving an **underworld**.

SELF, WILL (1961–). British writer of literary fiction whose work is often flamboyantly grotesque. *Cock and Bull* (1992) is a graphic **erotic**

fantasy. *My Idea of Fun* (1993) has an element of **Faustian fantasy**. *Great Apes* (1997) is a **satirical/animal fantasy**. *How the Dead Live* (2000) has an element of **afterlife fantasy**. *Dorian* (2002) **transfigures** Oscar Wilde's *Picture of Dorian Gray*. The short stories in *The Quantity Theory of Insanity* (1991), *Grey Area and Other Stories* (1994), *Tough, Tough Toys for Tough, Tough Boys* (1998), and *Dr Mukti and Other Tales of Woe* (2004) include numerous **fabulations**.

SENDAK, MAURICE (1928–). U.S. illustrator who began writing texts for young **children** to accompany his more imaginative flights of fancy in *Kenny's Window* (1956). *Very Far Away* (1957) champions **escapism** as a existential necessity of childhood—a theme assertively carried forward by the classic *Where the Wild Things Are* (1963) and *In the Night Kitchen* (1970). *Outside Over There* (1981) is darker, **recycling** an **Orphean fantasy** preserved by the **Brothers Grimm**.

SENTIMENTAL FANTASY. Fantasy that supernaturalizes the affectionate emotions; the category includes a great many **erotic fantasies** in which the primary emphasis is on love rather than lust, but sentimental fantasies can also celebrate bonds between parents and children, siblings, humans and animals, and childhood friends. Sentimental fantasy is frequently heartrending and usually expresses a strong belief in the redemptive power of love, but it also includes relatively detached studies of the nature and power of bonds of intimacy. Notable examples of various types include **Théophile Gautier**'s *Spirite,* **George du Maurier**'s *Peter Ibbetson,* **Rudyard Kipling**'s *They,* F. W. Bourdillon's *Nephelé* (1896), **Barry Pain**'s *Going Home,* Daphne du Maurier's *The Loving Spirit* (1931), Edith Pargeter's *The City Lies Four-Square* (1939), Antoine de Saint-Exupéry's *The Little Prince* (1944), numerous works by **Robert Nathan**, **Peter S. Beagle**'s *A Fine and Private Place,* **Richard Matheson**'s *Bid Time Return,* Alan Brennert's *Kindred Spirits* (1984), **Nancy Willard**'s *Things Invisible to See,* and Lisa Carey's *The Mermaids Singing* (2001). **Paranormal romance** is a **commodified** form of sentimental fantasy; other subgenres conspicuously hospitable to it include **angelic fantasy** and **timeslip** fantasy.

SERIES. Sequels and series are of particular importance in fantasy, because the extrapolation of existing stories is an elementary form of story generation in oral culture, which was carried over into various kinds of fantasy literature based in **myth**, **legend**, and folklore. **Homer**'s *Odyssey* is a sequel to the *Iliad,* and much Greek drama carried forward the stories of heroes who fought at Troy. It is not entirely clear why early tragedies were grouped into trilogies, but Aristotle's *Poetics* pointed out that all stories have a natural tripartite pattern, in which the introduction, body and conclusion of the story have distinct functions to fulfil—an item of wisdom that remains fundamental to modern movie script-writing theory.

The natural tendency of stories set in the **secondary world** of "once upon a time" to extend into series usually gives rise to "expansive" series in which the careers of characters undergo profound changes. Commercial genres, by contrast, tend to be organized around endlessly repeatable narrative formulas, which give rise to "segmental" series like those typical of crime fiction, in which crime fighters are confronted with a potentially infinite sequence of antagonists to be outwitted, outfought, and ultimately defeated. Although the basic formula of **commodified fantasy** is, in a sense, the extrapolation of the crime fiction formula to its logical extreme, in which the antagonist is the embodiment of a pure evil that threatens an entire world, it is not conducive to repetition; this is one of the reasons why the most common "unit" of genre fantasy is the multivolume "miniseries." When genre fantasy first took root in the commercial arena such miniseries were usually trilogies, but later recruits became more inclined to plan on a larger scale—**J. K. Rowling**'s extrapolation of Harry Potter's career over seven volumes is a conspicuous example. Unplanned series like **C. S. Lewis**'s Narnia series typically struggle to maintain forward momentum and often resort to the incorporation of **prequels**.

The fantasy subgenres most conducive to segmental serialization are **heroic fantasies** that employ relatively modest antagonists—especially **sword and sorcery** adventures modeled on **Robert E. Howard**'s Conan series—and **humorous fantasies** of a **chimerical** stripe. Fantasized **detective** stories mimic the crime fiction formula most slavishly but are marginalized in consequence. All these kinds of series are, however, subject to the pressure of **melodramatic inflation**, which continually pushes them toward some sort of confrontation with an *ultimate* adversary, and they lack the grandiosity that is a key element of the appeal of **immersive fantasy**. The evolution of commodified **epic fantasy** has necessitated a considerable reduction in the power typically attributed to dark lords and more reliance on the strategy employed in naturalistic "family sagas," which repeat cycles of individual maturation and personal success by moving through the generations of a dynasty—a strategy that is more easily workable in fantasy worlds, where the pace of social change tends to be glacial, than it is in historical fiction. The close association between genre fantasy and genre **science fiction** has, however, encouraged some writers of series fantasy—notably **Terry Pratchett**—to incorporate the spirit of sf's "expansive" series wholeheartedly into their work, resulting in a steady increase in secondary worlds that become more progressive as they become more elaborate.

SEUSS, DR. (1904–1991). Pseudonym of U.S. writer Theodore Seuss Geisel, whose verses for **children** imported something of the **nonsense** tradition of **Edward Lear** but leavened it with strong does of **sentimentality** and **moralizing**. *To Think That I Saw It on Mulberry Street* (1937) is a straightforward championship of childhood imagination, but *The 500 Hats of Bartholomew Cubbins* (1938), *The King's Stilts* (1939), and *Horton Hatches the Egg* (1940) began a trend of increasing **surrealism** that climaxed in such works as *Bartholomew and the Oobleck* (1949), *Horton Hears a Who* (1954), *How the Grinch Stole Christmas* (1957), and the books starring *The Cat in the Hat* (1957), in which a careful restriction of vocabulary was taken to extremes in *Green Eggs and Ham* (1960). *Dr Seuss's Sleep Book* (1962) is his most wide-ranging fantasy project. Elements of **political satire** crept into some of his later books, including *The Lorax* (1971) and *The Butter Battle Book* (1984).

SEVERANCE, CAROL (1944–). U.S. writer based in Hawaii. Hawaiian legends form the background to the trilogy comprising *Demon Drums* (1992), *Storm Caller* (1993), and *Sorcerous Sea* (1993), in which a retired warrior is obliged to go back into action against exotic forces until his children can take up the cause.

SF. *See* SCIENCE FICTION.

SHAKESPEARE, WILLIAM (1564–1616). English poet and playwright. His early work includes a narrative poem **recycling** Ovid's story of *Venus and Adonis* (1593). The status won for him by his plays as the single most influential figure in the history of English literature lent tremendous impetus to the imagery of his two classic fantasy plays, *A Midsummer Night's Dream* (c1595) and *The Tempest* (c1611), whose derivatives form the core of the subgenre of Shakespearean fantasy. The former, which foregrounds Puck as a commentator on the transactions of Oberon and Titania's **fairy** court, had a uniquely powerful influence on literary treatments of fairy mythology, while the latter's central quartet of characters—the retired enchanter Prospero, his daughter Miranda, the captive sprite Ariel, and the monstrous Caliban—have become literary archetypes spawning countless derivative images.

The **witches** featured in *Macbeth* (1606) may have been added by other hands, but that has not diminished their influence as literary models. The ghost in *Hamlet* (c1600) is of a kind that was already stereotyped, but the manner of its deployment helped to encourage the development of **psychological fantasy**. Other ready-made images that Shakespeare recycled include the elements of the **classical fantasy** *Troilus and Cressida* (c1602). Characters from non-supernatural plays who number among his most memorable creations—notably Falstaff, Romeo and Juliet, and King Lear and his Fool—also serve as archetypes for dozens of characters in fantasy literature.

Notable examples of Shakespearean fantasy include **Poul Anderson**'s *A Midsummer Tempest,* **Tanith Lee**'s *Sung in Shadow,* **Tad Williams**'s *Caliban's Hour,* Rebecca Reisert's *The Third Witch* (2001) and *Ophelia's Revenge* (2003), **Sophie Masson**'s *The Tempestuous Voyage of Hopewell Shakespeare,* the title story of Robert Devereux's *Caliban and Other Tales* (2002), **Garry Kilworth**'s *A Midsummer's Nightmare,* and Deborah Wright's *The Rebel Fairy* (2002). In Sarah A. Hoyt's *Ill Met by Moonlight* (2001), a Dark Lady takes young Will into **Faerie**; *All Night Awake* (2002) and *Any Man So Daring* (2003) are sequels. Showcase **anthologies** include *Shakespeare Stories* (1982), ed. Giles Gordon, and *Weird Tales from Shakespeare* (1994), ed. Katharine Kerr and Martin H. Greenberg.

SHARED WORLD. A setting used by a number of different writers, usually presented in an anthology or **series**. Collections of **myths** or **folktales** are shared-world projects of a sort, and that is one reason why so many writers felt free to add to them. Late 19th-century Christmas annuals sometimes featured stories with a common setting by different hands, and **H. P. Lovecraft**'s Cthulhu mythos established a significant precedent in the pulp magazines; the extension by other hands of such projects as **L. Frank Baum**'s Oz series and **Robert E. Howard**'s Conan series also provided key exemplars.

Shared-world enterprises became firmly established in the market strategy of genre fantasy following the success of the Thieves' World series developed by **Lynn Abbey** and **Robert L. Asprin**, whose many imitations and variants include **Emma Bull** and **Will Shetterly**'s Liavek series, **C. J. Cherryh** and **Janet E. Morris**'s Hell series, and **George R. R. Martin**'s Wild Cards series. Such series are, by necessity, segmental and tend to exhaust their potential relatively quickly. All TV and **game/tie-in** fiction is, in effect, shared-world fiction; like shared worlds spun off from series created by a famous author, such works are usually produced on the "sharecropping" principle by which the originator retains the intellectual property rights and keeps a considerable share of the books' earnings.

SHEA, MICHAEL (1946–). U.S. writer. The **picaresque fantasy** *A Quest for Simbilis* (1974) borrows its central character and **far-futuristic** scenario from **Jack Vance**, but Shea substituted his own anti-hero in the adventures assembled in *Nifft the Lean* (1982), two of which feature journeys into a remarkably phantasmagoric **underworld**; the series continued in *The Mines of Behemoth* (1997) and *The A'rak* (2000), the latter remaining on the surface to present a more conventional **sword and sorcery** story. *The Color out of Time* (1984) is a **contemporary** sequel to **H. P. Lovecraft**'s "The Color out of Space," and much of Shea's subsequent short work is **horror** fiction, but *In Yana, the Touch of Undying* (1985) is another extravagantly **decadent** far-futuristic fantasy leading into a bizarre underworld.

SHELLEY, PERCY BYSSHE (1792–1822). British poet who was central to the development of the English **Romantic** movement. *Queen Mab, A Philosophical Poem* (1813) employs **fairy** mythology to celebrate the penetrative power of the imagination. Many of his poems employ the imagery of **classical mythology**, notably *Prometheus Unbound* (1820), which **transfigures** the elements of **Promethean fantasy** into an exercise in disguised **literary satanism**. He wrote the preface for his wife Mary's classic **Gothic fantasy** *Frankenstein; or, The Modern Prometheus* (1818) and wrote two Gothic novels of his own, although *St. Irvyne* (1811) is the only one with a supernatural element.

SHEPARD, LUCIUS (1947–). U.S. writer whose works include **sf** (refer to *HDSFL*) and **horror** fiction. His major fantasy project is a trilogy of novellas comprising *The Man Who Painted the Dragon Griaule* (1984), *The Scalehunter's Beautiful Daughter* (1988), and *The Father of Stones* (1988), in which the immobile body of a gigantic **dragon** is carefully explored by its human neighbors. Most of his other relevant works are set in remote regions of the world where fantastic encounters catalyze subtle transformations of character; they include the title stories of *The*

Jaguar Hunter (1987) and *The Ends of the Earth* (1989), and the novella *Kallimantan* (1990). The **vampire novel** *The Golden* (1993) is set in a symbolic edifice several orders of magnitude larger than **Mervyn Peake**'s Gormenghast. *Louisiana Breakdown* (2002) is a subtle **Faustian fantasy** involving the small town of Grail. *Colonel Rutherford's Colt* (2003) is a **dark** fantasy featuring the eponymous weapon. *Two Trains Running* (2004) collects items inspired by the urban legend of the secret society of Freight Train Riders of America.

SHERMAN, DELIA (1951–). Japanese-born U.S. writer and editor. *Through a Brazen Mirror* (1989) incorporates an ingenious **feminist** element into a **recycled** version of a traditional ballad. *The Porcelain Dove* (1993) is a **historical fantasy** set in 18th-century France; its sexual politics are similarly adventurous. Sherman wrote an "Introduction to Interstitial Arts" for **Terri Windling's** Endicott Studio website and collaborated with fellow Endicott associate **Ellen Kushner** on *The Fall of the Kings* (2002).

SHERMAN, JOSEPHA (?–). U.S. writer. *The Shining Falcon* (1989) and *The Horse of Flame* (1990) are **sentimental fantasies** based in Eastern European folklore. Similar elements are deployed in the **children's fantasies** *Child of Faerie, Child of Earth* (1992), *Windleaf* (1993), and *Gleaming Bright* (1994), where they are syncretically fused with elements of **Celtic fantasy** that are displayed in purer form in *A Strange and Ancient Name* (1993), *King's Son, Magic's Son* (1994), and the Prince of the Sidhe couplet, comprising *The Shattered Oath* (1995) and *Forging the Runes* (1996). *Son of Darkness* (1998) is a **contemporary fantasy**. Sherman has also contributed to several **shared-world** enterprises, written **tie-ins**, and compiled several anthologies, including *A Sampler of Jewish-American Folklore* (1992) and *Rachel the Clever and Other Jewish Folktales* (1993). *Merlin's Kin* (1998) recycles stories of magicians.

SHETTERLY, WILL (1955–). U.S. writer and proprietor of the **small press** Steeldragon Press. He created the Liavek series of **shared-world** anthologies with his wife, **Emma Bull**, and contributed to a similar series devised by **Terri Windling**. *Cats Have No Lord* (1985) is an offbeat **quest** fantasy; its sequel, *The Tangled Lands* (1989), reveals that the scenario is a computer-generated fantasy world. *Witchblood* (1986) features a hidden community of **witches**. *Dogland* (1997) is a quasi-autobiographical **historical fantasy**.

SHIEL, M. P. (1865–1947). Montserrat-born British writer. He was the most conspicuous British exponent of **decadent** style, extravagantly displayed in the exotic **detective** stories collected in *Prince Zaleski* (1895) and the items in *Shapes in the Fire* (1896), including the **Poesque** "Xélucha" and "Vaila" (abr. as "The House of Sounds"), the fantasy of reincarnation "Tulsah," and the **erotic fantasy** "Phorfor." Most of his nonmimetic fiction is **sf** (refer to *HDSFL*), although there is a substantial element of experimental **religious fantasy** in a loosely knit futuristic trilogy comprising *The Lord of the Sea* (1901), *The Purple Cloud* (1901), and *The Last Miracle* (1906); the middle volume is an **apocalyptic fantasy** that **transfigures** the **biblical** stories of Adam and Job. The fantasies in *The Pale Ape and Other Pulses* (1911) tend toward **horror** fiction. *This Above All* (1933, aka *Above All Else*) is a **Christian fantasy** investigating the contemporary situations of individuals gifted with **immortality** by Jesus.

SHINN, SHARON (1957–). U.S. writer who also writes **sf**. *The Shape-Changer's Wife* (1995) is a **theriomorphic fantasy**. The trilogy comprising *Archangel* (1996), *Jovah's Angel* (1997), and *The Alleluia File* (1998) **hybridizes** sf and **angelic fantasy**; *Angelica* (2003) and *Angel-Seeker* (2004) continue the series. *Summers at Castle Auburn* (2001) is a **paranormal romance**; *The Safe-Keeper's Secret* (2004) is similarly **sentimental** but not as stereotypical.

SHORT FICTION. Because of the centrality of **folktale** derivatives—especially **fairy tales**—to the evolution of fantasy literature from the Renaissance to the 19th century, the histories of fantasy and the short story have been intimately and intricately entwined. The fantasy writers associated with the Romantic movements used French *contes populaires* and German *märchen* as their primary models, finding their synoptic format useful as a means of covering narrative ground economically, and the presence of an explicit or implicit teller invaluable as a vehicle of expository explanation. Further variants of the *conte*—especially the ***conte cruel*** and the ***conte philosophique***—were closely associated with fantasy from their inception.

Some modern critics and writers—notably **Angela Carter**—have drawn a distinction between "tales" and "short stories," reserving the latter term for naturalistic works that adapt the narrative methods of the novel to the depiction of thin "slices of life," while claiming the former as the natural medium of modern **fabulation**. Even in the Romantic era, however, the narrative techniques of *märchen* and naturalistic fiction were being fused in the German *novelle,* developed by **Ludwig Tieck** and **Johann Musäus**, and the French *conte* was soon supplemented by the *nouvelle,* although the distinction between the forms was never entirely clear and the English "novella" is usually taken as an indicator of intermediate length rather than a distinct form of narrative. At any rate, the *novelle/nouvelle*/novella has always had a particular appeal to writers of supernatural fiction, partly because it offers more scope than the *conte*/tale without taking on the full burden of naturalistic representation conventionally required by the novel.

The spectrum of short fiction was further complicated by the development by Aloysius Bertrand and **Charles Baudelaire** of "poems in prose," which were hailed by J. K. Huysmans as the quintessential art form of **decadent** style. The further development of prose poetry gave rise to a tradition of brief, lyrical, and lapidary tales, to which early contributors included **Richard Garnett**, **Rémy de Gourmont**, Lady Dilke (author of *The Shrine of Death* [1886] and *The Shrine of Love* [1891]), and J. H. Pearce, author of *Drolls from Shadowland* (1893) and *Tales of the Masque* (1894). Its ambience was carried forward into the works of **Vernon Knowles**, **Frank Owen**, and Donald Corley (1886–1955), author of *The House of Lost Identity* (1927) and *The Haunted Jester* (1931); it still echoes in such works as Jay Lake's *Greetings from Lake Wu* (2003) and *Green Grow the Rushes-Oh* (2004) and Tim Pratt's *Little Gods* (2003).

SHWARTZ, SUSAN M. (1949–). U.S. writer who also writes **sf** (refer to *HDSFL*). The trilogy comprising *Byzantium's Crown* (1987), *The Woman of Flowers* (1987), and *Queensblade* (1988) is set in an **alternative history** in which the thriving eastern sector of the Roman Empire dominates the western sector in medieval times. *Silk Roads and Shadows* (1988) is an **Oriental fantasy** whose protagonists journey eastward from the **historical** Byzantium, which also features in *Shards of Empire* (1996) and *Cross and Crescent* (1997). *Imperial Lady* (1989 with **Andre Norton**) is another muted Oriental fantasy; Shwartz also collaborated with Norton on *Empire of the Eagle* (1993), set in the pre-Christian Roman Empire, and edited the homage anthology *Moonsinger's Friends* (1985). *The Grail of Hearts* (1992) features the **Wandering Jew**. Shwartz's other anthologies include *Hecate's Cauldron* (1982), two volumes of *Arabesques* (1988–89) featuring **Arabian fantasies**, and *Sisters in Fantasy* (1995).

SIEGEL, JAN (1955–). British author born Amanda Askew, whose early works—mostly thrillers—appeared under her married name, Amanda Hemingway; they include the novella "The Alchemist" (1981). *Prospero's Children* (1999) is an enterprising **Atlantean fantasy**; its sequel *The Dragon-Charmer* (2000) broadens its scope to embrace elements of **afterlife fantasy** and **Shakespearean** fantasy. *Witches' Honour* (2002; aka *The Witch Queen*) takes a similarly syncretic approach to the hybridization of British, **classical**, and **mythical** materials. She reverted to the Hemingway byline in the Sangreal trilogy, launched with *The Greenstone Grail* (2004).

SILVERBERG, ROBERT (1935–). U.S. writer best known for **sf** (refer to *HDSFL*). *Son of Man* (1987) is an **allegorical/far-futuristic fantasy**. *The Book of Skulls* (1972) describes a costly **quest** for magical **immortality**. The series comprising *Lord Valentine's Castle* (1980), *The Desert of Stolen Dreams* (1981), *The Majipoor Chronicles* (1982), *Valentine Pontifex* (1983), *The Mountains of Majipoor* (1995), *Sorcerers of Majipoor* (1997), *Lord Prestimion* (1999), and *The King of Dreams* (2001) is **planetary romance** of a calculatedly exotic kind. *Gilgamesh the King* (1984) **recycled** the Sumerian **epic** before Silverberg extended it in "Gilgamesh in the Outback" (1986), which was combined with two further stories in the **transfigurative** *To the Land of the Living* (1989). *Letters from Atlantis* (1990) is an **Atlantean fantasy**. *Lion Time in Timbuctoo* (1990) is a **historical fantasy**. *Legends* (1998) and *Legends II* (2003) are showcase **anthologies** of novellas linked to best-selling **series.**

SINCLAIR, UPTON (1876–1968). U.S. writer. *Prince Hagen: A Phantasy* (1903; play version 1909) is a **political satire** in which the central figure is borrowed from **Nordic** mythology. *Roman Holiday* (1931) is a politically loaded **timeslip** fantasy. *The Gnome-Mobile* (1936) is a **children's fantasy** incorporating an early environmentalist protest. The **delusional fantasy** *They Call Me Carpenter* (1922) and the **timeslip** fantasy *Our Lady* (1938) are earnest **Christian fantasies** with a pessimistic trend that is continued in the **messianic** fantasy *What Didymus Did* (1954, aka *It Happened to Didymus*).

SINGER, ISAAC BASHEVIS (1904–1991). Polish writer who wrote in Hebrew before embracing the Yiddish vernacular; he moved to the United States in 1935, where translations of his work sometimes preceded the originals into print. His work draws heavily on the folkloristic roots of **Jewish fantasy**—whose leading modern **recycler** and developer he became—but routinely combines such material with depictions of the **Devil** and **witches** that are more in keeping with the spirit of **Christian fantasy**. The novels *Satan in Goray* (1935; tr. 1955) and *The Penitent* (1983) both feature false messiahs, while *The Magician of Lublin* (tr. 1960) and *The Fools of Chem and Their History* (tr. 1973) are also **historical fantasies**. His short stories are collected in *Gimpel the Fool and Other Stories* (1957), *The Spinoza of Market Street* (1961), *Short Friday and Other Stories* (1964), *The Seance and Other Stories* (1968), *A Friend of Kafka* (1970), *A Crown of Feathers and Other Stories* (1973), *Passions and Other Stories* (1975), *Old Love* (1979), *The Image and Other Stories* (1985), *Gifts* (1985), and *The Death of Methuselah and Other Stories* (1988). His **children's fantasies** include *Zlateh the Goat and Other Stories* (1966), *When Schlemiel Went to Warsaw and Other Stories* (1968), *The Topsy-Turvy Emperor of China* (1971), *The Power of Light* (1980), *The Golem* (1982), and *Meshugah* (1994).

SITWELL, OSBERT (1892–1969). British writer, one of three sibling poets. The title novella of *Triple Fugue and Other Stories* (1924) is a **satire** featuring technologically merged souls. *The Man Who Lost Himself* (1929) is a **timeslip** fantasy. *Miracle on Sinai* (1929) describes the effect of a new Mosaic revelation on a cross-sectional band of tourists. *Collected Stories* (1953) reprints "The Glow-Worm," in which a journalist's spiritual condition is ironically reflected in the waxing and waning of his halo, and the **ghost** story *A Place of One's Own* (1941). *Fee Fi Fo Fum!* (1959) is a collection of cynically **transfigured** fairy tales; its long version of Cinderella is a **political** satire.

SMALL PRESS. A publishing company established for vocational rather than commercial motives. Small presses played a vital role in the evolution and presentation of fantasy throughout the 19th century, from **Walter Scott**'s imprint to **William Morris**'s Kelmscott Press. Small press magazines like *The Germ* and *The Savoy* were significant in providing arenas for literary experimentation, and private publishers like the Golden Cockerel Press and the Hogarth Press were usually hospitable to offbeat fantasy. The fan culture associated with the **sf** pulps took considerable inspiration from the Amateur Publishing Association, with which **H. P. Lovecraft** was involved and through which he met some of his correspondents. Lovecraftian fiction has always been associated with enthusiastic small-press activity since **August Derleth** and

Donald Wandrei established Arkham House; the most significant imprints include Roy A. Squires, **Jack Chalker**'s Mirage Press, Marc Michaud's Necronomicon Press, **Karl Edward Wagner**'s Carcosa Press, Harry O. Morris's Silver Scarab Press, Robert M. Price's magazine *Crypt of Cthulhu,* and John Navroth's Pentagram Publications.

A number of small presses were founded in the aftermath of World War II to reprint sf from the pulp magazines; several also salvaged material from ***Unknown***. Gnome Press reprinted **Robert E. Howard**'s Conan series for the first time, as well as reprinting **sword and sorcery** by **C. L. Moore** and **Fritz Leiber**. Such specialist presses became effectively redundant after 1960, but a few that survived by specializing in collectible editions were drawn toward fantasy because of its greater **illustrative** potential; Underwood-Miller produced handsome editions of many books by **Jack Vance**, and Donald M. Grant repackaged Robert E. Howard. While small-press books were in the doldrums, small-press magazines multiplied rapidly, taking up the slack as the commercial magazines died out. Significant fantasy titles included *Amra, Anduril, Dragonbane* (issued by **Charles de Lint**'s Triskell Press), *Kadath,* **Jessica Amanda Salmonson**'s *Literary Magazine of Fantasy & Terror,* Robert Weinberg's *Lost Fantasies, The Silver Web,* and the often-revived ***Weird Tales***.

When small-press books began to reappear in some quantity in the 1980s, many of their producers proved short-lived, including **Kristine Kathryn Rusch**'s and Dean Wesley Smith's Pulphouse and the British Kerosina Publications, but others continually emerged to take their places. Those whose output made significant contributions to the evolution of fantasy literature include John Pelan's Axolotl Press (which eventually morphed into Nightshade Books), Mark V. Ziesing, Phantasia Press, **Will Shetterly**'s Steeldragon Press, **Jeff VanderMeer**'s Ministry of Whimsy Press, and W. Paul Ganley's and Sean Wallace's Prime Press.

SMITH, CLARK ASHTON (1893–1961). U.S. writer. His poetry continued French-inspired traditions imported to the American West Coast by Ambrose Bierce and **George Sterling**, his imagination reaching its furthest extent in "The Hashish Eater; or, The Apocalypse of Evil" (1922), which extrapolates the theme and manner of Sterling's "The Wine of Wizardry." The Arkham House *Selected Poems* (1971) is the most comprehensive sampler. In a brief period of hectic productivity in the 1930s—when he was greatly encouraged by **H. P. Lovecraft**—his prose fictions developed **decadent** style and sensibility to their furthest extreme in the context of "cosmic horror fiction" (refer to HSDF and *HDHL*).

Smith toyed with **historical fantasy** set in the imaginary French province of Averoigne, **Atlantean fantasy**, and **prehistoric fantasy** set in Hyperborea before realizing that the **far-futuristic** setting of Zothique—which he began to explore in "The Empire of the Necromancers" (1932)—allowed his imagination its most extravagant and fatalistic expression. His stories were reprinted in the Arkham House collections *Out of Space and Time*(1942), *Lost Worlds* (1944), *Genius Loci* (1948), *The Abominations of Yondo* (1960), *Tales of Science and Sorcery* (1964), *Poems in Prose* (1964), and *Other Dimensions* (1970) before being sampled in numerous subsequent collections.

The Necronomicon Press volumes *Tales of Zothique* (1995) and *The Book of Hyperborea* (1996) include numerous restored texts. Previously unpublished materials were issued in *Strange Shadows: The Uncollected Fiction and Essays of Clark Ashton Smith* (1989), ed. Steve Behrends, with Donald Sidney-Fryer and Rah Hoffman. *The Black Diamonds* (2002) and the title story of *The Sword of Zagan and Other Writings* (2004) are **Arabian fantasy** novellas written when Smith was a teenager. Homages to his work include *The Last Continent: New Tales of Zothique* (1999), ed. John Pelan, and *The Sorcerer's Apprentices: New Tales in the Tradition of Clark Ashton Smith* (1999), ed. James Ambuehl.

SMITH, DAVID C. (1952–). U.S. writer. His work is **sword and sorcery** fiction in the tradition of **Robert E. Howard**, including two series featuring Howard characters and the series comprising *Oron* (1978), *The Sorcerer's Shadow* (1978), *The Valley of Ogrum* (1982), and *The Ghost Army* (1983). The **apocalyptic fantasy** trilogy comprising *Master of Evil* (1983), *Sorrowing Vengeance* (1983), and *The Passing of the Gods* (1984) adopts the premise that our world is just a poor copy of another.

SMITH, THORNE (1893–1934). U.S. writer best known for **humorous/intrusive fantasies** that reacted against the stern strictures of Prohibition in the same way that **F. Anstey** reacted against the stuffiness of English Victorian mores. In *Topper* (1926, aka *The Jovial Ghosts*), two fun lovers killed in a car crash find death no obstacle to their mission to loosen up the eponymous pillar of rectitude—a project continued in *Topper Takes a Trip* (1932). *The Stray Lamb* (1929) employs serial

theriomorphy as an educative device. *Turnabout* (1931) echoes Anstey's *Vice Versa* but exchanges the personalities of a man and wife. *The Night Life of the Gods* (1931) similarly echoes *The Tinted Venus* on a more generous scale. *Rain in the Doorway* (1933) follows the same formula without using supernatural devices, employing a department store as a cornucopia. The protagonist of *Skin and Bones* (1933) finds periodic metamorphosis into a skeleton inconvenient, but the fount of youth in *The Glorious Pool* (1934) is much more helpful. **Norman Matson** completed *The Passionate Witch* (1941) in a cautionary fashion of which Smith might not have approved.

Smith also wrote the earnest **hallucinatory fantasy** *Dream's End* (1927) before deciding that humor was his forte, and several earnest **detective** stories that may have inspired other crime writers to dabble in humorous fantasy similar to his; those who did include **Frederick Arnold Kummer**; **Robert Bloch**; Theodore Pratt, in *Mr Limpet* (1942) and *Mr Thurkle's Trolley* (1947); James Hadley Chase, in *Miss Shumway Waves a Wand* (1944); Raymond Chandler, in "Professor Bingo's Snuff" (1952); Manning Coles, in *Brief Candles* (1954) and *Happy Returns* (1955); and John D. MacDonald, in *The Girl, the Gold Watch, and Everything* (1962). The tradition was also carried forward by **Nelson S. Bond** and Charles F. Myers, but it died out in the 1960s as social mores became far less restrictive; there are few modern examples, although Jenna McKnight's *A Greek God at the Ladies' Club* (2003) retains something of its flavor.

SNYDER, MIDORI (1954–). U.S. writer. *Soulstring* (1987) extrapolates a familiar **fairy tale** motif into an adventure fantasy. The Oran trilogy, comprising *New Moon* (1989), *Sadar's Keep* (1990), and *Beldan's Fire* (1993), incorporates elements of **Celtic fantasy** into an account of the renewal of magic in a land where it has long been suppressed. *The Flight of Michael McBride* (1994) incorporates similar materials into a complex **contemporary fantasy**. *The Innamorati* (1998) is a **historical fantasy** set in Renaissance Venice. *Hannah's Garden* (2002) is a contemporary fantasy in which the heroine discovers her **Faerie** heritage. Snyder is a leading contributor to **Terri Windling**'s Endicott Studio, assisting with the *Journal of Mythic Arts*.

SOMTOW, S. P. (1952–). Thai writer who became a U.S. citizen. His early work, most of which is **sf** (refer to *HDSFL*), was bylined "Somtow Sucharitkul." His new byline first appeared on a series of revisionist

vampire novels, launched with *Vampire Junction* (1984), which lean more toward **horror** than many works of that kind. *The Shattered Horse* (1986) features an **alternative** Trojan War. The **historical fantasy** *Moon Dance* (1989), featuring a conflict between rival families of **werewolves,** is similarly **dark** (refer to *HDHL*), but *The Fallen Country* (1986), *Forgetting Places* (1987), and *The Wizard's Apprentice* (1993) are lighthearted **children's fantasies**. The trilogy comprising *Riverrun* (1991), *Forests of the Night* (1992, aka *Armorica*), and *Yestern* (1996 in the omnibus *The Riverrun Trilogy*) is a surreal **contemporary fantasy** in which protagonists are caught up in a battle to alter reality, with confusing effects. The fantasy element in *The Pavilion of Frozen Woman* is marginal, but the "modern Siamese tales" collected in *Dragon's Fin Soup* (1998) are mostly fantasies, as are those in *Tagging the Moon: Fairy Tales from L.A.* (2000).

SOUTHEY, ROBERT (1774–1843). British poet, the brother-in-law of **Samuel Taylor Coleridge**. *Thalaba the Destroyer* (1801) is a long **Arabian fantasy** in verse. *Madoc* (1805) is the story of a legendary **Celtic** prince who supposedly discovered America. *The Curse of Kehama* (1810) is a similar exercise in **Oriental fantasy**. More significantly, Southey wrote new English versions of *Amadis of Gaul* (1803) and *Palmerin of England* (1807), two Iberian **chivalric romances** that had been immensely popular in the 16th century, thus introducing colorful **heroic fantasy** to 19th-century Britain.

SPANISH FANTASY. Spanish literature's key contributions to the early evolution of fantasy included **chivalric romances** of a broader stripe than those popular in France (modern versions of the classic *Amadis of Gaul* are derived from Spanish versions, although its origin was probably Portuguese). It was, therefore, appropriate that Spain should have produced **Miguel de Cervantes**'s satirical requiem for the genre, *Don Quixote,* whose cautionary example may have damped down any conspicuous enthusiasm for **romanticism** two centuries later.

The leading Spanish fantasists of the 19th century, Pedro de Alarcón (1833–91)—author of the **posthumous fantasy** translated as *The Strange Friend of Tito Gil* (1852; tr. 1890, aka *The Friend of Death*)—and Gustavo Bécquer (1836–70), were active half a century after the Romantic movements of northern Europe. Notable 20th-century works include Wenceslao Flórez's *Las siete columnas* (1926), in which the **Devil** takes back the seven deadly sins and removes all purpose from human existence; Rafael Ferlosio's extravagant **children's fantasy** *Industrias y andanzas de Alfanui* (1951); and two collections of stories by Marcial Souto (1983; 1988).

Contemporary Spanish fantasists of note include Juan Miguel Aguilera, Elio Barceló, and the Catalan writer Joan Perucho. Notable recent works in translation include Gonzalo Torrente Ballester's historical fantasy *The King Amaz'd: A Chronicle* (1989; tr. 1996); Cuca Canals' *Berta la Larga* (1996; tr. 1998), in which a young woman's moods affect the weather; Federico Andahazi's *The Merciful Women* (1998; tr. 2000), in which John Polidori finds an unusual **muse**; Javier Garcia Sánchez's *The Others* (1998; tr. 2003); and Juan Goytisolo's *A Cock-Eyed Comedy* (2000; tr. 2002). *The Dedalus Book of Spanish Fantasy* (1999), ed. Margaret Jull Costa and Annella McDermott, is a useful showcase.

SPARK, MURIEL (1918–). British writer whose works often have a **surreal** or fantastic edge. *The Comforters* (1957) is a **metafiction** in which the protagonist comes to the conclusion that she is merely a character in a book. In *Memento Mori* (1959), the telephone becomes a conduit of insistent reminders of mortality. *The Bachelors* (1960) is a **spiritualist fantasy**. *The Ballad of Peckham Rye* (1960) features a practical joker who turns out to have cloven hooves. *The Hothouse by the East River* (1973) is a **posthumous fantasy**. Some of Spark's short fiction—assembled in *The Short Stories of Muriel Spark* (1987)—has similarly coy but insistent supernatural elements.

SPENCE, LEWIS (1874–1955). Scottish scholar specializing in **myths**, **legends**, and **folktales**, many of which he **recycled** in a straightforward fashion. His own poetry and fiction was mostly trivial, but the reckless syncretism of his **scholarly fantasies** provided a template for a great deal of early 20th-century fantasy derived from the same (mostly fantastic) sources as his *Encyclopedia of Occultism* (1920). He wrote several books attempting to illuminate *The Problem of Atlantis* (1924) and one on *The Problem of Lemuria* (1932), but his most ambitious project was a speculative reconstruction of *The Mysteries of Britain* (1928), extrapolated in *The Magic Arts of Celtic Britain* (1945), *British Fairy Origins* (1946), *The Fairy Tradition in Britain* (1948), *The Minor Traditions of British Mythology* (1948), and *The History and Origins of Druidism* (1949), which made a substantial contribution to the ideological background of **Celtic fantasy**.

SPENSER, EDMUND (1552–1599). English poet whose work made abundant use of **myth** and folklore, especially the unfinished **epic** *The Faerie Queene* (1590: exp. 1596; further exp. 1609), a massive mock-archaic fusion of **Arthurian/chivalric romance** with **fairy** mythology, allegorizing and idealizing the reign of Elizabeth I with the aid of considerable borrowing from **Lodovico Ariosto**. *The Faerie Queene* became an important exemplar in both manner and content, and a significant precursor of **romanticism**. **J. R. R. Tolkien**'s attempt to produce an "English epic" devoid of Norman intrusions obviously had it in mind as an idol to be cast down. **William Shakespeare**'s *A Midsummer Night's Dream* may be considered an example of "Spenserian fantasy," although Michael Drayton's tongue-in-cheek *Nymphidia* (1627) is more obviously derivative, as are **L. Sprague de Camp** and **Fletcher Pratt**'s "The Mathematics of Magic" and **Michael Moorcock**'s *Gloriana*.

SPIRITUALIST FANTASY. Spiritualism originated as a 19th-century fad—launched by the Fox sisters in New York State in 1848—for receiving gnomic messages from the dead, in the form of "rapping" and table tipping. In spite of being exposed as frauds, the Fox sisters became the archetypes of a vast number of "mediums," whose activities became the core of a new religion. Mediums receiving more lucid messages usually operate with the aid of "guides" or "controls" in the world of the dead, who institute contact with spirits, whose voices are "channeled" through the medium during "seances," so that information may be passed to participant clients.

Spiritualist seances became a significant form of confidence trickery, investigation into which provided an important boost to the development of private detective agencies, a significant sideline to the careers of stage magicians like Harry Houdini, and a core activity of the Society for Psychical Research, founded in England in 1882 (its investigators—including the physicists William Crookes and Oliver Lodge—proved more gullible than their U.S. counterparts). The regular exposure of fraud did not prevent mediumship from becoming one of the most popular modes of 20th-century **lifestyle fantasy** or a popular subject of credulous literary fantasy. Elizabeth Stuart Phelps's (1844–1911) series comprising *The Gates Ajar* (1868), *Beyond the Gates* (1883), *The Gates Between* (1887), and *Within the Gates* (1901) were among the most popular pioneering examples of the subgenre. Its best sellers included *Letters from Hell* (tr. 1884, bylined "L.W.J.S."), Mrs. Oliphant's account of *A Little Pilgrim* (1882), and Camille Flammarion's *Urania* (1889). U.S.

mediums sometimes claimed to be channeling the posthumous works of writers—O. Henry and **Frank Stockton** were both credited with collections of this kind—but only confirmed that literary ability dies with the flesh.

Violet Tweedale's *The House of the Other World* (1913) was well timed, in that the heavy losses of the early months of World War I greatly increased the appeal of spiritualism in Britain, launching a new boom—led by Elsa Barker's *Letters from a Living Dead Man* (1914)—that captured the interest and faith of numerous literateurs, most notably **Rudyard Kipling**, **H. Rider Haggard**, and **Arthur Conan Doyle**. Once the U.S. joined the war, such series as **Julian Hawthorne**'s began appearing in the pulp magazines; the manifestation of ectoplasm and messages spelled out by planchettes on ouija boards became staples of popular fiction thereafter. Propagandistic intent tends to override the imaginative ambition of credulous spiritualist fantasy, often reducing its literary quality to insignificance, but examples that retain a measure of aesthetic interest include Doyle's *The Land of Mist* and Aldous Huxley's *Time Must Have a Stop* (1944). Notable cautionary tales include Stuart Cumberland's *The Vasty Deep* (1890), Richard Harding Davis's *Vera the Medium* (1908), and Ronald Knox's *Other Eyes than Ours* (1926).

As the 20th century progressed, spiritualist mediums often became comic figures, as in Alan Griffiths' *Spirits under Proof* (1935; aka *Authors in Paradise*); a significant archetype was provided by Madame Arcati in Noel Coward's play *Blithe Spirit* (1941), an example that continues to echo in such novels as Elisa de Carlo's *Strong Spirits* (1994). The most sophisticated sector of modern spiritualist fantasy consists of **historical fantasies** that place the fad in its true cultural context; examples include Melissa Pritchard's *Selene of the Spirits* (1998), Sarah Waters's *Affinity* (2000), Kathleen Karr's *Playing with Fire* (2002), and **Richard Matheson**'s *Come Fygures, Come Shadows*.

SPORTS FANTASY. Sporting success is one of the most common conjurations of **daydreams**, at least among males, and it is hardly surprising that it extends into **wish-fulfillment fantasy** in such stories as **Dave Luckett**'s *The Best Batsman in the World,* or that such fanciful desires are mocked in **humorous** works like Robert Marshall's golfing comedy *The Haunted Major* (1902) and Maurice Richardson's *The Exploits of Engelbrecht* (1950), in which the vertically challenged hero embarks upon a highly unlikely series of sporting enterprises. There is, however, a further dimension to sports fantasy, by virtue of the fact that a sport may symbolize a set of values—not merely "sportsmanship" but also competitive commitment—and "national sports" thus become available for allegorical use in commentaries on the moral condition of a society.

The most abundant literature of the latter kind deals with baseball in America, key examples being **W. P. Kinsella**'s *Shoeless Joe,* **Michael Bishop**'s *Brittle Innings,* **Robert Coover**'s *The Universal Baseball Association Inc. J. Henry Waugh, Prop.*, **Nancy Willard**'s *Things Invisible to See,* **Michael Chabon**'s *Summerland,* and Darryl Brock's **timeslip** fantasies *If I Never Get Back* (1990) and *Two in the Field* (2002). This too lends itself to parody, in such works as Douglass Wallop's *The Year the Yankees Lost the Pennant* (1954, aka *Damn Yankees*)—a humorous **Faustian fantasy** that became a Broadway musical and that makes an interesting contrast with Harold Hobson's use of cricket in *The Devil in Woodford Wells* (1946).

Imaginary sports, participation in which requires magical skills, occasionally feature in fantasy fiction; the most notable is **J. K. Rowling**'s quidditch.

SPRINGER, NANCY (1948–). U.S. writer. *The Book of Suns* (1977) was revised as the second element of the **commodified** series of **sentimental fantasy** comprising *The White Hart* (1979), *The Silver Sun* (1980), *The Sable Moon* (1981), *The Black Beast* (1982), *The Golden Swan* (1983), *Wings of Flame* (1985), and *Chains of Gold* (1986). The Sea King trilogy, comprising *Madbond* (1987), *Mindbond* (1987), and *Godbond* (1988), is similarly inclined. The **contemporary fantasy** *The Hex Witch of Seldom* (1988) brings similar material closer to home, as does the combative anti-**religious fantasy** *Apocalypse* (1989), which prepared the ground for two flamboyant exercises in **literary satanism**, *Damnbanna* (1992) and *Metal Angel* (1994).

Springer produced two **children's fantasies**, *Red Wizard* (1990) and *The Friendship Song* (1992), before achieving a further breakthrough in the exuberantly uninhibited **psychological fantasy** *Larque on the Wing* (1994), which confirmed her situation at the genre's cutting edge. *The Blind God Is Watching* (1994) is a **dark fantasy** about a monstrous Frog Boy. *Fair Peril* (1996) is a **contemporary fantasy** in which a divorced writer's daughter is seduced into **Faerie** after she refuses to oblige a frog prince. *I Am Mordred* (1998) is a revisionist **Arthurian fantasy**, to which *I Am Morgan le Fay* (2001) is a prequel. *Sky Rider* (1999) is an offbeat **ghost** story. In *Plumage* (2000), people are seen as birds with the aid of magic **mirrors**. Springer's short fiction is sampled in *Chance and*

Other Gestures of the Hand of Fate (1987) and *Stardark Songs* (1993). She edited an anthology of **fairy tales** about frogs, *Ribbiting Tales* (2000).

STACKPOLE, MICHAEL A. (1957–). U.S. **game** designer and writer. The Dark Conspiracy trilogy, comprising *A Gathering Evil* (1991), *Evil Ascending* (1991), and *Evil Triumphant* (1992), is **dark fantasy**. *Once a Hero* (1994), *A Hero Born* (1997), *An Enemy Reborn* (1998, with William F. Wu), and *Eyes of Silver* (1998) are unorthodox **heroic fantasies**. *Talion: Revenant* (1998) is a fantasy of frustrated revenge. *The Dark Glory War* (2000) is a **military fantasy**, as is the DragonCrown War Cycle, comprising *Fortress Draconis* (2001), *When Dragons Rage* (2002), and *The Grand Crusade* (2003).

STARRETT, VINCENT (1886–1974). U.S. bibliophile and writer best known for homages to and pastiches of Sherlock Holmes. His enthusiasm for the work of **Arthur Machen** led to his publishing two samplers of Machen's work. He was an early contributor to ***Weird Tales***, some of his work in that vein being sampled in *Coffins for Two* (1924) and *The Quick and the Dead* (1965). In the episodic bibliophilic fantasy *Seaports in the Moon: A Fantasia on Romantic Themes* (1928), various literary figures obtain temporary custody of a draft from the fountain of youth but never manage to take advantage of it. More short fantasies are collected in *The Escape of Alice and Other Fantasies* (1995), volume 7 of "The Vincent Starrett Memorial Library," published by George Vanderburgh's **small press** The Battered Silicon Dispatch Box.

STASHEFF, CHRISTOPHER (1944–). U.S. writer. The **planetary romance** *The Warlock in Spite of Himself* (1969) launched a series of **chimerical/science fantasies** continued in *King Kobold* (1969, rev. as *King Kobold Revived*) and *The Warlock Unlocked* (1982), supplied with a **prequel** in *Escape Velocity* (1983) and further extended in *The Warlock Enraged* (1985), *The Warlock Wandering* (1986), *The Warlock Is Missing* (1986), *The Warlock Heretical* (1987), *The Warlock's Companion* (1988), *The Warlock Insane* (1989), *The Warlock Rock* (1990), *Warlock and Son* (1991), *M'Lady Witch* (1994), *Quicksilver's Knight* (1995), and *The Warlock's Last Ride* (2004). A spin-off series featuring the original protagonist's son includes *A Wizard in Bedlam* (1979), *A Wizard in Absentia* (1993), *A Wizard in Mind* (1995), *A Wizard in War* (1995), *A Wizard in Peace* (1996), *A Wizard in Chaos* (1997), *A Wizard in Midgard* (1998), *The Spell-Bound Scholar* (1999), *A Wizard and a*

Warlord (2000), *A Wizard in the Way* (2000), and *A Wizard in a Feud* (2001).

The Wizard in Rhyme series, comprising *Her Majesty's Wizard* (1986), *The Oathbound Wizard* (1993), *The Witch Doctor* (1994), *The Secular Wizard* (1994), *My Son, the Wizard* (1997), *The Haunted Wizard* (2000), *The Crusading Wizard* (2000), and *The Feline Wizard* (2000), is stamped from a very similar mold, as is the Star Stone couplet, comprising *The Shaman* (1995) and *The Sage* (1996). Stasheff assisted in the revival of **L. Sprague de Camp** and **Fletcher Pratt**'s Harold Shea series, coediting *The Enchanter Reborn* (1992) with de Camp and contributing *Sir Harold and the Monkey King* (separate publication 1993). His short fiction is sampled in *Mind Out of Time* (2003).

STEPHENS, JAMES (1882–1950). Irish writer. His most successful novel, *The Crock of Gold* (1912), is definitive of a quintessentially Irish strand of **humorous** and **sentimental Celtic fantasy**, which **Lord Dunsany** occasionally tried to recapture. *Deirdre* (1923), the mosaic *In the Land of Youth*, and the collections *Irish Fairy Tales* (1920) and *Etched in Moonlight* (1928) deploy similar materials in a muted and increasingly earnest fashion.

STERLING, GEORGE (1869–1926). U.S. poet associated with the Californian circle of Ambrose Bierce, who arranged publication of Sterling's extravagantly **decadent** poem "A Wine of Wizardry" (1907) in *Cosmopolitan,* where it caused a storm of controversy; many readers and critics loathed it, but it exerted a powerful influence on **Clark Ashton Smith**, inspired **Fritz Leiber**, and was reprinted by **Lin Carter** as a manifesto for modern fantasy literature. Sterling's other major fantasy work is the long narrative poem "Duandon" (1911), which is included in the performance repertoire of contemporary California poet Donald Sidney-Fryer. Sterling's collections include *The Testimony of the Suns* (1903), *A Wine of Wizardry* (1909), *The House of Orchids* (1911), and *Beyond the Breakers* (1914).

STERLING, JOHN (1806–1844). British writer, one of the most important pioneers of fantasy fiction in Britain. He was an early coproprietor of the *Athenaeum,* using its pages for such experimental works as the **visionary fantasy** "Zamor" (1828) and the **Promethean fantasy** "Cydon" (1829). He interpolated more fantasies in the text of the novel *Arthur Coningsby* (1833) and contributed a series called "Legendary Lore" to *Blackwood's,* including "The Palace of Morgana" (1837),

"Land and Sea" (1838) and the allegorical **fairy tale** "A Chronicle of England" (1840). The series concluded with the novel "The Onyx Ring" (1838–39), an earnest **philosophical fantasy** in which the protagonist undergoes a series of **identity exchanges** in search of the secret of happiness; a revised text appeared in the collection *Essays and Tales by John Sterling* (2 vols., 1848), ed. Julius Charles Hare.

STEVENS, FRANCIS (1884–?). Pseudonym of Gertrude Bennett, née Barrows, who wrote for the pulp magazines between 1916 and 1920 in order to support herself and her young children, giving it up as soon as her financial situation eased. *The Nightmare* (1917; book 2003) is a conventional adventure fantasy—the **lost-race** novella *Sunfire* (1923; 1996) must also have been apprentice work—but *The Citadel of Fear* (1918; 1970) is a dramatic **dark fantasy** anticipating themes and methods subsequently employed by **A. Merritt** and **H. P. Lovecraft**. *The Heads of Cerberus* (1919; 1952) equips a **hybrid/science fantasy** with an exotic **portal fantasy** frame. *Claimed* (1920; 1966) is another dark fantasy. The **psychological fantasy** *Serapion* (1920; 2003) employs the **doppelgänger** theme. The 1919 title story of *The Elf-Trap: Complete Short Fiction* (2003) is a notable **sentimental fantasy**.

STEVENSON, ROBERT LOUIS (1850–1894). Scottish writer, author of the classic **moralistic fantasy** *Strange Case of Dr Jekyll and Mr Hyde* (1888), which was equally important to the history of **sf** (refer to HDSF) and **horror** fiction (refer to *HDHL*). The work assembled in *New Arabian Nights* (2 vols., 1882) is baroque but not supernatural; his other **dark** moralistic fantasies, including the ironic **angelic fantasy** "Markheim," are mostly to be found in *The Merry Men and Other Tales and Fables* (1887). "Will o' the Mill" features a personification of **Death**, while the title story is a **hallucinatory fantasy** partly written in Scottish dialect. *Island Nights' Entertainments* (1893) **recycles** the **Baron de la Motte Fouqué**'s "The Bottle Imp" for the Samoans, among whom he had taken up residence; "The Isle of Voices" is likewise set in the South Seas.

STEVERMER, CAROLINE (1955–). U.S. writer whose historical mysteries are bylined "C. S. Stevermer." *The Serpent's Egg* (1988) is a **historical fantasy** set in 16th-century Europe. *Sorcery & Cecilia* (1988 with **Patricia Wrede**) is a Regency romance spiced with **magic**; *The Grand Tour* (2004 with Wrede) is a sequel. *A College of Magics* (1994) describes an early 20th-century education in magic, whose rewards are further exhibited in *A Scholar of Magics* (2004). *When the King Comes Home* (2000) is a polished **immersive fantasy** in which the **secondary world** has a Renaissance ambience.

STEWART, MARY (1916–). British writer whose major contribution to fantasy is the biography of **Merlin** contained in *The Crystal Cave* (1970), *The Hollow Hills* (1973), and *The Last Enchantment* (1979). *The Wicked Day* (1983) is an appendix detailing Mordred's rebellion, and *The Prince and the Pilgrim* (1995) a detour into one of Malory's many backwaters. Her other works include the marginal **Gothic fantasies** *Touch Not the Cat* (1976), *Thornyhold* (1988), and *Rose Cottage* (1997). Her **children's fiction** includes *The Little Broomstick* (1971), featuring a school for witches; the offbeat **astrological fantasy** *Ludo and the Star Horse* (1974); and the **timeslip** fantasy *A Walk in Wolf Wood* (1980).

STEWART, PAUL (?–). British writer for **children**. His fantasies include the **timeslip** fantasy *The Weather Witch* (1989) and the ecological parable *Adam's Ark* (1990). With **illustrator** Chris Riddell, he produced the Edge Chronicles, comprising *Beyond the Deepwoods* (1998), *Stormchaser* (1999), *Midnight over Sanctaphrax* (2000), *The Curse of the Gloamglozer* (2001), *The Last of the Sky Pirates* (2002), and *Vox* (2003), collectively an extravagant **Odyssean fantasy** set on the rim of a flat **secondary world**. *Cloud Wolf* (2001) is a spin-off from the series. Riddell also collaborated on *Muddle Earth* (2003), in which a **wizard** summons a schoolboy to be a hero.

STEWART, SEAN (1965–). Canadian writer. *Nobody's Son* (1993) begins where conventional **quest** fantasies end, tracking the consequences of claiming the promised reward. *Resurrection Man* (1995) is an **intrusive fantasy** in which magical leakage initiated by the Holocaust transforms the post–World War II history of the United States; *The Night Watch* (1997) and *Galveston* (2000) are future-set sequels. *Clouds End* (1996) is an offbeat **doppelgänger** story. *Mockingbird* (1998) is a **contemporary fantasy** in which social workers seize a **witch**'s child. *Perfect Circle* (2004) is a sophisticated **ghost** story.

STOCKTON, FRANK R. (1834–1902). U.S. writer. Stockton wrote many **children's fantasies**, beginning with those in *Ting-a-Ling* (1870, aka *Ting-a-Ling Tales*), which features the novella "The Magical Music." Many of his stories have a surreal edge that adds adult interest to some of the items in *The Bee-Man of Orn and Other Fanciful Tales*

(1887)—notably "The Griffin and the Minor Canon," in which a clergyman befriends an unfortunate monster—and *The Clocks of Rondaine and Other Stories* (1892), notably *The Great Show in Kobol-Land* (separate pub. 1891). The later collections *Fanciful Tales* (1894) and *The Queen's Museum and Other Fanciful Tales* (1906) were mostly composed of reprints.

Stockton helped pioneer the **humorous** ghost story in the United States, in such items as "The Transferred Ghost" and "The Spectral Mortgage" in *The Lady, or the Tiger? and Other Stories* (1884) and others in *Afield and Afloat* (1900), preparing the ground for such writers as **John Kendrick Bangs**. His other adult fantasies include the title novella of *Amos Kilbright: His Adscititious Experiences, with Other Stories* (1888), "A Borrowed Month" in *The Christmas Wreck and Other Stories* (1886, aka *A Borrowed Month and Other Stories*), "The Philosophy of Relative Existences" in *The Watchmaker's Wife and Other Stories* (1893, aka *The Shadrach and Other Stories*), and various items in *A Story-Teller's Pack* (1897). *The Vizier of the Two-Horned Alexander* (1898) is a facetious fantasy of **immortality**. *The Novels and Stories of Frank R. Stockton* (23 vols. 1899–1904) is definitive.

STODDARD, JAMES (1955–). U.S. writer and musician, originally "Jerry" Stoddard, whose early short fiction was bylined "James Turpin." In *The High House* (1998), a child loses the keys to a mystical dwelling that controls the balance of the universe and has doors to many worlds. In the sequel, *The False House* (1999), a rival establishes himself therein and a crucial contest begins.

STOKER, BRAM (1847–1912). Irish writer best known for the classic **horror** novel *Dracula* (refer to *HDHL*), a pivotal text in the tradition of modern **vampire** fiction. His earliest publications, including "The Crystal Cup" (1872), were also horrific, as were his later short stories; some of the **fairy tales** collected in *Under the Sunset* (1882) also have a sinister edge. He could not repeat the success of *Dracula*, although *The Jewel of Seven Stars* (1907) attempted something similar with a **mummy** as the alien threat and *The Lair of the White Worm* (1911; restored text 1986) employed a femme fatale in a similar capacity. *The Mystery of the Sea* is an ambiguous **occult fantasy**.

STORR, CATHERINE (1913–2001). British psychiatrist and writer for **children**; her husband, Anthony Storr, also a psychiatrist, wrote an influential analysis of *The Dynamics of Creation* (1972). Her psychiatric interests inform much of her work, including *Clever Polly and the Stupid Wolf* (1955) and *The Adventures of Polly and the Wolf* (1957), in which the Big Bad Wolf of **fairy tales** fails to adapt to 20th-century London, and the classic **hallucinatory fantasy** *Marianne Dreams* (1958; rev. 1964; aka *The Magic Drawing Pencil*). Her work for younger readers includes many **recycled folktales** and Bible stories, as well as such consolatory fantasies as *Finn's Animal* (1994). Her other fantasies for older readers include *The Mirror Image Ghost* (1994) and *The If Game* (2001), the latter featuring a series of keys to secret doors. Her short fiction is sampled in *Cold Marble and Other Ghost Stories* (1985).

STRAUSS, VICTORIA (1955–). U.S. writer. *The Lady of Rhuddesmere* (1982) is a claustrophobic **political fantasy**. *Worldstone* (1986) is a **portal fantasy** in which the heroine has extraordinary abilities. *Guardian of the Hills* (1995) is an archaeological fantasy drawing on native American **myths**. The couplet comprising *The Arm of the Stone* (1998) and *The Garden of the Stone* (1999) is founded on an **allegory** in which the world has been split apart by a conflict between Mind and Hand. In *The Burning Land* (2004), renegade shapers who oppose an organized religion—described in unusual detail—must go in search of the lost city of Refuge.

STRICKLAND, BRAD (1947–). U.S. writer in various genres, mostly for young **children**. The trilogy of **humorous fantasies** comprising *Moon Dreams* (1988), *Nul's Quest* (1989), and *Wizard's Mole* (1991) employs a **hallucinatory fantasy** frame. In *Dragon's Plunder* (1992), a boy is abducted by pirates because he can whistle up the wind. Strickland completed several fantasies left incomplete by **John Bellairs** and continued the series to which they belonged. He wrote *The Ghost Finds a Body* (2003) in collaboration with Thomas E. Fuller.

STURGEON, THEODORE (1918–1985). U.S. writer born Edward Hamilton Waldo, who chose a new given name when he adopted his stepfather's surname. He began to write **humorous fantasies** for ***Unknown*** in 1939, soon diverging into **sf** (refer to *HDSFL*) and **horror** (refer to *HDHL*). His ***contes cruels*** are often invested with a ferocious emotional intensity, which also infects longer stories like the neo-**Arthurian** "Excalibur and the Atom" (1951) and the neo-**Gothic** *The Dreaming Jewels* (1950, aka *The Synthetic Man*). He usually employed the sf jargon of "psi powers" in stories in which individuals granted supernatural powers must learn to use them responsibly, while his pure fantasies tended to the **sentimental**, as in "The Silken Swift" (1953) and "The Graveyard Reader" (1958).

In the harrowing **existentialist fantasy** "Need" (in *Beyond*, 1960), a man gifted with extraordinary empathy struggles to cope with the pain of others. *Some of Your Blood* (1961) is a **psychological fantasy** anticipating developments in revisionist **vampire** fiction. A nearly lifelong writer's block thereafter caused Sturgeon to leave the ambitious **messianic fantasy** *Godbody* (1986) far short of completion. Sturgeon's bibliography is complex, but *The Complete Stories of Theodore Sturgeon*—whose first nine volumes are *The Ultimate Egoist* (1994), *Microcosmic God* (1995), *Killdozer!* (1996), *Thunder and Roses* (1997), *The Perfect Host* (1998), *Baby Is Three* (1999), *A Saucer of Loneliness* (2000), *Bright Segment* (2002), and *And Now the News . . .* (2003)—is definitive.

SURREALISM. A term coined by **Guillaume Apollinaire** to describe the fantasizing effects he and **Alfred Jarry** themselves employed; it was taken up by André Breton in a *Surrealist Manifesto* (1924; exp. 1929), which proposed that the crudities of bourgeois rationalism—as reflected in mimetic literature—could and should be overwhelmed by art that disowned any allegiance to mere representation, mining the unconscious via the imagery of **dreams**. The movement achieved much greater success in the visual arts—via Salvador Dali, Max Ernst, René Magritte, and many others—than it did in literature, where surreal techniques often produced a fatal obliteration of narrative coherence.

With Paul Eluard, Breton wrote the exemplary prose poems making up *The Immaculate Conception* (1930; tr. 1990). Other notable examples of surrealist fiction include Pierre Albert Birot's *The First Book of Grabinoulor* (1919), Robert Desnos's *Liberty or Love!* (1924; tr. 1993), Robert M. Coates's *The Eater of Darkness* (1926) and René Daumal's *A Night of Serious Drinking* (1938; tr. 1979). Samplers include *The Dedalus Book of Surrealism: The Identity of Things* (1993); *The Dedalus Book of Surrealism 2: The Myth of the World* (1994), ed. Michael Richardson; and two Printed Head sets of chapbooks produced by the specialist **small press** Atlas (1990–91; 1992–93). Surrealist painters who produced literary fantasies include Dali, in *Hidden Faces* (1944; tr. 1947), and the British surrealist Ithell Colquhoun (1906–88), author of *Goose of Hermogenes* (1961). **Michael Ende** is the son of a surrealist painter.

A significant element of surrealism is preserved and productively deployed by many modern **fabulations**; it has been further encouraged by the **postmodernist** fascination with the uncertain relationship between representation—especially linguistic representation—and reality, as reflected in such works as Michael Cisco's *The Divinity Student* (1999), Brian Charles Clark's *Splitting* (1999), and Amanda Filipacchi's *Vapor* (1999). Fantasy novels about the surrealist movement include **Lisa Goldstein**'s *The Dream Years* and **Robert Irwin**'s *Exquisite Corpse*.

SWANN, THOMAS BURNETT (1928–1976). U.S. scholar and writer whose heartfelt **classical fantasies** could not find a domestic market at first, many of them appearing in the British **magazine** *Science-Fantasy*. "Where Is the Bird of Fire?" (1962; exp. as *Lady of the Bees* 1976; the 1970 book *Where Is the Bird of Fire?* is a collection) **recycles** and **transfigures** the legend of Rome's founding in a typically poignant and polished manner; *Queens Walk in the Dusk* (1977) and *Green Phoenix* (1972) are **prequels** to it. The elegiac *Day of the Minotaur* (1966) depicts the **thinning** of the world of Greek myth; *Cry Silver Bells* (1977) and *The Forest of Forever* (1971) similarly provided **prequels**. Other classical fantasies include the 1963 title novella of *The Dolphin and the Deep* (1968), *The Weirwoods* (1967), and *Wolfwinter* (1972).

The Minikins of Yam 1976) is set in ancient Egypt. *Moondust* (1968) and *How Are the Mighty Fallen* (1974) are **biblical fantasies**. *The Gods Abide* (1976) is an **allegory** comparing classical and Christian worldviews. *The Tournament of Thorns* (1976), *Will-o'-the-Wisp* (1976, featuring the poet Robert Herrick), *The Not-World* (1975, featuring Elizabeth Barrett Browning), and *The Goat without Horns* (1971) are **historical fantasies**. Swann's scholarly endeavors included a study of the **decadent** poet Ernest Dowson. His mother commemorated his passing by sponsoring a series of academic conferences, which provided the seed of the **International Association for the Fantastic in the Arts**.

SWANWICK, MICHAEL J. (1950–). U.S. writer best known for **sf** (refer to *HDSFL*) before he moved in the direction of what he called—in the essay "In the Tradition . . ." (1994; reprinted in *The Postmodern Archipelago*, 1997)—"**hard fantasy**." The move is symbolically recapitulated in the plot development of the **quest** fantasy *The Iron Dragon's Daughter* (1993), in which the heroine experiences a series of milieux mapping the conventional spectra of **science fantasy** and **urban fantasy**. *Jack Faust* (1997) is a **Faustian fantasy** in which the hero's

Mephistophelean informant enables him to see the Industrial Revolution from its beginning to its implicit end within the space of a single generation. Short stories in the same vein are collected in *A Geography of Unknown Lands* (1997).

SWIFT, JONATHAN (1667–1745). Irish satirist whose *Travels into Several Remote Nations of the World in Four Parts . . . by Lemuel Gulliver* (1726; aka *Gulliver's Travels*) defined the category of Swiftian **satire**. The first part, in which Gulliver visits the miniature civilization of Lilliput, is frequently echoed in modern fantasy; his second excursion to the land of **giants**, Brobdingnag, is similarly exemplary. The scathing fourth part, which inverts the roles of horses and humans, exerted a powerful influence on many **animal fantasies**. Swift's essays sometimes adopt fabular form, as in the frame story of *A Tale of a Tub* (1704) and the item familiarly known as "The Battle of the Books," from the same volume.

Modern spin-off from *Gulliver's Travels* includes **T. H. White**'s *Mistress Masham's Repose;* Willis Hall's series begun with *The Return of the Antelope* (1985; aka *The Secret Visitors*); Alison Fell's *The Mistress of Lilliput; or, The Pursuit* (1999), which tracks the adventures of Gulliver's wife; and the first and last stories in Adam Roberts's *Swiftly* (2004).

SWINBURNE, ALGERNON (1837–1909). British poet acquainted with the pre-Raphaelites, who became a significant influence on the French **Decadent** movement after spending some years in exile in Normandy. His verse dramas *Atalanta in Calydon* (1865) and *Erechtheus* (1876) are **classical fantasies**, and he used similar materials in some of the fervent **erotic** inclusions in *Poems and Ballads* (1866), including "Hymn to Proserpine." He addressed **Arthurian** subjects in such poems as the title piece of *Tristram of Lyonesse and Other Poems* (1882).

SWORD AND SORCERY. A term coined by **Fritz Leiber** in response to **Michael Moorcock**'s plea for a category label descriptive of the kind of fiction pioneered by **Robert E. Howard**'s Conan stories and gradually sophisticated by **L. Sprague de Camp**, **Fletcher Pratt**, Leiber, and himself. De Camp became the subgenre's most clamorous popularizer, editing the showcase anthology *Swords and Sorcery* (1963) and several successors; the success of the subgenre in the paperback book medium was an important element in the establishment of **commodified fantasy**. Sword and sorcery fiction overlaps **heroic fantasy** considerably but is differentiated by its unashamed emphasis on action/adventure elements and by its generous hospitality to **picaresque** elements—the latter being lovingly developed by Leiber, de Camp, **Jack Vance**, and **Michael Shea** and formularized by the Thieves World **shared-world** series.

The subgenre's focus on swordplay carried forward a swashbuckling tradition initiated by the French *feuilletonists* but routinely transplanted its highly skilled fighting men into imaginary **prehistoric** milieux where black **magic** and **demonic** activity are rife. Its practitioners took inspiration from **Edgar Rice Burroughs**'s uninhibited adventure fantasies and Lord Dunsany's neo-**chivalric romances** as well as Howard's definitive exemplars, and **Clark Ashton Smith** established **far-futuristic fantasy** as an alternative matrix. Many paperback sword and sorcery writers were encouraged by marketing considerations to employ **planetary romances** and **parallel worlds** as convenient frameworks, paving the way for Moorcock's construction of a generically omnivorous **multiverse**. **C. L. Moore** introduced the first female hero to the subgenre, founding a tradition carried forward by such writers as **Jessica Amanda Salmonson** and **Marion Zimmer Bradley**.

The flood unleashed when sword and sorcery fiction first became commodified—which included a great deal of rough-hewn, mechanically violent, formularized fiction—had abated somewhat by the end of the 20th century, when forms of heroic fantasy focusing on individual characters became noticeably less violent than the collective endeavors of **military fantasy**.

SYMBOLISM. A literary technique that makes objects, landscapes, or exemplary actions serve as signifiers of human emotions, ambitions, or endeavors. In all literary works, but especially in fantastic ones, weather tends to symbolize the moods and predicaments of the characters, and **dreams** are almost always symbolic of their psychological predicaments. Flowers, bodies of water, and timepieces are other favorite symbolically loaded items. A Symbolist movement, organized around the aesthetic theories of Stéphane Mallarmé and provided with a manifesto by Jean Morés, emerged out of the **Decadent** movement, but symbolism was so central to the literary methods associated with the decadent style that it was never fully differentiated. Because overt symbolism is the fundamental method of **allegory** and **satire**—and also because **chivalric romances** were often saturated with symbolism—the descendants of all these subgenres in modern fantasy carry similarly full cargoes, but there is no part of the fantasy spectrum that does not take full advantage of the opportunities offered by fantastic devices for symbolic display and resonance.

SYMONDS, JOHN (1914–). British writer. His nonfiction includes studies of **Madame Blavatsky** and **Aleister Crowley**, but the great majority of his own fantasies have been quirky **children's** books, including *The Magic Currant Bun* (1952), *Lottie* (1957), *Elfrida and the Pig* (1959), and *Dapple Grey: The Story of a Rocking Horse* (1962). His adult fiction includes the **allegory** *William Waste* (1947), the **occult fantasy** *The Guardian of the Threshold* (1980), and the **Shakespearean fantasy** play *Tower above the Clouds* (1994).

SYRETT, NETTA (c1870–1943). British writer associated with the circle surrounding *The Yellow Book,* whose belief in her own psychic powers infected some of her adult romances, including *Barbara of the Thorn* (1913) and the quasi-autobiographical *Angel Unawares* (1936). Her most important contribution to fantasy literature consists of **fairy tales** for **children**; her first collection, *The Garden of Delight* (1898), was followed by *The Magic City and Other Fairy Tales* (1903) and a collection of *Six Fairy Plays* (1904). Her conviction that **fairies** were real, though perceptible only to those with appropriate powers, is further reflected in her **Christmas** anthology *The Dream Garden* (1905) and her collection *Godmother's Garden* (1918). *The Castle of Four Towers* (1909) transforms an Italian town into a fairy realm. *Magic London* (1922; rev. 1933) uses **timeslips** to construct a wide-ranging **historical fantasy**. Her other story collections include *The Endless Journey and Other Stories* (1912) and *The Magic Castle and Other Stories* (1922). More plays were collected in *Robin Goodfellow and Other Fairy Plays* (1918) and *The Fairy Doll and Other Plays for Children* (1922).

– T –

TALL STORY. An oral narrative in which the speaker exaggerates, often increasing the level of exaggeration by degrees until the tale becomes ludicrous. Fishermen and travelers are notorious for such exaggeration, and tales repeated by a series of tellers tend to grow as their tellings proliferate. Most tall stories replicated in literary form are travelers' tales; the archetypal examples are the exploits of Menippus recorded by

Lucian and Baron Münchhausen's accounts of his adventures, as recorded by **R. E. Raspe**.

In the United States, where they were manufactured on a prolific scale in the 19th century, tall stories have a particular association with the myth of the western frontier; their literary exploitation was pioneered by **Mark Twain** and was carried forward in such texts as Vincent McHugh's sprawling **historical fantasy** *Caleb Catlum's America* (1936) and infecting a good deal of modern American **humorous** writing, including works by **Robert Bloch** and **L. Sprague de Camp** and **Fletcher Pratt**'s *Tales from Gavagan's Bar*.

British tall stories feature strongly in the tradition of **humorous fantasy** maintained by such writers as **R. H. Barham** and **Douglas Jerrold**; they frequently take the form of "club stories" narrated at convivial gatherings, like those reproduced in **Dryasdust**'s *Tales of the Wonder Club*. Regional variants include the northern tales exemplified in Eric Knight's *Sam Small Flies Again* (1942; aka *The Flying Yorkshireman*) and such examples of Irish "blarney" as those collected in Desmond Ryan's *Saint Eustace and the Albatross* (1935).

Sports fantasy is also hospitable to tall stories, as exemplified by the work in the subgenre of **W. P. Kinsella** and Maurice Richardson.

TAM LIN. A Scottish **ballad** in which the heroine encounters the eponymous kinsman from a former era, who was taken into **Faerie** as a lover of its queen—while time passed far more rapidly in the **primary world**—but will now be offered as a tribute to Hell if the heroine cannot save him. It is similar to various accounts of Thomas the Rhymer, who is cursed by the fairy queen with an inability to lie when he returns belatedly to the primary world. **Diana Wynne Jones**'s *Fire and Hemlock* combines the two stories. Other notable transfigurations include works by **Susan Cooper**, **Dahlov Ipcar**, **Patricia McKillip**, **Pamela Dean**, and **Gael Baudino**, Holly Black's *Tithe: A Modern Fairy Tale* (2002), and Janet McNaughton's *An Earthly Knight* (2004). Sally Prue's *Cold Tom* (2002) describes the tribulations of an **elf** who is the half-breed son of Tam Lin. **Jo Walton**'s *Tam Lin* is credited to **William Shakespeare**.

TAPROOT TEXT. A term defined in the Clute/Grant *Encyclopedia* with reference to pre-18th-century texts from which modern fantasy literature draws significant inspiration and imagery. Because fantasy literature is descended from oral traditions, with references to marvelous entities and events that take their authority from tradition, it routinely justifies its fantastic devices as things that were once commonplace but have long been subject to a **thinning** process. Many fantasy stories refer back to oral—or purely imaginary—sources, but there is a particular authority in the written word that makes ancient texts very useful as sources of raw material. It is for this reason that imaginary sources are often represented as hypothetical texts. The more fanciful an actual text is and the more its content resonates with an author's literary purpose and ambition, the more useful it becomes as a potential source of tappable nourishment. **Scholarly fantasies** and **lifestyle fantasies** are so dependent on taproot texts that a considerable industry is devoted to faking them, but fantasy literature has the advantage of not having to represent its taproot texts as works of "nonfiction."

TARR, JUDITH (1955–). U.S. writer whose historical fiction—including **historical fantasies**—is conscientiously detailed. The trilogy comprising *The Isle of Glass* (1985), *The Golden Horn* (1985), and *The Hounds of God* (1986) employs a rich medieval setting. The series comprising *The Hall of the Mountain King* (1986), *The Lady of Han-Gilen* (1987), *A Fall of Princes* (1988), *Arrows of the Sun* (1993), *Spear of Heaven* (1994), and *Tides of Darkness* (2002) is cast as **planetary romance**, but its backcloth is similarly detailed. *A Wind in Cairo* (1989) is set in medieval Egypt, *Ars Magica* (1989) in Europe, *Alamut* (1989) and *The Dagger and the Cross* (1991) in the Crusader Kingdom of Jerusalem. *His Majesty's Elephant* (1993) features Charlemagne's half-**witch** daughter.

Fantasy elements are marginal to *Lord of the Two Lands* (1993), *Throne of Isis* (1994), *Pillar of Fire* (1995), and *King and Goddess* (1996) but more central to the Epona trilogy, comprising *White Mare's Daughter* (1998), *The Shepherd Kings* (1999), and *Daughter of Lir* (2001); *Lady of Horses* (2000) is a **prequel**. *Household Gods* (1999 with Harry Turtledove) is a **timeslip** fantasy. *Kingdom of the Grail* (2000) integrates the story of Roland into the body of **Arthurian** legend. *Pride of Kings* (2001) deals with the seduction of England's King John by a magical youth from the East; its sequels *Devil's Bargain* (2002) and *House of War* (2003) feature Richard the Lionheart. In *Queen of the Amazons* (2004), Hippolyta's daughter meets Alexander the Great. In *Rite of Conquest* (2004), a sorceress joins the court of the magically talented William of Normandy before he invades England to defeat Harold in 1066.

TAYLOR, G. P. (?–). British writer. While serving as the vicar of Ravenscar in Yorkshire, he published the fervent, disguised **Christian fantasy** *Shadowmancer* (2002), which attracted enough attention to persuade a commercial publisher to release a new edition on the same day as **J. K. Rowling**'s *Harry Potter and the Order of the Phoenix*—a ploy that boosted it to best-seller status. *Wormwood* (2004) is a similarly encoded **historical fantasy** set in 1750s London.

TAYLOR, KEITH (1946–). Australian writer. A series of short stories bylined Denis More (1975–77) was revised into the novel *Bard* (1981), a **Celtic fantasy** in which the hero is equipped with a magical harp; Taylor published the **planetary romance** *Lances of Negesdul* (1982) before continuing the series in *Bard II* (1984, aka *The First Long Ship*), *The Wild Sea* (1986), *Raven's Fathering* (1987), and *Felimid's Homecoming* (1991), which also have elements of **Nordic fantasy**. The trilogy comprising *The Sorcerer's Sacred Isle* (1989), *The Cauldron of Plenty* (1989), and *Search for the Starblade* (1990) is an orthodox **quest** fantasy in a similar setting.

TAYLOR, ROGER (1938–). British writer. The Chronicles of Hawklan series, comprising *The Call of the Sword* (1988), *The Fall of Fyorlund* (1989), *The Waking of Orthlund* (1989), *Into Narsindal* (1990), and *The Return of the Sword* (1999), is formularized **commodified fantasy**. *Dream Finder* (1991) is set in a more civilized milieu reminiscent of Renaissance Italy. The couplet comprising *Farnor* (1992) and *Valderen* (1993) is an elaborate **heroic fantasy**; its conclusions about the costs of heroism are carried farther forward in *Ibryen* (1995). *Whistler* (1994) is a **satire** on religion and politics. *Arash-Felloren* (1996) and *Caddoran* (1998) reverted to stereotypy.

TELEVISION. TV's heavy dependence on segmental series—enforced by the necessity of making programs in batches to occupy regular time slots—makes it difficult to employ fantasy materials in drama, although the standard formula derived from crime fiction, in which virtuous heroes (or superheroes) work through a series of cases, edged into fantasy via the "vigilante **angel**" subgenre pioneered by *Highway to Heaven* and *Touched by an Angel*. In the early days of the medium, much greater success was enjoyed by **humorous fantasies** in the tradition of **Thorne Smith**, in such shows as *Bewitched* and *I Dream of Jeannie,* whose descendants—notably, *Sabrina the Teenage Witch*—gradually took on more dramatic tension. Dramas cast in a similar mold, like *Charmed,* were careful to retain an element of humor.

The first TV fantasy to spawn a successful line of **tie-in** books was the strikingly anomalous **timeslip** soap opera *Dark Shadows,* which made the most of its American **Gothic** ambience. When a new suite of special effects and the influence of nascent genre fantasy spawned a new generation of TV **heroic fantasy**—spearheaded by *Hercules: The Fantastic Journeys* and *Xena: Warrior Princess*—the trickle of TV tie-ins became a flood, but the most successful were those that retained a soap-operatic element, including *Charmed* and the **horror** series *Buffy the Vampire Slayer*. This is understandable, given that the visual medium requires no assistance in depicting the action-adventure component of the fiction, whereas emotional undercurrents benefit considerably from literary augmentation.

In the late 20th century, TV became the primary medium of animation, with limitations that were further constrained by tight regulation of the kinds of violence depicted in **children's** cartoons made for U.S. network TV after 1980. The primary effect of this restriction was that animations not subject to the restrictions took full advantage of their exemption, with results that were often **surreal** as well as calculatedly gross; the influence of such developments on literary fantasy has been muted and marginal but not entirely negligible.

TEMPLARS. An order of warrior-monks founded in the early 12th century to protect the pilgrims who flocked to the Holy Land following the capture of Jerusalem in 1099; its early headquarters were near the site of the Temple, from which it took its name. The order grew exceedingly rich, not only taking over the property of its members and receiving liberal gifts from supporters, but functioning as a bank, accepting deposits from pilgrims, and issuing letters of credit honored throughout Christendom. When the Christians were expelled from the Holy Land in 1291, the Templars lost their ostensible function; Philippe IV of France took the opportunity to raid their wealth in 1307, justifying the seizure by means of confessions of idolatry extracted by torture. The confessions became the seed of many tales of hidden treasure, of which the more imaginative were integrated into every notable **secret history** featured in modern literature and a great deal of **scholarly fantasy**, in which the Templars often feature as custodians of the Holy **Grail**.

Dramatizations of the Templars' fate are featured in Pierre Klossowski's *The Baphomet* (1965 in French; tr. 1988)—in which shades reenact the legend, illustrating the Nietzschean doctrine of eternal recurrence—and **Umberto Eco**'s *Foucault's Pendulum*. James D. MacDonald's *The Apocalypse*

Door (2002) features an **alternative history** in which the Templars fight on. **Katherine Kurtz** edited the anthologies *Crusade of Fire: Mystical Tales of the Knights Templar* (1997) and *On Crusade: More Tales of the Knights Templar* (1998).

TENNANT, EMMA (1937–). British writer whose literary fiction often has fantastic elements. In *Hotel de Dream* (1976), **dreams** that interact with one another eventually begin to affect the waking environment; *Wild Nights* (1979) is similarly **hallucinatory**. *The Bad Sister* (1978) and *Two Women of London: The Strange Case of Ms. Jekyll and Mrs Hyde* (1989) are **doppelgänger** stories based on classic models. *Alice Fell* (1980) is an **Orphean fantasy** in the style of **Lewis Carroll**. *The Magic Drum* (1989) is a **ghost story**. *Sisters and Strangers* (1990) has marginal elements of **biblical fantasy**. *Faustine* (1992) is a **transfigurative Faustian fantasy**. Her **children's fantasies** include *The Boggart* (1980) and *The Ghost Child* (1984).

TEPPER, SHERI S. (1929–). U.S. writer in various genres. Most of her work is **sf** (refer to *HDSFL*), but a good deal of it is cosmetically dressed as fantasy, including the three trilogies of the True Game sequence, the first comprising *King's Blood Four* (1983), *Necromancer Nine* (1983), and *Wizard's Eleven* (1984), the second *The Song of Mavin Manyshaped* (1985), *The Flight of Mavin Manyshaped* (1985), and *The Search for Mavin Manyshaped* (1985), and the third *Jinian Footseer* (1985), *Dervish Daughter* (1985), and *Jinian Star-Eye* (1986). *The Revenants* (1984) and the trilogy comprising *Marianne, the Magus and the Manticore* (1985), *Marianne, the Madame and the Momentary Gods* (1988), and *Marianne, the Matchbox, and the Malachite Mouse* (1989) are more wholeheartedly fantastic but similarly rule bound. *The Awakeners* (2 vols., 1987) was the first of several **planetary romances** with sf elements that emerge only in the later phases—a pattern also evident in *Beauty* (1991), which begins as a **transfiguration** of a familiar fairy tale but is eventually retransfigured. *A Plague of Angels* (1993) is a similarly hybridized **far-futuristic fantasy**.

THEATER. The mythical elements in Greek tragedy and the **satirical** manner of Greek comedy equipped the theater with sturdy and highly influential fantastic **taproot texts**, which continued to feed the medium throughout its history. The difficulty of contriving fantastic effects—which required such conventions as the god-lowering device that gave birth to the expression "deus ex machina"—was never allowed to stand in the way of representation. Mystery plays and miracle plays maintained the dramatic tradition while theaters were virtually obliterated; the rebirth of drama in the late Renaissance had such popular traditions as the **Italian** *commedia dell'arte* to draw on.

Despite the great strides it made toward naturalism, English Elizabethan drama retained a substantial fantasy component in various plays featuring the **Devil** and his minions, including Robert Greene's *Friar Bacon and Friar Bungay* (c1589; pub. 1594), Christopher Marlowe's *The Tragical History of Dr. Faustus* (c1593; pub. 1604), the anonymous *The Merry Devil of Edmonton* (1608), Thomas Dekker's *If This Be Not a Good Play, the Devil Is in It* (1610), and Ben Jonson's *The Devil Is An Ass* (1616). Once they had been introduced by **William Shakespeare**, **fairies** began to appear in other dramas, including Jonson's *The Satyr* (1603) and *Oberon the Fairy Prince* (1610), while **witches** were perennially popular, as in Jonson's *Masque of Queens* (1609); such subgenres as **wish-fulfillment fantasy** cropped up in comedies like Dekker's *Old Fortunatus* (1600). The 17th-century French theatrical tradition founded by Pierre Corneille and Jean Racine made extravagant use of **classical** materials.

In keeping with the general **thinning** of the literary tradition, fantasy elements became marginal even in comedies and **Gothic** melodramas during the 18th and 19th centuries, but they gained ground again in connection with the **Romantic** movement, becoming especiually prominent in such late products as the works of **Gerhardt Hauptmann** and **Maurice Maeterlinck**. The export of Maeterlinck's **allegorical** "**fairy** plays" was assisted by the popularity in England of "fairy extravaganzas"—spectacular tableaux featuring gorgeously attired fairy queens accompanied by courts of winged children. The tradition continued into the 20th century in pantomimes, and the "topsyturvydom" of **W. S. Gilbert** retained a more reverent fantasy component in the work of such playwrights as **J. M. Barrie** and and **Laurence Housman**.

W. B. Yeats founded the Abbey Theatre in Dublin—with backing from Annie Horniman, whom he had met via his interest in **Rosicrucianism**—with the express purpose of evoking "the spirit of the ancient Celt," in opposition to the pevailing trend toward naturalism, but his own plays were less popular than those of Lady Augusta Gregory—whose recyclings of Irish "folk history" were de-supernaturalized, although her fairy plays for **children**, including *The Golden Apple* (1916) and *The Dragon* (1917) were not—and the project eventually had to be rescued by the determined realism of Sean O'Casey and J. M. Synge. British and American drama went the same way, fantasy thriving mainly in work aimed specifically at children, as exemplified by the work of **Nicholas Stuart Gray**. The Gothic melodramatic tradition that had given birth to the French *Grand Guignol* theatre—which specialized in **horror**—and such classic **moralistic** fantasies as the **Erckmann-Chatrian**-based *The Bells* and E. Temple Thurston's *The Wandering Jew* (1920), similarly fell into terminal decline despite the efforts of impresario Todd Slaughter, who preserved it in England until the early 1950s. A healthy **satirical** tradition was maintained in Eastern Europe by such playwrights as **Karel Ĉapek** and **Slavomir Mrozek**, but it had little influence on English-language work.

Most 20th-century fantasy plays are nowadays best known through their movie versions, partly because the additional capacity for special effects makes for more effective production; such works as Ferenc Molnar's *Liliom* (1909; tr. 1921), Alberto Casella's *Death Takes a Holiday* (tr. 1930), and Harry Segall's *Heaven Can Wait* (1940) would be forgotten had they not been continually remade for **cinema** and **TV**. (*Liliom* was Americanized as the musical *Carousel,* and *Heaven Can Wait* became *Here Comes Mr. Jordan,* its title having already been borrowed for another movie.)

The kind of fantasy most amenable to stage production is **intrusive fantasy** featuring single supernatural visitors—including **ghost** stories and other accounts of revenants—as exemplified by Molnar's *The Devil* (1907), David Belasco's *The Return of Peter Grimm* (1911), and Noel Coward's *Blithe Spirit* (1941). **Timeslips** are also easy to contrive, as in **J. B. Priestley**'s time plays, John Balderston and J. C. Squire's *Berkeley Square* (1928; based on Henry James's unfinished novel *The Sense of the Past,* 1917), and Tom Stoppard's *The Invention of Love* (1997). Modern theater companies specializing in fantasy include Chris and Tim Britton's Forkbeard Fantasy company; its calculatedly **chimerical** productions include *The Fall of the House of Usherettes* (1995), *The Barbers of Surreal* (1998), and *Frankenstein: The True Story* (2001).

Although the intrinsic "**magic** of the theater" is far less widely celebrated than the magic of **music**, it is manifest in numerous works by **Angela Carter** and **Fritz Leiber**, and in **Michael Ende**'s *Ophelia's Shadow Theater*.

THEOSOPHICAL FANTASY. The Theosophical Society, founded in 1875 by **Madame Blavatsky**, survived and thrived throughout the 20th century, sometimes taking aboard other occultists whose own **lifestyle fantasies** were floundering, including **Dion Fortune** and **Mrs. Campbell Praed**, and occasionally spawning its own offshoots, like Rudolf Steiner's breakaway movement Anthroposophy.

Theosophy's associated **scholarly fantasies** became significant feeders of fantasy literature; elements of their account of prehistory, involving various "root races" and elaborate versions of **Atlantis** and Lemuria, were widely borrowed and modified, as in the works of **E. Charles Vivian**, **F. Marion Crawford**'s *Mr Isaacs,* Franz Hartmann's *The Talking Image of Urur* (1890), and Muriel Bruce's *Mukara* (1930). Many aspects of theosophical prehistory were incorporated into **sword and sorcery** fiction by **Robert E. Howard** and his successors. Madame Blavatsky's claim to have received the details of *The Secret Doctrine* from a Tibetan cadre of Hidden Masters whose Himalayan hideaway includes a vast library of occult lore has also been widely reflected in 20th-century fantasy, forming a background element of action/adventure fantasy by such writers as **Talbot Mundy** and **E. Hoffman Price**.

The most notable practicing theosophist to write a significant quantity of fantasy was **Kenneth Morris**, whose use of its doctrines is unusually delicate. **Michael Moorcock**'s fantasy frequently displays echoes of his education at a Steiner school. The most active of several theosophical publishing houses still extant is Quest Books, in the United States. It occasionally publishes such **recycled** fiction as John Matthews's *The Song of Arthur: Celtic Tales from the King's Court* (2002), and *The Song of Taliesin: Tales from King Arthur's Bard* (2003); the range of its nonfiction extends as far as Robert Ellwood's *Frodo's Quest: Living the Myth in* The Lord of the Rings (2002). Theosophical fantasies kept in print by the society's Madras center include Mabel Collins's *The Idyll of the White Lotus* (1919).

THERIOMORPHIC FANTASY. Fantasy featuring transmutations between human and animal form; the Clute/Grant *Encyclopedia* prefers the term "shapeshifting," which implies a degree of conscious control, or at least a regularity and reversibility. Control and reversibility are, however, by no means universal in theriomorphic fantasy, where transformations of humans into animals are often arbitrarily inflicted, perhaps by way of amusement or punishment—a notion deeply rooted in **classical myth** and reproduced in such stories as David Garnett's *Lady into Fox* (1922), **Franz Kafka**'s *Metamorphosis,* **Thorne Smith**'s *The Stray Lamb,* Geoffrey Dearmer's *They Chose to Be Birds*

(1935), Vercors's *Sylva* (1961), **Doranna Durgin**'s *Dun Lady's Jess,* Jerry Jay Carroll's *Top Dog* (1996), **Melvin Burgess**'s *Lady: My Life as a Bitch,* and **N. M. Browne**'s *Hunted*. The most popular pattern of transformation that invites description as shapeshifting is that associated with **werewolves**, whose literary exemplars mostly straddle the border between fantasy and **horror** fiction.

Folktales are rich in theriomorphic imagery, the "swan maiden" being one of the standard motifs identified by Edward Hartland; the frog that might turn into a prince if kissed provides the raw material of a popular modern metaphor. Other folkloristic theriomorphs widely featured in fantasy literature include selkies, or "seal maidens," as featured in Ronald Lockley's *Seal Woman* (1974), Paul Brandon's *Swim the Moon* (2001), and Peter Dickinson's *Inside Grandad* (2004). Accounts of educational theriomorphy include **Selma Lagerlöf**'s Nils series, **T. H. White**'s *The Book of Merlyn* and **K. A. Applegate**'s Animorphs series. More orthodox accounts of shapeshifting involving animals other than wolves include **Fred Saberhagen**'s *Dancing Bears,* **Robin Jarvis**'s Hagwood series, Kate Thompson's *Switchers* (1997), **Jane Lindskold**'s *Changer,* and Alanna Morland's *Leopard Lord* (1999).

THINNING. A term coined by John Clute in *The Encyclopedia of Fantasy* to describe the common assumption of fantasy texts that the **primary world** has become less magical over time. The assumption is inherited from folktales, in which narrative voices are often acutely conscious of the fact that the time is long gone when animals talked, the gods walked the earth, or the fairy folk held regular intercourse with humankind, an age nostalgically consigned to some **Arcadian** era or dreamtime. Notable accounts of thinning include **Anatole France**'s "Saint Satyr," **Richard Garnett**'s "The Twilight of the Gods," **Thomas Burnett Swann**'s *Day of the Minotaur,* Kerstin Ekman's *The Forest Hours* (1988 in Swedish; tr. 1998), and Lilian Nattel's *The River Midnight* (1999).

There is an interesting subcategory of stories in which thinning is represented as a deliberate process tidying up the **chaotic** residue of past magical conflicts. Notable examples include John Brunner's *The Traveller in Black* (1971; exp. 1987), **Orson Scott Card**'s *Hart's Hope,* Brian Stableford's *The Last Days of the Edge of the World* (1978), and **Sean Russell**'s *River into Darkness*.

THURBER, JAMES (1894–1961). U.S. writer and **illustrator**, famous as a humorist. His classic account of **escapist** fantasizing, "The Secret Life of Walter Mitty" (1939; reprinted in *My World and Welcome to It*, 1942), was followed by the similarly ironic *Fables for Our Time and Famous Poems Illustrated* (1940) and *Further Fables for Our Time* (1956), which wryly invert, subvert, or pervert the formal morals of traditional **fables**. Following precedents set by the picture books *Many Moons* (1943) and *The Great Quillow* (1944), his longer prose fantasies were marketed as **children's** books, but they are highly sophisticated and equally subversive. The **theriomorphic fantasy** *The White Deer* (1945) **recycles** familiar **folktale** motifs, but the **Gothic fantasy** *The Thirteen Clocks* (1950) is remarkably inventive, and the **sentimental fantasy** *The Wonderful O* (1955) is an exuberant exercise in wordplay.

TIECK, JOHANN LUDWIG (1773–1853). German writer, one of the central figures of German **romanticism**. *Abdallah* (1795), a graphic **Arabian fantasy** modeled on **William Beckford**'s *Vathek*, has never been translated, but many of the **transfigured** folktales included in *Volksmärchen* (1797) and *Phantasus* (3 vols., 1812–17) are well known. The bibliography of his translations is confused by misattributions, but his most notable short stories are included in *Tales from the Phantasus, etc.* (1845), including a striking **allegory** of **thinning**, "The Elves" (1811); the couplet comprising the verse/prose hybrid "The Faithful Eckhart" (1797) and "The Tannenhäuser" (1799, about the legend of the Venusberg), and the **delusional fantasies** "The White Eckbert (1796)," "The Runenberg" (1802), and "The Love-Charm" (1811). The last item in *The Old Man of the Mountains: The Lovecharm and Pietro of Albano* (1831)—first published in 1824—is a melodramatic **historical fantasy** novella.

TIE-IN. A book associated with a film, TV series, or **game**. Novelizations of successful silent movies first appeared in the 1920s, a notable fantasy example being Achmed Abdullah's *The Thief of Bagdad* (1924), but such items of spin-off did not become commonplace until the 1960s. Game tie-ins are by far the most significant within genre fantasy, where they complete a tight feedback loop; role-playing games like Dungeons and Dragons are extensions of conventional literary fantasy into narrowly confined **lifestyle fantasy**, which plunder almost all their raw material from fantasy literature, so books based on the games are effectively **recycling** that material. Tie-ins to computer games and war games have to be more inventive, because their literary spin-off has to add far more supplementary material to the basic image sequences and rule books.

TILTON, LOIS (1946–). U.S. writer in various genres. *Vampire Winter* (1990) is revisionist **vampire** fiction. *Darkspawn* (2000) is an **epic fantasy** with a vampire hero. *Written in Venom* (2000) is a **Nordic fantasy** in which the **god** Loki tells his own story.

TIME REVERSAL. Reversing the flow of time within a story is a common fantasy motif, featured in Albert Robida's *L'Horloge des siècles* [The Clock of the Centuries] (1902), **Eden Phillpotts's** *A Deal with the Devil,* **Michael Maurice**'s *Not in Our Stars* (1923), Malcolm Ross's *The Man Who Lived Backward* (1951), Oliver Onions's *The Tower of Oblivion*, Martin Amis's *Time's Arrow* (1991), Daniel Quinn and Tim Eldred's *The Man Who Grew Young* (2001), and Andrew Sean Greer's *The Confessions of Max Tivoli* (2004).

TIMESLIP. An arbitrary dislocation in time, usually—but not invariably—a "fall" into the past. The device is frequently used to facilitate transtemporal love affairs, as in **Théophile Gautier**'s "Arria Marcella," Robert W. Chambers's "The Demoiselle d'Ys," **A. Merritt**'s "Three Lines of Old French," **Gerald Bullett**'s "Helen's Lovers," and Erica Jong's *Serenissima* (1987), for which reason such stories are often described as "timeslip romances" and are now a staple element of **paranormal romance**. They also figure extensively in novelistic ***contes philosophiques*** like **Mark Twain**'s *A Connecticut Yankee in King Arthur's Court,* G. G. Coulton's *Friar's Lantern* (1906), **Katharine Burdekin**'s *The Burning Ring,* **Christopher Morley**'s *Thunder on the Left,* and **Terence M. Green**'s *The Shadow of Ashland,* where they facilitate arguments about historical cause and effect or assault nostalgic delusions.

A variant of the theme that involves protagonists slipping back to an earlier point in their own personal histories, as in **J. M. Barrie**'s *Dear Brutus,* Louis Marlow's *The Devil in Crystal* (1944), P. D. Ouspensky's *The Strange Life of Ivan Osokin* (1947), and **Thomas Berger**'s *Changing the Past,* is a kind of **wish-fulfillment fantasy**. Folktales in which abductions into **Faerie** involve severe time dislocations are timeslip fantasies of a sort, although the effective movement is forward rather than back. Timeslip romances are sometimes complicated by continual slippages, as in **Margaret Irwin**'s *Still She Wished for Company,* **Robert Nathan**'s *Portrait of Jennie,* **Ken Grimwood**'s *Replay,* and Audrey Niffenegger's *The Time Traveler's Wife* (2003).

Timeslips in **children's fantasy** are usually educational, as in Alison Uttley's *A Traveller in Time* (1939), W. Croft Dickinson's *The Eildon Tree* (1947), **Philippa Pearce**'s *Tom's Midnight Garden,* **Penelope Farmer**'s *Charlotte Sometimes,* Jill Paton Walsh's *A Chance Child* (1978), Robert Westall's *The Wind Eye* (1977) and *The Devil on the Road* (1978), and various works by **Margaret J. Anderson**, **William Mayne**, **Helen Cresswell**, **Jane Louise Curry**, and **Theresa Tomlinson**.

TOLKIEN, J. R. R. (1892–1973). British scholar and writer. An academic specializing in Old English, he regretted the usurpation of British **myth** and **legend** by Norman invaders, whose imported traditions of **romance** had spawned the **Arthurian** tradition and polluted the **Celtic** traditions echoed in the Welsh texts translated as the ***Mabinogion***. In the wake of World War I, when **re-enchantment** was in vogue, he began work on his own mythos to "replace" the lost heritage, in a body of work whose **epic** core was ultimately to become *The Silmarillion*. Along with Owen Barfield, he was co-opted by **C. S. Lewis** into the **Inklings** discussion group before he published *The Hobbit; or, There and Back Again* (1937), a **children's/quest** set against the backcloth of his English mythos, which became a key exemplar of modern **immersive fantasy**. The literary theory behind the work was elaborated in a 1939 lecture "On Fairy Tales," reprinted in *Essays Presented to Charles Williams* (1947), and revised as "On Fairy-stories" in *Tree and Leaf* (1964), where it appeared with the exemplary "Leaf by Niggle." This essay, which defined such terms as **secondary world** and **enchantment** and proposed that the three functions of fantasy were Recovery, **Escape**, and Consolation, became the foundation stone of modern fantasy theory.

Following the success of *The Hobbit,* Tolkien set out to write a sequel; this grew by degrees into *The Lord of the Rings,* whose three volumes were issued as *The Fellowship of the Ring* (1954), *The Two Towers* (1954), and *The Return of the King* (1955). Its reputation grew slowly until paperback reprints issued in the United States in the mid-1960s became huge best sellers, followed by a British paperback omnibus in 1968. Tolkien labored for the rest of his life preparing a version of *The Slmarillion* for publication but was never fully satisfied with it; the posthumous version of 1977 was edited by his son Christopher, who went on to publish numerous spin-off volumes, including *Unfinished Tales of Númenor and Middle-Earth* (1980) and a set of textual commentaries issued under the collective title of *The History of Middle-Earth*, comprising *The Book of Lost Tales 1* (1983), *The Book of Lost Tales 2* (1984), *The Lays of Beleriand* (1985), *The Shaping of Middle-Earth* (1986), *The Lost Road and Other Writings* (1987), *The Return of the Shadow: The History of the Lord of the Rings 1* (1988), *The Treason of Isengard: The History of the Lord of the Rings 2* (1989), *The War of the Ring: The History of the Lord of the Rings 3* (1990), *Sauron Defeated: The History of the Lord of the Rings 4* (1992), *The Later Silmarillion 1: Morgoth's Ring* (1993), *The Later Silmarillion 2: The War of the Jewels* (1994), and *The Peoples of Middle-Earth* (1996).

The other **children's fantasies** Tolkien published—all slight by comparison with *The Hobbit*—are *Farmer Giles of Ham* (1949), *The Adventures of Tom Bombadil and Other Verses from the Red Book* (1962), and *Smith of Wootton Major* (1967). Other posthumous publications include *The Father Christmas Letters* (1976), *Poems and Stories* (1980), *Mr Bliss* (1982), and *Roverandom* (1998). In the meantime, imitations of *The Lord of the Rings*—imitations that retained the **quest** element and most of the casual narrative trappings while ignoring its basis in a synthetic English mythos—were published in sufficient profusion in the United States as to constitute the core of a commercial genre. Although the reduction of the archetype to a repeatable formula is undoubtedly a degradation, the influence of the book and its accompanying literary theory is by no means restricted to that process of formularization; the measure of Tolkien's achievement has been its tremendous inspiration to other writers ambitious to develop the artistry of fantasy literature.

TOMLINSON, THERESA (1946–). British writer. A series of **timeslip** fantasies for young readers dramatizing the effects of the industrial revolution in Yorkshire comprises *The Errand Lass, Meet Me by the Steelmen, Night of the Red Devil,* and *Scavenger Boy* (all 2003). The Forestwife Trilogy, **transfiguring** the legend of Robin Hood, comprises *The Forestwife* (1995), *Child of the May* (1998), and *The Path of the She-Wolf* (2000). *The Moon Riders* (2003) and *The Voyage of the Snake Lady* (2004) are concerned with the involvement of **amazons** in the Trojan war. *Blitz Baby* (2004) features infectious **dreams**.

TOURNIER, MICHEL (1924–). French writer whose novels usually have marginal but complex elements of fantasy. The novel translated as *Friday; or, The Other Island* (1967; tr. 1969) is a **metafictional/transfiguration** of Daniel Defoe's *Robinson Crusoe*. *The Erl King* (1970; tr.

1972) is an account of a modern ogre's search for truth in a world seemingly overladen with signs and **symbols**. *Gemini* (1975; tr. 1977) is an extrapolation of the ***doppelgänger*** motif. *The Four Wise Men* (1980; 1982) is an elaboration of the account of the magi in the second chapter of the biblical book of Matthew. *Gilles & Jeanne* (1983; tr. 1987) is a **historical fantasy** about the relationship between Jeanne d'Arc and Gilles de Rais. Tournier's short fiction, sampled in *The Fetishist* (1978; tr. 1983) and *The Midnight Love-Feast* (1989; tr. 1991), makes more explicit use of fantasy material, establishing him as one of the principal **fabulists** of the late 20th century.

TRANSFIGURATION. The routine **recycling** of **folktales** and other well-established stories within fantasy literature inevitably gives rise to a measure of transfiguration, whereby such stories gradually mutate and the most successful mutations—in terms of audience appeal—become built into future recyclings. It seems probable that the versions of **folktales** that were first written down were themselves the products of some such selective process, but the historical record tends to preserve all subsequent variants, making far more copies of some than of others. The potential scope of transfigurative exercises was demonstrated at the end of the 19th century by such far-ranging exercises as Jules Laforgue's *Six Moral Tales* (1887; tr. 1928), in which **erotic fantasies** are drawn from **myth**, **legend**, and literature in a flamboyantly parodic fashion.

Fantasy writers routinely recast old stories in order to extract presently relevant morals, import presently relevant metaphors, update or culturally revise the settings, demonstrate artistic virtuosity, or simply because they have licence to do it and it saves creative labor. Frequently transfigured stories often give rise to whole subgenres, including such portmanteau subgenres as **Arabian fantasy**, **fairy tales**, and **classical fantasy**, as well as more narrowly defined ones such as **Odyssean**, **Orphean**, and **Promethean** fantasies.

TRAVELER'S TALE. One of the oldest forms of narrative discourse, ever prone to exaggeration and—especially in its **tall story** variants—fantasization. Journeys, or **quests**, of discovery that provide a crucial tempering of the mind and spirit are central to **hero** myths and are often narrated in the form of traveler's tales. **Allegories** of maturation presented in this form retain a significant role in modern fantasy literature.

A key example of the fantasized traveler's tale is *The Voyage of St. Brendan* (c850), whose Latin original—presumably written in

Ireland—was widely translated into French, English, and Welsh as vernacular languages began to spawn natural literatures; it describes a series of marvelous islands culminating in the paradisal Island of Promise and may be regarded as the archetype of the modern tradition of fantastic sea voyages spawned by **Rabelais** and **Swift**. Its terrestrial equivalent, *The Marvellous Adventures of Sir John Maundeville, Kt.* (c1355 in French; tr. 1385), took considerable inspiration from a letter widely circulated between the 12th and 14th centuries, allegedly from a Christian emperor of India named Prester John, inviting the Byzantine emperor Manuel to visit his domain. Descriptions of this fabulous land varied as the letter was copied and transfigured, and the kingdom migrated from Asia to Africa; it may be regarded as an archetype of the moderrn **lost-race** story.

TRAVERS, P. L. (1899–1996). Stage name and pseudonym of Australian actress and writer Helen Lyndon Goff. She is best known for a series of **children's fantasies** about a magically gifted nanny, initially comprising *Mary Poppins* (1934), *Mary Poppins Comes Back* (1935), *Mary Poppins Opens the Door* (1943), and *Mary Poppins in the Park* (1952). After several volumes of trivial spin-off, the series resumed with *Mary Poppins in Cherry Tree Lane* (1982) and *Mary Poppins and the House Next Door* (1989). Her other works include the **historical fantasy** *Friend Monkey* (1971), the **recycled** materials collected in *About the Sleeping Beauty* (1975) and *Two Pairs of Shoes* (1980), and several essays on literary uses of **myths** and **folktales**, some of which are assembled in *What the Bee Knows: Reflections on Myth, Symbol and Story* (1989).

TREMAYNE, PETER (1943–). Pseudonym of British scholar and writer Peter Beresford Ellis. His nonfiction—issued under his own name—includes a great deal of material about **Celtic** history and **legend**, including *a Dictionary of Irish Mythology* (1987) and *A Dictionary of Celtic Mythology* (1992). His fiction includes **horror**, medieval mysteries, and **sf** as well as three prequels to **Bram Stoker**'s *Dracula* (1977–80) and a sequel to **H. Rider Haggard**'s *She,* entitled *The Vengeance of She* (1978). The trilogy comprising *The Fires of Lan-Kern* (1980), *The Destroyers of Lan-Kern* (1982), and *The Buccaneers of Lan-Kern* (1983) is a Celtic fantasy set in Cornwall, while *Ravenmoon* (1988, aka *Bloodmist*) and *Island of Shadows* (1991) employ an Irish setting. *Raven of Destiny* (1984) is a **historical fantasy** set in the 3rd century B.C. His short fantasies are sampled in *The Lady of Hy-Brasil* (1987).

TURGENEV, IVAN (1818–1883). Russian writer. His relevant works are mostly in the borderland between fantasy and **horror**, often making use of the **ambiguity** identified by Tzvetan Todorov as the definitive characteristic of the ***fantastique***. The 1864 title piece of *Phantoms and Other Stories* (1904) is an ambitious, didactic **timeslip** fantasy. "The Dream" (1877) is a **visionary fantasy**. "Clara Militch" (1882) is a languidly **philosophical ghost** story. Some of the poems in prose he published in 1878–82, translated in *Dream Tales and Prose Poems* (1897), also have fantasy elements.

TWAIN, MARK (1885–1910). Pseudonym of U.S. writer Samuel Langhorne Clemens, best known as a **humorist**. The classic **timeslip** fantasy *A Connecticut Yankee in King Arthur's Court* (1889) examines with a sardonic eye the career of a 20th-century handyman in 6th-century England. The various manuscripts cobbled together by Twain's literary executor as *The Mysterious Stranger* (1916; restored text as *Mark Twain's Mysterious Stranger Manuscripts*, 1969) is an eccentric **metaphysical fantasy**. Twain's comic fantasies are mostly **satires** on religion, including *Extracts from Adam's Diary* (1893; book 1901) and *Eve's Diary* (1905; book 1906)—assembled with others in *The Diaries of Adam and Eve* (1997)—and the **afterlife fantasy** *Extract from Captain Stormfield's Visit to Heaven* (1907; book 1909). He also wrote some notable **tall stories**, including "The Canvasser's Tale" (1876) and "A Horse's Tale" (1906).

– U –

UNDERWORLD. A term that once referred to the world of the dead and is nowadays used metaphorically to refer to the society of professional criminals. It retains its literal implications in fantasy literature, which makes extravagant use of subterranean spaces of various kinds, but associations with death and deviance remain common features of the underworlds of fantasy, as in the subgenre of **Orphean fantasy**. In works that deal in the **dualism** of Light and Dark, underworlds belong to the latter side, often constituting havens of primitive ignorance contrasted with enlightened cities that overlie them. The underworlds most likely to escape this kind of stigmatization are those that play host to miniaturized populations like **Elisabeth Beresford**'s wombles and **Mary Norton**'s Borrowers.

The common use of caves and tunnels as **portals** in **folktales**—reflected in such literary works as **Lewis Carroll**'s first *Alice* book and Herbert Read's *The Green Child* (1935)—identifies many **secondary worlds** as underworlds. Although **Faerie** was less frequently represented as an underground realm after its **Shakespearean** makeover, certain fairy races—especially dwarfs—retained their reputation as dwellers underground. Underworlds have become markedly more various and more versatile in recent times, as illustrated by the phantasmagoric extrapolations of **Michael Shea** and such subtly various versions as Gert Hoffman's "A Conversation about Balzac's Horse" (1981), **James Morrow**'s *City of Truth,* **Nick O'Donohoe**'s Gnome series, Jessica Rydill's *Children of the Shaman* (2001), David Herter's *Evening's Empire* (2002), Suzanne Collins's *Gregor the Overlander* (2003), and **N. M. Browne**'s *Basilisk*.

UNICORN. A mythical species of horse equipped with a single horn, often helical in form, projecting from the forehead. One legend alleges that a unicorn can be gentled only by a virgin, lending the motif considerable **symbolic** power in such **erotic fantasies** as **Theodore Sturgeon**'s "The Silken-Swift." Its reputation for extreme rarity justifies its crucial roles in such **quest** fantasies as **Alan Garner**'s *Elidor* and **Peter S. Beagle**'s *The Last Unicorn*. When a unicorn's head was adopted as the symbol of **Lin Carter**'s **Ballantine Adult Fantasy series**, however, unicorns soon became extremely common in fantasy **illustration**. They were integrated into the standardized apparatus of **commodified fantasy**, appearing in such **series** as **Bruce Coville**'s Unicorn Chronicles, the one begun with John Lee's *The Unicorn Quest* (1986), and **Meredith Ann Pierce**'s Firebringer trilogy. Such was their popularity that Jack Dann and Gardner Dozois's anthology *Unicorns!* (1982) required supplementation by *Unicorns II* (1992); similar items include *The Unicorn Treasury* (1988), ed. Bruce Coville, and *Peter S. Beagle's Immortal Unicorn* (1995), ed. Beagle and Janet Berliner.

UNKNOWN. U.S. pulp magazine founded as a companion to the **sf** magazine *Astounding* (refer to *HDSFL*) in 1939. It published 39 issues before wartime paper shortages killed it in 1943, shortly after its name had been expanded to *Unknown Worlds*. It developed a highly distinctive character by exploiting the narrative energy derivable from unashamedly absurd confrontations of sceptical and pragmatic protagonists with **magical intrusions** or **secondary worlds**. Such **humorous**

fantasies—foreshadowed in the work of **Thorne Smith**—were brought to a new level of sophistication and considerably broadened in scope by **L. Sprague de Camp**, sometimes in collaboration with **Fletcher Pratt**, **L. Ron Hubbard**, Anthony Boucher, and **Henry Kuttner**. The method was also employed in such wry **contes philosophiques** as **Robert A. Heinlein**'s "The Devil Makes the Law," **Jack Williamson**'s *Darker than You Think,* and **Fritz Leiber**'s *Conjure Wife*. Leiber also published his early **sword and sorcery** stories in *Unknown,* while other action-adventure fiction was provided by Hubbard and Norvell W. Page. *Unknown* thus provided an invaluable laboratory for experimentation with **chimerical** fantasies, although its example was not extensively followed up until the advent of genre fantasy reignited interest in the 1970s.

URBAN FANTASY. A fantasy with inclusions that carefully transfigure apparatus traditionally associated with rural settings in order to adapt it to modern cities, often redesigning it to fit specific locations. The core of the subgenre consists of **contemporary fantasies** and 20th-century **historical fantasies**, although the definition given in the Clute/Grant *Encyclopedia* also admits stories set in **secondary world** cities that are intended as archetypes of urban sprawl and urban decay. The development of urban fantasy was pioneered by **Fritz Leiber** in such stories as "Smoke Ghost" and "The Girl with the Hungry Eyes," but the subgenre was given more definitive form in the work of **Charles de Lint** and such individual items as **Mark Helprin**'s *Winter's Tale,* **Megan Lindholm**'s *The Wizard of the Pigeons,* **Emma Bull**'s *The War of the Oaks,* **Michael Moorcock**'s *Mother London,* **Kara Dalkey**'s *Steel Rose,* Richard Bowes's *Minions of the Moon* (1999), **Tanya Huff**'s *Gate of Darkness, Gate of Light,* Neal Shusterman's *Downsiders* (1999), and **Paul Brandon**'s *The Wild Reel* (2004).

– V –

VAMPIRE. A supernatural predator that feeds on human blood; humanoid versions are often alleged to arise by means of a method of reproduction in which the victims of vampires are subjected to a form of resurrection after death. The motif is widely featured in **horror** fiction (refer to *HDHL*), but the vampire's status as a **monster** is dependent on the conviction that resurrection as a vampire is a fate worse than death—a conviction that was never entirely safe and was subject to an extraordinarily strident challenge in the fantasy literature of the 1970s.

Literary vampires are derived from two distinct folkloristic traditions; the Greek *lamia* appeared as a seductive female, whose femme fatale quality always recommended her for use in many **erotic fantasies**, while Eastern European superstitions regarding cannibalistically inclined reanimated corpses seemed to have no such potential until the notion was usurped by John Polidori in his demonization of **Lord Byron** as *The Vampyre* (1819). So powerful was the influence of *The Vampyre* that Byron's **Gothic** image was firmly stamped on subsequent images of male vampires, whose powers and limitations were cobbled together from Eastern European folklore. The two sources were casually fused by **Théophile Gautier**'s "Clarimonde," **Paul Féval**'s *The Vampire Countess,* and J. Sheridan le Fanu's "Carmilla" (1872) before the combination was definitively formularized in **Bram Stoker**'s *Dracula*.

Although many subsequent writers of horror fiction strove to confine vampires to monstrous roles, the charismatic qualities derived from Byron and lamias could not be suppressed, and the vampire's qualified **immortality** became increasingly unconvincing as a form of eternal damnation. Tentative experiments like **Jane Gaskell**'s *The Shiny Narrow Grin* (1964) were followed a decade later by a drastic change of attitude manifest in such flamboyant **historical fantasies** as Pierre Kast's *The Vampires of Alfama* (1975; tr. 1976), **Fred Saberhagen**'s *The Dracula Tape,* and **Anne Rice**'s *Interview with the Vampire,* which gave birth to a **hybrid** species of vampire fiction in which the erotic and horrific elements added spice to exercises in baroque **existentialist fantasy**. Notable examples of this "revisionist" vampire fantasy include Susan Petrey's Varkela series (1979–83), **Chelsea Quinn Yarbro**'s Saint-Germain series, **Suzy McKee Charnas**'s *The Vampire Tapestry,* Geoffrey Farrington's *The Revenants* (1983), **Barbara Hambly**'s *Immortal Blood,* **Storm** Constantine's *Burying the Shadow,* Poppy Z. Brite's *Lost Souls* (1992), Anne Billson's *Suckers* (1993), **Lucius Shepard**'s *The Golden,* and the various series begun by Nancy Collins's *Sunglasses after Dark* (1989), **Kim Newman**'s *Anno Dracula,* **Freda Warrington**'s *A Taste of Blood Wine,* and—triumphantly completing the circle—**Tom Holland**'s *The Vampyre*.

Yarbro and Warrington demonstrated that the new breed of male vampire was not only amenable to recruitment to generic romantic fiction but perfectly adapted to that environment, where he began to flourish in such series as those launched by Maggie Shayne's *Twilight Phantasies* (1993), Nancy Gideon's *Midnight Kiss* (1994), and Christine Feehan's *Dark Prince* (1999), and such anthologies as *Strangers in the Night* (Silhouette, 1995) and *After Twilight* (LoveSpell, 2001). Despite the implicit eroticism of the motif, it was also adapted to **children's fiction** in successful series by Willis Hall and "Darren Shan" (Darren O'Shaughnessy).

A significant variant of the motif is the "psychic vampire" that renews its youth and strength by feeding on the "life force" of others—examples are featured in **Jean Lorrain**'s "The Egregore," **Sabine Baring-Gould**'s "Margery of Quether," **Arthur Conan Doyle**'s *The Parasite,* and **George S. Viereck**'s *The House of the Vampire*—but its fashionability waned in the 20th century; blood has far more **symbolic** force than any mere pseudoelectrical fluid.

VANCE, JACK (1916–). U.S. writer best known for **sf** (refer to *HDSFL*), although he would undoubtedly have written more fantasy had he been able to find magazine markets for the exotic **far-futuristic fantasies** making up *The Dying Earth* (1950); they eventually became exemplars as significant as **Clark Ashton Smith**'s Zothique series. Vance extended the series in the **picaresque** stories collected in *The Eyes of the Overworld* (1966) and *Cugel's Saga* (1983), and in the conscientiously **decadent** *Morreion* (1973; book 1979) and *Rhialto the Marvelous* (1984); he gave permission for a further extension by **Michael Shea**. *The Last Castle* (1967) offers a more carefully hybridized image of the far future.

Vance had earlier imported similar decadent elements into many of his exotic **planetary romances**, including *Son of the Tree* (1951; book 1964), *Big Planet* (1952; book 1957; restored text 1978), *The Houses of Iszm* (1954; book 1964), and *The Dragon Masters* (1963); he made a key contribution to the stylistic and ideative sophistication of **science fantasy** between 1950 and 1980, after which the establishment of genre fantasy reduced the necessity for such compromises. His most significant contribution to genre fantasy thereafter was an exuberantly exotic trilogy set in Lyonesse, comprising *Suldrun's Garden* (1983), *The Green Pearl* (1985), and *Madouc* (1989). Fantasy stories are included in many of his collections, most notably *Eight Fantasms and Magics* (1969; abridged as *Fantasms and Magics*) and *Green Magic: The Fantasy Realms of Jack Vance* (1979).

VANDERMEER, JEFF (1968–). U.S. writer and **small press** publisher. His Ministry of Whimsy Press (founded 1984) issued numerous avant-gardish fantasy books and the **magazine** *Jabberwocky*. *The Book of Frog* (1989) and *The Book of Lost Places* (1996) mingle fantasies with **horror** stories. The novella *Dradin in Love* (1996) launched a striking series of **decadent** fantasies set in the exotic city of Ambergris; it was collected with others in *City of Saints and Madmen: The Book of Ambergris* (2001; exp. 2002; further exp. 2004). Other **surreal fabulations** are included in *The Day Dali Died: Poetry and Flash Fiction* (2003) and *Secret Life* (2004). VanderMeer's anthologies—most notably *The Thackeray T. Lambshead Pocket Guide to Eccentric and Discredited Diseases* (2003, coedited with Mark Roberts)—offer further testimony to the range and innovative spirit of his imagination; they include the Leviathan series, coedited with Forrest Aguirre (4 vols., 2001–2004) and *Album Zutique 1* (2003).

VANDE VELDE, VIVIAN (1951–). U.S. writer in various genres whose work for **children** always displayed a mordant maturity that became increasingly conspicuous over time. *Once upon a Test* (1984) is a collection of subversively transfigured **fairy tales**; further examples are assembled in *Tales from the Brothers Grimm and the Sisters Weird* (1995) and *The Rumpelstiltskin Problem* (2000). The novel *A Hidden Magic* (1985) is similar in spirit, as are the **timeslip** fantasy *A Well-Timed Enchantment* (1990); *User Unfriendly* (1991), in which the protagonists are trapped in a **game**; *Dragon's Bait* (1992), whose heroine befriends the **dragon** to which she is sacrificed; the revisionist **vampire** story *Companions of the Night* (1995); and the **theriomorphic fantasy** *The Changeling Prince* (1998).

In *The Conjurer Princess* (1997), a princess apprentices herself to a **wizard** in order to undertake an **Orphean quest**. *A Coming Evil* (1998) is a dark **historical fantasy** set during World War II. *Ghost of a Hanged Man* (1998) is a fantasy western. *Never Trust a Dead Man* (1999), *There's a Dead Person Following My Sister Around* (1999), and *Magic Can Be Murder* (2000) are **dark**-edged **hybrid** mysteries. *Heir Apparent* (2002) is a hectic **satirical** quest fantasy. The protagonist of *Wizard at Work* (2003) is heavily stressed by the demands of his clients. More short fiction is collected in *Curses, Inc. and Other Stories* (1997) and *Being Dead* (2001).

VAN LUSTBADER, ERIC (1946–). U.S. writer who dropped the "van" from his byline in the 1980s, when he specialized in martial-arts thrillers, but reclaimed it in 2001. The **science fantasy** *The Sunset Warrior* (1977) served as a prelude to a trilogy comprising *Shallows of Night*

(1978), *Dai-San* (1978), and *Beneath an Opal Moon* (1980), which adapted **sword and sorcery** to an **Oriental** setting. He returned to more stylized adventures in a similar setting in the Pearl Saga, comprising *The Ring of Five Dragons* (2001), *The Veil of a Thousand Tears* (2002), and *The Cage of Nine Banestones* (2003).

VANSITTART, PETER (1920–). British writer. His first venture into **Arthurian fantasy**, *Lancelot* (1978), minimizes its fantasy component, but *Parsifal* (1988) allows its hero to survive from the Middle Ages to World War II. In *The Death of Robin Hood* (1981), another legendary hero becomes an abiding presence through the centuries, into the depression of the 1930s. In the far more playful *Hermes in Paris* (2000), the **classical** deity takes a holiday at Napoleon III's court.

VIERECK, GEORGE S. (1884–1962). German-born U.S. journalist whose fiction attempted to import the spirit of the European **Decadent** movements. *The House of the Vampire* (1907) is a homoerotic account of psychic **vampirism**. In the calculatedly scandalous best-selling trilogy of **erotic fantasies** he wrote in collaboration with Paul Eldridge, comprising *My First Two Thousand Years: The Autobiography of the Wandering Jew* (1928), *Salome, the Wandering Jewess* (1930), and *The Invincible Adam* (1932), the **Wandering Jew** and his female counterpart are heroic warriors against "the Great God Ennui," he **questing** for the ever-elusive secret of "unendurable pleasure indefinitely prolonged," she seeking to liberate womankind from the yoke of male domination. A similar combination of prurience and eccentric **feminism** features in *Gloria* (1952), in which the eponymous **goddess** alleges that the supposedly great lovers of history and legend were all woefully inadequate. *My First Two Thousand Years* had the rare distinction of inspiring a parody, *The Memoirs of Satan* (1932), by William Gerhardi and Brian Lunn, that is of considerable interest in its own right as a witty exercise in **literary satanism**.

VISIONARY FANTASY. A fantasy presented in the form of a **dream** that retains some pretence of being a "true" revelation; dream fantasies that do not are here categorized as **hallucinatory fantasies**. **Religious fantasies** routinely make the assumption that prophetic and **allegorical** revelations are often delivered as visionary fantasies, after the fashion of the biblical book of Revelations and much apocryphal literature; the most notable literary recapitulations of the notion include **Dante**'s *Divine Comedy* and **John Bunyan**'s *The Pilgrim's Progress*.

Less orthodox visionary fantasies aspiring to **oracular** quality are usually to be found in such fields as **spiritualist** and **theosophical fantasy**.

The notion that artists and writers might be blessed with a quasi-oracular genius was sustained by such examples as Simeon Solomon's "A Vision of Love Revealed in Sleep" (1871), Olive Shreiner's *Dreams* (1891) and **W. B. Yeats**'s *A Vision*, but after the advent of **surrealism** dreams were more often used as sources of incoherence than vehicles of revelation. The kinds of fantasy most likely to adopt visionary frames thereafter were **moralistic fantasies**—especially **Christmas fantasies** modeled on **Charles Dickens**'s templates—and **erotic fantasies** slightly ashamed of their own self-indulgence and ponderous **satires**.

VIVIAN, E. CHARLES (1882–1947). Pseudonym of British editor and writer Charles Henry Cannell. He published a few fantasy stories in *Flying* while he was its editor in 1917–18, sometimes using the byline "A. K. Walton," and produced similar works in the 1920s when he worked on early British pulp magazines. The fantasy novels he wrote as Vivian are mostly **lost-race** stories, some of which—notably *City of Wonder* (1922)—have elements of **theosophical fantasy**. *Fields of Sleep* (1923) features a remnant of the Babylonian empire in **bondage** to addictive scent, while its sequel *People of the Darkness* (1924) features an **underworld** inhabited by nonhuman descendants of an **Atlantean** race. *The Lady of the Terraces* (1925) features survivors of a pre-Incan civilization, whose heyday is described in *A King There Was* (1926).

Cannell also introduced fantastic elements into some volumes of a series of detective stories that he wrote as "Jack Mann." *Grey Shapes* (1937) features **theriomorphic** relics of an ancient race whose memory is preserved in the **Celtic** mythology of the Sidhe, a **secret history** further extrapolated in *Nightmare Farm* (1937)—which borrows its key motif from *City of Wonder*—*Maker of Shadows* (1938), *The Ninth Life* (1939), *Her Ways Are Death* (1939), and *The Glass Too Many* (1940).

VOLSKY, PAULA (?–). U.S. writer. *The Curse of the Witch-Queen* (1982) is a **humorous fantasy**. The **secondary world** featured in the trilogy comprising *The Sorcerer's Lady* (1986), *The Sorcerer's Heir* (1988), and *The Sorcerer's Curse* (1989) is modeled on 17th-century Venice. *The Luck of Relian Kru* (1987) is a comedy featuring a series of

quests. *Illusion* (1991) is a story of **thinning** featuring an **alternative** French Revolution. *The Wolf of Winter* (1993) is a **dark fantasy** whose plot recalls **Shakespeare**'s *Macbeth*. *The Gates of Twilight* (1996) is set in an alternative world where the end of the British raj is confused by the real existence of the Hindu gods; its sequel, *The Grand Ellipse* (2000), features an around-the-world race. *The White Tribunal* (1997) is an offbeat **Faustian** revenge fantasy.

VOLTAIRE (1694–1778). Pseudonym of French historian and philosopher François-Marie Arouet, one of the leading intellectuals of the 18th century. He invented and popularized the ***conte philosophique***, some of whose early examples employed tales modeled on those in **Antoine Galland**'s *Arabian Nights* as vehicles for rationalistic rhetoric. The protagonist of "The World as It Is" (1746) is conducted on an educational tour by the **angel** Ituriel. "Zadig, or Destiny" (1748), the prototype of all tales of deductive detection, employs an angel as a deus ex machina. "Memnon, or Wisdom" (1747) and "Barabec and the Fakirs" (1750) are similar, but the fantasy element was minimized in subsequent endeavors until Voltaire began to produce more playful tales, including "The Princess of Babylon" (1768), in which the heroine travels the world in search of her lost love under the guidance of a sarcastic **phoenix**, and the **biblical fantasy** "The White Bull" (1774). Voltaire's *contes philosophiques* were enormously influential, their form and method being adopted into numerous **moralistic** tales, sceptical **allegories**, and social **satires**. He demonstrated conclusively that fantasy, far from constituting an insult to rationality, might be a uniquely useful instrument of thought in an Age of Reason.

VORNHOLT, JOHN (1951–). U.S. writer. In the trilogy comprising *The Troll King* (2002), *The Troll Queen* (2003), and *The Troll Treasure* (2003), trolls in servitude to ogres attempt to bridge the Great Chasm that separates them from the land of the **elves**, in the hope of facilitating their liberation. *The Fabulist* (1993) is a fanciful biography of Aesop. *The Witching Well* (1995) is a **wish-fulfillment fantasy**.

– W –

WAGNER, KARL EDWARD (1945–1994). U.S. writer best known for **horror** fiction (refer to *HDHL*). His early works were **sword and**

sorcery novels of an exceptionally **dark** stripe, including the series comprising *Darkness Weaves with Many Shades* (1970; rev. 1978 as *Darkness Weaves*), *Death Angel's Shadow* (1973), *Bloodstone* (1975), *Dark Crusade* (1976), and various short stories in *Night Winds* (1978) and *The Book of Kane* (1985). The influence of **Robert E. Howard** is more directly displayed in novels extending Howard's Conan and Bran Mak Morn series. *Killer* (1985 with **David A. Drake**) is a **historical fantasy** set in the Roman Empire. Wagner's short fiction is collected in *Exorcisms and Ecstasies* (1997).

WAGNER, RICHARD (1813–1883). German composer whose operas setting **epic** poems to music **recycled** and reinvigorated many legendary motifs, exerting a strong influence over their subsequent redeployment. *The Fairies* (1833) is minor, but *The Flying Dutchman* (1843), *Tannhäuser* (1845), *Lohengrin* (1850), the Ring cycle—comprising *The Rhinegold* (1853), *The Valkyrie* (1856), *Siegfried* (1856–71), and *The Twilight of the Gods* (1869–74)—*Tristan and Isolde* (1859), and *Parsifal* (1882) made important contributions to such subgenres as neo-**chivalric romance**, **Nordic fantasy**, and **Arthurian fantasy**.

WAITE, A. E. (1857–1942). British occultist, a leading figure in the late 19th-century occult revival, especially in connection with the Order of the Golden Dawn and various **Rosicrucian** organizations, for which he wrote a good deal of ritual material. His **scholarly fantasies**—the most notable of which are *The Real History of the Rosicrucians* (1887), *The Occult Science* (1891), *Devil-Worship in France* (1896), and *The Hidden Church of the Holy Graal: Its Legends and Symbolism* (1909)—were strongly influenced by those of **Éliphas Lévi**, whose translator he was; in his turn, he exerted a powerful influence on the work of his friend **Arthur Machen**, whom he published—along with **Edgar Jepson**—in the unlikely venue of *Horlick's Malted Milk Magazine* while he was its editor in 1904.

Waite published several volumes of poetry, beginning with *Israfel: Letters, Visions and Poems* (1886). His anthology *Elfin Music: An Anthology of English Fairy Poetry* (1888) has a useful introduction; his own attempt at an **art fairy tale** was *Prince Sunbeam* (1889). *The Quest of the Golden Stairs: A Mystery of Kinghood in Faerie* (1893) fuses similar materials with a portentous **allegory**. The calculated impenetrability of *The House of the Hidden Light* (1904 with Machen; reprinted 2003) was emphasized by restricting its first edition to three copies.

Waite's longtime associate Evelyn Underhill (1875–1941) wrote numerous books on mysticism and religion as well as two novels featuring ritual magic: *The Lost Word* (1907) and *The Column of Dust* (1909). **Charles Williams** was also temporarily numbered among his disciples.

WALL, MERVYN (1908–1997). Irish writer. *The Unfortunate Fursey* (1946) is a polished **humorous fantasy** with elements of **literary satanism**; its sequel, *The Return of Fursey* (1948), is an ironic **Faustian fantasy**; *The Complete Fursey* (1985) is an omnibus. *The Garden of Echoes: A Fable for Children and Grown-Ups* (1982; book 1988) is a children's **Christmas fantasy**. His short fiction is sampled in *A Flutter of Wings* (1974).

WALTON, EVANGELINE (1907–1996). U.S. writer. Her elaborate **Celtic fantasy** *The Virgin and the Swine* (1936) was reprinted by **Lin Carter** as *The Island of the Mighty* (1970), inspiring her to **recycle** the other branches of the ***Mabinogion*** in *The Children of Llyr* (1971), *The Song of Rhiannon* (1972), and *The Prince of Annwn* (1974). Two stories written even earlier—"Above Ker-Is" and "The Mistress of Kaer-Mor"—were also reprinted in showcase anthologies edited by **Kenneth Zahorski** and Robert Boyer in 1978–80, and she resumed work on a long-abandoned novel about the **classical** hero Theseus, *The Sword is Forged* (1983). *Witch House* (1945) is an **occult** detective story. The historical novel *The Cross and the Sword* (1956, aka *Son of Darkness*) has marginal fantasy elements.

WALTON, JO (1964–). Welsh writer resident in Canada. The Tir Tanagiri trilogy, comprising *The King's Peace* (2000), *The King's Name* (2001), and *The Prize in the Game* (2002), employs a quasi-**Celtic** setting. In *Tooth and Claw* (2003), a Victorian mindset borrowed from Anthony Trollope is built into the biological imperatives of **dragon** existence. Her play *Tam Lin by William Shakespeare* is displayed on her website at bluejo.demon.co.uk.

THE WANDERING JEW. A legendary figure, usually called Ahasuerus, whose story was first written down in the 13th century; he was reputedly a shoemaker who rebuked Jesus for stumbling outside his shop on the way to Golgotha and was cursed to wander the world until Christ's return. Known in English via a **ballad** printed in Thomas Percy's *Reliques,* the legend was frequently **recycled** in various literary forms throughout Europe, becoming a key motif of cautionary accounts of **immortality**.

Ahasuerus's literary history, comprehensively detailed in George K. Anderson's *The Legend of the Wandering Jew* (1965), is summarized, exemplified, and further extended in *Tales of the Wandering Jew* (1991), ed. Brian Stableford. Literary fantasies employing him as a symbol include William Godwin's *St. Leon* (1799), Edgar Quinet's **epic** drama *Ahasvérus* (1833), **Hans Christian Andersen**'s epic poem *Ashasverus* (1844), Eugène Sue's vast novel *The Wandering Jew* (1844–45), **Paul Féval**'s *The Wandering Jew's Daughter,* E. Temple Thurston's play *The Wandering Jew* (1920), **George S. Viereck** and Paul Eldridge's *My First Two Thousand Years,* Par Lagerkvist's *The Death of Ahasuerus* (1960; tr. 1962), and Stefan Heym's *The Wandering Jew* (1981). He is rarely encountered in genre fantasy; **Susan Shwartz**'s *Grail of Hearts* is a notable exception.

WANGERIN, WALTER, JR. (1944–). U.S. writer of religious texts, mostly for **children**, including the allegorical **animal fantasy** *The Book of the Dun Cow* (1978) and its sequel *The Book of Sorrows* (1985). *Elizabeth and the Water Troll* (1991) and *Branta and the Golden Stone* (1993) are more orthodox **moralistic fantasies**; the latter is reprinted with *Probity Jones and the Fear-Not Angel* (1996) and others in *The Fear-Not Angel and Other Stories* (1998). *The Crying for a Vision* (1995) is a **contemporary fantasy** with a Native American protagonist. *The Book of God: The Bible as a Novel* (1996) is the quintessential **biblical fantasy**; *Paul: A Novel* (2000) is its **Christian fantasy** sequel.

WARNER, MARINA (1946–). British writer and mythographer specializing in analyses of the manner in which ancient **myths** and their literary descendants continue to influence perceptions and attitudes, especially with regard to gender issues. They include *Monuments and Maidens: The Allegory of the Female Form* (1985); the essay collection *Managing Monsters: Six Myths of Our Time* (1994); the couplet *From the Beast to the Blonde: On Fairy Tales and Their Tellers* (1995) and *No Go the Bogeyman: Scaring, Lulling, and Making Mock* (1998); *Fantastic Metamorphoses, Other Worlds* (2002); and *Signs & Wonders: Essays on Literature and Culture* (2003). Her anthology *Wonder Tales: Six Stories of Enchantment* (1994) features new versions of 17th- and 18th-century French **fairy tales**. Some of her own **recycled** fairy tales and legends are included in *The Mermaids in the Basement* (1993). Her earlier novels avoided supernatural materials, but *Indigo* (1992) and *The Leto Bundle* (2001) are time-spanning fantasies drawing on myth and folklore.

WARNER, SYLVIA TOWNSEND (1893–1978). British writer. *Lolly Willowes; or, The Loving Huntsman* (1926) is a wryly **sentimental/Faustian fantasy**. *The Cat's Cradle-Book* (1940) embeds transfigured **fairy tales** in an **animal fantasy** frame. *The Kingdoms of Elfin* (1977) is a remarkably ornate and effective collection of **moralistic fantasies** set in a uniquely elaborate and sophisticated version of **Faerie**. A few other fantasies are included in *Selected Stories of Sylvia Townsend Warner* (1988).

WARRINGTON, FREDA (1956–). British writer. The series comprising *A Blackbird in Silver* (1986), *A Blackbird in Darkness* (1986), *A Blackbird in Amber* (1987), and *A Blackbird in Twilight* (1986) accomplished a seamless fusion of genre romance and action-packed **immersive fantasy** some time before such **hybrids** became fashionable in the United States; *Darker than the Storm* (1991) is set partly in the same milieu, which it relocates in an **alternative** world. *The Rainbow Gate* (1989) is a **contemporary fantasy**.

The trilogy comprising *A Taste of Blood Wine* (1992), *A Dance in Blood Velvet* (1994), and *The Dark Blood of Poppies* (1995) is a flamboyant exercise in revisionist **vampire** fiction, one that makes much of the erotic potential of the motif. *Sorrow's Light* (1993) is a **dark fantasy**, as is the couplet comprising *Dark Cathedral* (1996) and *Pagan Moon* (1997), which features a continuing conflict between pagan witchcraft and the Christian church. *Dracula: The Undead* (1997) is a centenary sequel to **Bram Stoker**'s classic. The Jewelfire trilogy, comprising *The Amber Citadel* (1999), *The Sapphire Throne* (2000), and *The Obsidian Tower* (2001), has elements of **theriomorphic fantasy**. *The Court of the Midnight King* (2003) is an alternative history fantasy in which the War of the Roses mirrors the battle between a Mother **Goddess** and a patriarchal **God**.

WATT-EVANS, LAWRENCE (1954–). U.S. writer in various genres. The series comprising *The Lure of the Basilisk* (1980), *The Seven Altars of Dûsara* (1981), *The Sword of Bheleu* (1982), and *The Book of Silence* (1984) is lighthearted **heroic fantasy**, as is the Eshkar series, comprising *The Misenchanted Sword* (1985), *With a Single Spell* (1987), *The Unwilling Warlord* (1989), *Blood of a Dragon* (1991), *Taking Flight* (1993), *The Spell of the Black Dagger* (1993), *Night of Madness* (2000), and *Ithanalin's Restoration* (2002). The couplet comprising *The Cyborg and the Sorcerers* (1982) and *The Wizard and the War Machines* (1987) is **chimerical/science fantasy**. *The Rebirth of Wonder* (1992) features a magical **theater** troupe. *Split Heirs* (1993 with **Esther Friesner**) is a **humorous fantasy**. The trilogy comprising *Out of this World* (1994), *In the Empire of Shadow* (1995), and *The Reign of the Brown Magician* hybridizes **portal fantasy** with **sf**. The protagonist of *Touched by the Gods* (1997) is reluctant to fulfill his heroic destiny. The Obsidian Chronicles series, comprising *Dragon Weather* (1999), *The Dragon Society* (2001), and *Dragon Venom* (2003), is a revenge fantasy employing **dragons** as adversaries.

WEBB, CATHERINE (1987–). British writer. At the age of 14 she wrote *Mirror Dreams* (2002), in which the Lords of Nightkeep plot to ensnare dreaming souls left temporarily defenseless; *Mirror Wakes* (2003) is a sequel. In *Waywalkers* (2003), the Son of Time (the **Devil**) is living incognito in London, working at a university, when the gods go to war over ownership of the Earth; the sequel, *Timekeepers* (2004), moves in the direction of **apocalyptic fantasy**, but the author had to take a break thereafter to complete her "A levels" (examinations for the Advanced Certficate of Higher Education).

WEIRD TALES. U.S. pulp magazine founded in 1923; it folded a year later but was resuscitated under the editorship of Farnsworth Wright and the pervasive influence of **H. P. Lovecraft**, whose circle adopted the magazine as the principal vehicle for its literary experiments. Although he foregrounded **horror** fiction, Wright was exceptionally generous in his editorial policy, accommodating **sf** until the specialist sf magazines had demonstrated their durability, as well as **Dunsanian** fantasies and **lost-race** stories. Its most vital contribution to the history of fantasy was the hospitality it extended to the **sword and sorcery** fiction originated in 1929–37 by **Robert E. Howard**—and quickly taken up by **C. L. Moore**, **Henry Kuttner**, and Clifford Ball—and its provision of a market for **Clark Ashton Smith**'s **decadent**, **prehistoric**, and **far-futuristic fantasies**. Its horizons became much narrower when Wright was sacked in 1939; his successor, Dorothy McIlwraith, was instructed to banish sword-and-sorcery and decadent fantasy from its pages.

Weird Tales folded again in 1954 but was resurrected several times over in the 1970s, 1980s, and 1990s by editors keen to recover the boldly eclectic spirit of the early 1930s; the publishers of its sixth incarnation, George Scithers and **Darrell Schweitzer**, resuscitated it yet again in 1998. *The Weird Tales Story* (1977), ed. Robert Weinberg, proved to be an interim report.

WEIS, MARGARET (1948–). U.S. writer who became a best seller when she was recruited by the retailers of the role-playing game Dungeons and Dragons to work with game designer Tracy Hickman (1955–) on a groundbreaking series of **tie-ins**, the DragonLance Chronicles. The series was launched with the trilogy comprising *Dragons of Autumn Twilight* (1984), *Dragons of Winter Night* (1985), and *Dragons of Spring Dawning* (1985); it was subsequently extended by the anthologies *DragonLance: The Second Generation* (1994) and *DragonLance: The Dragons of Krynn* (1994) and also by the novels *Dragons of Summer Flame* (1995) and *The Dragons at War* (1996). The spin-off trilogy of DragonLance Legends, comprising *Time of the Twins*, *War of the Twins,* and *Test of the Twins* (all 1986), was similarly supplemented by anthologies and other associational items released between 1987 and 1994, alongside tie-in works by many other authors.

Weis and Hickman then began to produce non-tie-in novels of a similar stripe, including the trilogy comprising *Forging the Darksword*, *Doom of the Darksword,* and *Triumph of the Darksword* (all 1988), which was further augmented by *Legacy of the Darksword* (1997), and the **Arabian fantasy** trilogy comprising *The Will of the Wanderer*, *The Paladin of the Night,* and *The Prophet of Akhran* (all 1989). The more extensive Death Gate Cycle comprises *Dragon Wing* (1990), *Elven Star* (1990), *Fire Sea* (1991), *Serpent Mage* (1992), *The Hand of Chaos* (1993), *Into the Labyrinth* (1994), and *The Seventh Gate* (1994).

Much of Weis's solo work is **sf**, but *Mistress of Dragons* (2003) and *The Dragon's Son* (2004) began the Dragonvarld series, featuring **amazon** priestesses, continued in *The Dragon's Son* (2004). Anthologies she edited include *Fantastic Alice* (1995), featuring further adventures of **Lewis Carroll**'s heroine, *A Magic-Lover's Treasury of the Fantastic* (1997, with Martin H. Greenberg), and *Treasures of Fantasy* (1997, with Hickman and Greenberg).

WELCH, JANE (1964–). British writer. The Runespell trilogy, comprising *The Runes of War* (1995), *The Lost Runes* (1996), and *The Runes of Sorcery* (1997), served as a prelude to the more adventurous Book of Önd trilogy, comprising *The Lament of Athlone* (1998), *The Bard of Castaguard* (1999), and *The Lord of Necrönd* (2000), in which a talisman called the Druid's Egg contains the souls of creatures banished to an Otherworld. In the Book of Man trilogy, comprising *Dawn of a Dark Age* (2001), *The Broken Chalice* (2002), and *The Allegiance of Man* (2003), **dragons** conspire with other creatures to oust humankind from its dominant status.

WELLMAN, MANLY WADE (1903–1986). Angolan-born U.S. writer in various genres, including **sf** (refer to *HDSFL*) and **horror** fiction. He was a regular contributor to ***Weird Tales,*** sometimes using the byline "Gans T. Field," under which name he wrote a series featuring **occult** investigator Judge Pursuivant, reprinted along with the similar John Thunstone series in *Lonely Vigils* (1981). The novels *What Dreams May Come* (1983) and *The School of Darkness* (1985) also feature Thunstone. Other pulp fiction, including some fantasy, is sampled in *Worse Things Waiting* (1973), which includes several items developing Wellman's enthusiasm for synthesizing an American folklore; a collection stressing this aspect of his work is *The Valley So Low: Southern Mountain Tales* (1987).

"Frogfather" (1945) introduced the character who was to be the mainstay of Wellman's subsequent career: "Silver John," a wandering minstrel who encounters all manner of arcane phenomena in the hills of North Carolina. A sampler issued as *Who Fears the Devil?* (1963) was further expanded as *John the Balladeer* (1988); the novels in the series—*The Old Gods Waken* (1979), *After Dark* (1980), *The Lost and the Lurking* (1981), *The Hanging Stones* (1982), and *The Voice of the Mountain* (1985)—elaborated a syncretic mythology based in an imaginary **prehistory** of the United States.

WELLS, H. G. (1886–1946). British writer, the pioneer of the British tradition of scientific romance that ran parallel to American **sf** until 1950 and the leading 20th-century writer of **utopian** fiction (refer to *HDSFL*). Wells used fantasy materials in the cause of **moralistic fabulation**, his work in the genre becoming progressively darker as his utopian ambitions were frustrated. His liveliest fantasies are short ***contes philosophiques,*** including the classic **wish-fulfillment fantasy** "The Man Who Could Work Miracles" (1898), the wry **humorous fantasies** "The Story of the Inexperienced Ghost" (1902) and "The Truth about Pyecraft" (1903), and the **allegories** "The Magic Shop" (1903) and "The Door in the Wall" (1906).

The Wonderful Visit (1895), a **satirical** allegory featuring an **angel**, has the same ebullient spirit, but the mermaid story *The Sea Lady* (1902) is considerably darker in tone. *The Undying Fire* (1919) **recycles** and updates the **biblical** story of Job. *Mr Blettsworthy on Rampole Island* (1928) is a **delusional** satire. *All Aboard for Ararat* (1940) is a bitter biblical fantasy exemplifying the terminus of Wells's disenchantment.

WELLS, MARTHA (1964–). U.S. writer. The **chimerical** Ile-rien trilogy, comprising *The Element of Fire* (1993), *City of Bones* (1995), and *The Death of the Necromancer* (1998), is unusually various in the settings used as an **alternative historical** backcloth for a conflict between "scientific **magic**" and **fairy** magic. The Fall of Ile-Rien series, launched by *The Wizard Hunters* (2003) and *The Ships of Air* (2004), takes the conflict to another level, featuring an assault from another dimension. *City of Bones* (1995) is an **Arabian fantasy**. *Wheel of the Infinite* (2000) employs a quasi-**Oriental** backcloth in a tale of an exile's return to deal with a crisis of magical renewal.

WEREWOLF. A human who turns into a wolf, usually involuntarily, and usually during the nights of the full moon. Werewolf stories form the core of **theriomorphic fantasy**. Werewolves are often used as **monsters** in **horror** stories but are also widely employed as symbols of the regrettable tendency of humans occasionally to be overwhelmed by the force of their darker emotions, in which light they are portrayed as victims rather than callous predators. Their long literary history extends back to Gaius Petronius's *Satyricon* (A.D. c65) via **Marie de France**'s *Bisclavret,* but they were repopularized by **Sabine Baring-Gould**'s *The Book of Were-wolves* (1865).

Significant werewolf stories that lean more toward fantasy than horror include **Alexandre Dumas**'s **Faustian fantasy** *The Wolf Leader,* Saki's ***conte cruel*** "Gabriel-Ernest" (1909), **H. Warner Munn**'s "The Werewolf of Ponkert," Guy Endore's *The Werewolf of Paris* (1933), **Jack Williamson**'s *Darker than You Think,* Anthony Boucher's "The Compleat Werewolf" (1940), Richard Lupoff's *Lisa Kane* (1976), **Peter S. Beagle**'s "Lila the Werewolf," and Patrick Jennings's *The Wolving Time* (2003). Although the earliest examples are Rachilde's *La Princesse des ténèbres* (1896) and **Clemence Housman**'s *The Werewolf,* recent years have seen a spectacular increase in stories by female writers that use the motif as a metaphor for female sexuality; notable examples include works by **Tanith Lee**, **Kelley Armstrong**, and **Alice Borchardt**, and Annette Curtis Klaus's *Blood and Chocolate* (1997).

WEST, MICHELLE (1963–). Pseudonym of Canadian writer Michelle Sagara, who published *Into the Dark Lands* (1991), *Children of the*

Blood (1992), *Lady of Mercy* (1993), and *Chains of Darkness, Chains of Light* (1994) under her own name before relaunching her career.

The couplet *Hunter's Oath* (1995) and *Hunter's Death* (1996) feature a journey to an ancient city once ruled by Lord of Hell; the same **secondary world** is the setting of the **epic** Sun Sword series, comprising *The Broken Crown* (1997), *The Uncrowned King* (1998), *The Shining Court* (1999), *Sea of Sorrows* (2001), *The Riven Shield* (2003), and *Sun Sword* (2004), in which the awakening of long-dormant ancient powers provokes **quests** to locate the lost Cities of Man before an **apocalyptic** battle. Her short fiction is sampled in *Speaking with Angels* (2003).

WESTON, JESSIE (1850–1928). British scholar whose strong interest in the possible pre-Christian origins of **Arthurian** legends—particularly the stories elaborated in *The Legend of Sir Perceval* (2 vols., 1906–1909), *The Quest for the Holy Grail* (1913), and several books about Gawain—led her to borrow inspiration from **James Frazer** in constructing the **scholarly fantasy** *From Ritual to Romance* (1920). Her decoding of Arthuriana in terms of fertility cults and long-obliterated matrilineal patterns of inheritance has inspired numerous fantasy writers, including **Marion Zimmer Bradley**, **Gillian Bradshaw**, **Tim Powers**, and **Alexander Irvine**; it is deftly parodied in David Lodge's novel *Small World* (1984).

WHITBOURN, JOHN (1958–). English writer specializing in enterprising **transfigurations** of his homeland. The **alternative** world fantasy *A Dangerous Energy* (1992), which is closely akin to **Keith Roberts**'s *Pavane,* won a competition sponsored by the BBC and the publisher Gollancz; *To Build Jerusalem* (1995) is a sequel. *Popes and Phantoms* (1993) is an equally elaborate but blackly humorous **historical fantasy**. In *The Royal Changeling* (1998), elves and a villainous version of **Arthur** help the Duke of Monmouth launch a rebellion following the death of Charles II in an alternative England. In the satirical trilogy comprising *The Downs-Lord Dawn* (1999), *Downs-Lord Day* (2000), and *Downs-Lord Doomsday* (2002), a 17th-century curate is transported to a **parallel world** where he builds an empire and becomes a god-king before being exiled by **angels**; his eventual return threatens to precipitate an **apocalypse**. The short stories making up *The Binscombe Tales* (1997) are **dark fantasy.**

WHITE, E. B. (1899–1985). U.S. **humorist** who wrote three **animal fantasies** for **children**: *Stuart Little* (1945), about a tiny child; the classic

Charlotte's Web (1952), about the friendship between a pig and a spider; and the offbeat success story *The Trumpet of the Swan* (1970).

WHITE, T. H. (1906–1964). Indian-born British writer. *Earth Stopped; or, Mr Marx's Sporting Tour* (1934) is a humorous **apocalyptic fantasy** paying homage to the works of R. S. Surtees, whose addiction to hunting, shooting, and fishing White shared; in the sequel, *Gone to Ground* (1935), survivors of the catastrophe take **psychological** refuge in fantasy stories. *The Sword in the Stone* (1938) is a classic account of the boyhood and education of the future King **Arthur**. It was followed by the more broadly humorous *The Witch in the Wood* (1939) and the more earnestly **sentimental** *The Ill-Made Knight* (1940), but the publisher refused to issue the projected fourth novel in the series, which would have revealed its **epic** dimension.

Once World War II was over, White published *Mistress Masham's Repose* (1946), in which a young girl defends descendants of Gulliver's Lilliputians from commercial exploitation by Hollywood; and *The Elephant and the Kangaroo* (1947), an **allegorical comedy** in which an atheist, forewarned by an **angel**, builds an ark in anticipation of a second Deluge. With **J. R. R. Tolkien**'s crucial precedent in place to prove that quintessentially English epics could form the backcloth of seemingly lighthearted **children's** books, White revised *The Sword in the Stone, The Witch in the Wood*—as *The Queen of Air and Darkness*—and *The Ill-Made Knight* for incorporation in *The Once and Future King* (1958) with the previously unpublished *The Candle in the Wind*. Once again, the publisher omitted a final section, although some sections of it were transplanted into the first part; it was eventually published as *The Book of Merlyn: The Unpublished Conclusion to* The Once and Future King (1977).

Several short stories from *Gone to Ground* were reprinted with later items in *The Maharajah and Other Stories* (1981).

WILDE, OSCAR (1854–1900). Anglo-Irish writer best known for the plays he wrote in 1891–95. He was the central figure of the English **Decadent** movement and its chief theorist; "The Decay of Lying" (1891) is a deceptively lighthearted tirade against the disenchanting effects of narrative realism. *Poems* (1881) is redolent with lush fantastic imagery, whose expression reached its zenith in that medium in *The Sphinx* (1894). "The Canterville Ghost" (1887), a classic fusion of **humorous** and **sentimental fantasy**, was reprinted in *Lord Arthur Savile's*

Crime and Other Stories (1891); its 1887 title story employs the sparkling wit for which Wilde became famous as a sarcastic gloss on the hapless protagonist's attempts to cheat destiny.

The **children's fantasies** in *The Happy Prince and Other Stories* (1888) are subtly embellished with a cynical irony most evident in "The Nightingale and the Rose." The four stories in *A House of Pomegranates* (1891) extrapolate this trend to its extreme; "The Young King" (1888) refuses the regalia of his office after discovering the hardships that his people endured in paying for his coronation, but no one respects his decision. In "The Birthday of the Infanta"(1889), a similarly ostentatious display of callous wealth is the background to a harrowing tale of disillusionment. In the **Hans Christian Andersen**–influenced "The Fisherman and His Soul," the soul the fisherman rejects in order to marry a mermaid soul returns periodically to tempt him with visions of a world full of exotic promise, but their eventual reunion is tragic. "The Star-Child" tracks the tribulations of an infant betrayed by delusions of grandeur.

Wilde's most extravagant decadent fantasy, *The Picture of Dorian Gray* (1891), is a **Faustian fantasy** involving a painted **doppelgänger**. He wrote the play *Salome* (1893; tr. 1894) in French, with stylistic assistance from **Marcel Schwob** and **Pierre Louÿs**; it was produced in Paris in 1896 after being refused a license for English production in 1892. The longest item in a cycle of *Poems in Prose* (1893–94; book 1905) is a curiously plaintive **Christian fantasy**. Following his imprisonment after the collapse of his libel case against the Marquess of Queensberry and his subsequent prosecution for gross indecency, Wilde wrote nothing except *The Ballad of Reading Gaol* (1898), although an intensely bitter **moralistic fantasy** he improvised orally was reproduced by **Laurence Housman** in *Echo de Paris* (1923). **Jeremy Reed**'s *Dorian,* Rick R. Reed's *A Face without a Heart* (2000), and **Will Self**'s *Dorian* update the story of Dorian Gray.

WILDER, CHERRY (1930–2002). Pseudonym of New Zealand–born writer Cherry Barbara Lockett Grimm. Most of her work is **sf** (refer to *HDSFL*), but the trilogy comprising *A Princess of the Chameln* (1984), *Yorath the Wolf* (1984), and *The Summer's King* (1986) is a polished **heroic fantasy**. Her short fiction, much of it cleverly hybridizing sf and **mythical** fantasy, is sampled in *Dealers in Light and Darkness* (1995).

WILKINS, VAUGHAN (1890–1959). Welsh writer. *After Bath; or, The Remarkable Case of the Flying Hat* (1945) is a **children's fantasy**, and the **lost-race** story *The City of Frozen Fire* (1950) was also marketed for children, although Wilkins always listed it with his adult novels. Its **Celtic fantasy** elements were more enterprisingly extrapolated in the elegiac **portal fantasy** *Valley beyond Time* (1955).

WILLARD, NANCY (1936–). U.S. writer and scholar. Much of her fiction and poetry is for younger **children**. Three delicately polished fantasies collected in *Sailing to Cythera and Other Anatole Stories* (1974) were supplemented by the novellas *The Island of the Grass King: The Further Adventures of Anatole* (1979) and the marvelously phantasmagoric *Uncle Terrible: More Adventures of Anatole* (1982). The same artful combination of literary style and visionary extravagance is displayed in *A Visit to William Blake's Inn: Poems for Innocent and Experienced Travelers* (1981); similar homage to other influences is paid in *The Voyage of the Ludgate Hill: Travels with Robert Louis Stevenson* (1987) and *Pish, Posh, said Hieronymus Bosch* (1991). The sentimental **sports fantasy** *Things Invisible to See* (1984) combines many of the author's favorite themes and images, including **angels**.

Firebrat (1988) is a children's **quest** fantasy similar in spirit to the Anatole trilogy. *Sister Water* (1993) is an adult novel in which fantasy elements are carefully muted into deft **symbolism**. Willard's **recycled** tales include *East of the Sun and West of the Moon: A Play* (1989) and *Beauty and the Beast* (1992). Her short fiction, some of which has fabular elements, is sampled in *The Lively Anatomy of God* (1968) and *Childhood of the Magician* (1973), and is combined with critical essays—some of which analyze and celebrate the literary uses of fantasy—in *Angel in the Parlor, Five Stories and Eight Essays* (1982), *A Nancy Willard Reader: Selected Poetry and Prose* (1991), and *Telling Time: Angels, Ancestors and Stories* (1993). The last title features two essays ingeniously cast as fables: "Danny Weinstein's Magic Book" and "How Poetry Came into the World and Why God Doesn't Write It."

WILLIAMS, CHARLES (1886–1945). British scholar and writer, an associate of **A. E. Waite** in connection with an early interest in occultism, subsequently a recruit to the **Inklings** and a significant influence on **C. S. Lewis**'s later works. His novels are key contributions to the tradition of **Christian fantasy**, ingeniously embedding theological and **metaphysical** arguments in formats borrowed from popular fiction.

War in Heaven (1930) recasts the **quest** for the Holy **Grail** as a thriller. The **intrusive fantasy** *The Place of the Lion* (1931) describes an invasion of Platonic archetypes. *Many Dimensions* (1931) describes attempts to save a powerful magical object from commercial exploitation. *Shadows of Ecstasy* (1933 but written before the others) features a dangerous pagan revival. *The Greater Trumps* (1932) is an elaborate allegorical **occult fantasy** involving **gypsies**. *Descent into Hell* (1937) is a powerful **visionary fantasy** with elements of **posthumous fantasy**. The latter were further extrapolated in *All Hallow's Eve* (1945), which describes the struggle against an ambitious Antichrist.

Williams's poetry, collected in *Taliessin through Logres* (1938) and *The Region of the Summer Stars* (1944), includes a good deal of **Arthurian** material.

WILLIAMS, MICHAEL (1952–). U.S. writer whose early works were game **tie-ins**. The trilogy comprising *A Sorcerer's Apprentice* (1990), *A Forest Lord* (1991), and *The Balance of Power* (1992) is in much the same vein, but the couplet comprising *Arcady* (1996) and *Allamanda* (1997) is very different, set in a world where **William Blake**'s works are canonical texts, serving as scripture and magical compendia.

WILLIAMS, SEAN (1967–). Australian writer whose early work was collaborative **sf** (refer to *HDSFL*). In the Books of the Change series, comprising *The Stone Mage and the Sea* (2001), *The Sky Warden and the Sun* (2002), and *The Storm Weaver and the Sand* (2002), children with magical ability are taken to the Haunted City for elaborate training. *The Crooked Letter* (2004) is a **contemporary fantasy**, the first in a **prequel** series, Books of the Cataclysm.

WILLIAMS, TAD (1957–). U.S. writer. *Tailchaser's Song* (1985) is a whimsical **animal fantasy** featuring cats. The **epic** Memory, Sorrow and Thorn trilogy, comprising *The Dragonbone Chair* (1988), *Stone of Farewell* (1990), and *To Green Angel Tower* (1993; in 2 vols. as *Siege* and *Storm*), sets out to criticize and correct aspects of **J. R. R. Tolkien**–descended genre fantasy that Williams considered problematic, including racist undertones and the easy separation of Good and Evil. Two novellas offer similarly considered responses to familiar themes: *Child of an Ancient City* (1992 with **Nina Kiriki Hoffman**) is a **vampire** story drastically **transfigured** by its removal into an **Arabian fantasy** scenario, while *Caliban's Hour* (1994) takes issue with **Shakespeare** by presenting Caliban's account of the events leading up to *The Tempest* and their consequences.

The Otherland series, comprising *City of Golden Shadow* (1996), *River of Blue Fire* (1998), *Mountain of Black Glass* (1999), and *Sea of Silver Light* (2001), is a hybrid **science fantasy** about a "private multiverse" constructed in virtual reality, controlled by the avaricious and sinister Grail Brotherhood. *The War of the Flowers* (2003) is an elaborate **portal fantasy** juxtaposing San Francisco with an industrialized **Faerie**.

WILLIAMSON, JACK (1908–). U.S. writer best known for **sf** (refer to *HDSFL*). His early sf, including **planetary romances** and **portal fantasies**, was strongly influenced by **A. Merritt**, but the fantasy elements in the hybrid **science fantasy** *Golden Blood* (1933; book 1964) were more closely akin to the **sword and sorcery** fiction then popular in the magazine in which it appeared, ***Weird Tales***. Similar inclinations are evident in his first wholehearted fantasy, the **classical fantasy** *The Reign of Wizardry* (1940; book 1964), which appeared in ***Unknown***. For the same magazine, he wrote the classic hybrid **theriomorphic fantasy** *Darker than You Think* (1940; exp. 1948), in which the hero becomes reconciled to his true nature—unlike the similarly challenged character of the earlier **werewolf**-featuring **horror** story "Wolves of Darkness" (1932). Although he remained firmly committed to sf thereafter, Williamson continue to adapt genre fantasy materials to firmly rationalized frames in such novels as *Demon Moon* (1994).

WILLIAMSON, PHILIP G. (1955–). British writer whose first two novels, *The Great Pervader* (1985) and *Dark Night* (1989)—both **satires**—were bylined "Philip First," as was the collection *Paper Thin and Other Stories* (1987). He reverted to his own name for the sardonically edged trilogy comprising *Dinbig of Khimmur* (1990), *The Legend of Shadd's Torment* (1993), and *From Enchantery* (1993). A second trilogy set in the same **secondary world** comprises *Moonblood* (1993), *Heart of Shadows* (1994), and *Citadel* (1995). The series comprising *Enchantment's Edge* (1996), *Orbus's World* (1997), and *The Soul of an Orb* (1998) is similar, leading to a stylized climax in the Tower of Glancing Memory.

WILSON, DAVID HENRY (1937–). British writer, primarily a playwright, long resident in Germany. His first novel for adults—an elaborate version of "Cinderella" cast as a sophisticated **animal fantasy**—was published in German translation in 1985 before appearing as *The Coachman Rat* (1987). His other works are for younger children; they include *Elephants Don't Sit on Cars* (1977), *Superdog the Hero* (1986), and *Gideon Gander Solves the World's Greatest Mysteries* (1993). *The Castle of Inside Out* (2002) is an enterprising **portal fantasy**.

WINDLING, TERRI (1958–). U.S. editor and artist who played a central role in establishing and defining genre fantasy, initially as fantasy editor for Ace Books, for whom she coedited a series of showcase anthologies, *Elsewhere* (3 vols., 1981–84) with Mark Alan Arnold. Her enterprising ventures in the 1980s included the MagicQuest **young-adult** fantasy series, a series of novel-length transfigured **fairy tales** and the Bordertown **shared-world** series, all of which eventually fell victim to an economic downturn. She became a freelance editor in 1987, helping Tor Books to develop a fantasy line. In the same year, she founded the Endicott Studio of "Mythic Arts," initially an actual artsts' studio in Boston, which became virtual when it moved online in 1990; it now hosts her *Journal of Mythic Arts* (founded 2003), to which **Midori Snyder** is consultant editor.

Windling collaborated with Ellen Datlow (refer to *HDSFL*) on an annual *Year's Best Fantasy and Horror* series, for which she handled the fantasy component from 1988 to 2003. Her introductions tracked the fortunes of the commercial genre and parallel developments in literary fantasy, and her eclectic selection of texts helped to make manifest the intimate kinship between the two, while demonstrating that the best writers operating in the commercial genre could produce works of very high quality. She also collaborated with Datlow in a editing a series of anthologies of transfigured fairy tales, comprising *Snow White, Blood Red* (1993), *Black Thorn, White Rose* (1994), *Ruby Slippers, Golden Tears* (1995), *Black Swan, White Raven* (1997), *Silver Birch, Blood Moon* (1999), and *Black Heart, Ivory Bones* (2000). *A Wolf at the Door and Other Retold Fairy Tales* (2000), *The Green Man: Tales from the Mythic Forest* (2002), *Swan Sister: Fairy Tales Retold* (2003), and *The Faery Reel: Tales from the Twilight Realm* (2004) are in similar vein. She produced a story of her own for her solo anthology *The Armless Maiden and Other Tales for Childhood's Survivors* (1995).

Windling's first novel, *The Wood Wife* (1996), was originally intended for another of her projects, dramatizing **illustrations** by the artist Brian Froud, but outgrew its original inspiration to become a complex **contemporary fantasy** drawing on Native American folklore. *A Midsummer Night's Faery Tale* (1999) is a brief **Shakespearean** fantasy.

WINTERSON, JEANETTE (1959–). British writer whose literary fiction often includes fantastic motifs. *Boating for Beginners* (1985) is a **transfigurative/biblical fantasy**. *The Passion* (1987) is a **historical fantasy** about Napoleon. *Sexing the Cherry* (1989) embeds transfigurations of several well-known **fairy tales** in a sophisticated historical fantasy. *The PowerBook* (2000) is a **postmodernist/contemporary fantasy** about the power of story. The short story collection *The World and Other Places* (1998) includes several fantasies.

WISH-FULFILMENT FANTASY. Narrowly defined, a wish-fulfillment fantasy is one in which expressed wishes are magically granted, often in sets of three; most such fantasies—which have deep roots in **folktales** and **fables**—are cautionary tales, and many are cast as **Faustian fantasies**. In a broader sense, any story that dramatizes a common **daydream** fantasy—such as becoming invisible, having a bottomless purse, or being able to fly—qualifies as a wish-fulfilment fantasy, especially if it examines the fulfilment of desire in a wryly sceptical fashion. Again, cautionary tales predominate, often using excessively literal interpretation of expressed wishes, after the fashion of **Douglas Jerrold**'s *A Man Made of Money*.

A strong **children's** tradition of cautionary tales extends from **E. Nesbit** to **Roald Dahl**, although the indulgent element remains powerful in such examples as Enid Blyton's *The Adventures of the Wishing Chair* (1937). Writers of wish-fulfilment fantasies for adults, from **James Dalton**, **William Gilbert**, and **Joseph Shield Nicholson** to **Thomas Berger**, tend to be far more critical of mere self-indulgence, although **erotic** variants like Nicholson Baker's *The Fermata* (1994) are often unrepentant.

A great deal of ingenious literary endeavor has been expended on the question of how best to employ a set of three wishes; Gerald Heard's "The Marble Ear" (1952) is a neat summary of problems to be avoided. Ventures in wish-fulfilment fantasy usually keep abreast of current fashion, wish lists in contemporary texts often featuring rapid weight loss. Notable recent examples include Franny Billingsley's *Well Wished* (1997), Christy Yorke's *Magic Spells* (1999), Daska Slater's *The Wishing Box* (2000), **John Vornholt**'s *The Witching Well,* Ann Rinaldi's *Millicent's Gift* (2002), Sally Prue's *The Devil's Toenail* (2003), and Elyse Friedman's *Waking Beauty* (2004).

WITCH. A practitioner of magic, usually an informally educated female of relatively low status (unlike **wizards**). Some modern writers use "warlock" to designate a male witch, although this is a recent coinage and warlocks usually take on the standard attributes of wizards, as illustrated by the works of **Christopher Stasheff**.

Although the official position of the Christian church has always been that witchcraft is implicitly evil, much that was thus condemned was folk medicine and divination practiced by "wise women" (including midwives), so the term always had a fringe of ambiguity, which confused the persecution of witches in the 15th, 16th, and 17th centuries. The reckless use of torture in extracting confessions from those accused of witchcraft—often for spiteful or cynical reasons—eventually made "witch hunting" a pejorative term and inhibited the use of witches as straightforward figures of menace in **horror** fiction.

Christendom inherited its witch images from pagan legends. **Classical** images are divided between femmes fatales like Circe and Medea and hagwives like Erichtho (in Lucan's *Pharsalia*) and Ovid's Dipsas; such images are parodied in the depiction of Pamphile in **Apuleius**'s *The Golden Ass*. Witches in Northern European mythology and **folktales** are mostly hagwives, ceaselessly employed in mixing potions in their cauldrons. Both traditions are echoed in **Shakespeare**'s *Macbeth* (c1606), the former via the invocation of Hecate. The inquisitors charged with rooting out heresy justified turning their attention to witches with a series of slanderous fantasies, charging them with making diabolical pacts and participating in active **Devil** worship at regular "sabbats." The myth of the sabbat was constructed by Pierre de Lancre in *Tableau de l'Inconstance des Mauvais Anges et Demons* (1612); notable literary dramatizations can be found in W. Harrison Ainsworth's *The Lancashire Witches* (1849) and Valery Briussov's *The Fiery Angel* (1908; tr. 1930).

Notable literary works inspired by the Christian witch hunt include Thomas Middleton's *The Witch* (c1620), one of several works produced in the wake of a 1612 trial, of which other fictional representations include Thomas Shadwell's play *The Lancashire Witches* (1681) and Ainsworth's novel. The fascination such trials exert is reflected in the fact that the only significant witch trial ever held in America (in Salem, Massachusetts, in 1692) gave rise to numerous literary works, ranging from Esther Barstow Hammond's credulous *Yesterday Never Dies* (1941) through **Nathaniel Hawthorne**'s ambiguous "Young Goodman

Brown" (1835) to Arthur Miller's scathingly sceptical play *The Crucible* (1953). Other dramatizations of actual cases include several versions of the 1634 trial of the French priest Urbain Grandier—including Eyvind Johnson's *Dreams of Roses and Fire* (1949), and Aldous Huxley's play *The Devils of Loudun* (1952), William Meinhold's *Sidonia the Sorceress* (1848), Thomas Wright's *The Blue Firedrake* (1892), J. M. Brodie-Innes's *The Devil's Mistress* (1915), and the third novella in Françoise Mallet-Joris's *The Witches* (1969). Intensively researched representations of fictitious witch prosecutions include Meinhold's *The Amber Witch* (1843), Edith Pargeter's *By Firelight* (1948), and Leslie Wilson's *Malefice* (1992). The near-unanimous judgment of fantasy literature is that witch hunters are infinitely more dangerous than witches ever have been or could be.

The image of the witch underwent a drastic overhaul following the publication of **Jules Michelet**'s **scholarly fantasy** *La sorcière* (1862), which argued that the church's malicious slanders uttered against innocent midwives and practitioners of folk medicine might easily have generated a counter-religion of justified pagan protest. Michelet's regret that no such counter-religion actually arose was echoed by others, including **Charles Godfrey Leland**, before **Edgar Jepson** and **Margaret Murray** used fertility cults described by **James Frazer** as models for "covens" of witches—redefined as practitioners of a pagan religion often called "wicca"—whose "sabbats" were entirely innocent of satanic involvement or intent. The model was extravagantly taken up by **lifestyle fantasists** eager to practice what Michelet had preached; pagan witchcraft became the most popular lifestyle fantasy of the late 20th century, often taking aboard feminist and environmentalist ideals in the cause of a more rounded opposition to and protest against the inheritors of clerical hegemony. The image of the unjustly victimized pagan witch has had a huge impact on modern genre fantasy, most witch images in which—including those of the witches inhabiting **secondary worlds**—are modeled on some version of this thesis.

Contemporary literary witches are extraordinarily various, as displayed in **Sylvia Townsend Warner**'s *Lolly Willowes,* **Fritz Leiber**'s *Conjure Wife,* John van Druten's play *Bell Book and Candle* (1956), Mary Savage's *A Likeness to Voices* (1963), **Keith Roberts**'s *Anita,* **Roald Dahl**'s *The Witches,* **Terry Pratchett**'s novels featuring Granny Weatherwax, John Updike's *The Witches of Eastwick* (1984), Martin H. Brice's *The Witch in the Cave* (1986), Rebecca Ore's *Slow Funeral*

(1994), **Alice Hoffman**'s *Practical Magic,* Judith Hawkes's *The Heart of a Witch* (1999), Sean Stewart's *Mockingbird,* **Anne Bishop**'s Tir Alainn trilogy, Sandra Forrester's *The Everyday Witch* (2002), and Anna Dale's *Whispering to Witches* (2004). The success of such TV representations as *Sabrina the Teenage Witch* and *Charmed* has generated a good deal of spin-off in addition to **tie-ins**, including Jean Thesman's *The Other Ones* (1999), Isobel Bird's Circle of Three series (15 vols., 2001–2002), and Cate Tiernan's Wicca series (15 vols., 2001–2003). Showcase **anthologies** include *Hecate's Cauldron* (1982), ed. **Susan Shwartz**, and *Witches' Brew* (2002), ed. Yvonne Jocks.

WIZARD. A practitioner of magic, usually a male of considerable academic attainment and social status (unlike **witches**). The term derives from the Middle English *wysard* ("wise man"), by which route it became associated with "cunning men"—whose exploits in divination and folk medicine often made them targets of witch hunters—and the prestidigators who were ancestral to modern stage magicians; more crucially, however, the term also became associated with scholarly practitioners of ritual **magic** (the term *magus* has parallel etymological roots and similar implications), **astrologers** and **alchemists**. These categories are conflated in literary images such as Walter Scott's influential depiction of his alleged kinsman Michael Scott in "The Lay of the Last Minstrel."

The wizards of modern fantasy literature are usually figures of great pretension, who maintain a quasi-aristocratic bearing while dressing like medieval monks. The archetypal model for most modern representations is **Merlin**, although **Shakespeare**'s "enchanter" Prospero is also a significant paradigm. Despite **J. R. R. Tolkien**'s resentment of Norman impositions, his Gandalf—the archetypal wizard of **commodified fantasy**—is little more than a carbon copy of Merlin, as are **Diana Wynne Jones**'s Chrestomanci and **Gene Wolfe**'s *The Wizard*. Such wizards usually remain behind thrones, but they occasionally exercise direct rule, as in **Robert Newcomb**'s **epic** series.

The pretentiousness of wizardry inevitably attracts parody, as in **Terry Pratchett**'s representation of Discworld's Unseen University and **Vivian Vande Velde**'s *Wizard at Work,* while **feminist** protest against the blatant discrepancy between the images of wizard and witch is partly expressed in mockery and partly in the extension of the term to embrace both sexes, as in **Barbara Hambly**'s *Stranger at the Wedding,* **Diane Duane**'s *So You Want to be a Wizard,* and **J. K. Rowling**'s descriptions of Hogwarts Academy.

WOLFE, GENE (1931–). U.S. writer best known for **hybrid** and **chimerical** works on the borders of **sf** (refer to *HDSFL*), although he has also written earnest **Christian fantasies** like "The Detective of Dreams" (1980), in the spirit of **G. K. Chesterton**. *Peace* (1975) is an intricate **posthumous fantasy**. *The Devil in a Forest* (1976) is a de-supernaturalized **historical fantasy**. *Free Live Free* (1984) is an **Odyssean fantasy**. The couplet comprising *Soldier in the Mist* (1986) and *Soldier of Arete* (1989) is a **classical fantasy** involving an amnesiac curse. *There Are Doors* (1988) is an elaborate **portal fantasy**. *Castleview* (1990) is a **contemporary fantasy** with **Arthurian** elements.

Wolfe began an extensive series of sophisticated **far-futuristic fantasies** with the Book of the New Sun, comprising *The Shadow of the Torturer* (1980), *The Claw of the Conciliator* (1981), *The Sword of the Lictor* (1982), and *The Citadel of the Autarch* (1983), subsequently adding several short stories, mock-explanatory essays, and a sequel, *The Urth of the New Sun* (1987), before extrapolating its themes in two further multivolume novels, one comprising *Nightside the Long Sun* (1993), *Lake of the Long Sun* (1994), *Caldé of the Long Sun* (1994), and *Exodus from the Long Sun* (1996) and the other *On Blue's Waters* (1999), *In Green's Jungles* (2000), and *Return to the Whorl* (2001). Brief fantasies spun off from the series include *The Boy Who Hooked the Sun* (1985) and *Empires of Foliage and Flower* (1987).

The couplet comprising *The Knight* and *The Wizard* (both 2004), both set in Mythgarthr, aspires to definitive status as a generic **heroic fantasy** with **picaresque** and **allegorical** elements; its **Nordic** elements predominate but are carefully hybridized, with Anglo-Norman elements as the roots of the English language. Wolfe's short fantasies are mingled with other materials in many of his short story collections, including *Gene Wolfe's Book of Days* (1981), *Storeys from the Old Hotel* (1988), *Endangered Species* (1989), *Young Wolfe* (1993), *Strange Travelers* (2000), and *Innocents Aboard* (2004).

WOOD, BRIDGET (1947–). British writer in various genres. *The Minstrel's Lute* (1987) and *Satanic Lute* (1987) are **dark fantasies**. The trilogy comprising *Wolfking* (1991), *The Lost Prince* (1992), and *Rebel Angel* (1993) is a **timeslip** fantasy with elements of **Celtic fantasy**. *Sorceress* (1994), set in a similar milieu, describes the **thinning** of Irish paganism in the face of Christian invasion. Her subsequent dark fantasies were bylined "Frances Gordon"; they include *The Devil's Piper* (1995), *The Burning Altar* (1996), the Rumpelstiltskin **transfiguration**

Changeling (1998), the Sleeping Beauty transfiguration *Thorn: An Immortal Tale* (1997), and the Little Red Riding Hood transfiguration *Wildwood* (1999).

WOODING, CHRIS (1977–). British writer in various genres. *Broken Sky* (9 vols., 1999–2000) is a manga-inspired "fighting fantasy" series. *Catchman* (1999) is a **dark** fantasy. *The Haunting of Alaizabel Cray* (2001) is a baroque **alternative history** story. *Poison* (2003) is a striking **Orphean fantasy** featuring "phaeries" and a spider queen. The Braided Path trilogy begun with *The Weavers of Saramyr* (2003) and *The Skein of Lament* (2004)—with *Ascendancy Veil* to come—has a quasi-**Oriental** setting and tracks the progress of an "aberrant" child raised as heir to an empire in spite of stern opposition.

WORLD FANTASY CONVENTION. An annual convention formed in calculated opposition to the World Science Fiction Convention. The WFC maintains a greater focus on literary materials than does its rival and usually attracts a higher proportion of professional attendees, thus making it a useful venue for business dealings. It instituted the multi-category World Fantasy Awards in 1975, decided by a jury (by contrast with the **sf** Hugo Award's popular vote), although convention members can vote items onto the short lists.

WREDE, PATRICIA C. (1953–). U.S. writer for **children** and adults. The series comprising *Shadow Magic* (1982), *Daughter of Witches* (1983), *The Harp of Imach Thyssel* (1985), *Caught in Crystal* (1987), and *The Raven Ring* (1994) is set in a **secondary world** where the amicable relations between humans, Shee (**fairies**), and the Wyrd (forest folk) are periodically threatened by the evil Shadow Born. *The Seven Towers* (1984) makes much of the mystical associations of the number seven. *Talking to Dragons* (1985; rev. 1993) is an extravagant **quest** fantasy featuring an Enchanted Forest, whose nature and history are elaborated in *Dealing with Dragons* (1990, aka *Dragonsbane*), *Searching for Dragons* (1991, aka *Dragon Search*), and *Calling on Dragons* (1993). *Sorcery and Cecelia; or, The Enchanted Chocolate Pot* (1988) and *The Grand Tour* (2004), with **Caroline Stevermer**) are set in Regency London. *Snow White and Rose Red* (1989) **transfigures** the well-known **fairy tale**. The couplet comprising *Mairleon the Magician* (1991) and *Magician's Ward* (1997) are mysteries set in an **alternative** Regency England. Wrede's short fiction is sampled in *Book of Enchantments* (1996).

WRIGHTSON, PATRICIA (1921–). Australian writer of **children's fiction**. She drew on aboriginal folklore in several fantasies describing consequences of the **thinning** of a native magical reality under the pressure of colonial settlement, including *The Crooked Snake* (1955), *An Older Kind of Magic* (1972), *The Nargun and the Stars* (1973), *A Little Fear* (1983), the stories in *The Old, Old Ngarang* (1989), and—most graphically—the Wirrun trilogy, comprising *The Ice Is Coming* (1977), *The Dark Bright Water* (1978), and *Behind the Wind* (1981, aka *Journey behind the Wind*). *Moon-Dark* (1987) is a **political fantasy** with elements of **animal fantasy**. *Balyet* (1989) is a **ghost story**.

WURTS, JANNY (1953–). U.S. writer and artist. While midway through the **hybrid science-fantasy** series comprising *Sorcerer's Legacy* (1982), *Stormwarden* (1984), *Keeper of the Keys* (1988), and *Shadowfane* (1988), she teamed up with **Raymond Feist** to produce *Daughter of the Empire* (1987)—which was eventually expanded into a trilogy by *Servant of the Empire* (1990) and *Mistress of the Empire* (1992)—set in one of the **secondary worlds** Feist had introduced in *Magician*.

The Mistress of White Storm (1992), which tracks the making of a legendary fortress builder, was followed by the *The Curse of the Mistwraith* (1993), whose sequels—*The Ships of Merior* (1994) and *Warhost of Vastmark* (1995)—were combined into a single volume under the former title in the United States; the series, which tracks the fortunes of two half-brothers victimized by a curse, was continued in *Fugitive Prince* (1997), *Grand Conspiracy* (1999), *Peril's Gate* (2001), and *Stormed Fortress* (2004). *To Ride Hell's Chasm* (2002) is an **epic** fantasy featuring a high-spirited princess. Wurts' short fiction is sampled in *That Way Lies Camelot* (1994).

WYLIE, JONATHAN. Pseudonym of husband-and-wife team Mark (1952–) and Julia (1955–) Smith. Their stereotyped accounts of plucky young protagonists operating in **secondary worlds** include three trilogies, one comprising *The First Named* (1987), *The Centre of the Circle* (1987), and *The Mage-Born Child* (1988); the second *Dreams of Stone, The Lightless Kingdom,* and *The Age of Chaos* (all 1989); and the third *Dark Fire* (1993), *Echoes of Flame* (1994), and *The Last Augury* (1994). Their subsequent work became more various, the couplet *Dream Weaver* (1991) and *Shadow-Maze* (1992) being followed by the **portal fantasy** *Other Lands* (1995) and the **dark fantasy** *Across the Flame* (1996). The **contemporary fantasy** *Magister* (1997) is set in a world where magic is a performance art.

The couple adopted a new **pseudonym**, “Julia Gray,” for the **dragon** fantasies *Ice Mage* (1998) and *Fire Music* (1999), *Isle of the Dead* (2000), and the Guardian Cycle, comprising *Dark Moon* (2000), *The Jasper Forest* (2001), *The Crystal Desert* (2001), *The Red Glacier* (2002), and *Alyssa's Ring* (2002), in which a prophesied heir turns out to be twins, one of whom is disfigured but either of whom might be the true Guardian.

– Y –

YARBRO, CHELSEA QUINN (1942–). U.S. writer. Her early work was mostly **sf** (refer to *HDSFL*). Her **detective** fiction sometimes has **occult** elements reminiscent of the “nonfictional” **spiritualist fantasies** *Messages from Michael* (1979), *More Messages from Michael* (1986), *Michael for the Millennium* (1995), and *Michael's People* (1998). *Ariosto* (1980) is an **alternative world** fantasy in which **Lodovico Ariosto** is an adventurer in a world of strangeness that inspires him to put even more imaginative effort into his **epic**. The **historical fantasy** *To the High Redoubt* (1985), the **humorous fantasy** *A Baroque Fable* (1986), and the **children's fantasy** *Monet's Ghost* (1997)—in which a girl who can project herself into paintings is trapped in a Monet—offer further testimony to her remarkable versatility.

Yarbro's most impressive literary enterprise is a long series of revisionist **vampire** stories, which use their relatively enlightened immortal protagonists as viewpoints from which to compile sombre panoramic chronicles of man's (and occasionally woman's) inhumanity to man and woman, only slightly alleviated by interludes of **erotic fantasy**. Those featuring the Comte de Saint-Germain are *Hotel Transylvania* (1978), *The Palace* (1978), *Blood Games* (1980), *Path of the Eclipse* (1981), *Tempting Fate* (1982), *The Saint-Germain Chronicles* (1983; exp. as *The Vampire Stories of Chelsea Quinn Yarbro*, 1994), *Out of the House of Life* (1990), *Darker Jewels* (1993), *Better in the Dark* (1993), *Mansions of Darkness* (1996), *Writ in Blood* (1997), *Blood Roses* (1998), *Communion Blood* (1999), *Come Twilight* (2000), *A Feast in Exile* (2001), *Night Blooming* (2002), *Midnight Harvest* (2003), and *Dark of the Sun* (2004). A spin-off series featuring Atta Olivia Clemens comprises *A Flame in Byzantium* (1987), *Crusader's Torch* (1988), and *A Candle for D'Artagnan* (1989).

The Sisters of the Night trilogy, spun off from **Bram Stoker**'s *Dracula,* stalled after *The Angry Angel* (1998) and *The Soul of an Angel* (1999). Other **horror** novels (refer to *HDHL*) with fantasy elements include *The Godforsaken* (1983) and *A Mortal Glamor* (1985), both featuring ardent **witch** hunters, and a **contemporary/theriomorphic fantasy**, *Beastnights* (1989).

YEATS, WILLIAM BUTLER (1865–1939). Irish poet whose deep interest in native **folktales** and the **occult**—in a spirit not dissimilar to that of German **romantics** in quest of the volksgeist—made him a leading figure of **Celtic** revivalism. He founded a Hermetic society in 1885 with the poet A.E. (George Russell) and joined the Order of the Golden Dawn, but he was expelled from the **Theosophical** Society. His **recycled** *Fairy and Folk Tales of the Irish Peasantry* (1888) is combined with *Irish Fairy Tales* (1892) in *Fairy and Folk Tales of Ireland* (1977). This work was further elaborated by *Stories from Carleton* (1889)—based on the work of folklorist and novelist William Carleton (1794–1869)—and *Representative Irish Tales* (1891). These materials resound continually in his poetry, particularly in the **epic** title piece of *The Wanderings of Oisin and Other Poems* (1889) and *Poems* (1895).

Yeats gave his folkloristic interests dramatic form in such plays as the **Faustian** *Countess Cathleen* (1892), *The Celtic Twilight* (1893, about a seductive **fairy** child), and *Land of Heart's Desire* (1894). He founded an Irish National Theatre Company in 1902, which acquired the Abbey Theatre in Dublin, in the hope of keeping the flickering flame of the Celtic revival alight; fantastic material never thrived there, although he did put on a five-play series telling the story of Cuchulain (1903–38). His prose fantasies include the two novellas assembled in *John Sherman and Dhoya* (1891) and the story collections *The Secret Rose* (1897) and *The Celtic Twilight* (1902); the former includes a series revised in collaboration with fellow folklorist and Abbey Theatre stalwart Lady Augusta Gregory as *Stories of Red Hanrahan* (1905). The two collections were combined as *Mythologies* (1959). In "Rosa Alchemica" (1896), Yeats introduced an adept modeled on one of the Golden Dawn's founders, who featured in the stories, essays, and plays collected in *Michael Robartes and the Dancer* (1921) and *Stories of Michael Robartes and his Friends* (1932). His other occult writings include an enigmatic account of *A Vision* (1925).

YEP, LAURENCE (1948–). U.S. writer in various genres, mostly for **children**. His fantasies include a **theriomorphic fantasy** (series with elements of **Oriental fantasy**) comprising *Dragon of the Lost Sea* (1982), *Dragon Steel* (1985), *Dragon Cauldron* (1991), and *Dragon War* (1992). The stories in *The Rainbow People* (1989) and *Tongues of Jade* (1991) **transfigure** Chinese **folktales**, as do *The Ghost Fox* (1994) and *Tiger Woman* (1995). In *The Magic Paintbrush* (2000), pictures come to life. The hero of *The Tiger's Apprentice* (2003) is recruited by a tiger to protect a talisman.

YOLEN, JANE (1939–). U.S. writer, extremely prolific producer of **children's fantasies** for all age groups; Harcourt Brace introduced a young adult imprint called Jane Yolen Books under her guidance in 1990. Much of her early work was short fiction, often in a delicately lapidary vein exemplified by *The Girl Who Cried Flowers and Other Tales* (1973), and many of her early works were episodic in nature; the most substantial include the cautionary fantasy *The Magic Three of Solatia* (1974); *The Transfigured Hart* (1975); the poignant parable *The Mermaid's Three Wisdoms* (1978); the trilogy comprising *Dragon's Blood* (1982), *Heart's Blood* (1984), and *A Sending of Dragons* (1987); the hybrid **science fantasy** *Cards of Grief* (1984); and *The Stone Silenus* (1984). Her strong interest in **Arthurian** legend, reflected in the collection *Merlin's Booke* (1986), the novel *The Dragon's Boy* (1990), and the anthology *Camelot* (1995), was further extended in the Young **Merlin** trilogy comprising *Passager, Hobby,* and *Merlin* (all 1997), and in *Sword of the Rightful King* (2003).

The Chronicles of Great Alta, comprising *Sister Light, Sister Dark* (1988), *White Jenna* (1989), and *The One-Armed Queen* (1998), is a **heroic fantasy** with **messianic** elements. *The Devil's Arithmetic* (1988) is a **timeslip** fantasy about the Holocaust. *Wizard's Hal* (1991) features a magician's apprentice. *Briar Rose* (1992) is the longest of several **transfigurations** of the folktale. *The Wild Hunt* (1995) is based in **Nordic** legend. The Tartan Magic series, comprising *The Wizard's Map* (1999), *The Pictish Child* (1999), and *The Bagpiper's Ghost* (2002), are **Celtic fantasies**, the first featuring the famous **wizard** Michael Scot. In *Boots and the Seven-Leaguers: A Rock and Troll Novel* (2000), a young troll gets a job as a roadie. The series written in collaboration with Robert J. Harris comprising *Odysseus in the Serpent Maze* (2001), *Hippolyta and the Curse of the Amazons* (2002), and *Atalanta and the Arcadian Beast* (2003) consists of **classical fantasies** featuring heroes in their youth.

Yolen's many short-story collections include *Tales of Wonder* (1983), *Dragonfield and Other Stories* (1985), *Dream Weaver* (1989), *The Faery*

Flag (1989), the Here There Be series featuring *Dragons, Unicorns, Witches, Angels* and *Ghosts* (1993–98), *Twelve Impossible Things before Breakfast* (1997), and *Sister Emily's Lightship and Other Stories* (2000). She edited the *Xanadu* series of showcase anthologies (3 vols., 1995–97) and the **transfigurative** *Not One Damsel in Distress* (2001).

YOUNG ADULT FICTION. The rapid sophistication of **children's fantasy** in the late 1950s brought several new subgenres into the field, most significantly **psychological fantasies** specifically adapted to the developmental phases of adolescence, as exemplified by **Catherine Storr**'s *Marianne Dreams* and **William Mayne**'s *A Game of Dark*. The effectiveness of such works in modeling teenage angst and mapping out useful processes of psychological adaptation encouraged the identification within the marketplace of a specific category of young-adult fiction, in which elaborate parables of maturation provided conceptual bridges between childhood and adulthood. The label was first introduced as a marketing ploy, attempting to free the books so designated from stigma (teenagers are notoriously determined to avoid being reckoned children), but it fooled no one; what it did accomplish, however, was to permit a considerable **darkening** of teenage fantasy, as well as the pioneering of children's **horror** fiction by such writers as John Gordon and Robert Westall.

Heroic fantasies involving **quests** were rapidly and cleverly adapted to the allegorical mapping of adolescence, while timeslip **romances** and **ghost stories** also became much more common as means of facilitating the conceptual breakthroughs necessary to the acquisition of adulthood. The marketing category ran into difficulty in the late 1980s, when many publishers came to the conclusion that teenagers much preferred reading "adult fantasy" on image grounds, but it made a spectacular return in the wake of the commercial success of **J. K. Rowling** and **Philip Pullman**, when the profits of adult fantasy nosedived because of the overproduction of stereotyped **epic** trilogies.

There was an enormous expansion of young-adult fantasy in the 1990s, greatly assisted by the fact that the young-adult market was much more hospitable to innovation and variation than were formula-addicted editors of adult lines. The inspirational potential of such material is reflected in the emergence of such young adult writers as **Catherine Webb**, **Christopher Paolini**, and the French 14-year-old Flavia Bujor. Notable writers of fantasy for young adults include **Anne Bishop**, **Francesca Lia Block**, N. M. Browne, Melvin Burgess, **Louise Cooper**,

Pamela Dean, **Diana Wynne Jones**, **Gwyneth Jones**, **Sherryl Jordan**, **Ann Lawrence**, **Louise Lawrence**, **Margaret Mahy**, **Sophie Masson**, **Geraldine McCaughrean**, **Jody Lynne Nye**, **Meredith Ann Pierce**, **Tamora Pierce**, **Susan Price**, **Celia Rees**, **Katherine Roberts**, **Jan Siegel**, and **Chris Wooding**. Showcase **anthologies** of young adult fantasy include *Firebirds* (2003), ed. Sharyn November, and *New Magics* (2004), ed. Patrick Nielsen Hayden.

YOURCENAR, MARGUERITE (1903–1987). Pseudonym of French writer Marguerite de Crayencour, the first woman elected to the Académie Française. The prose poems translated in *Fires* (1936; rev. 1968; tr. 1981) employ themes from classical **myth**. *Oriental Tales* (1938; exp. 1978; tr. 1985) is a series of **Oriental fantasies**. *The Abyss* (1968; tr. 1976) is an elaborate **alchemical fantasy** in which the protagonist, Zeno, combines elements of Leonardo da Vinci, Paracelsus, Copernicus, and Giordano Bruno.

– Z –

ZAHORSKI, KENNETH J. (1939–). U.S. scholar. In collaboration with Robert H. Boyer (1937–), he edited the showcase **anthology** *The Fantastic Imagination: An Anthology of High Fantasy* (2 vols., 1977–78), which attempted to set the agenda for the emergent genre. Zahorski and Boyer also edited *Dark Imaginings: A Collection of Gothic Fantasy* (1978), which similarly sought to distinguish "**high**" and "**low**" forms, and *Visions of Wonder: An Anthology of Christian Fantasy* (1986). The theory of the high/low taxonomy, with a detailed breakdown of subgenres, was set out in "On Fantasy," the introduction to *Fantasy Literature: A Core Collection and Reference Guide* (1979), which Zahorski and Boyer compiled with Marshal Tymn.

ZELAZNY, ROGER (1937–1995). U.S. writer. His early work, marketed as **sf** (refer to *HDSFL*), was almost all **hybrid/science fantasy** heavily impregnated with images and themes drawn from **mythology**. *This Immortal* (1966) was the first of many works dealing with godlike superhumanity; whole pantheons are **transfigured** in *Lord of Light* (1967) and *Creatures of Light and Darkness* (1969), while *Eye of Cat* makes extravagant use of Native American mythology. *Jack of Shadows* (1971) is a striking **chimerical** science fantasy set on a world that keeps the same face turned towards its primary; its day side is ruled by science and its dark side by **magic**.

Zelazny's most elaborate fantasy project was the series comprising *Nine Princes in Amber* (1970), *The Guns of Avalon* (1972), *Sign of the Unicorn* (1975), *The Hand of Oberon* (1976), and *The Courts of Chaos* (1978), subsequently augmented by a sequel series comprising *Trumps of Doom* (1985), *Blood of Amber* (1986), *Sign of Chaos* (1987), *Knight of Shadows* (1989), and *Prince of Chaos* (1991), in which members of the strife-torn ruling family of Amber—the archetypal original of a manifold of **alternative worlds** set up in problematic opposition to **Chaos**—gradually obtain a better understanding of their existential situation and its magical privileges. The second series is more formulaic, as are his other exercises in the same vein, which include the couplet comprising *Changeling* (1980) and *Madwand* (1981), and the series collected in *The Changing Land* (1981) and *Dilvish, the Damned* (1982). Most of his other collections include some fantasies; they are most prominent in *The Last Defender of Camelot* (1980; rev. 2002) and *Unicorn Variations* (1983). *A Dark Traveling* (1987) is a children's **portal fantasy**.

Much of Zelazny's late work was written in collaboration. *The Black Throne* (1990, with **Fred Saberhagen**) and *The Mask of Loki* (1990, with Thomas T. Thomas) are science fantasies, but a series of **humorous fantasies** he wrote with Robert Sheckley, comprising *Bring Me the Head of Prince Charming* (1991), *If at Faust You Don't Succeed* (1993), and *A Farce to be Reckoned With* (1995), play exuberantly with familiar motifs. The **metafictional** *A Night in the Lonesome October* (1993), set in Victorian England, is similar in spirit. **Jane Lindskold** completed works left unfinished at his death, including *Lord Demon* (1999).

ZETTEL, SARAH (1966–). U.S. writer. The Isalvalta series, comprising *The Usurper's Crown* (2002), *A Sorcerer's Treason* (2002), and *The Firebird's Vengeance* (2004), is an offbeat **historical/portal fantasy**. *In Camelot's Shadow* (2004; aka *Camelot's Shadow*) is an **Arthurian fantasy** featuring Gawain.

ZINDELL, DAVID (1952–). U.S. writer best known for **sf** (refer to *HDSFL*). The Ea cycle, comprising *The Lightstone* (2001; in 2 vols. as *The Ninth Kingdom* and *The Silver Sword*), *Lord of Lies* (2003), and *The Evening Star* (2004) is an **epic/messianic** fantasy in which the hero must vanquish a fallen **angel** and then withstand reprisals.

ZIPES, JACK (1937–). U.S. scholar who has written extensively on **fairy tales**, especially those collected by the **Brothers Grimm**, whose works he retranslated in *The Complete Fairy Tales of the Brothers Grimm* (1987). *Breaking the Magic Spell: Radical Theories of Folk & Fairy Tales* (1979) collects essays exploring the transition from folklore to literary form, analyzing its subsequent evolution as a process of bourgeois appropriation and ideological manipulation. *Fairy Tales and the Art of Subversion: The Classic Genre for Children and the Process of Civilization* (1983), the essays in *Fairy Tale as Myth/Myth as Fairy Tale* (1994) and *Happily Ever After: Fairy Tales, Children, and the Culture Industry* (1997), and *When Dreams Came True: Classic Fairy Tales and their Tradition* (1998) extend and elaborate the thesis. He edited *The Oxford Companion to Fairy Tales* (2000). *Sticks and Stones: The Troublesome Success of Children's Literature from Slovenly Peter to Harry Potter* (2001) collects essays examining the ideological downside of the commercial success of **children's fiction** in the 1990s.

Zipes's exemplary anthologies include an exhaustive study of *The Trials and Tribulations of Little Red Riding Hood* (1983; rev. 1993); a showcase of **feminist** variants, *Don't Bet on the Prince* (1986); the national samplers *Victorian Fairy Tales: The Revolt of the Fairies and Elves* (1987), *Fairy Tales and Fables from Weimar Days* (1989), *Beauties, Beasts and Enchantments: Classic French Fairy Tales* (1989), and *The Great Fairy Tale Tradition: From Straparola and Basile to the Brothers Grimm* (2000); the massive compendium *Spells of Enchantment: The Wondrous Fairy Tales of Western Culture* (1991, aka *The Penguin Book of Western Fairy Tales*); and the collection of modern fairy tales *The Outspoken Princess and the Gentle Knight* (1994). He has also collated editions of fairy tales by **Herman Hesse** and tales from the *Arabian Nights.*

ZIVKOVIC, ZORAN (1948–). Serbian writer whose work is strikingly **chimerical** (refer to *HDSFL*). Fantasy elements are very prominent in *The Fourth Circle* (1993; tr. 2004), in which the cast of characters includes Archimedes, Stephen Hawking, and Sherlock Holmes, and *Seven Touches of Music* (2001), in which **music** is a vehicle for divine revelation. The omnibus collection *Impossible Stories* (2004) includes the short fiction mosaics "Impossible Encounters" (2000), "Steps through the Mist" (2002–2003), and *The Library* (2002; separate pub. 2004).

Bibliography

CONTENTS

INTRODUCTION

Because fantasy literature is both very old and (as a labelled commercial genre) very new, its bibliography is unusually complex and fragmented. Very few textbooks have been published as yet that endeavor to cover the entire genre as it is now conceived, although there are a great many that cover narrower subgenres such as folktales, fairy tales, apocalyptic fantasy, Arthurian literature, children's fantasy, imaginary creatures (here listed under the heading "monsters"), and so on.

Almost all the extant books attempting to characterize fantasy as a genre have been written in English, sources in foreign languages mostly confining themselves to individual topics—especially literary extensions of indigenous myths, legends and folklore, and subgenres conceived with particular reference to literatures other than English, like magic realism. A great deal of the work done on these narrower fields and topics is excellent, but the relative dearth of overview texts has tended to occlude important thematic and historical connections whose mapping has been seriously undertaken only within the last 20 years.

Two subcategories of fantastic fiction whose names have been used as commercial labels for much longer—science fiction and horror fiction—have a much more extensive critical literature than is now covered by the generic label of "fantasy." Both these subcategories have their own volumes in this series: my own *Historical Dictionary of Science Fiction Literature* and John Clute's *Historical Dictionary of Horror Literature*. Some overlap between the following bibliography and those of the companion volumes is inevitable, especially where reference books attempt to embrace more than one of these labeled genres, but many books whose central relevance has restricted their listing to one of these volumes also contain material of some relevance to the others. This is especially true of surveys of the work of individual authors whose activity extends over all three commercial genres.

The best broad accounts of the fantasy genre as it is presently conceived, and the most useful first ports of call for the interested reader, are the *Encyclopedia of Fantasy,* edited by John Clute and John Grant, and the St. James Press *Guide to Fantasy Writers,* edited by David Pringle. The history of fantasy is too extensive to be comprehensively covered in any single volume, although Lin Carter's *Imaginary Worlds* is a convenient synoptic sketch, while Brian Attebery's *The Fantasy Tradition in American Literature* and Colin Manlove's *The Fantasy Literature of England* are excellent surveys of domestic traditions.

Attebery and Manlove are also among the leading aesthetic theorists of the genre; crucial work has also been done by Robert Scholes, Kathryn Hume, Marina Warner, and Jack Zipes, although the interested reader really needs to start with J. R. R. Tolkien's seminal essay "On Fairy-stories." Writers whose critical work is deftly leavened by firsthand experience of the highest caliber include Ursula K. Le Guin, L. Sprague de Camp, and Michael Swanwick.

Single author studies are, of course, extremely numerous and various, but the collection of essays on *Supernatural Fiction Writers* assembled by Everett F. Bleiler and Richard Bleiler offers more detailed critical summaries than the *St. James Guide* and therefore offers a useful starting point for in-depth studies of the fantasy writers included therein. Humphrey Carpenter's book on the Inklings is a good introduction to three of the most widely studied 20th-century fantasy writers, and Roger Lancelyn Green's *Tellers of Tales* is a highly readable and remarkably comprehensive survey of the most important children's fantasy writers.

The most useful journals dedicated to the field include the IAFA's *Journal of the Fantastic in the Arts,* the Mythopoeic Society's *Mythlore* and Terri Windling's *Journal of the Mythic Arts,* the last-named being based on her very useful *Endicott Studio* website. Other websites that provide rich mines of information for general readers and scholars alike include *Locus On-Line*—an invaluable source of news and bibliographical information—and the extraordinarily elaborate *SurLaLune Fairy Tale Pages*.

GENERAL REFERENCE WORKS

Barron, Neil, ed. *Fantasy Literature: A Reader's Guide*. New York: Garland, 1990; expanded and revised as *Fantasy and Horror: A Critical and Historical Guide to Literature, Illustration, Film, TV, Radio, and the Internet*. Lanham, Md.: Scarecrow.

Cawthorn, James, and Michael Moorcock. *Fantasy: The 100 Best Books*. London: Xanadu, 1988.

Bleiler, Everett F. *The Guide to Supernatural Fiction*. Kent, Ohio: Kent State University Press, 1983.

Clute, John, and John Grant. *The Encyclopedia of Fantasy*. London: Orbit, 1997.

Magill, Frank N., ed. *Survey of Modern Fantasy Literature*. 5 vols. Englewood Cliffs, N.J.: Salem, 1983.

Pringle, David. *Modern Fantasy: The Hundred Best Novels, an English-Language Selection, 1946–1987*. London: Grafton, 1988.

——, ed. *The Ultimate Encyclopedia of Fantasy: The Definitive Illustrated Guide*. London: Carlton, 1998.

Tuck, Donald H. *The Encyclopedia of Science Fiction and Fantasy through 1968: A Bibliographic Survey of the Fields of Science Fiction, Fantasy, and Weird Fiction through 1968*. 3 vols. Chicago: Advent, 1974, 1978, and 1982.

Tymn, Marshall B., and Mike Ashley, eds. *Science Fiction, Fantasy, and Weird Fiction Magazines*. Westport, Conn.: Greenwood, 1985.

Tymn, Marshall B., Keneth J. Zahorski, and Robert H. Boyer. *Fantasy Literature: A Core Collection and Reference Guide*. New York: Bowker, 1979.

Waggoner, Diana. *The Hills of Faraway: A Guide to Fantasy*. New York: Atheneum, 1978.

HISTORICAL STUDIES

Cailliet, Émile. *The Themes of Magic in Nineteenth Century French Fiction*. Translated by Lorraine Havens. Paris: Presses Universitaires de France, 1932.

Carter, Lin. *Imaginary Worlds: The Art of Fantasy*. New York: Ballantine, 1973.

Chalker, Jack L., and Mark Owings. *The Science-Fantasy Publishers: A Critical and Bibliographic History*. Westmister, Md.: Mirage, 1991; revised edition 1992. Four supplements were issued in 1992–96.

Filmer, Kath, ed. *The Victorian Fantasists: Essays on Culture, Society and Belief in the Mythopoeic Literature of the Victorian Age*. London: Macmillan, 1991.

Michalson, Karen. *Victorian Fantasy Literature: Literary Battles with Church and Empire*. Lewiston, N.Y.: Edwin Mellen, 1990.

Mucke, Dorothea E. Von. *The Seduction of the Occult and the Rise of the Fantastic Tale*. Palo Alto, Calif.: Stanford University Press, 2003.

Prickett, Stephen. *Victorian Fantasy*. Bloomington: Indiana University Press, 1979.

Rottensteiner, Franz. *The Fantasy Book: An Illustrated History from Dracula to Tolkien*. New York: Collier, 1978.

Sale, Roger. *Fairy Tales and After: From Snow White to E. B. White*. Cambridge, Mass.: Harvard University Press, 1978.

Smith, Elton E., and Robert Haas, eds. *The Haunted Mind: The Supernatural in Victorian Literature*. Lanham, Md.: Scarecrow, 1999.

Veldman, Meredith. *Fantasy, the Bomb, and the Greening of Britain: Romantic Protest, 1945–80*. Cambridge, U.K.: Cambridge University Press, 1994.

Weiner, Stephen. *Faster than a Speeding Bullet: The Rise of the Graphic Novel*. New York: NBM, 2003.

AESTHETIC AND THEORETICAL STUDIES

Alexander, Lloyd. "High Fantasy and Heroic Romance." *Horn Book* 47, no. 6 (December 1971): 577–84.

Apter, T. E. *Fantasy Literature: An Approach to Reality*. Bloomington: Indiana University Press, 1982.

Armitt, Lucy. *Theorizing the Fantastic*. New York: Arnold, 1996.

Attebery, Brian. *Strategies of Fantasy*. Bloomington: Indiana University Press, 1992.

Bettelheim, Bruno. *The Uses of Enchantment: The Meaning and Importance of Fairy Tales*. New York: Knopf, 1976.

Boyer, Robert, and Kenneth J. Zahorski, eds. *Fantasists on Fantasy: A Collection of Critical Reflections*. New York: Avon, 1984.

Brooke-Rose, Christine. *A Rhetoric of the Unreal*. New York: Cambridge University Press, 1981.

Burke, Edmund. *A Philosophical Enquiry into the Origin of Our Ideas of the Sublime and Beautiful*. London: R. and J. Dodsley, 1757.

Chesterton, G. K. "The Ethics of Elfland." In *Orthodoxy*. London: John Lane, 1909.

Clark, Beverly Lyon. *Reflections of Fantasy: The Mirror Worlds of Carroll, Nabokov, and Pynchon*. New York: Peter Lang, 1986.

Cook, Elizabeth. *The Ordinary and the Fabulous: An Introduction to Myths, Legends and Fairy Tales for Teachers and Story-Tellers*. Cambridge, U.K.: Cambridge University Press, 1969.

Elhin, Don D. *The Comedy of the Fantastic: Ecological Perspectives on the Fantasy Novel*. Westport, Conn.: Greenwood, 1985.

Erskine, John. "Magic and Wonder in Literature." In *The Moral Obligation to Be Intelligent and Other Essays.* 1915.

Forster, E. M. "Fantasy." In *Aspects of the Novel*. London: Edward Arnold, 1927.

Hume, Kathryn. *Fantasy and Mimesis: Resposes to Reality in Western Literature*. London: Methuen, 1984.

Hurd, Richard. *Letters on Chivalry and Romance*. London: A. Millar et al., 1762.

Irwin, Wiliam Robert. *The Game of the Impossible: A Rhetoric of Fantasy*. Urbana: Illinois University Press, 1976.

Jackson, Rosemary. *Fantasy: The Literature of Subversion*. London: Methuen, 1981.

Kenward, Jean G. *Number and Nightmare: Forms of Fantasy in Contemporary LIterature*. Hamden, Conn.: Archon, 1975.

Kroeber, Karl. *Romantic Fantasy and Science Fiction*. New Haven, Conn.: Yale University Press, 1988.

Lewis, C. S. *An Experiment in Criticism*. Cambridge, U.K.: Cambridge University Press, 1961.

Little, Edmund. *The Fantasts: Studies in J. R. R. Tolkien, Lewis Carroll, Nicolai Gogol, and Kenneth Grahame*. Amersham, U.K.: Avebury, 1984.

MacDonald, George. "The Fantastic Imagination." In *The Light Princess and Other Fairy Tales*. Vol. 8 of *Works of Fancy and Imagination*. 10 vols. London: Strahan, 1871.

Manlove, C. N. *The Impulse of Fantasy Literature*. Kent, Ohio: Kent State University Press, 1983.

———. *Modern Fantasy: Five Studies*. New York: Cambridge University Press, 1975.

Martin, Graham Dunstan. *An Inquiry into the Purposes of Speculative Fiction: Fantasy and Truth*. Lewiston, N.Y.: Edwin Mellen, 2003.

Mathews, Richard. *Fantasy: The Liberation of Imagination*. Boston: Twayne, 1998.

Mendlesohn, Farah. "Towards a Taxonomy of Fantasy." *Journal of the Fantastic in the Arts* 13, no. 2 (2002): 173–87.

Miéville, Cina. "The New Weird." *Locus* 515 (December 2003): 8, 70.

Mobley, Jane. "Towards a Definition of Fantasy Fiction." *Extrapolation* 15 (1973–74): 117–28.

Moorcock, Michael. *Wizardry and Wild Romance: A Study of Epic Fantasy*. London: Gollancz, 1987.

Nodier, Charles. "Du Fantastique en littérature." *Revue de Paris* 20 (November 1830): 205–26.

O'Keefe, Deborah. *Readers in Wonderland: The Liberating Worlds of Fantasy Fiction from Dorothy to Harry Potter*. New York: Continuum, 2003.

Olsen, Lance. *Ellipse of Uncertainty: An Introduction to Postmodern Fantasy*. New York: Greenwood, 1987.

Propp, Vladimir. *Morphology of the Folk Tale*. Translated by Laurence Scott. 2nd revised edition. Louis A. Wagner. Austin: University of Texas Press, 1968.

Rabkin, Eric S. *The Fantastic in Literature*. Princeton, N.J.: Princeton University Press, 1976.

Reeve, Clara. *The Progress of Romance*. 2 vols. Colchester, U.K., W. Keymer, 1785.

Sandner, David, ed. *Fantastic Literature*. Westport, Conn.: Greenwood, 2004.

Schlobin, Roger, ed. *The Aesthetics of Fantasy Literature and Art*. Notre Dame, Ind.: University of Notre Dame Press, 1982.

Scholes, Robert. *The Fabulators*. New York: Oxford University Press, 1967; revised as *Fabulation and Metafiction*. Urbana: University of Illinois Press, 1979.

Scholes, Robert, and Robert Kellogg. *The Nature of Narrative*. New York: Oxford University Press, 1966.

Sherman, Delia. "An Introduction to Interstitial Arts: Life on the Border." *Interstitial Arts,* www.endicott-studio.com/IA/IA-intro.html, 2003 [accessed 15 September 2003].

Spivack, Charlotte. "The Fantastic Imagination in Literature." *Paradoxa* 4, no. 9 (1998): 89–102.

Swanwick, Michael. *The Postmodern Archipelago*. San Francisco: Tachyon, 1997.

Swinfen, Ann. *In Defence of Fantasy: A Study of the Genre in English and American Literature Since 1945*. London: Routledge, 1984.

Timmerman, John H. *Other Worlds: The Fantasy Genre*. Bowling Green, Ohio: Bowling Green University Popular Press, 1983.

Todorov, Tzvetan. *The Fantastic: A Structural Approach to a Literary Genre*. Cleveland, Ohio: Press of Case Western Reserve University, 1973.

Tolkien, J. R. R. "On Fairy-Stories." In *Tree and Leaf*. London: Allen and Unwin, 1964. [Revised from an earlier version in *Essays Presented to Charles Williams*. Oxford, U.K.: Oxford University Press, 1947.]

Warner, Marina. *Fantastic Metamorphoses, Other Worlds: Ways of Telling the Self*. Oxford, U.K.: Oxford University Press, 2002.

——. *No Go the Bogeyman: Scaring, Lulling, and Making Mock*. London: Chatto and Windus, 1998.

Wilson, Colin. *The Strength to Dream: Literature and the Imagination*. London: Gollancz, 1961.

Wolfe, Gray K. *Critical Terms for Science Fiction and Fantasy: A Glossary and Guide to Scholarship*. Westport, Conn.: Greenwood, 1986.

Ziolkovski, Theodore. *Disenchanted Images: A Literary Iconology*. Princeton, N.J.: Princeton University Press, 1977.

MISCELLANEOUS ANTHOLOGIES AND ESSAY COLLECTIONS

Burgin, Victor, James Donald, and Cora Kaplan, eds. *Formations of Fantasy*. London: Methuen, 1986.

Collings, Michael R., ed. *Reflections on the Fantastic: Selected Essays from the Fourth International Conference on the Fantastic in the Arts*. Westport, Conn.: Greenwood, 1986.

Collins, Robert A., and Howard D. Pearce, eds. *The Scope of the Fantastic.* Vol 1: *Theory, Tecnique, Major Authors.* Vol 2: *Culture, Biography, Themes, Children's Literature*. Westport, Conn.: Greenwood, 1985.

Coyle, William L., ed. *Aspects of Fantasy: Selected Essays from the Second International Conference on the Fantastic*. Westport, Conn.: Greenwood, 1986.

Hassler, Donald M., ed. *Patterns of the Fantastic*. Mercer Island, Wash.: Starmont House, 1983.

Hokenson, Jan, and Howard Pearce, eds. *Forms of the Fantastic: Selected Essays from the Third International Conference on the Fantastic in Literature and Film*. Westport, Conn.: Greenwood, 1986.

Langford, Michelle K., ed. *Contours of the Fantastic: Selected Essays from the Eighth International Conference on the Fantastic in the Arts*. Westport, Conn.: Greenwood, 1990.

Le Guin, Ursula K. *Dancing at the Edge of the World: Thoughts on Words, Women, Places*. New York: Grove, 1989.

———. *The Language of the Night: Essays on Fantasy and Science Fiction*. New York: Putnam, 1979; revised New York: HarperCollins, 1992.

———. *The Wave in the Mind: Talks and Essays on the Writer, the Reader, and the Imagination*. Boston: Shambhala, 2004.

Lewis, C. S. *Of Other Worlds: Essays and Stories*. New York: Harcourt, 1966.

———. *On Stories and Other Essays on Literature*. New York: Harcourt, 1982.

Morse, Donald E., ed. *The Fantastic in World Literature and the Arts: Selected Essays from the Fifth Annual Conference on the Fantastic in the Arts*. Westport, Conn.: Greenwood, 1988.

Palumbo, Donald, ed. *The Spectrum of the Fantastic: Selected Essays from the Sixth International Conference on the Fantastic in the Arts*. Westport, Conn.: Greenwood, 1988.

Pharr, Mary, ed. *Fantastic Odysseys: Selected Essays from the Twenty-second International Conference on the Fantastic in the Arts*. Westport, Conn.: Greenwood, 2003.

Ruddick, Nicholas, ed. *State of the Fantastic: Studies in the Theory and Practice of Fantastic Literature and Film*. Westport, Conn.: Greenwood, 1992.

Saciuk, Olena H., ed. *The Shape of the Fantastic: Selected Essays from the Seventh International Conference on the Fantastic in the Arts*. Westport, Conn.: Greenwood, 1990.

Schweitzer, Darrell, ed. *Exploring Fantasy Worlds: Essays on Fantastic Literature*. San Bernardino, Calif.: Borgo, 1985.

——. *Windows of the Imagination: Essays on Fantastic Literature*. San Bernardino, Calif.: Borgo, 1998.

Slusser, George E., and Eric S. Rabkin, eds. *Intersections: Fantasy and Science Fiction*. Carbondale: Southern Illinois University Press, 1987.

Slusser, George E. Eric S. Rabkin, and Robert Scholes, eds. *Bridges to Fantasy*. Carbondale: Southern Illinois University Press, 1982.

Smith, Elton E., and Robert Haas, eds. *The Haunted Mind: The Supernatural in Victorian Literature*. Lanham, Md.: Scarecrow, 1999.

Travers, P. L. *What the Bee Knows: Reflections on Myth, Symbol and Story*. Wellingborough, U.K.: Aquarian, 1989.

Willard, Nancy. *Telling Time: Angels, Ancestors, and Stories*. New York: Harcourt Brace, 1993.

Yolen, Jane. *Touch Magic: Fantasy, Faerie & Folklore in the Literature of Childhood*. New York: Philomel, 1981. Little Rock, Ark.: August House, 2000.

BIBLIOGRAPHIES

Ashley, Mike. *Who's Who in Horror and Fantasy Fiction*. New York: St, Martin's, 1978.

Bleiler, Everett F. *The Checklist of Fantastic Literature: A Bibliography of Fantasy, Weird and Science Fiction Books Published in the English Language*. Chicago: Shasta, 1948; revised as *The Checklist of Science-Fiction and Supernatural Fiction*. Glen Rock, N.J.: Firebell, 1978.

Briney, R. E., and Edward Wood. *SF Bibliographies: An Annotated Bibliography of Bibliographic Works on Science Fiction and Fantastic Fiction*. Chicago: Advent, 1972.

Brown, Charles N., and William G. Contento. *The Locus Index to Science Fiction (1984–1998)*, combined with William G. Contento, *Index to Science Fiction Anthologies and Collections*. Oakland, Calif.: Locus, 1999 [CD-ROM].

Burgess, Michael, and Lisa R. Bartle. *Reference Guide to Science Fiction, Fantasy and Horror: Second Edition*. Westport, Conn.: Greenwood, 2003.

Collins, Robert A., and Robert Latham, eds. *Science Fiction & Fantasy Book Review Annual, 1988.* Westport, Conn.: Meckler, 1988.

Currey, Lloyd W. *Science Fiction and Fantasy Authors: A Bibliography of First Printings of Their Fiction and Selected Nonfiction*. Boston: G. K. Hall, 1979.

Dziemianowicz, Stefan R. *The Annotated Guide to Known and Unknown Worlds*. Mercer Island, Wash.: Starmont House, 1990.

Green, Scott E. *Contemporary Science Fiction, Fantasy and Horror Poetry: A Resource Guide and Bibliographical Dictionary*. Westport, Conn.: Greenwood, 1989.

Hall, H. W. *Science Fiction and Fantasy Reference Index 1879–1985: An International Author and Subject Index to HIstory and Criticism*. 2 vols. Detroit, Mich.: Gale, 1987.

Herald, Diana Tixier. *Fluent in Fantasy: A Guide to Reading Interests*. Englewood, Colo.: Libraries Unlimited, 1999.

Lynn, Ruth Nadelman. *Fantasy for Children and Young Adults: An Annotated Bibliography*. New York: Bowker, 1979. 2nd ed. 1983. 3rd ed. 1989.

Miller, Stephen T., and William G. Contento. *Science Fiction, Fantasy, & Weird Fiction Magazine Index (1890–1998)*. Oakland, Calif.: Locus, 1999 [CD-ROM].

Pflieger, Pat. *A Reference Guide to Modern Fantasy for Children*. Westport, Conn.: Greenwood, 1984.

Reginald, Robert. *Science Fiction and Fantasy Literature: A Checklist, 1700–1974*. 2 vols. Detroit, Mich.: Gale, 1979.

Schlobin, Roger C. *The Literature of Fantasy: A Comprehensive Annotated Bibliography of Modern Fantasy Fiction*. New York: Garland, 1979.

Searles, Baird, Beth Meacham, and Michael Franklin. *A Reader's Guide to Fantasy*. New York: Avon, 1982.

Summers, Montague. *A Gothic Bibliography*. London: Fortune, 1938.

Tymn, Marshall B., ed. *American Fantasy and Science Fiction: Towards a Bibliography of Works Published in the United States, 1948–1973*. West Linn, Ore.: Fax, 1979.

Tymn, Marshall B., and Roger C. Schlobin. *The Year's Scholarship in Science Fiction and Fantasy 1972–1975*. Kent, Ohio: Kent State University Press, 1979. Supplements: 1976–19 (1983); 1980 (1983); 1981 (1984); 1982 (1985). (Further supplements for 1983–88 in *Extrapolation* and for 1989 in *The Journal of the Fantastic in the Arts.*)

THEMATIC STUDIES

Allegory

Clifford, Gay. *Transformations of Allegory*. London: Routledge and Kegan Paul, 1974.

Honig, Edwin. *Dark Conceit: The Making of Allegory*. London: Faber and Faber, 1959.

Leyburn, Ellen Douglas. *Satiric Allegory: Mirror of Man*. New Haven, Conn.: Yale University Press, 1956.

Quilligan, Maureen. *The Language of Allegory: Defining the Genre*. Ithaca, N.Y.: Cornell University Press, 1979.

Amazons

Salmonson, Jessica Amanda. *The Encyclopedia of Amazons: Women Warriors from Antiquity to the Modern Era*. New York: Paragon House, 1991.

Wilde, Lyn Webster. *On the Trail of the Women Warriors: The Amazons in Myth and History*. New York: St. Martin's, 2000.

Animal Fantasy

Blount, Margaret. *Animal Land: The Creatures of Children's Fiction*. New York: Morrow, 1974.

Apocalyptic Fantasy

Bull, Malcolm, ed. *Apocalypse Theory and the Ends of the World*. Oxford, U.K.: Blackwell, 1995.

Clute, John. *The Book of End Times: Grappling with the Millennium*. New York: HarperPrism, 1999.

Dubanski, Ryszard. "The Last Man Theme in Modern Fantasy and SF." *Foundation* 16 (May 1979): 26–30.

Robinson, Douglas. *American Apocalypses: The Image of the End of the World in American Literature*. Baltimore: John Hopkins University Press, 1985.

Seed, David, ed. *Imagining Apocalypse: Studies in Cultural Crisis*. London: Macmillan, 2000.

Wagar, W. Warren. *Terminal Visions: The Literature of Last Things*. Bloomington: Indiana University Press, 1982.

Arabian Fantasy

Irwin, Robert. *The Arabian Nights: A Companion*. London: Allen Lane, 1994.

Nadaff, Sandra. *Arabesque: Narrative Structure and the Aesthetics of Repetition in the 1001 Nights*. Evanston, Ill.: Northwestern University Press, 1991.

Arthurian Fantasy

Goodman, Jennifer R. *The Legend of Arthur in British and American Literature*. Boston: Twayne, 1988.

Howey, Ann F. *Rewriting the Women of Camelot: Arthurian Popular Fiction and Feminism*. Westport, Conn.: Greenwood, 2002.

Loomis. R. S. *Arthurian Legends in Medieval Art*. Oxford, U.K.: Oxford University Press, 1938.

——, ed. *Arthurian Literature in the Middle Ages*. Oxford, U.K.: Oxford University Press, 1959.

Lupack, Alan, and Barbara Tepa Lupack. "Introduction: The Forgotten Tradition." *Arthurian Literature by Women*. New York: Garland, 1999: 3–30.

Mathis, Arthur E. *The King Arthur Myth in Modern American Fiction and Culture*. Jefferson, N.C.: McFarland, 2002.

Mediavilla, Cindy. *Arthurian Fiction: An Annotated Bibliography*. Lanham, Md.: Scarecrow, 1999.

Spivack, Charlotte, and Roberta Lynn Staples, eds. *The Company of Camelot: Arthurian Characters in Romance and Fantasy*. Westport, Conn.: Greenwood, 1994.

Starr, Nathan Comfort. *King Arthur Today: The Arthurian Legend in English and American Literature, 1901–1953*. Gainesville: University of Florida Press, 1954.

Thompson, Raymond H. *The Return from Avalon: A Study of the Arthurian Legend in Modern Fiction*. Westport, Conn.: Greenwood, 1985.

Atlantean Fantasy

de Camp, L. Sprague. *Lost Continents: The Atlantis Theme in History, Science, and Literature*. New York: Gnome, 1954.

Celtic Fantasy

White, Donna R. *A Century of Welsh Myth in Children's Literature*. Westport, Conn.: Greenwood, 1999.

Children's Fantasy

Crouch, Marcus. *The Nesbit Tradition: The Children's Novel in England, 1945–1970*. London: Benn, 1972.

Gose, Elliott. *Mere Creatures: A Study of Modern Fantasy Tales for Children*. Toronto: University of Toronto Press, 1988.

Higgins, James E. *Beyond Words: Mystical Fancy in Children's Literature*. New York: Teachers College Press, 1970.

Hunt, Peter, and Millicent Lenz. *Alternative Worlds in Fantasy Fiction*. New York: Continuum, 2001.

Lanes, Selma G. *Down the Rabbit Hole: Adventures and Misadventures in the Realm of Children's Literature*. New York: Atheneum, 1971.

Lochhead, Marion. *The Renaissance of Wonder in Children's Literature*. Edinburgh, U.K.: Canongate, 1977.

Zipes, Jack. *Sticks and Stones: The Troublesome Success of Children's Literature from Slovely Peter to Harry Potter*. London: Routledge, 2001.

Christian Fantasy

Manlove, Colin. *Christian Fantasy: From 1200 to the Present*. Notre Dame, Ind.: University of Notre Dame Press, 1992.

Sammons, Martha C. *A Better Country: The Worlds of Religious Fantasy and Science Fiction*. Westport, Conn.: Greenwood, 1988.

Urang, Gunar. *Shadows of Heaven: Religion and Fantasy in the Works of C. S. Lewis, Charles Williams and J. R. R. Tolkien*. Philadelphia: Pilgrim, 1971.

Ziolkowski, Theodore. *Fictional Transfigurations of Jesus*. Princeton, N.J.: Princeton University Press, 1972.

Decadent Fantasy

Birkett, Jennifer. *The Sins of the Fathers: Decadence in France, 1870–1914*. London: Quartet, 1986.

Constable, Liz, Dennis Denisoff, and Matthew Potolsky, eds. *Perennial Decay: On the Aesthetics and Politics of Decadence*. Philadelphia: University of Pennsylvania Press, 1999.

Fletcher, Ian, ed. *Decadence and the 1890s*. London: Edward Arnold, 1979.

Pierrot, Jean. *The Decadent Imagination, 1880–1900*. Translated by Derek Colman. Chicago: University of Chicago Press, 1981.

Stableford, Brian. *Glorious Perversity: The Decline and Fall of Literary Decadence*. San Bernardino, Calif.: Borgo, 1998.

Symons, Arthur. *The Symbolist Movement in Literature*. London: Constable, 1899.

The Devil

Russell, Jeffrey Burton. *Mephistopheles: The Devil in the Modern World*. Ithaca, N.Y.: Cornell University Press, 1986.

Doppelgängers

Herdman, John. *The Double in Nineteenth Century Fiction: The Shadow Life*. New York: St. Martin's, 1991.

Keppler, Carl F. *The Literature of the Second Self*. Tucson: University of Arizona Press, 1972.

Miller, Karl. *Doubles: Studies in Literary History*. Oxford, U.K.: Oxford University Press, 1985.

Miyoshi, Masao. *The Divided Self: A Perspective on the Literature of the Victorians*. New York: New York University Press, 1969.

Rogers, Ralph. *The Double in Literature*. Detroit, Mich.: Wayne State University Press, 1970.

Dragons

Hoult, Janet. *Dragons: Their History and Symbolism*. Glastonbury, U.K.: Gothic Image, 1987.

Huxley, Francis. *The Dragon: Nature of the Spirit, Spirit of Nature*. New York: Thames and Hudson, 1992.

Petty, Anne C. *Dragons in Fantasy: Scaly Villains and Heroes in Modern Fantasy Literature*. Cold Spring Harbor, N.Y.: Open Road, 2004.

Shuker, Karl. *Dragons: A Natural History*. New York: Simon and Schuster, 1995.

Erotic Fantasy

Djikstra, Bram. *Idols of Perversity: Fantasies of Female Evil in Fin-de-Siècle Culture*. New York: Oxford University Press, 1986.

Reed, Toni. *Demon-Lovers and Their Victims in British Fiction*. Lexington: University of Kentucky Press, 1988.

Fables

Newbigging, Thomas. *Fables and Fabulists, Ancient and Modern*. London: Elliot Stock, 1895.

Fairies

Briggs, K. M. *The Anatomy of Puck: An Examination of Fairy Beliefs among Shakespeare's Contemporaries and Successors*. London: Routledge and Kegan Paul, 1959.

———. *The Fairies in Tradition and Literature*. London: Routledge and Kegan Paul, 1967.

Keightley, Thomas. *Fairy Mythology*. 2 vols. London: W. H. Ainsworth, 1828.

Kirk, Robert. *The Secret Commonwealth of Elves, Fauns and Fairies*. 3rd ed. Stirling: Eneas Mackay, 1933. [Written 1691; first published by Andrew Lang, 1893.]

Paton, Lucy Allen. *Studies in the Fairy Mythology of Arthurian Romance*. Cambridge, Mass.: Harvard University Press, 1903.

Purkiss, Diane. *Troublesome Things: A History of Fairies and Fairy Stories*. London: Allen Lane, 2000.

Salmonson, Jessica Amanda. *Wisewomen and Boggy-boos: a Dictionary of Lesbian Fairy-Lore*. Austin, Tex.: Banned Books, 1992.

Silver, Carole D. *Strange and Secret People: Fairies and Victorian Consciousness*. Oxford, U.K.: Oxford University Press, 1999.

Fairy Tales

Anderson, Graham. *Fairytale in the Ancient World*. New York: Routledge, 2000.

Bernheimer, Kate, ed. *Mirror, Mirror on the Wall: Women Writers Explore Their Favorite Fairy Tales*. New York: Anchor, 1998.

Bettelheim, Bruno. *The Uses of Enchantment: The Meaning and Importance of Fairy Tales*. New York: Vintage Books, 1975.

Cashdan, Sheldon. *The Witch Must Die: How Fairy Tales Shape Our Lives*. New York: HarperCollins, 1999.

Davidson, Hilda Ellis, and Anna Chaudri. *A Companion to the Fairy Tale*. Woodbridge, U.K.: D. S. Brewer, 2003.

Duffy, Maureen. *The Erotic World of Faery*. London: Hodder and Stoughton, 1972.

Harries, Elizabeth Wanning. *Twice upon a Time: Women Writers and the History of the Fairy Tale*. Princeton, N.J.: Princeton University Press, 2001.

Haughton, Rosemary. *Tales from Eternity: The World of Faerie and the Spiritual Search*. London: Allen and Unwin, 1973.

Hazlitt, W. C., ed. *Fairy Tales, Legends and Romances Illustrating Shakespeare*. London: Frank and William Kerslake, 1875.

Hearne, Betsy. *Beauty and the Beast: Visions and Revisions of an Old Tale*. Chicago: University of Chicago Press, 1990.

Lüthi, Max. *Once upon a Time: On the Nature of Fairy Tales*. New York: Ungar, 1970.

Warner, Marina. *From the Beast to the Blonde: On Fairy Tales and Their Tellers*. London: Chatto and Windus, 1994.

Yearsley, Macleod. *The Folklore of Fairy Tale*. London: Watts, 1924.

Zipes, Jack. *Breaking the Magic Spell: Radical Theories of Folk and Fairy Tales*. Austin: University of Texas Press, 1979. Revised and expanded edition. Lexington: University of Kentucky Press, 2003.

———. *Fairy Tales and the Art of Subversion: The Classical Genre for Children and the Process of Civilization*. London: Heinemann, 1983.

———. *When Dreams Came True: Classic Fairy Tales and Their Tradition*. New York: Routledge, 1998.

———, ed. *The Oxford Companion to Fairy Tales*. Oxford, U.K.: Oxford University Press, 2000.

Far-Futuristic Fantasy

Broderick, Damien, ed. *Earth Is But a Star: Excursions through Science Fiction to the Far Future*. Crawley: University of Western Australia Press, 2001.

Faustian Fantasy

Butler, Eliza Marian. *The Fortunes of Faust*. Cambridge, U.K.: Cambridge University Press, 1952.

Dédéyan, Charles. *Le thème de Faust dans la littérature européenne*. 4 vols. Paris: Lettres Modernes, 1954–67.

Smeed, John Wiliam. *Faust in Literature*. London: Oxford University Press, 1975.

Testa, Carlo. *Desire and the Devil: Demonic Contracts in French and European Literature*. New York: Peter Lang, 1991.

Folktales

Aarne, Antti, and Stith Thompson. *The Types of the Folktale: A Classification and Biography*. Folklore Fellows Communication 184. Helsinki: Academia, Scientiarum Fenica, 1964.

Dorson, Richard M. *American Folklore*. Chicago: University of Chicago Press, 1959.

———. *Folklore and Fakelore: Essays Towards a Discipline of Folk Studies*. Cambridge, Mass.: Harvard University Press, 1946.

Thomspon, Stith. *The Folkltale*. New York: Dryden, 1946.

———. *Motif Index of Folk Literature*. Revised edition. 6 vols. Bloomington: Indiana University Press, 1955–58.

Gothic Fantasy

Andriano, Joseph. *Our Ladies of Darkness: Feminine Daemonology in Male Gothic Fiction*. University Park: Pennsylvania State University Press, 1993.

Becker, Susanne. *Gothic Forms of Feminine Fictions*. Manchester, U.K.: Manchester University Press, 1999.

Hoeveler, Diane Long. *Gothic Feminism: The Professionalization of Gender from Charlotte Smith to the Brontës*. Philadelphia: Pennsylvania State University Press, 1998.

MacAndrew, Elizabeth. *The Gothic Tradition in Fiction*. New York: Columbia University Press, 1979.

Mulvey-Roberts, Marie. *The Handbook to Gothic Literature*. London: Macmillan, 1998.

Punter, David. *Gothic Pathologies: The Text, The Body, and the Law*. London: Macmillan, 1998.
——, ed. *A Companion to the Gothic*. Oxford, U.K.: Blackwell, 2000.
Summers, Montague. *The Gothic Quest: A History of the Gothic Novel*. London: Fortune, 1941.

Grail Fantasy

Evans, Sebastian. *In Quest of the Holy Graal*. London: J. M. Dent, 1898.
Nutt, Alfred. *Studies on the Legend of the Holy Grail*. London: David Nutt, 1888.
Owen. D. D. R. *The Evolution of the Grail Legend*. Edinburgh, U.K.: Oliver and Boyd, 1968.

Hallucinatory Fantasy

James, Tony. *Dream, Creativity, and Madness in Nineteenth Century France*. Oxford, U.K.: Clarendon, 1995.

Frazerian Fantasy

Fraser, Robert, ed. *Sir James Frazer and the Literary Imagination*. London: Macmillan, 1990.
Vickers, John P. *The Literary Impact of* The Golden Bough. Princeton, N.J.: Princeton University Press, 1973.

Heroic Fantasy

Campbell, Joseph. *The Hero with a Thousand Faces*. New York: Pantheon, 1949.
Galinsky, G. Karl. *The Herakles Theme: The Adaptations of the Hero in Literature from Homer to the Twentieth Centuiry*. Totowa, N.J.: Rowman & Littlefield, 1972.
Leeming, David. *Mythology: The Voyage of the Hero*. New York: Lippincott, 1973.
Rank, Otto. *The Myth of the Birth of the Hero and Other Writings,* ed. Philip Freund. New York: Random-Vintage, 1959.

Invisibility

Journal of the Fantastic in the Arts 4, no. 2 (1992) [special issue].

Lifestyle Fantasy

Hutton, Ronald. *The Triumph of the Moon: A History of Modern Pagan Witchcraft*. Oxford, U.K.: Oxford University Press, 1999.

Magic Realism

Angulo, Maria-Elena. *Magic Realism: Social Context and Discourse*. New York: Garland, 1995.
Bowers, Maggie Ann. *Magic(al) Realism*. London: Routledge, 2004.
Chanadfy, Amaryll Beatrice. *Magic Realism and the Fantastic: Resolved versus Unresolved Antinomy*. New York: Garland, 1985.
Durix, Jean-Pierre. *Mimesis, Genres and Post-Colonial Discourse: Deconstructing Magic Realism*. London: Macmillan, 1998.
Mellen, Joan. *Literary Topics*. Vol. 5: *Magic Realism*. Farmington Hills, Mich.: Gale, 2000.

Metafiction

Hutcheon, Linda. *Narcissistic Narrative: The Metafictional Paradox*. New York: Methuen, 1984.
Waugh, Patricia. *Metafiction: The Theory and Practice of Self-Conscious Fiction*. London: Methuen, 1984.

Monsters

Andriano, Joseph D. *Immortal Monster: The Mythlogical Evolution of the Fantastic Beast in Modern Fiction and Film*. Westport, Conn.: Greenwood, 1999.
Barber, Richard W., and Anne Riches. *A Dictionary of Fabulous Beasts*. London: Macmillan, 1971.
Cohen, Daniel. *A Modern Look at Monsters*. New York: Tower, 1970.
Costello, Peter. *The Magic Zoo: The Natural History of Fabulous Animals*. New York: St. Martin's, 1979.
Gilmore, David D. *Monsters: Evil Beings, Mythical Beasts and All Manner of Imaginary Terrors*. Philadelphia: University of Pennsylvania Press, 2002.
Goetsch, Paul. *Monsters in English Literature: From the Romantic Age to the First World War*. Bern, Switz.: Peter Lang, 2002.
Lehner, Ernst, and Johanna Lehner. *A Fantastic Bestiary: Beasts and Monsters in Myth and Folklore*. New York: Tudor, 1969.
Nigg, Joseph, ed. *The Book of Fabulous Beasts*. Oxford, U.K.: Oxford University Press, 1999.

The Moon

Montgomery, Scott L. *The Moon and the Western Imagination*. Tucson: University of Arizona Press, 1999.

Myth

Brockway, Robert. *Myth from the Ice Age to Mickey Mouse*. Albany: State University of New York Press, 1993.

Campbell, Joseph. *Transformations of Myth through Time*. New York: Harper and Row, 1990.

Fredericks, Casey. *The Future of Eternity: Mythologies of Science Fiction and Fantasy*. Bloomington: Indiana University Press, 1982.

Shinn, Thelma J. *Worlds within Women: Myth and Mythmaking in Fantastic Literature by Women*. Westport, Conn: Greenwood, 1986.

White, John J. *Mythology in the Modern Novel*. Princeton, N.J.: Princeton University Press, 1971.

Mythopoesis

Slochower, Harry. *Mythopoesis: Patterns in the Literary Classics*. Detroit, Mich.: Wayne State University Press, 1970.

Nonsense

Sewell, Elizabeth. *The Field of Nonsense*. London: Chatto and Windus, 1952.

Orphean Fantasy

Linforth, Ivan M. *The Arts of Orpheus*. Berkeley: University of California Press, 1941.

Segal, Charles: *Orpheus: The Myth of the Poet*. Baltimore: John Hopkins University Press, 1989.

The Phoenix

Blake, N. F.. ed. *The Phoenix*. Manchester, U.K.: Manchester University Press, 1964.

Race and Ethnicity

Leonard, Elizabeth Anne, ed. *Into Darkness Peering: Race and Color in the Fantastic*. Westport, Conn.: Greenwood, 1997.

Religious Fantasy

Reilly, Robert, ed. *The Transcendent Adventure: Studies of Religion in Science Fiction/Fantasy*. Wetport, Conn.: Greenwood, 1984.

Romance

Frye, Northrop. *The Secular Scripture: A Study of the Structure of Romance*. Cambridge, Mass.: Harvard University Press, 1976.

Romanticism

Abrams, Meyer Howard. *The Mirror and the Lamp: Romantic Theory and the Critical Tradition*. Oxford, U.K.: Oxford University Press, 1953.
———. *Natural Supernaturalism: Tradition and Revolution in Romantic Literature*. New York: Norton, 1971.
Bush, Douglas. *Mythology and the Romantic Tradition in English Poetry*. New York: Pageant, 1957.
Praz, Mario. *The Romantic Agony*. Oxford, U.K.: Oxford University Press, 1933.
Railo, Eino. *The Haunted Castle: A Study of the Elements of English Romanticism*. London: Routledge, 1927.
Siebers, Tobin. *The Romantic Fantastic*. Ithaca, N.Y.: Cornell University Press, 1984.
Willoughby, L. A. *The Romantic Movement in Germany*. New York: Russell and Russell, 1966.

Satire

Hall, Ernest J. *The Satirical Element in the American Novel*. New York: Haskell House, 1970.
Hodgart, Matthew. *Satire*. London: Weidenfeld and Nicholson, 1969.
Knight, Charles A. *The Literature of Satire*. Cambridge, U.K.: Cambridge University Press, 2004.
Snodgrass, Mary Ellen. *Encyclopedia of Satirical Literature*. Santa Barbara, Calif.: ABC-Clio Press, 1996.

Sexuality

Fendler, Susan, and Ulrike Horstmann, eds. *Images of Masculinity in Fantasy Fiction*. Lewiston, N.Y.: Edwin Mellen, 2003.
Frederick, Candice, and Sam McBride. *Women among the Inklings: Gender, C. S. Lewis, J. R. R. Tolkien and Charles Williams*. Westport, Conn.: Greenwood, 2002.
Garber, Eric, and Lin Paleo. *Uranian Worlds: A Reader's Guide to Alternative Sexuality in Science Fiction and Fantasy*. 2nd ed. Boston: G. K. Hall, 1990.
Merrick, Helen, and Tess Williams, eds. *Women of Other Worlds: Excursions through Science Fiction and Fantasy*. Perth: University of Western Australia Press, 1999.

Notkin, Debbie, and the Secret Feminist Cabal, eds. *Flying Cups and Saucers: Gender Explorations in Science Fiction and Fantasy*. Cambridge, Mass.: Edgewood, 1998.

Palumbo, Donald. ed. *Erotic Universe: Sexuality and Fantastic Literature*. New York: Greenwood, 1986.

Weedman, Jane, ed. *Women Worldwalkers: New Dimensions of Science Fiction and Fantasy*. Lubbock: Texas Tech Press, 1985.

Spiritualist Fantasy

Kerr, Howard. *Mediums and Spirit-Rappers and Roaring Radicals: Spiritualism in American Literature, 1850–1900*. Chicago: University of Illinois Press, 1972.

Symbolism

Feidelson, Charles, Jr. *Symbolism and American Literature*. Chicago: University of Chicago Press, 1953.

Tindall, William York. *The Literary Symbol*. Bloomington: Indiana University Press, 1955.

The Templars

Partner, Peter. *The Murdered Magicians: The Templars and Their Myth*. New York: Oxford University Press, 1982.

Timeslip Fantasy

Westfahl, Gary, George Slusser, and David Leiby. *Worlds Enough and Time: Explorations of Time in Science Fiction and Fantasy*. Westport, Conn.: Greenwood, 2002.

Travelers' Tales

Adams, H. C. *Travellers' Tales: A Book of Marvels*. New York: Boni and Liveright, 1927.

Unicorns

Beer, Rüdiger Robert. *Unicorn: Myth and Reality*. New York: Van Nostrand Reinhold, 1972.

Hathaway, Nancy. *The Unicorn*. New York: Viking, 1980.

Vampires

Auerbach, Nina. *Our Vampires, Ourselves*. Chicago: University of Chicago Press, 1995.

Gelder, Ken. *Reading the Vampire*. New York: Routledge, 1994.

Gordon, Joan, and Veronica Hollinger, eds. *Blood Read: The Vampire as Metaphor in Contemporary Culture*. Philadelphia: University of Pennsylvania Press, 1997.

MacDonald, Beth E. *The Vampire as Numinous Experience: Spiritual Journeys with the Undead in British and American Literature*. Jefferson, N.C.: McFarland, 2004.

Senf, Carol A. *The Vampire in Nineteenth-Century English Literature*. Bowling Green, Ohio: Bowling Green State University Popular Press, 1988.

The Wandering Jew

Anderson, George K. *The Legend of the Wandering Jew*. Providence, R.I.: Brown University Press, 1965.

Conway, Moncure Daniel. *The Wandering Jew*. London: Chatto and Windus, 1881.

Witchcraft

Briggs, K. M. *Pale Hecate's Team: An Examination of the Beliefs on Witchcraft and Magic among Shakespeare's Contemporaries and His Immediate Successors*. London: Routledge and Kegan Paul, 1962.

NATIONS AND REGIONS

Australia

Collins, Paul, Steven Paulsen, and Sean McMullen, eds. *The MUP Encyclopedia of Australian Science Fiction and Fantasy*. Melbourne, Australia: Melbourne University Press, 1998.

Canada

Ketterer, David. *Canadian Science Fiction and Fantasy*. Bloomington: Indiana University Press, 1992,

England

Kincaid, Paul. *A Very British Genre: A Short History of British Fantasy and Science Fiction*. Folkestone, U.K.: British Science Fiction Association, 1995.

Manlove, Colin. *The Fantasy Literature of England*. London: Macmillan, 1999.

France

Lofficier, Jean-Marc and Randy. *French Science Fiction, Fantasy, Horror and Pulp Fiction: A Guide to Cinema, Television, Radio, Animation, Comic Books and Literature from the Middle Ages to the Present*. Jefferson, N.C.: McFarland, 2000.

Ireland

Morse, Donald E., and Csilla Bertha, eds. *More Real than Reality: The Fantastic in Irish Literature and the Arts*. Westport, Conn.: Greenwood, 1992.

Latin America

Tavares, Braulio. *Fantastic, Fantasy and Science Fiction Literature Catalog*. Rio de Janeiro: Biblioteca Nacional, 1993.

Portugal

Holstein, Alvaro de Sousa, and José Manuel Morais. *Bibliografia da Ficção Científica e Fantasia Portuguesa*. Lisbon: Black Sun, 1993.

Scotland

Manlove, Colin. *Scottish Fantasy Literature: A Critical Survey*. Edinburgh, U.K.: Canongate, 1994.

The United States

Attebery, Brian. *The Fantasy Tradition in American Literature, from Irving to Le Guin*. Bloomington: Indiana University Press, 1980.

STUDIES OF INDIVIDUAL AUTHORS

Collections

Bleiler, Everett F. *Supernatural Fiction Writers: Fantasy and Horror*. 2 vols. New York: Scribner's, 1985. Revised and expanded edition. Richard Bleiler as *Supernatural Ficton Writers: Contemporary Fantasy and Horror*. 2. vols, 2002.

Carpenter, Humphrey. *The Inklings*. London: Allen and Unwin, 1978.

de Camp, L. Sprague. *Literary Swordsmen and Sorcerers: The Makers of Heroic Fantasy*. Sauk City, Wis.: Arkham House, 1976.

Green, Roger Lancelyn. *Tellers of Tales: Children's Books and Their Authors from 1800–1968*. Norwich, U.K.: Kaye and Ward, 1969 [first ed. 1946].

Nicholls, Stan. *Wordsmiths of Wonder: Fifty Interviews with Writers of the Fantastic*. London: Orbit, 1993.

Pringle, David, ed. *The St. James Guide to Fantasy Writers*. Detroit, Mich.: St. James, 1996.

——, ed. *The St. James Guide to Horror, Ghost and Gothic Writers*. Detroit, Mich.: St. James, 1998.

Spivack, Charlotte. *Merlin's Daughters: Contemporary Women Writers of Fantasy*. Westport, Conn.: Greenwood, 1987.

Van Belkom, Edo. *Northern Dreamers: Interviews with Famous Science Fiction, Fantasy, and Horror Writers*. Ontario, Can.: Quarry, 1998.

Wintle, Justin, and Emma Fisher. *The Pied Pipers: Interviews with the Influential Creators of Children's Literature*. New York: Paddington, 1974.

Peter Ackroyd

Peck, John. "The Novels of Peter Ackroyd." *English Studies* 75 (September 1994): 442–52.

Lloyd Alexander

Jacobs, James S., and Michael O. Tunnell. *Lloyd Alexander: A Bio-Bibliography*. Westport, Conn.: Greenwood, 1991.

May, Jill P. *Lloyd Alexander*. Boston: Twayne, 1991.

Tunnell, Michael O. *The Prydain Companion*. Westport, Conn.: Greenwood, 1989.

Hans Christian Andersen

Bresdorf, Elias. *Hans Christian Andersen: The Story of His Life and Works*. New York: Noonday, 1975.

Grønbech, Bo. *Hans Christian Andersen*. Boston: Twayne, 1980.

Piers Anthony

Collings, Michael R. *Piers Anthony*. Mercer Island, Wash.: Starmont House, 1983.

Stephensen-Payne, Phil, and Gordon Benson Jr. *Piers Anthony*. Galactic Central Bibliographies for the Avid Reader, vol. 35. Leeds, Yorkshire, U.K.: Galactic Central, 1990.

Apuleius

Haight, Elizabeth. *Apuleius and His Influence*. New York: Cooper Square, 1963.
Tatum, James. *Apuleius and the Golden Ass*. Ithaca, N.Y.: Cornell University Press, 1979.
Walsh, P. G. *The Golden Ass*. New York: Oxford University Press, 1994.

Paul Auster

Barone, Dennis, ed. *Beyond the Red Notebook: Essays on Paul Auster*. Philadelphia: University of Pennsylvania Press, 1995.
Varvogli, Aliki. *The World That Is the Book: Paul Auster's Fiction*. Liverpool, U.K.: Liverpool University Press, 2001.

John Kendrick Bangs

Bangs, Francis Hyde. *John Kendrick Bangs: Humorist of the Nineties*. New York: Knopf, 1941.

Clive Barker

Barbieri, Suzanne J. *Clive Barker: Mythmaker for the Milennium*. Stockport, U.K.: British Fantasy Society, 1994.
Winter, Douglas E. *Clive Barker: The Dark Fantastic*. London: HarperCollins, 2001.

J. M. Barrie

Birkin, Andrew. *J. M. Barrie and the Lost Boys*. London: Constable, 1979.
Darton, F. J. Harvey. *J. M. Barrie*. London: Nisbet, 1929.
Green, Roger Lancelyn. *Fifty Years of Peter Pan*. London: Peter Davies, 1954.
———. *J. M. Barrie*. London: Bodley Head, 1960.
Ormond, Leonee. *J. M. Barrie*. Edinburgh, U.K.: Scottish Academic, 1987.
Rose, Jacqueline. *The Case of Peter Pan; or, The Impossibility of Children's Fiction*. London: Macmillan, 1984.

John Barth

Fogel, Stan, and Gordon Slethaug. *Understanding John Barth*. Columbia: University of South Carolina Press, 1990.
Harris, Charles B. *Passionate Virtuosity: The Fiction of John Barth*. Urbana: University of Illinois Press, 1983.

Joseph, Gerhard. *John Barth*. Minneapolis: University of Minnesota Press, 1970.
Tharpe, Jac. *John Barth: The Comic Sublimity of Paradox*. Carbondale: Southern Illinois University Press, 1974.
Waldmeir, Joseph J., ed. *Critical Essays on John Barth*. Boston: G. K. Hall, 1980.
Ziegler, Heidi. *John Barth*. London: Methuen, 1987.

L. Frank Baum

Dighe, Ranjit, ed. *The Historian's Wizard of Oz: Reading L. Frank Baum's Classic as a Political and Monetary Allegory*. Westport, Conn.: Greenwood, 2002.
Hearn, Michael Patrick, ed. *The Wizard of Oz*. New York: Schocken, 1983.
Moore, Raylyn. *Wonderful Wizard, Marvelous Land*. Bowling Green, Ohio: Bowling Green University Popular Press, 1974.
Nye, Russel, and Martin Gardner, eds. *The Wizard of Oz and Who He Was*. East Lansing: Michigan State University Press, 1957.
Rogers, Katharine M. *L. Frank Baum: Creator of Oz*. New York: St. Martin's, 2002.
Sale, Roger. "L. Frank Baum and Oz." *Hudson Review* 25, no. 4 (Winter 1972–73): 571–92.
Wagenknecht, Edward. *Utopia Americana*. Seattle: University of Washington Book Store, 1929.

Peter S. Beagle

Zahorski, Kenneth J. *Peter Beagle*. Mercer Island, Wash.: Starmont House, 1988.

Thomas Berger

Landon, Brooks. *Thomas Berger*. Boston: Twayne, 1989.

William Blake

Frye, Northrop. *Fearful Symmetry: A Study of William Blake*. Princeton, N.J.: Princeton University Press, 1947.

Jorges Luis Borges

Barrenechea, Ana Maria. *Borges the Labyrinth-Maker*. New York: New York University Press, 1965 [original publication 1957].
Bell-Villada, Gene H. *Borges and His Fiction: A Guide to His Mind and Art*. Chapel Hill: University of North Carolina Press, 1981.

Bloom, Harold, ed. *Jorge Luis Borges*. New York: Chelsea House, 1986.

Foster, David William. *Jorge Luis Borges: An Annotated Primary and Secondary Bibliography*. New York: Garland, 1984.

McMurray, George R. *Jorge Luis Borges*. New York: Ungar, 1980.

Rodriguez Monegal, Emir. *Jorges Luis Borges: A Literary Biography*. New York: Dutton, 1978.

Stabb, Martin S. *Jorge Luis Borges*. Boston: Twayne, 1970.

Wheelock, Carter. *The Mythmaker: A Study of Motif and Symbol in the Short Stories of Jorge Luis Borges*. Austin: University of Texas Press, 1969.

Lucy M. Boston

Rose, Jasper A. *Lucy Boston*. London: Bodley Head, 1965.

Ray Bradbury

De Koster, Katie, ed., *Readings on "Fahrenheit 451."* San Diego, Calif.: Greenhaven, 2000.

Johnson, Wayne L. *Ray Bradbury*. New York: Ungar, 1980.

Mogen, David. *Ray Bradbury*. Boston: Twayne, 1986.

Olander, Joseph P., and Martin H. Greenberg, eds. *Ray Bradbury*. New York: Taplinger, 1980.

Reid, Robin Anne. *Ray Bradbury: A Critical Companion*. Westport, Conn.: Greenwood, 2000.

Slusser, George Edgar. *The Bradbury Chronicles*. San Bernardino, Calif.: Borgo, 1977.

Touponce, William F. *Ray Bradbury*. Mercer Island, Wash: Starmont House, 1989.

———. *Ray Bradbury and the Poetics of Reverie: Fantasy, Science Fiction and the Reader*. Ann Arbor, Mich.: UMI Research, 1984.

K. M. Briggs

Davidson, H. Ellis. *Katharine Briggs: Story-Teller*. Cambridge, U.K.: Lutterworth, 1986.

Steven Brust

Chandler, Wayne A. "The Magic(s) of Steven Brust." *Journal of the Fantastic in the Arts* 9, no. 2 (1998): 157–65.

Edgar Rice Burroughs

Holtsmark, Erling B. *Edgar Rice Burroughs*. Boston: Twayne, 1986.
Kudlay, Robert R., and Joan Leiby. *Burroughs' Science Fiction*. Geneseo, N.Y.: School of Library and Information Science, 1973.
Lupoff, Richard A. *Barsoom: Edgar Rice Burroughs and the Martian Vision*. Baltimore: Mirage, 1976.
Mullen, Richard D., the Elder. "Edgar Rice Burroughs and the Fate Worse Than Death." *Riverside Quarterly* 4, no. 3 (1970): 186–91.
Roy, John Flint. *A Guide to Barsoom*. New York: Ballantine, 1976.

Lord Byron

Nicholson, Mervyn. "Disaster Fantasies: Byron as a Poet of the Fantastic." *Journal of the Fantastic in the Arts* 2, no. 4 (1990): 110–32.

James Branch Cabell

Davis, Joe Lee. *James Branch Cabell*. Boston: Twayne, 1962.
Duke, Maurice. *James Branch Cabell: A Reference Guide*. Boston: G. K. Hall, 1979.
Godshalk, William Leigh. *In Quest of Cabell: Five Exploratory Essays*. New York: Revisionist, 1976.
Inge, M. Thomas, and Edgar F. MacDonald, eds. *James Branch Cabell: Centenary Essays*. Baton Rouge: Louisiana State University Press, 1983.
Mencken, H. L. *James Branch Cabell: Three Essays in Criticism*. New York: McBride, 1932.
Morley-Mower, Geoffrey. *Cabell under Fire: Four Essays*. New York: Revisionist, 1975.
Riemer, James D. *From Satire to Subversion: The Fantasies of James Branch Cabell*. Westport, Conn.: Greenwood, 1989.
Tarrant, Desmond. *Cabell: The Dream and the Reality*. Norman: University of Oklahoma Press, 1967.
Wells, Arvin. *Jesting Moses: A Study in Cabellian Comedy*. Gainesville: University of Florida Press, 1962.

Italo Calvino

Cannon, JoAnn. *Italo Calvino: Writer and Critic*. Ravenna, Italy: Longo, 1981.
Carter, Albert Howard, III. *Italo Calvino: Metamorphoses of Fantasy*. Ann Arbor, Mich.: UMI Research, 1986.

Weiss, Bruno. *Understanding Calvino*. Columbia: University of South Carolina Press, 1993.

Orson Scott Card

Collings, Michael. *In the Image of God: Theme, Characterization, and Landscape in the Fiction of Orson Scott Card*. New York: Greenwood, 1990.

———. "Orson Scott Card: An Approach to Mythopoeic Literature." *Mythlore* 21 (Summer 1996): 36–50.

———. *Storyteller: The Official Orson Scott Card Bibliography and Guide*. Woodstock, Ga.: Overlook Connection, 2001.

Lewis Carroll

Fordyce, Rachel. *Lewis Carroll: A Reference Guide*. Boston: G. K. Hall, 1988.

Gardner, Martin. *The Annotated Alice:* Alice's Adventures in Wonderland *and* Through the Looking Glass. New York: Potter, 1960.

Guiliano, Edward. *Lewis Carroll: An Annotated International Bibliography 1960–77*. Charlottesville: University Press of Virginia, 1980.

Hudson, Derek. *Lewis Carroll*. Westport, Conn.: Greenwood, 1972.

Jones, Jo Elwyn, and J. Francis Gladstone. *The Alice Companion: A Guide to Lewis Carroll's Alice Books*. New York: New York University Press, 1998.

Kelly, Richard Michael. *Lewis Carroll*. Boston: Twayne, 1977.

Phillips, Robert. ed. *Aspects of Alice: Lewis Carroll's Dreamchild as Seen through the Critics' Looking-Glasses 1865–1971*. London: Gollancz, 1972.

Reichertz, Ronald. *The Making of the Alice Books: Lewis Carroll's Uses of Earlier Children's Fiction*. Montreal: McGill-Queens University Press, 2000.

Sigler, Carolyn, ed. *Alternative Alices*. Lexington: University of Kentucky Press, 1998.

Angela Carter

Bristow, Joseph, and Trev Lynn Broughton, eds. *The Infernal Desires of Angela Carter: Fiction, Femininity, Feminism*. London: Longman, 1997.

Day, Aidan. *Angela Carter: The Rational Glass*. Manchester, U.K.: Manchester University Press, 1998.

Gamble, Sarah. *Angela Carter: Writing from the Front Line*. Edinburgh, U.K.: Edinburgh University Press, 1997.

Jordan, Elaine. "Enthralment: Angela Carter's Speculative Fictions." In *Plotting Change: Contemporary Women's Fiction.* Edited by Linda Anderson, London: Edward Arnold, 1990: pp. 19–40.

Peach, Linden. *Angela Carter*. New York: St. Martin's, 1998.

Sage, Lorna. *Angela Carter*. Plymouth, U.K.: Northcote House, 1994.
———, ed. *Flesh and the Mirror: Essays on the Art of Angela Carter*. London: Chatto and Windus, 1994.
Tucker, Lindsay. *Critical Essays on Angela Carter*. Boston: G. K. Hall, 1998.

Lin Carter

Price, Robert M. *Lin Carter: A Look behind His Imaginary Worlds*. Mercer Island, Wash.: Starmont House, 1991.

C. J. Cherryh

Stephensen-Payne, Phil. *C. J. Cherryh: Citizen of the Universe—A Working Biography*. Galactic Central Bibliographies for the Avid Reader, vol. 43. Leeds, Yorkshire, U.K.: Galactic Central, 1992.

G. K. Chesterton

Boyd, Ian. *The Novels of G. K. Chesterton: A Study in Art and Propaganda*. London: Elek, 1975.
Clipper, Laurence J. *G. K. Chesterton*. Boston: Twayne, 1974.
Dwarakanath, K. *G. K. Chesterton: A Critical Study*. New Delhi: Classical, 1986.
Ffinch, Michael. *G. K. Chesterton*. London: Weidenfeld and Nicholson, 1986.
Hunter, Lynette. *Chesterton: Explorations in Allegory*. London: Macmillan, 1979.
Kenner, Hugh. *Paradox in Chesterton*. New York: Sheed and Ward, 1947.
Wills, Gray. *G. K. Chesterton: Man and Mask*. New York: Sheed and Ward, 1961.

Chrétien de Troyes

Loomis, R. S. *Arthurian Tradition and Chrétien de Troyes*. New York: Columbia University Press, 1949.

Samuel Taylor Coleridge

Richards, I. A. *Coleridge on Imagination*. London: Kegan Paul, 1934; in U.S. as *On Imagination: Coleridge's Critical Theory*. New York: Harcourt and Brace, 1935.

John Collier

Richardson, Betty. *John Collier*. Boston: Twayne, 1983.

Marie Corelli

Boswin, S. *The Writings of Marie Corelli*. Bombay: Examiner, 1907.

John Crowley

Andre-Driussi, Michael, and Alice K. Turner, eds. *Snakes' Hands*. Albany, Calif.: Sirius, 2001.

L. Sprague de Camp

Laughlin, Charlotte, and Daniel J. H. Levack. *De Camp: An L. Sprague de Camp Bibliography*. Columbia, Pa.: Underwood Miller, 1983.

Samuel R. Delany

Barbour, Douglas. *Worlds out of Words: The SF Novels of Samuel R. Delany*. Frome, Somerset, U.K.: Bran's Head, 1979.

McEvoy, Seth. *Samuel R. Delany*. New York: Ungar, 1983.

Slusser, George Edgar. *The Delany Intersection*. San Bernardino, Calif.: Borgo, 1977.

Weedman, Jane Branhan. *Samuel R. Delany*. Mercer Island, Wash.: Starmont House, 1982.

Stephen R. Donaldson

Barkley, Christine. "Donaldson as Heir to Tolkien." *Mythlore* 10 (Spring 1984): 50–57.

Senior, W. A. *Stephen R. Donaldson's Chronicles of Thomas Covenant: Variations on the Fantasy Tradition*. Kent, Ohio: Kent State University Press, 1995.

Lord Dunsany

Joshi, S. T. *Lord Dunsany: Anglo-Irish Writer*. Westport, Conn.: Greenwood, 1995.

Schweitzer, Darrell. *Pathways to Elfland: The Writings of Lord Dunsany*. Philadelphia: Owlswick, 1989.

Steve Erickson

Kincaid, Paul. "Secret Maps: The Topography of Fantasy and Morality in the Work of Steve Erickson." *Foundation* 57 (Spring 1993): 26–48.

———. "Defying Rational Chronology: Time and Identity in the Work of Steve Erickson." *Foundation* 58 (Summer 1993): 27–42.

Eleanor Farjeon

Colwell, Eileen. *Eleanor Farjeon*. London: Bodley Head, 1961.

Lewis, Naomi, ed. *A Book for Eleanor Farjeon: A Tribute to Her Life and Work*. New York: Walck, 1966.

Neil Gaiman

Rauch, Stephen. *Neil Gaiman's* The Sandman *and Joseph Campbell: In Search of Modern Myth*. Holicong, Pa.: Wildside, 2003.

Alan Garner

Philip, Neil. *A Fine Anger: A Critical Introduction to the Work of Alan Garner*. London: Collins, 1981.

Richard Garnett

McCrimmon, Barbara. *Richard Garnett: The Scholar as Librarian*. Chicago: American Library Association, 1989.

Kenneth Grahame

Graham, Eleanor. *Keneth Grahame*. London: Bodley Head, 1963.

Green, Peter. *Kenneth Grahame 1859–1932: A Study of His Life, Work, and Times*. London: John Murray, 1959; abridged as *Beyond the Wild Wood: The World of Kenneth Grahame,* Exeter, U.K.: Webb and Bower, 1982.

Prince, Alison. *Kenneth Grahame: An Innocent in the Wild Wood*. London: Allison and Busby, 1994.

Jakob and Wilhelm Grimm

Ellis, John S. *One Fairy Story Too Many: The Brothers Grimm and Their Tales*. Chicago: University of Chicago Press, 1983.

McGlathery, James M., with Larry W. Danielson, Ruth E. Lorbe, and Selma K. Richardson, eds. *The Brothers Grimm and Folktale*. Urbana: University of Illinois Press, 1988.

Michaelis-Jena, Ruth. *The Brothers Grimm*. London: Routledge and Kegan Paul, 1970.

Zipes, Jack. *The Brothers Grimm: From Enchanted Forests to the Modern World*. London: Routledge, 1988.

Neil M. Gunn

McCulloch, Margery. *The Novels of Neil M. Gunn: A Critical Study*. Edinburgh, U.K.: Scottish Academic, 1987.

H. Rider Haggard

Cohen, Morton N. *Rider Haggard: His Life and Works*. London: Hutchinson, 1960; revised London: Macmillan, 1968.

Ellis, Peter Berresford. *H. Rider Haggard: A Voice from the Infinite*. London: Routledge, 1978.

Etherington, Norman. *Rider Haggard*. Boston: Twayne, 1984.

Higgins, D. S. *Rider Haggard, The Great Storyteller*. London: Cassell, 1981.

Pocock, Tom. *Rider Haggard and the Lost Empire*. London: Weidenfeld and Nicholson, 1993.

Vogelsberger, Hartwig A. *"King Romance": Rider Haggard's Achievement*. Salzburg, Ger.: Universität Salzburg, 1984.

Whatmore, D. E. *Rider Haggard: A Bibliography*. London: Mansell, 1987.

Nathaniel Hawthorne

Crews, Frederick. *The Sins of the Fathers: Hawthorne's Psychological Themes*. Oxford, U.K.: Oxford University Press, 1966.

Russell Hoban

Wilkie, Christine. *Through the Narrow Gate: The Mythological Consciousness of Russell Hoban*. Rutherford, N.J.: Fairleigh Dickinson University Press, 1989.

E. T. A. Hoffmann

Röder, Birgit. *A Study of the Major Novellas of E. T. A. Hoffmann*. Rochester, N.Y.: Camden House, 2003.

Robert E. Howard

Cerasini, Mark A., and Charles Hoffman. *Robert E. Howard*. Mercer Island, Wash.: Starmont House, 1987.

de Camp, L. Sprague. *The Conan Reader*. Baltimore: Mirage, 1968.

de Camp, L. Sprague, Catherine Crook de Camp, and Jane Whittington Griffin. *Dark Valley Destiny: The Life of Robert E. Howard*. New York: Bluejay, 1983.

Herron, Don, ed. *The Dark Barbarian: The Writings of Robert E. Howard: A Critical Anthology*. Westport, Conn.: Greenwood, 1984.

Lord, Glenn, ed. *The Last Celt: A Bio-Bibliography of Robert Ervin Howard*. West Kingston, R.I.: Donald M. Grant, 1976.

Schweitzer, Darrell. *Conan's World and Robert E. Howard*. San Bernardino, Calif.: Borgo, 1979.

Weinberg, Robert. *The Annotated Guide to Robert E. Howard's Sword & Sorcery*. West Linn, Ore.: Starmont House, 1976.

Diana Wynne Jones

Rosenberg, Teya, Martha P. Hixon, Sharon M. Scapple, and Donna R. White, eds. *Diana Wynne Jones: An Exciting and Exacting Wisdom*. New York: Peter Lang, 2002.

Guy Gavriel Kay

Webb, Janeen. "Myth and the New High Fantasy: Guy Gavriel Kay's *Tigana*." *The Ringbearer: Journal of the Mythopoeic Literature Society of Australia* 8, no. 2 (1991): 161–77.

W. P. Kinsella

Murray, Don. *The Fiction of W. P. Kinsella: Tall Tales in Various Voices*. Fredericton, N.B.: York, 1987.

Stephen King

Furth, Robin. *Stephen King's* The Dark Tower: *A Concordance*. Vol. 1. New York: Scribner, 2003.

Rudyard Kipling

Amis, Kingsley. *Kipling and His World*. London: Thames and Hudson, 1975.

Birkenhead, Lord. *Rudyard Kipling*. London: Weidenfeld and Nicholson, 1978.
Carrington, Charles. *Rudyard Kipling: His Life and Work*. London: Macmillan, 1955.
Dobrée, Bonamy. *Rudyard Kipling: Realist and Fabulist*. London: Oxford University Press, 1967.
Harrison, James. *Rudyard Kipling*. Boston: Twayne, 1982.
Kemp, Sandra. *Kipling's Hidden Narratives*. Oxford, U.K.: Blackwell, 1988.
Moss, Robert F. *Rudyard Kipling and the Fiction of Adolescence*. London: Macmillan, 1982.
Rutherford, Andrew, ed. *Kipling's Mind and Art*. Edinburgh, U.K.: Oliver and Boyd, 1964.
Seymour-Smith, Martin. *Rudyard Kipling*. London: Macdonald, 1989.
Stewart, J. I. M. *Rudyard Kipling*. London: Gollancz, 1966.
Sutcliff, Rosemary. *Rudyard Kipling*. London: Bodley Head, 1960.
Wilson, Angus. *The Strange Ride of Rudyard Kipling: His Life and Works*. London: Secker and Warburg, 1977.

William Kotzwinkle

Lewis, Leon. *Eccentric Individuality in William Kotzwinkle's* The Fan Man, E.T., Doctor Rat, *and Other Works of Fiction and Fantasy*. Lewiston, Me.: Edwin Mellen, 2002.

Mercedes Lackey

Helfers, John, and Denise Little, eds. *The Valdemar Companion*. New York: DAW, 2001.

Andrew Lang

Green, Roger Lancelyn. *Andrew Lang: A Critical Biography*. Leicester, U.K.: Ward, 1946.

Tanith Lee

Cowperthwaite, David, ed. *Tanith Lee: Mistress of Delirium*. Stockport, U.K.: British Fantasy Society, 1993.
Haut, Mavis. *The Hidden Library of Tanith Lee: Themes and Subjects from Dionysus to the Immortal Gene*. Jefferson, N.C.: McFarland, 2001.
Heldreth, Lillian M. "Tanith Lee's Werewolves Within: Reversals of Gothic Tradition." *Journal of the Fantastic in the Arts* 2, no. 1 (Spring 1989): 15–24.
Larbaleister, Justine. *Opulent Darkness: The Werewolves of Tanith Lee*. New Lambton, Australia: Nimrod, 1999.

Ursula K. Le Guin

Bittner, James. *Approaches to the Fiction of Ursula K. Le Guin*. Ann Arbor, Mich.: UMI Research, 1984.

Bucknall, Barbara J. *Ursula K. Le Guin*. New York: Ungar, 1981.

Cummins, Elizabeth. *Understanding Ursula K. Le Guin*. Columbia: University of South Carolina Press, 1990.

DeBolt, Joseph W., ed. *Ursula K. Le Guin: Voyager to Inner Lands and Outer Space*. Port Washington, N.Y.: Kennikat, 1979.

Olander, Joseph P., and Martin H. Greenberg. *Ursula K. Le Guin*. New York: Taplinger, 1979.

Rochelle, Warren G. *Communities of the Heart: The Rhetoric of Myth in the Fiction of Ursula K. Le Guin*. Liverpool, U.K.: Liverpool University Press, 2001.

Selinger, Bernard. *Le Guin and Identity in Contemporary FIction*. Ann Arbor, Mich.: UMI Research, 1988.

Slusser, George Edgar. *The Farthest Shores of Ursula K. Le Guin*. San Bernardino, Calif.: Borgo, 1976.

Spivack, Charlotte. *Ursula K. Le Guin*. Boston: Twayne, 1984.

White, Donna R. *Dancing with Dragons: Ursula K. Le Guin and the Critics*. Columbia, S.C.: Camden House, 1999.

Fritz Leiber

Benson, Gordon, Jr., and Phil Stephensen-Payne. *Fritz Leiber*. Galactic Central Bibliographies for the Avid Reader, vol. 22. 2nd revised edition. Leeds, Yorkshire, U.K.: Galactic Central. 1990.

Byfield, Bruce. *Witches of the Mind: A Critical Study of Fritz Leiber*. West Warwick, R.I.: Necronomicon, 1991.

Frane, Jeff. *Fritz Leiber*. San Bernardino, Calif.: Borgo, 1980.

Staicar, Tom. *Fritz Leiber*. New York: Ungar, 1983.

C. S. Lewis

Arnott, Anne. *The Secret Country of C. S. Lewis*. London: Hodder and Stoughton, 1974.

Christopher, Joe R. *C. S. Lewis*. Boston: Twayne, 1987.

Christopher, Joe R., and Koan K. Ostling. *C. S. Lewis: An Annotated Checklist of Writings about Him and His Works*. Kent, Ohio: Kent State University Press, 1973.

Duriez, Colin. *The C. S. Lewis Encyclopedia: A Complete Guide to His Life, Thought and Writings*. Wheation, Ill.: Crossway, 2000.

Ford, Paul F. *Companion to Narnia*. New York: Harper, 1980.

Gibb, Jocelyn, ed. *Light on C. S. Lewis*. London: Bles, 1965.
Gibson, Evan K. *C. S. Lewis, Spinner of Tales: A Guide to His Fiction*. Grand Rapids, Mich.: Christian University Press, 1980.
Glover, Donald E. *C. S. Lewis: The Art of Enchantment*. Athens: Ohio University Press, 1981.
Green, Roger Lancelyn. *C. S. Lewis*. London: Bodley Head, 1963.
Green, Roger Lancelyn, and Walter Hooper. *C. S. Lewis: A Biography*. London: Collins, 1974; revised 1988.
Honda, Mineko. *The Imaginative World of C. S. Lewis: A Way to Participate in Reality*. Lanham, Md.: University Press of America, 2000.
Hooper, Walter. *Past Watchful Dragons: The Narnian Chronicles of C. S. Lewis*. London: Macmillan, 1979.
Karkainen, Paul A. *Narnia Explored*. Old Tappan, N.J.: Revell, 1979.
Lindskoog, Kathryn Ann. *The Lion of Judah in Never-Never Land: The Theology of C. S. Lewis Expressed in His Fantasies for Children*. Grand Rapids, Mich.: Eerdmans, 1973.
Manlove, C. N. *C. S. Lewis: His Literary Achievement*. London: Macmillan, 1987.
Murphy, Brian. *C. S. Lewis*. Mercer Island, Wash.: Starmont House, 1983.
Rossi, Lee D. *The Politics of Fantasy: C. S. Lewis and J. R. R. Tolkien*. New York, Bowker, 1984.
Shakel, Peter J. *Imagination and the Arts in C. S. Lewis: Journeying to Narnia and Other Worlds*. Columbia: University of Missouri Press, 2002.
———. *Reading with the Heart: The Way into Narnia*. Grand Rapids, Mich.: Eerdmans, 1979.
———. *Reason and Imagination in C. S. Lewis: A Study of Till We Have Faces*. Grand Rapids, Mich.: Eerdmans, 1984.
Shakel, Peter, and Charles A. Huttar, eds. *Word and Story in C. S. Lewis*. Columbia: University of Missouri Press, 1992.
Walsh, Chad. *The Literary Legacy of C. S. Lewis*. New York: Harcourt Brace, 1979.
Wilson, A,. N. *C. S. Lewis: A Biography*. London: Collins, 1990.

Wyndham Lewis

Kenner, Hugh. *Wyndham Lewis*. Norfolk, Conn.: New Directions, 1954.
Meyers, Jeffrey, ed. *Wyndham Lewis: A Revaluation*. London: Athlone, 1980.

Thomas Ligotti

Schweitzer, Darrell, ed. *The Thomas Ligotti Reader*. Holicong, Pa.: Wildside, 2003.

David Lindsay

Pick, J. B., Colin Wilson, and E. H. Visiak. *The Strange Genius of David Lindsay: An Appreciation*. London: John Baker, 1970.
Power, David. *David Lindsay's Vision*. Nottingham, U.K.: Pauper's, 1991.
Sellin, Bernard. *The Life and Works of David Lindsay*. Cambridge, U.K.: Cambridge University Press, 1981.
Wilson, Colin. *The Haunted Man: The Strange Genius of David Lindsay*. San Bernardino, Calif.: Borgo, 1979.
Wolfe, Gary K. *David Lindsay*. Mercer Island, Wash.: Starmont House, 1982.

Hugh Lofting

Blishen, Edward. *Hugh Lofting*. London: Bodley Head, 1968.

H. P. Lovecraft

Carter, Lin. *Lovecraft: A Look behind the Cthulhu Mythos*. New York: Ballantine, 1972.
Gatto, John Taylor. *The Major Works of H. P. Lovecraft*. New York: Monarch, 1977.
Joshi, S. T. *H. P. Lovecraft*. Mercer Island, Wash.: Starmont House, 1982.
———. *A Subtler Magick: The Writings and Philosophy of H. P. Lovecraft*. Gillette, N.J.: Wildside, 1999.
Joshi, S. T., and David E. Schultz, eds. *An H. P. Lovecraft Encyclopedia*. Westport, Conn.: Greenwood, 2001.
Schweitzer, Darrell, ed. *Discovering H. P. Lovecraft, Revised and Expanded*. Holicong, Pa.: Wildside, 2001.
———. *The Dream Quest of H. P. Lovecraft*. San Bernardino, Calif.: Borgo, 1978.

George MacDonald

Hein, Rolland. *The Harmony Within: The Spiritual Vision of George MacDonald*. Grand Rapids, Mich.: Christian University Press, 1982; revised Chicago: Cornerstone, 1999.
Raeper, Wiliam. *George MacDonald*. Tring, Herts., U.K.: Lion, 1987.
———, ed. *The Gold Thread: Essays on George MacDonald*. Edinburgh, U.K.: Edinburgh University Press, 1990.
Reis, Richard H. *George MacDonald*. Boston: Twayne, 1972.
Robb, David S. *George MacDonald*. Edinburgh, U.K.: Scottish Academic, 1987.
Wolff, Robert Lee. *The Golden Key: A Study of the Fiction of George MacDonald*. New Haven, Conn.: Yale University Press, 1961.

Arthur Machen

Gekle, William F. *Arthur Machen: Weaver of Fantasy*. New York: Round Table, 1949.

Starrett, Vincent. *Arthur Machen: A Novelist of Ecstasy and Sin*. Chicago: Walter M. Hill, 1918.

Sweetser, Wesley D. *Athur Machen*. Boston: Twayne, 1964.

Valentine, Mark, and Roger Dobson, eds. *Arthur Machen: Apostle of Wonder*. Oxford, U.K.: Caermaen, 1985.

Gabriel Garcia Márquez

McMurray, George R., ed. *Critical Essays on Gabriel Garcia Marquez*. Boston: G. K. Hall, 1987.

Ortega, Julio, ed. *Gabriel Garcia Marquez and the Powers of Fiction*. Austin: University of Texas Press, 1988.

George R. R. Martin

Stephensen-Payne, Phil, and Gordon Benson Jr. *George R. R. Martin*. Galactic Central Bibliographies for the Avid Reader, vol. 27. 2nd edition. Leeds, Yorkshire, U.K.: Galactic Central, 1989.

John Masefield

Fisher, Margery T. *John Masefield*. New York: Walck, 1963.

A. Merritt

Foust, Ronald. *A. Merritt*. Mercer Island, Wash.: Starmont House, 1989.

Moskowitz, Sam. *A. Merritt: Reflections in the Moon Pool: A Biography*. Philadelphia: Oswald Train, 1985.

Michael Moorcock

Bilyeu, Richard. *The Tanelorn Archives: A Primary and Secondary Bibliography of the Works of Michael Moorcock 1949–1979*. Manitoba, Can.: Pandora's Books, 1981.

Gardiner, Jeff. *The Age of Chaos: The Multiverse of Michael Moorcock*. Stockport, U.K.: British Fantasy Society, 2002.

Greenland, Colin. *Michael Moorcock: Death Is No Obstacle*. Manchester, U.K.: Savoy, 1992.

C. L. Moore and Henry Kuttner

Utter, Virgil S., Gordon Benson, Jr., and Phil Stephensen-Payne. *C. L. Mooore and Henry Kuttner*. Galactic Central Bibliographies for the Avid Reader, vol. 21. 4th edition. Leeds, Yorkshire, U.K.: Galactic Central, 1996.

Wiliam Morris

Aho, Gary I. *William Morris: A Reference Guide*. Boston: G. K. Hall, 1985.
Clutton-Briock, Arthur. *William Morris: His Work and Influence*. London, Williams, 1914.
Kirchhoff, Fredrick K. *William Morris*. Boston: Twayne, 1979.
Mathews, Richard. *Worlds beyond the World: The Fantastic Vision of William Morris*. San Bernardino, Calif.: Borgo, 1978.
Oberg, Charlotte. *A Pagan Prophet: William Morris*. Charlottesville: University Press of Virginia, 1978.
Silver, Carole. *The Romance of William Morris*. Athens: Ohio University Press, 1982.
Thompson, Paul. *The Work of William Morris*. London: Heinemann, 1967; revised London: Quartet, 1977.

James Morrow

"The Divinely Human Comedy of James Morrow." Special issue. *Paradoxa* 5, no. 12 (1999).

John Myers Myers

Lerner, Fred, ed. *A Silverlock Companion*. Center Harbor, N.H.: Niekas, 1988.

Robert Nathan

Bromfield, Louis. *The Work of Robert Nathan*. Indianapolis, Ind.: Bobbs Merrill, 1927.
Sandelin, Clarence. *Robert Nathan*. Boston: Twayne, 1969.

E. Nesbit

Bell, Anthea. *E. Nesbit*. London: Bodley Head, 1960.
Briggs, Julia. *A Woman of Passion: The Life of E. Nesbit, 1859–1924*. New York: New Amsterdam Books, 1987.
Streatfeild, Noel. *Magic and the Magician: E. Nesbit and Her Children's Books*. London: Benn, 1958.

Andre Norton

Stephensen-Payne, Philip. *Andre Norton*. Galactic Central Bibliographies for the Avid Reader, vol. 41. Leeds, Yorkshire, U.K.: Galactic Central, 1991.

Flann O'Brien

Clissman, Ann. *Flann O'Brien: A Critical Introduction*. Dublin: Gill and MacMillan, 1975.

Mervyn Peake

Batchelor, John. *Mervyn Peake: A Biographical and Critical Exploration*. London: Duckworth, 1974.
Gardiner-Scott, Tanya J. *Mervyn Peake: The Evolution of a Dark Romantic*. New York: Peter Lang, 1989.
Watney, John. *Mervyn Peake*. London: Michael Joseph, 1976.
Winnington, G. Peter. *Vast Alchemies: The Life and Work of Mervyn Peake*. London: Peter Owen, 2000.

Charles Perrault

Barchilon, Jacques, and Peter Flinders. *Charles Perrault*. Boston: Twayne, 1981.

Eden Phillpotts

Girvan, Waveney. *Eden Phillpotts: An Assessment and a Tribute*. London: Hutchinson, 1953.

John Cowper Powys

Brebner, John A. *The Demon Within: A Study of John Cowper Powys's Novels*. London: Macdonald, 1973.
Cavaliero, Glen. *John Cowper Powys, Novelist*. Oxford: Clarendon Press, 1973.
Collins, H. P. *John Cowper Powys: Old Earth-Man*. London: Barrie and Rockliff, 1966.
Fawkner, H. W. *The Ecstatic World of John Cowper Powys*. Rutherford, N. J.: Fairleigh Dickinson University Press, 1986.
Knight, G. Wilson. *The Saturnian Quest: A Chart of the Prose Works of John Cowper Powys*. London: Methuen, 1964.
Krisdottir, Morine. *John Cowper Powys and the Magical Quest*. London: Macdonald and Jane's, 1980.

T. F. Powys

Buning, Marcus. *T. F. Powys: A Modern Allegorist*. Amsterdam: Rodopi, 1986.
Coombes, Henry. *T. F. Powys*. London: Barrie and Rockliff, 1960.
Hunter, William. *The Novels and Stories of T. F. Powys*. Cambridge, U.K.: Frazer, 1930.
Mitchell, J. Lawrence. *T. F. Powys*. Minneapolis: University of Minnesota, 1982.

Terry Pratchett

Butler, Andrew M. *The Pocket Essential Terry Pratchett*. Harpenden, U.K.: Pocket Essentials, 2001.
Butler, Andrew M., Edward James, and Farah Mendlesohn, eds. *Terry Pratchett: Guilty of Literature*. Reading, U.K.: Science Fiction Foundation, 2000.

Philip Pullman

Squires, Claire. *Philip Pullman's His Dark Materials Trilogy*. New York: Continuum, 2003.

Howard Pyle

Nebitt, Elizabeth. *Howard Pyle*. New York: Walck, 1968.
Pitz, Henry Clarence. *A Plethora of Talent: The Creative Life of Howard Pyle*. New York: Potter, 1975.

François Rabelais

Bakhtin, Mikhail. *Rabelais and His World*. Tr. Hélène Iswolsky. Bloomington: Indiana University Press, 1984.

Anne Rice

Ramsland, Katherine. *The Vampire Companion*. New York: Ballantine, 1993.
——. *The Witches' Companion*. New York: Ballantine, 1994.

Keith Roberts

Stephensen-Payne, Phil, and Gordon Benson Jr. *Keith Roberts*. Galactic Central Bibliographies for the Avid Reader, vol. 45. Leeds, Yorkshire, U.K.: Galactic Central, 1993.

J. K. Rowling

Blake, Andrew. *The Irresistible Rise of Harry Potter: Kid-Lit in a Globalized World*. London: Verso, 2002.
Colbert, David. *The Magical Worlds of Harry Potter*. London: Penguin, 2002.
Heilman, Elizabeth E., ed. *Harry Potter's World: Multidisciplinary Critical Perspectives*. New York: Routledge, 2002.
Killinger, John. *God, the Devil and Harry Potter*. New York: St. Martin's, 2003.
Kroznek, Allan Zola, and Elizabeth Zola. *The Sorcerer's Companion*. New York: Broadway Books, 2001.
Schafer, Elizabeth D. *Exploring Harry Potter*. London: Ebury, 2000.
Smith, Sean. *J. K. Rowling: A Biography*, London: Michael O'Mara, 2001.
Whited, Lana A., ed. *The Ivory Tower and Harry Potter: Perspectives on a Literary Phenomenon*. Columbia: University of Missouri Press, 2002.

Salman Rushdie

Brennan, Timothy. *Salman Rushdie and the Third World: Myths of the Nation*. London, Macmillan, 1989.
Harrison, James. *Salman Rushdie*. New York: Twayne, 1991.

William Shakespeare

Darling, Benjamin. *Shakespeare on Fairies and Magic*. New York: Prentice Hall, 2001.

Isaac Bashevis Singer

Alexander, Edward. *Isaac Bashevis Singer*. Boston: Twayne, 1980.
Buchen, Irving H. *Isaac Bashevis Singer and the Eternal Past*. New York: New York University Press, 1968.
Friedman, Lawrence S. *Understanding Isaac Bashevis Singer*. Columbia: University of South Carolina Press, 1988.

Clark Ashton Smith

Behrends, Steve. *Clark Ashton Smith*. Mercer Island, Wash.: Starmont House, 1990.
Sidney-Fryer, Donald. *Clark Ashton Smith: The Sorcerer Departs*. West Hills, Calif.: Tsathoggua, 1997.
——. *Emperor of Dreams: A Clark Ashton Smith Bibliography*. West Kingston, R.I.: Donald Grant, 1978.
——. *The Last of the Great Romantic Poets*. Albuquerque, N. M.: Silver Scarab, 1973.

James Stephens

Martin, Augustine. *James Stephens: A Critical Study*. Dublin: Gill and MacMillan, 1977.

McFate, Patricia. *The Writings of James Stephens: Variations on a Theme of Love*. New York: St. Martin's, 1979.

Pyle, Hilary. *James Stephens: His Work and an Account of His Life*. London: Routledge and Kegan Paul, 1965.

Robert Louis Stevenson

Jones, William B., Jr. *Robert Louis Stevenson Reconsidered: New Critical Perspectives*. Jefferson, N.C.: McFarland, 2003.

Theodore Sturgeon

Stephensen-Payne, Philip, and Gordon Benson Jr. *Theodore Sturgeon*. Galactic Central Bibliographies for the Avid Reader, vol. 32. Leeds, Yorkshire, U.K.: Galactic Central, 1989.

Thomas Burnett Swann

Collins, Robert A. *Thomas Burnett Swann: A Brief Critical Biography and Annotated Bibliography*. Boca Raton: Florida Atlantic University College of Humanities, 1979.

James Thurber

Holmes, Charles S. *The Clocks of Columbus: The Literary Career of James Thurber*. New York: Atheneum, 1973.

Long, Robert Emmet. *James Thurber*. New York: Ungar, 1988.

Morberger, Robert E. *James Thurber*. Boston: Twayne, 1964.

J. R. R. Tolkien

Bassham, Gregory, and Eric Bronson, eds. *The Lord of the Rings and Philosophy: One Book to Rule Them All*. Chicago: Open Court, 2003.

Bates, Brian. *The Real Middle Earth: Exploring the Magic and Mystery of the Middle Ages, J. R. R. Tolkien, and* The Lord of the Rings. London: Sidgwick and Jackson, 2002.

Carpenter, Humphrey. *Tolkien: A Biography*. London: Allen and Unwin, 1977.

Challis, Erica, ed. *The People's Guide to J. R. R. Tolkien*. New York: Cold Spring, 2003.

Chance, Jane, ed. *Tolkien the Medievalist*. New York: Routledge, 2003.

——, ed. *Tolkien and the Invention of Myth: A Reader*. Lexington: University Press of Kentucky, 2004.

——. *Tolkien's Art: A Mythology for England*. Lexington: University Press of Kentucky, revised 2001. [Original edition London: Macmillan, 1979, as by Jane C. Nitzsche.]

Clark, George, and Daniel Timmons, eds. *J. R. R. Tolkien and His Literary Resonances: Views of Middle-Earth*. Westport, Conn.: Greenwood, 2000.

Crabbe, Katharyn F. *J. R. R. Tolkien*. New York: Ungar, 1981; revised 1988.

Day, David. *Tolkien's Ring*. London: HarperCollins, 1994.

——. *The World of Tolkien: Mythological Sources of* The Lord of the Rings. London: Mitchell Beazley, 2003.

Ellwood, Robert. *Frodo's Quest: Living the Myth in The Lord of the Rings*. Wheaton, Ill.: Theosophical Publishing House, 2002.

Evans, Robley. *J. R. R. Tolkien*. New York: Warner, 1972.

Flieger, Verlyn. *Splintered Light: Logos and Language in Tolkien's World*. Grand Rapids, Mich.: Eerdmans, 1983; revised Kent, Ohio: Kent State University Press, 2002.

Flieger, Verlyn, and Carl F. Hofstedder, eds. *Tolkien's Legendarium: Essays on The History of Middle Earth*. Westport, Conn.: Greenwood, 2000.

Foster, Robert. *The Complete Guide to Middle-earth*. New York: Ballantine, 1978 [revision of Mirage Press edition, 1971].

Garth, John. *Tolkien in the Great War: The Threshold of Middle-earth*. London: HarperCollins, 2003.

Giddings, Robert, ed. *Tolkien: This Far Land*. London: Vision, 1983.

Haber, Karen, ed. *Meditations on Middle-Earth*. New York: St. Martin's, 2001.

Harvey, David. *The Song of Middle-Earth: J. R. R. Tolkien's Themes, Symbols, and Myths*. London: Allen and Unwin, 1985.

Helms, Randel. *Tolkien and the Silmarils*. London: Thames and Hudson, 1981.

——. *Tolkien's World*. New York: Houghton Mifflin, 1974.

Isaacs, Neil D., and Rose A. Zimbardo, eds. *Tolkien: New Critical Perspectives*. Lexington: University of Kentucky Press, 1981.

——, eds. *Tolkien and the Critics*. Notre Dame, Ind.: University of Notre Dame Press, 1968.

Johnson, Judith A. *J. R. R. Tolkien: Six Decades of Criticism*. Westport, Conn.: Greenwood, 1986.

Jones, Leslie Ellen, *Myth & Middle-earth*. New York: Cold Spring, 2002.

Kocher, Paul H. *Master of Middle-earth: The Fiction of J. R. R. Tolkien*. New York: Houghton Mifflin, 1972.

Lobdell, Jared. *England and Always: Tolkien's World of the Rings*. Grand Rapids, Mich.: Eerdmans, 1981.

——, ed. *A Tolkien Compass*. Chicago: Open Court, 1975.

Mathews, Richard. *Lightning from a Clear Sky: J. R. R. Tolkien*. San Bernardino, Calif.: Borgo, 1978.

Nitzche, Jane C. *Tolkien's Art: A Mythology for England*. London: Macmillan, 1979. [Revised edition Lexington: University Press of Kentucky, 2001, as by Jane Chance.]

Noel, Ruth S. *The Mythology of Middle-Earth*. London: Thames and Hudson, 1977.

O'Neill, Timothy, R. *The Individuated Hobbit: Jung, Tolkien and the Archetypes of Middle-earth*. New York: Houghton Mifflin, 1979.

Petty, Anne C. *Tolkien in the Land of Heroes*. New York: Cold Spring, 2003.

Purtill, Richard L. *J. R. R. Tolkien: Myth, Morality, and Religion*. New York: Harper and Row, 1985.

Rogers, Deborah, and Ivor Rogers. *J. R. R. Tolkien*. Boston: Twayne, 1980.

Rosebury, Brian. *Tolkien: A Critical Assessment*. London: Macmillan, 1992; revised and expanded as *Tolkien: A Cultural Phenomenon: Revised Edition*, 2004.

Shippey, T. A. *J. R. R. Tolkien: Author of the Century*. London: HarperCollins, 2000.

——. *The Road to Middle-Earth*. London: Allen and Unwin, 1982; revised London: Grafton, 1992; further revised as *The Road to Middle-Earth: How J. R. R. Tolkien Created a New Mythology*. New York: Houghton Mifflin, 2003.

Smith, Mark Eddy. *Tolkien's Ordinary Virtues: Exploring the Spiritual Themes of* The Lord of the Rings. Downers Grove, Ill.: InterVarsity, 2002.

Stanton, Michael N. *Hobbits, Elves, and Wizards: Exploring the Wonders and Worlds of J. R. R. Tolkien's "The Lord of the Rings."* New York: Palgrave, 2001; expanded edition 2002.

Zimbardo, Rose A., and Neil D. Isaacs, eds. *Understanding the Lord of the Rings: The Best of Tolkien Criticism*. New York: Houghton Mifflin, 2004.

Jack Vance

Cunningham, A. E., ed. *Jack Vance: Critical Appreciations and a Bibliography*. Boston Spa, Yorkshire, U.K.: British Library, 2000.

Mead, David G. *An Encyclopedia of Jack Vance, 20th-Century Science Fiction Writer*. 3 vols. Studies in American Literature, no. 50. Lewiston, N.Y.: Mellen, 2002.

Rawlins, Jack. *Demon Prince: The Dissonant Worlds of Jack Vance*. San Bernardino, Calif.: Borgo, 1986.

Stephensen-Payne, Phil, and Gordon Benson Jr. *Jack Vance*. Galactic Central Bibliographies for the Avid Reader, vol. 28. Leeds, Yorkshire, U.K.: Galactic Central, 1988.

Tiedman, Richard. *Jack Vance: Science Fiction Stylist*. Wabash, Ind.: Coulson, 1965.

Underwood, Tim, and Chuck Miller, eds. *Jack Vance*. New York: Taplinger, 1980.

Margaret Weis and Tracy Hickman

Little, Denise, ed. *Realms of Dragons: The Universes of Margaret Weis and Tracy Hickman*. New York: HarperPrism, 1999.

T. H. White

Crane, John K. *T. H. White*. Boston: Twayne, 1974.

Warner, Sylvia Townsend. *T. H. White: A Biography*. London: Jonathan Cape, 1967.

Charles Williams

Cavaliero, Glen. *Charles Williams: Poet of Theology*. Grand Rapids, Mich.: Eerdmans, 1983.

Hadfield, Alice Mary. *Charles Williams: An Exploration of His Life and Work*. Oxford, U.K.: Oxford University Press, 1983.

Howard, Thomas T. *The Novels of Charles Williams*. Oxford, U.K.: Oxford University Press, 1983.

Shideler, Mary McDermott. *The Theology of Romantic Love: A Study in the Writings of Charles Williams*. Grand Rapids, Mich.: Eerdmans, 1962.

Sibley, Agnes. *Charles Williams*. Boston: Twayne, 1982.

Soencer, Kathleen. *Charles Williams*. Mercer Island, Wash.: Starmont House, 1986.

Gene Wolfe

Andre-Driussi, Michael. *Lexicon Urthus: A Dictionary for the Urth Cycle*. San Francisco: Sirius, 1994.

Gordon, Joan. *Gene Wolfe*. Mercer Island, Wash.: Starmont House, 1986.

Stephensen-Payne, Phil, and Gordon Benson Jr. *Gene Wolfe.* Galactic Central Bibliographies for the Avid Reader, vol. 19. Leeds, Yorkshire, U.K.: Galactic Central, 1991

Wright, Peter. *Attending Dedalus: Gene Wolfe, Artifice and the Reader*. Liverpool, U.K.: Liverpool University Press, 2003.

Roger Zelazny

Krulik, Theodore. *Roger Zelazny*. New York: Ungar, 1986.

Lindskold, Jane. *Roger Zelazny*. New York: Twayne, 1993.

Stephensen-Payne, Phil, and Gordon Benson Jr. *Roger Zelazny*. Galactic Central Bibliographies for the Avid Reader, vol. 38. Leeds, Yorkshire, U.K.: Galactic Central, 1991.

Yoke, Carl B. *Roger Zelazny*. West Linn, Ore.: Starmont House, 1979.

WRITING GUIDES AND MANUALS

Budrys, Algis. *Writing Science Fiction and Fantasy*. Eugene, Ore.: Pulphouse, 1990.

Card, Orson Scott. *How to Write Science Fiction and Fantasy*. Cincinnati, Ohio: Writer's Digest, 1990.

Stableford, Brian. *Writing Fantasy & Science Fiction*. London: Teach Yourself Books, 1997.

Tuttle, Lisa. *Writing Fantasy and Science Fiction*. London: A&C Black, 2001.

SCHOLARLY FANTASIES

Blavatsky, Helena P. *Isis Unveiled: A Master Key to the Mysteries of Ancient and Modern Science and Theology*. 2 vols. New York: J. W. Bouton, 1882.

———. *The Secret Doctrine: The Synthesis of Science, Religion, and Philosophy*. 2 vols. Adyar, India: Theosophical Publishing House, 1888. Expanded edition 4 vols. 1910; further expanded to 6 vols. 1938.

Crowley, Aleister. *Magick in Theory and Practice by the Master Therion*. Paris: Lecram, 1929.

Donnelly, Ignatius. *Atlantis: The Antediluvian World*. New York: Harper, 1882.

Fortune, Dion. *Spiritualism in the Light of Occult Science*. London: Rider, 1931.

———. *The Training and Work of an Initiate*. London: Rider, 1930.

Frazer, James G. *The Golden Bough*. 2 vols. London: Macmillan, 1890; expanded 3rd edition 12 vols. London: Macmillan, 1911–15.

Freud, Sigmund. *The Interpretation of Dreams*. London: George Allen, 1913. [Original German publication 1900.]

Gardner, Gerald B. *The Meaning of Witchcraft*. London: Aquarian, 1959.

———. *Witchcraft Today*. London: Rider, 1954.

Geoffrey of Monmouth. *The History of the Kings of Britain*. Translated by Lewis Thorpe. Harmondsworth, U.K.: Peguin, 1966. [First published c1136.]

Grant, Kenneth. *Hecate's Fountain*. London: Skoob, 1992.

———. *Magical Revival*. London: Muller, 1972.

———. *Outside the Circles of Time*. London: Frederick Muller, 1980.

Graves, Robert. *The White Goddess*. London: Faber and Faber, 1948.

Hay, George, ed. *The Necronomicon*. London: Skoob, 1992.

Hubbard, L. Ron. *Dianetics: The Modern Science of Mental Health*. New York: Hermitage House, 1950.

Hughes, Ted. *Shakespeare and the Goddess of Complete Being*. London: Faber and Faber, 1992.

Jennings, Hargrave. *The Rosicrucians: Their Rites and Mysteries*. 2 vols. London: John C. Nimmo, 1887.

King, Francis. *Ritual Magic in England: 1887 to the Present Day*. London: Spearman, 1970.

Leland, Charles Godfrey. *Aradia: The Gospel of the Witches*. London: David Nutt, 1899.

——. *Gypsy Sorcery and Fortune Telling*. London: T. Fisher Unwin, 1891.

Lévi, Éliphas. *Dogme et rituel de la haute magie*. Paris: Germer Ballière, 1856. Translated by A. E. Waite as *Transcendental Magic: Its Doctrine and Ritual*. London: Rider, 1896.

——. *Histoire de la magie*. Paris: Germer Ballière, 1860. Translated by A. E. Waite as *The History of Magic*. London: Rider, 1913.

Michelet, Jules. *La Sorcière*. Paris: Dentu, 1862. Translated by A. R. Allinson as *Satanism and Witchcraft*. New York: Citadel, 1939.

Murray, Margaret. *The God of the Witches*. Oxford, U.K.: Oxford University Press, 1931.

——. *The Witch-Cult in Western Europe* Oxford, U.K.: Oxford University Press, 1921.

Ovason, David. *The Secrets of Nostradamus: The Medieval Code of the Master Revealed in an Age of Computer Science*. London: Century, 1997.

Powys, John Cowper. *Homer and the Aether*. London: Macdonald, 1959.

Rohmer, Sax. *The Romance of Sorcery*. London: Methuen, 1914.

Sinclair, Andrew. *The Discovery of the Grail*. London: Century, 1998.

——. *The Sword and the Grail*. New York: Crown, 1992.

Spence, Lewis. *British Fairy Origins*. London: Watts, 1946.

——. *An Encyclopedia of Occultism*. London: Routledge, 1920.

——. *The History and Origins of Druidism*. London: Rider, 1935.

——. *The History of Atlantis*. London: Rider, 1926.

——. *An Introduction to Mythology*. London: Harrap, 1921.

——. *The Mysteries of Britain; or, The Secret Rites and Traditions of Ancient Britain Restored*. London: Rider, 1928.

——. *The Occult Sciences in Atlantis*. London: Rider, 1943.

——. *The Problem of Atlantis*. London: Rider, 1924.

Starhawk. *The Spiral Dance: A Rebirth of the Religion of the Great Goddess*. San Francisco: Harper and Row, 1979.

Summers, Montague. *The History of Witchcraft and Demonology*. London: Routledge and Kegan Paul, 1926.

Waite, A. E. *The Book of Ceremonial Magic*. London: Rider, 1911.

——. *The Brotherhood of the Holy Cross*. London: Rider. 1924.

——. *The Hidden Church of the Holy Graal: Its Legends and Symbolism*. London: George Redman, 1909.

——. *The Occult Sciences*. London: Kegan Paul, Trench and Trubner, 1891.

——. *The Real History of the Rosicrucians*. London: George Redway, 1887.

Weston, Jessie. *From Ritual to Romance*. Cambridge, U.K.: Cambridge University Press, 1920.

——. *The Legend of Sir Perceval*. 2 vols. London: David Nutt, 1906.
——. *The Quest of the Holy Grail*. London: G. Bell, 1913.

JOURNALS

Arthuriana: The Journal of Arthurian Studies. Dallas, Tex.: Southern Methodist University.
The Cabellian: A Journal of the Second American Renaissance. New York: Cabell Society.
Extrapolation. Brownsville: University of Texas at Brownsville and Texas Southernmost College.
Foundation: The International Review of Science Fiction. Reading, U.K.: SF Foundation.
Journal of the Fantastic in the Arts. Boca Raton: College of Arts and Letters, Florida Atlantic University.
Journal of Mythic Arts. Endicott Studio website, www.endicott-studio.com.
Journal of William Morris Studies. Kelmscott House, London W6 9TA.
Locus: The Magazine of the Science Fiction & Fantasy Field. Locus Publications, P.O. Box 13305, Oakland, CA 94661.
Marvels and Tales: Journal of Fairy Tale Studies. Detroit, Mich.: Wayne State University Press.
Mythlore: A Journal of J. R. R. Tolkien, C. S. Lewis, Charles Williams, and the Genres of Myth and Fantasy. Alhambra, Calif.: Mythopoeic Society.
New York Review of Science Fiction. Pleasantville, N.Y.: Dragon.
Journal of Myth, Fantasy and Romanticism. Brisbane, Queensland: Mythopoeic Literature Society of Australia.
Science Fiction Studies. Greencastle, Ind.: SF-TH, Inc., at DePauw University.
SFRA Review. Eau Claire, Wisc.: Science Fiction Research Association.
Wormwood: Literature of the Fantastic, Supernatural and Decadent. Leyburn, U.K.: Tartarus.

WEBSITES

The Alien Online (news): www.thealienonline.net.
Asociación Española de Fantasia y Ciencia Fiçción (Spanish fantasy): www.ae-fcf.es.
Charles Williams Society: www.geocities.com/charleswmssoc/.
Elfwood (fantasy art): elfwood.lysator.liu.se.
Emerald City (reviews): www.emcit.com.
Encyclopedia Mythica: www.pantheon.org.

Encyclopedia of Arda (reference guide to Tolkieniana): www.glyphweb.com/arda.
The Endicott Studio ("an interdisciplinary organization dedictated to the creation and support of mythic art"; the host of Journal of Mythic Arts and other information): www.endicott-studio.com.
Faery Lands Forlorn (poetry and art): www.ragnarokpress.com/faerie/.
Fantastic Fiction (author bibliographies): www.fantasticfiction.co.uk.
Fantastic Metropolis (articles, interviews and fiction): www.fantasticmetropolis.com.
Fantasy Art Gallery: www.artpromote.com/fantasy.shtml.
The George MacDonald Society: www.macdonaldsiociety.org.
The Golden Key (site devoted to George MacDonald): www.george-macdonald.com.
The Green Man Review (reviews and news): www.greenmanreview.com.
Heren Istarion (New York Tolkien Society): www.herenistarion.org.
The Infinite Matrix (news, articles, and fiction): www.infinitematrix.net.
Infinity Plus (news, articles, and fiction): www.infinityplus.co.uk.
International Arthurian Society (North American branch): smu.ed/arthuriana/.
International Association for the Fantastic in the Arts: ebbs.english.vt.edu/iafa/.
International SF Database (author bibliographies, including fantasy): www.isfdb.org.
Interstitial Arts Foundation: www.artistswithoutborders.org.
The Labyrinth: Resources for Medieval Studies (has subsections on Arthurian Studies, Magic, and Alchemy, etc.): labyrinth.georgetown.edu.
Lamhfada: An Online Magazine of Myth & Story: www.lamhfada.com.
Lewis Carroll Home Page: www.lewiscarroll.org.
Locus On-Line: www.locusmag.com.
Mythic Imaginations Institute (Organizers of annual Mythic Journeys conference): www.mythicjourneys.org.
Mythopoeic Society: www.mythsoc.org.
Página Portuguesa de Ficção Cientfica e Fantasia (Portuguese SF): www.geocities.com/Area51.Vault/1077.
Science Fiction and Fantasy Research Database (bibliography of secondary sources): library.tamu.edu/cushing/sffrd.
Science Fiction and Fantasy Writers of America: www.sfwa.org.
Science Fiction and Fantasy Writers of Japan: ww.sfwj.or.jp.
SciFan (bibliographies and web links): www.scifan.com.
SurLaLune Fairy Tale Pages (includes many annotated texts with variants and bibliographies, a useful chronology, reviews, etc.): www.surlalunefairytales.com.
Tolkien Society: www.tolkiensociety.org.

About the Author

Brian Stableford (B.A., University of York; D.Phil., University of York) is a part-time lecturer in creative writing at University College, Winchester. He has been a professional writer since 1965, publishing more than fifty novels and two hundred short stories, as well as several nonfiction books, thousands of articles for periodicals and reference books, several translations from the French, and a number of anthologies. His fiction includes *The Empire of Fear* (1988), *Young Blood* (1992), *Year Zero* (2000), *The Fountains of Youth* (2000), and *Salome and Other Decadent Fantasies* (2004). His nonfiction includes *Scientific Romance in Britain* (1985), *Opening Minds: Essays on Fantastic Literature* (1995), *Teach Yourself Writing Fantasy and Science Fiction* (1997), *Glorious Perversity: The Decline and Fall of Literary Decadence* (1998), and the *Historical Dictionary of Science Fiction Literature* (2004). Reference books to which he has made major contributions include the Salem Press *Survey of Modern Fantasy Literature* (1983), Neil Barron's *Fantasy Literature* (1990), the Clute/Nicholls *Encyclopedia of Science Fiction* (2nd ed., 1993), *The St. James Guide to Fantasy Writers* (1996), the Clute/Grant *Encyclopedia of Fantasy* (1997), David Pringle's *Ultimate Encyclopedia of Fantasy* (1998), Everett F. Bleiler and Richard Bleiler's *Supernatural Fiction Writers* (2002), and the *Cyclopedia of Literary Places* (2003).